Chaucer and the Imagery of Narrative

THE FIRST FIVE CANTERBURY TALES

V. A. KOLVE

Chaucer and the
Imagery of Narrative

THE FIRST FIVE
CANTERBURY TALES

STANFORD UNIVERSITY PRESS

Stanford, California 1984

Published with the assistance of the
National Endowment for the Humanities

Stanford University Press
Stanford, California
© 1984 by the Board of Trustees of the
Leland Stanford Junior University
Printed in the United States of America
ISBN 0-8047-1161-5   LC 80-50907

THIS BOOK IS FOR LARRY

Acknowledgments

IN RETROSPECT, it seems to me this book had its beginning in a series of masterly lectures delivered by Edgar Wind as Professor of Art History at Oxford in the late 1950's. Though none of them concerned medieval art in particular, it was there I first learned that pictures often carry meaning other than the purely representational. A seminar in pictures and texts, taught jointly by Wind and John Sparrow, deepened that interest, as did classes with Douglas Gray on the medieval religious lyric and with Christopher Woodforde on religious iconography. The friendship of Nevill Coghill and his great love for all things medieval had something to do with it, as did, no doubt, my choice of the English medieval religious drama as the subject of my doctoral research and ultimately of my first book. Something hereditary may even be involved: though I never met her, I learned on a visit to my ancestral Norway that Rosemund Tuve was a cousin twice-removed. Whatever the logic of such a history may be, what began as an incidental pleasure has become no small part of my profession. It has led to the kind of book this is, a book in which pictures and texts are seen to cast a mutual light.

Because my researches from the beginning have concerned *The Canterbury Tales* as a whole—only a part of them is represented in the pages that follow—the book has been long in the making. The list of debts I have incurred, to both persons and institutions, is of corresponding length, and it is a pleasure to acknowledge them here.

The book was begun at Stanford and finished at the University of Virginia, and my students at both universities will recognize in these pages many ideas they have heard earlier in briefer, more tentative form. They will recognize too how much I have learned from them over the years. I am grateful to Thomas Moser for much kindness as my chairman at Stanford, not least for a quarter's research leave that allowed me to begin looking at illuminated manuscripts at the Pierpont Morgan Library in New York. And I owe much to the friendship and good counsel of Fredson Bowers, under whose chairmanship I was invited to join the Department of English at Virginia. A concurrent three-year appointment to the university's Center for Advanced Studies gave me a reduced teaching load and generous research support during the crucial first stages of this study. To the center and its director, W. Dexter Whitehead, I am deeply grateful. A Guggenheim Fellowship supported my first year of work with illuminated manuscripts in the great libraries of Europe; the Danforth Foundation's Harbison Award for Distinction in Teaching informally underwrote another year of the same. A six-week residency at the Rockefeller Foundation's Villa Serbelloni on Lake Como provided me the most perfect period of concentrated writing I have ever experienced. And for extended periods of hospitality in England, I must thank especially the Fellows of St. Edmund Hall, Oxford, as well as my friends Julian Mitchell and Toby Eady, for long visits to London working at the British Library and the Warburg Institute.

Among the many friends in medieval studies to whom I have turned for assistance in the writing of this book, I wish to thank most particularly Rachel Jacoff, Hoyt Duggan, John Leyerle, and Donald R. Howard, all of whom read the manuscript in its last-but-one stage with great sympathy and care. The book is better for their attention, in ways I hope will please them. James Wimsatt first invited me to make some public statement of my ideas on Chaucer and the visual arts at an MLA meeting in New York in 1972, and Derek Brewer soon after asked me to develop those ideas at greater length for a collection of essays he was editing on backgrounds to Chaucer. I am grateful to both for providing occasions valuable to the growth of this book. Jeannine Alton, R. E. Alton, Gay Clifford, J. W. Conley, Robert F. Cook, Patricia Eberle, J. Martin Evans, John Fleming, Gabriel Josipovici, Robert Kellogg, Jeanne Krochalis, Keith Moxey, Barbara Nolan, Derek Pearsall, Austin Quigley, A. G. Rigg, Fred C. Robinson, Murray Roston, Jon Whitman, and Chauncey Wood have all contributed something of value to the book—information, expertise, correction, support—as has a veritable roll call of former students, now medievalists in their own right: John Bowers, David Burchmore, Thomas Cannon, Roger Dahood, Penelope Doob, Louise Fradenburg, Allen Frantzen, Donald Fritz, Gail McMurray Gibson, Susan Hagen, Lisa Kiser, Charlotte Morse, Glending Olson, Thomas Reed, and Robert Yeager. I am grateful to them all. John Bowers, Annette LeClair, Beverly Seng, Kevin Grimm, Richard Barney, and Roger Hillas have all, at one stage or another, labored generously as research assistants to make this book more accurate and orderly. Julie Bates has done most, seeing it through the press with remarkable diligence and good humor; she has contributed the

Index as well. Jess Bell, of Stanford University Press, has waited for this book a long time; I am grateful for his patience and impatience in equal measure. In the crucial last stages, Helen Tartar has taught me how valuable a good editor can be.

But finally it is to a circle of friends that I owe the most. I have no words to express to Loy Martin, Jeanne Martin Vanecko, Rachel Jacoff, and Lawrence Luchtel all they have meant to the book and to me.

Many museums, galleries, libraries, and other institutions have supplied photographs and given permission to reproduce in this volume illustrations from works in their possession. Detailed acknowledgments appear in the list of Illustration Sources and Credits at the back of this book. I am grateful to the Early English Text Society for permission to quote extensively from their publications, and to Bell & Hyman Ltd., London, and the Ohio University Press for permission to reprint substantial portions of my essay "Chaucer and the Visual Arts," first published in *Geoffrey Chaucer: Writers and Their Background*, edited by Derek Brewer (1974). The National Endowment for the Humanities has made a generous grant to aid the publication of this book.

Charlottesville   V. A. K.
September, 1983

Contents

Three Notes to the Reader

ENDNOTES

The endnotes to this book are discursive and often lengthy: they carry the evidence upon which my argument rests, some of it little known, some of it complex; and they seek to provide a certain amount of bibliographical guidance to students who might wish to explore a given subject more fully. They are not intended to be read in tandem with the text. The notes that I consider essential to its understanding have been printed at the foot of the page.

PRIMARY TEXTS

Quotations from Chaucer are taken from *The Works of Geoffrey Chaucer*, edited by F. N. Robinson, second edition (Boston: Houghton Mifflin, 1957). Biblical texts are quoted from the Latin Vulgate and (in most cases) its Douay translation.

MEDIEVAL ORTHOGRAPHY

Two letters of the English alphabet current in Chaucer's time but now obsolete are regularly modernized in present-day editions of Chaucer. They occur frequently, however, in many of the other texts quoted in the pages that follow. Since I hope this book will interest not only professional Chaucerians but students not yet widely read in his contemporaries, together with still others whose primary concern is with the medieval visual arts, some brief information concerning those letters may be useful.

þ: called "thorn." A runic letter that stands for the voiced and voiceless sounds now represented by *th* in *this* or *thin*. Examples (and their modern equivalents): þe, *the*; þan, *than*; þridde, *third*; wheþer, *whether*; þynkeþ, *thinketh*.

ʒ: called "yogh." This derives from the Old English script form of the letter *g* and represents a group of spirant sounds:

1. In initial position, it is sounded like our *y* in *yoke* or *year*, even where that sound has changed to *g* in modern English. Examples: ʒow, *you*; ʒelde, *yield*; ʒeue, *give*; ʒonge, *young*; ʒate, *gate*; forʒetful, *forgetful*.

2. In medial or final position, it represents the guttural or palatal spirant, lost in modern English pronunciation but still spelled in words like *night, high, through*. The modern silent *gh* in such words was written ʒ and pronounced like the German *ch* in *ich* or *ach*. Examples: myʒt, *might*; bouʒte, *bought*; tauʒte, *taught*; ryʒt, *right*.

Sometimes in medial position but chiefly at the end of words, and distinct from the above in origin and sound although identical in script form, ʒ can be equivalent to modern *z* or *s*. Examples: clyffeʒ, *cliffs*; Goddeʒ, *God's*; spekeʒ, *speaks*; ʒateʒ, *gates*; profeʒies, *prophecies*.

Abbreviations of Chaucer's Works

ABC Poem	*An ABC*, or *La Prière de Nostre Dame*	LGW	*The Legend of Good Women*
		PF	*The Parliament of Fowls*
BD	*The Book of the Duchess*	RR	*The Romaunt of the Rose*
CT	*The Canterbury Tales*	TC	*Troilus and Criseyde*
HF	*The House of Fame*		

Chaucer and the Imagery of Narrative

THE FIRST FIVE CANTERBURY TALES

Introduction

LTHOUGH this book will bring together many images from literature and the visual arts, it is not my purpose to make stylistic comparisons between them—nor is my subject *ut pictura poesis* as that phrase from Horace's *Ars poetica* is usually defined. The idea that poetry can imitate the effects proper to painting, or painting those proper to poetry, has a real history, extending from Homer, Virgil, and Ovid to the present day, and has proved itself, on occasion, a source of creative renewal and stylistic innovation. But in the last analysis, such goals have always been more fanciful than real. As Ralph Cohen has reminded us, words are finally nothing like pigments; extension in time is not the same as extension in space; verbal and visual organization are not interchangeable.[1] The "sister arts" of poetry and painting are not, and cannot ever be, the same.

My interest instead is in the visual contexts of *The Canterbury Tales*—most especially, in how a knowledge of the symbolic traditions current in the visual arts of the later Middle Ages can clarify and deepen our response to his narrative poems. In a series of extended essays—Chapters III through VII—I assemble the visual materials and their literary analogues that seem to me most helpful in understanding the first five *Canterbury Tales*, a sequence I argue is intended formally to inaugurate the literary pilgrimage. Those essays constitute the core of the book, and readers chiefly interested in a critical reading of the *Tales* may proceed directly to them, for Chapters I and II, though related, are rather different in kind. They are intended to serve as a preface not only to those five essays, but to others already published or in hand: they seek to discover a coherent medieval rationale for the care with which Chaucer makes one visualize the action and setting of his poems, the powerful claim such images make upon the memory, and the affiliation they tacitly imply with similar images known from elsewhere in medieval tradition. In Chapter I, I explore a range of medieval ideas concerning the nature of mental

imagery and the role of the visual imagination in the moral and cre-
ative life of man, in ways potentially applicable to any poet of the
later medieval period. In Chapter II, I refine the terms of that descrip-
tion to suggest the ways in which Chaucer most characteristically
sought to exercise the visual imagination of his audience in the larger
enterprise of his art. Chapters I and II ask in general terms the ques-
tions Chapters III through VII will ask in particular, one tale at a
time: together they constitute an inquiry into what Chaucer asks his
audience to "see"—in what manner, and to what ends—as well as
into the cultural resources his first audiences might have brought to
that activity.

My focus throughout will be upon the imagery of narrative: not
the passing metaphor or simile ("As leene was his hors as is a rake"),
not the local iconographic detail ("Wel loved he garleek, oynons, and
eek lekes");[2] but those larger images created by the narrative action
itself, which it invites us to imagine and hold in mind as we experi-
ence the poem, and which later serve as memorial centers around
which we are able to reconstruct the story and think appropriately
about its meaning. They are images that Chaucer moves his story to
or through, and which he expected a significant part of his audience
to recognize in their iconographic dimension—as images possessing
public meanings independent of the narrative in which he uncovers
them. It is that double identity that makes them central to the man-
ner and meaning of his art. As I shall argue in Chapter II, they serve
both to forward the fiction and to formulate, in a nondiscursive way,
its truth.

This book, in short, will have little to say about imagery as rhe-
torical decoration, about brief metaphors or discrete similes used to
ornament a poetic theme. Those are important, to be sure, and any
full-scale study of Chaucer's imagery or any comprehensive account
of Chaucer's iconography would need to pay them systematic at-
tention. But they are not my subject here. If the medieval arts of
rhetoric and poetry are chiefly concerned with the management of
language, word by word, in figure and trope—with poems on the
page—then this book is concerned with something rather different,
with the life that poems have in the mind. It is interested in the way a
poem by Chaucer engages the literary and visual culture of its time,
both at the moment of its making (the poet in the act of conceiving
the larger outlines of his poem) and in its public life thereafter, as it is
experienced by an audience and thought about when it is over. Alain
de Lille approached the meaning of *ut pictura poesis* in just this way
when he declared, "A poem is a word picture of a mental image."[3] It
is in that sense only that this book will explore the ways in which a
poem can be like a picture, or a picture like a poem.

There are not many precedents to guide us. In English medieval studies, an intensive use of material drawn from the visual arts in the interpretation of literary texts dates back only two decades, to the publication in 1963 by D. W. Robertson, Jr., of *A Preface to Chaucer*—an epoch-making book that has greatly enriched my thinking about the poet, while leading me to conclusions rather different from its own. In the years between, important work from several hands has followed,[4] but the inquiry remains in many ways still young. Whereas art history offers venerable models of how to use literary texts in recovering the meaning of pictures—Erwin Panofsky, Edgar Wind, Meyer Schapiro, and E. H. Gombrich, to name just four, have charted the road from picture to text and back with brilliance and authority—traffic in the other direction remains infrequent and unsure. We are only beginning to understand the issues involved in using pictures as a means of recovering the meaning of literary texts, only beginning the hard tasks of historical scholarship, methodological refinement, and sympathetic imagination necessary if we would restore what was once a vital and viable relation between the two. In an essay entitled "Chaucer and the Visual Arts," published in 1974, I suggested in brief some new reasons for thinking such a subject might imply more than mere synchronicity, more than the simultaneous flourishing of several distinct arts in a single historical period. In the first two chapters of this book, I present that argument deepened and at its proper length, with a good deal of evidence drawn from the visual arts themselves. In them I inquire anew into the grounds upon which we may appropriately employ images from the visual arts in thinking about a work of medieval literature, and into the rules that may best guide us in that use.

Those chapters, let me say clearly, are intended as a point of departure, not as a statement of thesis to which the rest of this book will relate simply as proof or demonstration. I use them to put forward the largest generalizations I have been able to frame concerning medieval ideas of the image, and to suggest what seems to me Chaucer's most distinctive practice within those terms. But I mean to complicate, refine, and enlarge those generalizations as we move with the pilgrim company tale by tale toward Canterbury.[5] Chaucer did not write to a thesis, or limit himself to a single style, or use narrative imagery in only one way. *The Canterbury Tales* brings together poems written over a period of some twenty years; though all of them differ profoundly from the dream-vision poems that distinguish his early career—those would require a rather different introduction[6]—they also differ significantly from each other. The variety of Chaucer's later poetry is immense, and any reading that would seek to describe it accurately must be itself inclusive and nondogmatic, as attentive to complexities, contradictions, and discontinuities as it is to whatever continuities permit the generalizations with which it begins. The introductory chapters of this book are meant to make possible a sequential and cumulative definition. They do not seek to anticipate it—or account for it—in every detail.

Even within the first five *Canterbury Tales*, such variety is richly and quite deliberately represented. I can perhaps best make that point, and since the book is long, give my reader some guidance as to what lies ahead, by sketching the outlines of my larger reading here. The life of the argument is in its detail; it will not be made redundant by an advance summary.

The Canterbury Tales is a poem incorporating other poems, a fiction enclosing other fictions. The larger, inclusive poem is special: a fiction that claims to be the chronicle of a journey involving a specific number of pilgrims, some with real-life London names, who meet at a well-known tavern on a day and year that will be specified, and set off together on a conventional Canterbury pilgrimage, a spring-time excursion to worship the sainted martyr Becket at his shrine. But the work becomes less specific and "occasional" as it proceeds. It chronicles no inns along the way, no resting places for the night, no second- or third-day divisions, no arrival at Canterbury, no return journey. It becomes instead, in the prologue to its final tale, a poem governed by a grander idea of pilgrimage, in which all human life is viewed allegorically as a pilgrimage toward death and God's just judgment.* The literal journey (the journey that begins on April 18, 1387) is part of the larger pilgrimage, but only a part. In either sense, the first tale told on the journey is, I think, meant to occasion some surprise. For Chaucer inaugurates what we might call the "literary" pilgrimage—the sequence of tales that will lead *us* toward Canterbury and its allegorical equivalent—with a chivalric romance, *The Knight's Tale*, set mainly in pagan Athens, long before the incarnation of Christ. In Chapter III, I study the sense of limitations that characterizes that long and otherwise elaborate poem in terms of the architectural settings within which its most decisive actions take place—for they are images of the kind I have described above, created with such care and under such imaginative pressure that in their terms are posed the deepest philosophical questions of the poem. The prison/garden and the tournament amphitheatre are made to embody those questions, and it is their density as images that reveals the inadequacy of the answers a pagan culture is able to return. In the respect and sympathy with which it imagines the pagan condition, *The Knight's Tale* emerges as a great humanist poem, but only as part of a pilgrimage sequence that judges it even in the act of making its values accessible

---

*See especially Howard, *Idea of the Canterbury Tales* and *Writers and Pilgrims*, on the literal pilgrimage, and Baldwin, *Unity of the Canterbury Tales*, on its allegorical transformation. In Chapter VI, I offer further evidence concerning the absence of day divisions.

and real. It does so through the affiliations of its largest and most sustained images, which Chaucer works in his most characteristic manner: they summon to mind truths intrinsic to their occurrence elsewhere in medieval tradition.

The Knight's Tale, we have reason to believe, was written before The Canterbury Tales was begun, without a pilgrim teller or a pilgrimage frame in mind. Together with the Troilus,[7] it testifies to Chaucer's early discovery that the images of tradition, images that address hierarchical truth,* could be adumbrated discreetly and without sententiousness just below the surfaces of a verisimilar fiction—that poetry could imagine action and declare meaning in one indivisible act. But when the Knight concludes and the pilgrim company has expressed its general approval, we are moved abruptly to The Miller's Tale (Chapter IV), which uses imagery in a wholly different way. Abandoning for a time the hierarchical use of imagery (along with the assumptions about human experience it expresses, chief among them the belief that a distinction between "higher" and "lower" is important), Chaucer creates what might be called instead a "field image" in something like its modern sense: a tapestry of bird, beast, and flower similes without discernible symbolic center. This in turn is made background to a fabliau seduction that appropriates the imagery of Noah's Flood in playful disregard of the hierarchical meanings, moral and eschatological, that lie potential within it. Though the tale presents us with an iconic action—a rehearsal of preparations for the Flood—the differences between the fabliau and the icon turn out to matter more than the similarities, and no lessons higher than social prudence are implied. Both the field image and the Flood parody are untouched by the generalizations about Chaucer's use of imagery that I frame in Chapters I and II of this study and first illustrate in my reading of The Knight's Tale. But that is precisely their point. In The Miller's Tale, Chaucer explores the reverse of his customary artistic procedures, and its imaginative daring and freedom can be most fully savored when set against those norms. The first two Canterbury tales establish the alpha and omega of an alphabet in which the other Canterbury tales will be written.

In The Reeve's Tale (Chapter V), Chaucer presents us with a different sort of innovation, no less boldly original, though it does not separate itself in so total a way from the claims of hierarchical truth. He becomes interested instead in what happens to the hieratic image when its claims are subordinated to those of the individual human

*By hierarchical truth, I mean in sum those truths that bore the greatest sort of authority in medieval culture: truths most often theological, moral, philosophical, or astrological, which were perceived as making claims higher and more dignified than (let us say) the truths of everyday experience as formulated in the proverbs of popular speech, or of experience not brought into contact with generalizations of any sort at all.

consciousness—when a prejudicial vision of experience is allowed to manipulate for its own purposes the imagery of Truth. Here we will discover imagery of Death-as-a-Tapster and The Horse Unbridled made integral to the fabliau performance, but Chaucer's final purpose is less the uncovering of those images within the Reeve's fiction than a discovery of the Reeve through the way he uses those images in his fiction. Again, Chaucer can be seen extending the boundaries of what is possible in medieval poetry: new subjects and modes are being charted, with the narrative image serving as a means of exploration.

A study of *The Cook's Tale* (Chapter VI) cannot, in the nature of things, really be about imagery at all. Since it is only a fragment— little more than a preface to an action never written—it does not work its way to the sort of narrative image that is our subject elsewhere. And so I use pictorial evidence in this chapter rather differently: to speculate on what *The Cook's Tale* might have added to the sequence before us and—on several grounds, including a new interpretation of *The Man of Law's Introduction*—to take issue with the common assumption that the Cook's fragment marks the end of Chaucer's opening design in *The Canterbury Tales*. In what follows, I seek to demonstrate that *The Man of Law's Tale* is its true conclusion.

The Man of Law's Tale (Chapter VII) is a product of Chaucer's full maturity, but it works in a mode almost archaic in comparison with what has gone before: a mode in which two closely related images from medieval tradition, the rudderless ship and the sea, are made to express a complex allegorical truth, multivalent and polysemous, whose dignity is not limited to poetry and which renders certain kinds of judgment, both implicit and explicit, on the narratives the pilgrims have heard so far. Drawn from chronicle rather than fiction and sustained by the formal grandeur of a high rhetorical style, *The Man of Law's Tale* demonstrates the power of the narrative image at its most elevated and austere. Its power to conclude a sequence—to "correct" and reorient a longer poem—grows in no small part out of its relationship to historical truth, uncompromised by the ambiguities of fiction; it unfolds other truths from within a text that itself lays claim to that status.

At the end of *The Man of Law's Tale*, tale order becomes uncertain, and with it any sense of Chaucer's exact design for the middle journey. But in the opening sequence Chaucer marks out the boundaries of an imaginative field within which the entire enterprise of *The Canterbury Tales* will take place. That enterprise is, among other things, a great experiment in poetry, and pilgrim tellers become artists within it—surrogate poets through whose voices and visions Chaucer explores the possibilities of narrative art.[8] The pattern of pilgrim performance and pilgrimage interaction becomes, in the technical sense of the word, a poetic: it demonstrates the several ways in which a poetry of fiction can relate to the poetry of truth. But I do not mean to imply that these tales are about art alone. The grand images of medieval iconographic tradition, like the particular fictions in which Chaucer discovers them, address human experience directly, and I have tried never to lose sight of that fact. These chapters are intended as formal critical readings of the poems, linked by their approach through imagery but not limited solely to that subject: images of this size and importance cannot finally be separated from the poems that incorporate them without falsifying both their nature and their function.

In my concluding chapter, I return to the theory of imagery put forward in Chapters I and II, to think about it anew in the light of these examples and to suggest for the first time the relationship between the pattern they make and the pattern of *The Canterbury Tales* as a whole. In this reading of the poem, the tales of the Knight, Miller, Reeve, and Cook stand to *The Man of Law's Introduction and Tale* as *The General Prologue* and all the tales that follow stand to *The Parson's Prologue and Tale* at the journey's end. Both sequences—the one contained within the other—move from innovation to retraction, from imaginative ambition to its negation, from exploration and risk taking to consolidation and retreat. The pattern is so profoundly Chaucerian, reflecting both the continuing strength of medieval culture and the birth of something new, that even in a study limited to the first of these sequences, the tales that begin the journey, we may hope to approach the work at something near its imaginative and ethical center.

Before that argument begins, however, I should perhaps offer, like R. S. Loomis in his *Mirror of Chaucer's World*, an "apologia, but without apologies" for the range of pictures presented in these pages. As he says in his introduction, "critics may justly observe that not all the sources are contemporary, that, in fact, a considerable number belong to the fifteenth century or later. . . . and to this extent users of the book may be misled." To this criticism I would offer (with him) several replies. "The legend accompanying every illustration indicates its precise or approximate date, and no one need be deceived. Most of the fifteenth-century illustrations, including the Ellesmere miniatures, were executed in the first decade when little change had taken place since Chaucer's death, and to exclude these miniatures and the *Troilus* frontispiece would be a *reductio ad absurdum* of the principle of contemporaneity." He goes on to remind us that, in art or life, "a king, clad in crown and breechcloth, does not look very different, whether portrayed in the twelfth or the fifteenth century; and Becket's shrine . . . was not subject to changes of fashion." He likewise defends occasional exceptions to the rule of contemporaneity "when the application to Chaucer's text is particularly apt." I have allowed myself such freedom as well, partly because much fourteenth-century material has been lost and we must use the next best thing, partly because I wish to interest my readers in the continuity of these traditions, as well as in their specific late-fourteenth-century manifestations. The "first audiences" I assume for Chaucer's art necessarily include those of the early fifteenth century, when the earliest manuscripts that survive to us—quite possibly the earliest manuscripts ever to collect his works together—were first written and "published" at large. In every instance, even when I have preferred a later illustration, or (more rarely) when no fourteenth-century illustration was known to me, I have taken pains to document the occurrence of the symbolic tradition in fourteenth-century texts known to Chaucer and his audiences. I make no claim that Chaucer looked upon any of these pictures, only that he would have understood them, and that he could have counted on some substantial part of his audience to share with him that skill.

I. Audience and Image

SOME MEDIEVAL HYPOTHESES

The FUNDAMENTAL premise of this book—the claim that literature can offer an experience that is in some sense "visual"—must seem problematic to anyone familiar with the investigations of modern philosophy and psychology. We have learned to approach such metaphors with skepticism and to recognize the great diversity of ways in which people imagine. But medieval writers described literature in visual terms without embarrassment or equivocation. Such a description contributed to their larger, theoretical understanding of the creative imagination, and seemed in turn to be confirmed by it. In about the year 1330, for instance, Guillaume de Deguileville announced his poem *The Pilgrimage of Human Life* as the account of a dream he had one night after "I hadde in wakinge rad and considered and wel seyn the faire romaunce of the Rose."[1] He claims to have visualized the earlier poem—to have "seen it well"—and his first two verbs, "reading" and "considering," move quite naturally to that third, in which they are subsumed. The interrelationship of these three activities in medieval accounts of literary response is intimate and profound, though it has had relatively little attention from modern scholars. It explains not merely the many statements from the earlier period that explicitly link those activities, but also the passages (even more numerous) that move from one verb to another in transpositions that seem almost unconsidered—possessing a logic so much taken for granted that no explanation is necessary. Again Guillaume can provide us with an example, for when (in the sentence following) he says that he will *tell* us his dream in turn—using the verb *nuncier*, "to speak" or "to pronounce"—his English prose translator has him promise instead a "showing" of the dream: "this swevene which I wole after shewe yow."[2] He offers the work in English as something addressed to the eye of the mind.

As a fourteenth-century illumination to Richard de Fournivall's *Li Bestiaires d'amours* will make clear (figure 1), it is unlikely that any-

1. A man reading (from the *Bestiaires d'amours*). Lorraine, second quarter of the fourteenth century. Note 3.

one in that age would have thought the Englishman guilty of a mistranslation. The picture shows us a man reading a book and simultaneously "seeing" in his mind's eye the knights in armor that he reads about. Richard's text straightforwardly explains the process: "When one hears a tale read, one perceives the wondrous deeds as if one were to see them taking place."[3] Descriptions of this kind indeed span the medieval centuries. St. Augustine, for instance, in a letter to Nebridius written before the end of the fourth century, offered a similar account of the experience of narrative, referring to "images of things we imagine to have been so or to be so, as when, for the sake of an argument, we build up a certain case not repugnant to truth, or when we picture a situation to ourselves while a narrative is being read, or while we hear or compose or conjecture some fabulous tale. When it pleases me or when it comes to my mind, I can picture to myself the appearance of Aeneas, or of Medea with winged serpents yoked to her chariot, or of Chremes or of some Parmeno."[4] Chaucer too, in *The Legend of Good Women*, speaks of the reader who "wol beholde / The storye of Tereus, of which I tolde" (2242), and in a later work has the Man of Law say of that collection as a whole (italics added):

> "Whoso that wole his large volume seke,   (II.60)
> Cleped the Seintes Legende of Cupide,
> *Ther may he seen* the large woundes wyde
> Of Lucresse, and of Babilan Tesbee;
> The swerd of Dido for the false Enee;
> The tree of Phillis for hire Demophon"

and so on, in a veritable table of contents for the poem.

About such activity men in the Middle Ages held theories a good deal more confident than our own, and failed to make many distinctions we would now think necessary.[5] But they called their best understanding science, as we do ours, and it found expression both in the technical language of the schoolmen and in the formulas of popular understanding. My purpose in these pages is not to frame a logical critique that will move from "medieval error" to some version of modern "truth," but to offer a historical description of the model by which medieval men explained such processes to themselves, and then to investigate the consequences of that model for medieval poetry. Since poets at work in a culture that believes propositions X, Y, and Z about images are likely to use words and create rhetorical structures in ways that at once reflect those assumptions and seek goals intrinsic to them, attention to the model must be paid. It was no trivial invention, but the product of great minds at work over many centuries. Coherent and interesting in its own right, it may claim our respect on one other ground as well, for great art was made in its terms.

The way in which the human mind perceives external reality (the physically proximate) is even today far from clear. And the way in which it conceives of things or events not present and proximate is more mysterious still. In the course of this chapter, we shall have occasion to explore the medieval understanding of this mystery and the functions attributed to mental images within it—images conceived as a means of knowing, of poetic making, and of Christian remembering. An investigation of these three functions will furnish the essential structure of this chapter. But let us begin with the medieval audience itself, because a heightened sense of its variety and range, its characteristic privileges and problems, is necessary if we are to estimate properly the importance of these ideas. Within such a context, we may hope to understand better some neglected aspects of late-medieval poetic, and to think in some new and historically appropriate ways about the narrative art of one of its masters, Geoffrey Chaucer.

In any account of Chaucer's sense of his audience, we must allow an important place for the solitary reader—like the man pictured in the illumination we have just examined (figure 1) or like Chaucer himself, whom the Eagle in *The House of Fame* rebukes for habitual bookishness, even after days spent over "rekenynges" at the customs office:

> Thou goost hom to thy hous anoon;   (*HF*, 655)
> And, also domb as any stoon,
> Thou sittest at another book
> Tyl fully daswed ys thy look.

Chaucer was a learned man who found in books the poetry he valued most, and he was demonstrably concerned about the lettered transmission of his own work. His worries at the end of the *Troilus* (V, 1793) about the instability of the English language give evidence of this ("ther is so gret diversite / In Englissh and in writyng of oure tonge"), as does the witty curse he lays upon his scribe Adam, should Adam continue to work so carelessly:

> Adam scriveyn, if ever it thee bifalle
> Boece or Troylus for to wryten newe,
> Under thy long lokkes thou most have the scalle,
> But after my makyng thou wryte more trewe;
> So ofte a-daye I mot thy werk renewe,
> It to correcte and eek to rubbe and scrape;
> And al is thorugh thy negligence and rape.[6]

These are not the concerns of a minstrel, much less those of an "oral singer" in the tradition defined by Parry and Lord—poets or rhymers for whom poetry was exclusively process, a series of performances responsive to changing circumstance and changing audience. These are concerns urgent only to a poet for whom a poem is a communication made once and for all, which finds its finished expression before being offered to an audience, and whose future integrity as a text must elicit his care. Chaucer was a writer, as most portraits of him implicitly remind us in showing a pen-case attached to his gown.[7] He thought poetry the key of remembrance, our most vivid and authentic record of the past, and he wanted us to *read* him, to open ourselves to the progress of his narratives in ways that are uniquely the privilege of readers, just as he himself had done with *The Romance of the Rose*, or with Ovid, Virgil, Dante, Alain de Lille, Guillaume de Deguileville.

But we cannot speak of readers only. The well-known miniature (figure 2) that shows Chaucer reciting to a courtly company in the grounds of a castle[8] reminds us that he had another audience simultaneously in mind. Here we see him concerned not with the transmission of his work to a predicated posterity, but with its publication to his own contemporaries: the poem as process, as literary event, in a social setting. How different a situation that could be, how much

2 (*opposite*). Chaucer reading to a courtly audience.
English, early fifteenth century. Note 8.

more intimate and immediate, these lines from the story of Ariadne, in *The Legend of Good Women*, make clear:

> This Theseus of hire hath leve take,   (2137)
> And every poynt was performed in dede,
> As ye han in this covenaunt herd me rede.

There are several other places in his writing where he addresses listeners exclusively, but more common by far are statements that imply a double sense of audience, those who will hear a living voice and those who will read. He would address them all.

Such a division of audience in the Middle Ages was not based purely, or even primarily, upon literacy. Chaucer's first audiences included, to be sure, the nobly born and socially privileged: his status as court poet, his annuities, the sophisticated response his art required, all lay within their gift.[9] But even among that early privileged group there would have been many who read with difficulty or not at all. Fewer women would have read than men, and few persons of either sex would have had significant access to manuscripts. The most splendid occasions on which Chaucer read his work to the court would, in all probability, have taken place in a great hall, with the nobility sitting upon the raised dais, others less grand filling the body of the hall, and (we may surmise) servants standing at the back, listening too. Hearing a tale in company was one of the great ceremonial pleasures of medieval society, and it was valued at all levels— by kings as well as commoners, by monks and lay, by "lernyd and lewyd." Even extremely technical knowledge was taught and transmitted in this way. Though it may surprise us to find Chaucer speaking of clerks "that han hir bookes herd" (*CT*, v.235), referring to works on optics by Aristotle, Alhazen, and Vitulon, we remark as well that his own *Treatise on the Astrolabe* addresses both listeners and readers: "Now wol I preie mekely every discret persone that redith or herith this litel tretys to have my rude endityng for excusid" (Prologue, 41–43).

The pleasures of hearing poetry in company, however, are special, and the changing verbs Chaucer uses to define his narrative mode at the beginning of the *Troilus* show how vividly he sensed a listening audience even in the act of writing (italics added):

> The double sorwe of Troilus *to tellen*,   (*TC*, I, 1)
> That was the kyng Priamus sone of Troye,
> In lovynge, how his aventures fellen
> Fro wo to wele, and after out of joie,
> My purpos is, *er that I parte fro ye.*
> Thesiphone, thow help me for t'endite
> Thise woful vers, that wepen *as I write.*

In the first five lines, the poet thinks of himself as speaking in an au-
dience's presence,[10] and in the two that follow, as writing a poem. At
the poem's end, he invokes its double future in similar terms: "And
red wherso thow be, or elles songe" (V, 1797). Both instances enforce
a single recognition: Chaucer's is a lettered art shaped by, and con-
tinually responsive to, an oral-audial environment.[11] Even those royal
or noble patrons whose favor was most important to him as a profes-
sional poet could be found now listening to his work in company,
now reading alone.

Two miniatures showing a bishop preaching in the open air, painted
ca. 1419, can make more vivid our sense of the medieval audience
(figures 3, 4). The bishop's listeners, one notices, are for the most
part attentive, though some few are shown concerned with other af-
fairs: in one picture, an old man has fallen asleep; in the other, some-
one reads a book, apparently in preference to the sermon, and a young
man with his hat pulled over his eyes is odd indeed.[12] As images, they
are witty, candid, and urbane, worthy to stand comparison with the
painting of Chaucer and his audience already examined (figure 2).
There, too, one noticed a diversity of listening styles, some persons
lost in thought, some focusing on Chaucer, some looking at each
other. Behind this group, other courtly activities establish the larger
social context of such events, being at once ceremonial, like the
obeisance to a queen and nobleman shown in the middle distance,
and leisured, like the descent of the brightly costumed figures mov-
ing down a path in the top left corner of the landscape. These three
miniatures taken together bear witness to the overwhelming domi-
nance of the aural, the communal, and—not to oversimplify—the
various in the literary experience of the age.

That such facts are important in late-medieval poetic, and to Chau-
cer's poetry, is self-evident: medieval culture conceived of a poem
as a communication between poet and audience that is meant to do
work; its ends are not in itself. Although modern critics may some-
times without penalty write as though there were no immediate au-
dience for these poems, no medieval poet could afford to do so. The
problems inherent in creating narrative art addressed to an audience
of this dual kind remain in many ways—perhaps even the most im-
portant ways—obscure to us. In this chapter I will focus upon just
one of the many questions that arise: what role does narrative imag-
ery play in such a communication? To what deliberate ends might
a medieval narrative poet invite his audience to make images in their
minds?

Let us begin by noting some formal differences in the way listen-
ing and reading audiences experience poems. Listeners, in exchange
for special kinds of pleasure and assistance, submit to a process strictly

3, 4. A bishop preaching to a congregation. Burgundy, ca. 1419. Note 12.

controlled by a reader/reciter who, on behalf of the poet, exercises a maximum power over their experience of the whole. Emphasis, attack, variety of pace and tempo, volume and musical accent, all lie exclusively within his power. He can use his voice to create character, to point meaning, and to suggest, or even enact, appropriate emotional response. He benefits from his professional identity—they become an audience, rather than a random assembly of private persons, because they wish to hear him—and from that occasion's semiritual nature, for it imposes upon them all a certain kind of role, a certain kind of good manners. Chances are, for instance, no one will interrupt, or leave before the end, for one may not (without boorishness) allow purely private difficulties, whether of attentiveness or understanding or memory, to intrude upon the public experience of the work. (We know these manners best from the theatre or concert hall.) Members of such an audience take part in an event, a happening, and one price they pay is the forfeiture of certain freedoms. Once the poet or reciter begins, they are his until he finishes. For them the work *is* the performance.

A reader, on the other hand, has access to the book as a physical object, in which all the words of a poem coexist at any given moment. Even though the words of any sentence must be read in sequence if they are to yield sense, and though knowledge of the narrative in its full sequence remains a major goal of his endeavor, nevertheless a book allows him the freedom that objects allow their admirers. There is no external control over occasion, pace, or emotional response. The poem may be picked up or put down at any time, at any point in the story. It may be read slowly or quickly, one time or many times, from beginning to end or in any other sequence that seems attractive: "turne over the leef and chese another tale." The reader may pause to meditate upon some single line or event, or he may move about in the text at will, paging ahead to learn a story's outcome, passing over something that fails to hold his interest, or turning back to recover details of story or language he failed to understand or remember the first time. Problems of attentiveness, memory, and comprehension attend readers as well as listeners, but a reader has certain options a listener does not: he himself controls the way he receives the poet's poem. A reader can know *all* the words, in their exact sequence and in their most objective and neutral identity—ink on vellum, ciphers on a page—whereas a listener's knowledge is of a performance, in which his sense of what the poem is about is intimately linked with a vivid sense of voice and place and other persons. Lapses in a listener's attention are more or less irremediable, for although his mind will catch, rest, or wander every now and then, the performing voice moves on.

Listeners and readers, then, each have proper to themselves certain kinds of pleasure and privilege. We must not minimize the differences between these two groups, nor underestimate the difficulties that confront a poet who would address his art to both of them. And yet such differences are not absolute. When the poet/reciter's voice ceases, or the manuscript is put away, listener and reader alike possess only memories, through which alone the poem and the meanings intrinsic to the poem can be reconstructed.

One does not often find any very lively sense of this latter situation in the pages of modern critical writing on Chaucer—or on any other medieval poet, for that matter. In recent decades we have perhaps learned most from critics interested in a "close reading" of Chaucer's narratives—critics who have mastered the poem in its full verbal and structural detail, through many intensive readings over a long period of time. Such attention is by no means improper: every word that we read and reread in this manner is part of the poem we are offered. But such an experience is available to readers fairly exclusively. If approaches to such meaning were available to medieval listeners, or to medieval readers away from their books, they have been little charted by modern critics. The bridges a medieval poet might have constructed between the two sorts of poetic experience have in recent times been little used.

And so I wish to examine the role of narrative imagery—the images we form in our minds as we attend to the progress of a story—as a major link between the activities of a solitary reader, like Guillaume de Deguileville reading *The Romance of the Rose*, and those of a listening audience, like that assembled before Chaucer in a palace garden. I shall seek to define a kind of imagery, at once "mental" and "memorial," that provides for their common need to possess that experience richly and significantly after the book is closed or the story telling ends. The presence of such images must be noted, their function assessed, and their consequence within any specific tale understood if we would receive a poet's art at its fullest. Though a listening audience may have constituted the most urgent original necessity for the elaboration of such images, they are in the reader's poem as well,[13] and in memory were understood to serve him in equally important ways. As we shall see in the chapters that follow, in the hands of a great master such images could be made to transcend their own pragmatic necessity; they became instrumental to some of the deepest and most searching purposes of Chaucer's art.

The question of how and what an audience remembers is crucial, if one would inquire further into this matter. We may begin with matters of verbal memory, by noting that a particularly striking line of verse may fasten itself in the mind, available for instant recovery. Not everyone remembers in this way, and even those who do will not necessarily recall the same line or lines. But the aptitude is not uncommon, and such memories have their own kind of defining power. Often they are verbal epitomes, possessing a special conciseness or centrality that anchors them in the memory, calling upon that faculty we all share, however faintly, with the medieval minstrel or the modern actor—the skill of learning something "by heart." Some lines from such a minstrel have come down to us, in which he claims to know with that maximum skill *all* the chansons de geste: "De totes les chançons de geste . . . / Sai ge par cuer dire et conter."[14] But that was the boast of a professional. Most persons, then as now, are unable to manage long poems or even many lines *par cuer*, least of all upon a single hearing.

Two other kinds of remembering are more important by far. The first allows us to recall, with varying degrees of skill and accuracy, a story we have read or heard, taking as our goal the recreation of that story in sequence, as process. It was particularly valued in an age when social pleasure (as on the Canterbury pilgrimage) often centered on an amateur telling of tales. In the words of the Pardoner, "lewed peple loven tales olde; / Swiche thynges kan they wel reporte and holde" (VI.437). But no medieval storyteller who thought of himself as an artist would have been content to have his tale remembered in only that way. An itinerant tavern minstrel maybe, but not a professional like the Pardoner, and certainly not his creator—a poet who earlier sent forth his *Troilus* with instructions on how it was to behave if it should meet with "Virgile, Ovide, Omer, Lucan, and Stace" (*TC*, V, 1792). Chaucer thought of himself as a "makere," not an amateur teller of tales, and his work is finished, integral, self-reflexive, self-aware.

Chaucerian narrative, as a result, offers something more complex than story per se, and carries an implicit invitation to its audience to go beyond memories of the narrative action, asking them to seek a sense of the whole that is discursive in mode yet responsive to the narrative's full artistic complexity. Chaucer asks us to think about the narrative, to draw wisdom from it, to find "fruyt" within the "chaf" of fable. In Chapter II, I shall define carefully the terms in which I think Chaucer invites his audience to that activity. Here let me suggest merely that such an artist would have wished his audience to discover in his fiction, and to hold in their memories, a construct of ideas and feelings more complex than the terse truths of fabliau proverb, more subtle than notions of cupidity and charity stated at their most general, and more central than even an accurate précis of the action itself.

It is in this regard that another kind of memory becomes of commanding importance to the enterprise of medieval narrative. For if, in respect to a medieval narrative poem, we put to ourselves the question "What is remembered?" and limit our answer to what comes to mind immediately and intact, requiring no linear reconstruction of the narrative itself, the answer most often concerns things seen with the eye of the mind, things the narrative has caused us to imagine with particular force as we attended to the verbal process, which are instantly accessible *as images* to the memory. Francis Beaumont, father to the dramatist, wrote of Chaucer: "One gifte hee hath aboue other Authours, and that is, by the excellencie of his descriptions to possesse his Readers with a stronger imagination of seeing that done before their eyes, which they reade, than any other that euer writ in any tongue."[15] It is a testimony many have echoed, before and since. The author of a courtesy book printed by William Caxton praised Chaucer for the same power: "His langage was so fayr and pertynente / It semeth vnto mannys heerynge / Not only the worde / but verely the thynge."[16] *Verba et res*: word becoming thing, in an act of visual imagining. In the Middle Ages, poetic narrative—which even an early printed book, we might note, assumed to be addressed to "man's hearing"—sought a response from the inner eye: it became, at some mysterious juncture in its progress, "visual."

Already it must be clear, even from these brief and to some degree speculative remarks about audience, that an inquiry into medieval conceptions of the imagination—the faculty that can form an image independent of immediate visual stimulus—and into medieval ideas concerning the nature and status of such images may provide useful insight into medieval narrative art. I wish now to bring together evidence from several different areas of medieval thought, all of which converges upon one central fact: the dignity and importance of the *mental image* for any discussion of literary affect, and thus of probable artistic intention, in poems of the late medieval period. The progress of my argument for a time must become something other than linear: we shall have to make several independent journeys from the circumference to the center, reaching each time a similar conclusion, but in a sequence that I trust will become steadily richer and more comprehensive. The images that will be our subject are located "in the head" rather than in paint or wood or stone, and they are created by the mind's inner eye, shown in figure 5 imagining five different scenes—the Tower of Babel, Tobias and the angel, an obelisk, a ship in a storm, and the Last Judgment—as part of a memory system. In Latin this faculty was most often called the *oculus imaginationis* or *acies animi*. Chaucer employed an English plural, "thilke eyen of [the] mynde." [17]

If we would understand how, in medieval thought, "the vertu ymaginatif schapith and ymagineth," we may best begin by putting some questions to medieval faculty psychology, for we must know first of all how the imaginative faculty—that "vertu" or power— was understood to relate to the other distinctive capacities of man. Boethius's *Consolation of Philosophy* furnished one authoritative answer, the more important for us because Chaucer translated that work into prose, and used its ideas pervasively in his poetic fictions.

Boethius comes to the matter in attempting to explain how man's free will and God's foreknowledge can coexist, since either term would seem to rule out the possibility of the other. The solution to the problem, Boethius tells us, lies in making proper distinctions between ways of knowing. We can know by our "wits" (the five outer senses), which tell us about phenomena in their material form: we can see a loaf of bread, touch it, taste it, smell it, hear it fall to the floor. By virtue of our "ymaginacioun," the faculty most central to these pages, we can call to mind the image of a loaf of bread we have eaten in the past or, by combining diverse such memories, invent an image of a loaf we have never known—a loaf, let us say, of gold, or a loaf larger than a castle. This kind of knowing retains the form or figure of a thing, but divorces it from matter, and in that important sense is a higher faculty than the five "wits": it comes nearer to being

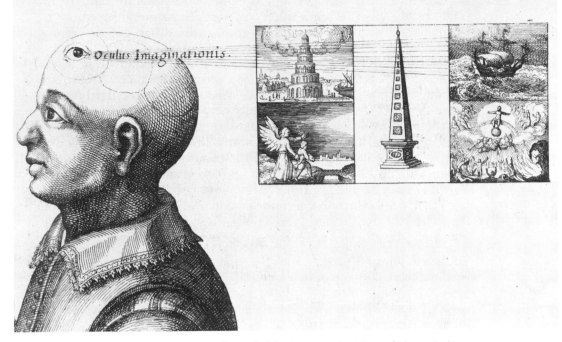

5. The eye of the imagination. Robert Fludd, *Ars memoriae* (Oppenheim, 1619). Note 17.

free of the phenomenal world. The faculty of "resoun" is higher still, for it is capable of relating the image, divorced from matter, to all other associated images, conceiving the universal class of which it is a species. The workings of reason are ultimately free not only of matter, but of images as well, and its power is unique to man among earthly creatures. The fourth way of knowing is possessed only by divine Providence, whose unique faculty—called "intelligence"— knows a thing not only as it exists within the world of matter, and as image, and as universal class, but as that thing exists in perpetuity within the divine thought—the "symple forme" (close kin to the forms postulated by Plato) that exists in advance of, and will endure beyond, the material creation and the categories that man's reason is able to discover there.[18]

In this hierarchy of faculties, each power comprehends all that is proper to the power(s) below it, but the lower has no access to anything higher. In the language of Chaucer's translation, a man is a thing "sensible" and "ymaginable" and "resonable." This is to say he shares with animals that do not move (like oysters and mussels) a knowledge derived from the senses. With animals capable of movement ("remuable bestis"), he shares the power to transform sense experience into mental images, and to remember by their means, for all such creatures, on seeing a thing, are inclined to seek it or shun it. But he is decisively separated from these other orders by his rationality: "Resoun is al oonly to the lynage of mankynde, ryght as intelligence is oonly the devyne nature" (V, pr. 5). Of these four faculties—*sensus, imaginatio, ratio, intelligentia*—the first three are proper to man's nature. Memory (*memoria*)—a subject no less crucial to our present inquiry—was understood to receive their product in sum.

Medieval faculty psychology explained our ability to remember in terms of a cellular model of the human brain that varied to some degree across the centuries, and from writer to writer. But even the variant models have a good deal in common, and that described by Bartholomaeus Anglicus in his great encyclopedia, *De proprietatibus rerum*, written before 1250 and translated into English near the end of the fourteenth century by John Trevisa, is not only important in its own right, but for our purpose sufficiently representative:

The innere witte is departid aþre by þre regiouns of þe brayn, for in þe brayn beþ þre smale celles. Þe formest hatte *ymaginatiua*, þerin þingis þat þe vttir witte apprehendiþ withoute beþ i-ordeyned and iput togedres withinne. . . . Þe middil chambre hatte *logica* þerin þe vertu estimatiue is maister. Þe þridde and þe laste is *memoratiua*, þe vertu of mynde.[19]

When the inner senses are so described, *ymaginativa* includes both the power to recall the forms of sense experience as images, separate from their material identities, and the power to combine such forms into forms of things never experienced. In Augustine's famous example, he can picture in his mind Carthage, which he knew, but also, in some approximate way, Alexandria, which he had never seen. This creative aspect of the imagination was often called *phantasia*, from Plato onwards. Medieval attitudes toward it are sometimes ambiguous: it was understood to be a higher power, but it could also mislead, presenting the unreal as though it were real.[20]

The second cell of the brain, in the Bartholomaeus version quoted above, houses *logica*, the estimative power, which in other models is sometimes called the particular reason, sometimes the cognitive power, sometimes opinion. Its various functions include judging the forms (testing their reliability and correctness as images) and discovering their "intentions" (estimating their tendency to help or harm). Of this I shall have much to say later; for now, this explanation by Murray Bundy will suffice:

The faculty of opinions (*aestimativa*) . . . from the forms retained in the imagination seeks out the "intentions" (*intentiones*) which were never in the original impressions, but are not separate from them. It is this power which enables one to decide whether a given individual is desirable or not, friend or enemy. Through this same faculty working with images the sheep recognizes its own offspring, flees from the wolf, and follows the dog as its guard. Opinion, in this version of the Aristotelian distinction, goes beyond imagination, for the latter begets no emotional experience. Imagination results in neither joy nor sadness, but opinion does. Imagination acts merely as a mirror for sensory images; opinion, working with these, determines upon courses of action, what to choose, and what to avoid. It is opinion, not imagination, which impels to action. It is to the brute what intellect is to man.[21]

This cell presents its findings to a third, *memorativa*, which stores the images, forms, and intentions,[22] and presents them upon demand—we have been speaking of the so-called Animal or Sensible Soul—to the Intellectual Soul, a still higher aspect of man's nature, also understood in terms of a tripartite model, comprising reason (proper), intellect or understanding, and the will.

This three-cell tradition goes back at least as far as Galen, in the second century A.D., and it has a number of variants. The most complex divides the cells into two parts each, locating the *sensus communis* (the meeting place of the five outer senses) and *imaginativa* in the first, *phantasia* and *aestimativa* in the second, with the third sometimes put in charge of motion or impulse (*motiva*) as well as *memoria*. The earliest-known Western illustration of brain function, from the eleventh century, shows the brain divided simply into *fantasia*, *intellectus*, and *memoria*, but I choose to reproduce instead (figure 6) a drawing made in about 1400 of a "disease man" (with the names of diseases inscribed around his head), which divides the head into four compartments. The *sensus communis* is shown foremost, and then the three cells, labeled *cellula imaginativa*, *cella aestimativa rationis*, and *cella memorativa* in that order. Figure 7, a woodcut from an anatomy book published in Italy in 1503, illustrates the continuity of the medieval tradition in its fullest form: the *sensus communis* and *ymaginativa* share the first cell, *fantasia* and *extimativa* the second, and *memoria* and *motiva* the third.[23]

Technical and difficult though even so abbreviated a discussion must be, what matters to our larger investigation is relatively simple: the importance of mental images in human understanding, and the role that memory plays in making them (and their intrinsic consequence) accessible to reason and thence to the will.

That Chaucer knew the three-cell doctrine of the brain can be readily demonstrated. St. Cecilia, in *The Second Nun's Tale*, wishing to instruct the pagan Tiberius in the mystery of the Trinity, uses an example of three-in-one that he already understands:

> Right as a man hath sapiences three,   (VIII. 338)
> Memorie, engyn, and intellect also,
> So in o beynge of divinitee,
> Thre persones may ther right wel bee.

Memory, imagination, and reason are here named out of their usual order, but in witness to their currency as a concept, and in assertion of their ultimate inseparability. Like the Trinity, their threefold nature is mysteriously one.[24]

We have been examining the role of imagery in the processes of understanding—images as a means of knowing—within a learned, scientific tradition. But there were other traditions—more broadly based, more widely accessible, some taking as their province very different sorts of knowledge—that also attributed this functional importance to the image. To these we may now turn and, by way of transition, note that both the learned and the popular traditions tend to value sight above the other senses. It becomes the paradigm, even though the word "image," in medieval writings on psychology, must be construed to mean what can be recollected of any sense experience: our ability to remember sound, smell, taste, and touch as well.[25]

The records go back as far as Plato (*Timaeus*, 45b–47), who held sight and hearing to be the most important senses, with sight preeminent—an idea whose first premise survives into the pages of Gower's *Confessio amantis* in the form of a Latin epigram, "Visus et auditus fragilis sunt ostia mentis," sight and hearing are the doors of

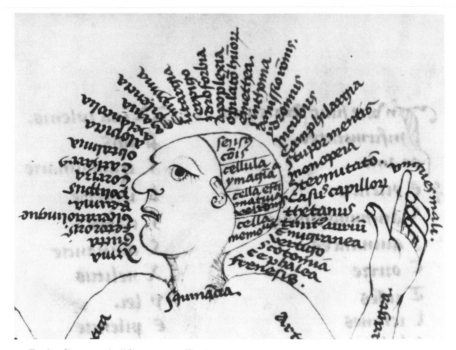

6. Brain diagram (a "disease man"). Paris, ca. 1400. Note 23.

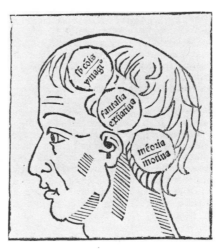

7. Three-cell diagram of the brain. Triumphus Augustinus de Anchona, *Opusculum perutile de cognitione animae . . .* , rev. Achillini (Bologna, 1503). Note 23.

the frail mind.[26] An elegant miniature from the beginning of the fourteenth century (figure 8), illustrating the opening of Richard de Fournivall's *Li Bestiaires d'amours*, turns that metaphor into a picture: it shows Lady Memory, holding a green branch and standing before a castle with two golden doors. One door bears the image of an ear, the other that of an eye, illustrating a discussion of the precise role played by each in bringing within Memory's castle, equated with knowledge, any man who would enter there. The text tells us that all men desire knowledge ("toutes gens desirent par nature a savoir"), but because knowledge is cumulative—in significant part an inheritance from those who have lived before—some means of access to the prior experience of others is necessary.

And therefore God, who so loves man that he wishes to provide him with all that he needs, has given to man a power and force of the soul that is called memory. This memory has two doors, sight and hearing, and to each of these doors there is a path by which one can reach them; these paths are painting and speech. Painting serves for the eye, speech for the ear. And the manner in which one may make one's way to the house of memory, both by painting and by speech, is thus made clear: the memory, guardian of the treasure won by man's senses through the excellence of the imagination, makes what is past seem as if it were present. And to this same end, one can come either by painting or by speech. For when one sees a story painted, whether a story of Troy or of some other thing, one sees the deeds of the brave men who were there in past times as if they were present. And so it is with speech. For when one hears a tale read, one perceives the wondrous deeds as if one were to see them taking place. And since what is past is made present by those two means, that is by painting and by speech, therefore it is clear that by these two things one can come to remembrance.[27]

8. Lady Memory and the doors of sight and hearing. French, early fourteenth century. Note 27.

Whether Richard is speaking of paintings or words, his preferred verb is "to see"—*on voit, on veïst*. The fact that the two sources of such images are very different is not for him of the first consequence. They share the same epistemological status as mental images once they enter the memory.[28] And seeing readily becomes a metaphor for higher kinds of knowing as well.

Christianity's particular emphasis on vision is, of course, rooted in those moments in Old Testament history when God showed himself to man, directly or in figure, as when Moses saw God in the burning bush or on Mount Sinai at the Giving of the Laws (Exodus 3:2, 19:20–21). To these the new religion added history specifically its own, as when the Angel of the Annunciation appeared to the Virgin Mary in bodily form, or in the fact that the priest Simeon was allowed to live until he had seen his Savior.[29] Christian eschatology, moreover, promised a seeing of God as one of the joys of heaven. St. Paul's vision of the happiness to come, "For now we see through a glass, darkly, but then face to face" (I Cor. 13:12), is echoed in this response from the Office of the Dead: "And in my flesh I shall see God, my Savior. It will not be some other being, but I myself who see Him: my own eyes shall look upon Him."[30] Chaucer himself, in the penultimate sentence of *The Parson's Tale*, describes heaven as a place where "every soule [is] replenyssed with the sighte of the parfit knowynge of God" (x.1079). Though his version is less literal—here sight is a way of talking about perfect knowing—the tradition is firm in both its modes.

But the Neoplatonic inheritance of Christianity, especially the conviction that sight is more spiritual than the other senses, is more to our present point—a survey of ideas concerning the nature and status of mental images in the Middle Ages. St. Thomas Aquinas, for example, praised sight above the rest because it alone neither alters the thing perceived nor is altered by it. Its operation is uncompromised by matter.[31] That fact in turn points to a more general truth, already noted in our discussion of medieval faculty psychology. Just as mental images were held to be superior to immediate visual images, so the constructive power of the imagination was understood to be superior to its reproductive power: the constructive power is able to transcend not only sense experience but also the particular mental images by which it enters the memory. Hugh of St. Victor speaks of this second kind of knowing in a dialogue, *De vanitate mundi*, in which Reason says to the Soul (whom it is setting out to teach through a number of grand meditational images):

So when you hear yourself invited to "see," it is not the sight of this eye [of the flesh] that I would have you think about. You have another eye within, much clearer than that one, an eye that looks at the past, the present, and the future all at once, which sheds the light and keenness of its vision over all things, which penetrates things hidden and searches into complexities, needing no other light by which to see all this, but seeing by the light that it possesses of itself.[32]

Hugh wrote as a mystic, a calling to which relatively few may aspire and which ultimately involves the negation of all images. I include him here, and will briefly discuss that graver discipline, because the writings of the mystics throughout the Middle Ages often discuss with exceptional clarity and beauty of expression the place of imagery in the ordinary Christian life. The guidebooks to mysticism were seldom written to be read by mystics only, but are part of a quest, recurrent in the period, for a new and deeper spirituality, less dependent on institutions, more direct in its knowing of God. In the nature of their subject, the advice they give is often most full and most confident about the preliminary stages of the mystic's way, stages that might be explored by Christians of any calling. In Hugh's version, "thinking, meditating, and contemplating are the rational soul's *three ways of seeing*" (italics added). Contemplation indeed leaves behind all objects of sense, all images derived from sense, and all processes of intellectual reason: "Contemplation is the piercing and spontaneous intuition of the soul, which embraces every aspect of the objects of understanding." Its goal is an inexpressible union with the Godhead. But the two earlier stages of the way are humbler by far, and exemplary to the ordinary Christian life. To both of those stages, the role of images is central. Hugh defines them so: "Thinking occurs when the mind becomes aware of things passing through it, when the image of some real thing, entering through the senses or rising up out of the memory, is suddenly presented to it," whereas "meditation is the concentrated and judicious reconsideration of thought, that tries to unravel something complicated or scrutinizes something obscure to get at the truth of it."[33] The literary images presented by Reason to the Soul in the dialogue just quoted are of the second kind, as is a magnificent series of meditations upon the image of Noah's Ark (from another work by Hugh) that later in this book will help us understand better the art and meaning of *The Man of Law's Tale*.

In this accommodation of a basically Aristotelian, empirical psychology to a mystical doctrine of illumination and transcendence, Hugh is typical of the Victorine school and many other mystical writers besides. One might say that theories of empirical knowledge interested the mystics chiefly as a way of defining its opposite: contemplation of the highest kind, in which all images fall away.[34] Yet such writers remained aware that meditation upon images was spiritually necessary to the mystic as a preparation for the higher ascent, as well as to those whose earthly journey would never seek that ultimate end: one climbed the ladder of perfection to whatever rung one's capacities and God's will allowed. The *scala perfectionis* was footed in ordinary Christian earth, and images as a means of knowing remained important to it. In the fourteenth century, the greatest period in the history of English mysticism, the lower rungs of that ladder had a great deal in common with other traditions that never named so high an end, the traditions of Franciscan meditation and popular devotional practice.

9. *Imago pietatis*, illustrating "O man unkynde." English, first half of the fifteenth century. Note 36.

To these traditions Rosemary Woolf's study *The English Religious Lyric in the Middle Ages* offers a deeply learned guide,[35] and a manuscript from the British Library (MS. Add. 37049), which links lyric poems and cursive drawings, can represent them in their most popular and influential form. The poem included in figure 9, an address to the sinner/reader spoken by Christ, begins "O man unkynde / hafe in mynde / my paynes smert / Beholde & see / þat is for þe / percyd my hert," to which the drawing alongside offers a double image, of speaker and thing spoken about. The banderole near Christ's head reads "þies woundes smert bere in þi hert" (etc.), and the cult image of the heart is inscribed "þis is þe mesure of þe wounde þat our jhesu crist sufferd for oure redempcion."[36] The bottom half of the page versifies man's proper response and illustrates his proper devotional posture in the face of all that lies above. As Christ asks him to "behold & see," he replies "O lord right dere / þi wordes I here," in a transposition as natural as the doubling of the Gates to Understanding in the *Bestiaires d'amours* illumination (figure 8). Words become pictures, pictures give birth to words. In the Middle Ages to be audience to an "image" (whether verbal or visual) implied activity, not passivity. It called one to thought, to feeling, to meditation. Indeed, numerous lyrics of this kind survive in manuscripts without illustrations: of the five manuscripts containing this very poem, three provide it with a drawing, two do not.[37] But all ask their audiences to "look" and to "see," confident that the words of the poem, along with the audiences' prior experience of similar images in other places, will lead them to a fully imagined devotional response.[38] The relation of such meditation to mysticism is limited but precise: in the words of Walter Hilton, one of the great mystical writers of the age, "A man schal nouȝt comen to gostli delit in *contemplacion* of [Cristes] godhede but he come in *ymaginacioun* bi bitternes and [be] compassion . . . of His manhede" (italics added).[39] The mystical experience (contemplation) might be likened to the ascent of a great mountain which, after rising slowly across many miles, suddenly soars to a peak so steep and sheer that few will ever climb it, but which can be reached only by traveling its entire length. We may imagine that Chaucer and his audiences lived, so to speak, mainly in the lower ranges, the mountain valleys; but all of these ideas were part of the cultural environment they shared. These ideas conferred upon the meditated image yet another kind of dignity and status, and they established certain habits of literary response that even a secular author might exploit to his art's advantage.

One other tradition of seeing as a way of knowing, the dream vision, must also concern us, though I shall do little more than mention it here. Its relevance to literary criticism is more apparent, and its central documents better known. Medieval dream theory, in the categories of Macrobius (cited by Chaucer in his own fictions), distinguished five sorts of dreams. Two of them are said to be empty and meaningless: the *insomnium* arises from derangements of the body or oppressions of the waking mind, and the *phantasma* or *visum* from the confused reverie that precedes sleep. But three sorts of dreams tell truth and may be trusted, of which only one—the *oraculum*, in which a relative or some sacred person appears to foretell a future event—centers upon words. The other two, the *visio* and the *somnium*, are largely visual, the *visio* showing things in the form in which they will come to pass, and the *somnium* showing the future in ambiguous ways, through signs that must be interpreted correctly.[40] In Chaucer's English, true dreams warn us of "aventures" (things about to happen) "be avisions, or be figures" (*HF*, 47). Going beyond medieval faculty psychology, this theory of cognition postulates an intelligence external to the dreamer that causes his dream,[41] but again the material is predominantly visual, something "seen" in sleep. The dream vision as a literary genre, which begins effectively with Cicero's *Dream of Scipio*,[42] became for the Middle Ages the most convenient of all pretexts for an allegorical fiction—for a narrative that could claim to be "true" without requiring credence as a literal history. In that genre Chaucer's waking imagination first fully expressed itself; we owe to it *The Book of the Duchess*, *The Parliament of Fowls*, *The House of Fame*.

This brief account of some of the ways in which mental images were honored in medieval thought as a means of knowing—of coming to knowledge—has hardly more than surveyed the outer boundaries of that subject. But such a survey is sufficient to suggest that literary images, being mental images, share some part of this functional importance. For literary images likewise reflect a reality not limited to the present and the material; they too present the suprasensual in the form of a figure to be contemplated with the inner eye. A passage from Deguileville's *Pilgrimage of Human Life* can make that point with maximum concision. Before the pilgrim sets out upon his journey, Grace Dieu, his instructress and guide, promises to give him the necessary bread and scrip and staff, but she says she must do one other thing first—she must put eyes in his ears! In Lydgate's translation:

> Thyn Erys muste haue Eyen clere
> Taparceyve, in this matere,
> And to conceyven euery thyng.[43]

There is no other way he will be able to *see* the scrip and staff she gives him, which turn out to be Faith and Hope respectively. (In the manuscript illuminations, they are shown, of course, in perfectly lit-

eral ways.) To understand only the visible is to see with an inferior
eye: the inner sight, the meditated vision, sees deeper, and its object
is truth.

Not only were medieval readers and listeners asked to respond to
literature in this way—to "see" what they heard described—but the
act of literary composition itself was often represented as an act of
visual imagining: the author at his desk sees the subject of his work,
often a personified idea, standing before him. In manuscripts of the
collected works of Guillaume de Machaut, whose poetry Chaucer
knew and borrowed from, the Prologue is sometimes adorned with
pictures that show Machaut being introduced by Dame Nature to her
children, *Sens*, *Rhétorique*, and *Musique*, and by the God of Love to
his children, *Douce Penser*, *Plaisance*, and *Esperance*. Figure 10, from a
manuscript made in about 1370,[44] illustrates the passage in which the
God of Love explains that his purpose in presenting these three is to
furnish the poet material for his verse ("pour toy donner matere"):

> Or pues tu ci prendre grande sustance
> Dont tu porras figurer et retraire
> Moult de biaus dis. . . .[45]

They are to furnish the substance, the great matter, from which Guil-
laume may draw forth (*retraire*) and make the images of (*figurer*)
many lovely poems. Those poems follow. In the miniature he is
shown seeing the children of Love as naturally and as clearly as he
might see the boy or the horse or the rabbits in the field beyond,
though those children stand for Sweet Thought, Pleasure, and Hope
respectively. We see illustrated an idea about how poems are made. In
another manuscript of his poems, made ca. 1360, he is shown sitting
within a walled park, simultaneously writing on a scroll and gazing
into space in a contemplative way (figure 11): what he sees in his
mind's eye is painted in the compartment below, a vision of Fortune
and her wheel that he is making into a complaint-poem ("comment
lamant fait une complainte de fortune et de sa roe"), part of his *Re-
mede de Fortune*.[46]

Boccaccio, too, in the *De casibus virorum illustrium*, describes his
material as presenting itself to him in the form of visual imaginings,
and, as a result, deluxe manuscripts of that work depict in perfectly
literal ways his meeting with Lady Fortune (for instance) at the be-
ginning of Book VI: "I was taking up my pen again . . . when sud-
denly there appeared that horrible monster, administrator of all mor-
tal affairs, Fortune. Oh God, how tall she was, what an extraordinary
appearance!" In figure 12, her several hands indicate that she raises
up and casts down many men. The man gazing out the window is
the illuminator's own invention, perhaps intended merely to increase

10. The God of Love presents his children to Guillaume de Machaut. French, ca. 1370. Note 44.

Comment lamant fait une complainte defortune. et de sa ra

11. Guillaume de Machaut writes a poem about Lady Fortune and her wheel. French, ca. 1360. Note 46.

12. Boccaccio writes about
Lady Fortune. Bruges,
ca. 1475. Note 47.

13. Boccaccio writes about
Adam and Eve. French,
late fourteenth century.
Note 48.

14. A Christian and a Jew discuss their faiths. French, ca. 1440. Note 49.

15. St. John writes the book of Apocalypse. French, early fifteenth century. Note 50.

the verisimilitude of the scene, perhaps meant to represent someone heedless of Fortune and thus potentially her victim. In any case, the idea of Fortune has become quite as "real," quite as literally seeable as he. Elsewhere in the same manuscripts, Boccaccio is shown sharing his study with a throng of the historically great who fell from Fortune's favor in the past and now press to have their stories told.[47] The first and greatest of those who fell, Adam and Eve, are also part of his material, and in figure 13 he is shown outside Paradise garden sitting at his book and contemplating our first parents, who approach, aged and grieving, to enter yet again a work of literature.[48] A more informal notion of "literary making" is illustrated in his *Decameron*, where the second story of the First Day concerns a Christian and a Jew discussing their respective religious faiths. In figure 14, from a manuscript made ca. 1440, Christ and Moses are depicted above the

16. Dante and the landscape of his book. Italian, 1465. Note 51.

two men, though they bear no relation to the picture's verisimilar space. They are mental images, at once the sources for and the projections of that discourse, ideas being exchanged. A companion picture shows the Jew being baptized, for after a visit to Rome to view the Pope and the papal clergy, he decides that any religion that can flourish in spite of such corruption and degeneracy must have God on its side.[49]

Further illustrations of the idea that imagery can serve as a means of literary making attach themselves to the figure of St. John on the Isle of Patmos, writing the *Apocalypse* and seeing again in full waking "vision" the things he was shown before, whether in mystical transport (on the authority of the book itself: "I was in the spirit"), or, according to a variant tradition, in a dream during the Last Supper when he fell asleep upon Christ's bosom. Neither of these versions of the visionary moment is the subject of figure 15, which concerns instead the moment of writing. The seven candlesticks, "the seven lamps that are the seven spirits of God," and the dragon with seven heads are all memorial images, being seen again as part of the process by which they became sacred literature.[50]

A well-known painting by Domenico di Michelino in the north aisle of the Duomo in Florence (figure 16) shows the end result of such a process. With one hand Dante holds open the book of his *Commedia*, and with the other indicates the three eschatological realms that constitute the landscape of his work: Hell; Purgatory mountain; and Paradise, represented by the banded heavens, with sun, moon, and Ptolemaic planets luminous therein. The city of Florence, whose moral and political history figures so large in the poem, is shown to his left. The painting tells us that the book holds those images, and that its author wants his readers to visualize them in turn.[51]

More problematic, but important nonetheless, is the tradition that presents St. Luke as portrait painter of the Virgin. First recorded in the sixth century, it caused St. Luke to become patron saint of painters, and is represented in a number of paintings of the late Middle Ages and early Renaissance, the earliest of them in the West dated 1368. The tradition is based on nothing in Scripture: indeed, it ignores the Biblical testimony (Col. 4:14) that Luke was a physician, a text sufficiently well known to make him patron saint of doctors as well. The full history of "St. Luke as painter" is obscure, but it is almost certainly related to the fact that from his gospel we derive most of our knowledge of the life of the Virgin: he was her *literary* portraitist. In the words of *The Golden Legend*, "And specially . . . the blessed Luke had recourse to her like as to the ark of the Testament, and was certified of her many things, and especially of such things as appertained to her, as of the salutation of the angel Gabriel, of the nativity of Jesu Christ, and of such other things as Luke speaketh only."[52] There were in some churches, to be sure, pictures of the Virgin attributed to St. Luke—possibly through confusion with an eleventh-century Florentine painter named Luke, and nick-named *il santo* because of his piety. And that means that in the later medieval centuries, at least, the legend was also believed to be liter-ally true. But the two explanations are not necessarily exclusive of each other. Figure 17, a French illumination from the late fifteenth century, shows the Virgin and Child sitting before the saint, who completes a portrait of them; beneath the text, he is shown again, writing his gospel and gazing at the ox who is his symbol as Evange-list, but who is here sheltered in a real stable, and is thus conflated with another ox, the ox of the Nativity.[53] As this picture shows clearly, the activities of portraying and writing could be as readily equated in the visual arts as they were in the vernacular language it-self (Chaucer constantly uses "portray" and "write" as synonyms). In a variant of the same tradition, the Book of Hours of Juana of Cas-tile shows St. Luke writing the gospel with a finished portrait of the Virgin and Child before him.[54] The historicity of St. Luke as writer could not be doubted, and the historicity of his identity as a portrait painter must have seemed to those who might doubt it relatively un-important. It was, at the very least, a way of talking about truth.

I have saved for last the most interesting visual evidence of this idea that I have come upon, the opening illumination of a late-fifteenth-century manuscript of Boethius's *Consolation of Philosophy* in both Latin and French (figure 18). If I read it correctly, it shows Boethius with his book before him, seated in a library, viewing him-self and Lady Philosophy in a large picture that hangs from a golden chain on the opposite wall. Since medieval pictorial convention al-lowed artists to depict sequential action within the same picture space, one might expect Boethius to be shown at his book in one cor-ner of the building, and through open archways or windows (per-haps) another room in which Lady Philosophy begins the instruction that will be his cure. Indeed, a manuscript made some twenty years later, modeled upon this one, preferred that alternative: the wall is cut away in a huge arch, and one looks through it to another build-ing, where Lady Philosophy attends the philosopher in his despair. But our illuminator has chosen to frame the scene not with an arch but as a literal picture, a painted image. And it has programmatic consequences for the images that follow. The picture before us adorns the first of five prologues to the work as a whole; thereafter each of the five books of the *Consolation* is introduced with a minia-ture of comparable size and beauty, illustrating a subject central to each book, the first and last of which (Books I and V) recapitulate the image here hung as a picture in a frame. Book I shows Boethius in

17. St. Luke as painter and
writer. French, late fif-
teenth century. Note 53.

18. Boethius and Lady Philosophy. French, 1476. Note 55.

bed with books, prostrate with sorrow, self-pity, and error, attended by the Muses of poetry, which Lady Philosophy (also present) will drive from the room and from his mind. It begins the first stage in his cure. Book V opens with a similar scene of Boethius lying in bed, but above the covers this time, without books, in what I take to be a posture of meditation—essentially that of *ego dormio, cor meum vigilat*—with Lady Philosophy seated beside him, his cure complete.[55] This twofold return to the opening image, each time with significant variation, suggests how we are to understand the images that introduce the other books as well: they are "pictures" the books "contain," pictures the books are meant to present to the reader's inner eye, as they are present to Boethius as author in the picture before us.[56]

Such pictures are, I believe, properly part of the history of medieval literary theory.[57] They illustrate the idea that authors "invent" their material—in the root sense of finding it, discovering it—by conceiving that material visually; and they testify to the potency of literary art to make readers (here illustrators) see that material in turn. We may note another poet so construing the process of invention in the *Prison amoureuse*, when Froissart (whom Chaucer is likely to have known, and some of whose works he used in the making of his own) expresses his eagerness to communicate in verse to his patron, Wenceslas of Brabant, *pluiseurs ymaginations* (several images/imaginings) he has recently conceived on the subject of love.[58]

Stephen Hawes, the most medieval of early Renaissance poets, for whom Chaucer, Gower, and Lydgate constituted the true English tradition, explains this process in some detail in his *Pastime of Pleasure*, written between 1496 and 1509. In the early part of the poem, as part of a survey of the Seven Liberal Arts, he meets Lady Rhetoric, who instructs him concerning her nature—an account that preserves medieval tradition without significant change. Hawes's larger subject determined that Rhetoric must be her name and that she must speak of an orator, since the formal art of poetry developed as a branch of rhetoric and was never raised to membership in the Seven Liberal Arts on its own. But it is poetry, Hawes's own professional art, that seems to be chiefly on his mind. By "oratoure" I think we are meant to understand *all* rhetoricians—narrative poets as well as orators—or so the word "tales" for their inventions and the long concluding commendation of Gower, Chaucer, and Lydgate would seem to require. If we so construe the word, and if we take the trouble to search out the meaning that lies behind the aureate abstraction of Hawes's diction, we may read there a remarkable statement of the role of the mental image in the making of narrative art:

> Yf to the orature / many a sundry tale
> One after other / treatably be tolde

Than sundry ymages / in his closed male
Eche for a mater / he doth than well holde
Lyke to the tale / he doth than so beholde
And inwarde / a recapytulacyon
Of eche ymage / the moralyzacyon
Whiche be the tales / he grounded pryuely
Vpon these ymages / sygnyfycacyon
And whan tyme is / for hym to specyfy
All his tales / by demonstracyon
In due ordre / maner and reason
Than eche ymage / inwarde dyrectly
The oratoure / doth take full properly
So is enprynted / in his propre mynde
Euery tale / with hole resemblaunce
By this ymage / he dooth his mater fynde
Eche after other / withouten varyaunce.[59]

It is pertinent instruction in how a writer was understood to stock his mind, "find" his material, and remember that invention: images are the means.

Let me conclude this section with an example drawn from the work of the poet whose art is the larger subject of my study, for Book I of *The House of Fame* offers especially interesting evidence concerning the way in which the verbal, the visual, and the memorial were linked in Chaucer's mind. More than 330 of its 508 lines are devoted to the story of Virgil's *Aeneid*, described as "graven" on the walls of Venus' temple—a long section remarkable not for any particular poetic eloquence or power (the *Aeneid* does not readily reduce to 330 lines of verse) but for the ambiguity with which it registers the mode of the experience being described. The beginning is clear enough: the narrator finds the opening lines of the poem ("I wol now singen, yif I kan, / The armes, and also the man"; *HF*, 143) engraved upon a tablet of brass. But his account of the story proper is narrated in terms of seeing rather than reading—"First sawgh I the destruction / Of Troye, thurgh the Grek Synon" (151)—a change so disorienting that when Chaucer returns to the verb "graven" ("And aftir this was grave, allas!"; 157) one no longer knows whether we are to understand "engraved with letters" or "with pictures." We return to a series of "I saugh" events, clearly intended to make us "see" in our turn, and then are moved into experience not accessible to sight alone, whether in written words or pictures, as he hears the sorrow of Creusa's ghost ("hyt was pitee for to here"; 180). The narrator briefly returns to a "saugh I," then specifies a new medium altogether as he describes a fearful tempest "peynted on the wal," and then resumes the "graven" designation until that point at which he identifies his own act of poetic composition with those temple decorations, by using a verb that belongs to neither poets or "gravers" by first right:

"What shulde I speke more queynte, / Or peyne me my wordes peynte / To speke of love?" (*HF*, 245). Rhetoric, too, has its colors, and they are used to create another event, which, since it cannot be painted, must be understood as either "heard," read, or remembered—the long complaint spoken by Dido after she has been betrayed. The verb "graven" then governs the narration of the story until the very end, when what the narrator has been seeing is defined unequivocally as pictorial rather than verbal:

> "A, Lord!" thoughte I, "that madest us,   (*HF*, 470)
> Yet sawgh I never such noblesse
> Of ymages, ne such richesse,
> As I saugh graven in this chirche;
> But not wot I whoo did hem wirche."

This redaction of the *Aeneid* begins with words on brass and ends with pictures, perhaps on brass, perhaps on glass, perhaps painted on the wall; between those two points we have at best a shifting sense of what mode of artistic experience is being reported. Reading, seeing, hearing, remembering, and even writing (see lines 381–82) are rendered as interchangeable. To describe this passage simply as an instance of *ut pictura poesis* is inadequate and finally off the point. If its aim were to demonstrate that poetry can do what painting does, it would seek descriptive effects more ambitious by far—in fact, its only real intensity is in the speeches, read or "heard"—and it would move far less swiftly through the story. It seems to me to concern instead a process of intellectual recall and imaginative response—to concern exactly what the poem's title would lead us to expect, narrative art as a "hous of fame" capable of preserving within men's memories the famous deeds of the past. In effect, we are shown a poet remembering a poem he has read as a series of pictures, by way of creating a new poem that describes those pictures as though they were real.[60] The narrator's experience of the *Aeneid* in Book I of *The House of Fame* offers a medieval paradigm of how narrative poems are made, responded to, and after that remembered.

We have returned to a subject already central to these pages—the problem of memory, which our survey of medieval faculty psychology revealed to be closely allied to the imagination, the image-making faculty of the mind. Having explored the mental image as a means of knowing and as a means of poetic making, we need now to consider it under one final rubric, as a means of Christian remembering. Our best approach will be through the formal art of memory, which the Middle Ages inherited from classical rhetoric (especially the *Rhetorica ad Herennium*), but which it made distinctively its own. Our new subject is not so much the act of memory as it was understood in the Middle Ages—we have already examined that—as it is the techniques that can create an "artificial" memory, a memory trained by art to capabilities beyond the ordinary. The original purpose of the *ars memoriae* was to help an orator remember the materials of a speech—an essential skill in the conduct of civic life. But the medieval context in which that art found its most characteristic home assumed for it, as we shall soon see, a goal more elevated by far.

The *Rhetorica ad Herennium*, whose true author is unknown, was in the Middle Ages believed to be by Cicero, to be indeed his lost "second rhetoric." But the legendary beginnings of the art of memory go back further, to one Simonides who lived in the fifth century B.C. According to Cicero in his authentic *De oratore*, Simonides alone survived a feast in which the roof of the banqueting hall collapsed, killing everyone beneath it; Simonides had been called outside some few moments earlier. So badly mangled were the corpses that even their relatives could not identify them for burial, but Simonides remembered where each person had been sitting at table, and thus effected the identification of the dead. According to Cicero, Simonides drew this conclusion:

He inferred that persons desiring to train this faculty [of memory] must select places and form mental images of the things they wish to remember and store those images in the places, so that the order of the places will preserve the order of the things, and the images of the things will denote the things themselves.[61]

The essentials of the art are here already formulated, though further recommendations, sometimes extremely complex, were to be developed in the treatises themselves. Common to them all is the teaching that one should invent images (*imagines*) for things one wishes to remember and then dispose them in images of places (*loci*), real or imaginary, that imply a single order of movement. A temple with entrance, side chapels, and high altar will do nicely, or the windows of a familiar room, to be scanned (let us say) from left to right. In such a way, the orator will be able to remember not only the topics of his discourse, but those topics in their proper order. A rote memory for words was understood to be both more difficult and less necessary than a memory for things held in the mind through images. Everywhere one finds this same assumption: that suitable words will follow in the train of the image.

Frances Yates's study of these memorial arts is a work rich in learning and surmise, and to it, for further information, I must refer my reader. Our present interest is probably not usefully directed toward the more extravagant refinements of the memory systems, though it is important to note the continued currency they gave to certain underlying Aristotelian axioms: "The soul never thinks without a mental picture," for instance, or "No one could ever learn or understand anything, if he had not the faculty of perception; even when he thinks speculatively, he must have some mental picture with which to think."[62] It is indeed possible that Chaucer may have read and studied such a treatise: he knew the allegory *On the Marriage of Philology and Mercury*, by Martianus Capella, which concerns the Seven Liberal Arts and includes a brief art of memory; Thomas Bradwardine, who was Archbishop of Canterbury at his death in 1349, had written a treatise thereon; Petrarch had begun another.[63] Furthermore, if Chaucer had access to the full text of Geoffrey de Vinsauf's *Poetria nova*—the matter is under dispute—he found there a substantial section on memory, mindful of the *Ad Herennium* rules but refreshingly independent of them. Geoffrey—Chaucer's "deere maister soverayn"—thought the systematic rules a bit subtle and not likely to suit all persons. Use them if they seem comfortable, he says, but keep in mind that the memory ("the little cell that remembers") is "a cell of delights," and must be treated kindly, not overburdened. After giving some brief rules for the verbal memory, he concludes with his easier version of the rules then ascribed to Cicero, a method more generally useful:

> To these methods add others which I make use of—and which it is expedient to use. When I wish to recall things I have seen, or heard, or memorized before, or engaged in before, I ponder thus: I saw, I heard, I considered, I acted in such or such a way, either at that time or in that place: places, times, images, or other similar signposts are for me a sure path which leads me to the things themselves. Through these signs I arrive at active knowledge. Such and such a thing was so, and I picture to myself such and such a thing. . . . Fashion signs for yourself, whatever kind your own inclination suggests.[64]

Some such generalized understanding of the relation between memory and mental images or visual signs is all we need postulate for Chaucer, not an interest in the art of memory per se.[65] He would have noticed, for instance, that Boccaccio's *Teseida*, the source of his *Knight's Tale*, devotes the last part of its eleventh book to a "pictorial" recapitulation of everything that has gone before, as prelude to the marriage between Palemone and Emilia, which will be celebrated in the concluding book. Palemone orders that a temple be built on the spot of Arcita's funeral pyre, and that wall paintings within the building depict the story of their friendship, imprisonment, love, and combat, along with Arcita's death. Each stage of the story is narrated again in its essentials, but this time as the description of a picture: the images are being impressed upon the mind, in some twenty stanzas of verse.[66] Cato's ancient advice to the orator applies to the reader/auditor as well: *rem tene, verba sequentur*; hold fast to the thing (the image of the thing); the words will follow.[67]

But the formal art of memory acquired a second house in the Middle Ages, reflecting other kinds of importance attributed to the memorial image in medieval culture. The *ars memoriae* continues to inhabit the handbooks of rhetoric and poetry, but it suddenly makes its appearance as well in treatises on ethics, written for the Christian who would save his soul. Cicero's *De inventione*, his genuine "first rhetoric," in suggesting the four cardinal virtues as subjects especially suitable to the orator had named *memoria* as one of the three parts of Prudence. The great scholastic treatises that incorporate an art of memory, the *De bono* of Albertus Magnus and the *Summa theologica* of St. Thomas Aquinas, follow that lead, but with man's needs as an orator no longer chiefly in mind.[68] They found the rules of the art in the *Ad Herennium* but transmitted them in the light of the *De inventione*,[69] in learned parallel to the emphasis the medieval church had long placed upon a less systematic use of images in teaching its faithful, the vast majority of whom were illiterate, but all of whose souls Christ had declared incomparably valuable. He promised at the end of time a magnificent exaltation of the truly humble—the last shall be first, the mighty shall be put down from their seats—and across the medieval centuries images were made, and defended against iconoclasts, as the "books" of the unlearned (*libri laicorum*), whether in wood or stone, pigment or stained glass. They were considered essential in that role. In the words of Gregory the Great, "what a book is to those who can read, a picture provides to even the unlearned who look at it carefully, for in it the unlearned see what they should follow, and those who cannot read books read it. Hence a picture especially serves as a book to the common people."[70]

When Albertus Magnus and St. Thomas Aquinas detail the formal procedures of the artificial memory, they do not write for the unlettered. But they add to their definitions of the memorial image a new element, responsive to the traditional importance of imagery within the Christian Church. The speculations of medieval faculty psychology and the systems of artificial memory combine in a conception of the trained memory as a repository not just of forms or images (the product of the imagination), but of the intentions discovered within them by the second cell of the brain. The memory receives not only the image but its consequence for the perceptor. In Yates's example,

An image to remind one of a wolf's form will also contain the *intentio* that the wolf is a dangerous animal from which it would be wise to flee; on the animal level of memory, a lamb's mental image of a wolf contains this *intentio*. And on the higher level of the memory of a rational being, it will mean that an image chosen, say, to remind of the virtue of Justice will contain the *intentio* of seeking to acquire this virtue.[71]

Because an image contains both a likeness and an intention, it has the capacity both to remind and to move the soul. The language of these treatises takes on overtones of medieval piety, even in very technical passages, as in this defense of the memory systems by St. Thomas Aquinas:

It is necessary in this way to invent similitudes and images because simple and spiritual intentions slip easily from the soul unless they are as it were linked to some corporeal similitudes, because human cognition is stronger in regard to the sensibilia.[72]

He is explaining why Cicero properly thought Memory to be part of the cardinal virtue of Prudence. In these scholastic works, the formal art of memory acquired a doubled relevance, *ad ethicum et rhetorem*,[73] useful to the moral man as well as the public speaker.

This moving power of the image is by no means restricted to religious images alone. In Gower's *Mirour de l'omme*, Reason tries to direct the Body by intellectual means ("Resoun la Char aresonna") but is often defeated by Temptation, who shows the Body the delights of sin, in images capable of depriving it of reason ("et tieux delices luy moustra . . . par quoy la Char desresonna").[74] Gower implies the need for an art that combines the two, that will use images to move man's soul toward rational ends. That Chaucer too was aware of such a doctrine of the image and its power, his *Legend of Lucrece* bears witness: one form that Tarquin's obsession takes is "Th'ymage of hire recordynge alwey newe" (*LGW*, 1760); it shakes him as a tempest shakes the sea. And in *The Miller's Tale*, so vividly does old John "image" Nicholas's narrative of a flood to come, that he forgets all ordinary common sense:

> Lo, which a greet thyng is affeccioun!　　　　　(I.3611)
> Men may dyen of ymaginacioun,
> So depe may impressioun be take.
> This sely carpenter bigynneth quake;
> Hym thynketh verraily that he may see
> Noees flood come walwynge as the see
> To drenchen Alisoun, his hony deere.

It is Chaucer's own testimony to the importance of my subject in this book.

But Dante, perhaps better than any other, can instruct us in the affective power attributed to mental images within medieval culture—even to those images born of sense experience within the secular world. In the *Vita nuova*, which he terms "my book of memory," the sight of Beatrice is the beginning of his true impulse to poetry. His memory allows him to keep her image before his eyes, even in her absence, exciting his passion and directing his will. The destructive capability of the imagination is sometimes recorded, in phantasms and false imaginings, but the true image of Beatrice is the center of his "new life": when he first saw her, his "animal spirit" said to the spirits of the sight, "Now your bliss has appeared" (*apparuit iam beatitudo vestra*).[75] It is her image that, in the *Commedia*, conducts him into the realm of Paradise. In that poem, he creates images of heaven meant to draw one's love and desire, along with images of hell meant to cause one to fear. They seek, by moving the soul, to alter the way one lives one's life. Yates has suggested that the great structural images created in the *Inferno*, *Purgatorio*, and *Paradiso* are themselves intended as memorial systems;[76] to complete the account, we need only add that the images located within those great structures are af-

19. Dante and Virgil contemplate images of humility. Italian, third quarter of the fourteenth century. Note 77.

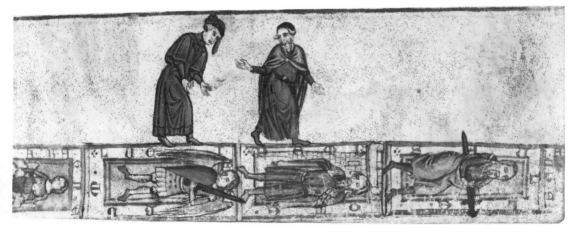

20. Dante and Virgil tread upon images of the proud. Italian, third quarter of the fourteenth century. Note 77.

fective in their power. In *Purgatorio* X, for instance, the first terrace on the mountain, the Terrace of Pride, has walls sculptured with examples of humility (figure 19): Mary at the Annunciation, David dancing before the ark of the Lord while enduring Michal's scorn, the Emperor Trajan detained by the grieving widow. To look upon these—to be moved by them—is part of the essential process of purgation, enjoined upon all the souls who travel that terrace; so too the necessity to tread upon other images set in the pavement like tomb slabs in a church floor, images of the proud cast down (Canto XII). In figure 20, Dante and Virgil are shown walking across four such images, which depict (from left to right): Arachne, who was turned into a spider; Lucifer, who fell from heaven; Nimrod before the Tower of Babel; and Saul pierced with his own sword.[77] These canti are central to Dante's theory of imagery—the mystery he names in X, 95, as *visibile parlare* ("visible speech")—as are others near the end of the *Purgatorio*, where Beatrice commands that he write what he has seen for the good of the world that lives so ill (XXXII, 103–5), and that he bear away at least the picture of what he has seen, if her speech has proved too lofty for his understanding (XXXIII, 73–78).

Obviously, the problem of memory within a purely literary experience is a great deal less urgent for man's soul than the need to hold the great truths of the Church (historical and doctrinal) in mind, ready to be summoned for guidance, clarification, meditation, sorrow, or joy. The need to experience narrative art richly, in memory as well as in the event, is a lesser need. But for an audience most of whose members could not read or had relatively little access to books, it is a closely related need, and in the Middle Ages it found its solution in techniques already evolved to meet the greater, morally more consequential problem. Medieval narrative calls upon the "inner eye" to a maximum degree, not because everything worth remembering can be visualized, but because the visual memory is very strong, and to images can be attached many details otherwise not readily accessible to the verbal memory. The words can be found through them. Perhaps the clearest explanation of the process comes from Albertus Magnus, in considering the objection that since *propria* (the literal details) represent a thing more accurately than can *metaphorica* (similitudes, metaphors), why should we not prefer the *propria* in a memory system? His answer is in three parts: (1) images by their very nature assist the memory; (2) many *propria* can be remembered through a few images; and (3) images are able to move the soul, a power that makes them more memorable still.[78] The formal arts of memory, which we too easily dismiss as virtuoso merely, were perceived in the Middle Ages to be ethical in significant ways; and less "artificial" uses of imagery for the sake of remembrance indeed dominated much of the experience of the age.

These two traditions—the learned and the popular—come together in a particularly interesting way in an image from the *Speculum humanae salvationis*, a work that links picture and text, New Testament event and Old Testament prefigurations, in a narrative sequence. Written in 1324, it became one of the most important works of popular devotion in the later Middle Ages; manuscripts and block books survive in the hundreds.[79] Its thirty-fifth chapter concerns the life of Mary after Christ's Ascension, and describes her as visiting the places made sacred by the Incarnation and Passion of her son, reliving that history with prayers, kisses, and tears, remembering joy and sorrow. But only one manuscript known to me (and that from the late fifteenth century) illustrates this chapter in a straightforward way, the way one might expect: Mary, accompanied by followers, stands holding a rosary before the door of a house that represents, in generalized fashion, one of these places.

Far more common is a representation like that I reproduce here from a fourteenth-century Italian manuscript (figure 21), in which the sacred places are ranged round the figure of Mary in what I think must be described as a memory system.[80] The images are to be read from top to bottom, left column then right. We see the room of the Annunciation, with Mary's lectern and rays of the sun representing the Holy Spirit by whom she conceives; the stable at Bethlehem, with ox and ass; a human leg and chalice, representing the washing of the disciples' feet and the institution of the Eucharist on Maundy Thursday; another chalice, holding the Instruments of the Passion; the pillar of the scourging, with the crown of thorns; the cross with nails, lance, and sponge; the empty tomb and banner; and the mount of the Ascension, with Christ's footprints still visible. Mary is shown contemplative in their midst; she meditates upon these images, and her spirit is moved by them. In this version of her life after the Ascension, there is no need to revisit the sacred places—the picture does not perfectly accord with its text—for she possesses these images free of time or space, in her memory. Her meditative posture is exemplary to the viewer of the manuscript, and the images that surround her recapitulate the *Speculum* itself, which has previously shown in word and picture the events that took place within those settings. We should note that these settings are empty of people, and, in the case of the Maundy Thursday image, strikingly unrealistic: they call the viewer to activity. He must repeople them in his own mind, and each pictured detail has the power to call forth many other memories in its train, profitable for the Christian to think on. Many *propria* can be associated with a single image, as well as many meanings that cannot otherwise be visualized. For instance, the lectern recalls Mary's childhood in the Temple, where her special study was the Psalms; the ox and ass may be understood as the New and Old Testaments, joined

21. Mary revisits in her mind the sacred places. Italian, mid-fourteenth century. Note 80.

by Christ's birth; the triumphal banner indicates Christ's victory over death. In this particular work, moreover, each scene invites memory of the (usually three) Old Testament events that foreshadowed it, which have been presented alongside it, in words and pictures, on previous manuscript pages.

As we have already noted, the importance of Mary's memory as authority for the events narrated in the Gospels to which the Evangelists themselves could not have been eyewitnesses was considerable. Jacobus de Voragine, in *The Golden Legend*, says of that crucial authentication (here in Caxton's translation):

For the blessed Virgin Mary kept and heled diligently all these things in her heart, as it is said, Luce secundo, to the end that she should afterward show them to the writers, as the gloss saith, that all things that were done and said of our Lord Jesu Christ she knew and retained them in her mind. So that when she was required of the writers or of the preachers of the incarnation and of all other things, she might express them sufficiently, like as it was done and were in deed. . . . This is she that fully from the beginning was instructed of the celestial mysteries, and it is to be believed that the evangelists enquired of her many things, and she certified them truly.[81]

In the illumination before us, Mary as custodian of memories is assimilated to both popular devotional tradition (these are the great scenes familiar to any medieval Christian from his experience of churches), and to certain prescriptions for the use of *loci* and *imagines* in a memory system, which descended from classical rhetoric, but were Christianized by the great scholastic philosophers of the Church. Medieval faculty psychology, popular devotional tradition, and the formal arts of memory join together at the single point they share in common: a sense of the importance of the mental image, for both the intellectual and spiritual life of man. Such images can be communicated in pictures, or words, or (as in the present instance) both together. But their life is not limited to those modes only: they can remain with the viewer, listener, or reader even after the closing of the book.

Because it is rare to find images whose explicit subject is the use of images, I have reserved for last the most important such sequence that I know. Two passages from Guillaume de Deguileville's *Pilgrimage of Human Life*, taken together, can summarize and make vivid—for I must not miss the lesson of my own material—much of what has been said so far. They do so in two kinds of image, those he created in words, and those that manuscript illuminators made in response, as pictures on a page.

The first concerns the vision of the Heavenly Jerusalem that the poet is shown, as though in a large and shining mirror, at the beginning of his dream. The vision is of such surpassing beauty that it moves him to become a pilgrim and seek that city. The verbs employed emphasize the affective power of imagery, as well as its skill to teach and to clarify. Here is Lydgate's translation (italics added), together with the original text; both will bear careful reading:

The seyde yer (ho lyst take kep)	En lan que iay dit par deuant,
I was *avysed* in my slep,	Auis me fut en mon dormant,
Excyted eke, and that a-noon,	Que daler iestoye excite
To Ierusalem for to goon.	En iherusalem la cite,
Gretly *meved* in my corage	La ou estoit tout mon couraige.
ffor to do my pylgrymage,	Dy faire le pelerinaige
And ther-to *steryd inwardly*.	Fichie du tout entierement
And to tell the cause why,	La cause estoit et mouuement
Was, ffor me thouht *I hadde a syht*	Pource que la cite veoie
With-Inne a merour large & bryht,	En ung beau miroer quauoye,
Off that hevenly ffayr cyte,	Qui de loing la representoit

Wych representede vn-to me   Dedens luy, et la me monstroit.[82]
Ther of holy the manere,
With Inne the glas *ful bryht & cler.*

For most of this immense poem—18,123 lines in Guillaume's second version—that initial image is the goal, the spur, the meaning of the quest. We are reminded of this again at the poem's end, as the pilgrim is about to die, and Grace Dieu tells him he has come to the door of the place he has so long been seeking:

> thou art come to the wyket
> which, in gynnyng of thy labour,
> thow beheld in a myrrour,
> whan thow were ful tendre of age,
> at gynnyng of thy pilgrymage.[83]

Most illuminated manuscripts show a very literal mirror in his room, hanging on a wall or standing on a column at the foot of his bed, with the image of the city visible within it. But I choose to reproduce (figure 22) a more interesting version from a manuscript made ca. 1430–40 in which, on the left, the poet dreams his dream, and on the right, recites his poem to a listening audience. The two activities are linked by the mirror, suspended in space between them. The source of what the poet first "saw" and what he makes the audience "see" differ, but the thing seen is the same. Lydgate's "translator's prologue" makes exactly that point in speaking of the poem and its audience: "Ther they may, as in a merovr, se / holsom thynges, & thynges full notable."[84]

In some later manuscripts and early printed editions, this opening image is augmented in an important way: the pictures that follow show a smaller mirror, shining clear or with the Holy City depicted thereon, at the top of the pilgrim's staff. Though no early illuminations known to me incorporate this detail, its authority is textual. Guillaume describes the top pommel of the staff ("bordoun") as being a mirror that reflects not only the surrounding countryside but the heavenly city as well:

> And in that myrour dyde I se
> The maner hool off the cyte
> To the wych I was so bent
> ffor to gon, in myn entent.
> ffor wych (in myn oppynyoun)
> I preysede gretly the Bordoun,
> And louyd also wel the bet.

A mirror has no literal function or probability at the top of a pilgrim's staff. But in reflecting the immediate countryside, it doubtless functions as a mirror of Prudence, and in reflecting Jerusalem ce-

22. Guillaume's dream: the image in the mirror. French, ca. 1430–40. Note 84.

lestial, tells us that the motivating image accompanies the pilgrim throughout his lifelong journey. Figure 23, from the late fifteenth century, represents this tradition; there are fine examples in the early printed books as well.[85] A related episode in the poem's first version has the pilgrim's Staff of Hope stolen from him during the attack by Gluttony and Venus. The result is, by definition, despair, and in the English prose translation he cries out: "Oo thou citee of jerusalem to which I was excited to goo. How shal I excuse mee to thee and what answere shall I make thee. I hadde bihight thee in my corage that I wolde do the viage to thee for that I sigh thee in the faire mirrowr cleer and polisshed. Now I am beten now I am hurt soo that on my sides it is seene. In euele time forueyed I. I trowe I shal neuere seen thee." Figure 24 shows him prostrate with his eyes closed, as Grace Dieu bends down from above to restore the staff to him. The recovery of the staff signifies his recovery of true vision, and movement again becomes possible.[86]

The progress of the poem is in fact a veritable progress through images. We might look once more at figure 23 in this regard, for it is typical of the poem's method. In it, the pilgrim meets Envy, Treason, and Detraction, in the guise of three women. The poet tells us that Envy, the eldest, thin and haggard, glides along the grass like a serpent, bearing her daughters on her back, with two spears emerging from her eyes. One spear is called Wrath at Other Folks' Prosperity, the other Joy at Their Adversity; they are poisonous spears, and they make her gaze as deadly as that of the basilisk. The young and beautiful woman who sits foremost on her back is Treason, whose face is in fact false; she carries a knife in her right hand, which she hides behind her back, and a jar of ointment in her left, at once a cosmetic to cover her ugliness and a flattering unguent with which to blear men's eyes. Behind her sits her sister Detraction, carrying a spear made of human ears (she pierces them with hostile speech), who gnaws unceasingly at a bone in her mouth. The text tells us that she devours a man's good name like raw flesh, and makes of it a broth that her mother uses as medicine "whan she hath any malladye."[87] The encounter in which these hags declare their natures and attack the pilgrim occupies 769 lines in Lydgate's translation—lines that invite the attentive reader or listener to frame just such an image in his mind. Around it, and by its means, a good deal of the episode's iconographic detail, illustrative story, proverb, and moral counsel can later be reconstructed; as a "visual" nucleus, it can be recalled with considerable ease.

Such an understanding of the text lies behind every illumination in the standard manuscript cycle, and such a description might be made of every major event in the poem. It is intensely visual. Indeed, an earlier sequence of images—the scene in which Grace Dieu arms the pilgrim for his journey—explores at length the process by which

23. Guillaume's pilgrimage: Envy, Treason, and Detraction. French, late fifteenth century. Note 85.

24. Guillaume's dream: Grace Dieu restores the Staff of Hope. Paris, 1393. Note 86.

such imagery works and by which it becomes valuable in the defense of the soul. We will examine its representation in a Parisian manuscript dated 1393.

The great command of Ephesians 6:11, "Put you on the armor of God, that you may be able to stand against the deceits of the devil," is here developed in a remarkable fashion. Grace Dieu shows the pilgrim a suit of armor that has been laid out in readiness for him (figure 25), and explains its necessity—attaching moral meanings to each part of it, often with a great deal of ingenuity. She brings forward the gambeson of Patience (figure 26: a gambeson is just a quilted coat, but this one has a steel anvil on its back to receive blows); the habergeoun (coat-of-mail) of Fortitude; the helmet of Temperance; the gorger (throat-piece) of Sobriety; the gloves of Continence; the sword of Righteousness (all of these are shown in figure 27); the scabbard of Humility; the girdle of Perseverance, with its buckle of Constancy; the shield of Prudence; and so on. In Lydgate's version, nearly a thousand lines of verse are devoted to explaining this spiritual armor,[88] lines made lively by the pilgrim's occasional reluctance—must he be burdened with such things?—and by his sinful size: when he complains that the gambeson is too tight, he is told rather sharply to reduce his diet until he fits it. When at last he has the armor on, he suddenly declares he will not have it at all. Whatever dangers may lie ahead, it is so heavy and so painful that he throws it off in a fit of petulant anger (figure 28):

> Thys armure may me nat profyte,
> In wych I do me nat delyte. . . .
> That ye gaff me, off armure,

25 (*left*). Grace Dieu shows the pilgrim a suit of armor. 26 (*right*). She offers him the gambeson of Patience. Paris, 1393. Note 88.

> Me streyneth so on euery syde,
> That I may nat ther-with a-byde.[89]

Grace Dieu disappears as a result, not being one to stay around when treated with discourtesy.

> And fro me she gan declyne,
> And entrede in, in hyr courtyne.
> And disarmyd I a-bood,
> And fulle nakyd so I stood.[90]

In that desolate condition, the pilgrim repents his error, and Grace Dieu returns to offer him help in carrying the armor. He dares then to hope for a pack cart, but is told instead that he already has a servant capable of carrying all that gear, whose name is Lady Memory. Turning to see her, he is shocked by her appearance, for at first glance she seems to have no eyes at all:

> I sawh that eyen hadde she noon,
> Ne mor than hath a stok or ston;
> Wych was to me a thyng hydous;
> She sempte a best monstruows,
> Outward, by hyr contenaunce.[91]

The Lady's eyes, in fact, are at the back of her head (as in figure 29). Grace Dieu identifies her as the Treasurer of Experiences, who holds the past in mind, and urges that all his armor be committed to her charge; she will accompany him on his journey (figure 30).[92] The images derived from a suit of armor will be with the pilgrim in his

27 (*left*). Grace Dieu offers the pilgrim further armor. 28 (*right*). The pilgrim throws off his suit of armor. Paris, 1393. Notes 88, 89.

29 (*left*). The pilgrim is introduced to Lady Memory. 30 (*right*). She takes up his armor. Paris, 1393. Note 92.

mind's eye, and the things they stand for, which he holds in his intellect, and which those images will help him to recall, will protect him from the spiritual enemies he will meet before his life comes to its end.

And so too they are meant to protect the medieval reader or listener. He would know, either from prior experience or the poem's own schematic instruction, the essential parts of a suit of armor, and the ordinary sequence in which a knight would put such armor on. As a result, he could in memory work his way back through such an image—it becomes a memory system—to reconstruct in some detail the moral counsel the poet has figured through its means. Such a memory is first "visual," then verbal—the image brings words with it—and each piece of it constitutes an invitation to meditation thereafter, as part of the armor the reader or listener knew himself to need in his own pilgrimage of earthly life.

Chaucer's aims in poetry are not identical with those of Guillaume de Deguileville—or with those of Langland, Gower, or the *Pearl* poet, to name only his most gifted English contemporaries. But as poets they shared a common ambition—to create literature that is valuable in ways extending beyond the pleasure of narrative for its own sake, the pleasure of narrative as process. And their first audiences, most urgently their listening audiences, shared certain common needs as well. Answering to both, there existed a legacy of ideas concerning the mental image—as a means of knowing, of poetic making, and of Christian remembering—whose consequence for literary art was far greater than that of *ut pictura poesis* as it is customarily defined.

Christianity gave to certain of these ideas a special inflection and nuance—particularly in its emphasis upon the power of an image to move the soul toward good or evil. But it did so in no exclusive way: we have not been constructing a theory of religious poetry only. The theory of *intentiones* is ultimately psychological rather than moral and was born of the need to explain animal behavior (attraction or repulsion) as well as human experience: all images function so, the theory tells us, whether they are the product of immediate sense perception, imaginative invention, or memorial recall. In the hands of a poet, they could serve God indeed, but also the world, the flesh, the devil. They have a central place in medieval poetics, taken at the large.

The materials we have surveyed in this chapter are pertinent in varying degrees to most late-medieval narrative verse. But every medieval century must finally be assessed in terms of its own evidence, and every medieval poet who was ambitious as an artist, in terms of his own particular practice. I have preferred to bring forward evidence for one poet, Geoffrey Chaucer, somewhat more often and on a greater variety of subjects than any other. But so far he has remained a figure among other figures in a background. We have been able to inquire into what makes his use of such images "medieval"—an essential place to begin. In the following chapter, I shall try to answer a different question: what makes him, in such use, the poet Chaucer and no other?

II. Chaucerian Aesthetic
THE IMAGE IN THE POEM

N THE LAST CHAPTER, we examined a number of me-
dieval propositions concerning mental imagery and the
role it could play in the enterprise of literature. They are
ideas of consequence for the whole of the medieval period and, in
varying ways, for the practice of virtually every major poet within it.
In the pages that follow, our inquiry will become more particular as
we attempt to locate Chaucer's own practice within the terms that
survey has provided. But first we must ask ourselves, as twentieth-
century persons who wish to imagine Chaucer's narratives as richly
and with as much historical accuracy as is possible, what problems
and what privileges will attend us in that quest.

It is, above all, our modern privilege to be readers. We can pur-
chase a volume of Chaucer's works expertly edited, glossed, and an-
notated, for relatively little money. We can study the poems, consult
their sources, and learn from generations of scholars who have en-
gaged in the same quest—to know the "poet's poem," the poem on
the page. These are advantages of an important kind and must not
be forgone. But in the preceding chapter I have suggested that we
should interest ourselves in the experience of his first audiences as
well, especially his listening audiences, not in perverse preference to
our own privileged access to books, but because the techniques that
Chaucer used to meet the needs of his first audiences—listeners as
well as readers—shaped profoundly and pervasively the poems that
readers read. Not least among these strategies is the importance he
attached to the image in the poem.

So let us begin with the simple recognition that, in Chaucer's art,
as in that of most of his contemporaries, there is much that is "vi-
sual," that invites the audience to "see," to image, to imagine. In a
manner consonant with rhetorical precept, both classical and medi-
eval, he sought imaginative vividness (*enargeia*) as a special goal.
Again and again the rhetoric books offer the counsel "ante oculos
ponere" (set it before the eyes),[1] and any description of Chaucer's aes-

thetic must include a place for this achievement. No one in English before him had admitted so generously into poetry the sights, sounds, and smells of daily life—the rich variety of its texture and detail—and it is important that we join his first audiences in responding fully to that rhetorical act, to that comprehensiveness and sympathy of vision. He did not disdain the surfaces of his fiction, and we should trust no critic who advises us to do so.

Because some six centuries lie between us and the empirical world reflected in those narratives, our first task must be to train our eyes on artifacts of a kind that were familiar to his contemporary audiences. We must achieve some accuracy of medieval imagining on all levels, even that of incidental, characterizing detail. When Chaucer describes Nicholas's bedroom, for instance, we would do well to have some sense of what a bourgeois house in fourteenth-century Oxford might have looked like—its architecture and furnishings, its style and size. A number of recent picture books have been helpful in meeting this kind of need. Joan Evans's *The Flowering of the Middle Ages*, elegantly produced and richly illustrated, may stand as perhaps the finest general example; books by R. S. Loomis, Maurice Hussey, Ian Seraillier, F. E. Halliday, Nevill Coghill, and Derek Brewer have sought specifically to illustrate the persons Chaucer knew, the places he visited, and the things he refers to.[2] If we would know the shape of a fashionable fourteenth-century shoe or the look of an astrolabe, a tally stick, a pilgrim's badge, or a walled city gate, we need look no further.

But visual information of this kind, on its own, is not sufficient. There was also current a learned language of visual sign to which we must educate our eyes, and in that undertaking the books named above are only sporadically useful. Loomis's *A Mirror of Chaucer's World*, for instance, in this second matter not only disappoints, but to some degree misleads, for its choice of pictures to illustrate Chaucer's poems is often merely antiquarian or (in the root sense of the word) eccentric. It is worth knowing the design of the rose window in old St. Paul's cathedral if we would form some accurate notion of Absolon's fine shoes, and perhaps even the look of the Holy Cross of Bromeholm if we would savour to the full a casual oath sworn by the Trumpington miller's wife—but only if other help, more central and significant in kind, has been provided.[3]

Both sorts of image, the mimetic and the iconographic, are important to Chaucer's poetry. But it is the argument of this book that at crucial places in his mature art they represent more than complementary modes of the imagination. As the chapters that follow will seek to demonstrate, the iconographic image is instead characteristically assimilated to the verisimilar and mimetic texture of the whole; it is discovered *within* the images one forms in attending to the narrative action itself. Among all the narrative material that is vividly imagined by Chaucer in the act of invention and "set before the eyes" of his audience in turn, it is this special kind of narrative image—which does a double kind of work, and of which there are seldom more than one or two in any tale—that is the subject of my study. They are images that the auditor/reader is invited to recognize as being *like*— as being in "approximate register" with[4]—symbolic images known from other medieval contexts, both literary and visual, where their meanings are stipulative and exact, unmediated by the ambiguities and particularities of fiction.

Such meanings, we would say now, must be attributed: only through a history of human use, both intellectual and artistic, can images acquire an iconographic dimension. The raw flux of experience, the total multiplicity of phenomena, contains no meanings in advance of our ruminations upon it. Certainly the images most central to the late Middle Ages carried with them a weight of accumulated cultural meaning—historical, religious, moral, and psychological. They are images with a human past. But they have their beginning in an assumption very different from our own—the belief that meaning is inherent in the material creation, because of the Divine Intelligence who created it, in rational ways and to rational ends. In the words of Aquinas, "Things signified by the words have themselves also a signification."[5] Such a statement attributes to God the Creator the intentional meaning of signs, and enjoins upon man the spiritual task of understanding their meaning, of deciphering them as part of a symbolic code. The universe was celebrated as a book for reading, in which one might find a plenitude of resonant things, as these lovely verses by Alain de Lille would instruct us:

Omnis mundi creatura	All creation, like a book or a pic-
Quasi liber et pictura	ture, is a mirror to us—a true
Nobis est in speculum;	figure of our life, our death, our
Nostrae vitae, nostrae mortis,	condition, our lot.
Nostri status, nostrae sortis	
Fidele signaculum.[6]	

As with creatures, so too with things, relationships, and events. When Hugh of St. Victor describes the universe as a dwelling made by God for man, his catalogue of its furnishings becomes (by no accident) a kind of handlist of medieval imagery, of things that attract meaning:

It is the house of God, it is the city of the King, it is the body of Christ, it is the bride of the Lamb. It is the heaven, it is the sun, it is the moon, it is the morning star, the daybreak and the evening. It is the trumpet, it is the mountain, and the desert, and the promised land. It is the ship, it is the way across the sea. It is the net, the vine, the field. It is the ark, the barn, the stable, and the manger. It is the beast of burden, and it is the horse. It is the storehouse, the court, the wedding-chamber, the tower, the camp, the battle-front. It is the people, and the kingdom, and the priesthood. It is the flock and the shepherd, the sheep and the pastures. It is paradise, it is the garden, it is the palm, the rose, the lily. It is the fountain and the river; it is the door, it is the dove, it is the raiment, it is the pearl, it is the crown, it is the sceptre, and it is the throne. It is the table and the bread, it is the spouse, the mother, the daughter and the sister.[7]

This radiant catalogue of things that are signs is introduced by the statement "God is become everything to you, and God has made everything for you." He may be approached through what he has made, and the spiritual meanings discovered there will create a second house within the Christian heart, where he may be received in his turn.[8]

To this task of reading the created universe and its history there were many guides. Christ's life and death was understood to be, among other things, a gloss upon the Hebrew Bible, revealing the hidden sense of many of its literal events: they were seen to be mysterious prefigurations of his life to come. And all holy writ contained clues to the significance of things. The great encyclopedias of the thirteenth century represent a scientific tendency that was to grow increasingly important in the later Middle Ages—an interest in more accurate classification, in direct observation, in the literal. Yet an older inheritance of moralized observation, descending through the bestiaries, the lapidaries, the etymological dictionaries, and so on, is neither forgotten nor made consciously separate, as though it bore an entirely different relation to the phenomenal world.[9] The encyclopedias, by incorporating this traditional material, became themselves symbolic handbooks to the universe, contributing to a public language of sign being fed from many other sources as well.

In this medieval language of sign, three major categories may be distinguished. There is first of all a vocabulary of *attribute*, which allows the ready identification of certain historical or pseudohistorical persons: the crown and harp that indicate King David, for example, or the wheel of St. Catherine, or the gridiron of St. Lawrence. Such objects mean themselves literally, but their significance derives from a history or legend that must be learned. There is also a vocabulary of *symbol*, in which things mean something other than themselves: the Holy Ghost is not a dove, but a dove, in painting or in literature, can stand for the Holy Ghost. And finally there are complex *allegorical figures*, most often abstract ideas expressed in a human form, sometimes accompanied by conventional symbols: Fortune as a woman beautiful on one side, ugly on the other, blindfolded and turning a wheel in the midst of the sea; or Avarice as an old man wearing torn clothes and sitting at a counting table stacked with money.[10]

Even ordinary members of Chaucer's audience would have known a whole repertory of such signs; they saw them in paintings, carvings, and stained glass; they heard them explained as signs in sermons, confessional teaching, and didactic literature; and they heard them used, sometimes openly, sometimes in covered, ingenious ways, in narrative and lyric poems not primarily didactic in intent. As modern readers, we can perhaps never recover an adequate sense of the visual richness of medieval culture,[11] or of the importance its pictures and signs held for a population mostly illiterate. Such signs constituted one of the major vocabularies with which medieval man sought to make sense of his daily experience. In the Middle Ages, it was the only language (in the sense of a body of abstract signs) that everyone could, to some degree, read. Only the very ignorant or indolent among Chaucer's first audiences would have been oblivious to the possibilities of such meaning in his art.

Such persons existed, of course. In our attempt to join the medieval audience in certain aspects of its experience, we may choose what part we wish to join: the attentive or the drowsy, the interested or the bemused. On the evidence of the prologue to *The Tale of Beryn*, a fifteenth-century continuation of *The Canterbury Tales* describing the pilgrims in Canterbury and their visit to the cathedral, we can ignore—by merry choice or through innocent lack of information—the meanings of the images to be seen there. In either case, the experience would still have legitimate claim to being called "medieval." But my reader would not have stayed with this book so long if he wished in the company of Chaucer to imitate the old man sleeping through a sermon, or in the nave of Canterbury Cathedral to imitate the Miller, interested in the stained glass only for the sake of boisterous jokes.* In the earliest of his major poems, *The Book of the Duchess*, Chaucer casts himself as "obtuse" auditor to the narrative of a man in black who tells, under the figure of a game of chess, how he has lost his wife to death.[12] The chess imagery is wholly conventional and was widely current, but the poem's dreamer/narrator persists almost to the end in hearing everything in a literal way. The larger purposes of the strategy, in a poem of lament and consolation, cannot occupy us here, but we may be certain that the excessively literal-minded auditor is not offered as exemplary to Chaucer's own au-

---

*The account in *The Tale of Beryn* (p. 6) reads:

> The kny3te went with his compers toward þe holy shryne,   (145)
> To do þat they were com fore, & aftir for to dyne;
> The Pardoner & þe Miller, & oþir lewde sotes,
> Sou3t hem selff[en] in the Chirch, ri3t as lewd[e] gotes;
> Pyrid fast, & pourid, hi3e oppon the glase,
> Countirfeting gentilmen, þe armys for to blase,
> Diskyueryng fast the peyntour, & for þe story mourned,
> And a red [it] also right as [wolde] Rammys hornyd.

diences. He intended them to understand the icons, the traditional language of symbol, through which he sometimes spoke even in his fictional art. Every art remains itself alone, yet painting and poetry often speak about common subjects through a language of things, and iconography is the study of that common tongue. If we would train ourselves in it, we may go still to the same school as his first audiences, to the manuscript illuminations, wall paintings, carvings and stained glass of the period, along with the sermons and treatises and literary texts that shaped, and themselves continued to transmit—as verbal images—these traditions of symbolic meaning. Our pleasant task is double: we must educate our eyes to the period at large, to the ordinary fourteenth-century world the literature assumes and reflects; and we must learn the symbolic language used in that period, sometimes in a fashion formally explicit, sometimes in a manner covered and complex.

Though material for both sorts of training survives in abundance, students of Chaucer labor under one notable disadvantage: no surviving manuscript of his work illustrates the narrative action of any of his poems. Indeed, were it not for a splendid chest front, carved in about the year 1400 with scenes from *The Pardoner's Tale* and only recently come to public notice (figure 31),[13] we should lack any such contemporary imaging at all. One need hardly say how valuable more evidence of this kind would be, not because any single such image would be definitive in its authority (the mental images formed by readers/auditors agree only in essentials: a white crow in a gilded cage, not absolutely identical crows in absolutely identical cages), but because such images offer evidence free from anachronism, and because they can sometimes tell us, through their choice of subject, what "places" in a literary text exerted the greatest pressure upon one member of that tale's first audience to make images in his mind. Such evidence could tell us what constituted the dominant images of a narrative poem by Chaucer for one medieval artist at least, or for that artist's patron or master, if some such other person dictated the places and scenes to be illustrated.[14]

Apart from *The Pardoner's Tale* carved in three scenes on a chest front, we have only images of the pilgrims, made in response to the word portraits of *The General Prologue* rather than to the tales they tell. Those in the Ellesmere Manuscript are deservedly famous; the six that survive (from a set once complete) in a manuscript in the Cambridge University Library (MS. Gg.iv.27) are nearly unknown.[15] That obscurity is undeserved, for although the Ellesmere portraits are skillfully done and have a special interest in having been made within a decade or so of Chaucer's death, the Cambridge portraits (from the mid-fifteenth century) exhibit at least as imaginative a response to Chaucer's text and have a peculiar energy all their own.

31. Scenes from *The Pardoner's Tale*. English, ca. 1400. Note 13.

They depict the Wife of Bath, the Pardoner, the Manciple, and the Monk, as well as the Reeve and the Cook (whose portraits are reproduced as figures 101 and 126 in the present volume). The manuscript also contains three pictures of personified Vices and Virtues from *The Parson's Tale*: there once were seven, but again vandals have cut out the rest. (I reproduce these pictures as figures 66–68.) Three other early pilgrim portraits are known, one presently in the Rylands Library (the Miller), and two in the possession of the Rosenbach Foundation (the Cook and Manciple). Several other manuscripts offer portraits of Chaucer as author; one depicts a friar; another has a small picture perhaps meant to represent Melibeus; and there is a fine mythographic depiction of Mars, Venus, and Jupiter, in a manuscript containing *The Complaint of Mars* and *The Complaint of Venus*. But the census remains brief,[16] a meager body of visual material that can be directly connected to our author's works, and none of it, except for the chest front, illustrating narrative per se. There might have been more, even of this second kind, had time or despoilers or the fortunes of patrons allowed. The magnificent Corpus manuscript of the *Troilus*, for example, whose frontispiece we have already had occasion to examine (figure 2), has spaces ruled in the text for some ninety narrative images. But they were never made.[17]

This paucity of surviving Chaucerian image, though a cause for regret, is no matter for surprise. Illuminated books were very expensive, and as a result were commissioned chiefly for religious or ceremonial use.[18] So popular a poem as *Piers Plowman* survives today in more than fifty manuscripts, but only one of these is illustrated, in drawings without artistic pretension of any kind. With two exceptions, the manuscripts of Gower's *Confessio amantis* likewise yield little information concerning what its audiences "saw" as they listened to its narratives: a standardized confession scene or the figure seen in Nebuchadnezzar's dream normally suffices to decorate even a deluxe manuscript of the poem. The *Gawain* manuscript (Cotton Nero A.x.), to whose chance survival we owe our only texts for four of the supreme poems of the age, is remarkable in having twelve illustrations, but they are somewhat crude in their design and coloring, and in several important details bear no relation to the texts they accompany.[19] Even the few earlier vernacular poems that had attained, already in the fourteenth century, a kind of classic status and had, therefore, evolved fairly elaborate programs of illustrations—especially the *Divine Comedy*, *The Romance of the Rose*, and Deguileville's *Pilgrimage of Human Life*—offer less evidence of how such texts were being read and imagined *across* the medieval decades than one could wish.[20] Most often, the picture cycle was simply copied from one manuscript to the next, with only changes in costume, setting, or painting style to indicate updating. The "new" response is as likely to be to the picture cycle itself as to the text it illustrates. The hand of tradition lay heavy on the productions of the ateliers. On almost every artistic level, sometimes including the highest, it was an age of the pattern book and the copy recopied.[21]

And so the lack of numerous and well-wrought contemporary images for Chaucer's narratives is by no means anomalous, nor does the lack of such material significantly separate us from his earliest audiences. Few of those who knew how to read would have had access to manuscripts richer than those that have survived, and most of his audience would have had no access to manuscripts at all. Yet these poems demonstrably ask their audience to imagine that they see what they hear described. I have drawn heavily upon manuscript illuminations in this book, even though many of the manuscripts I use would have been accessible in their own time only to persons of great wealth or learned privilege, because for us the illuminator is as close as we can get to a member of a medieval audience in the act of imaging a story. His pictures can show us—in ways that are free of large-scale anachronism and permit some degree of generalization—how other members of that audience might have imagined a given narrative. At the least, such pictures can show us the conventional images a given artist held in his mind, to be summoned to memory and replicated by his hand in response to a thematic cue—a red-ink rubric, let us say, directing him to show "Here the lover kneels before Lady Fortune and her wheel."[22] At most, such pictures can show us an artist adapting a traditional image of this sort to the details of the specific text before him, working from a store of conventional imagery to specific textual detail, refining what he knew of the tradition into an individual reader's response. Both kinds of evidence are valuable.

And so our steady recourse in this study must be to two special categories of image. (1) We must go to whatever illuminated manuscripts can be found of the sources and analogues to Chaucer's narrative poems, even though such illustrations—by definition—cannot be responsive to the changes in plot, character, or emphasis that are, so far as we know, Chaucer's own. (2) We must make judicious use of the vast store of conventional imagery, mostly religious, some secular, that served to illustrate the major ideas of the time and would have been known to Chaucer and his first audiences from other texts and other places. These images involve collective values and were publicly accessible; they are central to the visual arts of the age as well as to its literature; and in a fashion that is characteristic of the mature Chaucer, they are discovered in—uncovered by—the narrative as it moves naturally from beginning to end, in scenes that remain in our mind's eye through long actions or descriptions. Whether the image is that of an architectural setting, a landscape, a costume, or a significant event, its function in the story is so essential as to confer upon it a certain "covered" quality. The image does not call attention to itself in specifically symbolic ways, but instead signals its ultimate function through the rhetorical care with which it is created; through the way it is remembered, coming readily to mind as something "seen" in the course of the tale; and through its suggestive likeness to images known from elsewhere, in contexts not fictional in kind.

This matter of a suggestive likeness is crucial, for most narrative images, even in Chaucer, are not iconographic in their potential. For instance, in the three scenes from *The Pardoner's Tale* that we have seen carved upon a contemporary chest front (figure 31), the scene on the left—in which one of the "riotoures thre" buys poison from an apothecary to poison his fellows—is without iconographic dimension. Though it is an event crucial to the story, and one that Chaucer invites us to see in our mind's eye, it is a narrative event merely. The other two scenes, however, both in the carving and in Chaucer's tale, perform a double function. Because they bear a suggestive likeness to certain other images in medieval tradition—the iconography of "Death at the Feast"—they not only forward the story in essential ways but can guide us in thinking more deeply upon its meaning as a whole.

The knowledge necessary to read these images in their symbolic dimension is almost never essential to the surface coherence of the story. The Miller would not have understood *The Reeve's Tale* in precisely the same way, or with the same learned range of information, as would (in their different ways) the Friar, the Franklin, the Clerk, and the Knight. But the Miller was a vital and welcome member of the audience. Chaucer's art does not address itself to learned and sophisticated persons only, but for those with the training and intelligence to respond most fully, his narratives characteristically possess an intellectual, artistic, and imaginative coherence, deeper than the linear continuities of plot, to which these images are central. This assimilation of the iconographic to the mimetic is a technique which he brought to greater perfection than any other poet of his time.

For the critic who would respect the conditions of oral performance characteristic of much late-medieval narrative, but who is nevertheless in quest of what medieval audiences (including readers) might have received at a maximum from that art, these images offer an important conceptual bridge, suggesting how even a listener might move from a simplified recreation of the narrative as process to the richer, more complex vision that critics trained in the close reading of literature have found there. As we have seen in Chapter I, on the authority of many witnesses, the image is at once simple and easy to remember, but to it many other details adhere, and by its means those other details (narrative in sequence, verbal in nature) can be recalled. And that makes possible a special kind of literary response. Because such an image can bring to mind others like it that are symbolic rather than mimetic in their relation to truth, it invites a meditation upon what is remembered that is unrelated to narrative in terms of mode, but central to it in terms of meaning.

Though the textures of Langland's art are very different, a memorial use of images is fundamental to his work as well—as the importance he gives to the character "Ymagynatyf" makes clear.[23] He seems characteristically to have begun by inventing a magisterial image—a Field Full of Folk spread out between a Tower of Truth and a Dungeon of Falsehood, the Wedding of Lady Mede, a vision of Middle Earth, the Barn of Unity—and then to have invented actions and dialogue that explore the complexity of the image's potential meaning.[24] Langland's poem is written in the voice of one sorting out experience—judging, exhorting, searching, pondering—and to it these grand, enigmatic, and troubling images are central. Without them the poem would have no base. Chaucer's own early practice, in the dream-vision poems, bears a certain kinship to this. The dreamer/narrator is often "shown" images—places, sights, things— that are expressly suprareal, expressly symbolic, which the speeches and the action seek to define. But the mature Chaucer of the *Troilus* and *The Canterbury Tales*, so far as we know, invented few or none of his stories. He preferred to seek within a received fiction such details as could be made to address a generalized truth and then to work them, through an exercise of rhetorical skill, into commanding narrative images—memorial centers of meaning and meditative suggestion for the entire poem.

What we may best call such constructs is not easy to resolve. Chaucer and his first audiences would, I think, have called them "images" simply, for they used this term to designate the products of the visual imagination in any medium whatsoever, including stone, glass, paint, poetry, and thought. Just as Chaucer could use the verb "portrey" to describe the activity of those who paint pictures on walls, those who make verses, and those who think about something previously seen ("He purtreyed in his herte and in his thoght," *CT*, IV. 1600),[25] so he used the word "images" to stand for sculpture in stone or wood, as well as for visual memories.[26] The latter signification was common in the age, and could be extended quite naturally to literature: "Ffor as Chaucer saiþ in this prologe of the xxv. good wymmen. Be wryteng haue men of ymages passed for writyng is þe keye of alle good remembraunce."[27] Interesting evidence for this semantic interrelationship can be found in the *ars moriendi* that Thomas Hoccleve, who called Chaucer both master and friend, translated near the end of his life. In that work, Wisdom teaches her disciple how to die a good death by ordering him to imagine in his mind the speaking likeness of a dying man (figure 32 illustrates the scene):

> "Beholde now the liknesse and figure
> Of a man dyynge and talkyng with thee."
> The disciple, of þat speeche took good cure,
> And in his conceit / bysyly soghte he,
> And ther-with-al / considere he gan, & see
> In him self put / the figure & liknesse
> Of a yong man of excellent fairnesse,
>
> Whom deeth so ny ransakid had, & soght,
> þat he withynne a whyle sholde dye.[28]

These lines describe how the disciple is able to imagine such a figure, in ways that invite the reader/listener to do so in turn. Thus "made," the image begins to act. It speaks to the disciple, who answers it, and in the long colloquy that follows, it is referred to simply as "the ymage": "Than spak thymage / answerynge in this wyse." This "gastful sighte" addressed to the "myndes ÿen" offers an object lesson in medieval literary response: speak to the image, let the image speak to you, meditate upon it in your mind. The request of the image, "Let me be your ensaumple and your mirour," is not directed to the disciple alone: in the image's death scene, which is quite horrible, we are meant to see something potential in our own, and from

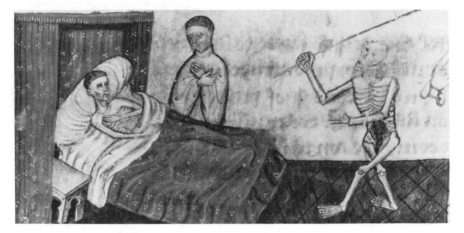

32. Hoccleve's dialogue with the image of a dying man. English, ca. 1430.
Note 28.

that experience to be moved (by the *intentio* of the image, as explained in Chapter I) toward a way of living that can prepare us for a patient and willing death.[29]

All of which is to say that if we define the word "image" with careful regard to medieval usage—that is, in ways inclusive of the visual arts, the art of literature, and certain ordinary processes of thought and memory—it necessarily claims central place in the critical vocabulary of this book. But the word has been used in such a variety of ways in the literary criticism of this century[30] that some further specification seems necessary if I would indicate clearly the sort of image that is my subject here. Let me name some possible supplementary terms, and in doing so, acknowledge as well my debt to several scholars who have helped me understand this subject better.

The first of these terms comes from Charles A. Owen, Jr. In his fine essay "The Crucial Passages in Five of the *Canterbury Tales*: A Study in Irony and Symbol," he examines as "crucial" several "passages that foreshadow the outcome in the unwitting speech of a character" and that "perform also a symbolic and unifying function." He sometimes terms these passages "controlling images" as well, and is careful to stress their "unobtrusive" nature: "nothing in the tale forces them to the symbolic level," though he shows how they ultimately function in that way.[31] This is a view of Chaucer's art that I seek to confirm and to extend. John Leyerle has worked with similar material, and in an essay entitled "The Heart and the Chain" has suggested the term "poetic nucleus" for symbols of that kind, as a way of indicating their function within Chaucer's work. He explains the term in a particularly felicitous way: "Nucleus means both seed, im-

plying origin and growth, and center, implying a surrounding struc-
ture."[32] I am happy with both Owen's "crucial passages" and Ley-
erle's "poetic nucleus" as critical formulas: they focus upon the text
as literature, as a construct of words, and they point to the tale's sym-
bolic center as a place of prime importance for the meaning of the
whole. But because the examples in Chaucer to which I would lay
common claim are so closely linked with visual images—both as an
experience of narrative and through the widespread currency of
those traditions of imagery within the visual arts—I wish also to name
them in ways that will steadily incorporate the word "image" itself.

Rosemund Tuve described with great learning the way some of
these medieval traditions (both literary and pictorial) survived into
Renaissance poetry, and termed them "allegorical imagery" in a dis-
tinguished book by that name.[33] She goes beyond Owen and Leyerle
in using pictures to talk about texts, and in that sense comes nearer
to furnishing a model for this study. But the term "allegorical
imagery"—appropriate both to her materials and to the Renaissance
poems that inherited and transformed them—is less useful for my
purposes than for hers. The poems of Chaucer that I shall write
about are not allegories. The images, as such, are allegorical in po-
tential, but they are uncovered in the course of fictions whose larger
decorum of the literal (the verisimilar) Chaucer took great pains to
preserve. Since that is what is most distinctive in his use of traditional
imagery, I wish to describe these images in ways that steadily honor
the fact.

Erwin Panofsky, in a brilliant study of Flemish painting in the fif-
teenth century, termed some related procedures in the visual arts
"concealed or disguised symbolism,"[34] a phrase that could be used to
describe Chaucer's technique as well, even though the poet's "con-
cealed images" are generally more popular in their provenance and
more insistent in their claims upon the reader/listener's attention
than are those of the Flemish painters. But Panofsky's subject is, in
other and more important ways, different from my own: he investi-
gates the way certain religious symbols, in response to a changing
sense of artistic decorum, were given "natural" (verisimilar) place
within religious paintings. He focuses on religious symbols within
religious contexts; my concern is with images that bring generalized
meaning into highly particularized fictional scenes—most often, sec-
ular fictional scenes—and apparently address no history more im-
portant than their own.

Panofsky terms such images "iconographic" as well, a term that
has been given a significant place in medieval literary criticism by
D. W. Robertson, Jr., and F. P. Pickering, among others.[35] In bor-
rowing that term from the art historians, we implicitly extend its

original meaning—the symbolic representation of ideas, persons, and history in pictorial form—as a means of describing verbal compositions that invite the imagining of symbolic pictures in the mind.

All of these books and essays have kept me good company in my researches, and have contributed to the critical vocabulary of this book. But for the most part I have preferred to term the passages I shall study "narrative images," by which I seek no more than to indicate their true kinship with visual traditions—which requires that they be called images—and their true mode of occurrence, within narrative that is self-sufficient in its own right. In that role, they satisfy certain other criteria as well: they are central to the tale that uncovers them (Owen would say "crucial," Leyerle "nucleic"); they are symbolic in their potential meaning (Tuve would say "allegorical," Robertson and Pickering "iconographic"); and their symbolic meaning is characteristically subordinate to the verisimilar surfaces of the fiction within which they await discovery (a symbolism that Panofsky would describe as "disguised" or "concealed"). In brief, they are symbolic images integral to the action that encloses them, in fiction that is itself neither symbolic nor allegorical in nature. In Chaucer's mature art, such images serve to forward the story in an easy and natural way. But if I have understood the matter correctly, his recognition of their potential provided him as well, in the act of composition, with cues to the thematic shaping and rhetorical elaboration of his story, and they can still serve to provide his readers with suggestions toward an appropriate and richly meditated response. My subject is the iconography of narrative, as practiced by a great medieval poet.

And so two things will especially concern me in the chapters that follow: these images in their iconographic identity, that is, in relation to similar images in literature and the visual arts; and these images in their contextual identity, that is, in relation to the narrative by which they are communicated, in its full, empirical, "covering" detail. Each imposes its special obligation: first, that we be willing to learn the symbolic language Chaucer is using; second, that we respect the artistic decorum with which he uses such signs, giving proper value always to the narrative context within which, for him, such images have their hidden but most authentic life. By what rules, then, shall we proceed?

We must, first of all, take account of the fact that iconography, as a language of things, lacks any comprehensive dictionary. Although certain ambitious projects concerned with Christian iconography are under way and shorter projects have been completed, the secular iconography of the Middle Ages still awaits systematic attention.[36] And no one, to my knowledge, has even contemplated a dictionary of sign in which both categories are intermingled—arranged on a basis no more prejudicial than the order of the alphabet—although the categories are less exclusive of each other than most such books assume. As a result, the critic who would write about such images as background to another subject—in the present case, *The Canterbury Tales*—must seek to establish, as best he can, a representative range of contexts in which a given image was current, as an essential step prior to thinking critically about the poem that has made that survey necessary. Only then will nonspecialist readers be able to judge his conclusions independently, or to reach better conclusions on their own, and only then will they be able to respond to that art out of an experience of imagery in some measure comparable to that of the medieval audience. I have sought in the chapters that follow to accept a discipline of the likely, the demonstrably available, seeking always to document, from his other writings, Chaucer's clear knowledge of the tradition under discussion. This has led me to avoid, for instance, the more remote corridors of the *Patrologia Latina* or the mythographic treatises, not because the reports we receive from the modern scholars who have made themselves most at home there lack claim to being possible "medieval" readings, but because I prefer to approach Chaucer's art and audience somewhere nearer its popular center. I have not attempted to provide an exhaustive chronological history of these images, tracing their full origins and lines of descent across the Christian centuries, since that would require a separate monograph devoted to each image, and the book on Chaucer would remain unwritten. But I offer for every image a brief account of its origins and main lines of development, so far as I have been able to discover them, and then proceed with the task that is to our present study more germane: a demonstration of the currency of that image in the fourteenth and early fifteenth centuries, with attention to the variety of contexts in which it occurs, as a preliminary to the close reading of a tale by Geoffrey Chaucer.

A survey of the full range of contexts in which an image was current is not only necessary in terms of *lexis*, but entails a procedural benefit as well: it can protect us from simplistic notions of how imagery functions and from reductive definitions that would summarily divorce images from all that surrounds them. The analogy with verbal language is again to the point: few words are complete sentences in their own right, and even those few—Stop! Help! Alas!—can mean vastly different things according to situation and tone of voice. (Stop!, for instance, articulated in a certain way, can be an invitation to continue.) Similarly, few visual signs or their verbal equivalents constitute independently precise communications. Not all doves represent the Holy Spirit: some indicate the soul; others identify Venus; some signify just themselves, doves and nothing more. Context alone turns a sign into a communication, limiting its possibilities, defining its exact and immediate intent.[37] And context alone can release the richness and subtlety potential in the sign. Though a devotional cross is among the least ambiguous of symbols, a crude cross of wood communicates something about Christ's death quite different from the expressive meaning of an elaborately decorated, highly worked cross of gold and jewels. A cross above the rood-screen in a great cathedral expresses something different from a cross in a private home, or a cross by Cimabue now to be viewed only as a part of the fine arts collection of a great museum. A cross without a figure on it or a cross that displays the regnant Christ of the Romanesque period, a cross displaying the tortured bird-flesh Christ of the Isenheim altarpiece or the "black" Christ of the Andes, all communicate different ideas, meanings, and emotions, though in terms of the lexicography of images all signify Christ's sacrifice. (And the cross of a modern telephone pole, or two sticks laced together by children in play, must not be confused with them.) Any sign in use is inseparable from context. In advance of use, no signification bears any priority over any other; all possibilities of meaning remain in suspension, potential merely. Geoffrey de Vinsauf begins his theory of determinations (the use of adjectives and adverbs) by expressing an analogous truth, "Dictio quae sonat una est quasi mater hyle; quasi res rudis et sine forma," which Margaret Nims has paraphrased: "A word standing alone has an element of un-definedness analogous to that of prime matter."[38]

The images of literature—mental images—likewise do not, and cannot, function in lexicographically neutral ways. They are at once delimited and increased by the words that create and surround them.[39] The sound of those words, their level of diction, the harmony of rhyme and meter, the emphasis conferred by accent and rhythm and pause, along with the genre in which the poem is made and the social milieu in which it is experienced, all are part of the sign properly understood. They are intrinsic to the real existence of signs in literature, and cannot be severed from any sign without its falsification, loss of potency, loss of life. What is at issue is more than the fact that an image can have different—even contradictory—meanings, *in bono* and *in malo*. That had long been recognized by the exegetes of sacred texts: a lion may stand for Christ or Satan. I am speaking instead of all the other factors that lie within the control of the author and constitute the complex language through which he speaks.* Through them we discover, and if his art is successful come to share, what he thinks and how he feels about his larger subject.[40]

---

*The author even controls, to some degree, the social milieu in which his work is read or heard, for he invites his audience to think of themselves in certain ways, to become a certain kind of audience. Pickering, *Literature and Art*, p. 56, stresses the importance of genre as a part of context; so does Gombrich, *Symbolic Images*, p. 5, following the lead of E. D. Hirsch, Jr.

The lexicographical survey, though essential, is only a preparation for the critical act (it is itself based upon a series of such acts), whose goal is to discover which of the possible meanings is most forcibly implied by the total context in which the image occurs, and how that context in turn mediates, complicates, and enriches the simplified lexicographical meaning (the sense *a*, *b*, *c*, or *d*) of the image.

And so I would argue that anyone concerned with the mental image as a vital link between Chaucer and the visual arts of his time must take as his subject whole poems, for that is where such images have their only real existence. By way of example, it has been demonstrated that bagpipes, whose shape can be made to look something like male genitalia (cf. figure 33, a fifteenth-century misericord from Rouen Cathedral), are part of an iconography of "the old song"—the carnal life that must be given over before the spiritual life ("Sing ye to the Lord a new song") can begin.[41] Indeed, they function so in my figure 85. But we may not conclude that bagpipes are therefore always and invariably a sign for that idea. The great Apocalypse tapestries at Angers, made in the late fourteenth century, show in their borders the music of the heavenly host—angels playing harps, viols, portative organs, and even (figure 34) bagpipes. No carnal meaning is implied: the designer of the tapestry was thinking of bagpipes as musical instruments only. So was Thomas Arundel, Archbishop of Canterbury, when he defended in 1407 the propriety of pilgrims choosing to leave a town to the sound of bagpipes played by one of their number: he affirmed, against arguments to the contrary (likewise perfectly literal), that such music was a respectable source of pleasure, which could lighten the burdens of a journey made in honor of God and His saints.[42] We must take care in our lexicography of signs not only to survey the full range of demonstrable symbolic meaning, but also to allow for the literal meaning of things—respecting both the possibility and the dignity of literal meaning. Context governs.

Indeed, certain medieval genres are defined by their refusal to grant privileged status to hierarchical truth. Parody, for instance, flourished in the Middle Ages, and could be valued for the pleasures of laughter and virtuoso display alone.[43] There existed as well a considerable literature that declared its chief purpose to be the relaxation and refreshment of the human spirit, as a goal both pragmatically necessary and theoretically defensible.[44] But the vast body of artistic narrative produced within the medieval period was shaped by the conviction that literature should possess a value beyond the pleasure it can give—that it has serious business with truth. This view expressed itself in English in several alternative formulas—"fruyt and chaf," "doctrine and delit," "sentence and solaas"—used to designate the two major elements that literature was expected to bring together

33. A bagpiper with small dogs. French, fifteenth century. Note 41.

in some viable union.[45] These formulas still provide us with an important and appropriate way of thinking about medieval poetry. But they must be used with care, for the Middle Ages is far from homogeneous as a period. It covers several centuries, which saw enormous changes in man's ability to dominate the physical universe and in his thought about the nature of his existence and the place of art within it. The quest of criticism for the radically singular truth about any single medieval narrative must be attentive to these changes. It must attempt to define, work by work, author by author, period by period, the exact—but multiple and shifting—relationship between these two quantities. This can only be discovered through a close look at actual artistic practice, for the formulas survive through the whole period largely unchanged, and in their brevity—their lack of specificity—can cover almost any balance struck between the two, almost any relationship established between them. Such formulas, separated from a critical engagement with texts, can tell us next to nothing. They exist to invite that engagement, not to render it unnecessary.

Chaucer's most extensive discussion of that duality is to be found at the end of his tale of Chauntecleer and Pertelote:

> But ye that holden this tale a folye,   (VII.3438)
> As of a fox, or of a cok and hen,
> Taketh the moralite, goode men.

For seint Paul seith that al that writen is,
To oure doctrine it is ywrite, ywis;
Taketh the fruyt, and lat the chaf be stille.

This brief passage has often been taken as a key to Chaucer's aesthetic, but all too often without close attention to what it actually says.[46] However great the medieval authority of the statement—and learned authors may be adduced in plenty, across the several medieval centuries—those authors are not speaking here, and certainly not speaking in their own contexts or out of their own moments in historical time. We must be alert to the place in which Chaucer introduces these terms, at the end of some six hundred lines of his most brilliant and audacious poetry, all of it (except for two "moralities" expressed in the preceding seven lines) in these terms "chaf"—a fable in which two chickens and a fox are allowed to speak and behave as though they were human beings, as though they were indeed lovers, villains, and tragic heroes. We must respect as well the clause that introduces the distinction, for what follows is no prescription to the general, but instead (as with most defenses of poetry) an address to those in Chaucer's audience who may be disposed to think such fictions empty and a waste of time: "ye that holden this tale a folye."

34. An angel with bagpipes. French, ca. 1375–80. Note 42.

For them—that possible subgroup within any audience—this advice. They, too, have been provided for. But we may doubt that Chaucer himself read (much less wrote) literature in so exclusive and austere a way, or that he wished his larger audience to value only the formulaic truths that he deduces in the preceding seven lines: keep your mouth shut; keep your eyes open. The real morality of *The Nun's Priest's Tale* (as E. T. Donaldson has persuasively argued) is inseparable from its surfaces, from the letter of its fiction, in which we are made to contemplate our customary assumptions concerning the grandeur, dignity, and meaningfulness of the human condition in a new and ironical light.[47] The tale seeks to alter our habitual gestures of self-regard and self-aggrandizement, and in its capacity to achieve that effect lies its greatest potential for the moral transformation of its audience. The formulaic morals are valid and useful, to be sure, but they do not necessitate six hundred lines in which the highest human questions are raised within a barnyard misadventure. You may, Chaucer tells us, throw all that away, if you can find no worth in it. But this is surely a witty challenge, not a sober directive concerning audience duty. The reference to St. Paul, outrageously too grand for the context, seems meant to amuse, rather than to send us scurrying to the tomes of the Fathers. No one, I think, has ever argued that Chaucer wrote *The Miller's* and *Reeve's Tales* only in order that we should skip them, though there too he says we may, if we fear we will be offended, "turne over the leef and chese another tale" (I.3177). Again he provides liberty for some, not a moral imperative for all: "whoso list it nat yheere" will find other tales more to their liking. It is the generosity of a host, not the didacticism of a teacher. Meanwhile he will get on with his own version of truth, the "greet mateere" (x.28; cf. I.3175) of the pilgrimage, to which the Miller and Reeve, quite as much as the Knight or Clerk, bring both their persons and their visions of experience—a complex truth whose claims are higher than those of literary decorum narrowly defined, and which he declares he will not "falsen" or betray (I.3175).

Just as we must accept Chaucer's own definition of what constitutes his "mateere," so must we accept his own definition of himself as artist. Nowhere in his work does he call himself "poete," a grandly evaluative word that he reserves for the great masters of classical antiquity—Homer, Ovid, Virgil, Lucan, Statius—and for only two medieval contemporaries, Dante of the divine imagination and Petrarch "lauriat," both of them authors of significant works in Latin as well as in the vernacular.[48] For himself and most of his kind, a simpler word: "makere." He describes himself so even at the end of his longest and most ambitious poems. The *Troilus*, for instance, concludes (italics added):

> Go, litel bok, go, litel myn tragedye,   (*TC*, V,1786)
> Ther God *thi makere* yet, er that he dye,
> So sende myght *to make* in som comedye!
> But litel book, no *makyng* thow n'envie,
> But subgit be to alle *poesye*;
> And kis the steppes, where as thow seest pace
> Virgile, Ovide, Omer, Lucan, and Stace.

Envy no other "makyng" (he instructs his poem) and before the higher seriousness of "poesye," stand humble. Throughout his writing, the verbs he characteristically uses to describe the process of composition are "to make" and "to endyte," [49] and in the *Retraction* to *The Canterbury Tales*, possibly the last thing he ever wrote, he presents the same modest self-estimation: "Heere taketh the makere of this book his leve." That there was room for pride and self-respect within the craft goes without saying: he saluted a French contemporary in these words, "Graunson, flour of hem that make in Fraunce," and he was himself remembered by William Dunbar in a moving lament as "the noble Chaucer, of makaris flour." [50] It was the ordinary, expected term, but certain of its implications are worth further thought.

The Middle Ages lacked any coherent theory of what we would call "the fine arts." Painters, for example, often belonged to the same guild as saddle-makers (fine saddles then were carved and painted), [51] and poets, too, were understood to be purveyors of something useful. Poetry preserved the memory of the past; it could shape man's conduct for the better; it could restore and refresh his spirit. But it was also artificial—a thing "made" of human speech worked into harmonious patterns of stanza, meter, and rhyme. Chaucer was an artisan, and like many of his greatest contemporaries sometimes made poems to order, on commission from a patron. *The Book of the Duchess* certainly, and *The Second Nun's Tale* probably, are poems of this kind. [52] Such a poetic prized learning and valued skill, but did not normally lay claim to the higher sorts of inspiration. [53] Alceste, in *The Legend of Good Women*, defends Chaucer's art by claiming for him (and, implicitly, for writers like him) a modesty of intent that falls short of the wish always to serve ultimate truth: "He useth thynges for to make; / Hym rekketh noght of what matere he take" (*LGW*, [F] 364).

A fourteenth-century miniature illustrating the sixth book of Aristotle's *Ethics*, which contains a brief but influential discussion of art as making, can instruct us in the classical antecedents of this tradition and in their Christian metamorphosis. The *Ethics* was one of the set texts of the medieval university curriculum, and had been translated into French by Nicole Oresme, whose version is illustrated here (fig-

35. Art and Wisdom (illustrating Aristotle's *Ethics*). French, ca. 1372–74. Note 54.

ure 35). We are shown Art as a man at his forge and anvil, whereas
Sapience is depicted as a man who contemplates truth, represented
by Christ and the angels, visible above.[54] For Aristotle, art (*techne*)
meant simply "practical thinking which is not divided from the mak-
ing in which it issues,"[55] in contrast to the several kinds of wis-
dom that can exist independent of things made—for example, "sci-
entific knowledge, practical wisdom, philosophic wisdom, intuitive

reason"[56]—which the medieval illuminator has replaced with knowledge of the Christian God. The enterprises of art and wisdom are quite properly shown side by side, but they are also distinct from each other: two people are engaged in them, as it were in different rooms.[57]

In such a schema, the artist is not seer, philosopher, or priest—not in his capacity as artist. When Chaucer spoke as a philosopher or preacher, it was, significantly, in other voices than his own. His two tales of "wisdom"— *The Tale of Melibee* and *The Parson's Tale*—both explicitly reject art (rhyme and verisimilar fiction) to offer "doctryne" unambiguous in its means.[58] And his *Boece*, his *Treatise on the Astrolabe*, and the attributed *Equatorie of the Planets* are prose works all. It is worth remarking that in translating Boethius's *Consolation* as a whole—as a book of wisdom—he chose to translate even the poems into prose; whereas in his fictions, notably *The Knight's Tale* and the *Troilus*, he versifies Boethius's poems and proses alike, as it suits him, but uses them to utterly different ends. In verse his characters are as likely to misunderstand or misrepresent these texts as to get them right, and the purposes of Truth are served only by indirection.[59]

Some of his poems, of course, touch more closely on Truth than do others; those that come nearest, whose narrative mode is least ambiguous and whose submission to phenomenal detail is least compromising, are also those in which he stays closest to his textual source. In *The Man of Law's Tale* or *The Second Nun's Tale*, for example, his "making" involves almost no invention of primary material, but instead translation, and the artistic elaboration of rhetoric and image. *The Man of Law's Tale*, which will be examined in Chapter VII, offers (in a certain sense) the "highest" poetry we shall consider in this volume. But even there Chaucer does not come before us as theologian or philosopher or even moral guide; he comes as maker, demonstrating his art in one of its most powerful modes.

The Parson's rejection of art, in his Prologue, is absolute, and it is expressed in the sort of formulaic language—"fruyt and chaf"— with which this part of my discussion began: "Why sholde I sowen draf out of my fest, / Whan I may sowen whete, if that me lest?" (x.35). He need not, and he does not. As the sun sets in Libra, the last of the tales—a prose treatise on the Seven Deadly Sins and the sacrament of Penance—is given respectful pilgrim audience. Chaucer might, of course, have made the same literary decision all his life long, but he characteristically chose instead to sow wheat and chaff together—despite all the pious treatises, worthy of translation or elaboration into English, that might (in those other terms) more fruitfully have claimed his attention. He worked relatively seldom within genres that sought Wisdom or Truth as their characteristic end: wisdom, yes, and truth, yes, but of a more tentative and modest kind, not only discovered through, but inevitably qualified by, the letter of fiction. All of his tales are in an important sense Christian—certainly none of them sets up a countertruth, not even the tales that take place in pagan times. But the degree to which—and way in which—they reflect that highest truth varies: not all of the imaginative worlds he created are Christian "worlds." *Troilus and Criseyde*, *The Knight's Tale*, *The Franklin's Tale*, and the fabliaux invoke sets of values and obligations different from those of, say, *The Second Nun's Tale* of St. Cecilia. Those differences must concern us, or literature itself becomes unnecessary and unprofitable. We need otherwise only read some theory of "the medieval possible," and waste no time in exposing ourselves to the complexities, ambiguities, and surprises of medieval art.

Our task is not to substitute an explicitly Christian context for every other sort of context Chaucer created, but instead to understand those contexts, too, as accurately and fully as we can; to ask why a Christian poet might have chosen to create them; and to ask concerning the Christian truths that he introduces into his fiction—most often through narrative images iconographic in their import—how they fare within it. I believe such images constitute the major way Chaucer sought to make a fictional construct coterminous with, but not the same as, a literature of wisdom. And I would argue further that the purpose of those images is seldom narrowly didactic. They are used rather to illuminate human experience in its full range and variety—sometimes tragic, sometimes comic, at times perplexing, at times magnificently clear. *The Canterbury Tales* presents no univocal statement, but rather some twenty-three pilgrim voices, out of a company of nine-and-twenty, bearing witness to their understanding of life through the fictions they tell. To read the whole of *The Canterbury Tales* in the light of *The Parson's Tale*, as though all the other narratives were merely partial expressions of its truth, intended only to summon its full truth to mind, is at once to underread and overread the larger work—to render it, against its nature, monotonous in intent and narrow in its sympathies, and to credit it in all its parts with a higher seriousness than it possesses.[60] We may need now and then to invoke such standards in order to determine the contextual limits of an image or a theme in a given tale, but we shall do so without trying to "remedy" its art by drawing it beyond those limits, making of it something other than what it is. There can be no question ever about the priority or superior dignity of the Christian truths (or their expression in images) for the culture in which Chaucer lived and which he served. But he used those images in fictional contexts less in order to reassert that priority (it needed no such defense or assertion) than as part of an assault upon the otherwise inexpressible: those areas of experience for which we have no single word, no adequate formula (a defense of metaphor that goes back to Cicero)[61] and which the "mirror of wisdom" on its own cannot adequately reflect. In such an undertaking, the fruit and the chaff, the doctrine and the delight, the moral and the matter are inseparable. The work as a whole is held together by the idea of pilgrimage and the image of the pilgrim, not by some neat and tidy moral equation.

And so I end this introduction with something of a paradox. In the essays that follow I shall be fairly steadily concerned with symbolic meaning—with the iconographic content of certain mental images that are created by Chaucer's narrative and anchored in his audiences' memory. But I wish to argue with equal vigor for the primacy of the *letter*: the authority of the whole poem, line by line, in which fiction and truth are voiced simultaneously. My goal is not to shrink the narrative to an icon, but rather to explore the icon as the vital center of a work vivid and valuable as a whole. In Chaucer's aesthetic, we must define the "chaf" as fiction, to be sure, but not as worthless falsehood, and the "fruyt" (more conventionally) as generalized truth freed of its fictive particularities. But the second emerges from the first, and most powerfully so through a meditation upon its dominant images; it does not make of the fiction something contemptible, to be disposed of or put out of mind as soon as a paraphrasable moral lesson can be discerned.

Beryl Smalley, in her remarkable studies of medieval Biblical exegesis and the activities of English fourteenth-century friars, has documented there a comparable interest in the literal meaning of texts, discovering it where it was perhaps least to be expected—in the glosses (*postilla*) to sacred texts themselves: "The words and events of Scripture retain all their symbolic value. But the [thirteenth-century] postillator has diverted his attention. He is treading on earth, with occasional upward glances, instead of floating above it, descending only now and then." The recovery of a text's most literal (often historical) meaning became a serious goal of Biblical scholarship.[62] R. W. Southern's revisionist essays arguing the existence of a "medieval humanism" are also to the present point: taking as the essential criteria for humanism belief in the dignity of human nature, the dignity of the natural world, and the human intelligibility of the universe, he demonstrates a coherent development of these ideas from the twelfth through the early fourteenth centuries. They have consequence for theology, philosophy, science, and the arts.[63] Within specifically literary studies, Judson Allen's important investigations into the "spiritual sense" as it was understood by fourteenth-century English exegetes have led him to suggest that, as medieval poetry became more "realistic," more verisimilar, its audiences became more likely, not less, to approach it alert to the possibilities of a spiritual

sense behind the letter: Biblical exegesis, from the very begin-
ning, had assumed (and required) a firmly literal base.[64] As Morton
Bloomfield has reminded us in an eloquent essay, only the literal
sense of fiction is truly profound, for it alone contains the possibility
of other meanings.[65]

Chaucer's art was responsive to these new currents of thought and
feeling, but it remained conservative in temper as well. Although the
surfaces of many of his fictions are as "modern" as Boccaccio's in the
Decameron, he ultimately never sought so great a freedom from the
hierarchies of truth, if Charles Singleton has correctly described Boc-
caccio's intention in deciding to take his narrative art out of the
plague-ridden city. Singleton writes: "The framework of the *De-
cameron* is the effort to justify and protect a new art, an art which sim-
ply in order to be, to exist, required the moment free of all other
cares, the willingness to stop *going anywhere* (either toward God or
toward philosophical truth)."[66] Chaucer, in his last great work, sim-
ilarly frees a diverse company from the exigencies of their real and
daily lives. But unlike Boccaccio's elegant young people, virtually in-
distinguishable from each other and unmarked by the lives they've
lived so far, Chaucer's pilgrims bring with them living evidence of
who they are and what they've been. He places them on a long road
to a cathedral, and creates for them tales that, in terms of the history
of style, simultaneously look forward (in the apparent autonomy of
their surfaces) and backward (in the symbolic images uncovered by
the action, which govern the making and meaning of the tale that
embodies them). Those images allow truth to speak through fable.
They join, in a more natural and organic way than anyone had ever
managed in English literature before, the *visibilia* and the *invisibilia* of
the universe, and the human lives lived out within it. If Boccaccio's
art in the *Decameron* is the more audacious and new,[67] it is also less
rich, less substantial, less resonant in the mind. Chaucer invented for
English literature a new decorum in the artistic use of symbol, able to
incorporate both the clarity of Truth and the common light of day.

III. *The Knight's Tale* and Its Settings

THE PRISON/GARDEN AND

THE TOURNAMENT AMPHITHEATRE

 H A U C E R's pilgrims journey toward the most important Christian shrine in England, the tomb of St. Thomas à Becket in Canterbury Cathedral. A great variety of motive has brought them together, and we hear from them as they "talen" along the way a great diversity of story, ranging from bawdy fabliaux to a miracle of the Virgin, from metrical romance to prose sermon, from Ovidian myth to a saint's legend. Because *The Canterbury Tales* exists only in fragments, some more fully articulated than others, our guesses about its internal organization must always remain to some degree tentative. In the great middle of the work—the record of the middle journey—it is very difficult to talk about formal intention, for we are dealing with material that Chaucer, had he lived, might later have revised, replaced, or repositioned. And we know nothing of the plans that never found their way into verse at all.

But the larger "idea" of *The Canterbury Tales*, in Donald Howard's phrase, can be investigated more confidently, for we have from Chaucer the first tale and the last—those of the Knight and the Parson—and incremental to each a series of tales that together create a substantial frame for the whole. The first of these groups is the subject of this volume, which will argue that the tales of the Knight, Miller, Reeve, Cook, and Man of Law formally begin the journey, constituting a narrative sequence at once coherent in its own right and prophetic—typologically anticipatory—of the shape of the literary pilgrimage as a whole. This sequence of tales looks toward three distinct historical periods—the pagan world of classical Greece, the transitional world of sixth-century Europe, and the contemporary world of late-fourteenth-century England. It does so through the lenses of three literary genres—romance, fabliau, and artistically elaborated chronicle—each capable of registering a particular area of human experience with maximum precision. But the larger design is also self-reflexive, concerned with the nature of poetry itself. The beginning of the journey offers a carefully structured demonstration of the several ways in which poetry can relate to truth.

The tale the pilgrim company hears first on its journey is dignified, eloquent, and serious in its intent,[1] but it is, for all that, a strange choice of tale to begin a Christian pilgrimage. Within such a story, set in pagan Athens, centuries before the birth of Christ and the continuing witness of his saints, the deepest truths known to the teller and his audience—the very truths they have become pilgrims to honor—cannot be expressed. In this chapter I shall argue that Chaucer chose it as his first tale precisely for its exclusion of Christian material, and for the self-limitation that such a choice entailed for him as poet. A sense of human limitation, apprehended on many levels, is at the heart of the tale, and constitutes its essential contribution to the first day's pilgrimage.

Chaucer's subject is nothing less than the pagan past at its most noble and dignified, imagined from within. As in the *Troilus*, generally thought to have been written at about the same time in his career, his purpose is to discover—through an act of the sympathetic imagination—what it was like to be human then, and what kinds of poetry can be made of that experience. In *The Knight's Tale*, he communicates his vision of the pagan past most powerfully through two great images essential to the narrative, the prison/garden and the tournament amphitheatre, settings that the poetry invites us to visualize in our minds and that rise readily to memory when we think about the tale. Around them it is possible to reconstruct and meditate upon the narrative experience as a whole. Let us look first at the prison/garden, for within that setting the love story has its beginning. As an image it undergoes a grave and beautiful metamorphosis in the poem.

The facts are initially very simple. Palamon and Arcite have been condemned by Duke Theseus "to dwellen in prisoun / Perpetuelly,— he nolde no raunsoun" (1.1023). They are held captive in a tower, "in angwissh and in wo," and it is from that prison some years later that they first see Emelye:

> . . . in the gardyn, at the sonne upriste,   (1.1051)
> She walketh up and doun, and as hire liste
> She gadereth floures. . . .

The action requires that the garden be within sight of the prison tower, but Chaucer (following his original, the *Teseida* of Boccaccio)[2] goes beyond that, to insist on their architectural contiguity. He joins them in an emblematic way:

> The grete tour, that was so thikke and stroong, (I.1056)
> Which of the castel was the chief dongeoun,
> (Ther as the knyghtes weren in prisoun
> Of which I tolde yow and tellen shal)
> Was evene joynant to the gardyn wal
> Ther as this Emelye hadde hir pleyynge.

In this striking juxtaposition of structures, the prison and garden are "evene joynant": they share a common wall. The setting is reminiscent of, and may ultimately have been suggested by, the House of Fortune in *The Romance of the Rose*, one part of which is high-towered and gorgeously decorated, with walls of gold and silver set with precious jewels; the rest is low and crumbling, with walls of mud and a thatch roof falling into ruin. Figure 36, from about 1400, shows Lady Fortune turning her wheel within.[3] That dual structure is analogous to the prison joined to a garden in *The Knight's Tale*, for both are ways of talking about the "wele" and "wo" of human life, about the bewildering range of experience that lies within Fortune's gift.

A remarkable manuscript painter, known after his patron as the Master of René of Anjou, responded vividly to this double setting in a miniature he made around 1455 for a French translation of the *Teseida*. It is part of a remarkable sequence of illustrations (some by a less gifted artist), which we shall examine closely in this chapter. He shows us, in figure 37, Emilia in the pleasure garden,* sitting on a turfed bench and weaving a garland of flowers, while the two knights look out upon her through the bars of their prison window.[4] The room behind them is in darkness, whereas the garden, delicate in its colors and open to the heavens, is washed by the light of spring. The double setting immediately establishes the *ethos* of the action, the themes the action will explore. The same may be said of a handsome presentation tray that Mariotto di Nardo, a Florentine painter, decorated sometime in the first quarter of the fifteenth century, or of a drawing illustrating the scene in a Florentine manuscript from about 1450.[5] The contrast between the two places, for these artists as well, serves as an entry into the meaning of the event, not merely a transcription of narrative detail. And that contrast suggested to Chaucer—as the first in a series of transformations he would work upon this image—a new approach to the young knights' discovery of passionate love, an approach more searching than anything in the *Teseida* or in these pictures based upon it.

---

*In order to distinguish between Chaucer's characters and those of Boccaccio's poem (whether in his original text, the paintings that illustrate its medieval French translation, or McCoy's modern English translation) I refer to Boccaccio's characters by their Italian names: Teseo, Palemone, Arcita, Emilia.

36. The House of Fortune (from *The Romance of the Rose*). Paris, ca. 1400. Note 3.

In Boccaccio's poem, the two knights at this moment are moved above all by the beauty of Emilia's person and her song. On seeing her, Arcita exclaims, "She is from paradise!" and Palemone echoes, "Surely, this is Venus!" (III, vv. 12, 14). They have never seen anyone so beautiful, so pleasing, so gracious—the usual superlatives, given a certain force by the skill of Boccaccio's rhetoric and by the correlative beauty of the *giardino amoroso* in which she is seen. These attributes of Emilia—including the conviction she must be a goddess ("But Venus is it soothly, as I gesse")—are important to Chaucer's version as well. But he works with something distinctive besides, narrating the process by which they fall in love in terms of a formula based on the verb "to roam," which owes nothing to Boccaccio and is repeated so often as to shape decisively our understanding of the event. In Chaucer's version (italics added), Palamon, by leave of his jailor,

> Was risen and *romed in a chambre an heigh,*   (I.1065)
> In which he al the noble citee seigh,
> And eek the gardyn, ful of braunches grene,
> Ther as this fresshe Emelye the shene
> Was in hire walk, and *romed up and doun.*
> This sorweful prisoner, this Palamoun,
> Goth in the chambre *romynge to and fro,*
> And to hymself compleynynge of his wo.

When Arcite notices his friend grow pale, Palamon explains the cause:

> "The fairnesse of that lady that I see (I. 1098)
> Yond in the gardyn *romen to and fro*
> Is cause of al my criyng and my wo."

A moment later Arcite is at the barred window:

> . . . with that word Arcite gan espye (I. 1112)
> Wher as this lady *romed to and fro*,
> And with that sighte hir beautee hurte hym so,

that he speaks of being wounded as deeply as Palamon.

> "The fresshe beautee sleeth me sodeynly (I. 1118)
> Of hire that *rometh in the yonder place*."

There are few places in Chaucer's writings where a single word is used so insistently. The repetition is surely a key to something central in the poem.

The convention of love at first sight that lies behind this fiction needs no apology. Then as now, such love has been known to hap-

37. Emilia in the pleasure garden; Palemone and Arcita in prison. French, ca. 1455. Note 4.

pen, and medieval love theory taught that erotic love enters the soul through the eyes (I.1096–97). Two illustrations of this scene indeed emphasize that tradition by showing the God of Love shooting an arrow of desire into the young knights' eyes.[6] But I think we can see Chaucer here seeking to reinforce those conventions with another sort of psychological truth—perhaps because there is something disproportionate, even potentially comic, about this event as a cause of everything that will follow. Love at first sight by two men for the same woman at exactly the same time makes a somewhat distant claim to credibility, as does the later moment when they stand ankle-deep in blood fighting over her, without Emelye even knowing they exist. Chaucer allows for all that is ridiculous in the situation through Theseus' response: "Now looketh, is nat that an heigh folye? / Who may been a fool, but if he love?" (I.1798). But beneath their apparently hopeless passion, Chaucer shows a deeper movement of the spirit as well—a compulsion not comic, arbitrary, or trivial. The two young knights fall in love with Emelye for her beauty, unmistakably, but for the beauty of her freedom most of all. They cannot describe her—for they cannot see her—apart from the liberty and ease of her movement. From within prison they fall in love with a creature who seems to incarnate a condition the exact opposite of their own.

Indeed, we are made to see this gratuitous decision to love—this act of pure will—as their only available expression of something within them still free, not limited by prison walls, leg-irons, or exile.[7] The affirmation of some freedom, no matter how tenuous, is essential to their survival as fully human beings. In the words of Arcite, returned from exile in the disguise of a servant, as he raises his sword against Palamon in the grove:

> "What, verray fool, thynk wel that love is free,   (I.1606)
> And I wol love hire maugree al thy myght!"

Their prison decision to love, and if necessary to die in affirmation of that love, enacts, in a way that becomes important later in the tale, a woefully distorted version of a truth taught by Lady Philosophy to Boethius in another prison: the fact that the mind and spirit can be free, even if the body is in chains. Being young knights, not philosophers, they choose to make their ultimate commitment to Emelye. But that decision is informed by values not limited to its choice of object alone, affirming both the freedom of the heart's affections, in despite of circumstance, and the power of man's will over his animal instinct merely to survive, on any terms at all. Central to man's nature as it is conceived in this poem are his need to seek freedom and his need to seek love. Palamon and Arcite in prison, looking out upon Emelye in the garden, blend these two compulsions into a single "entente." It is only in retrospect that we realize Emelye in her "romynge" is, in subtler, less apparent ways, as constrained as they.

Thus the way the two knights fall in love in this tale is far more deeply rooted in its physical setting than is the version offered by the *Teseida*, and it prepares us for even more complex manipulations of the image to come. What has been to this point essentially a poetry of stasis, permitting only the barest minimum of physical movement within a formal architectural tableau, suddenly becomes animated, opening out into a realm of contingency and change. Perotheus obtains Arcite's freedom, Palamon escapes, and the opening icon of the prison/garden—now left behind as a literal place, but lodged in our memory as a mental image—is redefined through a series of metaphors and used to illuminate the significance of the action in new and deeper ways.

Released "frely to goon wher that hym liste over al" (I.1207), Arcite feels no joy. He is in a world turned "up-so-doun," in which words and the things to which they point are perversely, if poignantly, reassessed:

> He seyde, "Allas that day that I was born!   (I.1223)
> Now is my prisoun worse than biforn;
> Now is me shape eternally to dwelle
> Noght in purgatorie, but in helle.
> Allas, that evere knew I Perotheus!
> For elles hadde I dwelled with Theseus,
> Yfetered in his prisoun everemo.
> Thanne hadde I been in blisse, and nat in wo.
> Oonly the sighte of hire whom that I serve,
> Though that I nevere hir grace may deserve,
> Wolde han suffised right ynough for me.
> O deere cosyn Palamon," quod he,
> "Thyn is the victorie of this aventure.
> Ful blisfully in prison maistow dure,—
> In prison? certes nay, but in paradys!
> Wel hath Fortune yturned thee the dys."

This extravagant reversal of values, in which freedom has become prison and prison freedom, yields a rueful sort of comedy, but the larger interest is psychological and fully serious. The way the young knights choose to assert their freedom from within the literal prison—electing to love another human being totally, making their entire happiness contingent upon someone other than themselves—is here revealed to be its own kind of bondage, a *prison amoureuse* at once bitter and sweet, painful but preferred. So cruelly perplexing is this new imprisonment that when they next meet (in a wooded grove), the encounter is described in language that recalls their former incarceration: Palamon hides in a bush, while Arcite "rometh up and doun" (I.1515). Even outside the prison tower, their experience is characterized as captivity and constraint.

In Boccaccio's poem, the metaphor of the love prison is established much earlier, when the knights see Emilia for the very first time. Referring to the God of Love, Palemone says "I tell you His captivity already weighs on me more heavily than that of Teseo. . . . I see myself imprisoned here and stripped of all my strength."[8] Chaucer chose instead to reserve the love metaphor for the moment of release from the literal prison, as did the Master of René of Anjou in his splendid sequence of illustrations. Figure 38 shows Arcita at the gate of Teseo's castle, as iron fetters are removed from his ankles; his friends stand ready with horses to accompany him home to Thebes, and the prison tower, with its high-barred window, is visible behind. Arcita is at the picture's center—everything is organized around him—but his head is turned sharply to the side, and we necessarily follow the direction of his glance. The deflecting gesture tells us *his* center is not within himself: he has eyes only for what lies behind him, the castle with its prison and that prison's single privilege, to see daily in the garden his lady Emilia.[9]

38. Arcita released from prison. French, ca. 1455. Note 9.

39. Lady Lechery and her manacles. Paris, ca. 1295, by the painter Honoré. Note 11.

We must note, however, one point of difference between this painting, Chaucer's poem, and the Boccaccio source. The painter illustrates the moment in the *Teseida* when Arcita, just before his release, prays to God (*Dio*) that he might see Emilia on the balcony, and has his wish granted him.[10] But I suspect both the painter and Chaucer before him thought that brief comfort a trivial invention. Chaucer suppressed it entirely, whereas the painter chose to show the moment of prayer rather than its issue, or, if indeed it is the later moment, not to let us see what Arcita sees. In terms of the picture space, Emilia is absent; only Arcita's love for her is shown. Though the open country lies before him, Arcita can only look back: he is in another prison, the prison of love.

That Chaucer displays a similar interest in the theme of psychological freedom and imprisonment any attentive reader can discover from the text alone. But it is also necessary to recognize that this thematic invention is not exclusive to Chaucer or to his source—that he here seeks to uncover for us, from just below the surface of his fiction, a generalized truth widely known and richly formulated in medieval tradition. Some knowledge of that tradition may help us discover what judgment he means for us to reach in thinking about this love as an experience of imprisonment.

There is space in my text for only a schematic survey of the image, though I shall document it more richly in the notes. We may begin with a picture showing Lechery (*Luxure*) as a beautiful woman who holds in one hand a veil and in the other a pair of manacles (figure 39).[11] This picture, from a manuscript of the *Somme le roi*, a widely known treatise on the vices and virtues, shows carnal love as un-equivocal bondage, and neither it nor the text it illustrates admits any qualification of that view. Lady Lechery with her manacles represents one end of an iconographic continuum within which we must locate as well Alain de Lille's *De planctu naturae*, a twelfth-century work Chaucer drew upon in making his own *Parliament of Fowls*. Alain de-fines this kind of love through a catalogue of paradoxes, among them "sorrowful paradise, pleasant prison." Like the author of the *Somme*, he writes out of an explicitly moral tradition, but he allows the expe-rience a degree of integrity within its own terms: "paradise" and "pleasant" seem to him appropriate words, however necessary their supplementation.[12] Andreas Capellanus, whose treatise *De arte hon-este amandi* is best understood as a scholastic comedy about such love ideas, also uses the metaphor in passing,[13] occupying some ambigu-ous middle ground between the theological and the profane, as does an important passage from *The Romance of the Rose*. In what may be Chaucer's own translation, the God of Love explains how his ser-vants endure their sufferings through hope of change alone:

> . . . as man in prisoun sett,   (*RR*, 2755)
> And may not geten for to et
> But barly breed, and watir pure,
> And lyeth in vermyn and in ordure;
> With all this yitt can he lyve,
> Good hope such comfort hath hym yive,
> Which maketh wene that he shall be
> Delyvered, and come to liberte.
> In fortune is [his] fulle trust;
> Though he lye in strawe or dust,
> In hoope is all his susteynyng.
> And so for lovers, in her wenyng,
> Whiche Love hath shit in his prisoun.[14]

If these lines are meant to recommend to the reader the adventure of erotic love, they are counterproductive, to say the least. But this is not the only vision of love in the poem. In recent years, the exact auctorial intent of the *Romance* has become once again a matter of controversy—just as it was in the early fifteenth century—and no new consensus has emerged. But whatever problems remain in the interpretation of this particular text, there can be no doubt that else-where in the literature of the thirteenth through fifteenth centuries the tradition of the love prison had become predominantly secular and nonmoralistic in tone. It is found chiefly in the literature of pas-sionate love, rather than in the literature of wisdom, and was used less to impose perspectives upon the love experience from the out-side than to clarify and celebrate the mysteries of that experience from within. This third major sense of the image, which presents the same psychological facts in ways that affirm the love that is their cause, is, in my judgment, the sense that governs Chaucer's treatment of the young knights' experience of love throughout most of *The Knight's Tale*. For Chaucer the tradition probably descends from an allegorical poem of Baudouin de Condé, *Li Prisons d'Amours*, written sometime between 1240 and 1280, and reaches him through two writers highly important to his own early development as a poet: Guillaume de Machaut in his ballades, and Jean Froissart in his *Prison amoureuse*.[15]

Baudouin's poem, 3,131 lines long, explores love in terms of life within a great castle prison, making steady reference to a love affair of the poet's own that is currently underway. The prison's foundations are allegorized, as is its tower, along with the movements of the lover's psyche that impel him toward such captivity, and its potential to cause him either happiness or despair. Figures 40–42 are taken from a northern French manuscript of the poem (second quarter of the fourteenth century)[16] that contains 43 miniatures in all, none especially beautiful, and none very generous in illustrating textual detail, but worth our brief attention, if only to clarify the symbolic underlay of Teseo's castle as represented in figure 38 or in the verses of Chaucer's poem.

Figure 40 shows the prison with its two floors (*estages*), the lower of which, in Baudouin's text, is a place of sorrow, complaint, and suffering, inhabited by those unfortunate in love, whereas the upper is high-walled and beautifully ornamented, suitable for those allowed to experience love's joy. The whole is raised on a foundation of precious stones, which are identified as beauty, wisdom, courtesy, generosity, and so on—the very qualities the poet praises in his beloved. (The manuscript illuminator has chosen to show, on his own initiative, a surrounding park in which rabbits go in and out of their holes, in witty suggestion that some other values may also be involved.) Figure 41 depicts the lover walking the road to that prison— a road built (the poem tells us) by his own eyes and ears, the senses through which he fell in love. Figure 42 depicts the torments a lover may endure in such a place. Although Fortune raises some lovers to the upper tower and its joys, others she hurls down to the place represented here—the *cartre* of desire, self-torment, and despair, shown as small dragonlike monsters afflicting a lover's mind.[17] Baudouin is both knowing and fearful in his treatment of the pathology of love suffering—indeed, he will discuss five means by which one can escape such incarceration—but his poem is, for all that, in honor of his lady and in praise of the *douce prison*.

Though other pictures from this manuscript would repay our attention, I shall draw my primary gloss on *The Knight's Tale* use of the image from Froissart's *Prison amoureuse*, since Chaucer and some part of his earliest audience may have known that work firsthand. Like Baudouin's poem, it involves more than a passing verbal metaphor or conceit: the prison is the dominant image in an epistolary exchange between Froissart and his patron, Wenceslas of Brabant, written while the latter was held prisoner in the castle of Niedeck in 1371. Just as Chaucer in *The Knight's Tale* used the materials of Boccaccio's story, so Froissart used historical circumstance, taking a literal prison and giving it an iconographic significance through art.

Froissart's treatise incorporates an extensive Art of Love and several long allegorical pieces, including the dream that gives the whole work its name. Wenceslas asks from the poet an *exposition nouvelle* of that dream, and receives in reply a veritable compendium of love-prison ideas. (It is also, alas, a celebration of rhetorical synonymity.)

Dear friend, I understand by that prison in which you are placed and shut up, the languor in which you dwell when you are banished and rejected by your lady, or have from her replies and looks that are not pleasant toward you, or are beaten with the rods and assaults of jealousy, which are exceedingly hard and cruel to feel and know, and you cannot then live without great lamentations and complaints. . . . You dwell and live in prison, for a fair and loving heart that loves in the form and manner you do cannot live or reign without being imprisoned. And this prison is fair and beloved [*jolie et amoureuse*] to you because, thank God, there is between your sovereign and you no discord or care; rather your two hearts are in quite perfect unity. . . . Hence such a life should be called both *amoureuse* and a prison, and (I would add) most suitably so: because clearly you are captured and imprisoned in the service of your lady, all favors notwithstanding, if you cannot excuse yourself from being her prisoner. . . . Though I languish in this prison awaiting the favor of my lady, yet is my life and hope so joyful to me that indeed I [too] should call it at once beloved and also a prison, because I deliver myself over to my lady and hold myself her prisoner. Wherefore it seems to me that I do not do wrong in giving your little book a title signifying as much.[18]

Froissart's "exposition"—only a small part of which is represented here—is charming, studied, comprehensive. But the figure of the love prison and the love prisoner could be met with as readily in polite conversation as in formal works of literature (witness *The Book of the Knight of the Tower*, written in French ca. 1371). And it continued well into the fifteenth century, notably in the poems of the knight-prisoner Charles d'Orléans ("Martir am y for loue and prisonere").[19]

In short, the image of a prison could be used to render a variety of judgments upon love, and there can be no doubt that some part of that tradition is actively in service in *The Knight's Tale*. Arcite's complaint upon his release from prison is drawn from it, as is Palamon's "double soor and hevynesse" (1.1454): the prison tower itself re-

40 (*above*). The Prison of Love (illustrating Baudouin de Condé).
41 (*right*). The lover walking the road to the prison.
42 (*below*). The torments of the Prison of Love. French, second quarter of the fourteenth century. Note 17.

sounds with the "youlyng and clamour" of his jealous desire; the fet-
ters at his ankles are wet with his love-tears (I.1277–80).[20]

But we have reached only the middle term, as it were, in the devel-
opment of an image that is almost coextensive with the poem. The
prison figure occurs once more, on a wholly new and significantly
deeper level of generalization, in the final consolation Theseus speaks
concerning the death of Arcite:

> "Why grucchen we, why have we hevynesse,   (I.3058)
> That goode Arcite, of chivalrie the flour,
> Departed is with duetee and honour
> Out of this foule prisoun of this lyf?"

The literal prison where the knights first fall in love expands into a
metaphoric prison that includes all human life.[21] Chaucer's prepara-
tions for this final transformation of the image go back almost to the
tale's beginning, and involve a number of striking alterations in his
source.

In Boccaccio's poem, Teseo deals courteously with the newly cap-
tured knights, and has their wounds attended to. On his return to
Athens, he decides not to kill them, since they are not traitors; but
because they remain a threat to his state, he condemns them to eter-
nal prison (II, v. 98). Chaucer's handling of the event to this point is
analogous, though slightly less detailed. But here important changes
begin. Boccaccio's Teseo orders the jail-keeper to guard the young
knights carefully, and to treat them with honor: "These two were set
apart to allow them greater comfort [ease], because they were born
of royal blood. And he made them live in the palace and kept them in
this way in a room where they were served at their pleasure."[22] They
are allowed servants of their own, who move about freely, and even
Palemone's escape from prison, once he desires it, seems not difficult
to arrange.

Chaucer retains none of these chivalrous and courtly details, in-
venting for the young knights an imprisonment harsher by far. In his
version, they are chained and fettered in the tower that is chief dun-
geon to the castle, where they live out a "martirdom" beyond his
power to rhyme, "in derknesse and horrible and strong prisoun"
(I.1460, 1451). And Chaucer insists upon a fact possibly implied but
not specified by Boccaccio: that in condemning them to prison on
these terms, Theseus has decided he will accept no ransom—that
great escape clause that enabled medieval man to regard warfare as a
chivalrous undertaking, suitable to the well born, the powerful, and
the wealthy. "He nolde no raunsoun"; "ther may no gold hem quite"
(I.1024, 1032). In short, Chaucer suppresses much that is courteous
and gentle in Teseo's treatment of the knights, while emphasizing,

and adding to, all that is savage and cruel. Henry J. Webb, in an essay published in 1947 and too seldom noticed since,[23] has called attention to that change, noting how ill it accords with the poem's larger celebration of Theseus as "worthy," "gentil," "noble," and its praise of "his wysdom and his chivalrie" (1.865). These discordant details are not easy to explain. Webb suggests only that they may indicate, on Chaucer's part, an ironic view of Theseus. I shall borrow some of his evidence, and add some of my own, to reach a different conclusion.

I do not mean to suggest that noblemen imprisoned in medieval times customarily received, or expected to receive, treatment as courtly as that offered the two young knights in the *Teseida*. As Christine de Pisan, with a welcome acerbity, reminded her readers in *The Book of Fayttes of Armes and Chyualrye* (ca. 1408), any prisoner, before risking capture in battle, "ought to haue bethoughte in hym self that pryson was not a place of dysporte nor of feste."[24] But an honorable treatment of captives might be at least hoped for, and to that the question of ransom was central. One of Christine's sources, the *Arbre des batailles* of Honoré Bonet, the most important book on the conduct of war written in the fourteenth century (ca. 1387), addresses the subject in these terms:

Mercy is indeed due to a prisoner, and his captor must give it to him and prevent discourteous treatment of him while he is in his power. He must give him reasonable food as far as he can, and must bear himself companionably and charitably towards him for the love of our Lord; and if he does not wish to let him go free, let him ask reasonable and knightly ransom, such as is possible for the prisoner to pay and according to the usage of arms and of his country, and not such as to disinherit his wife, children, relations and friends; for justice demands that they should have the wherewithal to live after the ransom has been paid. If he do otherwise he is not a gentleman but a tyrant, and no knight.[25]

Elsewhere, Honoré states that a knight-prisoner may legitimately seek to escape prison if the treatment accorded him is inhumanly cruel, and cites a refusal to accept reasonable ransom as just such a cause.[26] Christine declares in turn that a prisoner must be furnished "lodgyse not ouere strayte" (quarters not overly cramped) and that his captor must be willing "to treatte wyth hym for a reysonable raunson"; a captor must not "tormente or make hys prysonners to langwysshe in pryson," but should treat them "goodly and humaynly," never giving them cause "to dyspeyre hem self"—that is, never so destroying all hope of release that they are driven to suicide or some other desperate action.[27]

Though these exact texts may or may not have been known to someone hearing *The Knight's Tale* late in the fourteenth century or early in the fifteenth, they seek merely to describe and regularize approved sorts of real conduct. Certainly the conspicuously chivalric treatment of noble prisoners was not confined to books. Froissart's account of how the Black Prince took the King of France prisoner on the battlefield of Poitiers in 1356 offers vivid testimony to the way men in the late Middle Ages sometimes sought to make actual a vision of ideal human courtesy. Although Froissart's pages doubtless bear their own imaginative and idealizing relation to real history, a brief abstract from those pages (here in Lord Berners's translation) will be helpful.

The same day of the batayle at night the prince made a supper in his lodgynge to the Frenche kyng and to the mooste parte of the great lordes that were prisoners. . . . and alwayes the prince served before the king as humbly as he coude, and wolde nat syt at the kynges borde for any desyre that the kynge coulde make: but he sayd he was nat suffycient to syt at the table with so great a prince as the kyng was. But than he sayd to the kyng, Sir, for Goddessake make non yvell nor hevy chere, though God this day dyde nat consent to folowe your wyll: for sir, surely the kynge my father shall bere you as moche honour and amyte as he may do. . . . Therwith the Frenchemen began to murmure and sayde among themselfe howe the prince had spoken nobly. . . . Whan supper was done, every man wente to his lodgyng with their prisoners; the same nyght they putte many to raunsome and belyved them on their faythes and trouthes, and raunsomed them but easely, for they sayd they wolde sette no knyghtes raunsome so hygh, but that he myght pay at his ease and maynteyne styll his degree. . . . The Frenche kynge rode through London on a whyte courser, well aparelled, and the prince on a lytell blacke hobbey by hym: thus he was conveyed along the cyte tyll he came to the Savoy, the which house pertayned to the herytage of the duke of Lancastre; there the French kyng kept his house a long season, and thyder came to se hym the kyng and the quene often tymes and made hym gret feest and chere.[28]

In the course of time a truce is made between the kings, and the terms of the imprisonment become even more generous and courtly:

Anone after, the French kyng was removed fro the Savoy to the castell of Wyndsore, and all his householde, and went a huntyng and a haukyng ther about at his pleasur, and the lorde Philypp his son with hym: and all the other prisoners abode styll at London, and went to se the kyng at their pleasure, and were receyved all onely on their faythes.[29]

This was still living history at the time of the writing of *The Canterbury Tales*. It is likely that the Black Prince had been acquainted with Chaucer, and it is possible that Chaucer was in attendance at the great feast given at Windsor in 1358 by Edward III, in honor of the King of Cyprus and the prisoner Kings of Scotland and France.[30] The honorable treatment of high-born prisoners by high-born captors was probably nearer the rule than the exception: all knew themselves to be equally at fortune's mercy in war.[31] Chaucer himself was captured by the French in late winter of 1359, and was ransomed by the King some two or three months later for the sum of £16. He is not likely to have attributed this cruelty to Theseus in an unconsidered way.

Let us not mistake the matter: Theseus, for the greater part of the poem, treats his two prisoners ("they that weren of the blood roial / Of Thebes") in a manner fully consonant with the courtly ideal. When he releases Arcite "withouten any raunsoun," out of his own love for Perotheus (1.1205), he begins a movement back into the fully chivalric, and from that moment on there is no irony in the terminology of praise that attends his actions. He is noble, magnificent, magnanimous: he forgives the knights their breaking of exile and prison, he arranges the great tournament in their honor, he deems either of them worthy of Emelye. He is to the literature of England in the late Middle Ages what the Black Prince—if Froissart reports true—was to its history on the battlefield of Poitiers: a man seeking consciously to embody the highest chivalric ideals of his civilization.

But Chaucer does present Theseus rather differently at the beginning of the Palamon-Arcite action: let us not mistake that either. Having introduced Theseus into the poem first as the heroic conqueror of "the regne of Femenye," and then as the avenger of the Theban widows—thus establishing his valor and his virtue—Chaucer was willing to show him for a time in a morally dubious light in order that a harsh imprisonment (as a basis for later metaphoric redefinition) might become one of the terms of his literal story. The poem's larger strategy requires a maximally powerful contrast between the prison and the garden since not only do those places need to represent two opposing possibilities of human life, as they do near the poem's beginning, but one of them, the prison, must also at the poem's end serve to expose all human life as wretched and brutal bondage— whatever its appearances, and however much our perceptions may be lulled into thinking that prison sweet, into thinking it in fact a garden. From such imprisonment no ransom is possible: its walls are coextensive with human life.

To express that sense of the world, Chaucer needed stronger material than the prison experience of the French king could provide, or his contemporary, Honoré Bonet, was willing to sanction as lawful, or he found in his source—even at the risk of making Theseus seem, for a time, "nocht gentill, na courtas, na worthy man of were, bot . . . ane unconnand tyrane man, unworthy to be amang gude men of armes."[32] Chaucer attributes this initial cruelty to him, and intensifies it far beyond any cue in Boccaccio, so that when the prison image is expanded to encompass every human life, its first reference is to a captivity so terrible, so like the worst of prisons, that in it even death can be affirmed:

> "Why grucchen heere his cosyn and his wyf   (1.3062)
> Of his welfare, that loved hem so weel?"

Theseus's use of the word "welfare" comes with a certain shock, but the word is fully intended, in the sense of both "well-being" and "well-faring." However mysterious the death journey of a pagan soul, it is at least an exit from this world of contingency and constraint. Arcite has departed honorably "out of this foule prisoun of this lyf."

Chaucer's version of the literal prison supplies, from within the work itself, the only necessary gloss on this final transformation of scene into metaphor. But here too, as with the love prison, Chaucer was working out of a tradition so rich that some sense of its provenance and authority in the Middle Ages is a proper part of our response to the poem's intrinsic meaning. We are not asked to imagine Theseus improvising a new and tentative consolation over the dead Arcite, but rather to recognize that a truth long honored in the courts of men has once again been rediscovered and confirmed.

I shall postpone until later in this chapter discussion of the single most important text within this tradition, Boethius's *Consolation of Philosophy*. It has a special importance, touches upon many other issues, and furnishes the closest model for Chaucer's development of the prison image in this poem. But there are texts from the classical period itself that would have made Theseus's use of the image seem appropriate, the most important being Cicero's *Dream of Scipio*, written in imitation of the Vision of Er that concludes Plato's *Republic*, and Macrobius's encyclopedic *Commentary on the Dream of Scipio*, which draws heavily on Plato's *Timaeus* and *Phaedo* for its conception of universal order and the nature of the soul. Both *Dream* and *Commentary* were well known to Chaucer, and he found there ideas like these: "For a creature to have existence, it is necessary that a soul be confined in the body; for this reason the Greek words for body are *demas*, that is a 'bond,' and *soma*, a *sema*, as it were, being a 'tomb' of the soul. Thus you see that Cicero, by the words *those who have flown from the bonds of their bodies, as if from a prison*, means both that the body serves as fetters and that it is a tomb, being the prison of the entombed." [33] There were Old Testament sources for the tradition, as well, not the least of them David's great cry, "Bring my soul out of prison, that I may praise thy name" (Psalm 141:8), or the messianic prophecy of Isaiah 42:7, "thou mightest open the eyes of the blind, and bring forth the prisoner out of prison, and them that sit in darkness out of the prison house." Christianity found the figure congenial to its own theology, emphasizing the soul's imprisonment within the body and its bondage to sin. Chaucer translates a Pauline text in *The Parson's Tale*—"Allas, I caytyf man! who shal delivere me fro the prisoun of my caytyf body?" (x.344)[34]—having already explored that "thraldom" at length, through other texts drawn from St. Peter, Ezechiel, Seneca, and St. Augustine (x.136–53).[35] The currency and authority of this figure rested upon many works in the medieval vernaculars as well, in a range so great, and bearing so wide a range of contextual meaning, that I must content myself with footnote reference rather than textual illustration.[36] What matters to our present argument is the sheer weight and richness of the tradition, and the fact that Chaucer in *The Knight's Tale* does nothing to individuate it as a philosophic or religious idea. In those terms, he seizes it at its most formulaic and conventional—a single line brings it into the poem— offering instead what belongs to the office of a poet: an individuation through fiction and literary form, a figure emerging from the fabric of a long and highly worked poem. It is related to other works in the same tradition, but it is not the same as, or reducible to, any other.

Let me summarize what I take the larger development of the image in this poem to be. In the beginning, the imprisonment of the two young knights seems merely the result of bad fortune. Their condition is harsh and cruel, but other conditions are possible. The physical contiguity of prison tower and pleasure garden makes that fact seem to them (and us) self-evident: the joined structure epitomizes two kinds of human living, at two extremes. But when the young knights see Emelye and commit themselves to loving her, everything is suddenly changed. The prison takes on the values of the garden, it becomes the pleasant *prison amoureuse*. That such happiness is based upon a distorted perception is most clearly figured in the tale by Arcite's reluctance to leave the real prison when offered his freedom. But from the moment Theseus decides to convert their battle in the wooded grove into a formal tournament, their love is never again treated as trivial or foolish, not even briefly. Chaucer accepts their passion as urgent and authentic, and invites us to do so with him, as he opens out the action of his poem into a freer and more spacious world, characterized, one might say, by the garden values: a world of music and ceremony, ornate temples and magnificent wall paintings, beautiful women and magnanimous rulers, gorgeous tournaments and high marriages. It is a world chivalrous, well born, and privileged, though (as the action will show, and as the tournament theatre will make emblematic) it remains a world still subject to fortune, planetary influence, and destructive desire, a world not entirely conformable to man's highest aspirations and dreams.

This second version of the image, in which the garden is the dominant element of the prison/garden structure, governs most of the poem. It is decisively a romance—not an epic, or philosophical treatise, or moral exemplum. The two knights are young, vigorous, attractive, and most of the time untroubled by introspection; the love prison is sweet to them, approved by their society, and meant to be approved by us as audience:

> To fighte for a lady, *benedicitee*!   (1.2115)
> It were a lusty sighte for to see.
>
> "Do now youre devoir, yonge knyghtes proude!"   (1.2598)

But in one important sense, the mood of even this long section of the poem is overshadowed by the initial terms of the knights' imprisonment. Whatever action may be underway at any given time—whether it be talk of love, preparations for a tournament, or descriptions of the gods—we are never far from the language of violence, confusion, limitation, and death. While celebrating a world of romance and chivalry, the narrator is also preparing us for the moment in which the world itself will be called prison, this time in a way totally inclusive, the term no longer limited to an architectural structure within the real world but adumbrating instead the metaphysical structure of that world.*

Chaucer at this point works out of a tradition so central to Western culture, and with a conviction so sure, that the grammatical forms he uses imply more than likeness. They offer no ordinary simile ("this world is like a prison") or conventional metaphor, in which tenor and vehicle are kept distinct ("the foul prison of this life"), but instead the odd and powerful "out of this foule prisoun of this lyf." The demonstrative "this," twice repeated, blurs priorities and destroys the tenor-vehicle distinction. Life and prison are presented as coextensive and on a single plane. One is not likened to the other; they are understood to be identical.[37] The garden, in short, is finally seen as prison; the "evene joynant" wall falls away, revealing the garden as merely a part of that larger structure. As a moral treatise of the time instructs us, we may sleep and dream that we are "at weddynges and grete festes,"[38] but we are in prison all the time. The literal image—a specific mise-en-scène—is transformed into a secular metaphor, the prison of love, and from that into a metaphysical image of the world as prison, an image deeper, more inclusive, and (under the aspect of eternity) more true.

But the final meaning of the poem is not identical with the final development of this image, for all its structural and thematic impor-

---

*In Boccaccio's poem, the physician who treats the dying Arcita is able to advise only that they "keep him happy and comfortable so that he may depart with as much contentment as possible *to the eternal prison*, where Dis keeps every light extinguished, and where we shall follow him when we cannot live here any longer" (*Teseida*, X, v. 14; italics added). In Boccaccio, those on earth see the afterlife as prison, whereas in Chaucer, death is said to offer release from the prison of this world.

tance to the whole. The concluding business of the poem is not with a dark similitude but with a wedding, and that must impose upon all we have been examining one further perspective, which we shall need to approach with equal care. The final definition of the prison/ garden setting is granted less than total authority, but to estimate it properly we must first examine the other dominant narrative image of the poem.

✤

The amphitheatre that Theseus builds for the tournament between Palamon and Arcite is to the theme of order in the poem what the prison/garden is to the theme of freedom. It allows Chaucer to assess, in an unusually comprehensive and exploratory way, the possibilities of creating human order within a world apparently governed by chance.[39] His elaboration of Boccaccio's theatre into a major narrative image involves changes so bold and interesting that we are able, as in the earlier example, to sense his thematic intention with unusual confidence. We know what changes he made, and it is possible to guess why.

The most important change, from which all the others follow, is the decision Theseus makes to build an amphitheatre specifically for the tournament. In the *Teseida*, Teseo finds the knights fighting in the woods and orders them to come together a year later "for combat in our theater" (V, v. 97), referring without emphasis to a structure already in existence. We learn nothing in detail about it until the tournament begins,[40] when it is described in these verses:

> The round theater was situated a little outside the land and was not a finger less than a mile around. Its marble wall, of impeccable workmanship, rose so high toward heaven that the eye almost tired of gazing at it. It had two entrances with strong, well-made doors.
>
> One of these, on its great columns, turned toward the rising sun. The other, built like the first, looked toward the west. Everyone entered through these, for there was no other entrance anywhere. In the middle there was a plain as round as a compass, with room enough for every great celebration.
>
> Circular terraces rose up from it in more than five hundred tiers, I believe, and ascended up to the height of the wall by means of wide steps of splendid stone. People used to sit on these steps to watch cruel gladiators or others engage in some game, without getting in one another's way anywhere. (VII, vv. 108–10)

Boccaccio probably had the Roman Colosseum in mind while writing these lines, at once imagining it in its original perfection and adding to its grandeur of scale. I reproduce as figure 43 a model of the Colosseum as modern archaeology imagines it to have looked, for that model comes closer to Boccaccio's and Chaucer's descrip-

43. A modern model of the Roman Colosseum. Note 41.

tions of Theseus's theatre than any medieval pictures I am able to
supply, and we shall need some such image on which to center the
analysis that follows.[41] (For those interested in such matters, The-
seus's amphitheatre would have occupied approximately 51 acres; the
Colosseum occupies some 23.)

As the reference to gladiatorial combats and games makes clear,
Teseo's theatre holds an accustomed place in the public life of the city.
The theatre of *The Knight's Tale*, in contrast, is something wholly
new, which Theseus commissions, and whose decoration he super-
vises closely (1.1881–84, 2089–92). The love conflict of Arcite and
Palamon calls into being not only a tournament of the greatest splen-
dor, but the very structure in which it will take place. The creation of
the amphitheatre is itself a heroic achievement, and is celebrated
as such:

> . . . swich a noble theatre as it was,   (1.1885)
> I dar wel seyen in this world ther nas.
> The circuit a myle was aboute,
> Walled of stoon, and dyched al withoute.
> Round was the shap, in manere of compas,
> Ful of degrees, the heighte of sixty pas,
> That whan a man was set on o degree,
> He letted nat his felawe for to see.
>   Estward ther stood a gate of marbul whit,

Westward right swich another in the opposit.
And shortly to concluden, swich a place
Was noon in erthe, as in so litel space;
For in the lond ther was no crafty man
That geometrie or ars-metrike kan,
Ne portreyour, ne kervere of ymages,
That Theseus ne yaf him mete and wages,
The theatre for to maken and devyse.
And for to doon his ryte and sacrifise,
He estward hath, upon the gate above,
In worshipe of Venus, goddesse of love,
Doon make an auter and an oratorie;
And on the gate westward, in memorie
Of Mars, he maked hath right swich another,
That coste largely of gold a fother.
And northward, in a touret on the wal,
Of alabastre whit and reed coral,
An oratorie, riche for to see,
In worshipe of Dyane of chastitee,
Hath Theseus doon wroght in noble wyse.

There is more to this theatre than architecture, whereas Boccaccio's amphitheatre, for all the splendor of its materials and the grandeur of its scale, is finally no more than a place in which to stage a tournament or games, a function customarily served by timber scaffolding in the Middle Ages. In figure 44, which illustrates a treatise on the conduct of tournaments written by King René of Anjou, ca. 1460–65,[42] such lists consist of two wooden fences or barriers, separated by an alley for the squires and servants of those who tourney within. The inner fence defines the combat space; the outer excludes spectators from the staging area. Viewing galleries for the judges and the ladies are constructed on one side. In figure 45, interestingly enough, a painter in René's employ substituted an even simpler version of such a structure for the marble amphitheatre in illustrating Boccaccio's poem.[43] I reproduce these images chiefly by way of contrast: though they will not help us to imagine Chaucer's poem, they can emphasize the importance the theatre holds within it. Chaucer may have lacked Boccaccio's interest in the classical amphitheatre per se, but he made of that theatre something even grander, a structure that incorporates other sorts of art, a structure that becomes itself a complex work of art. By locating within it temples to the gods, decorated by human hands, he is able to test within it human purposes and capacities beyond those of Theseus alone.

Our best clue to Chaucer's intention in making these changes can be found in a related detail likewise without precedent in his source. In the *Teseida*, the location of the amphitheatre is only vaguely indicated—it lies "poco fuori della terra," a little outside Athens—

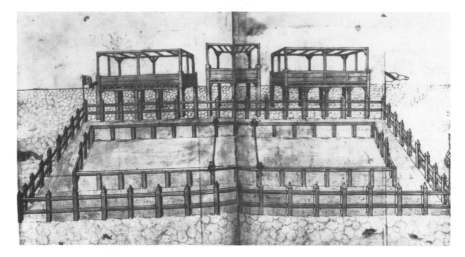

44. A medieval tournament lists. French, ca. 1460–65. Note 42.

whereas Chaucer's Theseus decides to build his theatre in the place where he finds the two knights fighting:

> . . . with sharpe speres stronge   (I.1653)
> They foynen ech at oother wonder longe.
> Thou myghtest wene that this Palamon
> In his fightyng were a wood leon,
> And as a crueel tigre was Arcite;
> As wilde bores gonne they to smyte,
> That frothen whit as foom for ire wood.
> Up to the ancle foghte they in hir blood.

In the contexts of heraldry, chronicle, and most romance, such images would require no special comment. A warrior-knight was supposed to fight fiercely, and such animals furnish appropriate similes. But the combat of Palamon and Arcite is not socially sanctioned and serves no human purpose: it is covert and irrational, and it destroys a sworn bond of brotherhood. They seek each other's death like savage beasts in a wooded grove symbolically appropriate to those passions.[44] It is a wild place, inhabited by animals only, where (like Palamon) an escaped prisoner can hide by day without fear of being found, or where (like Arcite) a person exiled from the country on pain of death can cast aside disguise and lament his fate, far from human ears. Both knights identify themselves with untamed nature, Arcite weaving a garland of woodbine and hawthorn in honor of the May, and Palamon crouching like an animal among the "buskes thikke," from which he leaps with murderous intent. When they meet to fight the battle described above, they look (Chaucer tells us) as terrified as Thracian hunters who hear the lion or bear come rushing at them, breaking boughs and leaves, and who know in that moment that they must kill or be killed.

Theseus, Ypolita, and Emelye enter this grove because they are hunting a hart, but what they find there is a fiercer sort of beast, two men fighting as savagely as wild boars. Figure 46 shows Boccaccio's Emilia riding out from the castle with companions, dogs, and a falcon at her wrist, pursuing a pastime as civilized and ceremonious as the architecture of the castle (in the upper left corner) from which she issues.[45] Figure 47 is painted on the following page of the manuscript, and offers a powerful contrast: the two knights fight within a forest glade luxuriant in its vegetation, random in its growth, unshaped by human hand.[46] Theseus's anger, instantaneous and absolute, focuses on the offense against social order:

45. Palemone and Arcita kneel before Teseo at the tournament lists. French, ca. 1455. Note 43.

"... telleth me what myster men ye been,   (1.1710)
That been so hardy for to fighten heere
Withouten juge or oother officere,
As it were in a lystes roially."

On learning their identities, he not only commands that they submit their enmity to the forms of tournament, but decides that the tournament will be held in that very grove, and that he himself will serve as referee, to enforce the rules essential to any civilized resolution of conflict: "The lystes shal I maken in this place"; "I shal evene juge been and trewe" (1.1862, 1864).

Bartholomaeus Anglicus, in his encyclopedia description of woods and forests, can confirm our sense of this place as we first meet it in the poem: "*saltus*, *silua*, and *nemus*," he writes,

beth wyde places, waste, and deserte, þat many trees groweþ inne wiþoute fruyte and fewe wiþ fruyte. . . . In þese woodes wiþ so dyuerse names beþ

46. Emilia rides out hunting. French, ca. 1455. Note 45.

47. Palemone and Arcita fight in the grove. French, ca. 1455. Note 46.

ofte wilde bestes and fowles. . . . In woode is place of deceipte and of hunt-
ynge, for þerinne wilde bestes beþ yhunted and [many] wacches and de-
ceytes arrayed and ysette of houndes and of hunters. There place [is] of
hydynge and of lurkynge, for ofte in wodes þeues beþ yhudde and oftere in
here awaytes and deceytes passynge men comeþ and beþ yspoyled and
yrobbed and ofte yslawe. Also for many and dyuerse weyes and vncerteyn
straunge men ofte erreþ and goth oute of þe weye.[47]

Bartholomaeus is careful to note details of another kind as well, for
woods contain medicinal herbs and timber useful for defense. They
offer shade against the sun, and often constitute important bound-
aries. But those facts do not cancel out the other (and perhaps deeper)
medieval sense of such places as potentially perilous, beyond law, an-
tithetical to human values. Chaucer's version of the grove identifies it
with almost every negative feature enumerated above: two men who

have made of themselves criminals fight within it like beasts in the service of a fruitless love (the lady does not know they even exist) and in an act that bears no real relation to any goal; they have lost their way.

When Theseus declares "The lystes shal I maken in this place," he proposes to lay down upon these woods a vast circle of marble, measured and shaped by the human mind, within whose perfect form he will ordain the most ceremonial and highly structured of all forms of human combat. The fighting in the wild wood, without ceremony, rules, or judge, is transformed into a tournament involving two hundred evenly matched knights—all "for love and for encrees of chivalrye" (1.2184).

Though the strife of Palamon and Arcite furnishes the tournament's necessity and occasion, it is only briefly seen as antagonistic to the values of Theseus and courtly society as a whole. Even within the grove, where they give free rein to all that is most wild and selfish within them, vestiges of their courtesy and breeding remain. Arcite refuses to fight Palamon while the latter is unarmed, promising to bring instead, on the following morning, "harneys right ynough for thee; / And ches the beste, and leef the worste for me" (1.1613). At that time, lacking squires, they courteously arm each other, though words between them are few:

> Ther nas no good day, ne no saluyng,   (1.1649)
> But streight, withouten word or rehersyng,
> Everich of hem heelp for to armen oother
> As freendly as he were his owene brother;
> And after that, with sharpe speres stronge
> They foynen ech at oother wonder longe.

The "lion," "tiger," and "wild boar" images follow immediately, naming something always potential in their natures, now become dominant as they surrender utterly to their passion. But even in this most disgraceful moment, their observance of some of the forms of chivalry makes them recognizably the knights we have known: the poet's language briefly evokes the sworn brotherhood that once bound them to each other. When Theseus has recalled them to their senses, and their truer natures, he not unfittingly makes a tournament in their honor, with Emelye as prize. And so the theatre that Theseus builds for this tournament is made consciously to stand at the furthest possible distance from all that is disorderly and self-destructive in man. It incorporates not only the abstract, intellectual skills of the master builder ("geometrie" and "ars-metrike"), but the arts of representation as well: painters and sculptors decorate three temples, dedicated to Venus, Mars, and Diana, placed within the amphitheatre walls. Just as man's intellectual nature separates him from the beasts,

48. Arcita, Emilia, and Palemone pray to the gods. French, ca. 1455. Note 48.

so does his religious nature, and both are given expression in this structure erected against the wildness within.

In the *Teseida*, the temples where Palemone, Arcita, and Emilia make offerings and pray are given no precise location. They are situated somewhere in Athens and, like the amphitheatre, have an accustomed place in the life of that society. The Master of René of Anjou, in illustrating Boccaccio, has placed them side by side, and shown the prayers as simultaneous (figure 48), with a tree and a gentle mountain in the left margin to indicate an open setting.[48] The picture is very beautiful, and its statues are of some use to us in imagining those Chaucer places in the amphitheatre temples.* But the two most important facts about *The Knight's Tale* temples are not repre-

*Diana is shown seated upon the moon (in the character of Luna), and Venus, less characteristically, is shown as a huntress—a tradition that goes back to the *Aeneid*, I, 314–17, where she appears to Aeneas in that guise. (Chaucer narrates that meeting in *LGW*, 970–1001.) Mars, in full armor, carries spear and shield.

sented here, for they grow out of changes that Chaucer made in his source. Chaucer places the temples within the walls of the amphitheatre, and he decorates them with wall paintings as well as sculpture, making them artistically elaborate beyond anything in the *Teseida*. In that earlier poem, indeed, the temples of Mars and Venus are not described at all.[49] We might note, with respect to the first of these changes, that Chaucer places the temples dedicated to Venus and Mars above the two great gates to the amphitheatre that he found described in Boccaccio. Palamon and his hundred knights will enter through one, Arcite and his hundred through the other. Chaucer might easily have created a third gate for the temple of Diana—a half line of verse would have brought it into being—but he locates it instead "northward, in a touret on the wal" (1.1909), thereby suggesting that one may enter the arena of passionate experience by the gates of Mars or Venus, but not through dedication to Diana, not through chastity.

It is the second change, however, the invention of the wall paintings, that most enlarges Chaucer's theatre as an iconographic narrative image, converting it from an emblem of reason and restraint into a comprehensive image of human life both rational and impassioned. For housed within the theatre are symbolic mansions dedicated to the gods, whose decoration brings into the geometric purity of its line all the energies and appetites to which the planetary gods gave their names, and which they were believed to foster: wrath and aggression, sexual passion, and scornful or hesitant virginity. The temples complicate, in ways both symbolic and prophetic, the idealism of Theseus's intent. Most of the *pars tercia* of the poem is given over to their description.

Chaucer's temples are more richly furnished than those of the *Teseida* partly because he transfers to them details that in the other poem describe the "houses" of the gods, their distant mythological dwellings to which the personified prayers of the young knights travel, and where those prayers are heard. Although Boccaccio's planetary gods will influence what happens at the theatre, just as they do in Chaucer, their houses bear neither spatial nor symbolic relationship to it. The house of Mars, for example, is "set in the Thracian fields, under wintry skies, storm-tossed by continuous tempest," whereas that of Venus is "on Mount Cithaeron . . . shaded among very tall pines" (VII, vv. 30,50). These prayer-journeys, which contribute to the epic scale of the *Teseida*'s action, are omitted in the English poem. Chaucer chooses to bring all this symbolic material into the theatre itself, concentrating it into a single narrative image that is more dense with suggestion and more potent in the memory. And whereas Boccaccio describes first the landscape in which the house is located, then a company of personified abstractions who inhabit it,[50] and only then a few generic or mythological scenes painted on the walls, Chaucer describes all of this material as painted—"wroght on the wal"—behind the statue of the god. The temple decoration is the work of "portreyours" and "kerveres of ymages," artists whose labor is ultimately related to Chaucer's own, for poetry causes us to frame such images in our mind. That relationship will concern us later in this chapter. First let us look more closely at the images themselves.

Nothing that survives from the visual arts during Chaucer's lifetime furnishes adequate equivalents to these temple paintings, nor can any example from the tradition we are about to consider rival their density of specification. A combination of sources is necessary to account for Boccaccio's "houses of the gods" and Chaucer's transformation of them into temple paintings. Those sources include earlier poems, especially the *Thebaid* of Statius; mythographic manuals explaining the significance of the pagan gods, both euhemeristically and morally;[51] and astrological texts deriving from Arab writings of the ninth and tenth centuries, especially the works of Abu Ma'sar and Alcabitius. Although mythological and astrological traditions cannot be separated absolutely, Chaucer's statues of the gods express, for the most part, their role in mythology, whereas his wall paintings chiefly depict planetary influence, and owe more to astrological belief. Because the wall paintings dominate this section of the poem, the astrological tradition will concern us chiefly.

The Arab texts mentioned above describe the "qualities" of the planets—hot, cold, dry, wet—together with the kinds of human occupation each governs and the kinds of event each characteristically brings about. From these seminal texts, which were translated into Latin between 1120 and 1180, there grew in time an important tradition in the visual arts: the "children of the planets," or *Planetenkinder*, whose earliest surviving examples date from the end of the fourteenth century, but whose most characteristic form (the one that comes closest to illustrating Chaucer's verse) did not take shape, so far as we know, until a few years after his death. What had begun in the Arab tradition as a row-on-row, serial depiction of trades or professions governed by each planet developed into something richer by far, as Western artists and their patrons sought to "group together the men ruled by the planets in a kind of lively 'genre' picture which appeared socially and psychologically more coherent. This involved, in the first place, a reduction of the chaotic variety present in the original 'tables' to a limited number of inherently related types; secondly, the assembling of these types in coherent surroundings and in the same perspective. The picture of Jupiter must illustrate the nature and way of life of men blessed with culture and property, Mercury that of scholars and artists," and so on.[52]

Chaucer's wall paintings either are in this tradition—if it predates the surviving examples—or they anticipate it by a few years. The fit is not exact, and we shall have to pay as much attention to the differences as to the similarities. But if we would imagine clearly just what the paintings bring into the symbolic structure of Theseus's great amphitheatre, recourse to such images will prove helpful. I shall represent the tradition in its most elegant and detailed form, a series of drawings made ca. 1480 for a German *Hausbuch*, though mid-century examples from several countries in Europe might equally well have been chosen, and a handsome German manuscript dated 1404 (now in Tübingen) makes a stronger contemporary claim.[53] In these pictures the planet-god is characteristically shown riding through the sky or in a roundel above; the world of occupation and event that he or she governs is depicted below.*

Figure 49 shows "the children of Mars" in a landscape full of violence, Mars riding triumphantly across the sky above. In the lower left corner, a pilgrim is set upon and killed, presumably for his money; reading clockwise, one sees a fleeing man seized by a mounted soldier to the anger and grief of two women, one of whom waves a jug in the air, ready to do battle; several persons take sanctuary in the steeple of a church while a house is set aflame by soldiers; a herd of cattle is driven off by a man on horseback, pursued by a woman with distaff in hand; in the center a man stands under arrest, threatened by another; and, at the lower right, there is a closely organized scene of cheating and domestic murder.[54] Of all the *Planetenkinder* pictures we shall examine, this comes closest to approximating the painting in Chaucer's poem. If one could multiply even further the number and variety of its incidents, one would have a suitable picture to place behind the statue of Mars in the temple where Arcite prays. Chaucer devotes some eighty lines to describing that painting, only a small part of which I represent here:

> The smylere with the knyf under the cloke;   (I.1999)
> The shepne brennynge with the blake smoke;
> The tresoun of the mordrynge in the bedde;
> The open werre, with woundes al bibledde;
>
> .   .   .
>
> The careyne in the busk, with throte ycorve;
> A thousand slayn, and nat of qualm ystorve;
> The tiraunt, with the pray by force yraft;
> The toun destroyed, ther was no thyng laft.
> Yet saugh I brent the shippes hoppesteres;
> The hunte strangled with the wilde beres;

---

*These verses from *The Squire's Tale* suggest that Chaucer knew of the planet-children tradition in at least its written form: "Now dauncen lusty Venus children deere, / For in the Fyssh hir lady sat ful hye, / And looketh on hem with a freendly ye" (v.272). The "Fyssh" is Pisces, the house of Venus's "exaltation"; the pictorial tradition, in contrast, characteristically shows the houses that a planet rules (in figure 50, for instance, we see Venus with Taurus and Libra).

49. The children of Mars. German or Dutch, ca. 1480. Note 54.

> The sowe freten the child right in the cradel;
> The cook yscalded, for al his longe ladel.
> Noght was foryeten by the infortune of Marte.

Chaucer's detail is richer and more inventive than that of the German drawing, but its incident is of the same violent kind.

Figure 50 shows "the children of Venus," a picture more pleasant by far. One sees an amorous couple in a bathhouse, attended by an old crone, while young people make music on fife and tabor, sack-horn and rustic lyre; some play cards (Venus's children do well at games of chance), and two boys practice tumbling; to the right we see a hasty copulation in the bushes, and a table spread with sweet-meats and wine (Venus's children include confectioners); at the bot-tom, a company of elegant young people followed by musicians moves in procession two by two, conversing and possibly dancing.[55] The painting Chaucer invents for Venus's temple includes some of the same material—"Festes, instrumentz, caroles, daunces, / Lust and array, and alle the circumstaunces / Of love" (I. 1931)—but we are asked to imagine the following details as well in the 36 lines of verse that describe the whole:

> The broken slepes, and the sikes colde,   (I. 1920)
> The sacred teeris, and the waymentynge,
> The firy strokes of the desirynge
> That loves servantz in this lyf enduren;
> The othes that hir covenantz assuren;
> Plesaunce and Hope, Desir, Foolhardynesse,
> Beautee and Youthe, Bauderie, Richesse,
> Charmes and Force, Lesynges, Flaterye,
> Despense, Bisynesse, and Jalousye,
> That wered of yelewe gooldes a gerland,
> And a cokkow sittynge on hir hand.

These verses remind us that suffering is often the price of becoming one of "Venus's children" (in the mythographic sense of the term). In Chaucer's version, as distinct from that of the *Hausbuch* Master, the psychopathology of erotic love claims at least equal place with "Ple-saunce and Hope," "Beautee and Youthe," and all that is most attrac-tive within the planet's influence.

Figure 51 shows "the children of Luna" (Diana/the Moon), whose influence governs all who earn their living by water—hence the wa-termill at the far left, with persons bringing grain to be ground and boys swimming in its stream, as well as fishermen with boats and nets in the lake behind. Luna is planetary goddess of traveling schol-ars as well, one of whom is shown bottom left, and of medicine men, jugglers, and popular entertainers: a shell game, a musician with a trained monkey, and a banner advertising acrobatic tricks are all

50. The children of Venus. German or Dutch, ca. 1480. Note 55.

51. The children of Luna. German or Dutch, ca. 1480. Note 56.

shown at bottom right.[56] In the landscape immediately behind, a young man rides out with falcon on wrist, and a fowler enters a forest in search of birds. Though the picture has virtually no relevance to Chaucer's poem, its very difference can help us understand the poem and its traditions better, through the two hunting scenes (the falconer and fowler) that constitute its sole link with the wall paintings in Diana's temple. In the *Planetenkinder* series, Luna presides over hunting for pleasure and as occupation, whereas the hunting scenes with which Chaucer decorates Diana's temple work "vengeaunce" and "care and wo" upon human victims. There we see Callisto changed into a bear, Daphne into a laurel tree, and Actaeon into a stag pursued and eaten by hounds, along with Atalanta (whose chastity cost many young men's lives) and Meleager, hunting the monstrous boar. All this demonstrates Diana's power, the power of virginity. Diana's statue, which stands in front of the painting, casts its eyes downward into hell, the region where she rules as Proserpina, Pluto's queen, and carved before her is the image of a woman in difficult labor, calling upon her as Lucina, goddess of childbirth, "for hir child so longe was unborn" (1.2084).

In the case of Diana, Chaucer invents almost entirely out of the mythological rather than the planetary tradition. He is more interested in the triplex goddess and her legends than in the influence of the planet, although the statue (cf. figure 48) has a moon "undernethe hir feet"—"Wexynge it was and sholde wanye soone" (1.2078). The painting in Venus's temple, as we have seen, draws almost equally on both traditions—a difference important to any account of Chaucer's sources, and to their perceived consequence within the tale. But more significant in terms of immediate poetic effect is Chaucer's nearly exclusive emphasis on all that is destructive or unhappy in either tradition.[57] There are no swimmers, fishermen, millers, or even ordinary hunters shown within his temple of Diana; there is precious little of love's delight shown within his temple of Venus; and we will hear nothing from Saturn in his turn about those of his children who till the earth, harvest crops, or live as hermits in devotion to God. Among the *Hausbuch* pictures, the drawing of the "children of Mars" alone reflects a similar concentration on the evil aspects—the "infortune"—of a planet's influence. But even there one must remark a modal difference that makes our experience of *The Knight's Tale* temple paintings more disquieting than anything intended by the *Hausbuch* Master.

I refer to the fact that Chaucer's descriptions of the wall paintings pile scene upon scene without any indication of spatial relationships. The result is a serial imagining that the reader/auditor performs confidently enough in each of its stages, but which is chaotic and uncertain in relation to the space he is asked to imagine as containing it. A classic instance, we might say, of one difference between the arts of poetry and painting—*ut pictura non poesis*—but which here expresses a theme that the poem's action will soon develop: the fact that an ordered system can contain disorder, without falsifying or fundamentally altering it. The *Hausbuch* pictures, which depict only planetary influence, display the beneficent and neutral as well as malign aspects of any planet's influence and offer for each a design that, if a bit more crowded and irregular than is common in medieval pictorial tradition, is nevertheless located firmly in two-dimensional space. Chaucer's temple paintings, on the other hand, combine mythographic and astrological traditions, emphasize malign planetary influence above all else, and are experienced as modally indeterminate, spatially unfixed, and devoid of any clear internal structure. Like the human experience that is their subject, they can be imagined in their parts but not as wholes. Chaucer's amphitheatre contains, at three points within the perfect geometry of its circle, a menacing potential for disorder, communicated to us in a peculiarly turbulent and disquieting way. As a narrative image it at once summarizes the causes of the action so far and intimates that its resolution will come only at some appalling cost.

Though the young people are explicitly linked to the planet-gods, their natures and allegiances are more complex than any one-to-one equivalence. Both of the knights are warriors and hence children of Mars; both are lovers and hence children of Venus; and Emelye worships Diana not as a dedicated virgin or a nun bound to chastity but as a young girl not yet awakened to love, who will consent to marry in the fulness of time. The energies originating from within the temples of the amphitheatre animate them all.[58]

Even in their choice of gods to whom to pray, Chaucer is less interested in telling us what may distinguish Palamon from Arcite—and thus suggest an answer to the question of why Arcite earns death and Palamon earns Emelye—than he is in focusing on the human difficulty of knowing what to wish for if one would be happy, and how to frame that wish without invoking disaster. The story, in this respect, more resembles a folk tale that grants three wishes to teach one the peril that may lie in answered prayers than a moral fable in which the prize goes to the more deserving. In Arcite's words,

> "We witen nat what thing we preyen heere: (I.1260)
> We faren as he that dronke is as a mous.
> A dronke man woot wel he hath an hous,
> But he noot which the righte wey is thider,
> And to a dronke man the wey is slider.
> And certes, in this world so faren we;
> We seken faste after felicitee,
> But we goon wrong ful often, trewely."

(As if to demonstrate his point, he says all this while bitterly lamenting his release from Theseus's prison.) The poem is finally less about questions of personal worth and moral value than about epistemological and teleological darkness.

It is so, however, in characteristically medieval ways. It would measure the darkness, chart its boundaries, throw light upon the obscurity at its center. Chaucer does so by introducing two further figures from the planetary tradition who, although no temples are built to them within the amphitheatre walls, are fully as important as Mars, Venus, and Diana to what will happen there. The first is Saturn, who describes his own nature in ways rhetorically parallel to the description of the temple paintings concluded just a few lines before:

> "Myn is the drenchyng in the see so wan; (1.2456)
> Myn is the prison in the derke cote;
> Myn is the stranglyng and hangyng by the throte,
> The murmure and the cherles rebellyng,
> The groynynge, and the pryvee empoysonyng;
> I do vengeance and pleyn correccioun,
> Whil I dwelle in the signe of the leoun.
> Myn is the ruyne of the hye halles,
> The fallynge of the toures and of the walles,"

and so on. Earlier in the tale, Arcite and Palamon have attributed their imprisonment to Saturn,* and some sense of what he will bring to the tournament action can be gauged from the *Hausbuch* drawing of his children (figure 52), who inhabit a world nearly as harsh and malevolent as that of which he boasts in Chaucer's poem. At its center hobbles along an old woman, poor and on crutches: poverty, injury, and deformity all lie within Saturn's influence. She moves in front of two men being punished in the stocks at the mouth of a cave (one of them is also in fetters), while in the distance a criminal hangs from the gallows and another, stretched on a wheel, is pecked at by crows. Nearby a hermit or mendicant friar watches a man being led captive before a troop of soldiers, probably to execution, while the rest of the picture is devoted to the flaying of a decrepit horse and to several sorts of agricultural labor: the tilling of a field, the ditching of an orchard.[59] Apart from its relationship to agriculture and to solitary wisdom—the latter figured by the hermit—Saturn's influence is largely baleful and malign. His self-portrait in Chaucer's poem is firmly within a tradition, since it is against his nature—"agayn his kynde"—to work toward the creation of order and harmony. But in *The Knight's Tale* he does just that, in an action whose hidden logic

---

*See 1.1087–91 and 1328–29. An Italian engraving of Saturn's children, from the second half of the fifteenth century, includes a prison scene, as well as a man in the stocks outside the prison's barred window. (See Klibansky et al., *Saturn and Melancholy*, fig. 39.)

52. The children of Saturn. German or Dutch, ca. 1480. Note 59.

derives from astrological lore, which Chaucer deftly incorporates into his narration of the strife among the planet-gods:

> And right anon swich strif ther is bigonne,   (1.2438)
> For thilke grauntyng, in the hevene above,
> Bitwixe Venus, the goddesse of love,
> And Mars, the stierne god armypotente,
> That Juppiter was bisy it to stente;
> Til that the pale Saturnus the colde,
> That knew so manye of aventures olde,
> Foond in his olde experience an art
> That he ful soone hath plesed every part.
> As sooth is seyd, elde hath greet avantage;
> In elde is bothe wysdom and usage;
> Men may the olde atrenne, and noght atrede.
> Saturne anon, to stynten strif and drede,
> Al be it that it is agayn his kynde,
> Of al this strif he gan remedie fynde.

To understand what has happened one must know that Jupiter is a beneficent planet, exercising a benign influence upon other planets that come within its range—even upon Saturn, the deadliest of all. In *On the Properties of Things*, Bartholomaeus Anglicus explains:

Þis Iubiter his cercle is next coniunct to Saturnus his cercle. . . . [and] by his goodnes abatiþ þe malice of Saturnus whanne he is in þe ouir partye of his cercle. . . . And þerfore poetis feynen þat he putte his fadir out of his kyngdome. . . . Þis Iubiter coniunct with goode planetis makeþ goode and profitable impressiouns. . . . he counfortiþ þe goodnes of alle þe signes, and tokeneþ in hem good whanne he is ifounde þerinne.[60]

(Dante, as well, describes Jupiter as a "tempering" planet, ameliorating the cold of Saturn and the heat of Mars.)[61] In *The Knight's Tale*, it is Jupiter who is first moved to end the quarrel between Venus and Mars, and Saturn who becomes agent to his wish, finding for it the specific means—a fury summoned from hell to frighten Arcite's horse and cause the fall that eventually proves mortal.

In Boccaccio's poem, matters are much simpler. There Venus and Mars watch the battle from above, like elegant spectators at a tournament, and when Palemone's party is defeated, she says to her consort:

"You have answered Arcita's prayer well, for as you see, he is victorious; now it rests with me to fulfill Palemone's, since, as you observe, he is sad because he has lost."

Mars, become gentle, said to her, "What you say is true, dear; now do whatever gives you perfect pleasure." (IX, v. 3)

At this point Venus sends the fury. Chaucer, in contrast, involves two further planet-gods in the action because he is interested in questions of order far larger than any attempted by Boccaccio. In a Boethian paradox, the planet most disorderly becomes the efficient cause of order within the poem's larger action—though at a terrible price, reflecting the planet's more ordinary influence.

And so, if we would understand fully the emblematic significance of the amphitheatre and the philosophical meaning of the tournament action it encloses, we must read in that action the work of three "shapers" or "movers"—related to each other in a hierarchical chain. In it "Juppiter, the kyng," "prince and cause of alle thyng" (1.3035, 3036), stands supreme, in wisdom, power, justice, benevolence. He is "Firste Moevere of the cause above" (1.2987), and properly the first to seek a resolution of the strife between Venus and Mars. At the end of the poem, Theseus will name him as the ultimate source of order in the universe—a god who converts everything, even what is apparently evil and malign, "unto his propre welle / From which it is dirryved, sooth to telle" (1.3037). In some sense he presides over the deathbed reconciliation of Palamon and Arcite as well, as the god Arcite twice invokes in commending Palamon to Emelye as husband after his death: "And Juppiter so wys my soule gye"; "So Juppiter have of my soule part" (1.2786, 2792).*

Above Jupiter in the skies, but below him in the poem's scale of power, wisdom, benevolence, and control, stands Saturn, whose influence Jupiter can "convert to good" but whose nature he cannot alter or transform. As figure 53 makes clear,[62] Saturn moves toward the creation of order through a most comprehensive and costly disorder: the dead and injured lie heaped in the foreground while Arcite's horse, in the middle of the lists, falls backward upon its rider. It has seen the fury. Though Saturn's procedures may lack elegance, no one could fault their economy: he resolves the claims of two petitioners by killing one. Saturn is "conjunct" with Jupiter in the poem, but his nature is not fundamentally altered.[63]

Beneath Jupiter and Saturn, in this succession of "shapers" who

---

*Chaucer in this poem conflates Jupiter the planet and Jupiter the god, locating at the heart of Theseus's philosophy an internal contradiction upon which the whole of his speech of consolation ultimately depends. In the Ptolemaic universe, Jupiter is not even the outermost planet (a position claimed by Saturn), much less the *primum mobile* (the outermost sphere, whose movement is the ultimate source of motion for the rest). But Jupiter can be called "First Mover" through his mythographic identity as chief ruler among the gods. The commentator on *The Chess of Love*, for instance, explains the pagan poets' "figure of Jupiter" as standing for a number of things, among them "the God who is sovereign and first above all," as well as "the second planet after Saturn." Jupiter's throne, its location in the sky, his sceptre, his power over thunder and tempest, his eagle that snatches up Ganymede from the earth to the sky, all these (the commentator tells us) can be interpreted so as to "reconcile" this figure to the true God. But, he continues, since "Macrobius says that when one speaks of the high God . . . one ought not mingle fable or fiction . . . I do not wish to pause very long" over such an interpretation. (See pp. 116–18.) The conflation of the two traditions, though it makes nonsense of astrology, allowed Chaucer to suggest that some portion of Christian truth could be glimpsed, however obscurely, from within the philosophical and religious ideas of Theseus's culture. They offer a distant prospect of the truth.

53. The fury frightens Arcita's horse. French, ca. 1455. Note 62.

work to create or restore order, stands Duke Theseus himself, who bears an interesting relationship to both. He is placed above Palamon and Arcite in a position of mediation, just as Saturn is placed in the heavens, above Venus and Mars; and it is he who invents the means of resolving the impasse on earth, just as Saturn does among the planetary gods. But more significant is Theseus's relationship to Jupiter, in ways the *Planetenkinder* can illustrate well. Figure 54 shows "the children of Jupiter," who are good at marksmanship and hunting—the activities in the middle distance—but who above all are intellectuals, jurists, and peacemakers, as the scenes in the foreground make clear. On the left, we see scholars at their books, and on the right, a ruler deciding a case being pleaded before him.[64] At the end of the poem, Theseus's learned speech on the nature of the created universe links him to the world of speculative thought, just as his earlier responses, first to the grief of the Theban widows, and then to the conflict between Arcite and Palamon, relate him to the world of justice. The verses that accompany the *Hausbuch* engravings say of those who are "wholly Jupiter's children": "Often they go hunting

54. The children of Jupiter. German or Dutch, ca. 1480. Note 64.

with hounds. / They are judges, boatsmen and scholars, / Lawyers, clerks, and courtiers."[65]

Theseus is, in addition, related to Jupiter by certain patterns specific to the poem. His rule in Athens is all powerful, like that of Jupiter among the planet-gods, and he is often described in language that evokes a higher power, as when the young knights "hym of lordshipe and of mercy preyde, / And he hem graunteth grace" (1.1827). The poet sometimes speaks of him in rhetorical apposition to Jupiter, as in the following transition:

> And forth I wole of Theseus yow telle.   (1.1662)
>   The destinee, ministre general,
> That executeth in the world over al

and indeed Theseus himself sometimes speaks with the accents of such a deity: "ech of yow shal have his destynee / As hym is shape" (1.1842). At the poem's most crucial moment, just before the tournament that he has arranged, he shows himself at his palace window as though he were a god seated on a throne—one is reminded of Diana's oratory, "in a touret on the wal"—and receives the reverence of his people:

> Duc Theseus was at a wyndow set,   (1.2528)
> Arrayed right as he were a god in trone.
> The peple preesseth thiderward ful soone
> Hym for to seen, and doon heigh reverence.

When it is announced that he will "his firste purpos modifye" and forbid any combat to the death—a change of intention like the movement from the Old Law to the New[66]—the people cry out with one accord, "God save swich a lord, that is so good, / He wilneth no destruccion of blood!" (1.2563).

Both Theseus and Jupiter, king and god, are intelligences who work to create peace and harmony, to establish an order based on love. Theseus is a functionary of Jupiter the All-Mover, and is like him in some ways: this relationship constitutes the propriety, as I see it, of the godlike overtones with which he sometimes speaks, or with which he is sometimes described in the poem. But because he is himself subject to Fortune's caprice, and lacks absolute control, Theseus can only work *toward* order. His will can be frustrated, his best-laid plans miscarry. He cannot avenge widows without destroying a city; he cannot arrange a tournament to prevent bloodshed without losing a life all the same, because a higher mover—for reasons Theseus can neither know nor influence—has preferred death as *his* means. The poem, in short, shows us three movers, each above the other in an ascending scale of perfection and power—Theseus first, then Saturn, then Jupiter—all of whom work toward the creation of order. But the cost, on any level, may be high.

Theseus seeks in the tournament to create an *exclusive order*: he replaces the wooded grove with a magnificent theatre, adorned with temples to the gods, and creates within it a world of ceremony in which a love conflict can be resolved under rule of law. But he achieves at most an *inclusive order*.[67] For all the perfection of its form, his great amphitheatre can only encircle what is selfish, destructive, and violent in man's nature, released under the malign aspects of the planet-gods.* It is able to contain, but not to alter or exclude, the passions and influences that make us what we are: children of the planets, playthings of the stars.

After Arcite's death, Theseus commands that the funeral pyre be built upon the same site, and that the funeral games be held there—a decision Chaucer did not work out with perfect consistency on the literal level of his poem. Theseus's decision when he finds the young knights fighting in the grove—"The lystes shal I maken in this place" (1.1862)—locates very precisely the theatre and the tournament, and shapes one's understanding of the poem for the next thousand lines. But in choosing the grove as the site of Arcite's funeral pyre and sepulchre, Theseus makes a second decision that implies it is still standing (1.2860): he orders it felled. One can explain the contradiction in terms of source—in the first instance, Chaucer altered the *Teseida*, and in the second, followed it—but one cannot resolve it within the poem, not even by close calculations: a theatre a mile in circumference, made "in this place," must include the grove that a thousand lines later is felled again. One can only surmise that Chaucer wanted both events, at their separate places in the poem, and that what attracted him to both was their thematic potential. In a long rhetorical *occupatio* concerning the funeral pyre, he pays a new kind of attention to the grove, summarizing the far more lengthy verses of his Italian original (XI, vv. 13–29).

> But how the fyr was maked upon highte,   (1.2919)
> Ne eek the names that the trees highte,
> As ook, firre, birch, aspe, alder, holm, popler,
> Wylugh, elm, plane, assh, box, chasteyn, lynde, laurer,
> Mapul, thorn, bech, hasel, ew, whippeltree,—
> How they weren feld, shal nat be toold for me;
> Ne hou the goddes ronnen up and doun,
> Disherited of hire habitacioun,
> In which they woneden in reste and pees,
> Nymphes, fawnes and amadrides;

---

*Fierce animal imagery, like that used to describe the young knights fighting in the grove, recurs in the description of the tournament: Arcite fights like a tiger (1.2626), Palamon like a lion (1.2630); Palamon seeks Arcite's blood, he seeks to slay (1.2632–33). But this time such emotion is unleashed within forms.

Ne hou the beestes and the briddes alle
Fledden for fere, whan the wode was falle;
Ne how the ground agast was of the light,
That was nat wont to seen the sonne bright;

all that (and more) says Chaucer, "kepe I nat to seye" ("I do not care to tell"; 1.2960). It is another of the poem's major events in which order is created by means of an appalling disorder. The grief of those who mourn Arcite is given ritualized and suitably magnificent expression: the corpse is dressed splendidly in cloth of gold, with white gloves, a bright sword, and green laurel crown; his shield and spear and bow are borne upon three white horses caparisoned with his arms; the funeral cortege moves from the city to the grove along a street hung with black; golden vessels filled with honey and milk and blood and wine are carried for the ceremony, along with fire to set the wood alight. But all this entails the destruction of the grove, displacing the wild creatures—birds and animals and tree spirits (nymphs, fauns, dryads, the "gods" of the place)—whose native place it was, and whose life there "in reste and pees" is now destroyed. Disinherited by the human need for order, they run frantic, "up and doun," or flee for fear. The very ground is aghast at the light of the sun, which has never before penetrated the forest darkness.

Since Chaucer did not resolve the contradiction implicit in the location of these two large actions, we cannot resolve it either: we can only respond to his invention seriatim. But his larger emblematic intention is, I think, clear. Apart from the poem's beginning, which moves swiftly to the prison/garden setting, and apart from its end, a speech of consolation and renewed purpose delivered "in parlement," one piece of ground outside the city furnishes the setting for the entire action: a single place, whose nature changes in response to Theseus's shaping will. We see it first as a wooded grove, random in its growth, in which two fugitives seek each other's death; then as a marble amphitheatre with temples dedicated to the planet-gods, at the center of which 200 knights fight in chivalric tournament; finally as the site of a great funeral, in which the grove is felled and burned in mourning Arcite's death. The wild wood is transformed—by art and ceremony and rule of law—as Theseus seeks to translate human aggression, sexuality, and (finally) sorrow into forms that will allow civilized life to continue. But in a universe bounded by the *primum mobile*, and from out of a culture that knows nothing of the highest god beyond his function as First Mover, all such effort, all such intelligence, can create only limited forms. Chaos is at the center even of figure 55, which shows the tournament at its height, proceeding precisely as Teseo had planned.[68] Disorder is intrinsic to such a ceremony, and need not wait upon the fury sent from hell. Such forms, even at their most successful, can only contain. They do not ever transcend.

🦋

Boccaccio's poem, it should already be clear, is not so deeply concerned with the theme of order. His Teseo does not build an amphitheatre uniquely for the tournament, nor are temples to the planet-gods located within it. It does not replace a wooded grove, and Saturn (conjunct with Jupiter) plays no role in the poem's action. So much we have already examined. Let us turn now to the poet's own relationship to the materials of his poem, the way he locates his own deepest sympathies within it.

The *Teseida* is a worldly and sophisticated poem, conceived in the most ambitious terms. In its final verses, Boccaccio proclaims it the first epic poem in the Italian vernacular to sing "the toils endured for Mars" (XII, vv. 84–86) and names as his models Virgil and Statius; the poem's twelve books extend to nearly ten thousand lines of verse. If it is not finally the equal of *The Knight's Tale* as an achieved work of art,[69] it surely surpasses it in the richness of its invention and the scale of its undertaking. But the author's relationship to his story, as he establishes it in a long Dedicatory Epistle and resumes it in a sonnet at the poem's end, is peculiarly narrow and intense, in ways that run counter to this larger literary ambition. Whereas Chaucer's narrator offers his story of Palamon and Arcite to a company of pilgrims on the road to Canterbury—*The Knight's Tale* is from the beginning a public poem—Boccaccio offers his to a single lady, the beautiful "Fiammetta" to whom several of his early works are dedicated, whom he loves (he tells her here) as hopelessly as Palemone and Arcita ever loved Emilia—from the first moment he saw her, from as great a spiritual distance, and from a life of comparable suffering and ill fortune. The poem has been written in order to please her: "I recall having heard in other days, more blissful than long-lasting, that you yearned to hear and sometimes even to read some story or other, especially tales of love." But the poem has a more intimate purpose still, for he tells her that it reflects their former happiness, as well as his present misery. She will be able to recognize him in the character of one of the knights: "If you remember well, you will be able to recognize in what is related of one of the lovers and of the young lady who is loved, things said and done by me to you and by you to me. . . . Which of the two [lovers] it is, I will not reveal because I know that you will discern it. . . . You will be able to realize what my life was before and what it has been since you no longer wished me to be yours."[70]

55. The tournament underway. French, ca. 1455. Note 68.

The puzzle he sets is not very hard to solve: Boccaccio transparently identifies himself with Arcita, especially the Arcita of Book IV, who has broken his exile to return to Athens, compelled by love to serve his lady, though his service is neither recognized nor rewarded. Boccaccio introduces his twelve-book epic poem as though it were an extended lyric plea to Fiammetta, bearing at its emotional center the hope that "realizing my love, you will be able to discard the haughtiness you have assumed and having cast it aside you will be able to transform my wretchedness again into the coveted bliss."[71] The Master of René of Anjou captures perfectly the spirit of this dedication in figure 56, where he shows the author as young, fervent, and anguished—bearing indeed some facial resemblance to the Arcita of the later illuminations—kneeling before his cruel mistress to present her the book of his poem.[72]

The *Teseida* is, of course, more varied in its interests than the Dedicatory Epistle suggests. But that dedication is part of the public poem, and it invites us to attend most closely to a certain kind of

56. Boccaccio presents to Fiammetta the book of his poem. French, ca. 1455.
Note 72.

lyric voice, a certain kind of emotional intensity within it. Whoever
the mysterious Fiammetta may have been—if indeed she was a real
woman at all[73]—the dedication identifies the voice of the author with
that of a single figure within his poetic design, a figure of suffering
rather than of wisdom.

Chaucer's narrative voice in *The Knight's Tale* is very different. It is
not highly inflected or individual—it tells us little about a specific
knight-narrator—but it is grave, mature, and dignified, with as deep
a stake in the philosophical questions posed by the poem's action as in
the narrative outcome of the actions themselves. It sounds most like
the voice of Theseus, but since even Theseus is sometimes described
at a critical distance, we will do better to characterize it simply as
sharing a common core of identity—in the sense of wisdom, matu-
rity, and concern for order—with Jupiter, Saturn, and Theseus, all
three. Especially with Theseus: as Robert Jordan has eloquently said,
"the Knight's Tale asserts in the example of its own structure a cele-

bration of *homo faber*, a tribute to man's capacity to build—to build a social order, ethical conventions, splendid buildings, noble poems—and to endow these works with dignity and grandeur."[74]

Among such works the making of noble poems must concern us now, for I think it was precisely Chaucer's sense of himself as one who gave form to human experience through fiction and verse that led him to identify his own voice with those who shape experience in the poem. Within the privileged world of a fiction, he knew himself to be, like Jupiter, a "First Mover" from which everything derives. He knew that, like Theseus, he could invent on the grandest scale, and as surely as Theseus does within the world of the poem, he creates an amphitheatre and stages a tournament in our mind.[75] But because Chaucer customarily thought of his poetry in terms far less imposing, he incorporated into his fiction "makers" of a more modest kind—the "portreyours" and "kerveres of ymages" who decorate the theatre temples—with whom he identifies as well. Their image-making art is related to his own in terms we have examined in Chapter I, for painters and sculptors bring to Theseus's amphitheatre the arts of representation, to which the art of narrative poetry is related.

The building of the amphitheatre from within the fiction thus may be said to parallel Chaucer's own enterprise in the creation of the poem,* in matters small (its detailed invention and rhetorical decoration) as well as large (the major alterations he makes to his source, the reduction of its twelve books to four parts, the distribution of its material within those new structural units). *The Knight's Tale* is the most insistently "artificial" of all Chaucer's major poems, constantly calling attention to itself as a thing "made." The relationship of the planet-gods, for instance, is made to echo the central human relationships of the poem; the temple descriptions and temple prayers are all cut to the same rhetorical model; the wedding, conquest, and funeral that open the poem are answered by the tournament, funeral, and wedding that bring it to its close. In a grandly artificial simplification of the calendar, virtually everything in the poem is made to happen

---

*Certain events in Chaucer's own life made particularly intimate this act of self-identification with builders, painters, and carvers, for in 1390, as Clerk of the King's Works, he was put in charge of constructing scaffolds for two tournaments convened by Richard II in Smithfield, just outside the walls of London. The second of these lasted four days and was particularly splendid. Proclaimed by heralds across much of Europe, it attracted many foreign as well as English knights, with sixty specially chosen by the king to accept the challenge of all comers; sixty ladies were in their company. Froissart's account celebrates the ridings, feasting, and dancing fully as much as the combats themselves; see E. Rickert, ed., *Chaucer's World*, pp. 211–14. Robertson, *Chaucer's London*, p. 171, suggests that Chaucer may have had a hand in designing the pageantry of the occasion, as well as supervising the construction of the lists. If Chaucer wrote the poem in its present form before 1390, as seems likely, he came to the tournament task experienced in his imagination, at the least. If, as some conjecture, he later revised the poem for inclusion in the *Tales*, he did so out of an immediate experience of all that links together those who give shape to such an occasion, whether in life or in poetry.

"in honor of May," and in a comparable concentration of setting, two locations—the prison/garden as it is progressively defined and the wooded grove in its several transformations—serve for most of the action. Its narrative movement as well is heavily patterned, with a fivefold recurrence of strife* expressing, on a structural level, two of the poem's fundamental assumptions: that human nature is willful, and that contention and disorder are its natural products. We notice that all these conflicts are resolved by outside intervention, signifying the importance the poem places on external sources of order, authority, and control. And finally we notice the sheer number of actions performed by two or more people in much the same way, whether that action be responding to imprisonment, falling in love, praying to the gods, fighting in a tournament, mourning a death, or seeking to create order. This leveling of individual differences is one source of the philosophical generality of the poem: the questions that arise concern all participants equally, in their relation to the heavens as well as in their relationships on earth. Is man in any sense free? Is any purpose served by his attempt to create order, in a universe governed by Fortune and the planet-gods? The question concerning order emerges from a poetic work insistently ordered, and has implications for poetry itself. In the first two sections of this chapter, we have looked at those questions by examining the narrative images through which they are posed. Let us look now at the answers the poem returns.

Theseus's long concluding speech addresses those questions directly, and with steady reference to the fact of death, Everyman's as well as Arcite's. What he has to say is very complicated, both in terms of its propositions and as an official performance—a performance Shakespeare's Polonius might have categorized as "philosophical-consolatory-pragmatic." There is a tendency among modern critics, well read in *The Consolation of Philosophy*, to hear more music than is really there. Let us pay the speech very close attention.

Theseus begins on a level of great generality, concerned not with human values but with physical law. The "Firste Moevere," he tells the mourners and the parliament before him, bound together in a "faire cheyne of love" "the fyr, the eyr, the water, and the lond / In certeyn boundes, that they may nat flee" (1.2987). His emphasis, be it noted, is on bonds and boundaries: we will hear nothing more of

---

*I have in mind these actions—the Theban widows' claims against Creon, the love rivalry between Palamon and Arcite in prison, the combat between them in the wooded grove, the dispute between Venus and Mars in the heavens, and the tournament battle between Palamon and Arcite—as they are resolved in turn by Theseus, Perotheus, Theseus again, Jupiter (through Saturn), and Mars and Saturn. Even the mourning for Arcite's death is ended only by outside intervention: the consolatory speech of Theseus and his provision for a marriage.

love for a long time, and then on a different level altogether. Theseus here describes the physical order of the universe and declares that man is part of that order because he too is limited—he is bound to die.

> "That same Prince and that Moevere," quod he,   (1.2994)
> "Hath stablissed in this wrecched world adoun
> Certeyne dayes and duracioun
> To al that is engendred in this place,
> Over the whiche day they may nat pace,
> Al mowe they yet tho dayes wel abregge."

A few lines later, Theseus returns to this vision of universal order based upon mortality and decline to link man's lot with that of trees and stones, rivers and great cities. Man, too, waxes and wanes, flourishes and dies:

> "Loo the ook, that hath so long a norisshynge   (1.3017)
> From tyme that it first bigynneth to sprynge,
> And hath so long a lif, as we may see,
> Yet at the laste wasted is the tree.
>   Considereth eek how that the harde stoon
> Under oure feet, on which we trede and goon,
> Yet wasteth it as it lyth by the weye.
> The brode ryver somtyme wexeth dreye;
> The grete tounes se we wane and wende.
> Thanne may ye se that al this thyng hath ende.
>   Of man and womman seen we wel also
> That nedes, in oon of thise termes two,
> This is to seyn, in youthe or elles age,
> He moot be deed, the kyng as shal a page;
> Som in his bed, som in the depe see,
> Som in the large feeld, as men may see;
> Ther helpeth noght, al goth that ilke weye.
> Thanne may I seyn that al this thyng moot deye."

As the parallel conclusions to the two verse paragraphs suggest, the consolation implicit in this idea is based entirely upon natural law: "al this thyng hath ende"; "al this thyng moot deye." A comprehensive dance of death, claiming man and woman, king and page, is identified with certain physical principles of the universe itself, and is thus in a sense made harmonious with it, made less outrageous to the human spirit. But the spirit itself goes begging here, its destiny undifferentiated from that of trees and stones, rivers and great cities.

In the course of his speech, though in no very orderly fashion, Theseus offers two further consolations that seek better to answer the spirit's need, the first of which is also derived directly from experience. The First Mover, he tells his listeners, has ordained:

> "That speces of thynges and progressiouns   (I. 3013)
> Shullen enduren by successiouns,
> And nat eterne, withouten any lye.
> This maystow understonde and seen at ye."

This second idea of order, based upon generation and succession, carries with it a deeper consolation, for it speaks of life as well as death. Though nothing on earth is eternal, the species endures. Only individuals die.

But that, of course, has been the problem from the beginning: our selfish problem, as persons who must die, as well as the specific problem that occasions this speech, the death of Arcite in his youth and at the moment of his victory. In the third of his propositions Theseus seeks to invest this natural order with a spiritual significance by invoking certain ideas concerning its motive (and originating) power. Concerning the law of limitation and mortality he counsels:

> "Thanne may men by this ordre wel discerne   (I. 3003)
> That thilke Moevere stable is and eterne."

And concerning the dance of death seen as a dance of succession, he asks:

> "What maketh this but Juppiter, the kyng,   (I. 3035)
> That is prince and cause of alle thyng,
> Convertynge al unto his propre welle
> From which it is dirryved, sooth to telle?"

Such conclusions, of course, can in no way be derived from experience directly. Theseus here takes leave of propositions that can be seen "at ye," to enter the realm of logical induction, working from analogy:

> "Wel may men knowe, but it be a fool,   (I. 3005)
> That every part dirryveth from his hool;
> For nature hath nat taken his bigynnyng
> Of no partie or cantel of a thyng,
> But of a thyng that parfit is and stable,
> Descendynge so til it be corrumpable."

His claim is that the imperfection, disorder, and mutability that characterize earthly existence necessarily imply the real existence of their opposite qualities elsewhere, without which they could neither be named or understood. That we are mortal proves something must be immortal; that we are imperfect proves something must be perfect; that we cannot make sense of our lives except as part of something else proves there must be something that is whole. Theseus's speech locates this immortality, perfection, and unity in the outermost sphere of the universe, and characterizes in those terms the force that moves it—the "Firste Moevere," or "Juppiter, the kyng, / That is prince and cause of alle thyng." Since, by the same logic, the real existence of evil and malevolence here must prove the First Mover's goodness and benevolence, we may also believe that he converts to good—"his propre welle"—all the conflict, confusion, and chaos of earthly life. The order that is based upon generation and succession reflects that goodness and benevolence, which can be seen directly only through logical induction, through the processes of mind.

These last propositions, in suggesting an order beyond disorder, a purpose beyond our comprehension, are transcendent ideas, and they are asserted rather than proven by Theseus in his speech. What Boethius requires five books to demonstrate in *The Consolation of Philosophy* cannot readily be expressed in six lines of verse, any more than in my slightly longer paraphrase above. But these six lines of Theseus's speech use language so close to that of Boethius and his sources, and derive so obviously from the full system of his philosophical thought, that many critics have written as though the whole of that work had been uttered here, or as though the consolation offered by philosophy were adequate to the human perplexity this poem addresses. The first is an error more readily excused than the second. Even if we should choose to read these few lines as being intended to summon the whole of the *Consolation* to mind, with its full authority, we would still need a more accurate idea of that work than one can count on finding in much of what has been written about *The Knight's Tale*.

In my earlier discussion of some texts in the prison-of-the-world tradition, I postponed considering this work by Boethius, though it is the most important of all. Chaucer himself translated it, and it has never lacked attention in discussions of *The Knight's Tale*. But I wish to focus on some aspects of the relationship that have had less attention than they deserve, suggesting first that Boethius's development of the prison image furnished Chaucer the essential model for his transformations of the *Teseida* prison/garden, and then discussing certain limitations the two works share.

The *Consolation* begins with Boethius exiled and imprisoned, for no good cause and in danger of his life, and then turns that fact into a metaphor that becomes a way of talking about all human life. E. K. Rand, years ago, stated it succinctly: "The *Consolation of Philosophy* is prison-literature, and prison-literature often takes the form of a theodicy," the form, that is, of a discourse that seeks to reconcile the existence of evil with the goodness and sovereignty of God.[76] But Boethius moves swiftly from his own present circumstances to the more general human anxiety he speaks of so often in the work, the feeling that we are in chains. "This man," says Lady Philosophy, "that whilom was fre, to whom the hevene was opyn and knowen, and was wont to gon in hevenliche pathes, and saugh the lyghtnesse

57. Boethius writes his
book, behind a prison
window. Italian, 1312.
Note 77.

of the rede sonne. . . . Allas! now lyth he emptid of lyght of his
thoght, and his nekke is pressyd with hevy cheynes, and bereth his
chere enclyned adoun for the grete weyghte, and is constreyned to
loken on the fool erthe!" (I, m. 2, Chaucer's translation.) In one early
illumination, he is literally chained by the neck, with Lady Philoso-
phy tall and stately on his right, the muses of elegaic poetry on his
left. In figure 57, the portrait of the author at his book is framed by
the bars of a prison window.[77]

The treatise as a whole can be read as an exploration, on many lev-
els, of man's need to be free. Although it employs a close Aristotelian
dialectic to resolve intellectual difficulties, its larger method is poetic
as well as logical. Boethius uses his own circumstances to teach him-
self how to be free: from melancholy and self-pity; from intellectual
error; from false friends; from contingent desire. Only by seeking
the sovereign good itself, the desire for which subsumes all partial
desires, can we free the mind from the body's vulnerability and pas-
sions, and find security in a world otherwise governed by Fortune:

But wher schal men fynden any man that mai exercen or haunten any ryght
upon another man, but oonly on his body, or elles upon thynges that ben
lowere than the body, the whiche I clepe fortunous possessiouns? Maystow
evere have any comaundement over a free corage? (II, pr. 6)

All these are amplifications of the central impulse behind this prison
book, and their cumulative power is great. But they grow into larger
formulations still, into statements of the most profound human un-
ease and longing. The final book of the *Consolation* is devoted to de-
claring man's freedom from determinism—the "destinal cheyne" (V,

pr. 2) that error derives from God's perfect foreknowledge of everything that will happen—and from linear time itself. This demonstration that we are more than puppets in a play whose every line has been written, every move plotted, and every consequence foreseen by some superior puppet-master, is a statement concerning free will: it affirms our liberty to choose, and to stand morally responsible for our choice. Anything less is perceived as bondage. And so too with time, our mortal prison, which can be escaped only if a higher order called eternity exists, where we may find freedom from change, from the erroneous understanding of change, and (potentially) from death. Lady Philosophy demonstrates the logical existence of such an order.

By this stage in the argument one has moved a long way from the opening image, the literal fact, of Boethius in prison. But that image has been part of all those that follow. From its root grows a tree whose tallest branches reach into heaven, like the figure of Lady Philosophy herself, whose height in Boethius's cell seems to vary from human stature to something much greater. In *The Knight's Tale*, Theseus's final speech concerning the prison of this life stands at a comparable distance from the literal prison tower of the opening action. Although Chaucer moves the image through a declension uniquely his own, including most significantly the love prison, the larger strategy may well have been suggested by the Boethian paradigm. It is generally assumed that Chaucer was translating the *Consolation* and writing the poem of Palamon and Arcite at about the same time.

The parallel is important, formally and thematically, but I would not have it contribute to an impression, too easily gained from Chaucer criticism, that *The Knight's Tale* is essentially a fictive version of *The Consolation of Philosophy*. The differences are at least of equal consequence. I would not say, for instance, that "the long Boethian discourse of Theseus which begins, 'The Firste Moevere of the cause above,' contains the solution to the problems raised by the preceding action, and is hence very valuable to the audience of the poem,"[78] for that is either to disregard the limited nature of the problems addressed by Boethius in the *Consolation*, or to mistake the specific problem Theseus is shown confronting here. Let us look more closely at both.

Boethius's book is about the role of fortune and free will in human affairs, and it ends with its author liberated from certain errors (both of the mind and spirit) concerning the moral coherence of life on earth. There is no further mention at his book's end of imprisonment and exile, not because that had changed—he was indeed executed soon after—but because when man's real freedom has been understood, literal imprisonment or exile becomes a fact of lesser consequence. A mind that thinks philosophically has wings, Boethius tells us, and no tyrant can imprison it: in its highest flight, it can conceive of eternity and can understand human experience, even its own experience, from that height.

Such a journey of the mind, freed from earthly things and moving into the realm of pure intellection concerning their eternal causes, is the greatest journey of which Boethius' book will speak. It is illustrated in figure 58, together with Lady Philosophy attending him in prison, giving his mind wings.[79] The book knows nothing more of how man's spirit may "retourne hool and sownd" into its native country. Lady Philosophy holds it axiomatic that "the soules of men ne mowen nat deyen in no wyse" (II, pr. 4), and that the true country of the soul is heaven, from which it descends (III, m. 6) and to which it would return after the body's death (II, pr. 7). But when asked whether the souls of evil men are punished after death, Lady Philosophy can offer only a vague answer and this excuse: "My conseil nys nat to determyne of thise peynes" (IV, pr. 4). The only journey to God charted in the *Consolation* is for the mind of philosophic man, by means of axiom, logical induction, and contemplation. But because that journey can free man's mind, the prison and the prison metaphor fall away; they vanish into the realm of illusion and error.

Chaucer's *Knight's Tale*, in contrast, expands the prison image to make it totally inclusive, so that it furnishes the poem's final philosophic description of the world as well as its first substantial mise-en-scène. The scraps of philosophy we hear from within the prison of this world serve only to make it a little more bearable; they offer no release.[80] In *The Knight's Tale*, the problem of freedom is never resolved—the poem remains locked in apparent determinism*— and the problem of order reveals at its center nothing less than the problem of death itself. Neither Boethius nor Chaucer would have thought the *Consolation* a sufficient answer to that. The *Consolation* was believed to demonstrate, by axiom and logical deduction, the existence of eternity as the realm of God. But it predicated for man no clear and available means of movement, other than within his mind, between this kingdom of mutability and death, and that other,

---

*Even Theseus's desire to go hunting on the morning that Arcite and Palamon fight within the grove—a fortunate coincidence upon which the entire action of the poem will turn—is made the function of a determinist universe: "For certeinly, oure appetites heer, / Be it of werre, or pees, or hate, or love, / Al is this reuled by the sighte above" (I.1670). These lines deny all human freedom, in expressing the power of a shadowy "destinee, ministre general," which is said to execute "the purveiaunce that God hath seyn biforn." But all we know of destiny in this poem is the action of the planet-gods (itself a good deal more than the actors in the poem can know). The planet-gods put a roof on the theatre, so to speak, for if Jupiter and the First Mover are synonymous, then no Boethian Providence can be detected behind destiny, and no explanation can be offered of how the stars can cause all this and yet leave man responsible for his acts. The poem is a closed system, created not only by Palamon and Arcite's inability to think clearly (the mind that thinks clearly has wings), but by its paganism (the cultural condition that limits Theseus's thought as well).

58. Lady Philosophy and the mind's wings. Dutch, 1492. Note 79.

"stable and eterne." Boethius wrote *The Consolation of Philosophy* in ways that do not go beyond philosophy.

Boethius was a Christian as well as a philosopher; indeed, he was venerated in the Middle Ages as St. Severinus, and his tomb was honored at Pavia Cathedral. We know now that it was a popular canonization only: his cult apparently rested upon a confusion with Severinus of Cologne, and upon the fact that the emperor Theodoric, who sentenced him to death, held heretical (Arian) views on the nature of God the Son. But that Boethius had accepted the new faith was not in doubt, and we have from his pen several Christian treatises that outline the higher truths of theology (dependent upon Christian history, revelation, and exegesis) that he deliberately excludes from the *Consolation*.[81] He conceived his prison book in ways that betrayed neither his larger theological beliefs nor its specifically philosophical intention, and the book's extraordinary influence across an entire Christian millennium is intimately related to that fact. In reading the *Consolation* as implicitly or potentially Christian—a tradition of commentary that begins with Alcuin—the Middle Ages read it correctly. But even those commentators most determined to discover a comprehensive *interpretatio christiana* for the whole never really distorted its generic nature, simply because the problems it considers are generically limited. A commentator may relate Lady Philosophy to the Wisdom of Solomon or to Christ as the Wisdom of the Father, but Christ as Suffering Servant or as Redeemer can never substantially enter such glosses: the work provides no adequate occasion. Boethius's God cannot be called more than "governour of thinges," "prince and bygynnere of wirkynge," "soverein intelligence," just as his themes do not go beyond "purveaunce," "destyne," "hap," "predestinacioun," and "fre wil."[82] In establishing a philosophic component for Christianity, and in conferring Christian dignity upon the highest achievements of philosophy, the work does sufficient service. It does not speak of Christian salvation.

Manuscript illuminators, by a discreet use of attribute, occasionally exceed these limits, alluding to the further knowledge of God that came to man through the Incarnation of Christ. Not infrequently they show God with a crossed nimbus (halo), which must have suggested Christ to many, though, as F. P. Pickering has recently demonstrated in relation to other texts and pictures, this need identify him only as Wisdom (*Sapientia*), Second Person of the Father, who created the world. Sometimes God holds an orb topped by a small cross; in figure 58, indeed, he wears a papal triple crown; and in two instances known to me he is shown as three identical persons. Such images implicitly extend Boethius's consolation beyond philosophy, but they are comparatively rare, and admit of two possible explanations. Some doubtless are influenced by Christian commentaries, but others may represent nothing more than an artist's response to the instruction "paint a picture of God in the heavens," and thus bear no thoughtful relation to Boethius's text.[83] The central pictorial tradition offers simply the image of a ruler on high, bearing sceptre and orb, whom Lady Philosophy invites Boethius to contemplate with his mind. The Son on the cross, the dove of the Paraclete, indeed the very concept of a Triune God, are totally absent from the pages of Boethius, and are virtually absent from illuminations to that text.

They are likewise absent from Theseus's concluding speech in *The Knight's Tale*, though for a different reason. The speech is limited not by the exclusions of a genre (philosophy as distinct from theology), but by its imaginative moment in time. The essence of that moment, from a late-medieval point of view, was the separation of man culturally and historically from knowledge of the true God.[84] Chaucer cannot allow Theseus to know what Boethius (here tacitly) knew, or what these late-fifteenth-century illuminators knew Boethius knew. In its full context, Theseus's final speech expresses a pathos as dignified as the dying of Arcite or the final joy of Palamon, for his own intentions have been frustrated, his idealism rebuked: he does not stand outside the suffering and confusion he attempts to declare rational and purposive.

It is an easy error, in this respect, to credit Theseus's philosophy with an assurance and authority it does not in fact possess, simply because the poem has allowed us to hear the counter-claims of Mars and Venus on behalf of their suppliants and to watch Saturn, moved by Jupiter, work to resolve the conflict of their wills. In the context of the poem's total action, we know that Arcite's death has not happened by chance. Whatever moral uncertainty we may feel about those higher agents of causality—the question of justice, be it noted, is never raised in the heavens—Arcite's death has an intentional and explicit cause.

But a fact of equal importance is that Theseus does not know these things. He and the gods are characters in the same story, but their orders of existence are different: Theseus is not privileged to hear what we hear or see what we see, up where the gods live and the planets exert their influence on human affairs. To read Theseus's long concluding speech properly, we must remember that it is spoken from within the human condition, by one who stands high on Fortune's wheel and is himself subject to her overthrow. That fact was established at the poem's beginning by the grieving Theban widows—each of whom has been "a duchesse or a queene"—who hail his triumph and offer their own suffering as evidence that under the reign of Fortune "noon estaat assureth to be weel" (1.926). The scene (figure 59) is itself emblematic,[85] and casts its shadow across the whole poem, including Theseus's speech of consolation. That speech bears no direct relation to the action the poet has imagined for the planet-gods, but grows more simply out of what is needed if his subjects are to be freed of the past, if death is not to make a mockery of human life and purpose. In the poem's last scenes, we are shown men trying to make what sense they can of an event that, for anything they may confidently know, must continue to seem arbitrary, senseless, and cruel.

In Boccaccio's poem, Teseo addresses the question of the moral coherence of human life at the conclusion of the tournament, while Arcita is still alive. His purpose is to console the knights who have been defeated that day, and to that end he expresses certain ideas "some

59. The Theban widows interrupt Teseo's triumph. French, ca. 1455. Note 85.

hold to be true" ("la quale alcuni afferman che sia vera") but about which he declares himself uncertain: "I do not know whether this be true" ("Se ciò è ver non so"). The statement that follows is the closest equivalent in Boccaccio's poem to the "Firste Moevere" speech that Chaucer gives Theseus at his poem's end: Teseo suggests that "in creating the world divine Providence foresaw with perfect lucidity the purpose of every seed sown, whether of rational or of brute being therein, and by eternal decree ordained that what had been foreseen should come to pass" (IX, vv. 52, 53). Teseo claims for the idea no more than possible credibility,[86] and Palemone's followers understand his purposes clearly: "Teseo's talk pleased them, although they did not think all of it was true" (IX, v. 61). Chaucer allows his Theseus greater rhetorical certainty, but it exceeds the facts of the poem, and exceeds the facts available to any pre-Christian ruler: the consolation is made provisional by its context.

In fact, many "consolations" are offered by Theseus (and by Egeus before him) in response to Arcite's death—not all carrying comparable conviction, and not all deeply compatible with each other. What we hear is not really philosophy so much as a kind of medley of what men say on such occasions, what their experience of life seems piecemeal to confirm. Sad truths, mostly, brought forward in no special order: all who live must die; this world is a place of woe; death with honor is better than death with dishonor; the dead cannot thank us for our tears; the dead may be offended by our tears. Although Theseus might suitably have ended his meditation upon Arcite's death upon reaching his highest philosophical affirmation—the claim that Jupiter converts everything "unto his propre welle"—in fact he follows that with a series of smaller conclusions and pragmatic truths, advising resignation:

> "And heer-agayns no creature on lyve, (1.3039)
> Of no degree, availleth for to stryve.
>   Thanne is it wysdom, as it thynketh me,
> To maken vertu of necessitee,
> And take it weel that we may nat eschue. . . .
> And whoso gruccheth ought, he dooth folye,
> And rebel is to hym that al may gye."

Again he has reached a suitable ending, from which he might properly turn to the future of those who live on. But he continues to address the fact of death, now from a perspective more problematic still, since the death in question is of someone young:

> "And certeinly a man hath moost honour (1.3047)
> To dyen in his excellence and flour."

Theseus explores this most minimal of elegiac ideas through ten lines of verse, before concluding in the metaphor for which the literal prison/garden has prepared us:

> "Why grucchen we, why have we hevynesse, (1.3058)
> That goode Arcite, of chivalrie the flour,
> Departed is with duetee and honour
> Out of this foule prisoun of this lyf?"

For all its apparent confidence, Theseus's philosophy ultimately reduces to this despairing vision of human possibility. It is where his philosophy ends. Arcite has honorably escaped the prison.

I do not deny that at the beginning of his speech, Theseus attempts something more than a piecemeal reflection on death and grief, and borrows enough from the philosophers—chiefly Boethius, but also Macrobius and Cicero—to give those ideas a philosophic cast.[87] Because those ideas are reasonably harmonious with Christian truth, they possessed for Chaucer's original audiences a certain authority: they were understood to be grounded in more than inductive logic or human need. But Theseus is allowed to express such ideas only in part, and out of even less knowledge of what has happened than we possess as audience to the poem. In his description of the universe as consisting of things bounded or limited, governed by death and sustained by generation, he speaks as much as he can really know. Theseus's speech of "philosophical resolution," so often celebrated in the pages of Chaucer criticism, is preceded by a long silence (1.2981–86) and ends in a metaphor of despair. As an instance of human reason attempting to understand on its own the nature and purpose of human existence, it shows reason confounded, not triumphant. The movement out is pragmatic, not philosophic.

For just as too much Boethius can be read into Theseus's brief attempt at philosophy, so too profound an affirmation can be read into the concluding marriage:

> "What may I conclude of this longe serye,   (1.3067)
> But after wo I rede us to be merye,
> And thanken Juppiter of al his grace?
> And er that we departen from this place
> I rede that we make of sorwes two
> O parfit joye, lastynge everemo."
>   · · ·
> Bitwixen hem was maad anon the bond
> That highte matrimoigne or mariage,
> By al the conseil and the baronage.
> And thus with alle blisse and melodye
> Hath Palamon ywedded Emelye.

Much has been made of the fact that Theseus calls marriage a "bond," in saying to Palamon, "Com neer, and taak youre lady by the hond" (1.3093), for that word looks back to Theseus's description of the universe as a "faire cheyne of love," bounding and binding together all its parts. The love of Palamon and Arcite for Emelye, which has been shown as a threat to order on many levels in the poem, is finally made conformable to the larger pattern, the larger necessity. But the order in which that marriage takes its place, to give Theseus's language its proper weight, is precisely a chain. It binds past generation to future generation in a ceremony of succession, in which dying creatures give birth to other dying creatures. Marriage in this poem is social, ceremonial, even political—it confirms and regularizes the dominance of Athens over Thebes—but it is not sacramental. The love it regularizes remains the love that gave birth to the initial disorder, a love of "yonge, fresshe folkes, he or she." Unlike the love of Christ that Chaucer recommends in the palinode to the *Troilus*, it contains within itself the possibility neither of release nor of transcendence. It is at most a link in a chain.

When Theseus has spoken his several consolations and pauses to ask, "What may I conclude of this long serye?" (1.3067), the answer is implicit in his question, for the meaning of a series is serial order itself, one thing following another:

> ". . . speces of thynges and progressiouns   (1.3013)
> Shullen enduren by successiouns,
> And nat eterne, withouten any lye."

Theseus turns to what the new moment allows: joy after woe, and after mourning, marriage. The language in which he arranges the betrothal moves the tale back into the genre of courtly romance, but it is also tonally unrelated to the earlier part of his speech. Palamon's suffering is absorbed into a conventional concept of love's "adversitee," and Emelye is asked, equally conventionally, to show "wommanly pittee" and "gentil mercy" in return. Although the marriage arranged by Theseus declares an end to the mourning for Arcite's death, it does not constitute a philosophic resolution of that death's perplexity and sorrow. The dance of succession, like the dance of death, is forced upon us. They are prison dances.

As the *Troilus* likewise bears witness, Chaucer was profoundly interested in the pagan moment in history as a subject in its own right. No medieval author ever imagined it with greater human sympathy, or with a more vivid sense of what human life at its most dignified and noble might have been before the Incarnation of Christ. But unlike the *Troilus*, *The Knight's Tale* never breaks free of its historical moment in order to name, in the manner of palinode, an ultimate truth whose authority is derived from outside the narrative itself, and which can measure, judge, and remedy the partial truths of the poem. As a vision of the classical past, *The Knight's Tale* serves instead as a point to move out from, as one tale follows another in a literary pilgrimage to Canterbury. Its usefulness to the larger fiction depends upon a scrupulous respect for the integrity and limitations of the pagan experience within the tale itself, and upon those limitations being remarked by the tale's audience in turn. I think we must stop a good deal short of saying that the "chain of love" in this tale "transcends" the disorder of both gods and men, or that the poem, on its most profound level, expresses a "whole providential design for good."[88] The poem is tentative and incomplete on all such matters, in ways that are essential to its meaning. They should not be resolved, for instance, by writing a Christian commentary on the concluding marriage, attempting to make of that ceremony what others would make of Theseus's philosophy, a satisfactory solution to all the problems the poem has raised. However easy it may be to find "patristic authority for an exalted view of marriage,"[89] that is not the same as finding such a view expressed in a medieval poem concerning classical civilization. Though patristic commentary can help us take the precise measure of what a poem actually says, it must not become a substitute for the poem's statement.

For all its anachronistic detail, *The Knight's Tale* never blurs the distinction between the two cultures on any essential level. It conceives their fundamental difference as clearly as did the painter of a miniature from a French manuscript of St. Augustine's *City of God* (figure 60), in which pagans and Christians urge upon each other the truth of their respective faiths, one group pointing to a temple surmounted by the figure of a naked goddess, the other group gesturing toward a chapel whose tower is crowned by the cross of Christ.[90] *The Knight's Tale* measures pagan culture against a specifically Christian understanding of the needs and purposes of human life, rendering the limitations of the former with both clarity and compassion, in a manner comparable to that of an illuminated Advent page from a late-fifteenth-century manuscript of the *Légende dorée* (figure 61). Its conception of pre-Christian experience is expressed in several scenes, which show (from the bottom, left to right) persons in darkness, in peril of the sea, and in hell mouth; persons in a cave and in a prison house; and shepherds awaiting the announcement of Christ's birth, along with persons in yet another prison. All pray to God, though under many names—*Oriens, Rex gentium, Emmanuel, Radix Jesse, Clavis David, Sapiencia, Adonay*—asking that He aid them, lighten their darkness, make them free. The range of names by which they call on Him expresses not only the comprehensiveness of their need but the mystery of its answer before Christ's birth. *Veni ad liberandum nos* is the picture's central theme, and Christ's advent as a child bearing the cross, descending from God the Father beneath the wings of the Holy Spirit to the waiting Virgin, constitutes (at the top of the picture) the eighth and most essential subject: the illumination and liberation the other scenes so urgently beseech.[91]

This painting's references are, of course, Judaic, not Gentile, and the pre-Christian experience of the Jews is depicted with dignity and respect. It shows us persons who know there is something they need to know, who seek what they truly need to find. They lift up their hearts toward heaven, and Christ is sent down to them. Pagan civilization, in contrast, by deifying (in the euhemerist analysis) great men of the past, along with the forces of nature and the planets in the skies, discovered in the natural universe a pantheon of gods. Chaucer's Theseus offers his subjects the knowledge that system can yield, the comfort it can afford, but in everything he says a sense of limitation is paramount. In *The Knight's Tale*, "Jupiter" is not a name for the Christian God,[92] and even the material furnished by the *Teseida*

60. Pagans and Christians point to their different temples. French, ca. 1400.
Note 90.

concerning the destiny of Arcite's soul after death—the journey to
the eighth sphere that Chaucer gives to Troilus at the end of a greater
poem[93]—is suppressed. Chaucer refuses to go beyond what any-
one in Theseus's historical moment could confidently have known,
which is to say, almost nothing at all, silence and enigma:

> His spirit chaunged hous and wente ther,   (1.2809)
> As I cam nevere, I kan nat tellen wher.
> Therfore I stynte, I nam no divinistre;
> Of soules fynde I nat in this registre,
> Ne me ne list thilke opinions to telle
> Of hem, though that they writen wher they dwelle.
> Arcite is coold, ther Mars his soule gye!

In limiting his poem to what Theseus knows and is able to achieve—
the tournament, the funeral, the marriage, and the saying of what is

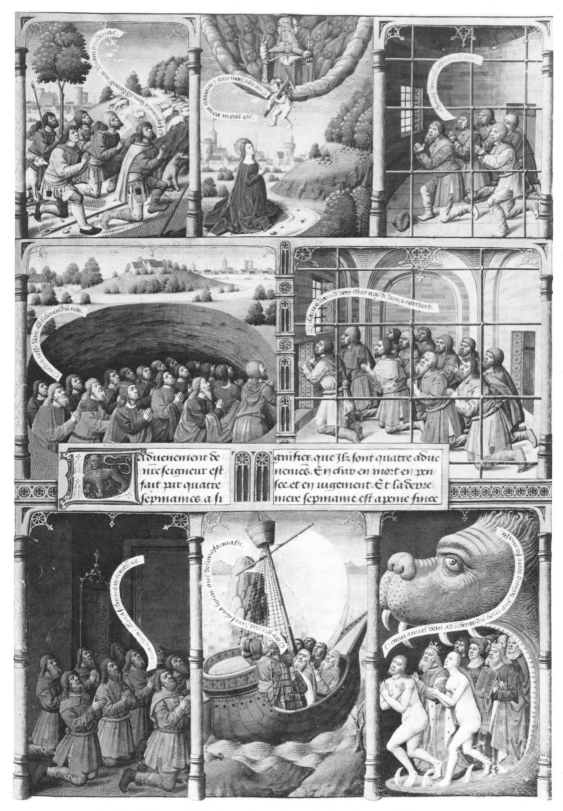

61. The Advent of Christ to those who wait in prison, in darkness, and in hell.
French, late fifteenth century. Note 91.

to be said on such occasions—Chaucer limits himself as artist, in kind. He represents through his own poetic predicament the larger subject of the poem.

The consequence of this self-limitation is nowhere more poignant than at the poem's end, where Chaucer joins the voice of his narrator to that of Theseus, as though no other option were available to him as poet. Though Theseus's periphrastic description of the proposed marriage—"I rede that we make of sorwes two / O parfit joye, last-ynge everemo" (I.3071)—is a beautifully expressed ideal, it offers a curious conclusion to a speech whose whole burden has been that no thing, no person, no joy, can last forever. Chaucer then brings the poem to an end in terms that echo and amplify these formulas:

> For now is Palamon in alle wele,   (I.3101)
> Lyvynge in blisse, in richesse, and in heele,
> And Emelye hym loveth so tendrely,
> And he hire serveth al so gentilly,
> That nevere was ther no word hem bitwene
> Of jalousie or any oother teene.
> Thus endeth Palamon and Emelye.

Chaucer's larger purpose is surely not the affirmation of such optimism. He has shown us too much of the world for that—not least in the temple paintings, which extend the evidence concerning human life beyond the immediate terms of the story and beyond the aristocratic milieu in which it was set. As Theseus and his subjects leave their grief behind,[94] moving on to create another union itself mortal and contingent, Chaucer honors their resolution by joining his voice with theirs. But he distances that resolution as well, in formulaic expressions that do not engage the issues of the poem on the level at which those issues have been raised. The world of the poem is not one in which people live "happily ever after."

The poem's action, then, is firmly located in pagan times, and insofar as the poem's wisdom adumbrates Christianity, it does so in ways that are, from the Christian point of view, insubstantially grounded and tragically incomplete. But the auctorial consciousness behind the poem allows its characters a vigorous, robust existence within those circumscribing limits, and that fact is of equal weight. Seen in a certain light, human life is a prison and Fortune the jailer of us all, and in that light Arcite's ending can be described as happy. But no one pretends he would not have preferred to live to enjoy Emelye, and no one would have wished on him his death. Certainly Arcite himself does not die glad of heart: "His laste word was, 'Mercy, Emelye!'" (I.2808.)

The distinctive ethos of the tale, in fact, can best be described in terms of its refusal to make final choices or determinations within its hierarchies. Its ending balances Arcite's "welfare" in death (I.3063) against Palamon's marriage "in alle wele" (I.3101). Two happy endings: in one, Palamon wins a wife but remains subject to fortune, mutability, disorder, and death; in the other, Arcite passes beyond all that to whatever destiny awaits the honorable among the pagan dead. It is helpful to recall at this point the conventional *démande d'amour* that ends Part I, the sort of elegant love question that had been fashionable in French and Italian courtly literature for some two centuries:

> Yow loveres axe I now this questioun: (I.1347)
> Who hath the worse, Arcite or Palamoun?
> That oon may seen his lady day by day,
> But in prison he moot dwelle alway;
> That oother wher hym list may ride or go,
> But seen his lady shal he nevere mo.

We know from many places, not least of them the proem to *Il Filostrato* (Chaucer's source for the *Troilus*), that such questions are meant to yield more than one answer, and that a person is likely to choose according to his or her present circumstances—a choice contingent, not absolute.[95] Though the love question in *The Knight's Tale* does not occur in the customary place—such a question concludes both *The Parliament of Fowls* and *The Franklin's Tale*—it comes naturally to one's mind there as well, for the ending closely recapitulates the earlier situation, in terms now metaphysically deepened: one knight is released from prison, the prison of this world; the other is in that sense prisoner still, but in sight of, and possessing, his beloved. Who has the better part? Whose destiny is most fortunate? The love question, one of the more trivial conventions of medieval love story, becomes in retrospect philosophical: it locates an unanswerable question at the heart of human experience after the Fall and before the birth of Christ. Christine de Pisan, in her *Epistre de la prison de vie humaine*, written in 1417, poses almost exactly the same *démande* in a work attempting to console the bereaved for the death of French noblemen at the battle of Agincourt.[96] But she writes about the death of Christians, and in the belief that there is a correct answer to such a question, however difficult to accept for those who live on. In *The Knight's Tale*, the question is no easier to answer at the poem's end than it was before, a fact of real importance in describing the nature and intention of this poem. "I noot which hath the wofuller mester" (I.1340): "Now demeth as yow liste, ye that kan" (I.1353). If one thinks of the *démande d'amour* in this concluding position, one does so in terms far deeper than those in which it was first posed. But the repetition is itself serial: no confident answer is possible in either place.

This is not to say, however, that the poem in its final verses be-

62. The marriage of Palemone and Emilia. French, ca. 1455. Note 97.

comes indecisive or incoherent as a work of art. Literature is distinctive as a mode of discourse and as a means of knowing precisely because it is able to explore propositions logically alternative to each other without having to make a choice between them. Unlike philosophy or theology, it is able to complete itself in ways other than the strictly dialectical; it can embody doubts and hesitations even in its endings. Narrative closure can replace philosophic resolution. The power of pattern is paramount, as one can see by analogy in the concluding illustration to King René's manuscript—which draws upon language specific to the visual arts to make a comparable end. In the final picture (figure 62), the wedding party is arranged in a circle—with Palemone and Emilia and the priest at its highest point—whose arc is repeated below by a verge of grass and flowers and completed above by the arch of Venus's temple in which the wedding takes place.[97] That arch, furnished with statues of Mars and Diana as well as Venus, forms a second circle with the hands that are being joined in marriage. This stable and harmonious design resolves in at least a formal way the disorder of the story's penultimate events. It takes its cue from Boccaccio: "And Arcita had already gone from everyone's mind, and he was remembered no more. Everyone concentrated on the festivities alone and waited for the day of the nuptials. . . . After a brief time, [Emilia] arrived at the great temple of Venus where she was received with splendid ceremony by the kings who praised her beauty as worth more than that of anyone else they had ever seen. . . . There was no delay; but when they had all formed a circle around the altar, which was decorated with leafy boughs and with flowers, they had the priests offer sacrifice. . . . The aid of Hymen was invoked with suppliant voices, and afterwards that of Juno most high."[98]

There is no comparable description of the wedding ceremony in *The Knight's Tale*, nor is Arcite's memory put so decisively to rest. But the answers to the problems of freedom, order, and death offered by Theseus, and by *The Knight's Tale* as a whole, likewise have less to do with philosophy or theology than with formal, ceremonial action: the rituals of tournament, funeral, and marriage, and the making of a narrative poem about such things. What cannot be answered from within the bounds of this poetic world can at least be ordered in a serial way, and responded to in whatever emotional terms immediate circumstance allows. The poem does not move through a hierarchy of truths in which only the most grave may ultimately be honored. It ends instead with a death and a marriage, both of which it affirms. The literal garden remains a garden, and a source of joy, even within the prison of this world.[99]

Although *The Canterbury Tales* is the story of a pilgrimage to a shrine and in the prologue to its last tale becomes, by allegorical extension, a pilgrimage to the heavenly Jerusalem, *The Knight's Tale* uses the idea of pilgrimage in a markedly different way. Old Egeus, speaking his best wisdom over the dead Arcite, reminds the mourners that

> "This world nys but a thurghfare ful of wo,   (1.2847)
> And we been pilgrymes, passynge to and fro.
> Deeth is an ende of every worldly soore."

All human life is a pilgrimage, he tells us, a street of sorrow along which we move restlessly "to and fro" until death releases us.[100] The adverbial phrase that characterizes that movement is, we recognize, heavy with associations from earlier in the poem, where it was used over and over to describe life lived in (or as though in) a prison. For a mind like Chaucer's—sophisticated, compassionate, Christian—the classical world, lacking any clear knowledge of the City of God, much less any means of access to it, must remain to the end a prison/garden/thoroughfare in which men "romen to and fro" without direction or clear purpose: pilgrims journeying toward no shrine, *peregrini sine patria*.

The richly medieval furnishings of the poem—its pervasive anachronism—would have suggested to Chaucer's original audiences another recognition as well: that men continue, even after the coming of Christ, to live willfully in confusion and error, prizing the world while holding it in contempt, disdaining their real freedom, preferring a plurality of truths in uncertain relationship to each other. Lines 1260–67, for example, implicitly link pagan (cultural) and Christian (individual) failures to discover and prefer the true path to man's true home. But the poem's primary purpose was not, I think, to enforce that recognition. Though Chaucer had written the story of "al the love of Palamon and Arcite" before he conceived of *The Canterbury Tales*, *The General Prologue* and its pilgrimage occasion serve as "Dedicatory Epistle" to *The Knight's Tale* fully as much as does Boccaccio's anguished dedication of the *Teseida* to Fiammetta. Each invites a special way of reading what follows.* *The Knight's Tale* became the first term in a long narrative sequence that was to enunciate in several ways and in several places all the further truths, some of them Christian, neglected here. Chaucer allowed his total fiction to make, as had history itself, a journey and a progress toward them.

---

* Alfred David has put it well: "At the time it was [first] written, the tale was Chaucer's last word in an ancient tradition. As the Knight's Tale it becomes the beginning of something new" (*Strumpet Muse*, p. 88).

IV. *The Miller's Tale*

NATURE, YOUTH, AND NOWELL'S FLOOD

IN *The Knight's Tale*, as we have seen, two images above all others—the prison that adjoins a pleasure garden, and the tournament amphitheatre—assume iconographic importance. The deepest questions that arise from the narrative action center upon them, and are explored in their terms. Although *The Knight's Tale* itself, in complex response to the pagan civilization that is its subject, eschews final philosophic determinations, art of this kind is always implicitly hierarchical; even within *The Knight's Tale* we recognize an ascending series of claims to propositional authority, moving steadily from the lower (the mimetic, the fictionally probable) to the higher (the philosophically universal, the theologically true) through all that may lie between. In that respect, the tale is perfectly suited to its teller,[1] for he is described as a man of feudal loyalties ("Ful worthy was he in his lordes werre"), of religious dedication ("For he was late ycome from his viage / And wente for to doon his pilgrymage"), and of sober living ("His hors were goode, but he was nat gay"; I.47, 77–78, 74). The Miller, in contrast, "nolde avalen neither hood ne hat, / Ne abyde no man for his curteisie" (I.3122)—a description immediately translated into action as he pushes himself forward, displacing the Monk, to insist that he tell the next tale: "For I wol speke, or elles go my wey" (I.3133). Just as he differs in temperament and social station from the Knight, so does the narrative art that he will offer: it will respect no hierarchies; it will doff its hat to nothing higher than itself. And its larger narrative images function, in consequence, very differently within it. Chaucer makes us privy to a miller's vision, though he does not express it beyond the prologue in anything resembling a drunken miller's voice. The connection between tale and teller is, as in *The Knight's Tale*, ideational, not mimetic.

Although the Miller sets out to "quite" *The Knight's Tale*—to offer a counter-vision of human experience—the fact that the Knight has chosen to address the Christian purpose of their journey only by indirection plays no part whatsoever in bringing the Miller to the fore.[2] The Miller's characters, to be sure, swear many a Christian oath, with even St. Thomas of Kent, toward whose shrine the pilgrims travel, twice pressed into service. But such oaths invite no close attention, and enjoy no privileged status within the fiction; they are simply part of the colloquial English speech that Chaucer imitates in this tale with a special felicity and accuracy of ear. When Gerveys the smith greets Absolon:

> "What, Absolon! for Cristes sweete tree,   (1.3767)
> Why rise ye so rathe? ey, *benedicitee*!
> What eyleth yow? Som gay gerl, God it woot,"

he uses three Christian formulas without intending a single one. They are part of his characteristic sound, no more, and other characters in the tale season their speech in similar ways.[3] We even hear a prayer in the course of the tale, but it is a night spell against elves and "wightes" so hilariously muddled as to end, almost logically, with a question for St. Peter's sister. The Christianity it brings into the tale is that of complacent superstition, imperfect in its forms, deficient in its understanding, but solemnly commended as a plain man's religion. "What! thynk on God, as we doon, men that swynke" (1.3491).

Christian reference of this sort requires little comment; its function is local and limited. But in addition, the action of the tale moves through two large narrative images of the kind that are my subject in this book, and which might properly be expected to address Christian truth: the one a ritual of religious adoration, the other a rehearsal of the preparations for Noah's Flood. That they are not meant to bear such weight in this instance seems equally clear. Chaucer warns us in the prologue in his own voice that "gentillesse, / And eek moralitee and hoolynesse" are not to be looked for in this story (1.3179), and nothing he says in the Miller's voice leads us to expect the contrary.* But between this expressed intent and the intrinsic tendency of his chosen material there is a radical disjunction that is not only central to the tale, but to the special challenge I think Chaucer set himself in its making: the witty and difficult business of writing about a second Flood without invoking, to any serious religious end, the meaning of the first. The means by which he sought to disengage this "new image" of the Flood from the moral and doctrinal significance that had accrued to its original text across centuries of exegesis involve matters of genre, imagery, and mode of action. Their complex interplay in relation to this great subject is as brilliant and audacious as anything in Chaucer's poetry, and constitutes, on a level far deeper

---

*The point of this qualification will become clear in Chapter V, where I interpret *The Reeve's Prologue* as preparing us for a very different relationship between his fabliau and the higher sorts of truth.

than the mimetic, the distinctive "voice" of the Miller in his tale.[4] Within a tale that recalls in its action the Flood with which God once cleansed the world of sin, and which was understood to prefigure the destruction of the world to come, Chaucer chose to explore the possibility of a purely comic, purely secular narrative art.

Our special interest will be in what happens to the narrative image in this enterprise, for, as I warned in my Introduction, such an intention runs directly counter to what I take to be the customary goals and procedures of Chaucer's mature poetic. The Miller's answer to *The Knight's Tale* not only presents a contrary view of human experience, but required of Chaucer the invention of a counter-art: nonhierarchic, nonhieratic, addressing no truth beyond itself. We shall need to look closely at certain techniques he uses nowhere else in his fiction: techniques intended to subvert the characteristic role of the image in mediating between fictional event and doctrinal or philosophic truth. In one case a "field image" is created, without a symbolic center; in two others, the action is cast in a parodic mode, with "game" as its exclusive intent. But we must speak first of genre, for much about the tale and its literary effect can be explained in terms of genre alone.

When Chaucer warns that what is to follow is a "cherles tale" in which "harlotrie" is "tolden," he raises in his audience certain expectations and dismisses others, addressing their prior literary experience as something he will confirm or revise in the course of the tale.[5] For the sake of convenience I shall call the genre "fabliau," though I do not mean to restrict the term to tales derived solely from the French tradition; many of the Italian *novelle*, especially Boccaccio's, imply a similar set of propositions about human experience, and that set as such is our present concern. In writing his "cherles tales," Chaucer drew upon both French and Italian sources, and for our present purposes we may likewise ignore distinctions of provenance in favor of the assumptions—the vision of life—they share.[6]

Characters in such stories live, for the most part, as though no moral imperatives existed beyond those intrinsic to the moment. They inhabit a world of cause and effect, pragmatic error and pragmatic punishment, that admits no goals beyond self-gratification, revenge, or social laughter—the comedic celebration of any selfishness clever enough to succeed. The exclusions of the genre are as decisive as its preferences, chief among them the fact that no one—not the characters, not the author, not the person that the reader or auditor is invited to think of himself as being—apprehends the action "under the aspect of eternity," in terms of good and evil, heaven or hell. If religious matters intrude, they are more likely to do so as a comic means of manipulation—as when a friar seduces a gullible woman by telling her that he is the angel Gabriel[7]—than as an adumbration of the divine. The end sought is laughter, not meditation on a counter-truth. The actions are swift, the stories short, and there is little room for detailed characterization: a person is what he does, and one or two actions tell us all we will ever learn about him; for the rest there is only his membership, already real or (by the end of the tale) at last begun, in a company of more or less grown-up people. The company is made up of familiar types—avaricious merchants, restless wives, suspicious husbands, bragging cowards, lecherous priests, clever clerks—all of them persons who have traveled a certain distance down life's road, show some dust from the journey, and are able to assimilate a further lesson or two without too serious a loss of social composure. In this world of winner and loser, duper and duped, life is a compromising business; it is no great shock to discover, in the course of the action, yet another way in which a person can use or be used.

The generic introduction to this "cherles tale" is meant to free Chaucer's art from certain demands we elsewhere legitimately make upon it. But, as we soon discover, he means nothing reductive thereby. In every one of his fabliaux—I include in this group the tales of the Miller, Reeve, Shipman, Summoner, and Merchant—Chaucer gives us more than the genre promises, or than most other examples had ever thought to provide. That something more or something other is a matter for description tale by tale, and must wait upon its proper occasion. (*The Reeve's Tale*, in which fabliau is worked to a very different end, is studied in Chapter V.) In the case of *The Miller's Tale*, we are offered not only the essential vision of truth that defines the genre—a fiercely comic respect for things as they are, and for the way folly will find its own punishment—but something imaginatively finer besides. Working with three fabliau motifs of a highly volatile kind—two of them coarsely obscene (the misdirected kiss and the arse branding), and a third that verges upon blasphemy (the parodic reenactment of Noah's Flood)[8]—Chaucer manages to create a narrative that is not only funny but also oddly innocent and imaginatively gay. *The Miller's Tale* represents the fabliau largely denatured of its indecency, brusqueness, and cynicism, although it recounts an action as outrageous as any in the entire corpus of such tales.

That of course is the work of a storyteller who is also a stylist, a rhetorician exploring the furthest possibilities of a genre. Charles Muscatine sees in this tale "fabliau at the stage of richest elaboration"—"in no other naturalistic poem of Chaucer is practical circumstance so closely tended, and practical detail so closely accounted for."[9] Muscatine's assessment of the stylistic consequence of this detail is deservedly well known, and will permit us to focus instead on the tale's richness of *figurative* specification, which I take to be of comparable importance: the series of images from the world of nature used to characterize, in highly specific and preferential ways, the energies that inform its action. They are brief similes, often proverbial, and sometimes arranged in catalogue form; yet I think Chaucer meant us to visualize them just as surely as he meant us to "see" certain functional details like the hole alongside Nicholas's door "ther as the cat was wont in for to crepe" (1.3441), or the larger scenes (soon to be considered) that potentially address a higher, extrafictional meaning. It was a commonplace of the rhetoric books, both classical and medieval, that metaphor and simile "set things before the eyes,"[10] and if we would respond to this tale in its full richness, we must allow ourselves to visualize both setting and simile; we must see "in our mind's eye" both literal and figurative detail.

Alisoun, as the object of all desires, may be said to stand at the tale's center; the way in which she moves, along with the way in which the others move toward her, decisively establishes its underlying ethos. Although the brief description used to introduce her in relation to her husband would suffice for most fabliaux,

> Of eighteteene yeer she was of age.   (1.3223)
> Jalous he was, and heeld hire narwe in cage,
> For she was wylde and yong, and he was old,

Chaucer soon presents her in a portrait 38 lines long, as finely crafted as any in *The General Prologue*. He takes the phrase "wylde and yong" and explores its meaning through a series of images drawn from the world of young animals and green, blossoming things—a landscape so attractively and exuberantly alive that the adjective "wylde" loses all moral connotations:

> *Fair was this yonge wyf, and therwithal*   (1.3233)
> *As any wezele hir body gent and smal.*
> A ceynt she werede, barred al of silk,
> A barmclooth eek as whit as morne milk
> Upon hir lendes, ful of many a goore.
> Whit was hir smok, and broyden al bifoore
> And eek bihynde, on hir coler aboute,
> Of col-blak silk, withinne and eek withoute.
> The tapes of hir white voluper
> Were of the same suyte of hir coler;
> Hir filet brood of silk, and set ful hye.
> And sikerly she hadde a likerous ye;
> *Ful smale ypulled were hire browes two,*
> *And tho were bent and blake as any sloo.*
> *She was ful moore blisful on to see*

Than is the newe pere-jonette tree,
And softer than the wolle is of a wether.
And by hir girdel heeng a purs of lether,
Tasseled with silk, and perled with latoun.
In al this world, to seken up and doun,
There nys no man so wys that koude thenche
So gay a popelote or swich a wenche.
Ful brighter was the shynyng of hir hewe
Than in the Tour the noble yforged newe.
But of hir song, it was as loude and yerne
As any swalwe sittynge on a berne.
Therto she koude skippe and make game,
As any kyde or calf folwynge his dame.
Hir mouth was sweete as bragot or the meeth,
Or hoord of apples leyd in hey or heeth.
Wynsynge she was, as is a joly colt,
Long as a mast, and upright as a bolt.
A brooch she baar upon hir lowe coler,
As brood as is the boos of a bokeler.
Hir shoes were laced on hir legges hye.
She was a prymerole, a piggesnye,
For any lord to leggen in his bedde,
Or yet for any good yeman to wedde.

The passages I have italicized, which liken Alisoun to various animals and birds, trees and blossoms, alternate with passages that detail her specifically human situation. We are shuttled back and forth between similes that suggest an animal nature—free, instinctive, sensual, untamed—and an inventory of the costume that is meant to contain those energies and cover all that beauty. Her clothing is insistently black and white—coal-black and milk-white—and is steadily registered as something that limits and confines: she is belted and girdled, with purse attached, brooch fastened, shoes laced high; her hair is held back by a headband and covered by a cap; a goodwife's apron is spread across her loins. The costume serves both to indicate Alisoun's status as a bourgeois wife and to suggest the constraints of that situation; it becomes an emblem of the narrow cage—less moral than social—within which old John seeks to confine all that is "wylde" within her.

The portrait of Absolon is fully as formal and nearly as long; it too greatly exceeds fabliau convention. As parish clerk, his duties at the mass would have included chanting the *Kyrie* and *Sanctus*, reading the Epistle, bearing the pax bread about the congregation, swinging the censer, and assisting at the Offertory.[11] Some of these duties are noted in the portrait, as is the way he converts them into occasions for casting loving glances at the ladies of the parish. But first we are told what he looks like, in a fashion stylistically related to the portrait of Alisoun:

> Now was ther of that chirche a parissh clerk,   (I.3312)
> The which that was ycleped Absolon.
> Crul was his heer, and as the gold it shoon,
> And strouted as a fanne large and brode;
> Ful streight and evene lay his joly shode.
> His rode was reed, his eyen greye as goos.
> With Poules wyndow corven on his shoos,
> In hoses rede he wente fetisly.
> Yclad he was ful smal and proprely
> Al in a kirtel of a lyght waget;
> Ful faire and thikke been the poyntes set.
> And therupon he hadde a gay surplys
> As whit as is the blosme upon the rys.
> A myrie child he was, so God me save.

His golden hair, combed out like a great "fanne" (possibly a basket for winnowing grain from chaff, more likely the "vane," or quintain, set up as a target for jousting with a lance), recalls that of his name-sake, King David's comely son, whose luxuriant hair brought about his death, and made him in medieval Scriptural exegesis an example of the effeminacy of sin.[12] But then we move to Absolon's face, which is described in an image as homely as certain of those employed for Alisoun: his cheeks were red, his eyes as gray as those of a goose. And just as the black and white of her dress loses all austerity in proximity to her body, so here the window of St. Paul's cathedral is asked to do no more than furnish a design cut into the leather of Absolon's shoes: it allows the red of his stockings to show through. The potentially moral notations are not allowed to signify; they do not become signs. In a similar fashion, we do not learn of the white surplice he wears as parish clerk until *after* we have focused upon his fashionable shoes and stockings, along with the blue tunic that is elaborately laced and closely fitted to his body. The ecclesiastical surplice covers (imperfectly) the clothing of a gallant; indeed, by means of rhetorical sequence, it is made to seem no more than that costume's elegant completion. Far from invoking some standard of devotion or chastity against which to measure Absolon's character, the white surplice is used to make us see him (in the concluding image) as a flowering branch—as "blosme upon the rys"—a part of the natural world burgeoning in the spring.

Since being parish clerk was only a part-time occupation, none too well paid, Absolon expends his energy and time in other ways as well—as barber-surgeon, legal aid, and tavern musician.[13] But our present concern is with what moves him toward Alisoun, and that is defined in a way by now familiar:

> I dar wel seyn, if she hadde been a mous,   (1.3346)
> And he a cat, he wolde hire hente anon.

Absolon himself has a fondness for such comparisons, courting her with food, bird, and animal images borrowed from the Song of Songs—its *sensus spiritualis* the last thing on his mind.

> "What do ye, hony-comb, sweete Alisoun,   (1.3698)
> My faire bryd, my sweete cynamome? . . .
> No wonder is thogh that I swelte and swete;
> I moorne as dooth a lamb after the tete.
> Ywis, lemman, I have swich love-longynge,
> That lik a turtel trewe is my moornynge."

Such imagery invites us to imagine the action of the tale not only as it occurs literally, in the streets of Oxford and within the rooms of a carpenter's house, but in a second way as well, against a country land-scape in which Absolon and Alisoun are seen as young animals—charming, instinctual, untamed—a spring landscape of whose natu-ral growth and issue they are part. Absolon dressed in his "gay sur-plys / As whit as is the blosme upon the rys" belongs to the same fecund world as Alisoun, softer than a sheep's fleece, her eyebrows black as sloeberries, more delightful to look on than a pear tree newly blossomed or flowers in a meadow.

The formal portrait of Nicholas is likewise lengthy and rich in de-tail, but its procedures are different and link him with another world. Instead of details concerning his person or his clothing, we are given an extended description of his room: the architectural space and its furnishings become an inventory of his inner "condicioun." He has "lerned art"—grammar, rhetoric, logic—as well as a bit of music and predictive astrology, and his room reflects those interests: along with bed and chest it contains books, an astrolabe, "augrym stones" for arithmetic, and a psaltery on which he accompanies himself in singing.[14] Nicholas is close and secretive, in every way an indoors man, but even he keeps his room strewn with green grasses and herbs:

> A chambre hadde he in that hostelrye   (1.3203)
> Allone, withouten any compaignye,
> Ful fetisly ydight with herbes swoote;
> And he hymself as sweete as is the roote
> Of lycorys, or any cetewale.

The last comparison gives him a characteristic "taste on the tongue"[15] —like Absolon, who chews "greyn and lycorys" and "trewe-love" in order "to smellen sweete" and be "gracious" (1.3690–93), and like Alisoun, the most delicious of them all, a honeycomb, a piece of cin-namon, her mouth as sweet as honeyed ale or apples laid up in hay.

But it also connects him, in its function as simile, to the metaphoric world of Alisoun and Absolon, fully as much as do the literal wild grasses and herbs that adorn his room. He does not live in the poem's "natural landscape" as fully as they; he is instead a shaper of fictions, a clerk "ful subtile and ful queynte" (1.3275), with some inclination toward theoretical studies. But Nicholas moves toward Alisoun under the same compulsion as does Absolon, in response to the same sort of instinctive desire, and the grasses in his room confer upon his person some share of their freshness and charm. Though "this sweete clerk," as Chaucer frequently calls him, is more intellectual and cunning than Absolon and Alisoun, he is ranged with them in these details, as well as in one of the central oppositions of the tale, the difference between young and old.

That "youthe and elde is often at debaat" is, of course, one of the fundamental propositions of fabliau (1.3230), and the youthfulness of Absolon, Nicholas, and Alisoun outweighs all differences between them when set against her husband John's old age. It is important, in our survey of the tale's natural imagery, to notice how Chaucer's rhetoric reinforces that fact. The similes that provide us with all we know of Alisoun's size, her singing, her movement, and her capacity for self-delight are either of very young animals, too young to be strictly applicable to a girl of eighteen, much less one already married—the images, for instance, of a calf or kid still with its mother—or else refer to animals so small and quick that we do not think of them in terms of age at all, like a mouse, a weasel, or a swallow. When Nicholas proffers his love and his roaming hands simultaneously, Alisoun springs back like a colt in a farrier's frame—"as a colt dooth in the trave" (1.3282)—an image that defines their common condition, for it concerns an animal only beginning to be tamed, an animal not yet made comformable to wills other than its own. Absolon, a "myrie child" (1.3325), is likewise made to seem younger than he is, weeping after his unfortunate kiss "as dooth a child that is ybete" (1.3759). His beauty, like Alisoun's, is compared to new blossom. And Nicholas, too, for all his skill at both fiction and lechery, presents a most youthful and innocent appearance. In the formal portrait surveyed above, only one line (out of 31) is devoted to telling us what he looks like, but it has a corresponding importance. He is "lyk a mayden meke for to see" (so meek he seems virginal, like a child; 1.3202).* Chaucer, in short, keeps steadily before us the youthfulness of his young people, and not infrequently, by a gift of rhet-

---

*In Middle English, the word "mayden" does not necessarily imply gender. It could mean anyone sexually inexperienced. Chaucer's use of the word here may remind us that students in the late Middle Ages customarily entered university at the age of fourteen. See Bennett, *Chaucer at Oxford and at Cambridge*, p. 22. Both universities petitioned Parliament in 1386, requesting that the minimum age be raised to sixteen.

oric, makes them seem even younger than they are. It is another of
the ways in which he extirpates from this fabliau plot the cynicism
and harshness latent in its materials—a potential that can be readily
assessed by a look at the tale's closest analogues, in which a seasoned
town whore with three impatient clients, or a promiscuous wife with
more than one lover, enact the misplaced kiss and its revenge. The
men usually include a lecherous priest or friar, a blacksmith, and
sometimes a miller, and the plot customarily turns on problems of
scheduling rather than erotic preference, since the woman expects to
favor all her suitors.[16] None of them is young, and their fornication,
though comic, is also coarse, urgent, and graceless. Chaucer's ver-
sion, in contrast, uses certain ideas about youth to reinforce the at-
tractiveness of the animal images we have been examining. Two con-
ditions are set in opposition to a third: "for she was wylde and yong,
and he was old."

The young, of course, do not stay young forever. They grow into
a moral life—into a knowledge of good and evil—and in the medi-
eval tradition that divided the life of man into six ages, this process
was understood to occur during the second age, between the seventh
and the fourteenth year.[17] But the condition of youth, more broadly
defined, was viewed with a certain indulgence, a certain freedom
from the strictest sorts of moral judgment, that can be demonstrated
even in the earliest monastic penitentials[18] and can be traced through
a good deal of later medieval thought and literature. Medieval writ-
ers on the ages of man,[19] like the authors of long allegorical poems on
human life, although they urge upon youth some lessons in caution,
courtesy, and religious devotion, also display a realistic sense of the
condition they are addressing. Because youth is an age in which the
rational powers are not fully developed, and the will not fully under
rational control, they tacitly acknowledge that wrong or thoughtless
choices will almost certainly be made within it, and emphasize instead
the fact that youth will pass and cares succeed it, including the most
urgent care of all, the salvation of one's soul. However hedged round
by those age-old admonitions that do eventually civilize, regulate,
and make conformable the energies of the young, the earlier state
was regarded with a degree of tolerance not accorded to man's matu-
rity. Peter Idley, for instance, in the *Instructions to His Son* written
about 1450, advises him to avoid seeking counsel from other young
people because

> . . . youthes counceill seldom availeth
> Wher as wysdom is not the meane.[20]

In the Middle Ages, youth was sometimes envisioned as a stage on
a turning wheel, like that the De Lisle Psalter uses to depict the ages
of man (figure 63). In its four corners, *Infantia* thrusts his hand up-

wards, aspiring to ascend; *Iuventus* is crowned and bears a sceptre; *Senectus* leans upon a staff; and *Decrepitus* adjusts his blanket (perhaps his winding sheet). Each figure governs his own segment of the wheel, which is divided into ten tondi, with the head of Christ at its center: the first shows an infant being held by his mother before a fire; the last shows simply a tomb. Man's full maturity is expressed by an image of kingship (the top of the wheel), whose accompanying verse reads "Rex sum; rego seculum; mundus meus totus" ("I am a king; I rule over this life; the whole world is mine"). But the medallions of special interest to us are second and third in the sequence, the second being assigned to *Infantia*, a youth gazing at his reflection in a mirror and combing his hair, and the third to *Iuventus*, a youth who holds a pair of balances, probably as a sign he is beginning to acquire judgment.[21] In the youth who combs his hair—he occurs in a Seven Ages sequence from the De Lisle Hours as well[22]—we have a veritable portrait of Chaucer's Absolon, and in the youth who holds the balances we see an icon of the prudential judgment into which both he and Nicholas grow (Nicholas perhaps a bit ahead of him) but which neither could yet be said to possess securely. The point of such a diagram is simple. It tells us that each age must be understood in appropriate ways. In *The Book of the Duchess*, Chaucer's Man in Black characterizes the time when he first saw and loved his lady in just such terms:

> "For hyt was in my firste youthe,   (*BD*, 799)
> And thoo ful lytel good y couthe,
> For al my werkes were flyttynge
> That tyme, and al my thoght varyinge.
> Al were to me ylyche good
> That I knew thoo; but thus hit stood."

In the words of the commentary on *The Chess of Love*, "No one should ever doubt that these ages sometimes cause great changes and diversity in morals. For the young have, by nature, different morals from the old."[23]

That commentary, which dates from late in the fourteenth or early in the fifteenth century, is worth further attention, for it goes on to distinguish (citing Aristotle as authority) six bad and six good "morals and conditions" toward which youth inclines by nature. Young people "willingly follow their passions and wills . . . especially those of sensuality. And this is because they have great natural warmth that moves them to do this, and makes them potent to accomplish their desires." "Secondly, the young are easily changeable . . . [because] the humors of [their] bodies are in themselves very changeable." Third, "they believe too easily, because they suppose that everyone is of good faith and without malice, as they are . . . [and] because

63. The Ages of Man. English, ca. 1308–10. Note 21.

[they] do not have, and cannot have by nature great sense or pru-
dence in them." Fourth, "they willingly cause injury to others . . .
because they [expect] to equal their teachers and to surpass and rise
above the others." Fifth, "they easily tell lies." And sixth, "they al-
ways, whatever they do and in all their works, willingly exceed. For
if they love, they love too much, and if they hate, they also hate too
much. . . . They do whatever they do at full speed without a reason-

able method and without any measure." The six good "morals and conditions" of youth tend to be simply the reverse of these defects: the young are liberal and generous, bold and optimistic, greathearted and courageous, credulous and without scepticism, easily moved to pity and mercy, modest and easily ashamed. (The "morals and conditions" of age, which differ greatly, are likewise related to the body's physiology, the mind's strength, and the degree of experience acquired in the world.) The author is careful not to suggest that these conditions *determine* behavior—that is the business of the will, upon which a moral judgment is possible—but that fact does not lessen their importance as the *inclinations* of youth and age.[24]

This commentary on *The Chess of Love* divides the human lifespan into Four Ages, two of which belong to Youth (the first extending from birth until the age of twenty, the second from twenty to forty), and two to Age (the first extending from forty to sixty, the second from sixty to death).[25] Whatever the exact ages of Absolon and Nicholas—they seem certainly no older than Alisoun, who is eighteen—all three seem securely located within the very first of these Ages. So they would have been for Dante as well, who extends the first of the Four Ages to man's twenty-fifth year:* "Because up to that time our soul is chiefly intent on conferring growth and beauty on the body, whence many and great changes take place in the person, the rational part cannot come to perfect discretion."[26]

Imaginative literature is, of course, less discursive than this. It is less about subjects than about style—about ways of seeing subjects—and we have been examining the ways in which Chaucer invites us to "see" the action of *The Miller's Tale*. By auctorial fiat, he makes the energies of his young people seem to arise outside of any moral system (the purpose of the images drawn from the world of nature), and in advance of any confident moral expectation (the reason he makes them seem even younger than they are). Out of these two related sets of images the energies that animate the tale's action are born. We are shown a world of the "wylde and yong," through which old John wanders at some risk.

Manuscript illuminations that show the character "Yowthe" in Guillaume de Deguileville's *Pilgrimage of Human Life* possess a special interest in this regard, for they bring together in visual form the same set of abstract ideas concerning youth's estate and man's animal nature. Figure 64, from a sumptuous manuscript now in Brussels, shows Youth bearing the pilgrim across the Sea of this World, a "sea" that will concern us later in this book. The wings and legs of Youth are literally feathered ("And lyke a dowue [as thoughte me] / She was

---

*So too perhaps for Chaucer, who describes the Man in Black (John of Gaunt) mourning his dead duchess as being 24 years old, "ryght yong" (*BD*, 454–55). Cf. the passage (*BD*, 799–804) quoted in my text above.

ffetheryd for to fle"), and her talk is entirely of freedom and pleasure ("Wyth wyldenesse I go to scole").[27] She personifies the pilgrim's own youth, still with him at the age of thirty, leading him all that time astray. Figure 65, from a manuscript of *The Romance of the Rose*, can bring this image into closer register with *The Miller's Tale*, for it illustrates the precise simile Chaucer draws on to describe old John's initial folly—his hope to keep his young wife "narwe in cage."[28] The text that the picture illustrates ("Li oisillons du vert bochage, / quant il est pris et mis en cage") testifies to Nature's "wondrous power":

When the bird from the green wood is captured and put in a cage, very attentively and delicately cared for there within, you think that he sings with a gay heart as long as he lives; but he longs for the branching woods that he loved naturally, and he would want to be on the trees, no matter how well one could feed him. He always plans and studies how to regain his free life.[29]

La Vieille (the old crone) is speaking, and in her worldly wisdom, the first application of the simile is to "women of every condition," the

64. Youth transports the pilgrim across the sea of this world. Flemish, ca. 1380–90. Note 27.

65. Bird in cage and monk in cloister. French, ca. 1380. Note 28.

second to "the man who goes into a religious order and comes to repent of it afterward," depicted in the next column of the manuscript page. Chaucer himself translated these lines for use in *The Manciple's Tale*, to end in this conclusion: "His libertee this brid desireth ay" (IX.174). In *The Miller's Tale*, what old John seeks to cage is youth itself, in its full wildness—the Guillaume de Deguileville image—and like the man admonishing the caged bird in our present picture, he becomes thereby a comic figure, a figure of futility. The difference between wild and tame is categorical, like that between young and old—as an aged man in a long poem called "The Mirror of the Periods of Man's Life" also experiences to his pain:

> "Now y am sixti ʒeere and ten,
> ʒonge folke Y fynde my foo,
> Where euere þei pleie, leepe, or renne,
> þei þinken in her weie Y goo."[30]

The young people of *The Miller's Tale* inhabit, in short, a special field of imagery that is responsible for much of the tale's charm and vivacity. I think it commended itself to Chaucer as a way of disarming certain kinds of potential response among his audience, as well as affording him a chance to write about a period of human life in which he took self-evident delight. Through the power of imagery, we find ourselves disinclined to think of the actions of these young people as immoral (or even, in our modern sense, amoral): the condition is too transitory, and *some* lessons are learned. Their actions become instead simply some things that young people do, which (as Helen Corsa has succinctly noted) no more invite stern moral judgment than do branches for putting forth blossom, calves and kids and colts for gamboling in meadows, birds for singing, lambs for wanting suck, or cats for playing with mice.[31] In such a world, farting, pissing, and the kissing of nether beards lose their power to offend, and even fornication is transformed into music:

> Ther as the carpenter is wont to lye.   (1.3651)
> Ther was the revel and the melodye.

Through a series of highly preferential images, not strictly justified by the facts, Chaucer invites us into a world seen in part as prior to, in part as outside of, morality: a world of creatures young and not wholly tame, whose nature cannot be held "narwe" in any cage at all.

I wish to move with special care at this point, lest I be thought to argue for an anachronistic view of the possibilities of fabliau, or in ignorance of the usual functions of animal imagery in the Middle Ages. Apart from beast fable, of no concern to us here, there are essentially three ways in which animals appear in medieval art and literature, and I shall briefly discuss each, in order to place Chaucer's use of such imagery in *The Miller's Tale* within what I take to be its proper tradition.

Animal imagery was widely used, first of all, as a way of helping man imagine the real nature of the Seven Deadly Sins. It furnished a vocabulary of similitudes with which to explore what man becomes in his spiritual nature when his own sin obscures further the likeness of God within him, already dimmed by Adam's fall. Chaucer's contemporary Walter Hilton writes powerfully about such transformations in *The Scale of Perfection*:

And thus wretchydly thyse þat done thus forshapen hemself fro the worthynes of man & torne hem into dyuers bestes lyckenes. *The prowde man is tornyd into a lyon for pryde* for he wolde be drade & worshypped of all men, & that no man ayenstonde þe fulfyllynge of his flesshly wyl nother in worde ne in dede. And yf ony man wolde lette his mysproude wyl he [wexyth] felle & wrothe, & woll be wroken of hym as a lyon wrekith hym on a lytyl beest. This man that dooth thus is no man for he dooth unresonably ayenst þe kynde of a man, & so he is tourned & transfourmed into a lyon. *Enuyous & angry men arne torned into houndes* thoroughe wrathe an[d] enuye þat brekyth [out] ayen her euen cristen & bytyth hem by wycked & malycyous wordes, & greuyth hem þat haue not trespassed with wrongfull dedes, harmyng hem in body & in soule ayenst goddis byddynge. *Some men arne for-*

shapen into asses þat arne slowe to þe seruyce of god, and euyl wylled for [to] do ony good dede to her euen crysten. . . . *Some are torned into swyne* for they are so blynde in wytte & so bestly in maners that they haue no drede of god, but folowen [onely] the lustes and lykynges of her flesshe. . . . *Some men are torned into wulfes* that lyuen [in] raueyn as fals couetous men done that thorough maystry & overledyng robben her even crysten of her worldly goodes. *Some men are torned into foxes* as fals men & deceyuable men that lyuen in trecherye & gyle. *Al thyse & many other moo* þat lyuen not in drede of god but breken his commanndementes *forshapen hemself fro the lyknes of god, & maken hem lyke to bestes—ye, & worse than bestes, for they are lyke to the fende of helle.*[32] [Italics added; punctuation mine.]

In the visual arts, personifications of the Deadly Sins are sometimes shown riding upon such animals. A mid-fifteenth-century painter, for instance, illustrated Chaucer's *Parson's Tale* (figures 66–68) by showing Envy as a man with a dagger astride a wolf that chews on a bone, Gluttony as a pot-bellied man mounted on a bear and feeding entrails to a kite, and Lechery as a fashionably gowned woman riding a male goat, with a sparrow on her finger.[33] The pertinence of these pictures is clear, but as Hilton emphasizes in his concluding sentence above, the true likeness of sin is demonic, not zoological. Animals, as creatures placed below man in the chain of being, offer useful signs—nothing more—for talking about the human degeneration worked by sin.

Two rough but vigorous drawings made ca. 1406 for a French manuscript of Boethius's *Consolation of Philosophy* can help us assess the stylistic consequences of such imagery. They face each other across the margins of the opened book (figures 69 and 70), illustrating Boethius's proof that for man bodily pleasure cannot be a source of true happiness.[34] I quote from Chaucer's translation:

But what schal I seye of delyces of body, of whiche delices the desirynges ben ful of anguyssch, and the fulfillynges of hem ben ful of penance? . . . Yif thilke delices mowen maken folk blisful, thanne by the same cause moten thise beestis ben clepid blisful, of whiche beestes al the entencioun hasteth to fulfille here bodily jolyte. (III, pr. 7)

In the first picture, Boethius gestures toward a man courting a woman; on the opposite page a boar is shown mounting a sow—an image intended to be as ugly as the former is graceful, and to alter the way in which one regards the human scene.

It is possible, of course, that the animal imagery in *The Miller's Tale* is meant to function in a similar fashion, that it points to something bestial in Nicholas, Absolon, and Alisoun. But before we proceed to that conclusion, we should notice that this kind of imagery characteristically draws upon animals that are mature and menacing, stupid, or generally despised. When the Manciple in his *Prologue* at-

66 (*top*). Envy.
67 (*center*). Gluttony.
68 (*below*). Lechery.
English, mid–fifteenth
century. Note 33.

69 (*left*). Boethius and two lovers courting. 70 (*right*). A boar mounting a sow. French, ca. 1406. Note 34.

tacks the drunken cook with a "Fy, stynkyng swyn! fy, foule moote thee falle!" (IX.40), he chooses an animal of that sort,[35] for he is painting a verbal picture of Gluttony. But Chaucer has seen the action of *The Miller's Tale* in terms of calves, kids, colts, cats, mice, lambs, and turtle doves—none of them images likely to make sin seem loathsome. I suspect they are not meant as a way of talking about sin at all.

A second major way that animals were used in medieval art and letters can conveniently be located in the bestiaries, those illuminated "books of beasts" for which English workshops were particularly renowned in twelfth- and thirteenth-century Europe. A double interest informs their most characteristic entries, which begin with an etymology or two, follow that with a certain amount of empirical detail about the animal, and then move on to draw a doctrinal or moral lesson based on one or more of those characteristics. The bestiaries take a significant interest in animals as they exist in their own right, being heir to a tradition of classification and study that goes back to the ancient Greeks, and they are as likely as not to frame morals that approve animal conduct. Here animals frequently become exemplary to man: "Let men learn to love their children from the example and from the sense of duty of crows," we read, or "Paul would like women to have that chastity which is kept by turtle-doves, but in other respects he urges the custom of matrimony, because mere women are seldom able to come up to the standard of doves."[36] As in

Nature's confession to Genius in *The Romance of the Rose*, or in Langland's great meditation on the beauty and plenitude of the natural world in *Piers Plowman*, these bestiary moralizations reflect the medieval belief that all creatures except man have remained true to their created nature, in perfect obedience to God.[37] In pictures showing the creation of the animals (figure 71), their attendance on the creation of Eve, or their witness to the marriage of Adam and Eve (figure 72), one finds as a kind of subtext the celebration of what those creatures in their kind remain.[38] It seemed to medieval observers that animals were notably moderate and orderly, especially in eating, drinking, and the engendering of kind. Langland makes this comparison, for instance, in reflecting on man's failure to observe any such rule:

> Ac þat moost meued me and my mood chaunged,
> That Reson rewarded and ruled alle beestes
> Saue man and his make.[39]

It is perhaps for this reason that bestiary moralizations *in bono* tend to outnumber those *in malo*, and that many entries have no moral attached at all, leaving at least a part of the animal world free of such encumbrance. The pictures that illustrate these books are most closely akin to the last sort of entry, for whatever comparisons the prose below or alongside a picture may suggest, the pictures themselves are never symbolic, nor do they address the moral life of man.[40] They amount to a picture book comprehensible in terms of natural history alone. We will examine below some bestiary images of animals Chaucer wishes us to summon to mind in the course of *The Miller's Tale* (figures 73–76).

This interest in animals for their own sake expresses itself most clearly in a third literary tradition, more leisurely and detailed in its natural description, which is to be found in the great encyclopedias of the thirteenth century. I shall draw upon the most influential of them all, Bartholomaeus Anglicus's *De proprietatibus rerum*, finished ca. 1260, in the English translation completed by John Trevisa two years before Chaucer's death.[41] The encyclopedists gathered together the opinions of many "auctoritees," from Aristotle and Pliny on, sometimes at sufficient length and with sufficient variety to communicate a sense of creatures drawn "from the life," or at least closely checked against it. In Bartholomaeus, for obvious reasons, this is especially true of animals neither foreign nor rare—the animals and birds of the English countryside—and it is to these entries that Chaucer's use of animal imagery in *The Miller's Tale* is most akin. Plants, birds, and animals are allowed to exist in the pages of the encyclopedia independent of our approval or disapproval, and to yield no lessons for our better conduct. When Chaucer tells us that if Alisoun had been a mouse, Absolon as cat would soon have had her, he asks

71. The creation of the animals. English, early fourteenth century. Note 38.

72. The wedding of Adam and Eve. French, ca. 1415. Note 38.

only that we respond out of our own experience of cats and mice. And if, at this great distance, we would check our experience of such animals against the medieval, it is to the writings of the encyclopedists we can best go—we will find there some uncommonly lively medieval prose into the bargain—and to pictures of those creatures in the bestiaries, the encyclopedias, and (not least) the manuscript borders of religious service books, where they began to appear in great number after the middle of the thirteenth century.[42]

Here, much abridged, is the Bartholomaeus (Trevisa) entry concerning the cat:

And he is a ful leccherous beste in ȝouþe, swyfte, plyaunt, and mery. And lepeþ [and] reseþ on alle þyng þat is tofore him and is yladde by a strawe and pleyeþ þerwiþ. . . . And whanne he takeþ a mous he pleyeþ þerwiþ and eteth him after þe pleye. And is as it were wylde and goþ aboute in tyme of generacioun. Among cattes in tyme of loue is hard fightynge for wyues, and

73. Cats and mice. English, late twelfth century. Note 44.

oon craccheþ and rendeþ þe other greuousliche wiþ bytyng and wiþ clawes. And he makeþ a reweliche noyse and horrible whan oon profreþ to fighte wiþ anoþer. . . . And whanne he haþ a fayre skynne he is as it were prowde þerof and goþ faste aboute; and whanne his skynne is ybrende þanne he abydeþ at home. And is ofte for his fayre skynne ytake of þe skynnere and yslayne and yhulde.[43]

We may properly compare this description to a picture of cats and mice from an English bestiary (figure 73),[44] for that image too is characterized by affectionate detail, utterly free of extrinsic significa-tion. It is in terms of just such an image that we are asked to imagine the desire of Absolon for Alisoun.* Let us sample some other entries. The kid

is a mylde beste and noyeþ nouȝt nouþer fighteþ, but he cheweþ his code and is clene and y-ordeigned to sacrifice in olde tyme. And lepeþ and skippeþ and is ful swift;[45]

and the lamb

among alle the bestes of þe erþe . . . is þe most innocent, softe, and mylde for he noþyng grieueþ nouþer hurteþ wiþ teeþ, nouþer wiþ horn, noþer with clawes. . . . In sowkynge tyme þe lomb bendeþ his knees, and for þe moder schulde ȝiue þe more mylke he þrusteþ and bussheþ at þe vdder of his moder . . . and sowkeþ neuere but he arst arere vp þe heed. . . . [He] is glad and ioyful of company of folk, and is elenge and sory and dredeþ ful sore whanne he is allone. The lombe hoppeþ and lepeþ tofore þe flok and playeþ, and dredeþ ful sore whanne he seeþ þe wolf.[46]

---

*Chaucer puts animal imagery to a very different use in *The Manciple's Tale* (IX.160–86), where the "Lat take a cat" passage is made moral by the explicit didacticism of what follows: "Lo, heere hath lust his dominacioun, / And appetit fleemeth discrecioun" (IX.181). I doubt that Chaucer steadily thought of his house cat in such a way.

Alisoun, as we have noted, is likened to "any kyde or calf folwynge his dame" (compare figure 74); Absolon longs for her "as dooth a lamb after the tete" (compare figure 75).[47] In his entry on the weasel, Bartholomaeus notes that it is "of double kynde, tame and wilde," for weasels were often domesticated and kept in houses, to kill mice and rats: "oon duelleþ in woodes . . . þe oþer goþ al aboute in hous." He pays special attention to the grace and quickness of its movement —"a swift beste of moeuynge an plyaunt of body and ful swyper and vnstable" (compare figure 76)[48]—as does Chaucer in inviting us to imagine Alisoun's beauty: "as any wezele hir body gent and smal." Though this encyclopedia tradition might pleasurably be represented in greater detail,[49] I shall limit myself to one further example, Bartholomaeus's entry describing the colt, for this animal, to which Alisoun is twice compared, will be important to our understanding of *The Reeve's Tale* as well:

While he is a colte he may touche his heed wiþ his hynder foot and may nouȝt so whan he is of age. And al þe while he is a colt he loueþ his moder wiþ wonder greet affeccioun and foloweþ hire whidereuer sche goþ. . . . The colte is nouȝt ylitered wiþ strawe, nouþer ycorrayed wiþ horse combe, nouþer yhight with trappynge and gay harneys, nouþer ysmyte with spores, nouþer ysadelid wiþ sadil, nouþer ytemed wiþ bridel, but he foloweþ his moder frikelich and eteþ gras. And his feet beþ nouȝt ypirled wiþ nayles, but he is ysuffred to renne hider and þider freliche. But atte laste he is ysette to worke and to trauayle and is yholde and ytyed and yladde wiþ haltres and reynes and ytake fro his moder and may nouȝt souke his dame tetes.[50]

The young people of *The Miller's Tale* are projected against a series of images from these graceful, early days—all animal energy, playfulness, and vulnerability—before the shoes are nailed to the hooves and the reins laid on (the reduced condition depicted in figure 77).[51] Among these many animal images, only one betrays a hint of the harshness elsewhere more characteristic of fabliaux. It describes Alisoun's later treatment of Absolon:

> And thus she maketh Absolon hire ape,   (I.3389)
> And al his ernest turneth til a jape.

But this image too stands outside any specifically Christian moral system. As H. W. Janson has remarked in his learned study of the ape as an image of the fool, the antonym of folly is wisdom, not virtue,* however "foolish" a life of sin may be. Neither the ape being put

---

*Janson, *Apes and Ape Lore*, p. 199. The second line of verse quoted above invokes yet another set of coordinates, "game"/"ernest," distinct from both folly/wisdom and vice/virtue: "jape" is part of the semantic field of "game." Since play as a mode of action is intrinsically neither wise nor foolish, neither sinful nor virtuous, it arises from an intention not readily evaluated within either of those systems.

74 (*top*). A cow and calf. English, second quarter of the thirteenth century. Note 47.
75 (*center*). Sheep and lambs. English, second quarter of the thirteenth century. Note 47.
76 (*bottom*). A weasel. French, second half of the thirteenth century. Note 48.

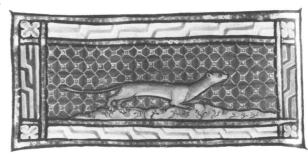

77. The shoeing of a horse. Flemish, 1344. Note 51.

78. A man training an ape.
East Anglian, ca. 1340.
Note 52.

through his tricks in a margin of the Luttrell Psalter (figure 78)[52] nor Absolon in the passage quoted above invokes ideas of vice or virtue. Translation into that other set of values is possible, of course, but the impulse to do so arises from outside the poem, and in disregard of the poem's own rhetoric.

To conclude this part of the analysis, we might note that even old John is once invited to imagine himself a member of this numerous and enfranchised "animal" group. In Nicholas's words:

> "Whan that the grete shour is goon away,   (1.3574)
> Thanne shaltou swymme as myrie, I undertake,
> As dooth the white doke after hire drake."

The image is derived from the departure of the animals from the ark, once the Flood is past (figure 79 reproduces that scene from the Bed-

79. The animals leaving the ark. French, ca. 1423. Note 53.

80. Ducks and geese swimming. Lorraine, first half of the fourteenth century. Note 54.

ford Book of Hours).[53] It offers old John a vision of himself and Alisoun swimming along together as duck and drake that is relaxing and seductive (compare figure 80),[54] and fully as important to Nicholas's persuasive strategy as the more daring promise that follows: "thanne shul we be lordes al oure lyf / Of al the world, as Noe and his wyf" (1.3581). Both images play a part in the carpenter's undoing as a victim of "ymaginacioun" (1.3612).

The action of *The Miller's Tale*, in short, is seen in two ways at once: as a series of literal events, and in terms of similes drawn from the world of animals, birds, flowers, and trees. Such images may properly be said to celebrate the beauty, plenitude, and particularity of the natural creation,[55] but they are untouched by any other idea, and invite no moral or doctrinal meditation. Because they are swift, specific, and unsystematic in their occurrence, they amount in memory to a field image, as free of any hierarchical principle of organization or meaning as are the pages of a late-fourteenth-century sketchbook, probably English, once owned by Samuel Pepys (see figure 81 for a representative example).[56] It is as though the idea of Nature (which Chaucer personified in a single commanding image as Dame Nature in *The Parliament of Fowls*) had been exploded into a series of discrete images drawn *from* nature, a plenitude of the merely "natural."[57] Chaucer uses such imagery to invoke a whole, and wholly attractive, category of life lived outside of morality, in order to locate his young people metaphorically within it: an animal world in which instinct takes the place that reason holds for man, a world in which instinct and necessity are one.

So far we have examined briefly the contribution of genre and, at greater length, the contribution of a special field of imagery to Chau-

81. Animals on a sketchbook page. Probably English, late fourteenth century. Note 56.

cer's immediate poetic purpose: the construction of a fiction perfectly counter to *The Knight's Tale*. Let us turn now to a third aspect of the poem, no less important than these—to the mode of its larger actions, as determined by the intentions that shape them. That mode prevents the narrative images of the tale from "governing" in the expected fashion, just as the tale's fragmentation of the idea of Nature into mere natural imagery excludes from it any sense of man's unique status or obligation, by virtue of his reason and the immortality of his soul, within a world of Nature hierarchically conceived.

This new subject constitutes yet another link between the allegorical versions of Youth examined earlier in this chapter and Chaucer's young people in *The Miller's Tale*. Beyond the shared animal images, quick energies, and wildness lies a community of interest that *The Romaunt of the Rose* incorporates into its own portrait of Youth:

> For yonge folk, wel witen ye,   (*RR*, 1288)
> Have lytel thought but on her play.

The winged and feathered "Yowthe" of Guillaume's *Pilgrimage* (figure 64) catalogues at great length her favorite pastimes; they include wrestling, climbing trees to steal fruit, playing ball and hockey, hunting, fishing, playing at bowls and dice and chess, and hearing songs and making music.

> "Wyth wyldenesse I go to scole;
> Now I sprynge, now I carole;
> I tryppe, I crye, synge & daunce,
> And euere ful off varyaunce." [58]

Her energies are great, and characteristically express themselves in games. For similar reasons, play and game become the governing modes of action in *The Miller's Tale*. From the very first moment in which "hende Nicholas / Fil with this yonge wyf to rage and pleye" (1.3272), there is about everything they do a certain arbitrary and extravagant quality, as though they could not move directly toward their goal without having first to satisfy the rules of a complex and delightful game in doing so. Every enterprise they initiate is cast in a game form that distances it from, and makes it something other than, a direct expression of desire. [59]

Game governs Absolon's wooing, too—an activity so public, so frequent, so multiple in its address ("sensynge the wyves of the parisshe faste"; 1.3341), that it runs little risk of success. What earnest trespasser upon a marriage would go sing to the wife at an hour when the husband lies beside her in their bed? Nicholas knows the need for secrecy in such matters, if success is what you're after. For Absolon the process is its own reward, an excuse for dressing up, combing out his beautiful long hair, and waking when others sleep:

> "Therfore I wol go slepe an houre or tweye,   (1.3685)
> And al the nyght thanne wol I wake and pleye."

Whatever his actual age, he seems in certain ways the youngest of the three, not least in his attempt to win Alisoun by another sort of game:

> Somtyme, to shewe his lightnesse and maistrye,   (I.3383)
> He pleyeth Herodes upon a scaffold hye.

There are, of course, better dramatic roles for a suitor to be seen in than that of a half-crazed, comic-grotesque villain: in the words of a Coventry stage direction, "Here Erode ragis in the pagond and in the strete also." (A roof boss from Norwich Cathedral, figure 82, which shows Herod tearing at his beard and being restrained by attendants, has been thought to reflect drama convention: "I stampe! I stare! I loke all abowtt! / . . . I rent! I rawe! and now run I wode!")[60] But it is all one to Absolon, whose pleasure is in roles as such. Even his tenderest wooing is expressed in the formulas of metrical romance, snatches of popular song, and a magpie raid upon the speeches of the bridegroom to the bride in the Song of Songs.[61] Alisoun seems initially little more to him than an occasion for extending his mastery of the games of courtship to some level comparable to his skill in dancing: "In twenty manere koude he trippe and daunce / After the scole of Oxenforde tho" (I.3328). Whatever he may be up to, sexual desire seems at most tangential to it.

Nicholas likewise proves himself no ordinary lecher. Between the intention and the act must fall the shadow of an elaborate and delightful invention, a game to earn him Alisoun:

> And hende Nicholas and Alisoun   (I.3401)
> Acorded been to this conclusioun,
> That Nicholas shal shapen hym a wyle
> This sely jalous housbonde to bigyle;
> And *if so be the game wente aright*,
> She sholde slepen in his arm al nyght,
> For this was his desir and hire also.

The conditional clause I have italicized above bears the impress of both their personalities. To increase their delight, they erect a barrier to the consummation of their desire—a game as elaborate as *The Knight's Tale* tournament by which a husband is found for Emelye. Nicholas must prove by his wit that he is worthy to lie with Alisoun, though simpler procedures lie readily to hand.

Here we must pause to note a curious thing. Although the tale occasionally terms old John "jalous" or speaks of his "jalousie," his actions do not support that characterization in the ways we might expect.[62] The marriage may indeed seem a cage to Alisoun, but it does so by definition, not by virtue of special bars or locks attached by a suspicious husband. (Chaucer will study that other kind of marriage in *The Merchant's Tale*.) John's folly, in truth, grows out of something quite different, an *excessive* love for his wife (a meaning well within the semantic range of the Middle English word "jalous")[63]—an overfondness that is no doubt a fault, but is at least generous in kind. Old

82. Herod ranting. Roof
boss, Norwich Cathedral,
ca. 1509. Note 60.

John is fond of Nicholas, too, and seems never to regard him with
suspicion, even though the carpenter's work takes him away from
home a good deal of the time. Old John is at Osney on the day that
Nicholas first seizes Alisoun "harde by the haunchebones" and pro-
fesses his love; he is there again on the Saturday when Nicholas goes
to his room to fall into his astronomical fit. We learn that people ex-
pect to see old John at that place, or at the grange even further away,
often for a day or two at a time, whereas Nicholas, the "nye slye,"
seems always to be about the house. Perhaps a fear of the servants
inhibits Alisoun and Nicholas from seeking immediate gratification;
perhaps not. Chaucer makes no point of it. All we can say is that on
two separate occasions detailed in the poem (and others are implied),
Nicholas has ample opportunity to lie with Alisoun without her hus-
band's knowledge. It is the advantage of a lodger, the "argument of
herbergage,"[64] but he chooses instead to earn her by means of a
"queynte cast," a parodic restaging of Noah's preparations for the
Flood. The difficult and elaborate game is invented for its own sake.

It requires that Nicholas spend two days alone in his room, ready
to gape at the moon should any visitor arrive; it calls into service his
finest arts of narrative persuasion; and it puts old John to no end of
trouble, what with the procuring and hanging of the tubs, and the
fetching of provisions for the great rain. These preliminaries are en-
tirely out of proportion to Nicholas's ultimate intent, unless one un-
derstands his object to be as much the witty exploration of an old
man's gullibility as the "swyvyng" of the wife that he will earn
thereby. Like Alisoun's merriment in inventing the arse kiss as a way
of getting rid of an unwelcome suitor ("Now hust, and thou shalt

laughen al thy fille"; 1.3722), it serves to alter our feelings about actions that in outline may seem scabrous in the extreme.[65] (Again I refer my reader to the analogues: they do not charm.) We witness a delight in game that is obsessive and pure in ways that young people manage best; and when the playing gets rough, they yowl in pain or "weep as dooth a child that is ybete." The complexity and indirection of their preferred means help to free our sympathy and laughter from notions (otherwise perfectly applicable) of adultery, aggression, and betrayal. All but Alisoun pay a certain price before the tale is over, but that price is not very great—nothing like the cost of the corresponding games of chivalry and *fin amors* in *The Knight's Tale*. The pervasive mood of game lessens to some degree even the carpenter's humiliation after his fall from the roof beam, for his neighbors refuse to take him seriously, ascribing his foolishness to an overwrought imagination ("fantasye"), and discounting anything he tries to say:

> The folk gan laughen at his fantasye;   (1.3840)
> Into the roof they kiken and they cape,
> And turned al his harm unto a jape.

Their laughter is at his expense, to be sure, but it is social laughter—less cruel by far than if they were to "make ernest" of the "game," contemplating within it the configurations of sin, charging him with pride or presumption. Though his wife has been "swyved," that is not public knowledge—it is possible he does not realize it himself—and anyone can admit, even before the neighbors, to a spell of foolishness now and then. Some tempered portion of his self-esteem will survive the event, just as surely as his arm will heal.

❧

The iconographic images that Chaucer's mature art characteristically uncovers just below the surface of a fiction are, as a rule, most serious when most hidden. They represent a gesture of accommodation toward an older, Augustinian aesthetic that defined poetic fiction as a kind of veil which the discerning reader would draw aside in order to gaze upon truth directly. In *The Miller's Tale*, however, the two larger iconographic images that most determine meaning emerge in their own names, without concealment or disguise, as the object of the narrative action. Nicholas's restaging of the preparations for Noah's Flood, like Absolon's translation of courtship into a ritual of religious adoration, emerges from a poetic matrix of animal simile, youthful high spirits, and instinctive desire, as games the young people play. Though both actions furnish narrative images of the kind that are my continuing subject in this book—images that Chaucer invites us to see in our mind's eye, and which call to mind other images in approximate register with themselves, known from other texts and other pictures—here the difference between the games and the actions they parody, rather than the similarity, carries both the laughter and the lessons of the tale. In both cases, I shall argue, Chaucer intended the implications of the image to extend no further than the boundaries of the game itself. We have examined the world of metaphor, simile, and motive out of which these larger images arise. Let us look now at the images themselves.

Twice in this tale an arse is extended out a window to be kissed, both times as an outrageous comic insult. Alisoun wants to make Nicholas laugh, as well as to get rid of Absolon; Nicholas wants to recover his position as master of the revels by "amending" (making even better) "al the jape." Though both actions are startling and memorable, the first—Alisoun to Absolon—is complicated by a poet's intention as well, finer than anything Alisoun intended. The cultural affiliations of the image that action presents to the mind reach well beyond the range of fabliau and deepen its comedy greatly. It alone, in the terms proposed by this book, invites analysis as an iconographic image.

But let us begin with what the two scenes share in common— what we may call "bum baring" as comic insult—for that constitutes Alisoun's intention in its entirety, and as such lays first claim both to our laughter and to an ineradicable place in our memories. It needs, of course, no prior status in the medieval repertory of images to do so: like Nicholas's variation on the theme, it possesses its own audacious power. But the baring of an arse has, in fact, its own humble area of provenance within medieval art—the borders of illuminated manuscripts—and it was doubtless not unknown as an insult within the world of ordinary life. In Trevet's *Chroniques*, for example (the source of Chaucer's *Man of Law's Tale*) King Alla's subjects, thinking him responsible for the banishment of Queen Constance, pelt him and his men with mud, stones, and filth upon their return from Scotland, while "women and naked children, in mockery, showed him their hindquarters."[66]

Since the border decoration of illuminated manuscripts is only rarely related in theme to the text it surrounds, the frequent depiction of bum baring there seldom expresses so unambiguous an intent. What are we to say, for instance, about an ape who exposes his buttocks to another ape in the pages of a Tournai psalter, or about an old man who bares his arse directly to the reader in the top margin of a page in the Gorleston Psalter?[67] Figure 83, in which a man bares his buttocks to a kneeling nun, is only slightly less enigmatic.[68] One may confidently label such a drawing "anticlerical"—as one does two other images from margins in which a mitred bishop and a Knight Templar kiss the arses of an ape and a tonsured cleric respectively[69]—

83. Arse baring, with kneeling nun. Flemish, 1344. Note 68.

but one cannot say whether her gesture expresses adoration or ab-horrence at what she sees. In yet another example, a woman at her spinning is favored with a similar spectacle, though again one can neither guess the young man's motives nor interpret confidently the hand she raises to her head in response.[70]

Other variations on the theme, likewise free of conceptual content, come readily to mind. Nicholas's improved version of Alisoun's jest, for instance—his decision to fart as loud as thunder at the moment of the expected kiss—may be compared to images in margins that show a man holding a long trumpet to his bared arse,[71] just as Absolon's revenge for his misplaced kiss—a red-hot colter aimed at this other orifice—can be seen as a variant on images in which persons shoot with bow and arrow at a bared bum, or attack such a target with spear or pole. Figure 84 shows archery of this kind, carved upon a roof boss in Sherborne Abbey.[72]

Most such imagery, whether in manuscript margins, misericord seats, or hidden high in the roofs of abbeys and cathedrals, precludes

84. Shooting at a bared arse with a crossbow. Roof boss, Sherborne Abbey, after 1485. Note 72.

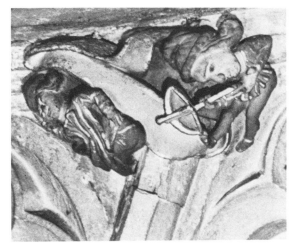

thematic explication. It is casual and haphazard, as obscure in its purposes as graffiti scratched on walls. *The Miller's Tale*, in contrast, is wonderfully lucid: we know what Alisoun and Nicholas intend as they extend their bottoms out the window, and we know, in precise interior detail, Absolon's response. But the first of these incidents, I have suggested, is complicated by an iconographic intention as well—the wish to explore what an action means in terms richer than narrative cause and effect. Chaucer is interested in Absolon not merely as the recipient of an insult, but as someone who creates the occasion for its delivery. He crosses the first of these scenes of bum baring with another image that at once makes available a further perspective upon it and deepens the laughter it evokes: it becomes of all possible insults the one most appropriate, the lesson this young parish clerk most needs to learn.

In contrast to Nicholas, who specializes in "deerne love" and roaming hands, free of idealization, Absolon at this moment is experimenting in love "paramours"—love in the French manner, the manner of romance literature—which at its most elevated became a highly self-conscious religion of love.[73] We have already noted his conduct in the church offertory when, for love of one lady, he puts himself in the service of them all:

> This parissh clerk, this joly Absolon,   (I.3348)
> Hath in his herte swich a love-longynge
> That of no wyf took he noon offrynge;
> For curteisie, he seyde, he wolde noon.

But his experience of women is not entirely posturing and fanciful—he knows the barmaids, the "gaylard tappesteres," of every alehouse in the city, and he knows some ways to delight them. The cat-and-mouse image that Chaucer uses to introduce his infatuation with Alisoun (I.3346) will be ultimately reaffirmed as the truth that underlies his courtship. But it pleases Absolon to dress up his desire in fashionable forms, to cast himself in the role of the idealized and idealizing lover, in a game as formal and, initially at least, as self-aware as anything Nicholas invents in the tricking of old John. Absolon is at Osney "with compaignye, hym to disporte and pleye" (I.3660) when he learns by chance that old John hasn't been seen for a while ("and axed upon cas a cloisterer / Ful prively after John the carpenter"). He goes to court Alisoun the same night in a similar mood:

> ". . . I wol go slepe an houre or tweye,   (I.3685)
> And al the nyght thanne wol I wake and pleye."

Such detail serves to undercut—and thus keep in proper balance—other moments that suggest Absolon has entirely lost himself in his own game: we see him try on all the feelings proper to the role, including "wo bigon" (1.3372, 3658). But he makes a fatal error in seeking to cast Alisoun as "the lady" in this fanciful courtship:

> "Now, deere lady, if thy wille be, (1.3361)
> I praye yow that ye wole rewe on me."

That role, which implies high birth and refined sensibility, is so far from Alisoun's secure sense of her own nature that it earns him a crude correction the next time around—when the love language he affects, and the posture from which he speaks it, become most intolerably elevated and grand. Three pictures will make my meaning clear. Figure 85 shows a man and woman on their knees before the God of Love[74]—a design that draws its power (and implicit blasphemy) from its likeness to another design, in which worshippers or donors kneel before a sacred personage, as in figure 86 (from the Gorleston Psalter), in which two monks kneel before Christ on the cross.[75] Figure 87, a fourteenth-century carving in ivory, can bring this tradition closer to *The Miller's Tale*: it shows a lover on his knees offering his heart to his lady, while she places a garland of flowers on his head, cradling a little dog in her arms.[76]

Such images furnish an appropriate background to our reading because Absolon first pleads for a kiss in precisely that posture:

> This Absolon doun sette hym on his knees (1.3723)
> And seyde, "I am a lord at alle degrees;
> For after this I hope ther cometh moore.
> Lemman, thy grace, and sweete bryd, thyn oore!"

What follows is quite possibly Chaucer's own invention, for in none of the contemporary analogues to the tale does the woman present her buttocks to be kissed—it is her male companion (most often a priest) who does so both times—and in none of them does the other suitor kneel to offer that devotion.[77] To make that posture possible Chaucer had to invent for the carpenter's house a street window very low indeed. A brief lyric dialogue, "De clerico et puella," places a similar pair in a more likely situation—"In a wyndou þer we stod we custe vs fyfty syþe"[78]—and figure 88 depicts a more likely architecture, illustrating the commandment against adultery by showing a young man climbing into a girl's chamber, assisted by a devil with a lascivious tongue who pokes him in the arse with a long golden rod.[79]

In Chaucer's tale there is no need for Absolon to step so high:

> He rometh to the carpenteres hous, (1.3694)
> And stille he stant under the shot-wyndowe—
> Unto his brest it raughte, it was so lowe.

And so it must be if he is to kiss his love while kneeling in the street. Absolon's posture is one of religious adoration—he intends it so— just as the language of his petition is charged with Scriptural and li-

85 (*above*). A man and woman kneel before the God of Love. Flemish, early fourteenth century. Note 74.

86 (*right*). Two monks kneel before the cross. East Anglian, ca. 1310–25. Note 75.

87 (*below*). A lover kneels before his lady. Ivory writing tablet, French, first half of the fourteenth century. Note 76.

turgical echoes from the Song of Songs. The extended arse that an-
swers his concluding plea for mercy and grace ("Lemman, thy grace,
and sweete bryd, thyn oore!") offers, in consequence, more than a
comic insult, which is all its masculine equivalent in the analogues
can provide. The poet's purpose is comic exposure, the creation of a
hilarious synecdoche in which the part is indeed the whole—the
whole object of Absolon's adoration and desire, once the mask of
manners and the language of fashionable love longing are stripped
away. (One may compare, in figure 89, the ape who reveres a pair of
lowered breeches and the arse they bare, the rest of the body notably
absent.) [80]

Absolon receives, almost exactly, what he didn't know he had been
asking for, and it works upon him a change that Chaucer describes
through a wonderful triple pun, "His hoote love was coold and al
yqueynt" (1.3754). The primary sense of "yqueynt," "extinguished,"
alternates with another, "foolish, fantastical," to end in yet a third,
the most devastating of all—the slang word for pudendum. [81] Though

88. A lover climbs in through the bedroom window, assisted by the devil. French,
1480. Note 79.

89. An ape reveres an arse and breeches. Franco-Flemish, mid-fourteenth century. Note 80.

the fastidious Absolon may (in this new definition of his purpose) have missed his mark by a few millimeters, the real nature of what he sought has been made unmistakably clear to him:

> For fro that tyme that he hadde kist hir ers,   (I.3755)
> Of paramours he sette nat a kers;
> For he was heeled of his maladie.
> Ful ofte paramours he gan deffie.

The hairy kiss restores him to his proper person, ending the make-believe and role playing, breaking the game. To this point he has cast his game as earnest, playing the woe-begone lover and half believing it himself; henceforth he casts his earnest in the form of game:

> "I am thyn Absolon, my deerelyng.   (I.3793)
> Of gold," quod he, "I have thee broght a ryng.
> My mooder yaf it me, so God me save;
> Ful fyn it is, and therto wel ygrave.
> This wol I yeve thee, if thou me kisse."

The red-hot colter is intended for Alisoun, not Nicholas.

🌿

To understand in its full richness the second of the major narrative images in *The Miller's Tale*—old John as new Noah, preparing for a second Flood—we shall need to look to the drama cycles that grew up in England around the feast of Corpus Christi in the 1370's. Like much other religious imagery of the time, they were intended to serve as "a tokene and a book to þe lewyd peple, þat þey moun redyn in ymagerye and peynture þat clerkys redyn in boke."[82] But they were very special, being living images in which speech, music, costume, setting, and impersonation came together so powerfully that some claimed religious painting could offer no comparison: "for þis is a deed bok, þe toþer a quick."[83] As Chapter I has demonstrated, however, medieval ideas of imagery pay relatively little attention to medium, to the fact, say, that "pleyinge" is different in its means from "peyntynge," or that narrative poems are different from either. In the medieval defense of images, distinctions in kind go largely unremarked; what matters is that all these arts yield images that may be "holden in mennus mynde" and thus "rehersid" (remembered and thought upon).[84] In this larger sense, certain images from the plays of Noah's Flood are intricately woven into the trick that Nicholas plays on his carpenter landlord. His invention is based upon what had become in medieval art an iconic action.

"Clerkes" that "redyn in the boke" were of course to be found among Chaucer's first audiences as well, and Nicholas proves himself a member of their fraternity. Knowing that the Scriptural Flood was sent to punish sexual sin—as Chaucer will tell us in *The Parson's Tale*, "by the synne of lecherie God dreynte al the world at the diluge" (X.839)—and knowing as well an exegetical tradition holding that marital intercourse had been prohibited in the ark while the waters covered the earth,[85] Nicholas creates a witty occasion on which to satisfy his own desire. The second Flood will serve to forward lechery rather than forestall it. Nicholas apparently knows as well the tradition that Noah was an astrologer who learned of the approaching deluge through his science,[86] for astrology is Nicholas's own avocation—he's good at predicting rain—and he reenacts the awesome moment of Noah's astrological discovery in a wonderfully comic way:

> This Nicholas sat evere capyng upright,   (I.3444)
> As he had kiked on the newe moone.

All this is part of a scholar's joke, and in its higher frequencies was probably heard only by scholars' ears. But the folly of old John, the material with which Nicholas works most directly, is quite another matter, and it is against an essentially popular understanding of the Flood, as developed by medieval drama, that the carpenter's actions can be best understood and most richly enjoyed.

Chaucer alerts us to the relevance of the cycle drama at several points in the tale, including the only two direct references to that

drama to be found anywhere in his works. Absolon's attempt to in-
terest Alisoun by playing Herod "upon a scaffold hye" has already
been noted, and to it we may add the prologue's description of the
Miller interrupting the Host "in Pilates voys," a reference to the
high, shrill, and pretentious voice apparently affected by those who
played Pilate on the scaffold-stage.[87] But the most important clue that
it is the drama's image of the Flood we are meant to hold in mind is
spoken by Nicholas when he reminds the carpenter of the marital
woes suffered by the last man to survive such waters:

> "Hastou nat herd," quod Nicholas, "also   (I.3538)
> The sorwe of Noe with his felaweshipe,
> Er that he myghte gete his wyf to shipe?
> Hym hadde be levere, I dar wel undertake
> At thilke tyme, than alle his wetheres blake
> That she hadde had a ship hirself allone."

Here the drama offers more than a necessary but isolated gloss: since
a recalcitrant Mrs. Noah belongs almost entirely to the stage, it fur-
nishes an essential subtext for the action that follows.

Though Noah's wife attracts no special attention in the Genesis ac-
count of the Flood, medieval illustrations of that event frequently
show her with Noah in the ark, along with the three sons, their
wives, and the animals—a composite image of the world Noah has
been commanded to save. In figure 90, for example, an English psal-
ter illumination of the late thirteenth century, the ark is highly sche-
matized and pyramidal in shape, with Mrs. Noah, prim and de-
corous, about to follow her husband on board. In figure 91, the
legend below serves as a guide both to the meaning of the event and,
more specifically, to the gestures Mr. and Mrs. Noah make within
the ark: "The ark of Noah which signifies peace" (*Larche Noel qui
senefie pes*). (In the adjoining space, in contrast, Moses is attacked by
wrathful men with clubs.) One notes the extreme stylization of this
ark—its perfect circularity—and the way its creatures, including our
second father and his wife, are visible through windows (or set in
compartments) probably meant to evoke church architecture, as is
the crenellated roof with towers above.[88] (On this motif, I shall have
more to say in Chapter VII; its figure 145 is also relevant here.) In
these pictures the relationship of Noah and his wife is harmonious
and seemly, as it is most everywhere else in medieval tradition. In the
Bible moralisée, for instance, Mrs. Noah participates in her husband's
typological importance: "Noe significat Christum, uxor eius beatam
Mariam." ("Noah signifies Christ, and his wife the blessed Mary.")[89]
Certainly the miniatures before us—their number could easily be
multiplied—portray in her countenance both dignity and concern.
An illustrated Anglo-Norman paraphrase of Genesis roughly con-

90. Noah and his family enter the ark. English, late thirteenth century. Note 88.

91. The ark and its inhabitants. French, ca. 1300. Note 88.

temporary with *The Canterbury Tales* even shows her receiving with Noah the command from God to build the ark.[90]

The troubles of Noah with his wife constitute a subject rarer by far. In the fourteenth century, it existed within two very different traditions, one of them quite possibly belonging to the drama alone. The first, and probably earlier, of these is thought to derive from a lost Gnostic text of the fourth century, the apocryphal *Book of Noria*. It diverges from the Genesis version of the Flood in the following details: God commands Noah to build the ark in secret; the devil corrupts Noah's wife, in order to find out what is going on; the wife uses a potion proposed by the devil to make Noah tell the secret; the devil enters the ark by construing Noah's order to the truculent wife (in some texts, a daughter-in-law) "Come on board, you devil" as a personal invitation; the devil exits from the ark as the waters recede by boring a hole in the ark's bottom, which the serpent then stops with his tail.

The full history of this legend, in which Mrs. Noah recapitulates the temptation of Eve rather than foreshadows the obedience of Mary, remains uncertain, though it has been diligently researched. It is found in a rhyming *Weltchronik* by one Enikel, from late-thirteenth-century Vienna; it is interpolated into late-medieval Russian versions of the Revelations of Methodius; Wogul folktales (from the Ural Mountains) demonstrate its currency in more recent centuries; the Koran refers to persons who scoffed at Noah and implies Mrs. Noah was among them; and several late-medieval wall paintings in Swedish churches portray Mrs. Noah with the devil at her side or on her shoulder, giving her husband trouble.[91] In the surviving evidence from medieval England this participation of the devil in the history of the Flood is limited to a Noah's play from Newcastle and (so far as I know) to just two illuminated manuscripts, both from the fourteenth century. One of them—Queen Mary's Psalter, English, ca. 1310–20—contains a substantial Flood sequence that I shall reproduce in its entirety, for the whole action, in its traditional iconic divisions, can represent for us the serial image against which Nicholas invents his Flood game. By its very difference, it can help us understand better the nondiabolic version of Noah's marital troubles invoked by Chaucer in his tale.

The Anglo-Norman prose below each picture in the sequence describes the action as follows. Figure 92: "Here the angel shows Noah how the world should be saved, and gives him his tools to make a ship in such a way that it can float upon the water and carry all things safely, and [tells him] that he should make it so secretly that no one should know of it." Figure 93 (upper register): "How the devil came in the form of a man to Noah's wife and asked where her husband was, and she said she knew not where. 'He is gone to betray thee and all the world. Take these grains and make a potion and give it him to drink, and he will tell thee all'; and she did accordingly." Figure 93 (lower register): "Here Noah begins to carpenter, and the first blow that he struck all the world heard it. And then came an angel to him, and he cried for mercy. The angel says to him, 'Thou hast done ill, but take these rods and wattles, and finish thy ship as best thou canst, for the flood is coming.'" Figure 94: "How Noah loads his ship, and carries his sons and his wife into the ship by a ladder, and of each thing male and female, as the angel of God had commanded him, in order to save the world." Figure 95: "How Noah sends a raven and a dove to learn if they find any land. The raven has found a horse's

92. The angel commands Noah to build the ark. East Anglian, ca. 1310–20. Note 92.

head, where it stops. . . . And the devil flees through the bottom of
the ship, and the serpent thrusts his tail into the hole."[92]

The Newcastle Flood play alone among the dramatic texts that
have come down to us works within this diabolic tradition. As in the
York cycle, two guilds were responsible for its production, with the
action divided into two parts, though in Newcastle only the first sur-
vives. We must pay it some attention, for it includes the command
to secrecy, the devil's potion, and, emerging from them, the trucu-
lence of the wife. In a characteristic speech, the devil promises her,
sotto voce:

> "Believe, believe, my own dame dere,
> I may no longer bide.
> To ship when thow shall fayre,
> I shall be [by] thy side."

When she learns her husband's secret, she responds with a curse:

> "The devil of hell thee take
> To ship when thou shalt go."

But Noah answers with a prayer:

> "God send me help in hy
> To clink yon nails twain;
> God send me help in hy
> Your hand to hold again."[93]

(Part I ends shortly thereafter, and with it all we know of the New-
castle play.)

This play and the drawings I reproduce from Queen Mary's Psalter
were long thought to be our only evidence that this version of the
Flood was current in medieval England.[94] To their number we may
now add a picture from the Ramsey Psalter, made near Peterborough
sometime between 1303 and 1316, which Gail MacMurray Gibson
has called to my attention. In a lively but economical design, it shows
the devil clinging to Mrs. Noah's back as the waters rise and Noah
urges her to enter (figure 96).[95] But even when augmented by this
further example, the diabolically inspired Mrs. Noah remains a fig-
ure for whom wide currency cannot be assumed. All other medieval
English versions of the Flood, in narrative poems, plays, or the visual
arts, either present Noah's wife as patient, obedient, and essentially
characterless, or root her antagonism to her husband in marital dis-
cord rather than diabolic alliance. The tradition of marital discord is
unequivocally represented only in the medieval drama, though it has
been suggested that stained-glass panels in Great Malvern Priory and
York Minster may reflect the drama tradition in turn.[96] In the non-
diabolic version of "the sorwe of Noe with his felaweshipe," an or-
thodox image of the Flood is crossed (as it were) by demotic images

Coment le diable voint en forme de feme a la feme Noe e demaunt v sun mary. Coment
e de visent qe de ne sout on il est ale pur toi revir z tote le mund: prefne ces greisnes
e sere vn aboynon e le voterz a boyre e il te dirra tore. E issint fist ele.

93 (*top left*). The devil and Mrs. Noah;
Mrs. Noah and her husband; the angel's
reprimand.
94 (*above*). The loading of the ark.
95 (*left*). The release of the dove; the
escape of the devil. East Anglian, ca.
1310–20. Note 92.

96. The devil on Mrs. Noah's back. English, ca. 1303–16. Note 95.

from manuscript borders and misericord seats (see figure 97), in which husbands and wives brawl simply because they are married to each other.[97] The stubbornness of Mrs. Noah is common to pageants from York, Chester, and Wakefield, as well as Newcastle, but in the first three the devil plays no role. It is surely to some version of this domestic tradition that Nicholas refers in his "Hastou nat herd" speech: his allusion is to the difficulties of marriage, not the danger of the devil.

The surviving plays of the Flood differ from each other, of course, and ideally one would refer to local traditions only—in this case to the Oxford plays, in which Absolon is said to have played Herod, and to the London plays, as the cycle best known to Chaucer and his first audiences. But too much has been lost to permit such economy and exactitude. Indeed, *The Miller's Tale* allusion to Herod "upon a scaffold hye" constitutes our only evidence that Oxford had plays in the fourteenth century, although, as J. A. W. Bennett has recently reminded us, that may be merely another way of saying that "its Guild records are few and Council records fragmentary."[98] (Professor Bennett's book establishes beyond question the intimacy of Chaucer's knowledge of that ancient university city.) The cycle text for London, too, has been lost, though chronicles record a five-day perfor-

97. A domestic quarrel. Misericord, Church of St. Mary, Fairford, Gloucestershire, late fifteenth century. Note 97.

mance in 1384, four-day performances in 1391 and 1409, and a seven-day performance in 1411.[99] Such length implies a Flood play of considerable elaboration, to which our best guide, however imperfect, is likely to be the extant drama of other English cities. Since my purpose is to elucidate Chaucer's tale rather than to attempt a reconstruction of the Oxford or London play, I shall offer no readings I think not demonstrable from his text alone. But I shall draw my evidence from the treatment of similar themes in the several play texts that do survive, which nondramatic treatments of the Flood either pass over in silence or fail to explore with comparable vigor. I wish to study the ways in which Chaucer prevents Nicholas's Flood game from bringing into the tale anything resembling the moral weight and doctrinal richness of its original—the Flood as recounted in the Book of Genesis, as understood in patristic commentary upon that text, or as represented (sometimes even in comedy, though ultimately toward a serious end) on the medieval pageant stage.

The most obvious means by which Chaucer seeks to prevent our thinking about this fiction from perspectives outside it—perspectives as awesome as Doomsday, which the Biblical Flood was understood to prefigure—turns upon the comic discordance of the image that Nicholas plants in old John's mind with the traditional image of Noah's Flood. The fit is so bad, the two images so comically out of register, that it is the differences that occupy our attention. This flood is going to be much worse than its original—more than twice as big (1.3518), and infinitely more swift. Instead of 40 days and nights of rain, after which the ark floated for 150 days before the waters began to abate, this time the world will be drowned in an hour and dry again by breakfast. There will be three arks, instead of the three-tiered ark of the theologians, and, replacing an architecture dictated by God (whose very numbers conceal sublime mysteries), brewing barrels and dough troughs will serve.[100] Haste is everything: unlike the medieval texts in which God instructs Noah to spend 120 years building the ark, so that any who amend may be saved,[101] Nicholas speaks this prophecy to John on a Sunday, one day before the Flood is due. Nicholas's use of the Mrs. Noah tradition is similarly free and improvisational, for unlike the drama's Noah, wedded to someone as old and cantankerous as himself—both he and she have a taste for battle—our carpenter loves his young and winsome wife too much. Finally, though it is no part of his plan, Nicholas in his own person experiences that part of Biblical prophecy old John forgets to remember, the promise that punishment will come by fire next time. Nicholas's game version of the Flood is so comic in its distortions, and (as we shall see) old John's performance as "second Noah" so remarkable in its omissions, that we should perhaps call it, as old John himself does, "Nowell's Flood."[102] The congruences are erratic and haphazard, emphasizing the witty difference rather than a significant similarity. Let us look at "Nowell's Flood" in some detail.

When old John first learns from Nicholas that "thus shal mankynde drenche, and lese hir lyf" (1.3521), he can think only of his mate:

> This carpenter answerde, "Allas, my wyf!   (1.3522)
> And shal she drenche? allas, myn Alisoun!"

The absence of any other concern will in time earn him a fall, but this care for her keeps him attractive and sympathetic as well. Overfondness for one's wife is, in fabliau terms, a mistake, but it is not ugly. To take its measure, one need only compare a late German analogue (1559) in which the husband, hearing destruction by water predicted in a Doomsday sermon, sets out to save himself, ordering a boat to be made and hung in the roof, where he sleeps night after night alone.[103] Old John is not so selfish: he loves at least one other creature as much as himself.

But if that makes him slightly more generous than his German counterpart, his failure to ask any other question ultimately earns him his humiliation and harm. He registers no surprise at all that God's inscrutable will should be communicated through his student lodger. He forgets God's promise never to destroy the world again by water, though he recollects having heard "ful yoore ago" the story of "hou saved was Noe" (1.3534). He neither asks why the world must be destroyed, nor gives any sign of comprehending God's purpose independent of such a question. Above all, he never wonders why God should have chosen to save *him*—and Nicholas, and Alisoun —from the universal catastrophe. The medieval drama offered a very different version of Noah's response.

In the York play, Noah's first speech in reply to this news recognizes his own unworthiness:

> "A! lorde, I lowe þe lowde and still,
> þat vn-to me, wretche vn-worthye,
> þus with thy worde, as is þi will,
> Lykis to appere þus propyrly." [104]

And he shows himself able to comprehend as an act of justice God's destruction of a world "that synne would nouȝt for-sake." The York Noah has a certain advantage over his fabliau counterpart—God appears in His own person to tell him his destiny—but when Mrs. Noah appears (a hundred years later) she views the ark with the sort of suspicion that might have saved old John some painful lessons. Learning for the first time of the deluge to come, and having only her husband's word for it, she declares the probabilities not sufficient. She will not leave "þe harde lande" to climb onto some precarious tower; she thinks, indeed, that Noah has lost his mind:

> "Now Noye, in faythe þe fonnes full faste,
> This fare wille I no lenger frayne,
> þou arte nere woode, I am agaste,
> Fare-wele, I wille go home agayne." [105]

The Wakefield play, in turn, begins with a speech of 72 lines in which Noah at prayer laments the world's sin, fears God's vengeance, and asks His mercy.[106] The N-Town play (edited under the title *Ludus Coventriae*, but now thought to have been written at Bury St. Edmunds), makes a similar point by other means: after a brief description of the world lost in sin, Noah introduces "my wyff and my chyldere here on rowe," each of whom pledges obedience to God in a ritual round of speeches, and then God speaks.[107] In both cycles, Noah's troubled response to the world's wickedness, and his sense that correction must be imminent, precedes God's message that He will send a Flood: the sequence of events serves to establish the righteousness of God's anger, and to distinguish the family of Noah, who will be saved, from all the others who will be destroyed. John the carpenter is not as thoughtful as the Noah of this second tradition, nor as self-knowing as the Noah of the first—the Noah who proclaims himself unworthy.

In this matter of self-knowledge, the drama and fabliau traditions inevitably meet, for the dramatists' Noah, often with less cause than old John, is able to see within himself a profound likeness to those who will be drowned. In most cycles, he acknowledges his age, his physical weakness, and his ignorance of boat building, and in speaking of man's need for grace exempts no one, not even himself:

> "god is sore grevyd with oure grett tresspas
> þat with wylde watyr þe werd xal be dreynt." [108]

Mrs. Noah, flesh of his flesh, is in some cycles used more boldly to this end. She is a "free" character, without Scriptural specification, and her sense of community with all that is flawed and found wanting becomes one of the major ways the drama authenticates the right of these survivors to be saved. In failing to see why God's grace should have fallen so remarkably on them, or to sense any great difference between themselves and the people who will be drowned, Mrs. Noah as matriarch expresses an important kind of humility, even in the versions that explore it through comedy. In Chester, for instance, she refuses to board the ark unless her gossips can come with her—"They shall not drowne, by sayncte John, / and I may save there life"—and when Noah forbids that, sits down on the bank with them for a last drink and a merry song before the waters rise.[109] In York, more decorously, she is allowed to ask why her friends and kinsmen cannot be saved, remembers them during the Flood, and asks after them again as the waters recede:

> "But Noye, where are nowe all oure kynne,
> And companye we knewe be-fore."[110]

In the comic versions, she brings to the ark an imperfect capacity for obedience, some shrewd common sense, and a special kind of humility no one would ever confuse with meekness. But she too has been chosen by God and is one of those who will be saved—however much her husband might have wished for her a ship alone.

Rosemary Woolf has argued that the comic Mrs. Noah must be understood allegorically, as representing "the recalcitrant sinner, perhaps even the sinner on his deathbed, who refuses to repent and enter the church" (which Noah's ark was understood to prefigure); to read it otherwise, she suggests, risks thinking Mrs. Noah's attachment to her friends "a sympathetic sign of human feeling, which the authors manifestly do not intend."[111] It is possible that Woolf is right, that the devil (so to speak) continues to sit on Mrs. Noah's shoulder, as in the picture from the Ramsey Psalter (figure 96), or to give her shrewd counsel, as in that from Queen Mary's Psalter (figure 93). But nothing in the dialogue invokes the Eastern diabolic tradition, and nothing urges us to see her as representative sinner rather than as representative wife. We know from the first that she will board the ark sometime—she is *uxor Noe*, after all—and what we see we understand as telling us something about those who will be saved, rather than about those who will be drowned. The lines from York quoted above make clear that sympathetic "human feeling" could be soberly expressed within this context—as do the texts already mentioned in which God orders Noah to spend 120 years constructing the ark, on the chance that other human beings will amend their lives, or in which Noah deliberately works slowly with this hope in mind, or prays from within the ark for the souls of those outside it, drowned in the waters.[112] The French cycle known as the *Mistère du Viel Testament*, conceived on a scale far grander than its English counterparts, includes the unavailing repentance and drowning of nine different sinners (each with a name and a speaking part), and calls for yet others to mime the same death, if more persons can be made available: "Here the waters will cover the entire place where one stages the play, and one might have there several men and women who do not speak but who enact being drowned."[113] Where before the cycle has shown us their sin, we now see their terror and hear them utter (too late) their regret and repentance; the mood of the moment is tragic and invites a fearful, temporary identification with the doomed as well as a continuing identification with those who are saved.

Mrs. Noah's contribution to this set of ideas within the English tradition throws no special light upon Alisoun, cast as *uxor Noe* in Nicholas's Flood game. Quite the contrary. Alisoun boards her ship without opposition or delay, simply that she may leave it the sooner: her husband has barely begun to snore before she is down the ladder and making music in the lodger's arms. The "image," in this respect as in so many others, is non-congruent. It is old John himself we will understand better for having "herd" some of these things about "the sorwe of Noe with his felaweshipe."

Chaucer, in short, invokes the popular image of the Flood in order to throw the strongest possible comic light upon old John's presumption. Complacent in his certainty that men "sholde nat knowe of Goddes pryvetee" (1.3454), he forgets they need some candid sense of their own. Given the prospect of universal destruction, he can think only of sweet Alisoun; invited to imagine their singular salvation, he never questions its probability. Like the first Noah he is found obedient, but to spurious authority and without self-knowledge. The rest of the world is no more to him than Robyn and Gille, the servants he sends off to London (and, by implication, their death by drowning) "upon his nede . . . for to go" (1.3632). Nicholas, to be sure, is the source of this "fantasye" of a second Flood, and, as Chaucer takes care to emphasize, the power of such images—mental images—can be enormous. John "sees" the coming Flood so clearly it makes him shake, weep, wail, and sigh:

> Men may dyen of ymaginacioun,   (1.3612)
> So depe may impressioun be take.
> This sely carpenter bigynneth quake;
> Hym thynketh verraily that he may see
> Noees flood come walwynge as the see

To drenchen Alisoun, his hony deere.
He wepeth, weyleth, maketh sory cheere;
He siketh with ful many a sory swogh;
He gooth and geteth hym a knedyng trogh.

Nicholas, I repeat, is the source of the image; but the assent to its
truth, and the translation of it into action, are entirely the carpenter's
own. His weary sleep in the kneading tub on high, snoring away in
expectation of a morrow when the three of them shall be "lordes al
oure lyf / Of al the world, as Noe and his wyf" (1.3581), offers a
comic image of intolerable presumption and complacency, from
which he must be cut down. In keeping with the decorum of fabliau,
it is his own hand, not God's, that lays axe to the rope and punishes
his folly: the tale concerns foolishness old and young, not sin.

A tale from the *Decameron* that turns on a similar trick but moves
to a moment of greater thematic tension can help us better estimate
the nature of this two-part image: old John asleep in the new ark
above, Nicholas and Alisoun making love below. Boccaccio's tale
(III.4) demonstrates the proposition "many are those who, whilst
they are busy making strenuous efforts to get to Paradise, unwit-
tingly send some other person there in their stead."[114] It tells of Friar
Puccio, a wealthy lay brother of the Franciscan order, who has so
dedicated his life to religious devotion that he neglects his young and
beautiful wife. His spiritual counselor, a monk named Dom Felice, in
order to sleep with her, recommends a spiritual exercise that he says
is so efficacious the papal court in Rome keeps it secret for itself. All
it requires is that for forty days Friar Puccio should fast, abstain from
sexual intercourse, place himself in open view of the heavens, and,
with his arms spread out in the posture of Christ on the cross, recite
paternosters and Hail Marys by the hundred. If he does this, he will
surely attain eternal salvation. The husband eagerly embraces the
penance, the monk embraces the wife, and she ends the story with a
bedroom compliment: "You make Friar Puccio do penance, but we
are the ones who go to Paradise."[115] Figure 98 shows Friar Puccio (in
the upper right corner) in an ordinary posture of prayer, unlike some
other illustrations that show him properly cruciform, but I choose to
reproduce it because it registers correctly the relationship of the ac-
tions "above" and "below"—*superior* and *inferior*—with the first
serving as occasion for the second.[116]

The equivalent action in *The Miller's Tale* juxtaposes two architec-
tural spaces and two sets of motives in equally disjunctive and comi-
cally volatile ways, but creates no comparable moral tension. Al-
though Friar Puccio's devotion is imprudent and excessive, he seeks
an end that, in other medieval contexts, might be affirmed: he prac-
tices genuine devotion in that upper room. Boccaccio, moreover,

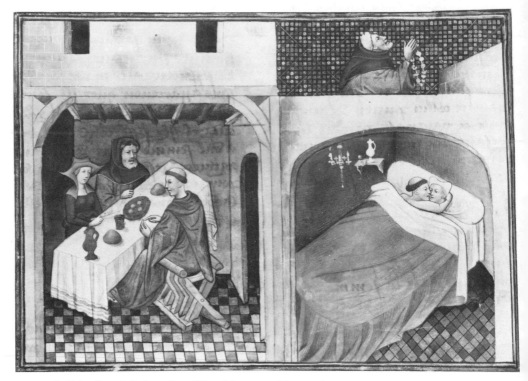

98. Friar Puccio's devotions. Flemish, 1432. Note 116.

ends the tale without formally exposing either the folly or the for-
nication, in an equivocation that may give special meaning to the
scene shown on the left:

The lady was of the opinion that she had never felt better in her life, and
having been compelled to diet by her husband for so long, she acquired such
a taste for the monk's victuals that when Friar Puccio reached the end of his
long penance, she found a way of banqueting with the monk elsewhere.
And for a long time thereafter, she continued discreetly to enjoy such
repasts.[117]

Chaucer, in contrast, seeks and achieves a more perfect equilibrium:
he shows us folly and complacency above, wit and carnality below,
and relates them by an even more elaborate contrivance, the Flood
game, which offers a commentary on the action too rich and many-
leveled to be summed up in a quip at the end. Indeed, I suspect that
the Flood play or plays Chaucer knew best created a stage image that
used music as part of its expressive means at the point of maximum
stillness in the action, the moment when the audience was to imagine
the ark afloat upon the waves. The N-town cycle, for instance, after

staging the death of Cain, ordains "Hic . . . intrat noe cum naui can-
tantes" ("Here . . . Noah enters in the ship singing"), though it does
not specify his song.[118] The Chester cycle, in contrast, gives some
fairly detailed information. After Noah has brought his whole family
on board, he notices the boat begin to move, and in four of the extant
manuscripts we find the stage direction "Then they singe, and Noe
shall speake agayne." That speech briefly introduces the action called
for immediately after: "Then shall Noe shutt the windowe of the
arke, and for a little space within the bordes hee shalbe scylent; and
afterwarde openinge the windowe and lookinge rownde about" he
thanks God for their salvation. The best of the Chester manuscripts,
however, conflates these two actions, creating a moment of utter
stillness in which all who will survive from the first world are hidden
within the ark, directing their whole attention toward God through
song. Its single stage direction reads:

Tunc Noe claudet fenestram archae et per modicum spatium infra tec-
tum cantent psalmum "Save mee, O God" et aperiens fenestram et re-
spiciens. . . .[119]

Then Noah will close the window of the ark and for a little while, concealed
within, they will sing the psalm "Save me, O God," and [after], opening the
window and looking about [Noah will say. . . .]

This image, iconographic in its power, links the death of one world
and the beginning of another, and it has a possible counterpart in *The
Miller's Tale*. Chaucer moves the action to a point of comparable fix-
ity, and then invites us to imagine music of three contrasting kinds:
the carpenter snoring above, Nicholas and Alisoun fornicating below
("Ther was the revel and the melodye"), and the special music of the
Church that marks the early hour of the day, the friars singing Lauds:

> And thus lith Alison and Nicholas,   (1.3653)
> In bisynesse of myrthe and of solas,
> Til that the belle of laudes gan to rynge,
> And freres in the chauncel gonne synge.

Professor Robertson has taught us to detect in many medieval con-
texts a witty juxtaposition of two musics, the "old song" of carnal
man and the "new song" of spiritual man, of man reborn.[120] But both
songs in the foreground of this tale are "old" songs—the snoring and
the fornication—and the other serves only to indicate the hour at
which Absolon comes to the window for his kiss: it lacks sufficient
rhetorical weight to invite a specifically religious judgment upon the
scene immediately before us.

    In place of such a judgment, Chaucer provides the logic and laugh-
ter intrinsic to the genre he called "cherles tales." Unlike Boccaccio's
tale adduced above, this narrative comes full circle: Absolon earns

a hairy kiss, Nicholas a burned arse, and old John a broken arm and the derision of his neighbors—the townfolk whose future death by drowning had troubled him not at all. Nicholas's anguished cry for "Water!" brings everything together and everything to an end: his revels with Alisoun, Absolon's revised game of courtship ("'Of gold,' quod he, 'I have thee broght a ryng'"), and the carpenter's expectations as second Noah. But it is fabliau justice only. The hand of an offended God is nowhere to be seen in this comic catastrophe, nor inferred from it against an idea of Doomsday to come. In the Miller's scheme of things, Absolon, Nicholas, and old John sin against common sense, not the deity, and their punishment is in every case poetically sufficient: exposure is cure, and we are not invited to think beyond it. Though the story has moved through two large narrative images that might have been worked poetically in such a way as to address religious truth—Absolon's ritual of misplaced adoration and old John's rehearsal of the Flood—in *The Miller's Tale* they are insistently parodic in mode,[121] comically out of register, and by means of genre made to short-circuit their highest kinds of potential meaning. The tale's energy is born of youth and natural instinct; it expresses itself in game; and it flows (so to speak) in a circle*—within a self-contained fabliau system—not outward toward a world of transcendental meaning and spiritual destinies.

The respect accorded Chaucer's "cherles tales" has increased markedly since the nineteenth and early twentieth centuries, when their sexual frankness excluded them from polite discussion. They are now generally ranked among his finest work in short narrative, even by those who believe that they express didactic versions of Christian truth. In this other reading of the tales, laughter is still admitted, but laughter of one kind only. It must be ironical and distant, a proper response to the spectacle of sin punishing itself. In *The Miller's Tale*, John the carpenter, Nicholas, and Absolon are seen primarily as exemplifications, intended to communicate through verisimilar speech and action some Christian truths about the nature of Avarice, Lechery, and Vanity—one man to one sin, in that precise order.[122] I wish to conclude this chapter by suggesting one further reason for thinking such a reading not only reductive but improper.

My argument turns upon the fact that the pride punished in fabliaux and the Pride (*Superbia*) warned against in sermons and moral treatises exist within wholly different conceptual structures and imply wholly different value systems. (So too with the other Deadly Sins.) Because fictions and moral treatises share a common subject, human life, it is of course possible to move from the first to the sec-

---

*The progress from "But sith that he was fallen in the snare, / He moste endure, as oother folk, his care" (I.3231), to "stonde he moste unto his owene harm" (I.3830) is, of course, no progress at all; the story confirms what it knows from the beginning.

ond in thinking about the meaning of a medieval story. But the artistic coherence of fabliau does not depend upon a reader doing so—not even as an act of historical criticism. The remedy for fabliau pride is exposure and a measure of self-knowledge, whereas the remedy for the sin of Pride is humility (*Humilitas*) in the manner of Mary Virgin or Christ, its great exemplars. The correction of fabliau pride, moreover, is a function of society, whereas the sin of Pride will ultimately be corrected—and judged—by Heaven's King. Unless a poet unmistakably invites us to superimpose one system upon the other, we should refrain from doing so—and in *The Miller's Tale*, the invitation seems to be in the other direction entirely. If we want morality, provision has been made: "Turne over the leef and chese another tale" (1.3177). Chaucer explores the world of moral meaning elsewhere.

In the Miller's preferred vision of the world, human actions are as free of such meaning, such weighty consequence, as are those of the birds, beasts, and flowers of the English countryside to which it pleases him to relate the instincts and necessities of his young people.[123] More is involved than a "barnyard version of courtly love," though that description has some relevance.[124] In sequel to *The Knight's Tale*, Chaucer sought a perfectly antithetical vision, a look at life through eyes uncomplicated by transcendent idea or ideal. It required a different artistic style—a breakup of the hieratic, the noble, the questing—through large narrative images whose meaning is never allowed to break free of their game mode and the genre's self-sufficiency as system, and through a cluster of similes, drawn from the world of nature, used to identify in a morally neutral way the energies that give rise to those larger images. As several pictures reproduced in this chapter have demonstrated, the animals and birds have an untroubled place within Noah's ark,[125] and Chaucer, who chose to make an ordinary fabliau seduction contingent upon a successful restaging of part of that medieval play, chose also to see his characters' intentions as no more accessible to high moral scrutiny than are the actions of that animal confraternity given its own necessary place on board.

In contrast to *The Knight's Tale* version of the world as palace/prison or prison/garden, both ultimately places of the spirit's captivity, the Miller invites us into a world of open streets and (through simile) country farmyards, where man's freedom and accountability are like those of the animals: consequence follows cause, not in eternity, but here and now, and in scale with his capacities. There is no cynicism in this vision, and no despair. It finds the physical world enough—its plenitude, its charm, its energy, its rules. Out of the law of gravity, the logic of cause and effect, and a respect for ordinary limits there is constituted an idea of order sufficient to man's needs. The deepest answers returned in this tale are not cosmic but prudential: "stonde he moste unto his owene harm." In celebrating human and animal likeness, the life of the instincts, and the company of youth and wit, Chaucer celebrates as well the possible sovereignty of comic order within the world of daily life, a world temporarily—by an act of imaginative exclusion—unshadowed by Last Things. The tale moves toward adjustment, not judgment, with an audacity fully the equal of its grace.

V. *The Reeve's Prologue and Tale*

DEATH–AS–TAPSTER AND THE HORSE UNBRIDLED

HE CANTERBURY TALES is neither the first collection
of stories to be enclosed by a larger narrative, nor the
first in which such stories are assigned to individual
characters within the narrative frame. But Chaucer put that tradition
to certain uses it had never served before, chief among them, as
Thomas F. Cannon has suggested, the creation of a symbolic Christian community, and the investigation of human personality in its
terms.[1] The second of these purposes will particularly concern us in
this chapter. No reader of *The Seven Sages*, for instance, has ever
thought to any purpose about what might distinguish one of those
sages from another, or in the *Decameron*, Pampinea (let us say) from
Filomena. They come nearer to being "named occasions" than "characters" or "voices." Though they are useful as a means of marking
narrative sequence, all we really know of them pertains to their
membership in a group. The sages must be wise, the young people
well born, attractive, and pleasure loving.

Chaucer's characters possess, as pilgrims, a group identity of similar importance,[2] and their portraits in *The General Prologue* associate
them with prior groups as well, for each of them is made representative, to some degree, of his or her profession or estate. Some of the
pilgrims, such as the Yeoman or the five Guildsmen, never become
more particular than that; most others, such as the Clerk or Franklin,
inhabit some middle distance of specification and individuating detail; a few, through the cumulative power of *General Prologue* portrait, personal prologue, and narrative act, become remarkably individual. The Prioress, the Wife of Bath, the Pardoner, and the Canon's
Yeoman lay unequivocal claim to that distinction, as does the pilgrim
who now steps forward to take his place in the opening design,
Chaucer's choleric Reeve, come from "biside a toun men clepen Baldeswelle" (1.620). For unlike Guillaume de Deguileville's single character called Pilgrim, whose experience is perfectly understood by his
author at every moment and who stands until the very end (when he

enters a religious order) universally for us all, Chaucer's pilgrim company is numerous and varied—a composite image of people bearing real English names and coming from real English places (Harry Bailly of Southwark, Alisoun of Bath, Hodge of Ware), known or knowable in varying degrees, and constituting a highly articulated demonstration of the many ways in which one can be a pilgrim on this earth. No single member of the pilgrim company will serve as a mirror to us all. We are meant to find parts of ourselves in many, through a series of discoveries as tentative and tactful as Chaucer's own.

Chaucer works within the tradition of the fallible narrator, but in a manner philosophically much deeper than does (say) the author of the poem called *Pearl*, whose narrator's mistakes are made for our better instruction, and whose experience in the poem is meant to move us along with him from error to truth—both conceived in absolute terms. Chaucer instead brings forward every pilgrim portrait under the shadow of the phrase "so as it semed me" (I. 39), and in that modest stipulation, at once apology and authentication, he invites us into a realm more problematic by far, more painful in its uncertainties and in its steady sense of human limitation. In *The Canterbury Tales* as a whole, no man's essence is ever free of accident, no human life entirely reducible to the clarity and consistency of idea, and no man's "privitee"—his deepest and most inward being—ultimately knowable except by God alone. By turning his central characters into narrators, Chaucer was able to investigate human personality in its fullest and richest detail, without in any sense violating its ultimate mysteries.

Chaucer clearly understood that one possible entry into any man's most hidden self is to ask him to tell you a story. The story that he chooses to tell, along with the way he chooses to tell it—his language, tone, emphasis, and choice of detail—can sometimes constitute a communication that goes beyond the story itself, and is not inferior in terms of interest. Chaucer's practice in this matter, as in the individuating detail within the formal portraits, varies from the perfunctory to the profound. Many of his tales, in the older fashion of *The Seven Sages* or the *Decameron*, are merely attached to their tellers; some, such as *The Nun's Priest's Tale* or *The Second Nun's Tale*, hint at character even without a formal (*General Prologue*) portrait to guide us; some few move upon a brilliant new frontier in medieval narrative, where Chaucer's art anticipates a set of discoveries central to modern science: that an observer is inescapably part of what he observes, that no simple distinction can be made between subject and object, perceiver and perceived, that man cannot separate himself from reality in order to observe reality. At this most innovative level of his art, Chaucer explores not only personality through tale-telling, but the many and divergent "truths" likely to coexist in any human company.

The tales in which narrative voice becomes most highly individual and self-revelatory require exploration by a rather different means than those that have governed this study so far. *The Canterbury Tales* is not an entirely homogeneous work, not all in Chaucer's mature style, not everywhere responsive to his latest interests and experiments in the art of narrative. No work so large and numerous in its parts would need to be; no work composed over a period of so many years (ca. 1387–1400), and incorporating pieces written before the Canterbury pilgrims were even imagined, is likely to be. Chaucer would have noted in that fact a happy verisimilitude—in real life, as in this collection, some people will tell stories "after the olde guise," some "after the newe," just as certain of them will reveal more of themselves than will others in the telling of a tale. Let me summarize my sense of the first two tales in this regard, as a preface to this study of *The Reeve's Prologue and Tale*, for in it (I shall argue) governing image and narrative voice become a single complex whole.

We know from *The Legend of Good Women* ([F] 420–21) that Chaucer had written a poem concerning "al the love of Palamon and Arcite" as an independent work before *The Canterbury Tales* was begun, and that it had not been widely circulated: "the storye ys knowen lyte." Although counter-arguments have been made, it continues to seem likely that the poem was incorporated into the later work without substantial change. We derive from the tale, it is true, a richer sense of the Knight's courtliness, his interest in love and philosophy, and his carefully judged respect for the pagan past. Yet these additions offer at most a completion of the *General Prologue* portrait, filling it out in some ways we might expect and offering aesthetic satisfaction in those terms. By virtue of its initial position, length, and artistic authority, the tale establishes one of the norms for the Canterbury collection as a whole—but its greatest interest is as a narrative, not as an act of narration.

The Miller, unlike the Knight, is given a prologue that extends our sense of him in significant ways. He becomes increasingly "Robyn," a particular miller we know by name—boisterously self-assertive, oddly patient in fending off the Reeve's attack, and not a little under the influence of ale: "That I am dronke, I knowe it by my soun" (I.3138). But the voice of the tale itself grows out of the Miller's class identity and in response to the high idealizations of the preceding tale rather than out of the Miller's own individuality. Although the Ellesmere portrait (figure 99) captures the pilgrim we meet in the two prologues tolerably well,[3] the image is entirely discordant with the narrative assigned. Nothing about that sullen figure hunched over his bagpipes, ruddy of complexion and with thumbs literally colored

99. The Miller (Ellesmere
MS.). English, ca.
1400–1410. Note 3.

gold (a sign of cheating), suggests a narrator capable of the high ener-
gies and genial affirmations of *The Miller's Tale*. Chaucer uses his
Miller as a means of confronting courtly culture with certain bour-
geois counter-truths, but the relationship is ideational and dialectic
rather than mimetic. The first two tales of the Canterbury sequence
are equally remarkable within their kinds, the one in an early style,
the other in a late; but it is chiefly the material that speaks, not in any
highly characterized way the tellers through the material. In the first
two tales, our interest is in narrative ethos, not in individual narrative
voice.[4]

The Reeve's Prologue and Tale, in contrast, is interesting as a perfor-
mance—as the act of a man revealing himself through the material
and manner of his story telling. By means of a lengthy self-portrait (a
prologue whose burden is "The Reeve Grown Old"), we are led well
beyond what *The General Prologue* and his preliminary skirmish with
the Miller in *The Miller's Prologue* have already taught us about him.
Between the Reeve's refusal to answer the Miller in fabliau terms—
"me list not pley for age"—and the beginning of a story offered ap-
parently in compliance with Harry Bailly's prohibition on any fur-
ther "sermonyng," the Reeve not only tells us a great deal about his
inner "condicioun," but colors the mood of the tale that follows and
fills in yet another area of late-fourteenth-century response to the
challenge of eternity. For the Reeve has more in mind than self-

presentation: he seeks to become, in his own person, a mirror to all who listen, moving tacitly from "I" to "we," and exempting no one who is old, or who hopes to live long, from his gloomy imperatives. He offers us portrait painting of a moral kind, capable of ending the pilgrimage fun and games altogether, or, at the very least, undermining the fun of those games. His performance is a signal event in Chaucer's larger design.

In *The General Prologue*, the Reeve is introduced as one whose special skill lies in adroitly serving those above him, terrorizing those below him, and doing himself some quiet good along the way: "Ful riche he was astored pryvely" (1.609). He discharges his duties as reeve with great exactitude and care—"Ther was noon auditour koude on him wynne"; "Ther koude no man brynge hym in arrerage" (1.594, 602)—but he brings to that office a severity of insight into the hidden motives and desperation of other men that seems excessive in the circumstances, a manner perhaps better suited to Doomsday than to the keeping of accounts on a medieval manor: "Ther nas baillif, ne hierde, nor oother hyne, / That he ne knew his sleighte and his covyne" (1.603). They fear him like the Black Death, not least because he is himself corrupt and sly. Figure 100, illustrating the labor of August from the calendar pages of Queen Mary's Psalter, can furnish us with an appropriate image for the Reeve in his professional aspect: it shows a field foreman or reeve standing behind three

100. The labor of August: a reeve in the field. English, ca. 1310–20. Note 5.

101. The Reeve (Cambridge MS.). English, midfifteenth century. Note 6.

reapers, supervising their work with a staff. They are within his view and under his power.[5] In a similar fashion, Chaucer's Reeve rides last among the pilgrim company, "hyndreste of oure route" (I.622), perhaps out of habitual preference for a place where he can keep an eye on others while being himself out of their sight.

But it is from two external details in the pilgrim portrait that the Reeve's self-portrait develops tonally and thematically: "His top was dokked lyk a preest biforn" and "Tukked he was as is a frere aboute" (I.590, 621). The Cambridge portrait (figure 101) is more faithful than its Ellesmere equivalent (figure 102) in this important respect:[6] its close-cut hair, clean-shaven beard, and simple, dark gown give the Reeve the look of a rather seedy priest or friar. Harry Bailly will invoke that very likeness in attacking the tenor of the Reeve's opening speech:

> Whan that oure Hoost hadde herd this sermonyng,   (I.3899)
> He gan to speke as lordly as a kyng.
> He seide, "What amounteth al this wit?
> What shul we speke alday of hooly writ?
> The devel made a reve for to preche,
> Or of a soutere a shipman or a leche."

Harry Bailly will hear no sermon from a reeve, thank you very much; that would be like turning to a shoemaker when you need a shipman or a doctor. Bailly's need to keep the game moving forward, his own social truculence, and perhaps even a sense of the Reeve's real

102. The Reeve (Ellesmere MS.). English, ca. 1400–1410. Note 6.

nature all move him to assert his rule. But the Reeve's sermon is in fact as suspect as its speaker. I wish to think more critically than is common about his version of old age and of life and death;[7] I imagine that Chaucer would have wished us to do so.

The Reeve presents himself to the pilgrim company in a series of swift, ugly, and humiliating similitudes, as concentrated as anything in Chaucer's poetry:

> "But ik am oold, me list not pley for age;   (I.3867)
> Gras tyme is doon, my fodder is now forage;
> This white top writeth myne olde yeris;
> Myn herte is also mowled as myne heris,
> But if I fare as dooth an open-ers,—
> That ilke fruyt is ever lenger the wers,
> Til it be roten in mullok or in stree.
> We olde men, I drede, so fare we:
> Til we be roten, kan we nat be rype;
> We hoppen alwey whil the world wol pype.
> For in oure wyl ther stiketh evere a nayl,
> To have an hoor heed and a grene tayl,
> As hath a leek; for thogh oure myght be goon,
> Oure wyl desireth folie evere in oon.
> For whan we may nat doon, than wol we speke;
> Yet in oure asshen olde is fyr yreke.
>   Foure gleedes han we, which I shal devyse,—
> Avauntyng, liyng, anger, coveitise;

> Thise foure sparkles longen unto eelde.
> Oure olde lemes mowe wel been unweelde,
> But wyl ne shal nat faillen, that is sooth.
> And yet ik have alwey a coltes tooth,
> As many a yeer as it is passed henne
> Syn that my tappe of lif bigan to renne."

He is, he tells them, like a horse in winter, whose only fodder is forage and dry hay; his heart is as moldy as his hair is white. He likens himself to an "open-ers" (the medlar fruit, called by a name that suggests the incontinence of extreme old age), waiting to "ripen" in refuse or in straw. But then the pronoun changes: "We olde men, I drede, so fare we: / Til we be roten, kan we nat be rype" (1.3874). The self-portrait suddenly becomes a genre scene including all men who are old, creatures hopping about gracelessly to the world's tune, persevering in lechery long after the power to achieve it is gone. We are like leeks, he says, our tails green, our heads white; we are like ashes in a burned-out fire, with just four coals (boasting, lying, anger, and greed) still lively enough to be raked into a final flame. He then draws together the self-loathing and despair, the sense of decay and exhaustion, that haunt these antecedent figures into an extended final image that exempts no one, young or old:

> "For sikerly, whan I was bore, anon   (1.3891)
> Deeth drough the tappe of lyf and leet it gon;
> And ever sithe hath so the tappe yronne
> Til that almoost al empty is the tonne.
> The streem of lyf now droppeth on the chymbe.
> The sely tonge may wel rynge and chymbe
> Of wrecchednesse that passed is ful yoore;
> With olde folk, save dotage, is namoore!"

As in *The Knight's Tale*, where the garden is seen ultimately as prison, here living is seen as a process of dying, whose end is grotesquely and painfully protracted. The beginning of life, the Reeve tells us, is the beginning of death.

Although Chaucer's program calls for us to hear two fabliaux in a row, he avoids a mere repetition of mood and material by altering almost totally the context in which we hear the second. We are forced, before the games resume, to contemplate the wretchedness of life and age and death in imagery of great power, and through language that invokes the moral sanctions of eternity—in its list of sins, and in the verse from St. Luke's Gospel that gives us "We hoppen alwey whil the world wol pype."[8] Since literary genres are defined as much by their exclusions as by their preferred subject matter, it is important to note that the central materials of the Reeve's prologue are almost entirely inimical to fabliau, a genre that cannot flourish in

103. A monk cellarer.
French, thirteenth century.
Note 9.

the presence of long perspectives, continuing pain, or the reality of death. In his self-portrait the Reeve implicitly rebukes the Miller's celebration of young people in a green and growing natural world, ever at odds with the cares and labor of age. In this revised version of human life, distinctions between age and youth make only superficial sense, and there is no innocence in the dancing: we are all willful and dying. The Reeve reminds us of all that has been excluded from *The Miller's Tale*, offers his own person as proof of its truth, and forces us in one final, comprehensive image to reconsider everything the Miller has invited us to enjoy—animal liveliness, bawdy laughter, youthful energy, aged gullibility—and see them as another thing. Death is the cellarer (compare figure 103)* who draws the tap of life.[9]

The Reeve's choice of metaphor has a special and perverse brilliance, for what we are made to see in our mind's eye—an opened cask of wine running freely—we associate with life at its most pleasurable and carefree. It is an image, on the face of things, especially harmonious with the world of fabliau, for many a merry tale allows its characters to take their pleasure over good wine, and many a fabliau would have been recited in a tavern or hall around just such a cask of the white or the red. Jean Bodel's *Le Jeu de Saint Nicholas*, for instance, sets an important scene in a tavern, where three thieves rejoice in their good fortune: "Ah, God! How wine restores the soul! /

---

*In this picture from a health manual, a monastic cellarer, holding the keys of his office, fills a pitcher presumably destined for the refectory or the refreshment of guests, while surreptitiously sipping some wine.

At last we're well provided for" ("Hé, Diex! con chis vins nous pour-
fite! / Or primes sommes assenés").[10]

The visual arts testify as well to the customary medieval connota-
tions of the image. Figure 104, for instance, shows six men, one of
them tonsured, holding a piece of music and singing across a barrel
of wine. Unlike Bodel's three thieves, they are neither drunken nor
disreputable, and we are probably meant to think of them as singing
the *rondeau* by Machaut that follows in the manuscript below, its bur-
den a courtly-love complaint: "Dearest heart, remember" ("Gentils
cuers, souveingne vous").[11] The company depicted in figure 105 per-
haps represents more accurately the social milieu assumed by fabliau.
It decorates the text of a Latin drinking song, "O potatores ex-
quisiti," and includes a number of churchmen, prosperous burghers,
a dog, and two chained monkeys, all making merry around a tun of
wine. (The manuscript was probably made for the Chapel Royal of

104. Singing around a wine cask. French, late fourteenth century. Note 11.

105. "O potatores exquisiti" (carousing around a wine cask). English, ca. 1450.
Note 12.

St. George, Windsor, ca. 1450.)[12] Chaucer himself, in *The Parliament of Fowls*, discussing how our daily cares determine the subjects of our dreams, has the rich man dreaming of gold, the lover of his lady, and the sick man of better times when "he drynketh of the tonne" (104).[13] In short, the relation of tun imagery to relaxation and joy is intrinsic, not stipulative, and carries with it always the probabilities of laughter, love making, and freedom from care. The Reeve uses it instead to remind us that even when our thoughts are furthest from death, we are dying. The young man who draws wine for the company in figure 105 is, so to speak, replaced in the Reeve's prologue by a tapster who is Death himself.

The Reeve's prologue, then, in its discussion of age and death must be understood as a preliminary requital of *The Miller's Tale*. In response to a world of play and game, where proverbial wisdom and the energy of young birds, beasts, and flowers establish the only significant moral coordinates, the Reeve offers his experience of old age and a vision of living as dying that yields a very different moral grid against which the human comedy is played out. That vision is compromised by the moral character of the Reeve, but it is also compromised by its own limitations and exclusions. They are the subtext, as it were, to the Reeve's prologue; let us examine them briefly.

There are distortions in the Reeve's view of life that anyone might easily remedy. In Cicero's *De senectute*, a dialogue concerning old age from which Chaucer quotes in *The Tale of Melibee*, Cato makes these points, among others, in explaining how he manages to be content in his old age:

To those who have not the means within themselves of a virtuous and happy life every age is burdensome; and, on the other hand, to those who seek all good from themselves nothing can seem evil that the laws of nature inevitably impose.

But, the critics say, old men are morose, troubled, fretful, and hard to please; and, if we inquire, we shall find that some of them are misers, too. However, these are faults of character, not of age.

I approve of some austerity in the old, but I want it, as I do everything else, in moderation. Sourness of temper I like not at all.[14]

I begin with a pagan text because medieval Christianity is not necessary to put all of the Reeve's distortions into true perspective. Certain late-medieval texts spoke of the matter with similar judiciousness, emphasizing the role of moral choice. The medieval bestiary, for example, taught that "Old Age brings with it many goods and ills. The advantages are that it liberates us from all-powerful urges, puts paid to the sensual pleasures, breaks the violences of lust, increases wisdom and gives maturer counsels. The bad things are that decline is very miserable with debility and hatefulness. Diseases and sad senectitude creep in."[15] Bartholomaeus Anglicus, too, noted that "this age haþ wiþ hym mony damages and also propirtees boþe goode and yuel. . . . Good for it delyuereþ vs out of þe power of myȝti men and tirauntis, and makeþ ende of lust, and brekeþ of fleischelich likinge, and haþ wit and wisdom, and ȝeueþ good counseile as mony olde men don. It is ende of wrecchidnes and of woo, and bigynnynge of welþe of ioye, and passinge out of perile and comynge in prise, parfitnes in medeful dedis, and disposicioun to be parfite."[16] *The Chess of Love*, too, is insistently bipartite and ultimately affirmative in its stance: like youth in the parallel passage that we examined in the last chapter, old age is an estate worthy of commendation and respect, though it too has some good aspects and some bad; six of each are explored seriatim.[17] Any of these texts can restore to proper balance the Reeve's version of old age, though none of them is explicitly or insistently Christian in its premises. But Christianity is necessary to name the most singular of the Reeve's omissions, for it is in that respect that his monologue becomes an important element in the structural design of the pilgrimage's beginning.

I do not mean that the Reeve lacks Christian antecedents in this matter. The eleventh-century antiphon, "Media vita in morte sumus" ("In the midst of life we are in death") merely gave new form to a paradox at least as old as Seneca, which St. Augustine had explored at great length in *The City of God*: "No sooner do we begin to live in this dying body, than we begin to move ceaselessly towards death." A treatise on the art of holy dying called "Toure of All Toures" expresses that idea most beautifully: "And Holy Writ telleth us that this life is but a passage, and for to live is not but for to die, and that is sooth as the Paternoster. For when thou beginnest for to live anon thou shalt begin for to die: and all thine age and thy time that is passed, death hath it conquered and holdeth."[18]

These texts speak with the voice of Christian authority, and the Reeve has borrowed their theme, though the figure of the wine cask in which he casts it is (as far as I know) entirely Chaucer's own. The theme belongs, by genre, to "sermonyng," as does the roll call of sin that precedes it:

> "Avauntyng, liyng, anger, coveitise;   (1.3884)
> Thise foure sparkles longen unto eelde."

But here the use of these themes amounts to bad sermon making—in ways that even the Pardoner's tale does not, though his life is far more vicious than the Reeve's—for a truth can be so partial that it is not even true. The Reeve has nothing to say of the possibility of virtue, or of the Christian fact of life after death, and in the context of those omissions, his bitter heart's-truth—if that is what he offers us—must be seen as an act of aggression, or as self-indulgent display, or both. In medieval terms, it is far less serious than he thinks, or than it seems.

For there is an essential structure to all Christian meditations on death, from which the Reeve offers us only a single dismembered limb. The antiphon "Media vita" quoted above concludes in hope of the comfort of Christ, "Holy and merciful Savior, deliver us not to bitter death" ("Sancte et misericors Salvator, / Amarae morti ne tradas nos"), and *The City of God* names in its very title the final destination of any true Christian, for whom death is merely part of a long journey home. Though evil men, Augustine tells us, may properly despair, for "never can a man be more disastrously in death than when death itself shall be deathless," the last phrase refers to eternal damnation, not to this other kind of dying that we endure daily, which he would have us confront with courage and equanimity. Indeed, the whole purpose of the "Toure of All Toures" is to help a man die well, which is to say die gladly, in hope of heaven.

I do not mean to suggest that the Reeve's meditation on old age and dying is not profound. It could not move us so if it were not— summoning from their secret places our deepest fears and vulnerabilities, and casting them in a series of mordant images that haunt the mind. But there can be no *Christian* meditation on death that stops short of Christ's victory over Death, no Christian discourse on sin that can entirely neglect the possibility of virtue and man's freedom to amend. The single text Chaucer seems to have raided more than once in the making of this prologue, the *Testament* of Jean de Meun, offers unequivocal evidence of this fact. It provided Chaucer with the idea of four sins that, like burning coals, can still kindle fire in old men—"Baraz et tricheries, haÿnes, trahisons. / Trop de gent sont espris de ces quatre tisons"—and perhaps as well with the theme of life as a long dying—"Tantost que li homs naist, il commence a mourir."[19] But I suspect Chaucer owed more to this poem in composing the Reeve's prologue than has been properly assessed, perhaps not least his immediate sense of a total discourse against which the piecemeal truths of the Reeve can be measured. For all the bitter realism with which Jean describes old age, and for all the satiric power with which he excoriates the corruption of the Church and of society, his *Testament* offers a steady counter-vision of the possibility of virtue, the corrigibility of institutions, and the availability of salvation.

Two other long medieval poems that Chaucer knew well— *The Pilgrimage of Human Life* of Guillaume de Deguileville and the *Confessio amantis* of his friend and fellow court poet John Gower—can likewise help us take the measure of the Reeve's meditation. Both see their protagonists into the indignities and sufferings of age, but it is unthinkable that either might have ended in mere complaint. At the conclusion of Gower's poem, Venus herself advises the poet to make a "beau retret," leaving behind carnal love to seek a life of wisdom. After Cupid has removed his fiery dart, Venus anoints Gower's heart and head and loins with a cold ointment, and then hands him a mirror in which he sees himself grow old:

> Wherinne anon myn hertes yhe
> I caste, and sih my colour fade,
> Myn yhen dymme and al unglade,
> Mi chiekes thinne, and al my face
> With Elde I myhte se deface,
> So riveled and so wo besein,
> That ther was nothing full ne plein,

> I syh also myn heres hore.
> Mi will was tho to se nomore
> Outwith, for ther was no plesance.

In answer to his distress, Genius, Venus's priest, grants him a lover's absolution, and Venus herself gives him a rosary gauded *Por reposer* ("that you may have rest"), as Gower takes his leave of passionate love. The poem moves beautifully to that close, achieving in its final pages a power and intensity of feeling it has not reached before, in part because its last lines are in praise of another love entirely, sufficient to reconcile man to his dying body and to earn him happiness beyond the grave:

> Bot thilke love which that is
> Withinne a mannes herte affermed,
> And stant of charite confermed,
> Such love is goodly forto have,
> Such love mai the bodi save,
> Such love mai the soule amende,
> The hyhe god such love ous sende
> Forthwith the remenant of grace;
> So that above in thilke place
> Wher resteth love and alle pes,
> Oure joie mai ben endeles.[20]

It is in the shadow of such a poem and against the fullness of its vision that we may best estimate the inevitability ascribed by the Reeve to his version of lechery and age. And it is in the shadow of the pilgrimage itself—Chaucer's governing image for *The Canterbury Tales* as a whole—that the Reeve's larger despair about human life may best be judged. For whether the figure of pilgrimage is understood in its literal sense, as it is at the poem's beginning (a group of pilgrims moving toward Canterbury Cathedral) or in its allegorical sense, as it is near the poem's end (a group of pilgrims moving toward eternity), the image is purposive and dynamic: it includes a sense of destination. One may meet one's own Infirmity and Age in the course of the journey—figure 106 shows Deguileville's pilgrim confronting that part of his life in the guise of two old crones—yet the teaching of Lady Grace Dieu, the efficacy of Prayers and Alms, and the comfort of Lady Misericord mitigate their terror, and see the pilgrim safely to his journey's end.[21]

The Reeve's image of human life as a tun of wine that Death taps at our birth claims to be similarly comprehensive, but it is expressive only of despair—it is an image that ends in depletion rather than completion, drawing no strength from any system of meaning larger than itself. Like the Reeve's prior image of fires that burn themselves out, leaving only coals and ashes, the emptied tun cannot express, to a medieval audience, all the possibilities of human life.[22] Even the tradition of *contemptus mundi*—the Christian tradition that comes nearest to the gloom and negativism of the Reeve—takes care not to be misunderstood on that score. The most famous text in that tradition, Pope Innocent III's *On the Misery of the Human Condition*, a work Chaucer once translated, begins by referring to the necessary counter-truth, which the author promises to provide in another book: "If your lordship approve it, I will henceforth, with Christ's favor, describe also the dignity of human nature; so that, as in the present work the proud man is brought low, in that the humble man will be exalted."[23] Chaucer's Monk, choosing as his theme *de casibus virorum illustrium*—a subject nearly as one-sided as *de contemptu mundi*—promises, for a similar reason, to narrate a saint's life as companion piece to those stories of men who fell from Fortune's favor: "I

106. The pilgrim meets Infirmity and Old Age. Flemish, ca. 1380–90. Note 21.

wol yow seyn the lyf of Seint Edward; / Or ellis, first, tragedies wol I
telle, / Of whiche I have an hundred in my celle" (VII. 1970).[24]

Chaucer does not deny the truth of the Reeve—indeed, his whole
art is invested in establishing the existential credibility of that speaker,
that voice. But he would deny, I think, the Reeve's version of the
truth. Because of its singular lacunae, the Reeve's prologue would
have been received by Chaucer's first audiences less as a tragic state-
ment of the human predicament than as ugly, self-indulgent poetry
of error. Anyone could have supplied his omissions, for the priorities
of truth that stand behind them bear the force of an entire civiliza-
tion. Harry Bailly does well to end it, even if his first reason for do-
ing so is the threat it poses to the pleasure of hearing tales along the
pilgrim way.

The Reeve is ordered to stop his "sermonyng," and, in a fashion
intrinsic to the man, he complies. We have already been told, in *The
General Prologue*, of the Reeve's skill at presenting the appearance of
submission and subordination while serving his own will unchecked,
and we discover that it is precisely in those terms that he agrees to
resume the game, to speak some "ribaudye" that will answer the
Miller in kind. On the surface of things, he keeps the bargain per-
fectly well: his tale, in its two central actions, is as ribald and comic as
any of its sources or analogues. But the laughter has a certain edge, a
darker side. The prologue with its gloom and despair remains part of
what we have heard in this voice—though Harry Bailly can stop it,
he cannot obliterate it from our minds—and, what is more, the "ser-
monyng" has not really ended. It goes underground, its expression
henceforth covered over and discreet. The Reeve will requite the
Host as well as the Miller in the way he plays the game.

As the two prologues have already made clear, the Reeve possesses
a comprehensive vision of corruption, whether in the workers on the
manor whose "sleighte and covyne" is an open book to him, or in
old men like himself, driven by envy and lust. The first 80 lines of his
tale derive their chief energy from the same moral vision. In telling
us that his story takes place in Trumpington and involves a miller and
his wife and daughter, the Reeve draws, as though in passing, a re-
markable anatomy of evil within an English village. Every detail is in
proper scale—local, quotidian, banal. Yet it steadily suggests the
moral universe of which it is part. We are shown, in the person of a
thieving miller with a monopoly on his craft, corruption among the
trades; there is nowhere else one can take one's grain, no alternative
to being cheated.[25] And we are shown viciousness in the village's so-
cial life, with the miller and his mate parading through it like two

characters from a moral play: Sir Anger, so to speak, and Lady Pride, the one all knives and daggers and glowering looks, the other scornful and insolent, dressed boldly in red, and demanding the salutation "dame."[26] (Their pride is very different from that punished in *The Miller's Tale*, for it is a matter of commission rather than omission: self-conscious, defiant, bullying, they think they are better than other people, whereas old John merely forgot at a crucial moment to wonder if he was.)

Above all, the Reeve sets out to show us corruption in the parish life of the Church. The first and ugliest sin in *The Reeve's Tale*, the sin that literally engenders other sin, is the proud lechery of the parson of the town, who fathered the miller's wife and who intends to make his granddaughter heir to all he has kept for himself of "hooly chirches good." In the rhetoric of the tale, the corrupt parson *becomes* Holy Church; he and his lineage are all that is to be known of it there. He has appropriated its wealth, and its blood, which ought to be the blood of Christ, descends (in a bitter pun) through his own loins. To Malyne and her mother, the sole and only too literal children of this Church, its whole treasury, here thought of as material wealth alone, is consecrated:

> For hooly chirches good moot been despended   (I.3983)
> On hooly chirches blood, that is descended.
> Therfore he wolde his hooly blood honoure,
> Though that he hooly chirche sholde devoure.

The last line is mysterious and terrible, for Holy Church resides ultimately in the souls of the faithful. It is the faithful he is willing to devour.

In sum, the parson's evil gives birth to the insupportable pride of the miller and his wife; it becomes an impediment to marriage for the daughter, twenty years old and still a spinster; and it is not without consequence (here only darkly suggested) for the congregation of Christ. Since Malyne's marriage dowry will not be negligible, the parson's purpose is "to bistowe hire hye / Into som worthy blood of auncetrye" (I.3981), which is to say, the gentry will be touched by it next, if his presumption flowers. Corruption starts at a center, here the pastoral life of the Church, and spreads. Langland described the phenomenon: "Right so out of holi chirche alle yueles spredeþ / There inparfit preesthode is, prechours and techeris."[27] Chaucer's Parson assesses the harm done by lecherous priests in a similar fashion: "For right as a free bole is ynough for al a toun, right so is a wikked preest corrupcioun ynough for al a parisshe, or for al a contree" (X.899). Sometimes he puts it even more simply: "if gold ruste, what shal iren do?" (I.500).

The eye that surveys this village scene is harsh, steady, and little prone to similitudes. In *The Miller's Tale*, as we have noted, a wealth of imagery is used to create a preferential view of the action, invoking sympathy, inviting delight. The few similes admitted here are, in contrast, ugly and degrading: a peacock's pride, an ape's behind, pigs in a poke, magpies and jays, stale water in ditches stinking to the skies. The Reeve prefers to call things by their simplest names, leaving no room for equivocation. None of the tale's possible sources or analogues offers anything like this vision of small-town evil, and only one of them has even a thieving miller. So far as we know, the setting has been invented by Chaucer for the Reeve—it has been found through his voice.

The scene-setting lacks, as did the Reeve's prologue, any corresponding vision of virtue or love or the life to come, but one registers those omissions less strongly here: the claims to truth made by fabliau are more modest and particular than those of moral homily. The Reeve pretends simply to describe for us some people in a town who will figure in a merry story. But the "naturalism" of this tale, its obsessive concern with literal fact, cannot be credited to the traditions of fabliau alone. It is rooted firmly in the Christian analysis of sin, especially as developed within the sacrament of penance, where a searching scrutiny of every individual life had long been enjoined upon both penitent and confessor. Every sin had to be recognized in its most precise particularity, if it were to be adequately repented and fully forgiven. The Reeve's "naturalism" owes at least as much to the heightened moral vision developed in response to that need as it does to the celebrated freedom of fabliau from the claims of social decorum and extrinsic meaning.

One can trace quite easily the separate influence of these two different ways of regarding human action and motive, for they account for relatively separate portions of the Reeve's narrative. Only at line 4002, with the introduction of the two clerks, does the action move into the language and mood of fabliau; only then do words like "play," "game," and "jape" become important. The clerks' decision to take the grain to the mill is "oonly for hire myrthe and revelrye" (I.4005)—a purpose as generic to fabliau as is the description of their character, "testif" and "lusty for to pleye" (I.4004). The combination will set off a train of events fully as outrageous as those of *The Miller's Tale*. But the opening 80-odd lines (there are only 403 in all) exist to communicate a sense of person and place with a richness of detail no French fabliau ever found necessary, and what is more, to register that sense in terms that derive from a specifically Christian understanding of the purposes of human life and community. Everything up to line 4002, for all its energy and comic detail, is "in ernest," a moral landscape with figures.

This then is one way in which the "sermonyng" of the prologue

invades the tale, one aspect of the continuity of voice that binds the
two together. I want to turn now to another such technique, more
easily passed over by readers not versed in the language of medieval
symbolism: the use of a narrative image that adroitly incorporates
moral truth of a scholastic kind into the very texture of the fabliau
action. It represents, I think, the Reeve's most hidden "sermonyng"—
his deepest continuing assertion of self-will within apparent obe-
dience to the ordinances of the Host, master of the pilgrims' game.

When the miller lets loose the clerks' horse, that horse is made the
subject of a fully developed, independent action, although the plot
requires no more than an occasion for the clerks' absence so the mil-
ler can steal their grain. We follow this horse in his wild running for a
very long time, in what becomes one of the richest "visual" events in
the tale:

> Out at the dore [the Miller] gooth ful pryvely,   (I.4057)
> Whan that he saugh his tyme, softely.
> He looketh up and doun til he hath founde
> The clerkes hors, ther as it stood ybounde
> Bihynde the mille, under a levesel;
> And to the hors he goth hym faire and wel;
> He strepeth of the brydel right anon.
> And whan the hors was laus, he gynneth gon
> Toward the fen, ther wilde mares renne,
> And forth with "wehee," thurgh thikke and thurgh thenne.
>
>   .   .   .
>
> The wyf cam lepynge inward with a ren.   (I.4079)
> She seyde, "Allas! youre hors goth to the fen
> With wilde mares, as faste as he may go.
> Unthank come on his hand that boond hym so,
> And he that bettre sholde han knyt the reyne!"
>
>   .   .   .
>
> Thise sely clerkes rennen up and doun   (I.4100)
> With "Keep! keep! stand! stand! jossa, warderere,
> Ga whistle thou, and I shal kepe hym heere!"
> But shortly, til that it was verray nyght,
> They koude nat, though they dide al hir myght,
> Hir capul cacche, he ran alwey so faste,
> Til in a dych they caughte hym atte laste.
>   Wery and weet, as beest is in the reyn,
> Comth sely John, and with him comth Aleyn.
>
>   .   .   .
>
> Thus pleyneth John as he gooth by the way   (I.4114)
> Toward the mille, and Bayard in his hond.

One of the actions for which this action becomes an emblem—the
miller's theft of a half-bushel of flour—takes place in the space indi-
cated by the second ellipsis above. Both actions are created with

107. Four horses (from a bestiary). English, second quarter of the thirteenth century. Note 28.

equal verisimilitude, and both are literally necessary to the story. But the first offers as well a moral commentary upon the other—and upon all the actions that will follow in its train.

Horses, whether they pull carts or bear kings, usually have no identity in art beyond their animal species, and figure 107, from an English bestiary, can represent for us the ordinary image of their kind.[28] They were as central to medieval and earlier civilizations as motor technology is to our own: essential to transportation, agriculture, and warfare, as well as to chivalric display and leisure. But they furnished in addition a central image through which man could imaginatively explore certain aspects of his own nature. Like the drowned horse being eaten by the raven in figure 108, a thirteenth-century miniature of Noah's Flood,[29] the horse in *The Reeve's Tale* is of a double kind, both literal and symbolic.

A great variety of sources—including Greek philosophy, Roman erotic poetry, late-classical textbooks in logic, Old Testament books of prophecy and wisdom, patristic exegesis, and countless medieval works in Latin and the vernaculars—all contributed to the range of symbolic meanings the horse had acquired in art and literature by this time. And almost all of them found equivalent expression in the visual arts, well into the late Renaissance: figure 109, for instance, a representation of Lechery (*Luxuria*) from Achille Bocchi's *Symbolicae quaestiones*, was engraved in 1574.[30] The documents are so numerous and their relationships so complex that a full history of the figure has never been written, and perhaps never can be. Certainly my goal in

108. The raven feeds on a horse (Noah's Flood). Paris, ca. 1250. Note 29.

these pages must be more modest. I shall do little more than suggest what seem to be the broad divisions of the subject, and then invite the reader to look with me at something of the variety of contexts, many of them visual, in which that image might have been known to Chaucer and his first audiences.

We may begin by noting that a verse from Psalm 31—"Do not become like the horse and the mule who have no understanding"— runs parallel in meaning to certain scholastic traditions centering upon the *Categories* of Aristotle. As a way of explaining the relationship of genus and species within the Aristotelian concept of substance, Porphyry's *Isagoge* (a third-century introduction to the *Categories* that became, in Boethius's translation, a standard university text throughout the Middle Ages) made a series of distinctions often expressed in diagrammatic form as the *arbor porphyriana*, or Porphyry's tree (see figure 110),[31] and in his explanation of those distinctions, Porphyry gave the horse special importance. Here is a concise seventeenth-century summary of the concept:*

Man is a Substance; but because an Angel is also a Substance; *That it may appear how Man differs from an Angel*, Substance ought to be divided into

─────────

*Figure 110 may be read by means of this summary, which describes the branches of the tree. One reads from top to bottom, from *Ens* ("Being") to *Substantia* ("Substance")—where our quotation begins—and so on, stopping at each branch along the way. At the very bottom, *Homo* ("Man") is subdivided into Peter and Paul, a final flourish owing nothing to Porphyry.

Corporeal and Incorporeal. A Man is a *Body*, an Angel *without a Body*: But a Stone also is a *Body*: That therefore a Man may be distinguished from a Stone, divide Bodily or Corporeal Substance into Animate and Inanimate, that is, *with or without a Soul*. Man is a Corporeal Substance Animate, Stone Inanimate. But Plants are also *Animate*: Let us divide therefore again Corporeal Substance Animate into *Feeling and void of Feeling*. Man feels, a Plant not: But a Horse *also feels*, and likewise other Beasts. Divide we therefore Animate Corporeal Feeling Substance into Rational and Irrational. Here therefore *are we to stand*, since it appears that every, and only Man *is Rational*.[32]

As Porphyry's own text puts it: "a man differs from a horse because of a specific difference, the quality rational," or "rational and irrational separate man and horse which are under the same genus, animal."[33]

This Porphyrian tradition in which the horse stands for all that is not rational or spiritual in man's nature is neither intrinsically nor exclusively negative. We might compare it to the patristic understanding of an exultant verse from the Old Testament (Exod. 15:1) concerning the destruction of Pharaoh's host in the crossing of the Red Sea: "the horse and the rider he hath thrown into the sea." This text necessarily concerns literal horses, horses in history; but its depiction in the visual arts (see figure 111) characteristically expresses the tradi-

109. Prudence controlling the horses of Lechery. Engraving, Achille Bocchi, *Symbolicae quaestiones*, CXVII (Italian, 1574). Note 30.

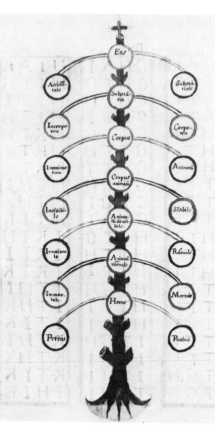

110. Porphyry's tree, German, first half of the seventeenth century. Note 31.

tional iconography of Pride as well—Pride shown as a man falling from his horse[34]—for as early as Philo Judaeus, in the first century, the horse in that text had been interpreted as a neutral figure for the human psyche. The horseman signifies the mind (*nous*); the horse is appetite or passion; and he who cannot control his horse is soon destroyed. (Philo, like Porphyry, may have had some knowledge of Plato's myth of the charioteer in the *Phaedrus*, 246–56, thus continuing the influence of a text unavailable to the Middle Ages directly.) The emphasis in Philo's commentary is on control, not denial or denunciation. Orthodox Christianity understood the flesh to be fallen through sin, but it could never wholly despise the body: God had fashioned it, Christ was born of it, man will be resurrected in it. And so in the dominant Christian tradition, the horse functions as a morally neutral sign. The Church Fathers often commented on the figure in this extended sense, as in these words of St. Gregory: "Indeed the horse is the body of any holy soul, which it knows how to restrain from illicit action with the bridle of continence and to release in the exercise of good works with the spur of charity," or in these from a fourteenth-century commentator on the Proverbs of Solomon, "Thus *moraliter* our flesh is the horse and the reason spirit is the rider."[35]

If we would discover such an idea among the works of imaginative literature known to Chaucer, we need look no further than the *Anti-claudianus* of Alain de Lille, its inspiration both Platonic and Christian. In that poem (written ca. 1181–84), the chariot Prudence rides into the heavens has been constructed by the Seven Liberal Arts, is pulled by five horses (the Outer Senses), and is driven by Reason. Figure 112, from a manuscript miscellany, illustrates the essential action, though unaccompanied by Alain's text.[36] An illumination from fourteenth-century Germany illustrating the *Concordantia caritatis* (figure 113) represents an allied tradition whose subject is the arming of *Anima* (the soul), mounted upon a horse labeled *Caro* (the flesh). Hope and Charity place a helmet upon *Anima*'s head, Perseverance hands her a spear, Faith proffers a shield, Continence holds the reins, and Abstinence adjusts the saddle. A crowd of retainers below— Love of God, Justice, Humility, Temperance, Patience, Love of Neighbor, Fortitude, and Prudence—tighten the cinch and examine

111. The drowning of Pharaoh's host. Paris, ca. 1250. Note 34.

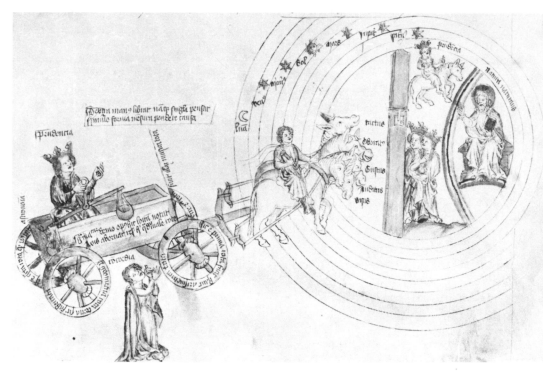

112. The chariot of Prudence. German, ca. 1420. Note 36.

113. The arming of the soul. German, mid-fourteenth century. Note 37.

114. *Ymago Prudencie*. Bavarian, 1424. Note 39.

the horse's shoes. The soul here puts on "the whole armour of God," and to her warfaring the horse (the human body) is an essential conveyance.[37] The picture could serve to illustrate almost as well a fourteenth-century English "Tretyse of Gostly Batayle" (Treatise of Spiritual Battle) long attributed to Richard Rolle, which likewise moralizes the various parts of a horse's gear and is careful to affirm both the necessity and potential dignity of all that the horse symbolizes.[38]

Figure 114, from the first quarter of the fifteenth century, exemplifies an ethical tradition, more limited in scope, that plays an important role in the literature of courtly loving (and can move us another step closer to Chaucer's use of the horse in *The Reeve's Tale*). It is an image of Prudence, shown as a man at a desk reading a book whose threefold text commands memory of the past, understanding of the present, and foresight concerning the future; he holds a horse by its bridle to indicate that prudence likewise requires control over one's carnal nature.[39]

When Chaucer's Criseyde explains to Troilus that she could not accept his offer of love service until she knew that his "resoun bridlede" his "delit" (*TC*, IV, 1678), she uses a figure that derives from this specifically moral tradition. The absence of the horse as explicit image elevates the tone and makes the metaphor more "dignified," but the

115. A lover presents his heart to his lady. Ivory mirror back, French, fourteenth century. Note 41.

expression depends on the full tradition for its sense.[40] Such language of the bridle is common in courtly love poetry as a means of "proving" that chaste erotic love—the so-called *fin amors*—is possible between men and women. In the visual arts, one often finds such imagery carved upon elegant articles intended for the use of ladies, especially the ivory mirror backs and writing-tablet covers made in fourteenth-century France and Germany. In figure 115, for instance, while a groomsman holds a pair of bridled horses and scourges them with a whip, a lover presents his heart to his lady and is crowned with a garland in return.[41] The horses and the attendant have no literal justification in a design so highly stylized (compare figure 87 of the present study, which shares the same theme). They are there to signify that these lovers are at once passionate (the horses) and chaste (the attendant, the reins and whip).

The *Troilus* not only uses several metaphors derived from this tradition, but includes very early in the poem Chaucer's only other horse to bear the name "Bayard."[42] The passage I refer to is explicitly psychological—it does not concern a literal horse at all—and it fills an entire stanza describing the love-stricken Troilus's new-found relation to the law of kind:

> As proude Bayard gynneth for to skippe   (*TC*, I, 218)
> Out of the weye, so pryketh hym his corn,
> Til he a lasshe have of the longe whippe;
> Than thynketh he, "Though I praunce al byforn
> First in the trays, ful fat and newe shorn,
> Yet am I but an hors, and horses lawe
> I moot endure, and with my feres drawe."

As Troilus looks upon Criseyde for the first time, all his former scorn of lovers is revealed as mere ignorance of self. He discovers the "horse" within.

In the fully moral tradition, the image of the bridle postulates man in control of his entire animal nature, of all his senses and their appetites. But in courtly contexts it furnishes most often a polite way of speaking of sexuality alone, and that may point us to a third aspect of horse imagery in the Middle Ages, which has its parallel in yet another verse from the Old Testament, describing the children of Israel in their fornications: "They are become as amorous horses and stallions: every one neighed after his neighbour's wife" (Jer. 5:8). For the horse is frequently associated with sexual prowess and freedom, in ways that may be seen at their most neutral in the "naturalist" data of the medieval encyclopedist (here Bartholomaeus, citing Aristotle): "And whanne þe hors bigynneþ to gendre þanne here voice is grettere, and so fareþ þe mares also and loueþ þe werk of generacioun more þan oþere bestes."[43] When William Langland, for instance, writes of false beggars in *Piers Plowman*, he castigates their lechery as a signal part of the evil of their lives (italics added):

> For þei lyue in no loue ne no lawe holde.
> Thei wedde no womman þat þei wiþ deele
> But *as wilde bestes with wehee* worþen vppe and werchen,
> And bryngen forþ barnes þat bastardes men calleþ.[44]

There is no ambivalence in this passage; the focus is upon the prohibited and ugly, with men copulating like horses, rearing up (the verb carries a sexual pun) and whinnying "weehee."

Several secular texts from the twelfth and thirteenth centuries, however, employ the figure in a morally ambiguous way. It is likely that Andreas Capellanus's so-called *Art of Courtly Love* (*De arte honeste amandi*) is finally of this unresolved kind,[45] as is perhaps the use of the horse in *The Romance of the Rose*, where the Old Woman (*La Vieille*) describes the natural desire of men and women for each other in an extended image invoking stallions and mares, and where Genius, speaking in praise of copulation, advises that we imitate our parents: "If it weren't for their chivalry [*chevalerie*, "horsemanship"], you would not be alive now." (He argues, we note, on behalf of a courtship not intended to lead to marriage.)[46] In the borders of one manuscript of this poem, a horse is shown walking away from a man copulating with a nun in the grass (figure 116), but whether the painter intended the beast as a clarification or a condemnation, it would be hard to say.[47] (The borders of this manuscript include many witty obscenities.)

If on this matter as on many others, these long, difficult, and obliquely scholastic works seem able to rest in ambivalence and

116. A horse walks away from a man copulating with a nun. French, fourteenth century. Note 47.

grand internal contradictions, other medieval texts deploy the horse in a manner as free of moral meaning as did Ovid in his *Art of Love*.[48] Consider, for instance, this lyric by the Provençal poet Guillaume d'Aquitaine (1071–1127), describing his vexed good fortune in being loved by two women:

> I have two splendid horses, and can mount either;
> Each has its points, each is a marvellous charger—
> And yet I cannot keep both, for they can't stand each other!
> If only I could tame them, as was my plan,
> I'd never change my battle equipment then,
> For I'd have better riding than any other man!

He concludes by addressing an audience of *cavallieri* like himself:

> Noble riders, resolve my predicament:
> Never has a choice caused such embarrassment—
> I don't know which to keep now—Agnes, or Ermensent![49]

The poem could be descended directly from Ovid, so distant is it from Christian moral concerns, but its figural language had been kept alive across the intervening centuries almost exclusively by moral uses. In one last witty text I wish to consider before returning to *The Reeve's Tale*—Henri d'Andeli's *Lay of Aristotle*, written in 1220, and perhaps the most brilliant of all French fabliaux—that distance is both real and not real. As in Chaucer's tale, a residue or echo of moral meaning remains.

In Henri's story, the young Alexander the Great, already the conqueror of many kingdoms, is himself conquered by love for Phyllis, a beautiful palace courtesan. For this, he is berated by his tutor, the philosopher Aristotle, who says to him, "Sire, . . . I believe that you are quite blind and that you could be led to pasture with the other dumb beasts. Your mind must be deranged if for some strange girl you have so utterly changed that one can find no vestige of reason in you." Phyllis and Alexander decide to teach the old tutor a lesson in return. When Aristotle falls victim to her seductive charms, she agrees to make love to him—if he will just grant her one little favor. "I have been seized with a great desire," she tells him, "to ride astride you over the grass in this garden. And I want you to wear a saddle, for so I shall ride more respectably." She rides him thus, triumphantly, as Alexander steps from his hiding place to confront the philosopher and make him admit the power that love and desire hold over us all. The image of Phyllis riding Aristotle is one of the most popular secular images in all of medieval art; it is to be found in manuscript margins, stone and wood carvings, tapestries, ivories, woodcuts, engravings. I choose to represent it carved upon a fourteenth-century ivory casket, French in origin (figure 117), which shows (at left) Alexander being taught by Aristotle from a book, and in the next panel, the philosopher being ridden as a horse, bridle in mouth and whip at flank, while Alexander, looking down from a high tower, prepares to throw a flower to make his presence known. The story could only have been invented by a learned man—Henri d'Andeli was an ecclesiastic, and a writer of some importance—and the full refinement of its wit requires a moderately learned audience in turn. For it does not, as scholars have tended to say, offer a figure of female domination only, though that is part of its subject. The joke ultimately turns upon the tradition of representing man's flesh and reason as a horse and rider, inverting that image here (sensuality rides reason) to tell a merry, accommodating fabliau truth. Henri concludes with a moralization that is tolerant and utterly lacking in didacticism: "Thus did Love constrain him and carnal desire, which has power over every man and woman. So it seems to me that the tutor was not guilty of any offense, for he did not do wrong by reason of his learning, but because of Nature, true and absolute."[50] Henri's art depends upon the moral tradition for its full effect, but it is not used to make a statement intrinsic to that tradition. It limits itself to fabliau, and is communicated in a voice genial and amused.

We are dealing then with a tradition whose beginning antedates Chaucer by many centuries, which was fed by many sources, and which was widely known throughout the Middle Ages. Not all of this material—not even the small part represented here—is directly relevant to Chaucer's *Reeve's Tale*. But it is all part of the figure's authority, and amounts to evidence that some part of a medieval audience would have been quick to detect emblematic significance in a runaway horse, in contexts both secular and religious. By surveying the tradition at large, I have attempted to represent fairly, and without oversimplification, a range of contextual meaning—not equivalences merely, but attitudes toward those equivalences—historically

117. Phyllis rides Aristotle. Ivory casket panel (detail), French, fourteenth century. Note 50.

associated with the figure, for somewhere within that range we must seek to understand what Chaucer has made of the horse that brings the grain from Soler Hall.

In the first half of the tale, the horse runs free, following the wild mares, while the miller grinds and steals, the wife bakes, and the clerks run up and down chasing their "capul," to end as wet and weary as he. Nightfall, however, brings a quick, circumstantial transition. Having outwitted the clerks with such easy, throwaway skill, the miller permits himself a generous condescension: since they can't return to the college that evening, but have money to pay for bed and board, his small room will serve to feast and lodge them all. As the miller simultaneously celebrates himself and dismisses them from his further attention, a second fabliau action begins, offering a swift calculus of sexual appetite and random probability: three beds, five per-

sons, one cradle; some changes to be rung. Two fifteenth-century il-
lustrations to Boccaccio's version of this story can reveal the energies
implicit in the design. The first of these (figure 118) by a visual con-
vention substitutes an open room for the narrow darkness in which
the Reeve's characters seek, grope, and find; and it shows the miller
and his wife twice within the same picture space, simultaneously
standing to one side and asleep in the bed on the right. But it suggests
well the potential volatility of this arrangement of persons and places,
for to fill any bed (the clerk is already sleeping with the daughter) is to
leave another half-empty, and that new space, like a vacuum, pulls
into itself some other person in turn, until a whole series of combi-
nations and couplings has been explored. Figure 119 sets the scene
in motion, focusing upon action rather than situation.[51] In fabliau,
proximity is destiny.

It is the image of the horse running wild in the fen, however, that
ultimately joins the two halves of the tale, for Chaucer makes us see
the revenge in its terms. Through metaphoric language that recalls it
to our minds as a literal event, other actions become associated with
it, and take on meanings that go beyond the traditional limits of
fabliau. By way of preface, Chaucer has the miller himself bind the
clerks' horse so that "it sholde namoore go loos" (1.4138)—an action

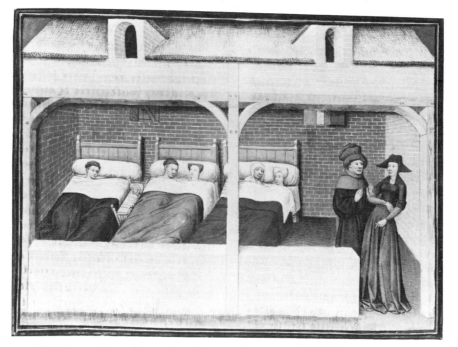

118. The Boccaccio analogue. French, second quarter of the fifteenth century.
Note 51.

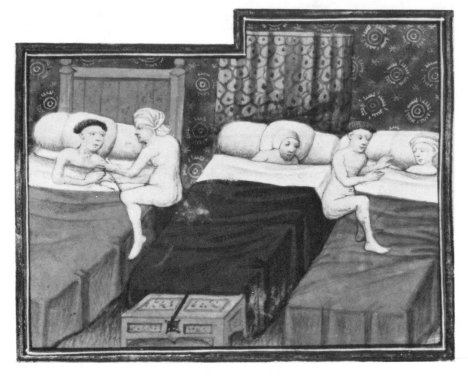

119. The Boccaccio analogue. French, ca. 1430. Note 51.

emblematic of his present complacency. He thinks, as the revenge action begins, that he has their Bayard safely under control.

The first in the series of actions that will be viewed in terms of horse imagery is the noisy sleeping of the miller and his family. In his drunkenness, the miller snores—or snorts—like a horse:

> This millere hath so wisely bibbed ale   (1.4162)
> That as an hors he fnorteth in his sleep,
> Ne of his tayl bihynde he took no keep.
> His wyf bar hym a burdon, a ful strong;
> Men myghte hir rowtyng heere two furlong;
> The wenche rowteth eek, *par compaignye.*

It is, in every possible sense, a carnal music—indeed, a snoring monk was once rebuked by St. Bernard for sleeping "according to the flesh"[52]—and the clerks are quick to term it "compline," the Church's night song as sung in the miller's house. In the course of that droning office, they are quick to take note of the horse's tail that this deep sleep has left vulnerable—the tails of his wife and daughter.* John's

---

*There is comparable punning at the end of *The Shipman's Tale* (VII.416–17): "I am youre wyf; score it upon my taille, / And I shal paye as soone as ever I may."

love making becomes itself a kind of horsemanship through punning language drawing on the same image: "he priketh harde and depe as he were mad" (1.4231). After a day spent trying to regain control of the runaway college horse, the clerks now let their own libidinous horses run free in the bedroom darkness—ending as weary and exhausted, having "swonken al the longe nyght" (1.4235), as they had been after their daylong chase of Bayard before.

But theirs are not the only horses (so to speak) now set free and running. In an action metaphorically parallel to Symkyn's untying of the college horse, Symkyn's wife is temporarily released from the confines of her marriage—no man has hitherto dared "rage or ones pleye" (1.3958) with the wife of a market bully so viciously armed with knives—and from the tedium of that marriage as well: "So myrie a fit ne hadde she nat ful yoore" (1.4230). The daughter too—unwed at twenty because of the family's preposterous pride—is at long last released from an oppressive chastity; she runs in those libidinous pastures freely and with joy. For both women, drink has loosened the bridles, but it is the clerks who slip them off and ride; it little matters whom. Gower had used a similar image in the *Confessio amantis* to describe people who wed within forbidden degrees of kinship, saying that such love is

> Bot as a cock among the Hennes,
> Or as a Stalon in the Fennes,
> Which goth amonges al the Stod,   [*stod*: breeding mares]
> Riht so can he nomore good,
> Bot takth what thing comth next to honde.[53]

In every sense except the symbolic, the events in the miller's bedroom darkness are similarly random and anarchic.

I do not mean to suggest the clerks are so witty as to shape consciously their revenge "horse for horse." But one of the pleasures in store for the reader as he reflects upon the tale is the realization that what is unloosed in the room, through drink and darkness, contiguity and error, is precisely the forces in man that the horse figure has traditionally symbolized in medieval art and thought.[54] And remembering that the horse is a way of talking about all of man's appetites and passions, not lechery alone, the reader finds himself thinking about the earlier action as well—the pride of Symkyn and his wife, the outrageous thievery, the drunken feasting—as well as about the violence in which the story ends. All represent passions and appetites indulged without restraint or measure. At the end of the tale, the wife and daughter are returned to the miller's control, reclaimed from their wild running, and he, like the clerks at the end of the tale's first action, is a slightly wiser man than before. All the "keepers" learn something, but only the clerks go off scot-free—

a bloody nose excepted—with horse and flour and cake, to say nothing of stories for the boys at Soler Hall. They don't even pay the cost of their supper. The horse links the two plots, the stealing and the swyving, just as surely as the cry "Water! water!" brings together the Flood trick and the arse kiss in *The Miller's Tale*. But the expressive purpose of the link is very different. It is used to characterize the Reeve, as well as forward the story he tells.

Though few of Chaucer's narratives are surrounded by so many possible literary sources or close analogues, in none of them does a horse function in the manner of Bayard in this tale.[55] There is no horse at all in Jean Bodel's *De Gombert et des II clers*, written ca. 1194, nor any horse that matters in the two German analogues from the thirteenth century. In Boccaccio's version (*Decameron*, IX, 6), the young men ride up on horses in order to pass themselves off as travelers, for without that excuse they could not plausibly lodge at a (sometime) guest house whose owner's daughter one of them has long desired. Their horses are not freed, nor does the story take note of them again. Only in the version known as *Le Meunier et les II clers* does a horse actually figure in the action. Its miller hides the mare and the grain in his barn, tells the clerks their horse has strayed, and causes them to spend the day searching for her in the woods. In a similar fashion he locks up his daughter in a bed-cupboard each evening, to protect her chastity against her generous and agreeable nature. Though the parallel enclosure of mare and daughter is not developed further, it may have suggested to Chaucer (if this was indeed the version he knew) the possibility of developing the role of the horse in a symbolic as well as literal way. But the exact invention—a horse running in the fens with wild mares—would seem to be Chaucer's own, as is most surely the brilliance with which it is made to function in the story.

Perhaps better than anyone else, Charles Muscatine has taken the measure of fabliau as a genre, writing (in *Chaucer and the French Tradition*): "The peculiar strength of the naturalistic style is, as we should expect, also a limitation. It is a style adjusted to a particular cosmos. Behind the comedy and the caricature there is a spirit of intense practicality, a myopic circumscription of the attention to clock time and local space, a reckoning with tangible force, concrete motive, physical peculiarity. It is a style designed to evoke a naturalistic, material world, and little more."[56] In *The Reeve's Tale*, Chaucer draws upon that tradition for some of its characteristic strengths—narrative speed, a functional spareness of detail, concentration on event—but only after anatomizing a village setting for its evil, and in the course of uncovering at the center of the action a hieratic moral image that illuminates, in ways uncharacteristic of fabliau, both the larger action and the character of its teller. We have moved from the Miller's world of the colt to the Reeve's world of the horse, and although both concern the "animal" in man, the Reeve registers it in harsher and more scholastic ways. The apples laid up in hay, sweet like Alisoun, have become medlar fruit, their ripeness coterminous with rot. The laughter lacks a little in terms of joy, the narrative image its full authority and traditional purpose. It serves only as a means of clarification—a half-muted revelation of what lies behind the action. It invokes no world of alternative human possibilities.

The Reeve does not let himself, or humankind, off lightly. In the prologue, he offers his own life as proof of the wretchedness of old age and the perverse longevity of sexual desire, and in two of the expressions he uses there—"Gras tyme is doon" and "a coltes tooth"—associates himself with all that the horse will come to stand for in the tale: avarice, gluttony, vengefulness, pride, fornication. He is his own first subject: in the prologue obviously, but also in the tale itself, where several of the characters seem clear projections of his own self-knowledge and embittered self-regard. It earns the college manciple, for instance, a sympathetic portrait (he is smart enough to keep the miller's thievery within reasonable bounds), for a manciple is to a college what a reeve is to a manorial estate. On the other hand, the portrait of the college warden (a learned man unable to do more than chide and fuss) betrays a condescension parallel to the Reeve's implicit scorn for his own lord, whom (*The General Prologue* has told us) he cheats with consummate ease.

For reasons concerning his own station in life, the Reeve likewise identifies with the miller against the clerks—just as long as the miller is more cunning than they. He shares with the miller a revenge formula ("blere hir ye")[57] and a common dislike of the clerks' bumptious self-confidence and educational privilege. He makes them, in terms of class and origin, conspicuously no better than himself, or perhaps a little worse. Their dialect is more "north country" than his, their wit less quick, and their favored "auctoritee" little more than folk proverb, wisdom of a kind no one ever had to go to university to learn. Indeed, the Reeve's discourse in his prologue is far more learned than anything we ever hear from their lips.[58] The Reeve likes these scholars little—until the miller overextends himself and relaxes his guard. At that point the Reeve's sympathies abruptly shift, and he makes common cause with the students in their revenge, until at the end, in a final gesture of characteristic disdain, all the characters are reduced to one level and held at one distance, like pigs in a poke, fighting in darkness.

The first and most mordant of the Reeve's self-portraits in the tale, however, remains to be accounted for. In the town parson's thefts from the Lord of Holy Church, the Reeve describes a pattern of stealing—secretive, hidden beneath the forms of service—that is the very pattern of his own relationship to the lord on whose manor he serves. Both the Reeve and his tale's parson are in charge of their "lordes sheep," the one literally, the other figuratively; both hold that charge "by covenant" and must give reckoning; and both cheat along the way, the Reeve as vigorously as the parson in his fiction: "Ful riche he was astored pryvely" (1.609). In creating the Reeve, Chaucer no doubt drew upon his own experience of such men, as well as upon the characteristic way they are portrayed (along with bailiffs and other officers of great lords) in the sermon and complaint litera-ture of the period.[59] But he did one greater thing besides: he took an available story and made it express a specific reeve's temperament in its own singular and subtle nuance. The effect is of a narrator finding his whole subject within himself—a narrator who is at once first cause and epitome of his tale.

It was never Chaucer's purpose to create for his pilgrims literal "voices" of the kind we now capture so easily with tape recorder or in stenographic transcription. He worked instead with a set of con-ventions designed to communicate the idea of a voice, and he doubt-less thought the role of art to be precisely the achievement of that more difficult thing, expecting his audience to construct in turn its sense of a pilgrim from the clues thus offered, clues that include (in the most highly developed instances) a *General Prologue* portrait, a self-portrait, and a narrative act.

The extent to which Chaucer explores the idea of a teller through the shaping of his tale therefore varies greatly, from pilgrim to pil-grim. The aesthetic of *The Canterbury Tales* is predicated at all levels upon articulation, variety, and degree, for Chaucer knew that just as a few spices will flavor a whole stew, so too a few such grandly elab-orate dishes will grace a whole feast, and make the simpler dishes welcome in their turn. In only the most complex performances is story filtered through a highly individualized sensibility; and to such performances a richly developed personal prologue furnishes the es-sential clue—whether the evidence offered by that prologue be chiefly stylistic, as in the case of the Prioress, or stylistic and auto-biographical together, as in the case of the Wife of Bath, the Par-doner, the Canon's Yeoman, and our present subject, the Reeve.

The Reeve's concluding moralization offers indeed a proof text in this matter. In most fabliaux it would give one little pause, but here it takes on a special force in the way it brings forward, one final time, a certain pattern of thought and sensibility one has noticed throughout the prologue and tale. After a narrative that has included the spiritual darkness of sin and the literal darkness of a small room in which no one knows for certain who pleasures or pummels whom, the Reeve can only conclude, in a fashion implicitly dismissive of Christ's vi-sion of a better kind of human living, "Hym thar nat wene wel that

yvele dooth" and "A gylour shal hymself bigyled be" (I.4320–21).
The Old Law stands affirmed, with human action locked in an end-
less cycle of aggression and counter-aggression, from which no
progress is possible. Christian schema and native wit together give
Chaucer's Reeve a fierce insight into human behavior, but it is per-
ception without purpose or future: it is not on the side of life. Like
the envious man anatomized in the *Somme le roi*, his heart and mouth
are envenomed—he is the basilisk whose glance withers everything
green that stands before it, grass and bush and tree.⁶⁰ The Reeve can
neither forgive himself for his life, nor imagine altering it. Like wine
from a barrel, it simply runs out.

Unpleasant men can tell good stories, can even tell, if required,
stories that amuse and elicit laughter. If I have spent little space at-
tempting to recreate the comic surfaces of *The Reeve's Tale*, it is be-
cause they communicate vigorously still, and because I have wanted
to get at something that lies just beneath. Among the many possible
kinds of laughter, and the many sorts of stance a comic artist may
take, we have been examining the highly specified kind Chaucer at-
tributes to his Reeve: the merriness of an unmerry man, the ob-
sessively moral vision of a man whose own life is not good. The
Reeve's art is scornful of his immediate audience, of his fellow Chris-
tians at large, and finally, for all his bitter self-sufficiency, of himself.
Like all the other narrators in this opening sequence of tales, the
Reeve concludes with a formulaic blessing on the pilgrim company:

> "And God, that sitteth heighe in magestee,   (I.4322)
> Save al this compaignye, grete and smale!"

But he alone cannot quite bring himself to end there. One last tribute
must be paid to revenge, one small further meanness of spirit find
expression:

> "Thus have I quyt the Millere in my tale."   (I.4324)

At the end of *The Miller's Tale*, we remember,

> Diverse folk diversely they seyde,   (I.3857)
> But for the moore part they loughe and pleyde,

but at the end of the Reeve's story, we are made to focus upon one
member of the audience alone:

> The Cook of Londoun, whil the Reve spak,   (I.4325)
> For joye him thoughte he clawed him on the bak.
> "Ha! ha!" quod he, "for Cristes passion,
> This millere hadde a sharp conclusion."

A work of art "creates" its audience by asking from it certain kinds of
response, and here, exemplifying that fact, we are shown the Cook

almost beside himself with pleasure at this comedy of gullibility, greed, strict justice, and exact revenge. The response seems out of control and uncomfortably singular, but it is entirely consonant with the Reeve's vision of human life. In place of the Miller's company as a whole—relaxed, amused, interested in the tale and in each other— the Reeve's art finds its definitive audience in Roger the Cook,* eliciting from him an oath by Christ's passion and a large but ungenerous joy.

*On the character of the Cook I shall have much to say in Chapter VI; figures 120 and 126 reproduce his Ellesmere and Cambridge portraits respectively.

VI. *The Cook's Tale* and *The Man of Law's Introduction*

CROSSING THE HENGWRT/ELLESMERE GAP

STUDY OF *The Canterbury Tales* that focuses upon the work's opening sequence—the tales that begin the journey—might properly be expected to end with this chapter; to end, indeed, with the first half of this chapter. *The Cook's Tale* breaks off after a mere 58 lines, at which point, as all modern editions make clear, the first stretch of "finished" road to Canterbury comes abruptly to an end.

There are two major reasons for accepting this description of the work's opening design. Fragment I, so distinguished, presents a sequence of tales introduced by a *General Prologue* and made fully ready for publication, whether in manuscript folio or to a listening audience, marred only by *The Cook's Tale*'s unscheduled termination. Fragment II, which comprises *The Man of Law's Introduction*, *Prologue*, *Tale* and *Endlink*, follows in all the best manuscripts,[1] but is, in contrast, a patchwork of uncertain intentions, imperfect cancellations,[2] significant discrepancies, and substantively variant manuscript readings. Certain lines in its *Introduction*, moreover, are commonly read as beginning the narratives of a second day.[3]

The prospect before us is, in one sense, disheartening. We cannot hope to finish what Chaucer left incomplete, or to resolve the problems he had not yet solved. But *The Man of Law's Tale* on its own stands free of those limitations, and forces us to confront both *The Cook's Tale* in its incompletion and *The Man of Law's Introduction* in its lack of a final revision. For all their problems, these two brief pieces stand between finished tales of such power—the Reeve's and the Man of Law's—that to them some attention must be paid, however speculative and provisional in kind.

Certain questions inevitably arise. What sort of narrator did Chaucer intend the Cook to be? What sort of tale did he intend for him to tell? What formal and ethical relationship might such an intention bear to *The Man of Law's Tale*, which follows? And why did Chaucer invent an attack upon his own poetic oeuvre in *The Man of Law's In-*

troduction? To some of these questions no real answer can be given; a survey of the possibilities and probabilities must suffice. Elsewhere a bolder response seems possible. In every case, I hope to extend the range of available speculation, or to return an answer at least in some part new. But my largest argument will extend over three chapters, for I wish to suggest that *The Man of Law's Tale* is integral to the opening design.

Although *The Cook's Tale* contains no narrative image as such for us to focus upon—the fragment is too brief to yield anything at once central to the narrative and iconographic in its import—pictures can serve us here in a different fashion, as a means of defining the voice and ethos of the tale. Two of the surviving Cook portraits, in particular, can help us think to good purpose about the sort of pilgrim-narrator Chaucer had in mind.

The more famous of them, the Ellesmere portrait of the Cook, is notable for its vigor and vulgarity (figure 120);[4] in emphasizing the sore on his shin—"But greet harm was it, as it thoughte me, / That on his shyne a mormal hadde he" (1.385)—it is also repellent in some of its detail. The red pustules and filthy bandage shown on his leg (more vivid by far in the manuscript's painted color) are not only repugnant in their own right, but would have suggested to at least some of Chaucer's contemporaries the style of life that, according to medieval medicine, fostered the disease: "uncleanly personal habits, such as lack of frequent bathing and the continuous wearing of soiled clothes, . . . the eating of melancholic foods and the drinking of strong wines, and . . . disgraceful association with diseased and filthy women."[5] The sore on the Cook's leg, like the coarseness of his visage, is certainly intended as a sign of his inner condition.

Such a portrait prepares us well for the quarrel that will spring up between the Cook and the Manciple in Fragment IX, when the Cook is so stupefied with drink he cannot reply to the Host's request for a tale, defend himself against the Manciple's verbal attack, or pick himself up after he has fallen, in impotent anger, from his horse. Such a portrait is consonant too with Harry Bailly's attack upon him as a vendor of pies and roast geese in his cookshop in London:[6]

> "Now telle on, Roger, looke that it be good;   (1.4345)
> For many a pastee hastow laten blood,
> And many a Jakke of Dovere hastow soold
> That hath been twies hoot and twies coold.
> Of many a pilgrym hastow Cristes curs,
> For of thy percely yet they fare the wors,
> That they han eten with thy stubbel goos;
> For in thy shoppe is many a flye loos."

120. The Cook (Ellesmere MS.). English, ca. 1400–1410. Note 4.

The Ellesmere artist portrays a man fully capable of offering his customers meat pies grown stale, scrawny goose, and fly-blown parsley. He looks, moreover, like the sort of man modern scholarship has discovered his real-life prototype (or witty referent) to have been—the "Roger of Ware of London, Cook," who twice figures in pleas of debt (the first dated 1377) and who pleaded guilty (as noted in the Ward Presentments of the city) to the charge of being a common "nightwalker," one who habitually wandered about the streets after curfew, in defiance of the law and in pursuit of illicit pleasure or gain. In an ordinance of 1340, "nightwalkers" are linked with thieves and keepers of bawdy houses as birds of a common feather.[7]

To whatever extent these charges may be appropriate to our reading of Chaucer's text, the Ellesmere portrait perfectly embodies them; and such a reading of Chaucer's Cook has become an unquestioned commonplace in Chaucer criticism. We think about him and the tale he begins in relation to these facts alone, discounting the "play and game" nature of the narrative contest through which we get to know him, and giving privileged status from the very beginning to his disgraceful appearance in *The Manciple's Prologue* just one tale before the Parson's somber close. As the Manciple puts it, "What eyleth thee to slepe by the morwe? / Hastow had fleen al nyght, or artow dronke? / Or hastow with som quene al nyght yswonke, / So

121. Portrait of a cook. Misericord, Kent, Minster-in-Thanet, ca. 1410. Note 8.

that thow mayst nat holden up thyn heed?" (IX.16). Though the Cook of Fragment I and the Cook of Fragment IX are clearly not contemporaneous creations—are not even a continuous creation *— it is in the light of that later appearance that we most appropriately search medical texts for information on the pathogenesis of "mormals" and most confidently infer the Host's expectations in Fragment I when he asks the Cook to tell the next tale.

Though I shall shortly call attention to certain aspects of the Cook's portrait and narrative voice that have gone unmentioned so far, I do so without wishing to deny or discredit any of the material brought forward above. It has its relevance. Indeed, the medieval visual arts offer ways of extending such an interpretation a pejorative degree or two further, should one wish to do so. A misericord seat from Minster-in-Thanet, Kent (figure 121), made ca. 1410,[8] for instance, shows a heavily bearded fellow, large of head and bony of brow, stirring vigorously in an iron pot and holding a basting ladle and an oven peel. The carving presents a figure wholly carnal in its energies and self-absorption, with two swans, perhaps destined for roasting, flanking him on either side.

Because cooks practice their craft above a fire and often serve (in

---

*In Fragment IX, the Host calls on the Cook to tell a tale without any suggestion that he has previously begun one; no other pilgrim receives a second invitation. If, as seems likely, Fragment IX was composed later than Fragment I—it is part of a final sequence every bit as carefully worked as the opening series of tales—then this must mean that Chaucer intended to cancel the Cook's fragment as we have it (and perhaps lighten his task as well, by having the Cook prove incapable of telling a tale). Because of these discrepancies, I think we would do best to read the Cook's two appearances as essentially independent of each other, interpreting each in terms of its immediate context. Since both derive from *The General Prologue* portrait, they have, of course, some things in common. But certain aspects of the Cook in Fragment I that I shall examine above go unexplored in Fragment IX, for the real subject of Fragment IX (never lost sight of) is the Manciple and his tale about ill-advised speech. The needs of that tale determine the Cook's characterization there.

omus ifrael fperauit in domino:
diutor corum + protector corum eft.
omus aaron fperauit in domino:
diutor corum + protector corum eft.
ui timent dominum fperauerunt

122. Kitchen scenes (from
the Luttrell Psalter).
English, ca. 1340. Note 10.

the medieval analysis of sin) the closely allied appetites of gluttony and lechery,[9] they are often depicted as corpulent ministers-to-the-body at work in a hot place, in an iconography that elsewhere takes on an explicitly demonic cast. The instruments of their craft—the boiling caldron and ladle, the fleshhook and flashing knives, as shown, for instance, in the borders of the Luttrell Psalter (figure 122)[10]—provide some of the furnishings most common in medieval imaginings of the tortures of hell. Figure 123, from a Paris manuscript of about 1400, shows devils boiling the damned in caldrons, poking at them with fleshhooks, basting them on spits over beds of burning coals, and opening up a carcass with a knife, as Satan gorges himself upon sinners at hell's center.[11] The cities of Chester and Beverley, indeed, charged their Cooks' guilds with staging Christ's Harrowing of Hell in the local drama cycle,[12] presumably because of the witty likeness between certain torments of hell and the ordinary enterprises of a large medieval kitchen.

Though the implement is not specified by Chaucer's text, the Ellesmere portrait of the Cook places a fleshhook in his left hand. Used especially to draw quarters of pork or beef out of pots cooking on the open fire, it offered the manuscript painter a ready way of identifying the cook's métier. But there is something sinister about it as well. In *Inferno* XXI and XXII, Dante describes the barrators—those who buy and sell public office—as being boiled in pitch and tended by devils with fleshhooks, who use them, he says, just as cooks' helpers do, poking the meat down into the caldron so that it does not float. (The punishment is illustrated in figure 124.)[13] Chaucer's Summoner evokes the tortures of hell in similar terms: "Ful hard it is with flesshhook or with oules / To been yclawed, or to brenne and bake" (III.1730). Elsewhere in medieval art, devils use such hooks to catch unwary souls while they are still on earth—as in the Holkham Bible Picture Book's scene preceding the Annunciation, in which Satan argues with Christ the terms of his dominion over sinners. Satan is

123. Demons torture the damned in hell. Paris, ca. 1400. Note 11.

124. Barrators punished in hell. Florentine, ca. 1390–1400. Note 13.

shown with a pack of them on his back and a fleshhook dangling from his arm (figure 125).[14] In figure 158 of the following chapter, a devil captures a sinner's soul by just such means.

There is, to be sure, an enormous iconographic distance between the merely carnal cooks of the Kentish misericord or the Ellesmere manuscript and these minions of hell with their kitchen accoutrements. But they are images on the same tonal spectrum. If Chaucer's Cook were to be understood solely in terms of his appearance in *The Manciple's Prologue*, little further comment on his character would be necessary. The Manciple attacks him as though he were a personification of gluttony itself, and the Cook in his own actions at that point—drunken, slovenly, incoherent—may reasonably be said to represent the human soul at something like its most bestial and debased, all spiritual light extinguished. This aspect of the Cook's personality is not absent from the tale he begins to tell, but there is more to him than this, and on its own it cannot account for his full narrative voice.

For "Hogge of Ware," the pilgrim Cook, is of course no literal devil, no singular personification of a vice. He joins the company as a Cook of London, and that part of his nature—the part chiefly noted in *The General Prologue*—is better represented by his portrait in the Cambridge MS. (figure 126) than by its Ellesmere equivalent.[15] Even here his face hints at energies and appetites of a troubling kind—the portrait is, for its time, remarkably individual—yet everything else about him suggests a significantly higher economic and social status. Instead of Ellesmere's fleshhook, soiled apron, torn slippers, and bandaged shin—the livery, one might say, of labor and poverty and disease—we are shown a comfortable, middle-class citizen on a highly decorated saddle, with covered legs (no mormal showing) and spurs upon his feet; he bears a short sword in an elaborate scabbard. His full-length gown is colored mauve and edged with brown fur at neck and sleeves, implying a lining of the same, and on his head he wears a draped green chaperon, curiously embroidered. He holds in his hand a well-turned whip-and-goad. Margaret Rickert, who made a special study of the illuminated manuscripts of *The Canterbury*

125. Disputation between Christ and Satan. English, ca. 1320–30. Note 14.

126. The Cook (Cambridge MS.). English, midfifteenth century. Note 15.

Tales, thought this picture in comparison to its Ellesmere equivalent a poor piece of work: its artist, she wrote, "neither follows the text nor shows any sign of realizing what manner of man he was supposed to represent."[16]

But a cavalier disregard for the text is not characteristic of the Cambridge portraits: indeed, they are sometimes more fully responsive to its detail than are their Ellesmere predecessors.[17] The Cambridge illuminator simply gave priority to other aspects of the Cook than those that were most to interest Rickert, and with her most critics after.

We might remark, first of all, the picture's suitability as an illustration to *The Cook's Prologue and Tale*, when the Cook of *The Manciple's Prologue* is a creature we have yet to meet—a creature, indeed, whom Chaucer may not have even yet imagined. It offers a highly plausible image of the skilled professional described earlier in *The General Prologue*, a cook who has been hired by five London guildsmen—a haberdasher, a carpenter, a weaver, a dyer, and a tapestry maker, all prosperous folk dressed in the livery of a common religious fraternity—to accompany them on their journey and see to the standard of their meals:

> A Cook they hadde with hem for the nones   (I.379)
> To boille the chiknes with the marybones,
> And poudre-marchant tart and galyngale.
> Wel koude he knowe a draughte of Londoun ale.
> He koude rooste, and sethe, and broille, and frye,

> Maken mortreux, and wel bake a pye. . . .
> For blankmanger, that made he with the beste.

The Cook's culinary skills, which include almost the entire repertory of medieval cooking techniques,[18] are the focus of his *General Prologue* portrait (I have omitted only the two lines that notice the mormal on his shin). Whatever else "Hogge of Ware" may be, or later become, he enters *The Canterbury Tales* as a cook worthy of the guildsmen's custom. The Cambridge illuminator has read his portrait chiefly with respect to that affiliation, and we should not neglect it.

Indeed, the character of the guildsmen is our first index to the character of their cook—"A Cook they hadde with hem for the nones"—and it is epitomized in the line "Wel semed ech of hem a fair burgeys" (I.369). For they are all, the Cook included, London citizens—*cives, burgenses*—members of the newly self-conscious class that earned its living through organized trades and crafts, and whose rise to dignity and power was one of the signal events in fourteenth-century English history. Had Chaucer lived to write tales for their telling, even the five guildsmen might have become particular pilgrims. But Jill Mann is surely correct in suggesting that what most interested Chaucer in *The General Prologue* is their common class, not their individuality or even their individual trades.[19] The Cook is doubtless less wealthy than these men he briefly serves, and he belongs to a newer and less important guild than any of theirs—the Cooks did not gain ordinances (become self-governing) until 1379.[20] But he is unequivocally of their political class: one could not be admitted to the freedom of the city (that is, become a citizen) or practice a trade within its limits except through guild membership.[21] The group portrait represents that new middle class in English society, and exemplifies especially its ambition, self-importance, and self-satisfaction. Just as their wives are pleased to be called "*ma dame*," to take precedence in church processions, and to have their mantles carried by servants "roialliche" (I.374–78), so the husbands bring with them on a pilgrimage their own cook—in emulation of the nobility and higher clergy, who customarily traveled with an entourage of servants. (Significantly, no pilgrim of higher rank travels on this pilgrimage thus attended, unless we think of the Knight and his Yeoman so.) The Cambridge manuscript depicts a Cook who seems adequate to the role, a cook who would do his new patrons credit—something no one would ever claim for his Ellesmere equivalent. A group of "new men" eager to advertise their prosperity and discriminating taste are not likely to have hired such a man for such a purpose. Any inn along the way would have furnished at least his equal.

If the Ellesmere artist was not "reading ahead" to *The Manciple's*

Prologue, he may have been reading too literally Harry Bailly's attack on the Cook in *The Cook's Prologue*—reading it as a statement of charges rather than as a bantering exchange. Though the Cook's response to the Reeve's tale ("For joye him thoughte he clawed him on the bak," 1.4326) gives us a flash of the Ellesmere cook (even perhaps a gesture with the fleshhook), he recovers his composure as soon as he begins to speak. He draws an appropriate moral, deriving it from Solomon:

> "'Ne bryng nat every man into thyn hous';   (1.4331)
> For herberwynge by nyghte is perilous."

And he offers, in a courteous fashion, to tell a related tale:

> "And therfore, if ye vouche-sauf to heere   (1.4340)
> A tale of me, that am a povre man,
> I wol yow telle, as wel as evere I kan,
> A litel jape that fil in oure citee."

When Harry Bailly replies, "I graunte it thee. / Now telle on, Roger, looke that it be good" (1.4344), he begins a comic attack *in a particular mode* ("A man may seye ful sooth in game and pley"), which is meant to govern our understanding of it. Roger replies in kind, and emerges (from this exchange at least) as Harry Bailly's equal in social confidence, urbanity, and self-control. His adroit use of the proverb "sooth pley, quaad pley" ("a true jest is no jest")[22] in warning Harry that if he comes too near the truth about cooks, he may have to hear some home truths about innkeepers before the journey is over, leaves "gentil Roger" untouched by charges of pies twice hot, twice cold. In treating such charges as a customary joke, to be answered with a joke in kind, he leaves us no way of knowing whether in fact they touch on truth. The wit and urbanity of the exchange is its point.* Though the Cook is clearly no pious lay-brother on leave from a monastery kitchen, neither is he (at this point in *The Canterbury Tales*) a moral grotesque, a certifiable threat to London's health, or a suppurating sore. The Cook is larger and more interesting than the mormal on his shin—and upon this point depends our ability to read his performance in something like its full tonal range.

The Cook begins with a formal portrait of his young hero, a London apprentice who forsakes his master to enter upon a life of riot and street crime—a portrait so celebratory in tone that only his nick-

---

*"Play and game," as the declared mode of the pilgrimage tale telling, imposes certain limits upon any psychological reading of the pilgrims' interaction. And we might note as well that a traditional opposition between cooks and innkeepers—as rivals for the same patronage, or for power when one is employed by the other—constitutes the public intelligibility of this exchange between the Host and the Cook. Their purpose is to amuse the company, not to defame each other's person—and they manage it with equal skill.

name, Perkyn Revelour, makes any gesture toward a moral system larger than the pleasures of the moment. As full of love as a hive full of honey, merry as a goldfinch in a grove, he is constantly in motion and in search of a good time:

> A prentys whilom dwelled in oure citee,   (1.4365)
> And of a craft of vitailliers was hee.
> Gaillard he was as goldfynch in the shawe,
> Broun as a berye, a propre short felawe,
> With lokkes blake, ykembd ful fetisly.
> Dauncen he koude so wel and jolily
> That he was cleped Perkyn Revelour.
> He was as ful of love and paramour
> As is the hyve ful of hony sweete:
> Wel was the wenche with hym myghte meete.
> At every bridale wolde he synge and hoppe;
> He loved bet the taverne than the shoppe.
> For whan ther any ridyng was in Chepe,
> Out of the shoppe thider wolde he lepe—
> Til that he hadde al the sighte yseyn,
> And daunced wel, he wolde nat come ayeyn—
> And gadered hym a meynee of his sort
> To hoppe and synge and maken swich disport;
> And ther they setten stevene for to meete,
> To pleyen at the dys in swich a streete.
> For in the toune nas ther no prentys
> That fairer koude caste a paire of dys
> Than Perkyn koude, and therto he was free
> Of his dispense, in place of pryvetee.

Even Perkyn's fondness for playing dice (a game endlessly denounced from the pulpit and in moral writings) is expressed in terms that seek our tacit approval: no one throws dice more gracefully, no one spends more generously whatever he has to spend.

In response to such detail, and lacking any analogues to a story not really even begun, Earl D. Lyon, in the chapter devoted to the tale in *Sources and Analogues*, brought together some London records of real-life criminals and rogues, and made this guess about what was to follow: "From the tone of the fragment itself we may be sure that the Cook was going to cap the fabliau of the Reeve with another not unlike it. . . . We may look, therefore, for a humorous tale." That guess has been seconded again and again by later critics: we are told that Chaucer here began yet another fabliau,[23] which he then abandoned or failed to finish.

But in fact the Cook's narrative voice changes completely in the lines that follow, when Perkyn's portrait is suddenly confirmed from the master victualler's point of view:

That fond his maister wel in his chaffare;   (1.4389)
For often tyme he foond his box ful bare.
For sikerly a prentys revelour
That haunteth dys, riot, or paramour,
His maister shal it in his shoppe abye,
Al have he no part of the mynstralcye.
For thefte and riot, they been convertible,
Al konne he pleye on gyterne or ribible.
Revel and trouthe, as in a lowe degree,
They been ful wrothe al day, as men may see.
     This joly prentys with his maister bood,
Til he were ny out of his prentishood,
Al were he snybbed bothe erly and late,
And somtyme lad with revel to Newegate.
But atte laste his maister hym bithoghte,
Upon a day, whan he his papir soghte,
Of a proverbe that seith this same word,
"Wel bet is roten appul out of hoord
Than that it rotie al the remenaunt."
So fareth it by a riotous servaunt;
It is ful lasse harm to lete hym pace,
Than he shende alle the servantz in the place.
Therfore his maister yaf hym acquitance,
And bad hym go, with sorwe and with meschance!
And thus this joly prentys hadde his leve.
Now lat hym riote al the nyght or leve.

The tone has suddenly become moral, though in a highly specific way. Its ethos is that of trade, its standards those of profit and respectability. Although no Christian priest would have dissented from the equation "Thefte and riot, they been convertible," that maxim here reflects, first and foremost, the world of business rather than of moral theology, as does the other proverb that guides the master victualler's decision: "One bad apple will rot a whole barrel." In *The Cook's Tale* as we have it, the bottom line is "For often tyme he foond his box ful bare." That is the intolerable event, which produces a variety of response and reflection. Only 24 lines—the first 24—celebrate what is attractive in Perkyn, while 34 lines (some not yet quoted) are spoken from out of a prudential, mercantile ethic, severely distanced from any pleasure in youth and carelessness and folly. The tale is continued, and its major action is begun, in the same bourgeois voice:

And for ther is no theef withoute a lowke,   (1.4415)
That helpeth hym to wasten and to sowke
Of that he brybe kan or borwe may,
Anon he sente his bed and his array
Unto a compeer of his owene sort,

> That lovede dys, and revel, and disport,
> And hadde a wyf that heeld for contenance
> A shoppe, and swyved for hir sustenance.

It is a voice able to assimilate even language from the streets—the plain verb "swyved"—without losing its essential decorum and composure. With that line, and in that voice, the fragment ends.

We do not have enough of the tale to tell whether the Cook comes by this "moral" voice honestly—that is, whether it is his own in the moments when he thinks of himself specifically as a tradesman and a citizen—or whether he here simply assumes such a voice, in an attempt to please and flatter the tradesmen-citizens who have hired him for the journey. What is certain is that this "moral" voice speaks in a language new to *The Canterbury Tales* so far.

Such language, however, constituted no novelty in the real world of late-fourteenth-century England, where economic success was systematically translated into ideas of social distinction and moral worth. As Sylvia Thrupp tells us in her remarkable study *The Merchant Class of Medieval London*, documents of the time characteristically refer to aldermen as the "more sufficient" (*pluis sufficeauntz*) or the "abler" or "more powerful" (*potentiores, pluis vaillantz*) sort of men, contrasting them to lesser folk (*de plebeis, inferiores*) in a manner that consciously blends moral, economic, and political considerations. Every citizen, by definition, had satisfied certain conditions establishing moral worth: he had sworn an oath of loyalty to the king and the government of the city, thereby proving himself politically responsible; he had provided evidence that he was of good reputation; and he had proved his competence to earn a livelihood in some recognized trade. Persons thus admitted to the freedom of the city were styled in contemporary records "good folk" (*bons gens*) and "men of probity" (*probi homines*), who elected their guild officials from "the moste wise and discrete," "the worthy and notable," *des meillours et pluis sufficeantz*. Lesser folk—the unenfranchised—were (in general) ignorant, unable to pay taxes and thus support city services, as well as inexperienced in public affairs.[24] The guilds governed the city through elected aldermen and a mayor, and controlled entrance to their ranks through the institution of apprenticeship. In order to understand more fully the action that comprises the Cook's fragment, as well as to hear more accurately the ethical component in the Cook's narrative voice, let us consider for a moment the nature of that institution.

The duration of an apprenticeship varied from trade to trade and from city to city, but most often it lasted seven years. In the words of Lujo Brentano, "it was the beginning of a kind of novitiate to citizenship," solemnly inaugurated in a ceremony at the town hall or at a meeting of the entire craft guild, where the new apprentice was instructed in his role. The bill of indenture that thenceforth bound him to his master often defined their relationship as being like that of father and son.[25] The master assumed responsibility for the apprentice's moral training as well as his instruction in the craft, and it was understood to be his duty, not merely his right, to chastise the boy—though an apprentice could make legal complaint if he had been punished beyond "reson and the comon usage."[26] At the end of the specified term, the master would present the apprentice to the guild as a candidate for citizenship.

Sylvia Thrupp explains the deeper logic of this institution so: "Since everyone knew that the preservation of the local civic liberties hung upon the continuance of orderly behavior, all emotional resources were drawn upon to secure this end," including (in master/apprentice relations) ideas of lordship and paternity. "Much of the moral teaching addressed to the young was focused upon the need of making what was considered prudent use of money. The wasteful character was undeserving."[27] Indentures of 1382 apprenticing a Cirencester youth to a goldsmith specified that he "should not commit fornication either in his master's house or elsewhere, that he should not marry, and that without his master's permission he should not even become engaged. Nor was he to play at tables or chess or other forbidden games or to go to taverns except on business for his master."[28] In another instance, permission to marry before he was of age was given to a grocer's apprentice only upon condition that he not become "a Comen Riotour" and that he restrict his expenses for pleasure to no more than 20s. a year—all as a way of keeping him "in awe and ffere to lose or mysspend his goods."[29] The guilds, even in their role of looking after members who had fallen upon hard times, specified that in certain cases charity was not to be extended: if the cause "be his foly, he schal nout han of ye elmes" ("alms"), any more than "ʒef he be a theffe proued" or if his ill fortune results from "his owne folye [or] ryotous lyuyng." (These examples are drawn from guild ordinances in Norwich.)[30]

Much of the time the system worked well,[31] and *The Cook's Tale* in one of its aspects represents that system from within, as seen by those who valued it most. The Cook's secondary subject, to this point in his narrative at least, is the world of the London guilds, a world of civic order at once moral and economic, like that idealized in figure 127, which shows, between two allegorical ladies representing Fortitude and Justice, a street of prosperous and attractive shops. They include, from the left, that of a farrier or shoeing smith, a grocer, a hat-maker, a cook (with cloth curtain to keep away flies), a tailor, and a candlemaker.[32]

The detailed representation of such a subject is as much a novelty in the visual arts of the later Middle Ages as it is in that period's literature. Previously, the visual arts had chiefly presented the city as a physical entity—as a complex of walls, houses, castles, and churches brought into being by an act of corporate or seignorial will. It enters the world of painting as a setting for religious processions and notable miracles, as background to calendar scenes showing the labors of the month, or (more rarely) in the form of a schematic map showing principal monuments.[33]

The earliest paintings known to me that formally celebrate the creation of a mercantile life *within* the city—the achievement of a system of trade and exchange—decorate a manuscript *Life of St. Denis* presented to Philip V of France on his coronation in 1317. Its great illuminated pages depict events in the saint's life, but include in their lower borders scenes of commercial life on the bridges of Paris, which are richly various and bustling with energy. Figure 128 is drawn from that sequence—there are 30 such borders in all—and shows a moneychanger, a goldsmith, a ragpicker, an apothecary, and a man in a boat fishing in the river.[34] From such beginnings (along

127. A street of shops, between figures representing Fortitude and Justice. Northern French or Flemish, ca. 1460–70. Note 32.

128. Commercial life on a Paris bridge. French, 1317. Note 34.

with the random, unprogrammed decoration of many other manu-
script borders) there slowly evolved an iconography of the trades
that culminated in civic documents like the Behaim Codex (ca.
1505), which pictures the various trades practiced in Cracow and re-
cords their privileges, regulations, oaths, and coats of arms.[35]

But in the fourteenth century such things were still piecemeal and
rare, the expression of a new economic class only gradually achiev-
ing a sense of identity, and with it, social and political confidence. In
the last quarter of the century, craft guilds in several English cities
decided to stage a history of the world from Creation to Doomsday—
the Corpus Christi play—as another expression of this nascent sense
of power and civic responsibility. Indeed, they sometimes signed
their work in highly ingenious ways. The Shipwrights, for instance,
often took charge of the Noah play, and in building the ark before the
audience's eyes, managed both to instruct the audience in Scriptural
history and to lay claim to Noah as master shipwright, founder and
father of their craft. The visual arts themselves occasionally reflect
such an idea, as in the Bedford Book of Hours (figure 129), where
Noah is shown as a person of great substance and authority, directing
a number of skilled workmen and apprentices as they frame the ark.[36]

Chaucer's Cook is on pilgrimage in the service of men who take
this new world of values very seriously—that is the point of their
General Prologue portrait—and it is possible that the Cook does so

129. Noah as master shipwright. French, ca. 1423. Note 36.

himself: the person of greatest power and moral probity in his tale is a master victualler, whose trade is allied to the Cook's own. The term "victualler" was generic, and included any guildsman who made or sold food supplies, especially members of the Grocers', Fishmongers', Vintners', and Brewers' companies, but embracing the Bakers, Piemakers ("pastelers"), Butchers, and Cooks, along with many others.[37] The part of the Cook's performance that projects an imaginative self-identification with the values of his master victualler is grounded in a linked professional and civic identity.

But *The Cook's Tale*, in its action so briefly begun, concerns an instance in which the institution of apprenticeship does not work as intended—in which bonds are breached, dangers preferred, paternalistic authority rejected—and the Cook betrays an imaginative identification with those wilder energies and destructive impulses as well. In this other act of sympathetic self-projection—one whose highest values are holiday, license, and freedom from care—he locates within the orderly institutions of the middle-class city an action contemptuous of law, moral code, and good reputation. He invites us for a walk on the wild side, whose intended destination no one can know for sure. The Hengwrt scribe, at the end of his work on the entire manuscript, returned to note in the present margin "Of this Cokes tale maked Chaucer na moore." In one sense, that is all there is to be said. But for any reader who has taken pleasure in the tale (and the *Tales*) to this point, this brief introduction to an action haunts the mind. Where was Chaucer going? What did he hope to make from what he had so interestingly begun? Let us survey some possibilities.

It is possible, of course, that Chaucer intended us to hear no more of the master victualler or his values. The extant text may be little more than a preface to a tale very different in kind—a fabliau celebration, perhaps, of ingenious fraud and the art of the narrow escape, a tale set in the alleys and hovels of low-life London, its only ethics an informal code of survival.[38] Modern critics indeed write as though this were the only possible continuation of the tale. But medieval scribes read the tale very differently, as the several spurious conclusions that have come down to us bear witness. Consider these doggerel verses, for example, surely the most abrupt denouement in the history of English narrative:

> And thus with horedom and bryberye
> Togeder thei vsed till thei honged hye
> For who so euel byeth shal make a sory sale
> And thus I make an ende of my tale.[39]

Another scribe fleshed out the tale with some forty lines of his own, most of them heaping moral maxim upon moral maxim, for example:

Revell ys ordeyned to hem þat mow pay
But prentise ne pore man þey mowe nat away,
Euelle sponne wolle at the laste wolle come oute
They þou kepe it neuer as prevey in a lytelle cloute.

. . .

He þat his Maister no profite wolle wynne
Y holde hym better out of þe hous þan with ynne.

The last 12 lines of this version are worth quoting in full, since they
resume and resolve the narrative directly:

What thorowe hym selfe and his felawe that sought
Vnto a myschefe bothe þey were broght.
The tone ydampned to preson perpetually,
The tother to deth for he couthe not of clergye.
And therfore yonge men, lerne while ye may,
That with mony dyuers thoghtes beth prycked al þe day.
Remembre you what myschefe cometh of mysgouernaunce:
Thus mowe ye lerne worschep and come to substaunce.
Thenke how grace and governaunce hath broght hem a boune
Many pore mannys sonn chese state of the towne
Euer rewle the after þe beste man of name
And god may grace þe to come to þe same.[40]

These scribes, rightly or wrongly—together with some others to
be considered soon—took their cue from the last 34 lines of the
Cook's performance. They finish the tale in a voice concerned to af-
firm a close connection between virtue and profit, decent living and
material reward. The emotional distance that characterizes the Cook's
own final comment on his young reveler—"Now lat hym riote al the
nyght or leve" (1.4414)—was for these medieval readers the key to
its intent. For them, death by hanging or some form of public
correction—whether gibbet, stocks, or pillory—was its most likely
end.[41] The medieval audience was interested in narratives of justice—
of civil crime and civic punishment—as well as fabliaux; they did not
call for the merry Chaucer on all possible occasions.

I make no larger claim for these fifteenth-century scribes as inter-
preters of Chaucer than I would make for their skill as poets. But
they read his text as immediate heirs to the culture of his age—an
advantage we do not have—and (as earlier pages in this chapter have
sought to make clear) their response does bear some real relation to
his text. If we neglect this aspect of the Cook's performance, we can
hardly be said to have read the tale at all.

Yet surely none of us would limit Chaucer so. Other possibilities
remain, among them the sort of narrative that would see Perkyn
through a painful career as reveler into repentance and amendment,
perhaps crowned by restitution to his former place in the master's
household. For one can see latent in the tale's beginnings a prodigal-

son story as well, which might have flattered the values of the guilds even better than a narrative of justice strictly conceived. It might have celebrated at the end, as it does at the beginning, the master victualler's patience and discretion, adding to those virtues a demonstration of his Christian capacity to forgive and be charitable of heart.

It would be a mistake, in this respect, to assume too great an ironic distance between Chaucer the poet and the public values of his tale. No organized society, whether lay or clerical, aristocratic or bourgeois, can tolerate a figure like Perkyn for very long. Chaucer was educated in a noble household, wrote poems on royal commission, married well, and rose to positions of the highest responsibility in government; but his father had been a prosperous vintner, his family name suggests shoe-trade antecedents, and his own *Tale of Melibee* suggests how deep the agreement between aristocratic and bourgeois values could be: its long section in praise of riches properly gained and put to proper use (VII.1551–655) is translated from a French treatise addressed specifically to noblemen.* Perkyn's values are most assuredly not Chaucer's own.

But neither would I associate him directly with the other voice in this tale. I think it likely Chaucer intended us to perceive the mercantile overtones of this *Cook's Tale* morality as differing, in some subtle ways, from other competing registrations of the goals of human life. An illustration to the eighth book of Aristotle's *Ethiques* (translated by Nicole Oresme in 1370) offers a useful distinction in this regard (figure 130), in showing the three kinds of friendship (*amistié*)† common among men. We see on the left two elegant young men walking arm in arm, in animated conversation, as an example of those who are friends for the sake of pleasure ("ceuls qui se entr'aiment pour delectacion"); at the center two merchants bargain at a counter with their wares spread out about them, as an example of those who are friends for the sake of usefulness or profit ("ceuls qui s'entreaimment pour chose utile ou pour proffit"); and on the right we see two Dominican friars in virtuous conversation—this is Aristotle Christianized—exemplifying those who love a friend for his own sake, and for what such friends are in themselves ("ceuls qui sont bons et semblables en vertu . . . [qui] veulent bien a leur amis pour la

---

*Written by Renaud de Louens, working from Albertano of Brescia's *Liber consolationis et consilii*, it is intended "au profit de mon tres cher seigneur . . . et de tous autres princes et barons qui le vouldront entendre" (Bryan and Dempster, eds., *Sources and Analogues*, p. 568).

† *Amistié* and "friendship" alike are somewhat inadequate versions of Aristotle's key term in this passage. A modern translator comments: "The subject . . . is *Philia*, the feeling which friends have for one another. Since this may run through the whole gamut of emotions between love and liking, it cannot be translated by any English word, though in general 'friendship' will serve. . . . The love between friends played a much larger part and reached a far greater intensity among the Greeks than it normally does among us." (Aristotle, *Ethics*, trans. Thomson, p. 227.)

130. Three kinds of friendship (illustrating Aristotle's *Ethics*). French, ca. 1450.
Note 42.

grace et pour le bien d'eulz"). According to Aristotle, the latter kind
of friendship alone is perfect. The other kinds, being based on acci-
dent rather than essence, are quickly and easily broken ("legierement
dissolubles et de legier desfaites"). Pleasure soon palls, and profit ul-
timately diminishes; what is "accidental" is subject to change.[42]

Aristotle thought friendship based on the quest for pleasure
slightly better than that based on the quest for profit, and it is possi-
ble Chaucer did so as well. He did not need to know Aristotle to
make such distinctions. *The Cook's Tale* sets out to explore the first
sort of friendship at its most difficult extreme. where pleasure be-
comes indistinguishable from crime; but it also chooses to express
the second sort of friendship at its most conventional and compla-
cent. (The third sort of friendship seems unlikely to figure in the
tale.) To whatever extent *The Cook's Tale* bids to become moral, it

does so in a way new to *The Canterbury Tales* so far. The finely nuanced morality of trade, as well as the ambivalent moral consciousness of one minor tradesman/pilgrim, seem likely to remain essential to its subject. What most interested Chaucer in *The Cook's Tale*, as I read it, was the self-conscious appropriation of moral values by a rising, trade-oriented middle class, and their compromised expression by Roger of Ware, cook of London, whose divided allegiance seems likely to constitute a subtext to the tale he tells. As the Pardoner stands to Christian religion, so the Cook stands to mercantile idealism: the energies that lead each of them to deny or evade are fully as strong as those that lead them to affirm.[43] Against the bourgeois values of trade are ranged the values of the body and its pleasure; the iconography of trade is, as it were, forced to assimilate the carnal iconography of the Minster-in-Thanet or the Ellesmere cook. *The Cook's Tale*, had it been completed, is likely to have demonstrated yet another compromised way in which narrative poetry can relate to truth.

However much we might wish to say to our poet, as the Cook says to the Reeve, "God forbede that we stynte heere" (1.4339), the fact remains that Chaucer, for whatever reason, did not finish *The Cook's Tale*.[44] And so the question of its possible continuations must give way to others. Specifically, what formal status are we to accord this apparently unprogrammed termination? What are we to make of this fragment in thinking about the continuity of *The Canterbury Tales* as a whole?

Eight of the 58 substantially complete manuscripts of *The Canterbury Tales* lack the Cook's fragment altogether, but since those eight manuscripts carry no great authority, that omission has never been thought significant. Four others have lost the leaves that would have contained it, an accident likewise without literary implication.[45] The two earliest manuscripts, however—Hengwrt and Ellesmere, upon which all modern editions have been based—both include the tale. They are thought to have been written by the same scribe, probably in the order named, sometime between 1400 and 1410—in the first decade, that is, after Chaucer's death.[46] Whether we think of that scribe or his director as someone working with many partial and imperfect manuscripts, seeking to make of them a consecutive whole (as Manly and Rickert require), or as someone working from an imperfect single manuscript arranged by Chaucer himself in the order represented by Ellesmere (as Larry Benson has recently argued),[47] it is clear that the texts as we have them are in certain places inconsistent, contradictory, or unrevised, and that they include at least one passage, germane to our present study, that Chaucer himself intended to cancel: *The Man of Law's Endlink*, so-called, which gives a false sense that Chaucer had determined, at the time of his death, what was to follow *The Man of Law's Tale* in the larger, developing design.[48] That earliest scribe or his director sought to make the best possible sense of what survived—as we do still—and so in both manuscripts he left space for the remainder of *The Cook's Tale*, obviously hoping to obtain its continuation later, from some other source. The manuscript pages demonstrate that fact clearly: in Hengwrt, the scribe left room for ten further lines at the bottom of the page (figure 131), conveniently the last page of a quire, to which further pages could easily be added without disturbing any of the writing that followed. In Ellesmere, he left blank not only the rest of the page but both sides of the following folio as well (figure 132): later owners or readers have since decorated it with signatures and fugitive quotations. (*The Man of Law's Tale* begins on the folio after.) It was only later, in a distinctive yellow-brown ink with which he completed the *Tales* and made final corrections, that the Hengwrt scribe returned to note in the manuscript's left margin the failure of his expectations: "Of this Cokes tale maked Chaucer na moore."[49]

Much in modern culture prepares us to accept such a conclusion in stoic fashion. We are at ease with fragments and amid ruins. We are indeed suspicious of closure, preferring open-ended forms on the ground that they bear a stricter mimetic relationship to current ideas of truth. And we are scholarly in our love for literature, cherishing every scrap of writing that can be associated with a great author's work, publishing the poems he or she ordered suppressed, resurrecting first versions despite later revisions, recording in definitive editions even the accidents and errata that afflict a work's textual history. We would lose nothing, no chip or shaving from the workbench of a master. And none of us, surely, would lose a word of *The Cook's Tale*. We find even the scribe's marginal notation rather beautiful and touching, for it reminds us that the poet who has been speaking through the pilgrims is gone; it offers a formal correlative to our lack of knowledge concerning Chaucer's last years and his death.

But medieval aesthetics had little room for such notions, and that fact must concern us too. Medieval theories of art derive chiefly from a conception of God as first artist—and of the created universe as the supreme work from his hand. Figure 133, for example, shows him as *artifex*, using a master mason's compass to make the universe into a perfect sphere.[50] He is at the stage of separating day from night and the earth from the waters—the earth at this moment still "without form and void."*

---

*God's compass implies the purely intellectual principles of number and proportion, whereas the work of his hand perhaps reflects the comparison of him to a potter, based upon Isaiah 29:16 and the fact that he molded the human body of clay. In the Book of Wisdom (13:1), he is called *artifex*.

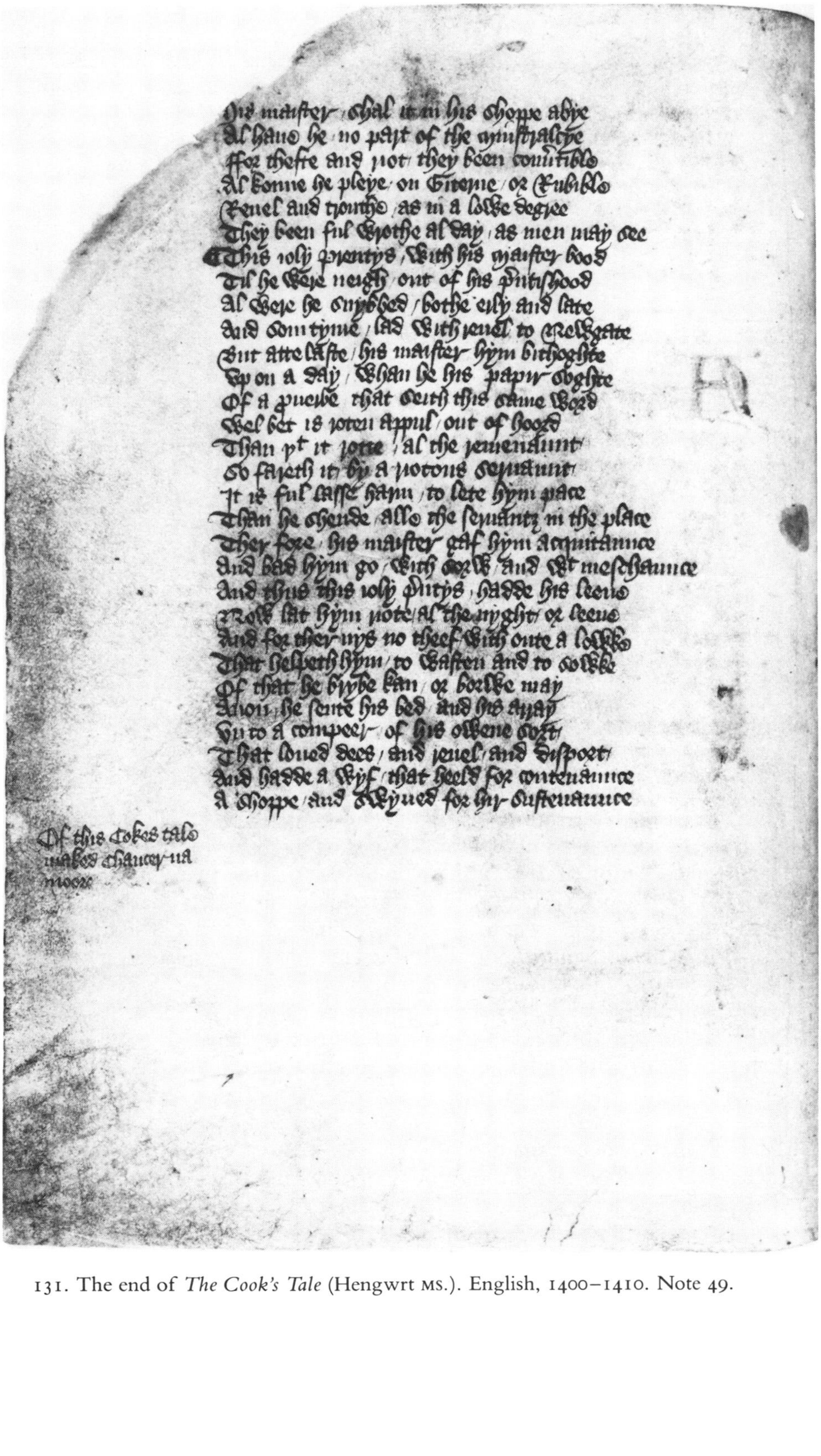

his maister shal it in his shoppe abye
Al haue he no part of the mynstralcye
ffor thefte and riot / they been couertible
Al konne he pleye on gyterne or Rubible
Reuel and trouthe / as in a lowe degree
They been ful wrothe al day / as men may see
This ioly prentys / with his maister boos
Til he were neigh out of his prentishood
Al were he snybbed / bothe erly and late
And som tyme / lad with reuel to Newegate
But atte laste / his maister hym bithoghte
vp on a day / whan he his papir soghte
Of a prouerbe / that seith this same word
Wel bet is roten Appul / out of hoord
Than pat it rotie / al the remenaunt
So fareth it / by a riotous seruaunt
It is ful lasse harm / to late hym pace
Than he shende / alle the seruantz in the place
Ther fore / his maister gaf hym acquitance
And bad hym go / with sorwe and with meschaunce
And thus this ioly prentys / hadde his leeue
Now lat hym riote / al the nyght or leeue
And for ther nys no theef with oute a lowke
That helpeth hym / to wasten and to sowke
Of that he bribe kan / or borwe may
Anon / he sente his bed / and his array
vn to a compeer / of his owene sort
That loued dees / and reuel and disport
And hadde a wyf / that heeld for contenaunce
A shoppe / and swyued for hir sustenaunce

Of this Cokes tale
maked Chaucer na
moore

131. The end of *The Cook's Tale* (Hengwrt MS.). English, 1400–1410. Note 49.

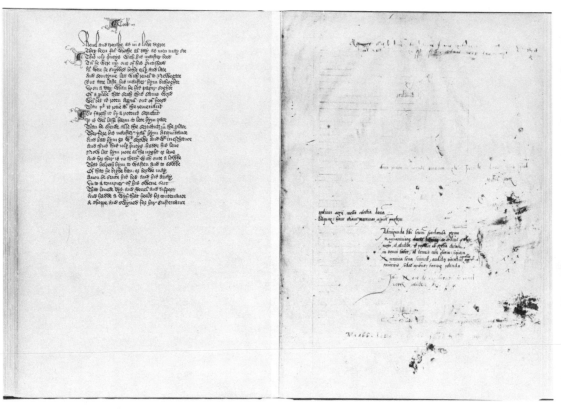

132. The end of *The Cook's Tale* (Ellesmere MS.). English, ca. 1400–1410. Note 49.

According to medieval theory, the principles by which God created the universe—principles of number, weight, proportion, clarity, plenitude, completion—are the principles an artist must imitate, so that his own work (however imperfect) may be at least analogous to that of the Creator in the Creation.[51] That idea had consequences both great and small, among them the fact that the shaping of a manuscript exemplar, a fair text from which others might be copied, was never guided by a love for the fragmentary or unfinished for its own sake. When circumstances permitted no more than that, the work ran the risk of amendment or completion by other hands. One thinks of the 78-line conclusion some near-contemporary wrote for Guillaume de Lorris's *Romance of the Rose*, for example, as well as Jean de Meun's massive continuation of it. And in respect to our present author, one thinks of the anonymous conclusion to *The House of Fame* that William Caxton printed in his edition to the poem; or the anonymous fifteenth-century *Tale of Beryn*, whose lengthy Prologue sees Chaucer's pilgrim company to Canterbury and its cathedral; or Lydgate's *Siege of Thebes*, whose Prologue sets the pilgrims on their homeward way, with Lydgate himself a member of their company, courteously invited to tell the first tale on the return journey.[52] Piety toward an author could be usefully expressed by "perfecting" his work—by finishing it for him.

We have seen evidence of this impulse already in the two spurious

133. God as *artifex*, creating the world. French, mid-thirteenth century. Note 50.

conclusions to *The Cook's Tale* quoted above, which abruptly rhyme Perkyn Revelour into prison or to a death by hanging. There is indeed more of the kind. Yet another manuscript abruptly announces in the Cook's voice a distaste for such low subject matter, and immediately begins something "better":

> Fye þer one, it is so foule, I wil nowe tell no forþere
> For schame of þe harlotrie þat seweþ after.
> A velany it were, þare of more to spell,
> Bot of a knyhte and his sonnes My tale I wil forþe tell.[53]

No fewer than 25 manuscripts (more than half of those that include *The Cook's Tale*) do conclude the fragment: they substitute for it the spurious *Tale of Gamelyn*. Eight do so without transition of any kind, though most employ some version of this couplet:

> But hereof I wol passe as now
> And of yong Gamelyn I wole telle yow.[54]

In short, the majority of Chaucer manuscripts do finish *The Cook's Tale*, at whatever violence to the verse or the authentic canon, and the Hengwrt and Ellesmere manuscripts make clear that the fragment first entered the received text because its incomplete state was uncertain. In such a matter, I think we may trust the scribes and their directors to represent the expectations of Chaucer's audience as a whole. Manly and Rickert conclude from the extreme degree of variation and correction in the copies that all manuscripts of this fragment "go back to the same archetype, which was Chaucer's unfinished MS,"[55] which he had not released for publication. Though we will never know just how the Hengwrt scribe or compiler came upon it, we may properly doubt that Chaucer intended him to preserve it in this fashion,[56] or (if so preserved) that Chaucer would have wished us to grant it the formal status it has assumed.

I do not argue that we should cancel—or even relegate to some editorial appendix—the Cook's fragment. Its connection to *The Reeve's Tale* is too intimate, its manner too achieved, its matter too interesting in its potential. (We have moreover the right to our own twentieth-century tastes and predilections.) But I would consign to critical oblivion the convention—necessary and appropriate to editors only—of dividing Chaucer's opening text into Fragments I and II, or Groups A and B[1], in which readers are asked to understand the Cook's incompletion as concluding the morning's tale telling, or (more misleading still) the pilgrimage's first day. Though the Hengwrt and Ellesmere pages may seem to offer a spatial equivalent to our modern editorial practice, they do so for reasons intrinsic to the process by which they were compiled; neither they nor any other manuscript of *The Canterbury Tales* divide the work into "Groups" or

"Fragments." The accident of the Cook's incompletion should not be read as an element in the larger artistic design. It is not mimetic.

The *Introduction* (or *Proem*) to *The Man of Law's Tale*, which seems so puzzling when taken as the beginning of a new Fragment or of the second day's journey, offers interesting evidence to support this view. When read in connection with the preceding tales, moreover, many obscurities in its own interpretation disappear.

❧

The opening lines of the *Introduction* describe the Host elaborately calculating by means of sun and shadow the hour and the day:

> Oure Hooste saugh wel that the brighte sonne   (II. 1)
> The ark of his artificial day hath ronne
> The ferthe part, and half an houre and moore,
> And though he were nat depe ystert in loore,
> He wiste it was the eightetethe day
> Of Aprill, that is messager to May;
> And saugh wel that the shadwe of every tree
> Was as in lengthe the same quantitee
> That was the body erect that caused it.
> And therfore by the shadwe he took his wit
> That Phebus, which that shoon so clere and brighte,
> Degrees was fyve and fourty clombe on highte;
> And for that day, as in that latitude,
> It was ten of the clokke, he gan conclude,
> And sodeynly he plighte his hors aboute.

It is April 18, and 10:00 in the morning. Although most editors and critics, as I have said, apparently take this to mark the beginning of a new day, some few (for the most part, a long time ago) for various reasons and to various ends have doubted at least part of that conclusion. They are a distinguished group—John Koch, Eleanor Hammond, Carleton Brown, Manly and Rickert, and C. A. Owen, Jr.— and certain of their arguments are worth recalling here.[57]

In a long poem, they have reminded us, a passage establishing the time and date of the action belongs, by logic and literary convention alike, at or near the beginning—as does the lengthy (signature) catalogue of the poet's previous work that the Man of Law offers a few lines later. Ten o'clock, moreover, seems too late in the morning to begin the tale-telling among a group of pilgrims who have been on the road since daybreak and who have agreed to spend the journey hearing stories. It is not, however, too early for them to be represented as having already heard the Knight's, Miller's, and Reeve's tales, for as a few calculations can readily demonstrate, Chaucer sought to imitate time's passage in only a broadly verisimilar way.[58] I would now take those arguments a step further, to argue that when Harry Bailly devotes the next sixteen lines to a homily against wasting time, he is not to be understood as criticizing the company's putative delay in beginning a morning's tale telling—as "governour" of the pilgrim group, he himself would be solely responsible for that—but rather as rendering a judgment in terms of literary profit on all they have heard so far. His central exhortation is "Lat us nat mowlen thus in ydelnesse" (II.32), but the critique he offers is interesting in its full detail:

> "Lordynges," quod he, "I warne yow, al this route,   (II.16)
> The fourthe party of this day is gon.
> Now, for the love of God and of Seint John,
> Leseth no tyme, as ferforth as ye may.
> Lordynges, the tyme wasteth nyght and day,
> And steleth from us, what pryvely slepynge,
> And what thurgh necligence in oure wakynge,
> As dooth the streem that turneth nevere agayn,
> Descendynge fro the montaigne into playn.
> Wel kan Senec and many a philosophre
> Biwaillen tyme moore than gold in cofre;
> For 'los of catel may recovered be,
> But los of tyme shendeth us,' quod he.
> It wol nat come agayn, withouten drede,
> Namoore than wole Malkynes maydenhede,
> Whan she hath lost it in hir wantownesse.
> Lat us nat mowlen thus in ydelnesse.
>   "Sire Man of Lawe," quod he, "so have ye blis,
> Telle us a tale anon, as forward is."

The Host is not saying "It's time we started telling tales," but rather, "It's time we heard a tale of a different kind." "Ydelnesse" in medieval English usage is far more likely to mean devoting one's time to trivial, morally dangerous things than to doing nothing at all.[59] Harry Bailly himself specifies two alternative definitions: "pryvely slepynge" (sleeping when we shouldn't) and "necligence in oure wakynge" (failing to do what we ought in our waking hours). The latter sense surely governs his exhortation. The pilgrims have not been idle in our modern sense, but they have failed so far to do the proper and fruitful thing: "'los of tyme shendeth us,' quod he." The speech in which "Ydelnesse" introduces herself in *The Romaunt of the Rose* can offer some guidance, as that beguiling young woman, gatekeeper to the Garden of Delight, declares her true nature:

> "Lo, sir, my name is Ydelnesse;   (*RR*, 593)
> So clepe men me, more and lesse. . . .
> For I entende to nothyng
> But to my joye and my pleyinge,

> And for to kembe and tresse me.
> Aqueynted am I and pryve
> With Myrthe, lord of this gardyn."

The Second Nun's Prologue uses the term in a context virtually identical to that of *The Man of Law's Introduction*, for it too raises the question of how we should spend our time, and what sort of tales we should hear:

> The ministre and the norice unto vices,   (VIII.1)
> Which that men clepe in Englissh ydelnesse,
> That porter of the gate is of delices,[60]
> To eschue, and by hire contrarie hire oppresse,
> That is to seyn, by leveful bisynesse,
> Wel oghten we to doon al oure entente.

The Second Nun's own answer ("my feithful bisynesse"; VIII.24) is to offer a devout narration of the life of St. Cecilia. For a final gloss on the Host's use of the word in *The Man of Law's Introduction*, we may adduce his later attack on the pilgrim Chaucer, when he cuts short Chaucer's own poor tale of *Sir Thopas* with "Thou doost noght elles but despendest tyme" (VII.931), and gets in return the highly moral, barely fictive *Tale of Melibee*—the very tale many scholars have thought originally intended for the Man of Law, meant to follow upon this Introduction.[61]

All these instances address the same two questions, at varying levels of seriousness and urgency: What is the profit of fiction? Can we afford it in a world of irrecoverable time? The problem of literary choice, here made urgent by the context of a religious pilgrimage, concerns not only the host and the pilgrims but the poet and his readers: it has consequence for the destiny of immortal souls. In *The Parson's Prologue*, as the shadows lengthen and the moon ascends in Libra (the sign of the Scales standing in for Christian imagery of Doom), Chaucer raises the question a final time, to agree at last that the price may be too high and time too exigent. In the character of the Parson, he concludes in prose and without benefit of fable.

In *The Man of Law's Introduction*, however, we stand at a great strategic distance from that final act of self-abnegation as artist and man. Though the Host's language is proverbial rather than explicitly Christian, that is appropriate to this earlier moment of transition, and what he means is defined both by the omissions in what we have heard so far—"Lat us nat mowlen thus in ydelnesse"—and by the story of Custance with which the Man of Law will answer his request: the story of a Christian life exemplary in its integrity and fortitude.

I reserve for the next chapter my most substantial case for thinking that *The Man of Law's Tale* stands in a dialectical relationship to the tales we have heard so far. But other details in the Host's exhortation may be usefully noted here, since they also alert us to the possibility that a redefinition of the pleasure and profit of literature is at hand. I refer to the way certain of the Host's present words and images invite a recollection of the Reeve's performance—the last finished tale in the sequence—and, at the same time, subject it to a critical revision. If I understand these correspondences correctly, they offer yet another reason for thinking that Chaucer intended us to read Fragments I and II as a single narrative unit, integral in design. In the introduction to "Fragment II," the Host, not yet the merry vulgarian of some later episodes, offers a dignified rebuke to the Reeve while tacitly correcting some of the errors and distortions in his version of human life.

The Host begins by offering an image for human time utterly opposed to that dominating the Reeve's prologue. He likens time to a river, running from the mountains into the plain—an image that evokes ideas of natural order and natural purpose, and through them a sustaining vision of "Kynde" (Nature). Chaucer explicitly glossed the image so in an earlier work, when the eagle in *The House of Fame* uses it to instruct Geoffrey in the mystery of how sound travels:

> "And for this cause mayst thou see   (*HF*, 747)
> That every ryver to the see
> Enclyned ys to goo by kynde,
> And by these skilles, as I fynde,
> Hath fyssh duellynge in flood and see,
> And treës eke in erthe bee.
> Thus every thing, by thys reson,
> Hath his propre mansyon,
> To which hit seketh to repaire,
> Ther-as hit shulde not apaire."

In this grand vision of natural order, everything moves to its proper place:

> ". . . every thyng that is   (*HF*, 835)
> Out of hys kynde place, ywys,
> Moveth thidder for to goo."

The emotional and intellectual implications of thinking of time as a river[62] differ greatly from those that follow upon thinking of human life (time made personal) as wine spilling from a barrel, unredeemed by any sense of purpose, its ending mere depletion, its constant attendant a cellar master named Death. In those terms the Reeve is able to affirm only selfishness, vice, humiliation, and despair. The Host's image allows for other possibilities:

> "Now, for the love of God and of Seint John,   (II.18)
> Leseth no tyme, as ferforth as ye may."

Though time runs from us, we may put it to some use: we may seize the day.

The Host next recalls a wise saying he attributes to Seneca,

> "For 'los of catel may recovered be,   (II.27)
> But los of tyme shendeth us,' quod he"

before moving to the homely comparison with which he concludes his call to order:

> "It wol nat come agayn, withouten drede,   (II.29)
> Namoore than wole Malkynes maydenhede,
> Whan she hath lost it in hir wantownesse.
> Lat us nat mowlen thus in ydelnesse."

The comparison of time misspent to lost virginity was not disdained even by St. Thomas Aquinas, who used it in his *Summa theologiae*.[63] But the present usage may be pointed as well as proverbial, since "Malkyn" evokes not only any low-born girl of easy morals— "Malkyn of hire maidenhed þat no man desiriþ"—but in its likeness to the name "Malyne" seems intended to call to mind the (recently deflowered) miller's daughter of *The Reeve's Tale*.[64] The loss of a silly girl's maidenhead, like time fruitlessly wasted, cannot be recovered, and the pilgrim group, in attending to the chronicle of such a loss, has been idle in Harry Bailly's most urgent sense of the word. Even the verb that carries his conclusion—"Lat us nat mowlen thus in ydelnesse" ("Let us not grow mouldy in such idleness")—invokes memories of the Reeve's prologue, with its mordant comparison of his aged but still lecherous heart to the gray in his hair: "Myn herte is also mowled as myne heris."

If to note so closely this shared vocabulary of word and image is not to overread the text—Martin Stevens, for one, has made some of these connections before me[65]—then the Host's chief purpose in this speech is to announce other possible choices, both in literature and in life, than those the pilgrim company has heard narrated so far. Charged by the company with the conduct of a large-scale entertainment, possessed of an innkeeper's sense of the need for variety of fare, he declares that they have had enough of a certain kind of fiction (at least for a while), and in particular, of the view of life expressed by the Reeve, both in his prologue and his fiction.* In reminding the pilgrim company that there are other ways of using time—and of growing old—he decisively isolates time past, along with all they have heard so far, in order to invite a new beginning. Chaucer here

---

*This assumes that Chaucer wrote *The Man of Law's Introduction* before beginning *The Cook's Tale*, thus addressing the Reeve's performance directly, or after having abandoned *The Cook's Tale*, intending its cancellation, which would amount to the same.

uses the Host to create the occasion for a tale that will confirm the ordered ends of human life, the possibility of human virtue, and the human need to use time well, if we would enter into the joy of heaven.

It is in a critical context, then, that Harry Bailly calls for the next tale, and he chooses, reasonably enough, the pilgrim who seems most capable of supplying what is needed, the one least given to frivolous thought and wasting time, the learned, sober, and dignified Sergeant of the Law (figure 134).[66] "Nowher so bisy a man as he ther nas," opines Chaucer the pilgrim in *The General Prologue*, "And yet he semed bisier than he was" (1.321). Recent criticism tends to read the latter line, and other fugitive suggestions like it, as demolishing utterly the statement it reflects upon, as though the ironic suggestion were the only meaning intended. But Chaucer's satire is usually subtler and more provisional in kind: it says two things in order to say two things, not to reduce them to one. (Jill Mann, to her credit, has argued for a decent uncertainty in this matter—the sort of uncertainty that is the soul of such wit.)[67] The other adjectives Chaucer applies to the Man of Law—"war and wys," "discreet," "of greet reverence"—call attention (I think largely without irony) to the qualities that have raised him to his present rank and riches: his learning, his practical sense, the force of his presence. For he is one of the most eminent lawyers in the kingdom, of a rank elected (after a minimum of sixteen years' service as a barrister) by writ of the king himself. The Ellesmere portrait prominently features the white silk cap of his office, which by custom Sergeants of the Law did not remove even in the presence of the king.[68] Chaucer's lawyer confers with his clients at the "Parvys" (the porch of St. Paul's Cathedral), argues their cases before the Court of Common Pleas in the Great Hall of Westminster Palace (figure 135)[69]—a court where only Sergeants of the Law might plead*—and often serves as judge in county sessions ("Justice he was ful often in assise"; 1.314). He knows by heart all the precedent cases upon which English law is founded: "caas and doomes alle / That from the tyme of kyng William were falle" (1.323).

In *The General Prologue* Chaucer has some fun, it is true, at the expense of a real-life Sergeant of the Law, one Thomas Pynchbek, and his formidable skill in acquiring lands.[70] A swift pun furnishes the

---

*In figure 135, seven judges sit above, hearing the case; nine clerks keep official record around a table in the middle; a court crier with staff stands at each end; and five sergeants of the law stand below, wearing their white caps and flanking a long-haired defendant in a short smock and an officer-of-the-court with a staff. The Court of Common Pleas dealt with legal actions between subject and subject, especially concerning land, and corrected errors of the lower courts. (The Court of the King's Bench, the only higher court, had jurisdiction in appeals in error, in criminal cases, and in all matters affecting the Crown.) Sergeants of the law had, in effect, a monopoly on pleading in the king's central courts.

134. The Man of Law
(Ellesmere MS.). English,
ca. 1400–1410. Note 66.

means of identification: "Ther koude no wight pynche at his writ-
yng" (1.326). Some members of Chaucer's first London audience
would doubtless have caught the reference, and some specific dislike
of Pynchbek (or even of lawyers as a professional class) may account
for the peculiar prologue to *The Man of Law's Tale*, in which wealth is
praised over poverty, and wealthy merchants are particularly ad-
mired. But the ironic wit of all this is far more carefully controlled in
Chaucer's text than it is in the pages of modern Chaucer criticism.
One may doubt the propriety of substituting the historical Pynch-
bek, about whom, in truth, we know very little, for the fictional
Man of Law, or of seeing in the specific fictional pilgrim only the ar-
chetypal figure of the lawyer familiar to us from sermon and com-
plaint literature of the period. Chaucer's *General Prologue* is infinitely
more urbane than either the records of the Rolls Office or the poems
of moral complaint. And he too, through his own energy, wit, and
learning, died richer and more grandly connected than he had been
born. On all these counts, and particularly on the evidence of the
story to come, we may doubt that Chaucer thought Pynchbek—or
intended us to think his Man of Law—a total fraud or an ignorant,
preposterous fool.[71] Harry Bailly, sensing the need for a story more
weighty, proper, and profitable than those the pilgrim company has
heard to this point, turns to the Man of Law. He cannot be said to
have mistaken his man.

135. The Court of Common Pleas, with Sergeants of the Law (coiffed) in the foreground. English, ca. 1460. Note 69.

What we witness, in short, is something like a rebeginning of *The Canterbury Tales*. We move from a sense of pilgrimage related simply to the turning seasons of the year ("Aprill with his shoures soote"), its energies ambiguous in both impulse and intention,[72] to a sense of pilgrimage rooted in historical time so precise that we can deduce, even now, the year (1387) in which this pilgrimage is to be understood as taking place. The world's time is at last made particular rather than seasonal, because that is how we waste it, and because the pilgrim company has been wasting it so: "The fourthe party of this day is gon." The Host's criticism focuses especially upon the Reeve, in response to the provocations studied in my last chapter. But the implications of that criticism reach back further still. It must include *The Miller's Tale* certainly, similar in kind if more generous in spirit, and perhaps even *The Knight's Tale* as well, an idealized romance centered upon pagan perplexities, interested in imagining human life within a civilization ignorant of Christ.* Chaucer now locates his pilgrims in historical time, as he brings forward the first of their tales to be set in such time: a tale that will recount a chapter in the conversion of England to Christianity (Alla is King of Northumbria) and will identify Alla's son as the Emperor Mauritius of Rome. He brings forward the Man of Law to narrate a life exemplary of fortitude and constancy in the love of God, a tale that can move the pilgrim audience into areas of human experience and Christian affirmation unexpressed until this moment in the pilgrimage journey. It is the sort of tale one might have expected to begin the pilgrimage, but it has been withheld, for reasons that concern the work's larger poetic, until now. In the medieval moral scheme that ranges the Seven Virtues and the Seven Vices against each other in opposing pairs, "Fortitude" (of which Constancy is a constituent virtue) is customarily set against "Sloth" (of which Idleness is a constituent vice),[73] a tradition that may consciously underlie Chaucer's decision to remedy the "ydelnesse" of the narrative sequence so far with a life of "Custance." The design of the whole at last addresses ordinary expectations: it is finally made responsive to the pressure of Christian truth.

If this account of the opening narrative sequence is not in substantial error, then what follows—the Man of Law's lengthy attack on Chaucer's previous writings, spoken as though the poet himself were unrecognized in the company—makes a special kind of sense. The Man of Law complains that since the poet Chaucer is so endlessly prolific in verse, any further telling of tales can only be redundant: Chaucer has used up all the stories. The Man of Law offers as proof a list of the subjects thus exhausted, each of them the story of a woman betrayed in love. They include Alcyone from *The Book of the Duchess*, Lucretia, Thisbee, Dido, and four others from *The Legend of Good Women*, along with still others (Helen, Laodamia) not represented in his extant writings, but of the same dolorous kind. This catalogue of Chaucer's prior works doubtless incorporates more coterie jokes than we have yet managed to understand, but its serious point lies surely in its omissions, which are categorical and very clear.[74] Every story named is classical and pagan; no Christian version of love or suffering is represented. The Man of Law's summary catalogue offers a partial and prejudicial version of Chaucer's works prior to *The Can-*

---

*I am guessing here at Chaucer's reasons for including *The Knight's Tale* in this condemnation. Harry Bailly might have added a further reason or two particular to his own sensibility. *The Cook's Tale*, had it been completed, would surely have been equally censurable in the Host's (temporarily rigorous) terms. It could have been begun before *or* after *The Man of Law's Tale* was chosen to follow, for in this reading of the larger context, only its incompletion is problematic.

terbury Tales, as a means of reminding us that if indeed that were all Chaucer had undertaken or accomplished, his oeuvre would offer a partial and prejudicial view of poetry's potential dignity and use. For poetry is not limited to the beautiful lie, the delightful falsehood; it can serve truth directly, without benefit of fiction.

The Man of Law's attack, in short, distorts Chaucer's achievement of several decades—that is its wit, in ways that Alfred David has made particularly clear[75]—but it is also cognate with the truth about *The Canterbury Tales* so far. Though the description is comically off-register, the categorical omissions are precisely perceived. It is, we might say, a mock-palinode—a parodic version of the retrospective judgment on his work (or works) that Chaucer offers in full serious-ness at the end of the *Troilus* and in the *Retraction* to *The Canterbury Tales*. It reminds us that Chaucer is the author of all these tales, the voice that speaks through all the masks. It acknowledges his sole re-sponsibility for all that has gone before, especially for the limitations of the first three tales in respect to full medieval truth—whatever their other merits. But it also shows him ready to demonstrate a fur-ther range of his powers, another reach of his art. The four finished tales that begin the journey offer a composite demonstration of what poetry is, and what the poet can do, through a series of poet/pilgrim performances. They explore four distinctively late-medieval ways in which poetry can relate to its civilization's deepest truths. (Had *The Cook's Tale* been finished, it would have interposed a fifth.)

From *The General Prologue*'s transcription of quotidian fourteenth-century Christianity—as common, confused, and compromised as the very inns in which pilgrims took their rest along the Canterbury road—we move backwards in time to a vision of that religion in its primitive purity and strength, when the constancy of a single person could convert kingdoms and when God suffered no mock. For the first time in the opening sequence of tales, Christian images give birth to explicitly Christian meaning, with that meaning unmediated by cultural exclusions, shorter perspectives, mundane complexities, or lived despair.

The Man of Law's Prologue (so-called), which follows his *Introduc-tion*, reminds us of those other human facts in its morally complacent praise of wealth over poverty—perhaps because Chaucer wished at this critical juncture to remind us that most serious works of art are morally superior to the lives of their makers,[76] that, in Milton's terms, few writers' lives can be called "true poems." It may be doubted that Chaucer really intended to begin the tale of Constance with both a *Man of Law's Introduction* and a *Man of Law's Prologue*,[77] but if that was his intention, I think we may best view the latter as yet another version of the modesty topos with which he characteris-tically separates his poetic persona (the voice through which, in that

poem, he will speak) from the highest seriousness of the poem that
he makes. One thinks, for example, of the narrator of *The Book of the
Duchess*, who until the poem's very end apparently cannot under-
stand the symbolism of the chess game and the loss of the "white
queen." Or one thinks of the book-dazed and reluctant accountant
seized in his dreams by an eagle who shows him the House of Fame
and the House of Rumor, or the genial pilgrim who is patronized by
Harry Bailly, and whose tale of *Sir Thopas* is the single tale told on
the pilgrimage deemed utterly worthless—"drasty rymyng . . . nat
worth a toord" (VII.930). And one thinks finally of the poet in his
Retraction, who asks in prose for our prayers and says that he "wolde
ful fayn have seyd bettre if I hadde had konnynge." In all of these,
Chaucer becomes, one might say, the "least person" in his poem.
And so too in *The Man of Law's Introduction*, when the poem's open-
ing design becomes at last explicitly serious, Chaucer speaks to his
own discredit through the voice of the Man of Law, and then in the
Prologue undermines the moral authority of this newly assumed
voice as well, mindful perhaps that not only lawyers in their own
lives, but also poets in theirs, seldom prefer poverty over pros-
perity,[78] or austere Christian virtue above a comfortable compromise
with the world.

William Langland, Chaucer's great contemporary, apparently did
live as a poor chantry clerk singing masses for souls, but even he rep-
resented himself, in relation to the deepest visionary experiences of
his poem, as an idler and wastrel, a man "mazed in his mind"—to the
world's eyes, at least, and sometimes even to his own.[79] At this im-
portant point in the design of *The Canterbury Tales*, the Man of Law's
unqualified praise of wealth over poverty serves less as an instance of
inadvertent self-exposure, intended to close our ears to what might
otherwise prove authentic in his tale,* than as a veiled and witty re-
minder that the life of any teller/poet often bears only a poor relation
to the truths of his art, though he may be able to narrate them in their
fullest power. With respect to Chaucer—the poet behind the poetry
created for the Man of Law—that is not an exclusively ironic pos-
ture; it expresses self-knowledge and Christian humility as well.

I have no wish to claim, either in this chapter or the next, that
Chaucer would have described *The Man of Law's Tale* as the most in-
dividual or distinctive tale he had offered so far in the literary pil-
grimage. In terms of English literature as a whole, the fabliaux pos-

---

*There are a few *Canterbury Tales* in which the teller remains for Chaucer a secondary sub-
ject throughout his whole performance—where a teller (e.g., the Reeve) is subjected to a *con-
tinuous* satiric examination. But in many others the teller interests Chaucer only for a while,
until the narrative itself claims his nearly exclusive attention. I would call that *discontinuous* sat-
ire, and I think the Man of Law a case in point.

sess greater novelty, and within their kind display at least as great a brilliance. But nothing previously written in English equals the power of the tale we are about to consider—within its own particular kind. The pilgrims move toward Becket's shrine hearing at last "storial" material as intimately rooted in history and truth as Becket's own martyrdom. *The Canterbury Tales* has found a new beginning, inaugurated (as the following chapter will demonstrate) by the only one of Chaucer's tales to create the kind of meaning that Dante had named as fundamental to allegory: a multivalent significance, here anchored in history, that not only acknowledges God as ruler of the heavens, but is able to touch upon those very regions through the mode and shape of the narrative itself.

VII. *The Man of Law's Tale*

THE RUDDERLESS SHIP AND THE SEA

HE Man of Law's tale of Custance answers to two kinds of pressure created by the design of *The Canterbury Tales* as Chaucer had determined it so far. There was a need to establish, within the developing fiction, the possibility of an uncompromised Christian life and true Christian society, in which the absolute power of God and his love for those who serve him would stand revealed. And there was a need to demonstrate, within a work governed by a multiple but hierarchical aesthetic, what poetry can do at its fullest dignity, in the service not of fable but of Christian truth.

The first of these pressures—the need to incorporate a vision of human life exemplary to, and corrective of, late-fourteenth-century Christianity—required, almost inevitably, a return to earlier history, as recorded in chronicles and the early lives of the saints. Chaucer here takes his audience back to a time when issues were more simple, right and wrong more clearly opposed, and the Church a shining article of faith rather than a massive, powerful, and corrupt institution. *The Man of Law's Tale* concerns the very period when England was converted to Christianity—often at a cost of blood and suffering and shame—and when men's commitment to Christ partook of a corresponding vigor and integrity. Such imaginative recourse to the distant historical past, like Langland's dream visions of Biblical past or apocalyptic future, always implies a contemporary criticism, and risks present despair. But I think the main impulse behind Chaucer's tale was less to offer criticism than to explore the past in ways exemplary to the present. The austerity and conviction of the early Church are at the center of this tale (as they will be again in the tale told by the Second Nun), and its purposes are clarification and renewal—for the *communitas* as much as for the individual Christian soul.

Modern criticism, for the most part, offers a very different description of the tale, preferring to examine it through the lenses of religious skepticism, a more accurate knowledge of early history, a

different conception of the purposes of history writing, and an en-
cyclopedic index of folktale motifs and story types, each with its
own identifying number. In telling us that Chaucer's audience "doubt-
less recognized the story as the widely known folk-tale of the accused
queen, of which more than twenty versions were in circulation in the
fourteenth century,"[1] or in offering us learned studies of how a "ro-
mance" or "tale of marvels" has been influenced by the conventions
of hagiography,[2] modern criticism confers the benefits of both our
skepticism and our scholarship upon Chaucer's first audiences.

As best I can judge, however, those audiences would not have
thought the story of Custance a fiction at all: they would have per-
ceived it as history. Those who had heard some version of it before
would most likely have known it from two works specifically con-
nected with the English court and widely current during the time of
Chaucer's writing: an Anglo-Norman chronicle written by Nicholas
Trevet sometime in the 1330's for an English royal nun, which fur-
nished Chaucer his direct source for the tale, and Gower's versifica-
tion of the same in Book II of the *Confessio amantis*, a poem whose
first version was completed in 1390 and was dedicated to Richard II.
(*The Man of Law's Introduction* makes playful allusion to the latter
work).[3] Neither of these presents the story as folktale, fiction, saint's
life, or "pathetic [i.e., sentimental] experiment." Some sense of
Trevet's and Gower's response to the same material should help us
move toward a more accurate estimation of Chaucer's own.

Trevet begins his version, in the *Chroniques écrites pour Marie d'An-
gleterre, fille d'Edward I*, with a historian's care, noting that there are
two contradictory traditions concerning the names and relationships
of the central personages involved: what "some chronicles tell" is
contrasted with what other "ancient chronicles of the Saxons say."
He chooses to follow the latter sources (*solom lestoire de Sessouns auant
dites*), and his story, which begins "in the time of this Emperor Ti-
berius Constantinus," concerns for the most part authentic historical
figures. Tiberius was made Emperor (though of Constantinople, not
Rome) in 578; Pope Pelagius held office from 555 through 560; King
Alla of Northumbria, who makes Constance his queen, died in 560;
Maurice succeeded Tiberius as Emperor in 582. (Trevet narrates the
life of Maurice immediately after that of Constance, with both lives
falling under the rubric "Les gestes des Aposteles, Emperours, et
Rois.")[4] This is history writing by one of the most learned and so-
phisticated men of the fourteenth century, an author with commen-
taries on Boethius, Livy, and Seneca's tragedies to his credit, along
with three historical works, two in Latin and a third—our present
subject—in the vernacular.[5] The *Chroniques* is more popular in tone
than the other two, more interested in picturesque detail and anec-
dote, but its genre is history, and it presents the story of Constance as

true. Gower's collection, more self-consciously literary and orga-
nized around the Seven Deadly Sins, uses the Trevet material to warn
against the sin of Detraction (malicious speech). But that larger
moral structure in no way diminishes the stressed historicity of the
narrative. Again and again Gower declares his dependence on source:
"as the Cronique seith"; "after that the bokes sein."[6] For both Trevet
and Gower, these are real personages inhabiting a real past, and they
confer upon the whole narrative an important kind of medieval cred-
ibility; moral meaning emerges from a historical narrative.[7]

It is likely that Gower's version predates Chaucer's, and that Chau-
cer was acquainted with it;[8] it is certain that Chaucer wrote with a
copy of Trevet's chronicle before him, for he sometimes translates it
word for word. I suggest that Chaucer went to the *Chroniques* pre-
cisely because it was a book of history, and that the story attracted
him (as it had Trevet and Gower) because it not only concerned a
chapter in the history of his own nation's conversion to Christianity,
but constituted part of an even larger true history—the spreading of
the faith, the Christianization of Europe. Whatever the point may be
of those lines in the *Prologue* in which the Man of Law says he learned
the story from a merchant—one of those "wise folk" who "knowen
al th'estaat / Of regnes" and "been fadres of tidynges / And tales,
bothe of pees and of debaat" (II.128)—it is clear that within the tale
proper, the Man of Law knows, and expects his audience to know,
that other books ("olde Romayn geestes") corroborate and supple-
ment what he chooses to tell:[9]

> This child Maurice was sithen Emperour   (II.1121)
> Maad by the Pope, and lyved cristenly;
> To Cristes chirche he dide greet honour.
> But I lete al his storie passen by;
> Of Custance is my tale specially.
> In the olde Romayn geestes may men fynde
> Maurices lyf; I bere it noght in mynde.

The historical ambience surrounding Constance's life is offered as au-
thentic (there is no reason to think that Chaucer, or his first audi-
ences, doubted it in its essentials), and its credibility devolves upon
the rest. Chaucer's fourth finished tale in the Canterbury sequence
represents a movement away from fiction, and that modal change is a
major part of its expressive meaning.

But I have suggested that Chaucer sought here to meet a second
need as well: the need to demonstrate, for the first time within the
opening sequence of tales, what poetry can do at its maximum dig-
nity, in the service of historical fact and Christian truth. The extreme
rhetorical stylization of the tale—the intrusiveness of the narrator,
with his apostrophes, similes, Biblical catalogues, and exclamations

of praise and blame—constantly calls attention to the fact that we are attending to history made into art, its vast detail sifted for significance and related to patterns of universal truth:

> Me list nat of the chaf, ne of the stree,   (II.701)
> Maken so long a tale as of the corn.
> What sholde I tellen of the roialtee
> At mariage, or which cours goth biforn;
> Who bloweth in a trumpe or in an horn?
> The fruyt of every tale is for to seye:
> They ete, and drynke, and daunce, and synge, and pleye.

The terms chaff, straw, corn, and fruit are all central to medieval discussions of the means and ends of poetry, and they are used here to emphasize the fact that we are being offered narrative of an ambitious, artistically self-conscious kind. The poet has separated the wheat from the chaff, the more profitable from the less: a single stanza will do for the wedding feast, another for the bridal bed and married life, after which we move immediately to the birth of Maurice ("Mauricius at the fontstoon they hym calle"; II.723). The poet does not seek to delight us with detail for its own sake, any more than he will divert us with other histories tangential to his own. The Scottish wars fought by King Alla (II.717–18), like the reign of Maurice as emperor, will be little more than noted.

In the Middle Ages, the ultimate "fruit" of both chronicle and poetry was understood to be wisdom that could be incorporated into one's own life, but poetry was permitted certain other ambitions as well, and they will be our major concern in the pages that follow. In the Man of Law's severe and often beautiful narrative, poetry is conceived as being by its very nature on the side of truth rather than fiction, and as having for its proper subject what is good rather than evil: Satan alone, we are told, could properly rhyme the treachery of a Donegild (II.778–81). Trevet's *Chroniques* is, of course, a literary work in its own right, with certain specifically literary ambitions. He knew the art of rhetoric as well as the materials of chronicle, and shared with his age the belief that since human history is shaped by the hand of God, it possesses an intrinsic design and structure that it is the historian's business to reveal. In matters of style, both large and small, Trevet's art is not meager. But he had no ambition to explore the possibilities of art beyond the boundaries proper to chronicle, whereas Chaucer, I shall argue, sought to demonstrate, using the same material, how poetry can communicate several truths at once, on several levels—even on that highest plane where the historicity of the *saeculum* is absorbed into the timelessness of eternity. The tale is firmly anchored in one specific period of history—that is its substantive contribution to the design of the first day—but it seeks as well to represent other periods and other lives, including Everyman's, through the polysemous nature of its art.

And so I shall structure my discussion of the narrative images of *The Man of Law's Tale* around a set of definitions borrowed from allegorical exegesis, even though I am in substantial agreement with the late C. S. Lewis and with J. A. Burrow that "nowhere in Chaucer do we find what can be called a radically allegorical poem," one that has its "main meaning in some sphere of signification other (*allos*) than that which the story itself literally occupies."[10] Instead of inventing an allegory in the formal, constructivist fashion of a Prudentius or an Alain de Lille, Chaucer worked poetically upon certain motifs and occasions in Trevet that allowed him to achieve an end closely akin: the creation of a work as literal as the conversion history of England in the sixth century, yet allegorical in its shape and resonance as well.

It would exceed the scope of this book, and be inappropriate to the tale, to attempt here any full account of medieval allegorical theory.[11] I wish only to suggest that in elaborating the story's central image, Chaucer drew upon a range of iconographic meaning associated with both ship and sea that can (for purposes of exposition) be conveniently ordered within the four categories of meaning most commonly postulated by medieval allegorical exegesis.[12] An often-quoted memory tag will serve our purposes well enough:

> Littera gesta docet; quid credas, allegoria;
> Moralis, quid agas; quo tendas, anagogia.[13]

In the terms of this formula, the "letter," the literal sense, informs us of deeds and events, and is communicated by the words and syntax. It is what the poem plainly says. The "allegory" (sometimes called the figural, typological, or mystical sense) teaches us what we must believe, and concerns the life of Christ, the Creed, the Sacraments, the Church on earth. The "morality," also called the tropological sense, instructs us in how to live, if we would do well and avoid evil, whereas the "anagogy," the anagogical sense, shadows forth mysteries concerning death and judgment, heaven and hell, the Church in eternity.

I shall use these commonplace verses, one at a time, to mark the internal divisions of this chapter. My purpose in each part will be to survey the iconographic materials that seem necessary if one would respond to the tale in its full richness and according to its proper nature, and then to suggest how those traditional materials are made particular within it. If classroom experience of the tale is any guide— it is, I suppose, a tale seldom read anywhere else—twentieth-century readers find it a distant, difficult, and uninvolving work. But that may simply be a way of saying that modern literary experience little prepares us for its peculiar mode, and that our modern experience of

texts and images includes little of the iconographic knowledge neces-
sary to receive the tale fully.

I shall begin with the simplest of questions—what is remembered?
what comes immediately to mind when one thinks of the tale?—and
proceed to the answer I think most readers would return: the image
of a woman in a rudderless boat, afloat on the sea. The tale that holds
this image at its center is episodic in the extreme, moving restlessly
from Rome to Syria, Syria to Northumbria, Northumbria to the
coast of Spain, Spain to Rome, Rome to England, England to Rome,
in a series of voyages specified by the historical source but trans-
formed by art into something else besides—into an image of life as a
passage that must be understood in many ways. The geography of
the poem becomes itself an icon, a mental image incorporating much
of what was known of the Western world. We shall need to consider
in some sequence the details by which this image of life as a passage is
enriched and its meanings explored—that is the use of the fourfold
scheme outlined above. But in fact it is the simultaneity of these
meanings that constitutes the beauty and complexity of the poem's
mode. The several significations of the image are present or potential
at all times, like overtones in music, but the story exploits them in
varying degrees at any given moment, and to its changes in emphasis
we must closely attend. By the tale's end, the image of ship and sea
will have invited us to think about the whole poem in a fashion free
of historical particularity, in ways that relate it to any human life, the
history of the universal Church, and the immortal destiny of any hu-
man soul. But a particular history is where it begins.

❧ LITTERA GESTA DOCET ❧

Since in a story the "letter" tells us simply what happened—"what
the deeds were"—details already noted concerning the tale in its his-
torical dimension properly belong under this rubric. King Alla and
Custance, the Emperors Tiberius Constantinus and Maurice of Cap-
padocia, lay claim to a different kind of being than do Palamon and
Arcite, Absolon and Alisoun, the Miller of Trumpington and his
wife: the claim to have been alive, to have lived the events recounted.
Though no one today would think Trevet's account trustworthy
history—the tradition he explicitly rejects is, in fact, the more ac-
curate one—what matters for our present purpose is that Trevet
thought the story true. He is able to tell us exactly when Constance
died (584) and where she is buried (St. Peter's), just as Gower and
Chaucer alike refer to other books of history ("the olde Romayn
geestes") for further corroborating details. It is the historical claim
that matters, not the accuracy of the history, although we might note
(with F. N. Robinson in his edition) one special kind of imaginative

achievement even within those terms: "The whole account of Roman Britain in the tale conforms to historic fact to a degree unusual in mediaeval stories."[14]

But the most characteristic elaboration Chaucer works upon the letter of his story is the interest he evinces in Custance as a human being, as someone valuable apart from her role in history and in advance of any literary program or allegorical design. Most of the story describes her in God's service, forged into an instrument entirely conformable to His will. But the fact that so singular a destiny is never of her own seeking represents on Chaucer's part a telling change of emphasis. In Trevet's version, her inclination, talent, and will center from the beginning on God's work and ministry: Constance preaches to the Syrian merchants and converts them *before* they return to Syria and before the Sultan asks for her in marriage.* But Chaucer suppresses that preliminary action, to create a story that begins small and ends on the same reduced and purely human scale. She goes to her marriage in Syria without gladness—"forth she moot, wher-so she wepe or synge" (II.294)—and near the end, asks for rest and quiet: "Now, goode fader," she says to the Emperor of Rome, "mercy I yow crye! / Sende me namoore unto noon hethenesse" (II.1111). Unlike the heroic conclusion to the *Chanson de Roland*, where the angel of God orders the aged, weary, and grieving Charlemagne to ready himself once more for battle against the pagan,[15] this story of Custance releases her at its end, in one among a series of small, unemphatic deaths, noted but not detailed: her husband's, her father's, her own.

Throughout the poem Chaucer allows us moments of insight into a woman's inner experience that are as fine as anything he ever wrote.[16] When she is cast up on the Northumbrian shore, for instance, she begs the constable who finds her to put her to death:

> In hir langage mercy she bisoghte,   (II.516)
> The lyf out of hir body for to twynne,
> Hire to delivere of wo that she was inne.

Though she soon recovers herself, kneels down "and thanketh Goddes sonde" (II.523), she has for a moment experienced and expressed total despair. It is the acknowledgment of this suffering that most gives life to the literal sense of the poem, for the poem otherwise sees

---

*"Then, when she had entered the thirteenth year of her age, there came to the court of her father Tiberius heathen merchants out of the great Saracenland . . . and Constance went down to them to look at their riches, and asked them about their land and their belief. And when she understood that they were heathens, she preached to them the Christian faith. And after they had assented to the faith, she caused them to be baptized, and perfectly taught the faith of Jesus Christ. Then they returned to their country." In defending their new faith, they praise Constance, and through that praise the Sultan falls in love with her. (Trevet, *Life of Constance*, trans. Brock, p. 4.)

the issues of personality far more starkly, without allowing for complexity of any kind: the choice it offers is between Christ *or* Satan, Christian *or* apostate, chaste mother *or* diabolic virago. It is a story in which "God uses men," and its narrative shape might be diagramed so:

Once Custance is called to her high destiny, her will hardly wavers, but she remains a natural woman proved constant under trial, a woman (in literary terms) at some life-giving distance from *Constantia* personified or from *Fortitudo* (Strength), the cardinal virtue to which Constancy is related in the medieval schema of the Seven Virtues.[17] Both constancy and strength are, of course, exemplified in her story—we will examine them below under the rubric of *quid agas*—but they are developed in such a way that on the level of characterization (the literal level) Custance is allowed to fear, to suffer, and once even to despair. There was Biblical precedent for this, to be sure. It was believed that Christ, in the mystery of His nature as both man and God, for a moment showed fear and doubt in His dying, and late-medieval images of Christ carrying the cross to Calvary may well come to mind when we read of Custance:

> Have ye nat seyn somtyme a pale face,   (II.645)
> Among a prees, of hym that hath be lad
> Toward his deeth, wher as hym gat no grace,
> And swich a colour in his face hath had,
> Men myghte knowe his face that was bistad,
> Amonges alle the faces in that route?
> So stant Custance, and looketh hire aboute.

But there should come to mind with even greater force the remembered face of any criminal, accompanied by a crowd on his way to the gallows. Chaucer's Custance is allowed to experience that ultimate fear, to know what it is to be forsaken.

An elegant manuscript illumination made in France, ca. 1450, may help us understand more precisely the choice Chaucer made. It shows *Fortitudo* (*Force* in the picture's French) as a woman surrounded by properties emblematic of her strength (figure 136). She stands on a winepress, bears on her head an anvil for receiving blows, holds in her arm a fortified tower, and strangles with her bare hand a dragon that signifies vice or the devil.[18] She is the sum, as it were, of the virtues that surround her: *Constance*, *Magnificence*, *Pacience*, and *Perseuerance*, represented as four young maidens. Their beauty, modesty, and apparent vulnerability may seem unsuited to a virtue whose chief characteristics are power and strength. But that

136. Fortitude, attended by Constancy, Magnificence, Patience, and Perseverance. French, 1450. Note 18.

paradoxical conjunction of image and meaning is very like the two aspects of Custance developed in Chaucer's tale. For Chaucer likewise asks us to contemplate the nature of power at its most mysterious, when what may appear to be weakness, passivity, defeat, or even death emerges victorious through its perfect alliance with God's will—in Christian terms, the only true source of power. The Crucifixion had offered a new definition of heroism, a new configuration of victory—that is the logic of such praise as "Humblesse hath slayn in hire al tirannye" (II.165)—and that Chaucer should choose to explore this fact in *The Man of Law's Tale* indicates not a "sentimental" intention (a word that haunts much of the published criticism of this tale), but instead his interest in a paradox central to Christianity and its heroes, men and women alike. The text below the illumination makes clear the difference between the two kinds of strength: "Et est assavoir que celle vertu de force n'est pas ditte proprement force corporelle mais est vertu de l'ame qui est espirituelle." ("And it is to be understood that this virtue of Fortitude is not, properly speaking, bodily fortitude, but is a virtue of the soul that is spiritual.")*

Chaucer's poem too is unmistakably about power: it celebrates a warfaring Christianity in which Satan and God are the commanders and champions, and men merely the weapons with which they fight—weapons that are tempered and tested, that hold or fail. As Custance says of Christ before her third seafaring, "As strong as evere he was, he is yet now" (II.831). But so deep is Chaucer's interest in the prior level of his poem's meaning that he allows the battle weapon, the Christian soul, full human dignity. He calls his heroine always "Custance"—not "Constance" as does Trevet or Gower—preferring, I would guess, a more domestic and intimate form of the name, distancing it just a little from the maximum power of personification it might otherwise so easily carry. That moral equivalence is never entirely suppressed, and it is never inappropriate—we will soon examine the chief means by which it is explored. But Chaucer's primary stress, in terms of narrative sequence and imaginative energy, is upon a human being chosen by God, taken up by Him, employed, released, and in her final days (though still subject to death) rewarded. Chaucer's primary stress is upon the letter of the story.

🌿 QUID CREDAS, ALLEGORIA 🌿

Chaucer might have contented himself with the historical aspect of Constance/Custance merely. There is no sustained allegorical heightening of her adventures in Trevet or Gower, though those authors would not have been ignorant of the traditions and possibilities I shall survey in the following pages. But they had other, more limited, literary ends in view. The only illustration of the Constance story known to me (figure 137, from a manuscript of the *Confessio amantis*)[19] communicates chronicle content only, without resonance of any kind.† But Chaucer worked his way to a richer, more deeply meditated sense of his material, and we may turn now to certain other meanings that he recognized as potential within it—meanings derived from the literal furnishings and actions of his story when they are thought of as signs. In matters that concern what we are to believe they point toward sacred personages and sacred histories other than themselves. The ship and the sea are made to suggest more than their identity in chronicle.

---

*"Vertu" in the French text means not only "virtue" as I have translated it here (since this is a text concerning the Virtues), but also "power" or "strength."

†The exact identity of the three figures standing on the gangplank to the larger ship is not clear, nor is the gesture of Constance in the foreground. Since she is on green land, she is perhaps giving thanks for safe arrival. The background scene showing her in the boat is of greater relevance.

137. Scenes from Gower's tale of Constance. English, second half of the fifteenth century. Note 19.

Our first sense that this may be so derives from the fact that the marriage contract is concluded despite the problems of *disparitas cultas*,[20] the "diversitee / Bitwene hir bothe lawes" (II.220) that makes Rome and Syria religious enemies:

> I seye, by tretys and embassadrie,   (II.233)
> And by the popes mediacioun,
> And al the chirche, and al the chivalrie,
> That in destruccioun of mawmettrie,
> And in encrees of Cristes lawe deere,
> They been acorded, so as ye shal heere:
>
> How that the Sowdan and his baronage
> And alle his liges sholde ycristned be,
> And he shal han Custance in mariage,
> And certein gold, I noot what quantitee.

The marriage is on behalf of Christendom, with great risks being run for Christ's sake; its sole justification is the willingness of the Sultan to convert, and to convert his kingdom with him: "Rather than I lese / Custance, I wol be cristned, doutelees" (II.225).

A strong sense of danger and sorrow attends the preparations for this journey to a husband Custance has never seen, in a country serving false gods. But she does not go alone. The first ship on which she travels is grand, and carries a large and significant company:

> Bisshopes been shapen with hire for to wende,   (II.253)
> Lordes, ladies, knyghtes of renoun,
> And oother folk ynowe, this is th'ende;
> And notified is thurghout the toun
> That every wight, with greet devocioun,
> Sholde preyen Crist that he this mariage
> Receyve in gree, and spede this viage.

The purpose of this voyage is defined by its ecclesiastical members—the marriage has been arranged "by the popes mediacioun, / And al the chirche, and al the chivalrie" (II.234)—and to it the Sultan's mother in her turn, faithful to the "hooly lawes" of the Koran, proposes a deadly counter-measure:

> "We shul first feyne us cristendom to take,—   (II.351)
> Coold water shal nat greve us but a lite!
> And I shal swich a feeste and revel make
> That, as I trowe, I shal the Sowdan quite.
> For thogh his wyf be cristned never so white,
> She shal have nede to wasshe awey the rede,
> Thogh she a font-ful water with hire lede."

The battle is decisively engaged—between God and Mahomet, the old rites and the new—as the bishops come to baptize the Syrians. Their journey has nothing to do with "romance adventure"; its serious and stately purpose is the spreading of the true faith, in the historical dispersion that Christ commanded of his disciples just before his Ascension: "Teach ye all nations: baptizing them in the name of the Father and of the Son and of the Holy Ghost." (Matt. 28:19; cf. Mark 16:15–20.)

In contrast to her later voyages, Custance's first ship journey is marked by purposiveness and splendor—"Arryved been this Cristen folk to londe / In Surrye, with a greet solempne route" (II.386)—and we are surely meant to associate it with the Ship of the Church, as that image was known and understood throughout the Middle Ages. The literal boat is subsumed within a larger icon, for its freight is not simply an emperor's daughter and her entourage, but the Christian faith itself going out across the waters; it is at once their protection, their treasure, and their charge.

One could wish to illustrate the iconographic tradition drawn upon here with a picture of the *nef* described in an inventory made in 1395 for Louis, Duke of Orleans, for that elegant artifact, a miniature ship model meant to grace a banquet table, was fashioned of gold and

precious stones, and included figures of the Virgin and the Angel
Gabriel on its forecastle and stern, the twelve Apostles on its deck,
and the four Evangelists on its bridge. Its mast and sail were made in
the likeness of a great cross, at the top of which was seated a figure of
God Almighty with orb and cross in hand. Other figures included an
emperor, a king, and eight "Adams and Eves," "enameled white, as
though naked," probably meant to represent Christian souls. But the
nef itself has been lost, doubtless melted down for the value of its
materials. Recent scholarship has failed to guess its subject,[21] though
clearly it was a Ship of the Church, part of a tradition rhymed by a
northern English poem "Of þo flode of þo world":

> But a shipe thorgh þo flode of þo world sayles,
> þat is laden ful of gods vitayles,
> in whilk are men þat of þo world are irke:
> & þat shippe is noght ellis but holy kirke.
> Þer-Inne are dyuerse men of religion,
> and mony oþer of grete deuocion,
> þat to þo trouthe of holy kirc are lele.
>   . . .
> In myddis þo ship stondis a mast,
> þat no storme may stir hit stondis so fast:
> þis ilk mast is noght ellis to telle
> but Crist, þat boght mon-kynd fro helle. . . .
> Þis mast has a brood saiel dight þerby:
> þat is noght ellis but his grace & his mercy,
> with þo wynde of his myght þat fayles noght,
> thurgh whilk þis shyp to þo hauen is broght,
> þat is to þo blisful londe of lyue,
> where endeles pees is with-outen stryue.
>   . . .
> Þese fisshers þat þus fisshen ouer þo ship borde,
> Arc noght but þo prechours of gods worde,
> þat to men prechen þat here wrong lyuen
> & to þo world & delytes of flesshe hom gyuen.[22]

These verses invite us to see, in our mind's eye, an image not un-
like that in a late Italian breviary (figure 138) in which the Ship of the
Church is crowded with the company of the saints, St. Peter is
helmsman, and Christ hangs crucified upon the mast; the Pelican of
Piety, above, feeds her children with blood from her breast, and
symbols of the four Evangelists surround it in the sky.[23] The picture
is later than Chaucer's poem by some fifty to eighty years, but I
reproduce it in part for the interest of its foreground. It shows
two groups of men: one consists of tonsured clerics, with a teacher
holding a book and pointing to the ship; the other is hostile or
unconcerned—one of its members shoots at the ship with a cross-
bow, another attacks it with a spear, and a third turns his back alto-

138. The Ship of the Church. Italian, third quarter of the fifteenth century.
Note 23.

gether. That foreground subject is Chaucer's as well: his story con-
cerns the diverse response of kingdoms and persons to the faith as it
is brought to them in the person of Custance, her teaching and her
example.

The earliest of such Christian journeys were, of course, less grand than the one Chaucer describes as originating in an emperor's court in Rome. But the iconographic meaning is the same. The legend of St. Mary Magdalen, for instance, prefaces her conversion of the kingdom of Marseilles with an account of a ship journey that touches in important ways on the several journeys of Custance:

In the fourteenth year after the Passion and Ascension of Our Lord, the disciples went out into the divers regions of the earth to sow the word of God; and Saint Peter entrusted Mary Magdalen to Saint Maximinus, one of the seventy-two disciples of the Lord. Then Saint Maximinus, Mary Magdalen, Lazarus, Martha, Martilla, and Saint Cedonius . . . together with still other Christians, were thrown by the infidels into a ship without a rudder and launched into the deep, in the hope that in this way they would all be drowned at once. But the ship was guided by the power of God, and made port in good estate at Marseilles. There no one would give shelter to the new-comers, who were forced to take refuge beneath the porch of a pagan temple. And when Mary Magdalen saw the pagans going into their temple to offer sacrifice to their gods, she arose with calm mien and prudent tongue, and began to draw them away from the worship of the idols and to preach Christ to them.[24]

The arrival in Marseilles of that company of saints, in a rudderless boat and preceded by angels, may be seen in a fresco in Assisi attributed to Giotto (figure 139).[25]

A variant tradition, closer in scale to the second and third of Constance's voyages, when she is put out to sea alone or with her infant son, may be represented by a German woodcut, which shows in a boat only the child Jesus, the Virgin, and angels (figure 140). It has a beautiful literary analogue from the same country, an anonymous lyric "Es kumpt ain schiff geladen" (ca. 1340–60) often attributed to Johannes Tauler:[26]

Es kumpt ain schiff geladen	There comes a ship all laden
recht vff sin höchstes port.	Right up to highest board.
es bringt vns den sune des vatters,	It brings the Son of the Father,
daz ewig wort.	The true eternal Word.
Vff ainem stillen wagen	Upon a calm still ocean
kumpt vns das schiffelin.	The little ship is borne
es bringt vns riche gäbe	It brings us richest treasure,
die herren kungeen. . . .	The noble Heaven-Queen. . . .
Daz schifflin, daz gät stille	Quietly the ship doth move,
vnd bringt vns richen last;	Rich burden unsurpassed,
der segel ist die mine,	The sail is tender Love
der hailig gaist der mast.	The Holy Ghost the mast.

Chaucer's Custance invokes the protection of Christ and Mary as she is put to sea from Northumbria in similar terms:

"In hym triste I, and in his mooder deere, (II.832)
That is to me my seyl and eek my steere."

A third example (figure 141, a Swiss woodcut made ca. 1470) will
repay our attention as well.[27] It shows St. Ursula surrounded by some
of her eleven thousand virgins, a pope, a bishop, and a monk, be-
neath a sail depicting the Crucifixion; they are rescuing (in a man-
ner already glossed for us by the verses from "Of þo flode of þo
world") a cleric and a lay man and woman from the waters. St. Ur-
sula's ship, like the ship of Custance, is a literal fact in her history; but

139. The arrival of St. Mary Magdalen and her fellows at Marseilles. School of
Giotto, first half of the fourteenth century. Note 25.

140. Mary and the Christ
Child aboard a ship. German,
ca. 1450–65. Note 26.

like Chaucer in his poem, the Swiss artist "saw" it simultaneously as
the Ship of the Church.

Preeminent among the many places in which Chaucer would have
met this tradition is Guillaume de Deguileville's *Pilgrimage of Human Life*. Near the end of that work, when the pilgrim is in despair
and weakened by sin, he sees approaching him a ship "riht gret and
wunderful." His lady-teacher Grace Dieu explains it to him: "The
ship, quod she, bi his name is cleped religioun. She is bounden
and bounden ayen, fretted with obseruaunces. As longe as it is so
bounden it may not perishe ne faile. . . . Of it am I gouernowresse,
maistresse, and conduyeresse. . . . The mast is the cros of Ihesu Crist
and the wynd is the holi gost."[28] Because salvation can be found only
on board that ship—most safely in one of its castle towers (the
houses of the religious orders)—the pilgrim's entry on board begins
his spirit's movement, so long delayed, toward a happy and holy
death. In figure 142, the pilgrim sees the ship for the first time, with
Fear of God on board trying to prevent his entry. The relationship of
the ship to cathedral architecture is clear.[29]

This conception of the Church as being (in Gower's phrase) "the
Schip which Peter hath to stiere" goes back at least as far as St. Hippolytus, in the third century,[30] but it was Augustine who gave the
figure its greatest early currency, developing it with special richness

141. St. Ursula rescuing
sinners. Swiss, ca. 1470.
Note 27.

in his sermons on Matthew 14:24–33, in which Christ walks on the
water, bears up Peter, and calms the storm. The theme was popular
in the visual arts (figure 143 is from a Franciscan missal of the mid-
fourteenth century, French in origin), and its importance grew in re-
sponse to the Black Death, as a beautiful painting by Andrea da Fi-
renze in Santa Maria Novella in Florence testifies.[31] But the most
famous rendering of the scene was a vast mosaic, the *Navicella*, de-
signed by Giotto, which decorated the facade of the old Basilica of
St. Peter in Rome; though it was destroyed in the seventeenth cen-
tury, early sketches of it survive.[32] In Augustine's commentary on
Matthew, the experience of the Apostles in the storm is like our lives
on earth, "exposed to waves and tempests; but we must needs be at
least in the ship. For if there be perils in the ship, without the ship
there is certain destruction." These are hard days for us, he says, be-
cause the Lord has gone up on a mountain (i.e., to heaven) and
"meanwhile the ship which carries the disciples, that is, the Church,
is tossed and shaken by the tempests of temptation . . . the devil her
adversary, rests not, and strives to hinder her from arriving at rest."[33]

Augustine's interpretation of this gospel text runs parallel to his ex-
egesis of the Flood in *The City of God*, XV.26, which sees in Noah a
figure of Christ and in the ark a figure of the Church, bearing the

142. The pilgrim sees the Ship of the Church. French, ca. 1400. Note 29.

faithful through destruction to salvation. This idea too had important consequence for the visual imagination of the Middle Ages, for Noah's ark is often depicted as a kind of church built on a ship's base. In figure 144, the foundations are clearly of stone; in figure 145, there is a superstructure ecclesiastical in design, and the boat lacks any visible means of navigation.[34] In figure 146, an illustration to *The City of God*, the City of Cain—the earthly city—is being built in the foreground, as those in the lineage of Cain (seven generations from Adam to Lamech) move toward it. In the background, those in the lineage of Seth (ten generations from Adam to Noah) move as pilgrims estranged from the earthly city toward the ark of Noah, which Augustine, shown as bishop alongside the ark, explains allegorically in the banderole he holds in his hand: "Archa noe cristum et eus sponsam ecclesiasm significat" ("Noah's ark signifies Christ and his spouse the Church").[35] Indeed the very word "nave," used to identify the largest space in a cathedral, the space where the laity hears mass, comes from the Latin *navis*, meaning "ship," and the "ship's keel" roof that characterizes certain church naves—a roof that looks like the inside of an upturned boat, and depends upon construction techniques related to boat building—may represent a translation of that

143. Christ, walking on the water, bears up Peter. French, mid-fourteenth century.
Note 31.

symbolism into architectural fact. Two fourteenth-century examples
in Verona are known to me—figure 147 shows that at San Zeno—as
well as two in Padua and three in other countries.[36] The Ship of the
Church, like the Church as ship, always points east, for the journey
is toward salvation.

All of this suggests that we are meant to recognize in the first voy-
age of Custance, the voyage to Syria, a journey of the Ship of the
Church bringing the true faith to "hethenesse." Though it is not
given an elaborately visual description, we need only imagine a boat
whose company includes bishops on a mission to baptize to recog-
nize the essentials of the tradition. The rudderless boat of Custance's
second journey, in which she drifts for three years before arriving at
the coast of Northumbria, gives precedence to a different meaning
(an alternative and more pressing likeness, soon to be considered),
but it remains a Ship of the Church as well, whose voyage will con-
vert another kingdom. That first identity is not forsaken, even
though Custance is no longer accompanied by bishops or lords. In-
deed we may be meant to see in it a clue to the identity of the "certein
tresor" (II.442) brought with her to Syria from Rome, whose exact
nature is never specified, but which accompanies her on all her jour-
neys. It may be a literal treasure, of silver and gold. It may be a cru-
cifix, if in the stanzas that follow we are meant to imagine her pray-
ing to a literal object ("hooly croys," "victorious tree"). Or it may be
a treasure greater still, the Christian faith she carries in her heart, of

144 (*above*). Noah's ark. French, late thirteenth century. Note 34.
145 (*right*). Noah's ark. English, mid-thirteenth century. Note 34.
146 (*below*). Noah's ark and the City of Cain. French, ca. 1473. Note 35.

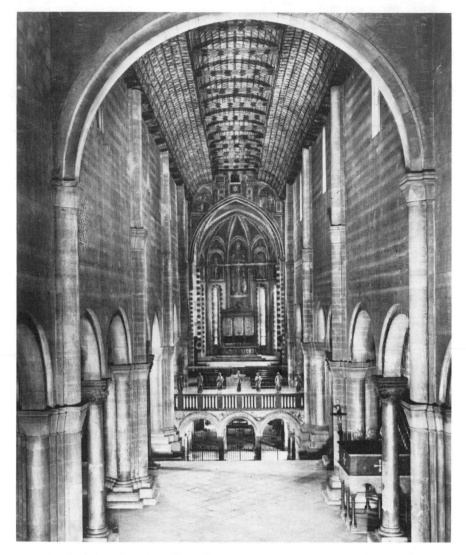

147. A "ship's keel" roof. Basilica of San Zeno Maggiore, Verona, fourteenth century. Note 36.

which a literal crucifix is merely a sign. That treasure, authenticated by the courage and constancy of her life, proves as potent to convert a constable and his wife, and later a king, as any shipload of bishops sent in highest splendor from Rome. She establishes Christianity in a second kingdom,[37] and earns thereby the formal title pronounced by God "in general audience" (II.673) after He has struck dead the knight who bears false witness against her: "Thou hast desclaundred, giltelees, / The doghter of hooly chirche in heigh presence."

In terms of *quid credas*, then—the sense that teaches what we must "believe"—the tale creates a residual image that is geographical: a map of Europe with a boat moving upon its waters. It shows us the Ship of the Church bearing its cargo of sacred truth and living witness to the several nations—with shipmen and priests and councillors in charge of its first journey, and thereafter (on an apparently reduced, but no less powerful scale) with the invisible Christ himself as helmsman: "He that is lord of Fortune be thy steere!" (II.448.)

This second kind of meaning proper to allegory often concerns the Sacraments as well, one of which is indeed central to this poem—baptism, the sacrament of conversion. "Unless a man be born again of water and the Holy Ghost, he cannot enter into the kingdom of God" (John 3:5). Custance's mission to Syria is defined by the Sultaness in those terms[38]—"Coold water shal nat greve us but a lite! . . . Thogh she a font-ful water with hire lede" (II.352)—and even the verses devoted to Custance's childbearing move directly to baptism: "Mauricius at the fontstoon they hym calle" (II.723). It is where real birth, as this poem conceives it, begins. Because the action of the tale so frequently involves the sea, both its literal events and the rhetoric through which they are communicated could readily be shaped into an exploration of the power of the sacrament itself.

Let us begin with the rhetoric. When the Man of Law would explain Custance's safety upon the sea, he invokes other histories no less remarkable:

> Who kepte Jonas in the fisshes mawe   (II.486)
> Til he was spouted up at Nynyvee?
> Wel may men knowe it was no wight but he
> That kepte peple Ebrayk from hir drenchynge,
> With drye feet thurghout the see passynge.

The story of Custance bears a figurative relation to that of Jonah (figure 148),[39] for she too is held and then released by the sea: "the wawe hire caste"; "Custance, and eek hir child, the see up caste" (II.508, 906). And she must likewise visit foreign and hostile kingdoms, as Jonah did Nineveh, to convert the people to better living. But the second history adduced by the Man of Law—the crossing of the Red Sea—must concern us more deeply, for it was the most important of the Old Testament prefigurations of baptism: the primary historical event through which God mysteriously revealed the nature of a sacrament to come. Tertullian's *De baptismo*, written in the third century, was read and quoted throughout the Middle Ages, and it carefully specifies the significant congruences (figure 149, from the Franciscan missal that furnished our figure 143, offers a visual parallel):[40]

when the people [of Israel] are set free from bondage in Egypt and by passing through the water are escaping the violence of the Egyptian king, the king himself with all his forces is destroyed by water. This is a type made abundantly clear in the sacred act of baptism: I mean that the gentiles are set free from this present world by means of water, and leave behind, drowned in the water, their ancient tyrant the devil.[41]

The sacrament is a rite of birth and initiation—the birth of the "new man," the spiritual man—but it is also a ritual of struggle and death: the death of the "old man," the carnal nature in which we descend from Adam. Though ideas of purification are important to the sacrament, its most essential actions concern things more elemental—death and rebirth experienced in a single rite of passage—as early baptismal ceremonies clearly reveal. The converts typically emerged naked before the congregation, stood on sackcloth awaiting the ceremony, and then descended three steps down into the baptismal font or well, where they were submerged or immersed three times, signifying the three-day death of Christ. When they ascended the three steps on the other side, it was as persons resurrected in Him, to be clothed in white garments signifying the cloak of glory. The devil had been left behind, drowned in the water.[42] Figure 150 shows the ancient baptistery at Poitiers,[43] parts of which go back to the fourth century, designed for such a ceremony. In the later Middle Ages, depictions of Christ's baptism in the river Jordan (figure 151) and of the baptisms of earlier kings and pagans, who are always shown naked

148. Jonah cast up by the whale. French, early fifteenth century. Note 39.

149. The crossing of the Red Sea. French, mid-fourteenth century. Note 40.

and waist-deep in the font (as in figure 152), kept current a sense of that symbolic submission to water, in both its power to destroy and its power to give and sustain life.[44]

Once the conversion of Europe was substantially complete, infant baptism became the more customary form, and its ceremonies communicate these ideas less vividly. But an illuminated initial for Trinity Sunday from a magnificent Carmelite missal made in England in the 1390's gives evidence of that fierce earlier theology operative still, even in the context of infant baptism (figure 153).[45] The writing on the scroll in the lower picture contains the Trinitarian formula used in baptism—*In nomine patris et filii et spiritus sancti amen*—as a means of establishing the relevance of a baptismal scene to the Trinity Sunday occasion. But the picture's special power derives from the way the lower picture is linked to the picture of the Trinity above, by a greatly elongated cross upon which Christ hangs dead. Its vertical beam touches the rim of the font, in a conjunction central to the picture's meaning. In the words of St. Paul (Rom. 6:3–4):

Know you not that all we who are baptized in Christ Jesus are baptized in his death? For we are buried together with him by baptism into death: that, as Christ is risen from the dead by the glory of the Father, so we also may walk in newness of life.

The picture reminds us that the infant, held as though he were about to be committed to the waters, will endure a sacramental death and be born to a new life thereafter.

Some such understanding of the theology of baptism is, I think, necessary if one would comprehend the logic of two major actions in *The Man of Law's Tale*: (1) the fact that baptism leads the Syrians (and all assisting Christians except Custance) to immediate death, and (2) the drowning of the apostate steward who attempts to rape Custance in her ship. The power of baptism to renew and to grant life is illustrated in the histories of Custance, Alla, and Maurice, but it is condi-

150. Interior. Baptistery of St. John, Poitiers; fourth, seventh, and thirteenth centuries. Note 43.

tional upon right motive. Its destructive power is figured in the two other episodes.

There is no indication that the newly converted Syrians die a sanctified death, martyrs glorious in the eyes of God, nor is the Sultan viewed favorably in the poem. Through the treachery of his mother, they are all "tohewe and stiked at the bord" (II.430)—killed at the tables of the wedding feast. Only Nevill Coghill (to my knowledge) has thought to wonder about the larger logic of that event, and I think his explanation probably correct: the Sultan's motive, Coghill writes, is "romantic love, as idolatrous as any he had rejected with his 'Mawmettrie'; he was adopting the love of Christ to gain the love of a woman."[46] The stages by which the Sultan reaches his decision reveal his true priorities:

> . . . this Sowdan hath caught so greet plesance   (II.186)
> To han hir figure in his remembrance,
> That al his lust and al his bisy cure
> Was for to love hire while his lyf may dure.

> And he answerde, "Rather than I lese   (II.225)
> Custance, I wol be cristned, doutelees."

151 (*top*). The Baptism of Christ. English, late fourteenth or early fifteenth century. Note 44.
152 (*center*). The baptism of pagans. French, after 1370. Note 44.
153 (*below*). Initial for Trinity Sunday, with infant baptism. English, ca. 1398. Note 45.

In strong contrast is the sequence of thought and feeling by which King Alla comes to love Custance and make her his queen. He is moved first to conversion, by a miracle God works on her behalf, and only thereafter to love and marriage, again by Christ's own will: "Jhesus, of his mercy, / Made Alla wedden ful solempnely / This hooly mayden" (II.690). In the language of theology, the Sultan places the love of a creature before love of the Creator; in the language of the story, the waters of the font for him, and for the Syrians who convert upon his order (in mere obedience to an earthly king), lead ultimately to death: their souls drown with Satan within it.

The second episode I wish to discuss, the attempted rape, demonstrates even more clearly the destructive power of water and (allegorically) of the sacrament. Custance's boat drifts to a heathen shore, apparently in Spain, where the steward of a nearby castle enters her ship one night intending rape. In terms of narrative cause and effect, the incident is abrupt and little prepared for: we learn only that the steward is lecherous and apostate. Once Christian, he has reverted to paganism—"A theef, that hadde reneyed oure creance" (II.915)—and from that detail alone the logic and importance of the action derive. Custance wrestles with him fiercely, until

> . . . with hir struglyng wel and myghtily   (II.921)
> The theef fil over bord al sodeynly,
> And in the see he dreynte for vengeance;
> And thus hath Crist unwemmed kept Custance.

It is Christ who takes vengeance here; His power, which is the source of her power, is once again proved greater than the power of the devil. But in relation to *quid credas*, one further meaning is shadowed forth. As Maxwell Luria has suggested, in this action we see Apostasy (the abandonment of true belief) lay hands on Holy Church and fail in its sacrilegious desire.[47] It is a necessary part of the history of the Church, allegorically rendered, though it may seem gratuitous to the life of Custance alone.

For in the early Church, whose theology informs Trevet's version, presumably through his own "Saxon" source, the principal sins were not seven in number but three: homicide, fornication, and idolatry (or reversion to paganism).[48] And the history of Custance, read allegorically, offers an image of the Church threatened by, and ultimately victorious over, them all. Two are involved in this episode of the renegade steward (*vn renee de la fei Cristiene* in the Trevet original).[49] His apostasy has already done violence to the Ship of the Church, and now, as he sets out to do sexual violence to a person within it, he is destroyed by the very element, water, that as sacrament once gave him his own place therein. A phrase from St. Augustine already quoted can describe the conclusion of this event with perfect fitness:

"For if there be perils in the ship, without the ship there is certain destruction." In terms of the literal story, the confrontation may well seem violent, melodramatic, excessive—an action equivalent to the poem's frequent recourse to high and emotionally charged rhetoric. But such action and language, I think, point to something far different from a lapse in literary taste on the part of our poet, or carelessness about probability, or a wish to establish ironic distance between himself and the Man of Law as pilgrim-narrator. I take such passages to indicate that Chaucer perceived in his story issues and identities much larger than the literal terms of the action, which these strange events and this artifice of language invite his audience to discover in turn. Both the Sultan and the apostate steward seek to enter the ship—one sacramentally, the other literally—for the sake of the woman it carries, rather than for the sake of the God she serves. They seek right entry, for the wrong reasons, and both are destroyed.

🌿 MORALIS, QUID AGAS 🌿

Larger issues and identities are involved in a moral/tropological sense as well—in the reading of an action that would instruct us in how to live in this world, choosing right and avoiding wrong. Whereas the first journey of Custance invokes the tradition of the Ship of the Church—a symbolic identity that remains relevant to every ship she journeys in thereafter—her second journey brings into prominence a new symbolic meaning, that of the individual soul journeying through the sea of this world, subject to the changes of fortune and the temptations of sin.

In her second ship, Custance sails at random "in a ship al steerelees," without company of any sort (II.439). She is set adrift as a person hateful to the Syrian community, a custom that has been traced back as far as the ancient Greeks, who thought the sea an arbiter of sin and innocence. In the words of J. R. Reinhard, "The notion seems to have been that the sea could not endure within itself or upon its surface anything that was sinful or impure"; at the same time "the sea would not injure the innocent, and [such] persons accidentally or purposely cast upon its surface were safely conveyed to shore."[50] Such an action should not be thought a "romance" motif in any sense that would restrict its seriousness or credibility to literature alone. English instances are documented, for example, in William of Malmesbury's *De gestis regum Anglorum*, and also in the *Flores historiarum*, which narrates the judgment imposed by King Edmund upon his huntsman Beorn for the murder of the Viking King Lothbrok. Edmund ordered that "the huntsman be placed in the small boat in which the said Lothbrok often sailed to England and that he be set loose alone in mid-ocean without any means of navigation, to dis-

154. St. Edmund sets Beorn adrift, in judgment for murder. English, 1433.
Note 52.

cover [*probetur*] whether God wished to free him from peril."[51] Figure 154 illustrates Lydgate's version of the same event, in his *Life of St. Edmund*:[52]

> Into that vessel, the story is weel knowe,
> Which nouther hadde oore, seil nor mast,
> Folwyng the cours what coost the wynd list blowe,
> This said Bern be Juggement was cast.

Persons were most often set adrift for one of three reasons: when guilt could not be conclusively determined by human investigation, when men wished to combine severity with some possibility of mercy, or when, as in the case of Custance, society wished to expel an unwanted person from its midst.[53] The Christian instances assume that God is sole arbiter of guilt and innocence, and the sea merely an instrument through which He expresses His judgment. But linking those two ideas is a special conception of fortune imaged in terms of the sea, which is older than Christianity and which the northern poem "Of þo flode of þo world" explains:

> for when richesse & welthe heghes a man,
> þo world as flowand hym vp-beris þan;
> but þo wawes of þo world weltren to & froo
> & kesten a mon now to wele nowe to wo;
> þo world bigynnes to ebbe & to withdrawe
> fro a mon when he fallis fro hegh state to lawe.[54]

The waves of the sea present a restless motion—a raising high and casting low—symbolically equivalent to that figured by Fortune's wheel.

Chaucer's knowledge of this tradition can be readily demonstrated, since several of the books most important to his work invited him to think about fortune as an island set in the midst of a tumultuous sea. In Alain de Lille's *Anticlaudianus*, for example, Lady Fortune inhabits an island rock lashed by waves, on which two rivers flow, one sweet and pleasant, the other dark and treacherous, with men both swimming and drowning therein. The two rivers ultimately join—to the corruption of the sweet, clear water—and on the cliffs above them stands the House of Fortune.[55] This elaborate image was borrowed and developed even further by Jean de Meun in *The Romance of the Rose*; his version is illustrated in figure 36 of the present text.[56] *The Romance of the Rose* in turn influenced Guillaume de Deguileville's *Pilgrimage of Human Life*, which, in its second version, narrates at length the pilgrim's experience of the Sea of the World, where he swims as best he can until he sees a green tree in the midst of the waves. Thinking it must be an island, he swims toward it, only to find himself caught on a wheel unseen beneath the waves:

> Off whiche to-fforne I sawgh no thynge;
> ffor the ffloodes, in ther fflowynge,
> Hadde with his wawes euerydel
> Ouere-fflowyd so that whel,
> That I toke no heede there-at,
> Tyl sodeynely there-on I sat. . . .
> And euere round, as thoughte me,
> This whel wente aboute the tre.

The wheel turns upon the tree—the tree of worldly life—and Lady Fortune stands beside it (or at its center) in her double aspect, at once beautiful and ugly, youthful and aged, handsomely gowned and in tattered rags. Figure 155 shows the pilgrim on the wheel, with the tree full of birds (persons of great estate) above, and persons hoping to rise high crowded into a knot in the tree below; a hand with a hook emerges from a knot in the middle of the tree and strikes at the birds' nests. Figure 156 shows Lady Fortune at the center of the wheel, explaining to the pilgrim her nature, as he seeks to rise from the waves and is cast down.[57]

The use of the sea as an image for fortune's variance often includes, in other texts and pictures, a symbolic boat as well. The opening miniature from a late-fifteenth-century French copy of Innocent III's *On the Misery of the Human Condition*, for instance, sees human life as a man naked in a boat tossed on a turbulent sea, its mast and rigging broken by storms. The boat has no rudder, and on its prow sits Lady Fortune, turning men upon her wheel (figure 157).[58] This image of a rudderless boat (like Custance's "ship al steerelees") develops from a much earlier tradition in which Fortune either holds or stands upon a rudder, as if to say that she alone directs human affairs. Examples

155. The sea of this world, with the tree of human life, and the pilgrim caught on the wheel of Fortune. English, fifteenth century. Note 57.

156. The pilgrim and Lady Fortune in the sea of this world. English, fifteenth century. Note 57.

may be found in Roman sculpture of the first centuries A.D., and in coins from the reigns of Vespasian and Domitian.[59] Although I have come upon no instances from the medieval visual arts that show just Lady Fortune and a rudder, the idea survives in literary texts very clearly—*Troilus and Criseyde*, III, 1291–92; IV, 274–82, for example—and surfaces again in the visual arts of the early Renaissance, heir to both classical and medieval traditions.[60]

157. Life as a storm-tossed ship. French, 1474. Note 58.

One possible response to the vision of the world as a perilous sea of fortune recommends a life of philosophical detachment and virtue. A Christian version of this can be seen in a miniature made in the fifteenth century for the *Livre de contemplation*, a treatise attributed to Jean Gerson, in which certain contemplatives, assisted by the virtues necessary to their undertaking (personified as young women), work their way to the top of a mountain in the midst of the sea and are rewarded by the sight of God's face; the rest of the world struggles in peril of shipwreck and drowning below (figure 158).[61]

But the rudderless boat, as image, requires a counter-truth of its own, and the journeys of Custance present it with absolute clarity. By refusing to will, by affirming God's governance and seeking no direction of her own, she allows God to become her steersman. The essential details are all in Trevet, where Constance is put to sea without sail or oar (*saunz sigle e sauntz neuiroun*), with only God as her mariner (*mes dieu estoit soun mariner*).[62] But Chaucer adjusts his translation slightly, to move the event more firmly into the tradition of the moral image. He specifies the lack of a rudder, and he names God in a special way—"O Emperoures yonge doghter deere, / He that is lord of Fortune be thy steere!" (II.447). It is as *Lord* of Fortune, the shaping intelligence and moral coherence behind the apparent anarchy of human life, that God is invoked, at once rudder to Custance's boat and shipman to her soul. A northern English poet contemporary with Chaucer, in a poem we call *Cleanness*, described Noah's ark in just such a way—rolling and driving upon the waters, without sail or tackle or rudder, apparently at the mercy of wind and sea—in order to end with this fine understatement concerning that ship's company: "Nyf oure lorde hade ben her lodeȝmon, hem had lumpen harde" ("If our Lord had not been their steersman, they would have fared badly").[63] Christ guides the ark of Noah, as in Chaucer He guides the ship of Custance, because in peril of the sea its passengers commit their lives and fortunes entirely to His hands, asking only that His will be done.

That will, of course, was understood to be mysterious, capable of purposing for those He loves both elevation ("And thus hath Crist ymaad Custance a queene"; II.693) and abasement (the two journeys in which she is set adrift, along with the suffering those journeys entail). And so the second voyage in the poem is emblematic above all of the role of fortune in any human life: "Yeres and dayes fleet this creature . . . as it was hire aventure" (II.463). But this new identification offers commentary upon the Ship of the Church as well, whose voyage through history is likewise a voyage through that sea. In Custance's first voyage, the relation of her grander ship to fortune was explored by other means—chiefly through the narrator's complaint against the stars, seen in retrospect to have been aligned un-

favorably toward the Syrian marriage. The second voyage will explore that relationship again, and provide a truer key to its understanding.

The narrator's earlier speech postulated a universe that is often cruel, but whose malevolent aspects—if we had sufficient knowledge and took sufficient care—we might avoid:

> Imprudent Emperour of Rome, allas!   (II. 309)
> Was ther no philosophre in al thy toun?
> Is no tyme bet than oother in swich cas?
> Of viage is ther noon eleccioun,
> Namely to folk of heigh condicioun?
> Noght whan a roote is of a burthe yknowe?
> Allas, we been to lewed or to slowe!

The Man of Law asks a series of rhetorical questions, raising the commonsense objections in order that they may be put to rest: Why wasn't a better time chosen for the journey? Was there no competent astrologer? Did they have no choice in the matter? But he answers those questions in a fashion not limited to the Romans who are his subject: "we been to lewed or to slowe." Our fortune is written in the stars, but we will never learn to read them correctly. What looks like misfortune here (the appalling slaughter of Christians at the feast, the exile of Custance on a rudderless boat) will be revealed as part of a providential design that, until the very end, can be known only by faith.[64]

Boethius's *Consolation of Philosophy*, which furnishes yet another central text from which Chaucer knew the sea as an image of fortune,[65] uses a parallel strategy. In Book I, Metre 5 (Chaucer's own translation) Boethius charges the Creator with governing all things except man in a rationally comprehensible way:

"We men, that ben noght a foul partie, but a fair partie of so greet a werk, we ben turmented in this see of fortune. Thow governour, withdraugh and restreyne the ravysschynge flodes, and fastne and ferme thise erthes stable with thilke boond by which thou governest the hevene that is so large."

For just as the entire argument of the *Consolation* must be read before this complaint can be wholly laid to rest, so we must know the entire history of Custance in order to answer fully these earlier rhetorical questions. Lady Philosophy will demonstrate to Boethius that Fortune is merely a name for Providence misunderstood, and that the apparent cruelty and caprice of human life are part of a larger providential order whose ends are good. But Chaucer, in his tale of Custance, does not pose the problem in philosophical terms or seek that kind of answer. Custance instead lives out the problem and its resolution—by submitting to time and refusing to become "shaper" of her own life.[66] In terms of *quid agas*, nothing in the story is to be explained as chance. Its shape is meant to teach us courage and trust in the face of mutability.

There are "historical" parallels to this second kind of ship journey as well, which again prevent us from dismissing Custance's voyages as merely "romance adventure" or evidence of a credulous and sentimental narrator. The records of these journeys, though the product of an earlier Celtic Christianity, became significant history for the Roman Church in turn, particularly in *The Voyage of St. Brendan*, a saint's life extant in more than a hundred Latin manuscripts.[67] Though it probably dates from the ninth century, it describes an eight-year voyage supposedly made from 565 to 573 by the saint and his companions in quest of visionary lands, while relying entirely on God's will for their provisions and destinations. One brief passage will illustrate the second of these matters:

"Have no fear," said Brendan, losing no time in encouraging the brethren, "for God is our helper. He is our captain and guide and will steer us out of danger. Just leave the sails and let Him do as He will with His servants and their boat." . . . From time to time the wind would fill their sails, though they knew neither whence it came nor whither it was taking them.[68]

Figure 159, from a late-fifteenth-century French manuscript, illustrates the mode of their journey. The Latin work was translated or adapted into many languages, among them Anglo-Norman in the twelfth century and English around 1300.[69]

We need to remind ourselves that saints' lives were then received as a kind of history, whatever our modern skepticism. But historical evidence of a stricter sort exists as well, involving the small Celtic boat known as a coracle, normally paddled or rowed, that is pictured in figure 160 (from a late-thirteenth-century manuscript of Giraldus Cambrensis's *Topography of Ireland*).[70] *The Anglo-Saxon Chronicle*, for instance, records in 891 the arrival of three Scots at the court of King Alfred "in a boat without any oars from Ireland, which they had left secretly, because they wished for the love of God to be in foreign lands, they cared not where . . . and they took with them enough food for seven days."[71] Still others (Snedgus and MacRiagail) set out to sea, saying, "Let us quit our voyaging . . . save the path that our curragh will take us . . . and let us leave our voyaging to God."[72] *The Book of Leinster* similarly records three young clerics setting out to sea on pilgrimage, taking only three cakes as provision, and saying, "In Christ's name, let us cast away our oars into the sea, and throw ourselves on the mercy of our Lord."[73] This form of sea journey or exile was conceived as a kind of pilgrimage, sometimes termed a *peregrinatio pro amore Dei* (or *propter nomen Domini*, or *ab amorem Christi*), and described as a "white martyrdom."[74]

159. The voyage of St. Brendan. French, late fifteenth century. Note 69.

On the level of moral allegory the story of Custance expresses an associated truth: all these persons discover the Providence that lies behind Fortune by abandoning themselves to Fortune, by refusing to will the direction of their journey. The Celtic monks chose their seafaring freely, as part of a religious vocation; Custance is chosen for it. But the ethos of the action is the same. In the tropological sense, the words of St. Brendan—"Is not the Lord our captain and helmsman? Then leave it to Him to direct us where He wills"[75]—are at one with those of Custance: "In hym triste I, and in his mooder deere, / That is to me my seyl and eek my steere" (II.832).

All literature, of course, impinges upon the moral life of man, implicitly or explicitly, whether the morality it advocates is conventional, is revisionist, or (as in *The Miller's Tale*) attempts to evade such categories altogether. But too often we proceed as if the moral aspect of medieval literature were located chiefly in rhetorical constructs that are unmistakable and unambiguous: in proverbs, *sententiae*, and explicit moralizations. In late-medieval literature, the matter is far more complex: we must "read" signs and identities as well as words, and the former can often be understood only by rethinking their traditional significance against the material of an entire poem.

160. Two Irishmen in a coracle. English, third quarter of the thirteenth century. Note 70.

In its moral sense—in its identity *quid agas*—the image of the ship and the sea possessed one further meaning available for poetic appropriation, which Chaucer likewise made functional in his tale.

In terms of how we ought to live and act, the image concerns sin and temptation as well—not the rule of Fortune merely—and again its first premise is a simple comparison: this sinful world is like the sea, full of perils, tempests, and the risk of drowning. It was described so by Church Fathers, theologians, preachers, and poets,[76] in a tradition that descends from two Old Testament sources, the first Proverbs 23:33–34:

Thy eyes shall behold strange women: and thy heart shall utter perverse things. And thou shalt be as one sleeping in the midst of the sea, and as a pilot fast asleep, when the stern is lost.

Psalm 68, *Salvum me fac, Deus*, is of equal importance:

Save me, O God: for the waters are come in even unto my soul. I stick fast in the mire of the deep: and there is no sure standing. I am come into the depth of the sea: and a tempest hath overwhelmed me. . . . Draw me out of the mire, that I may not stick fast: deliver me from them that hate me, and out of the deep waters. Let not the tempest of water drown me, nor the deep swallow me up: and let not the pit shut her mouth upon me.

This psalm is of great importance in the visual arts, for it is one of the eight customarily illuminated in manuscript Psalters, often with a picture showing King David praying to God from out of entirely literal waters of tribulation (figure 161).[77] The psalm specifically concerns David's sufferings at the hands of his enemies—they are sometimes shown taunting him from the shore[78]—and it is sometimes assimilated to the Ship of the Church tradition, with St. Peter in David's place, floating upon perilous waters (figure 162).[79] But the image could clarify certain kinds of inner experience as well. The

161. David amid the waters
of tribulation. French,
1357. Note 77.

verses from Proverbs concern temptation and sin exclusively, and
that aspect of the "sea of this world" tradition, in its rich medieval
development, can illuminate certain events in Chaucer's narrative
that otherwise have no adequate explanation.

To return to Guillaume de Deguileville's allegory of the pilgrimage
of this life, everyone alive must swim in the sea of this world, and is
in consequence constantly in danger of Satan the fisherman, who
casts his net to catch sinners. (Figure 163 shows him translated into a
fisherman, his face, alas, badly rubbed.) But the larger tradition does
not require that Satan be literally included: waves and tempests, as
symbolic signs, can be readily internalized, to suggest storms of pas-
sion and concupiscence within. Figures 155 and 156 show the pilgrim
swimming alone, though the equation of sea and threat of sin has al-
ready been made explicit.[80] Hugh of St. Victor wrote his magnificent
meditation on the Flood, *De arca Noe morali*, within the same tradi-
tion, after a discussion with his fellow monks about "the instabil-
ity and restlessness of the human heart."[81] The monks had wished
to know its cause and remedy, which Hugh explains in an ex-
tended image:

let a man return to his own heart, and he will find there a stormy ocean
lashed by the fierce billows of overwhelming passions and desires, which

swamp the soul as often as by consent they bring it into subjection. For there is this flood in every man, as long as he lives in this corruptible life, where the flesh lusts against the spirit. Or rather, every man is in this flood, but the good are in it as those borne in ships upon the sea, whereas the bad are in it as shipwrecked persons at the mercy of the waves.[82]

In Guillaume's version, sinners go under, tangle their feet in weeds and drown, whereas those "contemplatyffe" in heart, who love Christ above any earthly thing, "make hem whynges off vertu" to fly to the heavenly mansion. (Both destinies are illustrated in our figure 163.)[83]

Chaucer could have known this tradition from a variety of other texts as well, including an extended passage in *Piers Plowman* beginning "Lat brynge a man in a boot amydde [a] bro[o]d watre." The dreamer's despair at Piers' tearing of the pardon is there countered by the teaching that, even though man's body is like a ship afloat in the

162. St. Peter praying from aboard a ship. French, ca. 1325. Note 79.

163. Satan as fisherman in the sea of the world. English, fifteenth century. Note 80.

turbulent sea of this world, and even though a righteous man will sin seven times daily ("seuen siþes þe sadde man synneþ on þe day"), so long as Charity is man's steersman, he will not commit deadly sin and drown his own soul.[84] In translating Guillaume's ABC poem to the Virgin, Chaucer found expressed a similar urgency and fear:

> Loo, how that theeves sevene chasen mee!   (15)
> Help, lady bright, er that my ship tobreste![85]

Such poems concern an ordinary man, an Everyman, who will fall and rise and fall again, to be saved only by the mystery of God's mercy. Guillaume's pilgrim is such a protagonist, as is (collectively) the pilgrim company that Chaucer assembles at the Tabard at the beginning of *The Canterbury Tales*.

The story of Custance, on the other hand, concerns no ordinary "pilgrimage." She becomes literature precisely because her story lacks such moral dynamics. Custance never seriously doubts or falters, but because she is meant to be understood as a historical person (and it is important to Chaucer's larger design that this be so), she too is finally seen as one who must live "in the sea" in some compromise with perfect integrity. In Guillaume's version,

In the see thei ben, for thei mihten not elles liue bodiliche. But thei seechen not the gostly lyfe in the see. Wel thei witen that in oother place thei shule haue it, and therfore thei swimmen and gon up riht.[86]

Thus Custance's beauty arouses the lust of a knight, who out of his love "so hoote, of foul affeccioun" (II.586) murders her bedfellow, Hermengyld, and thus an apostate steward will later attempt to rape her on her boat. The knight and the steward represent one sort of peril endemic to the sea of this world, which she resists successfully, as both an outward threat and an internal possibility. The temptations that lead to fear, self-pity, despair, suicide, and self-will are likewise conquered: "She wolde do no synne, by no weye" (II.590).

But she is finally "Custance," not Constancy per se, and at the end of the poem Chaucer allows the other possibilities implicit in the image of the sea to surface, to become rhetorically explicit. In a passage very strange if one has not properly estimated the many meanings latent in the image, when Alla and Custance are reunited and returned to England, the sea is used one last time to illuminate their lives, first in relation to fortune, then in relation to passion, sin, and guilt. They return to England to live at last "in joye and in quiete"— the happy ending we would have expected for them—

> But litel while it lasteth, I yow heete,   (II.1132)
> Joye of this world, for tyme wol nat abyde;
> Fro day to nyght it changeth as the tyde.
>
> Who lyved euere in swich delit o day
> That hym ne moeved outher conscience,
> Or ire, or talent, or som kynnes affray,
> Envye, or pride, or passion, or offence?
> I ne seye but for this ende this sentence,
> That litel while in joye or in plesance
> Lasteth the blisse of Alla with Custance.

This passage could easily be judged inappropriate, for we have seen nothing of these sins in Custance, and Alla's life, one deed excepted,[87] seems as virtuous as hers. But now their story is adjusted rhetorically to accord with what we know about all human lives. The joy that is possible within this world, even for persons such as these, must prove finite, unstable, and impure. No exceptions are to be presumed.

Though Constancy as a virtue implies stability and nonmovement above all,[88] the life of Custance is, in appearance, nothing but movement and change, especially in the eight years she spends adrift on the seas, without rudder or willed destination. The power of Chaucer's material depends upon this fact: we are meant to recognize her steadiness as entirely inward, an aspect of the heart and its moral condition. Though the history of Custance is exemplary, the chronicle of even such a life must finally confront certain universal facts about man's experience of this world and his own mortality: "We han here no dwelling citee or place . . . we seeken þat is to come."[89] That too is accounted for at the end of Chaucer's poem.

🌿 QUO TENDAS, ANAGOGIA 🌿

Each of Custance's sea journeys could readily end in death, a fact that colors each leave-taking and brings mortality as a literal subject into the poem: "Ne shal I nevere seen yow moore with ye"; "After hir deeth ful often may she wayte" (II.280, 467).[90] But there are times when more seems to be involved than an ominous departure for a pagan country or the ordeal twice-repeated of being set adrift. In a final kind of allegorical enrichment—the anagogic, concerning that toward which we ultimately move—Chaucer shaped the loading and sending forth of the rudderless ship in ways that suggest the journey the soul makes after death, to its eternal home. In several traditions current in Chaucer's time, a corpse is described as being put out to sea, or the soul is understood to voyage to "the other world" across water. Though Custance will, in fact, survive her voyages, both ideas contribute to the symbolic resonance of Chaucer's poem.

To treat the matter fully, we would need to consider in detail the myth of the river Styx, which encircles Hades and across which Charon ferries the souls of the dead, particularly as it is described in Book VI of the *Aeneid*, where only Aeneas's golden bough allows him safe passage and return.[91] But the suggestiveness of this myth for the medieval imagination can best be demonstrated by turning to Dante's transformation of it in the *Divine Comedy*. In figure 164, for instance, a fourteenth-century Italian illustration to Canto III of the *Inferno*, the damned souls, weeping, groaning, and blaspheming, await a journey across dark waters to their eternal punishment.[92] This event has its counterpart in *Purgatorio* II, where the souls of the newly dead arrive by boat, driven by God's angel, without instrument, oar, or sail (figure 165): "He came on to the shore with a vessel so swift and light that the water took in nothing of it. On the stern stood the heavenly steersman, such that blessedness seemed written upon him, and more than a thousand spirits sat within. *In exitu Israel de Aegypto* they sang all together with one voice, with all that is written after of that psalm; then he made over them the sign of Holy Cross, at which they all flung themselves on the beach, and he went swiftly as he came."[93] These cantos concern groups of people rather than a single person, but together they kept current, and made explicitly Christian, the notion of a soul journey after death that traverses water.

These poems of Virgil and Dante were for Chaucer among the most important of the "olde feldes" out of which "cometh al this

164. Charon and the souls of the damned. Italian, second quarter of the fourteenth century. Note 92.

newe corn": *The House of Fame*, for example, draws heavily on both. But several other narrative traditions to which Chaucer and his first audiences might have had easy access also involve a corpse or a dying man put out to sea.

Three examples worth noting come from the realm of Arthurian romance. In the *Tristan* of Eilhart, for instance—the earliest complete account of the story (ca. 1170–90), thought by many scholars to resemble most closely the lost original—when Tristan lies wounded by the poisoned barb of the Morholt, he decides "that he wanted to set forth on the sea and did not care if he never came to land unless he improved. He asked to be placed in a small boat by himself to die, for he would rather perish alone on the water than endanger all the people with [the] stench [from his wound]." His wish is granted, though "there was great mourning when they carried him to the sea. The noble man asked (as I have heard) that only his harp and sword be put on the ship with him. They did this and pushed the craft from shore. . . . The boat went far out on the wild sea. . . . It drove him here and there, and, without a helmsman, he had to go as it wished, but he no longer cared where the ship sailed."[94] The essential configurations of judgment by setting adrift and a ship of fortune are present, but they are emotionally subordinated to a ship of death tradition: no outcome other than his death is to be looked for. The boat goes at random until it comes to the coast of Ireland, where Tristan is cured by Iseult (who alone has that power) and where the tragic love story has its true beginning. Figure 166 shows the King grieving as Tristan's ship is put to sea, without sail or rudder; it is from the Wienhausen Embroidery (ca. 1310).[95]

The motif is developed in the quest for the Holy Grail as well. When Percival's sister allows herself to be bled beyond recovery in order to heal the leprous lady, she says before dying (here in the version by Sir Thomas Malory, closely translating the thirteenth-century *Queste del Saint Graal*):

"Fayre brothir, sir Percivale, I dye for the helynge of this lady. And whan I am dede, I requyre you that ye burye me nat in thys contrey, but as sone as I am dede putte me in a boote at the nexte haven, and lat me go as aventures woll lede me. And as sone as ye three com to the cité of Sarras, there to enchyeve the Holy Grayle, ye shall fynde me undir a towre aryved. And the[re] bury me in the spirituall palyse." . . . Than sir Percivale made a lettir of all that she had helpe them as in stronge aventures, and put hit in hir [r]yght honde. And so leyde hir in a barge, and coverde hit with blacke sylke. And so the wynde arose and droff the barge frome the londe.[96]

165. Souls ferried to Purgatory. Italian, second quarter of the fourteenth century. Note 93.

166. Tristan put to sea. German, ca. 1310. Note 95.

The unhappy love of the Fair Maid of Astolat for Lancelot ends in a similar fashion. Dying of grief, she asks that her corpse, laid out on a sumptuous bed, be sealed in a ship and set afloat on the Thames, with a man to direct it toward Westminster. There Arthur and Guinevere chance to see it, cause it to be opened, and learn her story.[97]

These, of course, are secular romances. For a closer parallel to Chaucer's *Man of Law's Tale* we may turn to the death journey of St. James the Greater, the first of the Apostles to suffer martyrdom. He was beheaded by Herod Agrippa I in the year 44 (Acts 12:2). According to the legend, his followers put his body in a boat and set it out to sea to go where God willed, accompanying the body without guiding its journey. It arrived in Galicia in northern Spain, where its presence as a holy relic made the cathedral at Compostela the foremost pilgrimage shrine in western Europe (and St. James the patron saint of pilgrims). Though this part of his legend is unrecorded before the seventh century, it was credited by Christians throughout the Middle Ages.

Here, as narrated in *The Golden Legend* of Jacobus de Voragine, are the details most congruent with Chaucer's story of Custance:

After the apostle's death, his disciples, in fear of the Jews, placed his body in a boat at night, embarked with him, although the boat had neither rudder nor steersman, and set sail, trusting to the providence of God to determine the place of his burial.[98]

Figure 167, from a thirteenth-century collection of saints' lives in French, shows the corpse and its attendants floating on the sea. In an English alabaster retable given to the Cathedral of Santiago de Com-

167. The death ship of St. James the Greater. French, second half of the thirteenth century. Note 99.

postela in 1456 by John Goodyear, a priest from the Isle of Wight, the ship is attended by three angels, one watching over the body while the other two tend the sails.[99] As in Chaucer's tale, not only do ideas of the ship of death and the discovery of God's providence within the sea of fortune contribute to the richness of the image, but the narrative lays similar claim to being historically true.

The legend of another saint—that of Mary Magdalen as painted in her chapel at Assisi—incorporates an interesting variation on this tradition. According to the legend, the last thirty years of her life were spent in total reclusion in a mountain cave, where angels bore her aloft at the seven canonical hours every day so that she might hear the chanting of the heavenly hosts. She lived on that music, and needed no other food. When she knew her death was near, she had herself brought by the angels to Saint Maximinus, from whom she received last Communion. In illustrating the end of her life (figure 168), Giotto and his assistants show her watched by reverent churchmen as she kneels for the sacrament, and again above, supported by angels in an orange or umber-colored boat against a sky as dark blue as a sea. Since her daily contemplation of the joys of heaven is painted in a lunette elsewhere in the chapel, the boat image here must represent the death journey of her soul. In the words of *The Golden Legend*, "no sooner had she taken the Communion than her body fell lifeless before the altar, and her soul took its flight to the Lord."[100] The scene is painted by program on the wall directly facing our figure 139, the depiction of her ship journey to Marseilles.

Against such images, and others yet to be adduced, I wish to examine more closely Custance's later voyages and their conclusion. In Syria, she is set adrift:

> . . . in a ship al steerelees, God woot,   (II.439)
> They han hir set. . . .
>
> A certein tresor that she thider ladde,
> And, sooth to seyn, vitaille greet plentee
> They han hire yeven, and clothes eek she hadde,
> And forth she sailleth in the salte see.

In Northumbria, she is set adrift again, in a similar manner:

> "But in the same ship as he hire fond,   (II.799)
> Hire, and hir yonge sone, and al hir geere,
> He sholde putte, and croude hire fro the lond."
>
> Vitailled was the ship, it is no drede,   (II.869)
> Habundantly for hire ful longe space,
> And othere necessaries that sholde nede
> She hadde ynogh, heryed be Goddes grace!
> For wynd and weder almyghty God purchace,
> And brynge hire hoom! I kan no bettre seye,
> But in the see she dryveth forth hir weye.

When these passages are set against their source, what is most remarkable is their degree of generality: "a certein tresor"; "vitaille greet plentee"; "al hir geere"; "othere necessaries." Trevet's sultaness, in contrast, "caused a ship to be stored with victuals, bread which is called biscuit, peas, beans, sugar, honey, and wine, to sustain the life of the maiden for three years. And in this ship she caused to be placed

168. The soul of St. Mary Magdalen borne by angels to heaven. School of Giotto, 1314–29. Note 100.

all the riches and the treasure which the Emperor Tiberius had sent with the maid Constance, his daughter." [101] Chaucer never measures out the peas and beans, nor does he identify the treasure as being specifically wedding dowry. Instead there is a generalized lading— woman and food and treasure in a boat that will move at random on the waters—unburdened by specifications that would diminish the allegorical potential of the image. And in place of narrative detail concerning long years spent at sea, we are given highly rhetorical passages that name the Biblical antecedents for such protection from danger: Daniel in the lion's den, Jonah in the whale, the Israelites crossing the Red Sea, the stilling of the four winds in the Apocalypse, the feeding of St. Mary of Egypt, Susannah among the elders, David against Goliath, Judith in Holofernes' tent. [102]

All of these Chaucer has added to Trevet. Though no one has discovered a source that brings them together in precisely the same company, John Yunck has discovered in the liturgy one roughly parallel grouping: Daniel, Moses, David, and Susannah all figure in the *Ordo commendationis animae*, a ceremony of prayers for the dying, recited immediately before administering extreme unction. Indeed, one of Chaucer's lines takes its very syntax from that prayer: "Immortal God, that savedest Susanne / Fro false blame" (II.639) translates "Domine . . . qui liberasti . . . Susannam de falso crimine."[103] Such a recital serves both to celebrate and make historically credible the miracle of Custance's deliverance, but it may be meant to carry as well liturgical echoes attending the soul as it begins its death journey, the journey to eternal life.

Fully to trace the history of the ship of death tradition would require an excursus into ancient Egyptian beliefs about that journey, along with learned speculation concerning the transmission and transformation of such ideas, none of it to our present purpose.[104] Chaucer knew nothing of such distant origins. It is enough to note that early Christian culture borrowed and transformed those earlier pagan beliefs, and that ship symbolism became important to both the funeral liturgy and the tomb sculpture of the early Church. Death was conceived as a *migratio ad Dominum*, a journey of the soul to God.

Tombstones from the catacombs, for instance, often show a ship traveling to the right (indicating the east, and representing eternity), where the monogram *chi-ro* is often carved, signifying Christ; on top of the ship's mast there is sometimes shown a bird, representing the soul, which holds a branch in its beak. Other closely related tombstones depict the soul safely arrived in the harbor of eternity. Figure 169, a fourth-century stele from Terenouthis (in Christianized lower Egypt), offers a particularly expressive example.[105]

When Christianity came to northern Europe, it found there pagan death customs, at least for those of high rank, that shared some of the same configurations and could readily be converted to Christian meaning. From the pagan practice of setting a boat out to sea laden with everything necessary for the journey to the next world (including treasure meant to indicate the status of the dead person) Christianity apparently moved to, or chose to prefer among the ceremonies already available, the custom of ship burial, in which a similar lading took place upon a seacoast or riverbank, after which the ship was covered with earth to form a barrow. Such boat graves or cenotaphs (they do not all contain the remains of bodies) are numerous, and to them we owe much of our knowledge of the period's art and patterns of trade.[106] Elsewhere such customs were simplified; near Stockholm, for instance, the early burial ground at Badelunda is enclosed within the outline of a ship made by carefully placed upright stones.[107]

Uniting all these customs is a single idea: the notion of a ship trav-

169. A soul arrives in the harbor of eternity. Coptic, fourth century. Note 105.

eling through unknown perils, guided by the will of God, bearing as its greatest treasure the soul of someone dead. It can be found at its simplest in the Anglo-Saxon *Rune Poem*, where the death of Ing is described simply as the moment in which he *ofer wæg gewat*, "departed over the waves,"[108] whereas Cynewulf's runic signature at the end of *The Fates of the Apostles* (ninth century)—a meditation on the nearness of his own death—explores the full emotive power of the metaphor: "May he remember, who loves this lay, to ask for me God's comfort and aid. For I must go forth far hence alone, seeking a home, setting out on a journey—I know not whither—out of this world. Unknown are those dwellings, that region, and realm."[109]

The voyages in rudderless boats made by God's "pilgrims," the *pere-grini pro amore Dei* already discussed, also readily became emblem-atic of the journey man makes to the next world: in "Cormac's Choice," an Irish poem of the early tenth century, the simple boat made of hides in which Cormac sets sail for God's sake becomes in his meditation the "narrow boat" that will bring him to eternal judgment.[110]

Although Chaucer could not have known these early antecedents, they underlie the traditions already surveyed that kept the idea of a ship of death current in his own century. And there are others. In Guillaume de Deguileville's *Pilgrimage of the Soul*, for instance (the lengthy sequel to his *Pilgrimage of Human Life*), the earlier poem's rich imagery of the sea of the world and the Ship of the Church is completed by songs sung by the blessed souls as they enter heaven, declaring Paradise their goal, their port, their final shore ("Du tout leur pelerinage / Dont fin es, port et rivage").[111] Hoccleve, too, con-cludes his translation of an *Art of Holy Dying* by urging us to imitate the prudence of a merchant who readies a cargo ship for a long jour-ney and takes care to see it safely out of harbor, for

> Right as a Marchant stondynge in a port,
> His ship þat charged is with marchandyse
> To go to fer parties / for confort
> Of him self / lookeþ / þat it in sauf wyse
> Passe out . . .

so we too should prepare our soul for its departure hence:

> See to thy soule so / or thow hens weende,
> Þat it may han the lyf þat haath noon eende.[112]

Lydgate, in his "Testament," preparing his soul for death, derives his hope from "Crystes woundes five / Wherby we cleyme, of mercyful piete, / Thorow helpe of Iesu at gracious port taryve,"[113] a journey longer and a haven more gracious than anything the pagan Troilus was able to imagine in his suffering: "God wold I were aryved in the port / Of deth, to which my sorwe wol me lede!"; "Toward my deth with wynd in steere I saille. . . . My ship and me Caribdis wol de-voure" (*TC*, I, 526–27; V, 641, 644).

The wish to explore that final possible *significatio* of the tale's cen-tral image may explain yet another change that Chaucer made in his source; for whereas in Trevet a new boat is prepared for Constance when she is driven from Northumbria,[114] in Chaucer's version the forged letter orders the constable to send her forth "in the same ship as he hire fond." The third journey resumes the second, emphasizing the continuity of the whole *peregrinatio* and linking the two in ways that can be read anagogically, as the unitary death voyage of the soul.

As the story approaches its resolution, all journeys point toward Rome—that of Custance and her son, that of the Senator and his fleet, and that of Alla on penitential pilgrimage. Rome is the center of the poem's gravity, its geography, and its moral and spiritual meaning; and the poem's "numbers," which seem intimately connected with the decision to conflate two separate boats into one, reinforce this view. In Trevet, events are far more clearly located in time: the first boat is stored with provisions to last three years; Constance arrives in Northumbria in the eighth month of the fourth year; in the second year of the second journey she is attacked by the apostate steward; in the fifth year of that journey she encounters the Senator and his navy; and she lives for twelve years with the Senator and his wife before the final reunions take place.[115] Whereas Trevet's numbers have the specificity of chronicle, Chaucer's numbers invite a symbolic reading, for he suppresses all but two relating to her journeys: her first voyage lasts "thre yeer and moore," her second "fyve yeer and moore" (II.499, 902). Though their sum is made indeterminate by the phrase "and moore," they are linked by the single boat and the single "steerelesse" mode of voyage, and they associate her journey's end with the number eight. That too invites reflection.

For eight, in medieval exegesis, was understood to be the number of eternity, rebirth, and new beginnings: Christ had risen on the eighth day (the day after the Jewish Sabbath); eight persons had been saved in Noah's ark; and in St. Augustine's influential analysis, the history of the world divides itself into eight ages—six mark its historical sequence, the seventh is coeval with them all (the Sabbath of the dead, begun with Abel), and the eighth inaugurates eternity (with Doomsday its beginning). Thus it is that baptisteries and baptismal fonts are often octagonal, their geometry emblematic of the sacrament's meaning.[116] By choosing to retain just two numbers from all the history that separates Custance's journey from Syria and her return journey to Rome, Chaucer brings her to that city in one boat and in something like eight years. As in the many moralizations on the stories of the *Gesta Romanorum* that identify Rome allegorically with heaven and the Roman Emperor with God,[117] so Custance's journey to that city, and her reunion with her father the Emperor, are heavy with a consequence that cannot be limited to the literal.[118] Though the joy of this homecoming is on one level transitory— she still must die her literal death—nevertheless her homecoming adumbrates the joy of a further journey's end, in heaven. "And brynge hire hoom! I kan no bettre seye, / But in the see she dryveth forth hir weye." (II.874.)

Christian ideas about the afterlife have always given a significant place to the return to native country and the restoration of true community. Whether our life in this world be conceived as pilgrimage or

exile—the dominant medieval metaphors, sometimes interchange-
able—a sense of distance, peril, and alienation is paramount. It lies,
for example, behind the words of St. Augustine, "our pilgrimage [is]
in this world, although our community is in heaven,"[119] as it does
behind the prayer inscribed in a historiated initial from the Beaufort
Book of Hours (ca. 1399): "Mater ora filium ut post hoc exilium
nobis donet gaudium sine fine" ("Mother, pray to your Son that after
this exile He grant us joy without end").[120]

Because a similar anagogical reading of human experience under-
lies the conclusion of Chaucer's poem, we cannot adequately explain
it in the fashion common a generation ago, when it was simply la-
beled the kind of "recognition scene" to be expected in Greek ro-
mance, or its subcategory, the persecuted-queen cycle.[121] Chaucer, to
be sure, exploits the pathos intrinsic in the literal situation with great
skill. But because his first audiences were accustomed to hearing the
joys of heaven expressed in terms of reunion with family, royal
feasts, and restored community, he was able to use the language of
such things—under the pressure of the allegorical voyage—to speak
not only of joy in the present but of what is to come. As St. Cyprian
of Carthage expressed it:

What man after having been abroad would not hasten to return to his native
land? Who, when hurrying to sail to his family, would not more eagerly
long for a favorable wind that he might more quickly embrace his dear
ones? We account Paradise our country, we have already begun to look upon
the patriarchs as our parents. . . . A great number of our dear ones there
await us, parents, brothers, children. . . . To these, beloved brethren, let us
hasten with eager longing, let us pray that it may befall us speedily to be
with them, speedily to come to Christ.[122]

Chaucer's concluding paragraph to *The Parson's Tale*, describing the
joys of heaven, includes "the blisful compaignye that rejoysen hem
everemo, everich of otheres joye" (x.1077).[123] And Custance's re-
union with her husband is explicitly related to that happiness:

> And swich a blisse is ther bitwix hem two   (II.1075)
> That, save the joye that lasteth everemo,
> Ther is noon lyk that any creature
> Hath seyn or shal, whil that the world may dure.

In the visual arts, although heaven is most frequently filled with
symmetrical ranks of the blessed adoring God—an experience of
perfect oneness within multiplicity—sometimes there is shown in-
stead a communion of saints engaged in sober, graceful, intimate dis-
course, in numerous groups of two or three, with God above them
all. A beautiful miniature (figure 170) from a late-fifteenth-century
French manuscript of *The City of God* conceives Paradise as a place
in which the blessed have not lost human interest in one another,

170. Paradise. French, ca. 1473. Note 124.

though that interest is now sanctified in eternity, as does a version of
Paradise (figure 171) painted by Giovanni di Paolo ca. 1445—a paint-
ing deeply moving in its affirmation of human conversation and so-
ciety.[124] As Chaucer's Prioress will say of her "litel clergeoun" in a
concluding petition, "Ther he is now, God leve us for to meete"
(VII.683).

In the first of the feasts that conclude Chaucer's narrative, King
Alla sees his son for the first time, and is put in mind of the wife he
thinks he has lost forever. Their reunion follows. At the second feast,
to which her father the Emperor of Rome has been invited, the joy is
even greater.

> The morwe cam, and Alla gan hym dresse,   (II.1100)
> And eek his wyf, this Emperour to meete;
> And forth they ryde in joye and in gladnesse.
> And whan she saugh hir fader in the strete,
> She lighte doun, and falleth hym to feete.
> "Fader," quod she, "youre yonge child Custance
> Is now ful clene out of youre remembrance.

I am youre doghter Custance," quod she,
"That whilom ye han sent unto Surrye.
It am I, fader, that in the salte see
Was put allone and dampned for to dye.
Now, goode fader, mercy I yow crye!
Sende me namoore unto noon hethenesse,
But thonketh my lord heere of his kyndenesse."

The happiness of this final reunion, though its emotional complexity is great, is expressed in absolutely simple social terms:

171. Paradise. Giovanni di Paolo, ca. 1445. Note 124.

> The day goth faste, I wol no lenger lette.   (II. 1117)
> This glade folk to dyner they hem sette;
> In joye and blisse at mete I lete hem dwelle
> A thousand foold wel moore than I kan telle.

The passage brings together Senator, King and Queen, Emperor and heir—or to name them differently, father, daughter, husband, wife, son, and fellow Christian. It is a community based on an extended sense of family, on what Christ called a father's house in which there are many mansions. At the right of figure 172, from a *Biblia pauperum* dated ca. 1400, we see the company of saints through the windows of such a building[125]—illustrating the sense of community that, according to *The Book of Vices and Virtues*, explains why Christ taught us to pray in the *Pater noster* "fadre oure" instead of "fadre myn," and "ȝue vs" our daily bread instead of "ȝue me."[126]

Indeed the communal dinner itself asks to be read as part of an eschatalogical ending. To the left of the heavenly mansion on the same folio page is painted one of its Old Testament antecedents, the feasting of the children of Job (figure 172, left), a feast every bit as literal as that Chaucer asks us to imagine near the end of his tale.[127] These

172. The house of many mansions, right; and left, the feasting of the children of Job. Flemish or Rhenish, ca. 1400. Note 125.

173. The feasts of Ahasuerus and of Job's children. Dutch, first half of the fifteenth century. Note 128.

pictures in the *Biblia pauperum* serve to tell us that such earthly feasts were what the patriarchs were allowed to know of heaven—that they prefigured the joys of heaven—and it is through two such earthly feasts that the perilous journeys of Custance reach their happy end. In the *Speculum humanae salvationis*, written about 1324, another antetype is added: in figure 173, which illustrates the two in a fifteenth-century Dutch manuscript, the feasting of Job's children is shown on the right, and King Ahasuerus's 180-day feast on the left.[128] Giving authority to both these works, which were immensely popular and created a rich pictorial tradition, is the fact that Christ spoke of heaven as a feast—a figure the Apostle John developed in the Apocalypse into the great marriage supper of the Lamb. Figure 174 shows an English version from about 1350, in which the mystery of the Lamb is adored upon the altar but its essence is conveyed in terms of a very literal meal, including fish, being eaten by the saints below.[129]

Numerous examples might be cited of late-medieval vernacular texts in which heaven is so described—including the "blisful feste" of Chaucer's own *Second Nun's Tale* (VIII.241).[130] But finally Chaucer wishes to insist, with fully as much care as he created the proximate

174. The marriage supper of the Lamb. English, ca. 1350. Note 129.

likeness, that this earthly reunion, this earthly banquet, cannot last. The two feasting scenes serve as a foretaste and symbolic preenactment of the joy in heaven that alone never "changeth as the tyde," because it has already paid its dues to death. Our earthly feasts, in contrast, are celebrated under the shadow of fortune, mortality, sin, and error. Chaucer's insistence that even this reunion is not the end becomes almost unbearably moving after the suffering and separation his central characters have endured.[131] They still must die their real deaths, experience their final separations, before they can come together again in a new communion, in a stable and continuing place. Chaucer's poem avoids the happy ending characteristic of most such tales of wonder, for he would remind us that reunion and restoration here are impermanent. Even those constant in the faith must die to happiness, going a last journey to that place recorded by St. John in Apocalypse 21: "And I saw a new heaven and a new earth: for the first heaven and the first earth were passed away; and there was no more sea."

 CONCLUSION

Et mare iam non est.[132] The materials Chaucer found in his chronicle source he deepened in many ways, making them into a complex work of art. Though not every allegorical equivalence is the same, the larger process is very like that described by Hugh of St. Victor, after the first ten chapters of his remarkable *De arca Noe morali* already cited:

But look what has happened. We set out to talk about one ark, and one thing has so led to another that it seems now we have to speak not of one only, but of four. Of these, the two that are visible were built visibly and outwardly, but the two that are invisible come into being inwardly and invisibly, by an unseen process of construction. The first is that which Noah made, with hatchets and axes, using wood and pitch as his materials. The second is that which Christ made through His preachers, by gathering the nations into a single confession of faith. The third is that which wisdom builds daily in our hearts through continual meditation on the law of God. The fourth is that which mother grace effects in us by joining together many virtues in a single charity. . . . Let us call the first Noah's ark, the second the ark of the Church, the third the ark of wisdom, and the fourth the ark of mother grace. Nevertheless there is in a certain sense only one ark everywhere. . . . The form is one, though the matter is different, for that which is actualized in the wood is actualized also in the people, and that which is found in the heart is the same as that which is found in charity.[133]

Or, in the more technical language of St. Thomas Aquinas:

The multiplicity of these interpretations does not cause ambiguity or any sort of equivocation, since these interpretations are not multiplied because one word signifies several things, but because the things signified by the words can themselves be types of other things.[134]

Hugh of St. Victor began with simple narrative material—the Genesis account of the Flood—and demonstrated how the single can become multiple in meditation, without ever losing its essential unity and integrity of form. Chaucer does not include his own exegesis, but he suggests the directions in which that exegesis may properly proceed. His aim is not a set of equivalences, but a narrative enriched by the contextual possibility of such meaning. The story of Custance is by no means allegorical poetry in its purest form: her life does not disappear into its own explanation.[135] It is instead the record of a poet's meditation on a story found in history and honored always, even in those moments when its images become most general in their significance, as being literally true.

I have sought to document the sorts of material from late-medieval culture upon which Chaucer drew, and which would have allowed at least some part of his audience to follow him in the full enterprise of his art. My point is not that his earliest audiences necessarily thought about all these things when they thought about Custance, but rather that because they had thought about such things before and in other places—"seen" them imaged in pictures and in words—they would have heard her story in ways different from those of a modern reader innocent of such traditions. And they would have thought about it, in memory, in ways richer by far. The central link between their prior experience in literature and the visual arts and the experience of Chaucer's tale is an image, simple and absolute—a woman in a rudderless boat, afloat upon the sea.

To call such a tale "sentimental" is perhaps chiefly to declare our modern difficulty in imagining such terrible tests as true, or truly assented to. But there is no evidence that medieval authors or audiences responded in that fashion. The tale does indeed ask us to feel for and about its central character, but through its central narrative image, it also requires us to think, and in that thinking to discover the deeper kinds of logic that underlie the perils, the miraculous protection, the episodic journeys, the circularity of the whole.

In terms of the larger design, Chaucer chose to offer through this tale a vision exemplary to, and corrective of, late-fourteenth-century Christianity—the mostly casual, careless, "lived-in" Christianity so brilliantly explored in the majority of the *General Prologue* portraits and in the two fabliaux. He turns to the materials of a more primitive faith for something like a rebeginning of the literary pilgrimage as art, and for the first time in the sequence, shows us that historical truth can be made artistically elaborate and polysemously beautiful. We witness the conversion of time and journey themes, so important in the preceding tales, to new and purposive ends. Time is at last conceived as redemptive, and old Egeus's "pilgrymes, passynge to and fro" within the confines of the pagan world of *The Knight's Tale* (I.2848), are set free at last, under a Christian dispensation, to move toward true *patria, civitas, communitas*. And poetry itself, which to this point in the *Tales* has served chiefly to mediate between fictional contexts and iconographic truth, is allowed at last to speak in a complex but univocal way. The image most central to this tale inhabits its narrative context in a fashion new to the sequence thus far. Its purpose is not to suggest (as in *The Knight's Tale*) ideas of limitation that run counter to the idealism of the tale's major actions. It is not used (as in *The Miller's Tale*) as a means of evading, imaginatively, the categories and imperatives of moral life. Nor is it used (as in *The Reeve's Tale*) in cynical contempt of its own wisdom. Instead, context and narrative image yield everywhere the same meaning, pointing beyond themselves to a reality that can include the full literal text without disjunction or disharmony. "Al is to schewe vs þat þis lif nys not but a passage, and þe deþ nys but a passage, and to lyue here nys but a passage."[136] It tells us that if man will prove constant, in the end Christ will speak to the storm at sea, as He does in an illumination from the Bedford Book of Hours, masterful words suggesting more than the literal: "Cessez vent et torment et tempeste," "Let wind and torment and tempest cease."[137]

Conclusion

HEN I began the final version of this book I set myself two goals: first, to bring into the critical arena certain theories of imagery that I think important to the way Chaucer made poems and the way he expected his audiences to receive them; and second, to write about the art and meaning of the opening sequence of tales in a manner informed by those theories, introducing my reader as richly as I could to the traditions common to literature and the visual arts that seem to me vital to their meaning. We have examined several groups of images in relation to those tales—images sufficiently "in register" with each other, in terms of configuration and symbolic content, to constitute a tradition—not in search of some "reciprocal illumination of the arts," but simply in order to join the part of Chaucer's audience that knew these traditions from many other places, for whom such knowledge was part of the essential literacy they brought to his narrative art. Although the images studied in this book have long histories that antedate Chaucer, the renewal of such imagery within a literature interested in imitating the appearances and modalities of the natural world is a remarkable achievement, and Chaucer was in England its great originator. The brilliance with which he unites symbolic image and mimetic, verisimilar action is one of the most distinctive aspects of his mature art—as important, I suggest, as his preference for the easy and unforced comparison (whether simile or metaphor), which Charles Muscatine has declared intrinsic to the style of the man and the style of the work.[1]

In these readings I have sought to pay both elements, the mimetic and the symbolic, equal attention, taking as an important goal the need to "save the phenomena"—to respect the apparent intention and level of seriousness of the literal text, without constant recourse to ironic interpretations. I have argued that Chaucer's narratives characteristically confirm, and are illuminated by, general truths embodied in traditional images; and I have sought to demonstrate with equal force that they are never simply disguised statements of those truths. The extrinsic cultural affiliation of the image provides a cue for meditation, but it invites us to reflect upon the fiction in which it has been discovered, as well as its application to one's life. In this kind of late medieval art, context has become more than cortex. Truth inhabits detail, and cannot in the end be separated from it.

Robert Payne based his fine study of Chaucer's rhetorical art on two essential propositions. First, "tradition, in its common medieval sense, implied what was nearest to stability in human knowledge: the preserved record of what is constantly meaningful to all men in all times and places, and therefore a record of the way in which temporal events reflect eternal purposes." And second, "if [Chaucer's] poetry were to live at all, it had to grow out of the past in such a way as to keep the past alive in it."[2] It is in just such terms that I have sought to read the larger iconographic component of Chaucer's art. To join Chaucer's first audiences in discovering such images and thinking about their meaning is to be put in touch with a whole repertory of imagery, a repertory by that very act revived and renewed. It is to read in the visual library of an age, and—if I may express my highest hope—to read in *The Canterbury Tales* more richly.

But this book, for all that high intent, is finally no more than *a* reading of *The Canterbury Tales*: one reader's account of his experience. That experience has been enhanced by the privilege of examining, over a period of years and in many of the great libraries of Europe and America, hundreds of medieval illuminated manuscripts; and so it has emerged iconographic in its emphasis. But even within those privileged terms, it is finally personal, partitive, less rich than the text itself. My insights are limited to what I have been able to discover, and by the interests and accidents that have moved me toward these discoveries rather than others perhaps equally possible. I have described what seem to me the major images in Chaucer's opening tales: the ideomatic centers toward which the poems move, around which they organize many of their details, and by means of which they invite us to think about their actions on a level deeper than the continuities of plot or character alone.

In an effort to avoid idiosyncratic and anachronistic readings, I have documented in detail the texts and pictures that make these images seem charged with meaning for the larger narrative action. But I do not imagine these readings to be, in Milton's phrase, doctrinal to a nation, a definitive account of narrative imagery in *The Canterbury Tales*. The tales are too rich for that, and the interests of readers too various. Literature, it has been said, marks the intersection between subjective expression and subjective apprehension,[3] and there will be readers of this book, learned in texts and pictures other than those that have most interested me, who will discover in these tales images of comparable significance here passed over; still other readers will wish to interpret the images examined here as leading to conclusions different from my own. The possibility of supplementation I cannot, in any precise way, anticipate: it will be based on traditions I do not know or have failed to recognize. The possibility of divergent readings I have attempted to forward and assist, surveying in its full semantic range each iconographic tradition that has seemed relevant, without limiting my discussion to the part of it I think Chaucer most intended.

Because my meaning will be clearer now, this seems a good place to restate the grounds upon which I have declared poetic images of this kind central to an iconographic reading of *The Canterbury Tales*. We have focused upon images that (1) the tale invites us to imagine and hold in mind as the narrative action progresses; that (2) are recognizably akin to other images known from other medieval contexts, where they bear expressly symbolic meaning; and that (3) offer an appropriate and illuminating guide to our understanding of something substantial in the tale in which they occur. To put it another way, they are essential to the action, they are affiliated with other images in other texts, and they organize and clarify—on a level deeper than the linear continuities of plot—our experience of the narrative. Only when all three of these conditions are fulfilled do we have an image of the sort I have stipulated here.

An example or two of images that do not so qualify may make my meaning more clear. In *The Man of Law's Tale*, for instance, the scene in which a lecherous knight murders Hermengyld to revenge himself upon Custance is strongly visual:

> . . . pryvely upon a nyght he crepte   (II.594)
> In Hermengyldes chambre, whil she slepte.
>
> Wery, forwaked in hire orisouns,
> Slepeth Custance, and Hermengyld also.
> This knyght, thurgh Sathanas temptaciouns,
> Al softely is to the bed ygo,
> And kitte the throte of Hermengyld atwo,
> And leyde the blody knyf by dame Custance,
> And wente his wey, ther God yeve hym meschance!

The murderer arranges a criminal tableau in which the proximity of corpse and bloody knife suggest Custance's guilt, and leave her speechless in her own defense. As readers, we too imagine the scene— it meets perfectly well the first of the criteria outlined above— and it could be related, no doubt, to certain stereotypes in the depiction of murder in other medieval texts and pictures. But it lacks affiliation with images whose meaning is expressly symbolic—my second criterion—and thus does not satisfy my third: it invites no meditation beyond itself; it is a narrative image without iconographic dimension.

The same tale can provide another sort of image that is likewise excluded from this study. Consider the decision of the Sultan's mother to kill an entire Christian company—some newly arrived from Rome, others newly converted in Syria—under the guise of hospitality:

> The tyme cam, this olde Sowdanesse   (II.414)
> Ordeyned hath this feeste of which I tolde,
> And to the feeste Cristen folk hem dresse
> In general, ye, bothe yonge and olde.
> Heere may men feeste and roialtee biholde,
> And deyntes mo than I kan yow devyse;
> But al to deere they boghte it er they ryse.
>
> O sodeyn wo, that evere art successour
> To worldly blisse, spreynd with bitternesse!
> The ende of the joye of oure worldly labour!
> Wo occupieth the fyn of oure gladnesse. . . .
>
> For shortly for to tellen, at o word,
> The Sowdan and the Cristen everichone
> Been al tohewe and stiked at the bord,
> But it were oonly dame Custance allone. . . .
>
> Ne ther was Surryen noon that was converted,
> That of the conseil of the Sowdan woot,
> That he nas al tohewe er he asterted.

Again the scene is powerful and vivid, inviting us to imagine it in our mind's eye (criterion one). This time moreover (criterion two) the image *is* affiliated with a symbolic tradition—the imagery of Death at the Feast, widespread in late-medieval art—and is therefore able to suggest moral meaning of the sort rhymed in the second stanza quoted above: it expresses the idea that even in the midst of our greatest pleasure and good fortune, we are vulnerable; death will end the feast of life. The image satisfies two of my criteria, but not the third: it does not become a center of meaning for the entire poem. I think Chaucer employs this image in that maximum way elsewhere— I shall write about it as central to *The Pardoner's Tale*—but here it does not bear such emphasis.

In the four lines that follow, a greater image is begun:

> And Custance han they take anon, foot-hoot,   (II.438)
> And in a ship al steerelees, God woot,
> They han hir set, and bidde hire lerne saille
> Out of Surrye agaynward to Ytaille.

The image of a person adrift on the sea in a rudderless boat will recur several times in the action; it has already been anticipated by the ship that brought Custance to Syria from Rome; and it holds potential within it not only the theme of fortune's variance, but several other themes untouched by the imagery of Death at the Feast. The latter image, though it is powerful and iconographic, and though it could be said to serve as a negative antetype to the poem's concluding feast, does not occupy a comparable imaginative space. The subject of *The Man of Law's Tale* is finally not forgetfulness in the midst of life's pleasures.

In *The Reeve's Tale*, Chaucer's use of the mill as a witty figure for copulation is likewise subordinate to the image of the horse un-bridled. As Beryl Rowland has taught us, the expression *molere mulierem* had long been used to describe the sexual act, "the husband being the miller who grinds and the wife the mill."[4] That proverbial comparison no doubt underlies some of Chaucer's most audacious comic effects in the tale, as in its conclusion—"Thus is the proude millere wel ybete, / And hath ylost the gryndynge of the whete" (1.4313)—or even (perhaps) its description of the milling process:

> "By God, right by the hopur wil I stande,"   (1.4036)
> Quod John, "and se howgates the corn gas in.
> Yet saugh I nevere, by my fader kyn,
> How that the hopur wagges til and fra."

But the wit of the implied comparison is purely local in its effect; it invites no extended meditation. The image of the horse unbridled, in contrast, not only is developed at far greater length, but invades the rhetoric of the second half of the tale, links the two major actions, and becomes a key to the character of its teller, creating a distinctive narrative voice. It is far richer—both in medieval tradition and in Chaucer's usage—than the image of the mill as sexual metaphor: the latter is too limited in its suggestiveness to function in that greater way.

Our subject, in short, has been Chaucer's use of imagery at its maximum power, not as rhetorical ornament but as an iconographic possibility of narrative action itself. Chaucer was not a "painterly" poet; his iconographic descriptions are swift, spare, and concerned only with the essential. But they are descriptions, and they invite a certain activity in response. The degree of their indeterminacy— their lack of inessential specification—indeed facilitates iconographic recognition, for it is the outline and notional content of an image that ultimately relate it to other images in this powerful way, not style, artistic quality, or degree of circumstantial detail. The pictures re-produced in this book encompass an entire artistic spectrum, ranging from the sketchy and diagrammatic to the sumptuously decorated and detailed, but in terms of lexical meaning, their differences matter far less than their similarities. Chaucer individuates his most important images not by descriptive flourish, but by making them serve as the scene or object of an action; in Chaucer's art function, not degree of detail, gives an iconographic image its importance.

The images we have examined emerge from a meditation upon story rather than from the wish to exemplify an idea, and Chaucer, in working them poetically, observes a decorum intrinsic to their origins. He does not insist upon their symbolic dimension or make the surface coherence of the story depend upon that learned recognition. But he invites all who will to follow him in discovering these iconic centers of meaning within the heart of story, where ideas emerge from experience, and where tradition is honored by its rediscovery, by the confirming of its authority anew. Such imagery, for the most part, is mercifully removed from the bizarre, unnatural, or grotesque sort of invention the *ars memoriae* so frequently commended as being most easy to hold in mind[5]—the kind of image represented by our figure 23, showing Envy, Treason, and Detraction as three hags crawling along the ground. Chaucer instead took care that the narrative image should remain in scale with the action that encloses it, and in harmony with the verisimilar detail of its setting. Whatever the intellectual pressure he may bring to bear on such an image—at its greatest, in the present volume, in the prison/garden and the tournament amphitheatre of *The Knight's Tale*—that image remains rooted in the mimetic surfaces of his art.

So much then for the nature of these images. I have reserved for my final pages the hardest question that they pose as a sequence. If we read *The Man of Law's Introduction and Tale* not as a new beginning—the beginning of a putative "second day"—but instead as the conclusion to a sequence of tales designed to begin the journey, then its *Introduction* offers a rebuke to all that has gone before. More than a quarter of the day is spent, says Harry Bailly, and time is awasting: "Lat us nat mowlen thus in ydelnesse." He turns to the Man of Law for something more grave, more decorous, and more profitable, and is rewarded with the tale we examined in the last chapter: a tale that is part of the history of England's conversion to Christianity, that refers to Roman history for authentication, and that Chaucer translated from an Anglo-Norman chronicle written for a royal English nun. Taking leave of the fictive "lie"—which at its most dignified can do no more than convey a hidden truth—Chaucer turns to a story understood to be true, and shows us the further truths it carries within itself, accessible to poetry and meditation. It will be clear by now that I think *The Man of Law's Tale* worthy of the place it is given; it is a narrative of great richness and power, grand

and archaic in kind. But at its end a certain puzzlement remains. What value are we to ascribe to the tales of the Knight, Miller, Reeve, and (possibly) Cook, after such a dismissal? What is the economy of the larger design? In these concluding pages, I wish to suggest that the opening sequence furnishes the model upon which *The Canterbury Tales* as a whole is constructed.

For the Man of Law's performance is the first in a series of self-corrections that give the work its distinctive rhythm, its characteristic tone, and ultimately its largest structural shape—keeping it on course, yet allowing it to indulge in many sorts of curiosity along the way.[6] It is a return to cultural center after a series of explorations into literary territory less familiar by far. *The Knight's Tale* is above all a great humanist poem, a profoundly sympathetic account of pagan aspiration and failure that leaves unspoken its necessary Christian correction and supplementation. But this is also to say it is a poem highly problematic in the present context. The first and longest narrative heard on the pilgrimage to Canterbury addresses only by omission and indirection the purposes of pilgrimage and the faith that gave Canterbury Cathedral its importance as a goal. The literary pilgrimage begins (so to speak) in pagan Greece, ignorant of Christ, unsanctified by the witness and martyrdom of saints. It is a poet's beginning, and Theseus's amphitheatre, which is built by every "craft man" in his kingdom (master builders, masons, representational artists) becomes an emblem not only of the limits of our human capacity to create order, but also of the limited capacity of art to assist in that creation. The wall paintings in the temples are able to represent the chaos of life in this world—to arrange it by planetary influence, and give it shape and form—but they cannot transcend it. Even the story of the planet-gods—again, a poet's invention—finds in the heavens only a mirror reflecting the passions that move and trouble men below; our predicament is replicated there. The gods do not act more virtuously, or more wisely, or with greater control than do the human actors in the story, and the conflict at its center is not resolved, it is merely ended. Someone dies. This testing of the limits of human knowledge and power—one comes to see it as an entirely proper place for a literary pilgrimage to begin—is centered most profoundly on Theseus, but it is also enacted by the poet himself in his inability to declare the destiny of Arcite's soul. (This though his source detailed the soul journey explicitly.) In late-medieval England, the poet and his audience could extend to the classical past their imaginative sympathy, respect, and compassion, but they could not free it or redeem it, even within a fiction. If knowledge of the garden makes life in the prison nearly intolerable, the reverse is also true. *The Knight's Tale* is about ceremonies, not answers.

As a medieval poem interested in imagining a civilization alternative to that redeemed by Christ, *The Knight's Tale* needs to be supplemented, or corrected, immediately. And so it is, though not in the manner we might expect. The Miller, drunken and merry, holds *The Knight's Tale* up to his own understanding of life, and finds its idealism dubious, its courtly manners mere disguise, and the philosophic inscrutability of its universe preposterous. He answers the Knight's Boethian questions with an idea of justice stricter by far but mysterious not at all: the law of cause and effect, provocation and response, in a universe tolerant of everything except foolishness.

To follow *The Knight's Tale* with a fabliau is daring, purely in terms of literary decorum. To do so in a pilgrimage sequence is more audacious still. But to do so with *The Miller's Tale* is daring beyond all. Its reenactment of Noah's Flood—which every parish Christian had heard foreshadowed the end of the world and Doomsday—puts at great risk the precarious equilibrium of fabliau, a genre whose laughter depends upon the exclusion of any sense that human life is lived under the aspect of eternity, or is subject to any judgment more searching than the story's own brusque denouement. Alain de Lille's *Natura* here becomes the natural world merely, a metaphoric spring landscape alive with bird and beast and blossom, just as Noah's Flood becomes little more than a witty conveyance to lechery and a mechanism for its correction; it has nothing to do with God's punishment of that sin. Images of the sort that elsewhere in Chaucer's art invite sober meditation manage in *The Miller's Tale* to short-circuit it, in part by the play-and-game mode in which they are cast (the ideas are not directly engaged), and by the highly specific lessons they teach: social lessons that turn on the discrepancy between image and referent rather than on their similarity. Neither God nor his angel speaks to man in this new "play of the Flood," and no new world is born from it. But a new kind of narrative art comes into being. The hierarchical image that Chaucer worked so powerfully in *The Knight's Tale* makes possible the creation of a counter-art, in which the anti-hierarchical impulse is elevated to the status of a significant artistic genre and allowed to fill the greatest possible imaginative space. This "cherles tale" moves us one tale further on the road toward Canterbury, but it removes us still further from Christian truth.

Most of the pilgrims take pleasure in the tale, but the Reeve responds to it with anger, in a bitter "sermonyng" so presumptuous in its generalizations that he must be silenced by the Host—"What shul we speke alday of hooly writ?" (1.3902)—and told to begin his tale. Chaucer uses the occasion to invent yet another kind of "non-pilgrimage art," a prologue and tale in which hieratic images are elaborated with great care, but in contempt of their wisdom and in despair of their power to amend anyone's life. The laughter becomes ungenerous; pride and stupidity replace foolishness as the subject;

and the imagery of Christian truth is made to serve a private conscience so self-knowing and self-loathing as to become its own tale's most comprehensive subject. The Reeve offers himself as evidence that the wine of life runs out to no purpose and that the horse of our carnal nature can never be bridled, not even when it grows old and weak. On a road leading to a Christian shrine, he can affirm only the Old Law of revenge and counter-revenge: "'Hym thar nat wene wel that yvele dooth'; / A gylour shal hymself bigyled be" (1.4320). Again, although the spiritual pilgrimage moves forward without the Reeve—his tale does not advance us on that way—the tale establishes new possibilities for narrative art, an art in which narrator and narrative become one.

The contribution that *The Cook's Tale* was intended to make to the sequence must remain a matter of conjecture; we do not have enough of it to tell. I suspect that Chaucer intended a further experiment in the art of compromised narration, in which two opposed voices are heard, both identifiable with the Cook himself. There is the voice of a London guildsman, cautious and prudent, for whom moral behavior guarantees (among other things) financial profit and social respectability; it is the voice of the master victualler in the tale. And there is the voice of Perkyn Revelour, the tale's London apprentice, discharged for cause by his good master and last seen in the company of a pimp and a whore: it is a voice libertine and disorderly, careless of risk and eager for holiday. From what Chaucer tells us of the Cook outside his tale, we sense the Cook's self-identification with both those voices; and within the fragment we possess their disharmony is not resolved. Along with the medieval scribes who finished the tale by rhyming Perkyn to the gallows, I think it possible Chaucer meant to end its action morally, but I think he intended its ethos to be more complex by far, colored throughout (as in *The Pardoner's Tale*) by the radically divided personality of its narrator. Its version of Christian virtue is not only subtly mercantile in its inflections, but is simultaneously undercut by appetites and allegiances inimical to virtue of any sort at all. The tale seems intended to explore a kind of civic morality that even in its highest ideals never quite distinguishes between the City of Cain and the City of God.

That is the first claim I have made concerning this problematic juncture in the text of *The Canterbury Tales*—problematic because unfinished (*The Cook's Tale*) or imperfectly revised (*The Man of Law's Introduction*). A "moral" ending for *The Cook's Tale* is not, however, crucial to my argument: even if Chaucer intended simply another fabliau, merry in its conclusion, the tale would still leave the literary pilgrimage oddly begun. This fourfold series of tales has yet to address in any serious way the Christian truth that made pilgrimage a hallowed institution as well as a central metaphor for man's life on earth. (*The General Prologue* itself devotes just seven lines to the subject, of which only two are untouched by irony and ambiguity of motive.) And so my second claim is more important by far. I argue that we should not think the incompletion of *The Cook's Tale* structurally significant. The division of *The Canterbury Tales* into a number of fragments is the work of modern editors, in the service of modern scholarship; it reflects neither Chaucer's intentions nor the practice of medieval scribes. If we read *The Man of Law's Introduction and Tale* not as a new beginning but as the culmination of the opening sequence, we find it answers to the pressure of the developing design in some interesting and characteristically Chaucerian ways.

As I suggested at the beginning of this summary, the Host and the Man of Law are used to voice the first of Chaucer's self-corrections within the work—the first of what he called, at the end of his life, and in a significant plural, "my retracciouns." There is room in this moment to satirize both the Host and the Man of Law as literary critics—the one bourgeois and complacent, the other intellectual and severe, prone to make a case (as lawyers will) at some cost to objective truth. It amuses Chaucer to charge himself with those offenses, and to do so in the person of those particular pilgrims; but he does not mean us to dismiss what they say on *ad hominem* grounds. Either charge can be restated in terms both appropriate and true. Chaucer here looks back on the part of his writing that seems to us most brilliant and new to declare it trivial at best and dangerous at worst: work born of "ydelnesse."

At that moment the tales of the journey so far become a single unit of meaning—a sequence that must be grouped together, not because of what they share, but by virtue of what they omit. The act of retrospective self-judgment leads here to reorientation and supplementation, elsewhere to explicit correction and retraction; whatever its occasion and form, the reflex is profoundly medieval, and profoundly Chaucerian. Its definitive statement, of course, must wait for the *Retraction* to *The Canterbury Tales*—"heere taketh the makere of this book his leve"—but it is anticipated on a grand scale twice before: in *The Legend of Good Women*, whose programmed progress from Cleopatra to Alceste I have written about elsewhere;[7] and in the *Troilus*, whose palinode reduces to vanity all the joy and suffering of Troilus and Criseyde, as well as our own sympathetic identification with their story. In the *Retraction*, Chaucer reviews not merely the work at hand but his entire literary career—this last book reduced to just another book among many—and asks God's forgiveness for precisely the works we value most: "translacions and enditynges of worldly vanitees, the whiche I revoke in my retracciouns" (X.1084), among which he specifies the *Troilus* (its own "retraction" notwithstanding), *The House of Fame*, *The Legend of Good Women*, *The Book*

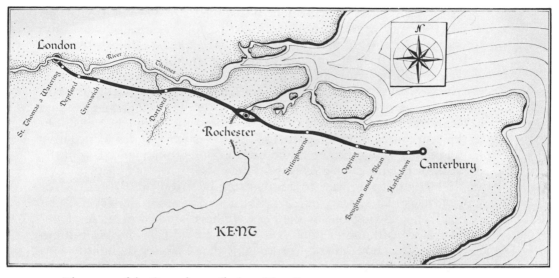

175. The route of the Canterbury pilgrims. Note 8.

of the Duchess, *The Parliament of Fowls*, and (the work grown self-reflexive once again) "the tales of Caunterbury, thilke that sownen into synne."

And so *The Man of Law's Introduction and Tale* should be read, I suggest, as a provisional palinode: the first "retraccioun" in a carefully articulated series within the pilgrimage collection itself. It is a retreat from innovation and partial truth—a retreat governed by ideas of withdrawal, submission, and self-negation that possessed in the Middle Ages a dignity and urgency denied to them in modern systems of value. A parallel movement, this time in ironic variation on the theme, will occur just outside Rochester, at the exact midpoint of the journey (see figure 175),[8] in the transition from *Sir Thopas* to *The Tale of Melibee*—the tales that Chaucer assigns to himself as pilgrim. (Harry Bailly's charge there, "Thou doost noght elles but despendest tyme" [VII.931], resumes his critique in *The Man of Law's Introduction* and makes clear that *The Canterbury Tales* has a structural middle as precisely calculated as its beginning and end.) *The Second Nun's Prologue and Tale* stand next in this series, likewise rejecting art that is made in "ydelnesse." That *Prologue*'s implicit rebuke to all that has gone before (the diverse tales of the middle journey) also serves to begin the concluding narrative sequence, "correcting" the work and pointing it once again toward its pilgrimage goal. But not until the Parson rejects both poetry and fiction does this recurrent impulse toward reflexion and retraction achieve its definitive expression. Again there takes place an explicit act of literary criticism, as Chaucer asks (through the Parson; X.35), "Why sholde I sowen draf out of my fest, / Whan I may sowen whete, if that me lest?" The intellectual and moral beauty of the sermon/treatise that follows mitigates to some degree the shock of that renunciation and makes it—in this place, at least, under this mounting pressure—acceptable and perhaps even welcome. But it also moves us steadily toward an even greater self-criticism, the final *Retraction*. There Chaucer takes leave of his book and his art altogether, in an act of penance ending in a prayer: "so that I may been oon of hem at the day of doom that shulle be saved." In the work of a moralist pure and simple, such a series of negative judgments would not be found puzzling or problematic. But in the work of Chaucer, what does it mean?

This is not the place to address that question in relation to *The Canterbury Tales* as a whole. A few generalizations, however, seem possible, growing out of the tales we have studied in these pages. First of all, although I think *The Man of Law's Tale* very beautiful in its kind, I do not think it—or imagine that Chaucer thought it—his highest achievement among the tales told at the beginning of the journey. I doubt indeed that comparative rankings were much on his mind. The work as a whole is governed by a multiple aesthetic, in which the retraction reflex (if we may so name it) serves as a means of ordering the various possibilities of art, without voiding or destroying any of them. Chaucer's retractions are published, after all, with the works that they retract, correct, or amend; they are part of the artistic strategy of those works, not failed attempts to suppress them. Unlike the witty machines Jean Tinguely designs to destroy themselves in single, unrepeatable, avant-garde events, books do not end in absence or combustion: whatever their strategies of self-criticism and self-consciousness, such artifacts are not literally self-consuming. *The Man of Law's Tale* does not end *The Canterbury Tales*, any more than it permanently corrects or realigns it. The tales that follow—the tales of the middle journey—resume an exploration of the possibilities of art as vigorous, robust, and locally autonomous as anything that has gone before. Whether the Wife of Bath or the Shipman is brought forward to tell the next tale—tale order becomes uncertain at this point—we find ourselves once again in a fictive world where chaos and confusion are more readily identified than goodness and evil, a world where art is (on the surface at least) often as compromised as its subject or the character of its teller. For all its seriousness, the art of *The Man of Law's Tale* is old-fashioned in kind, and I think it represented for Chaucer a "higher" art only in very specific ways. The "mateere" that he chose for his final work of art—the experience of a company of pilgrims on a journey to Canterbury—could not be wholly represented by it, or by any other single genre or mode. He used his opening sequence of tales to represent a number of possible relationships of poetry to truth, not to make a definitive choice among them.

I do not think that Chaucer prized *The Man of Law's Tale* and the poetic that informs it above his own most novel inventions and contributions to the art—above his exploration of the possibilities of fabliaux, for instance, or the positioning of an entire pilgrimage within the play-and-game mode of a narrative competition. But I think he may have valued those innovations less than we do, defining their goals within a spectrum of poetic possibility that at once emphasized their novelty and situated them critically in relation to Christian truth. It is possible to be serious without being solemn, and Chaucer's design in this opening group of tales, like his design for *The Canterbury Tales* as a whole, triumphantly achieves that end. If Gregory Bateson is correct in thinking that art is part of man's quest for grace—grace understood as a kind of integration, a sense of speaking and feeling from an integrated center[9]—then it is easy to see how that quest, in an age of faith and a theocentric culture, would often merge into, or return to, the religious quest itself. Chaucer was not merely a courtly poet, or an ironist, or a moral teacher. He was moved instead by all those impulses to create an aesthetic design on the grandest and most generous scale, in which they could speak in complex counterpoint until the very end. There the deepest truths of a civilization are once again reaffirmed—to the aesthetic advantage of the work, certainly, in providing so authoritative a sense of closure, but also, we may believe, in witness to the deepest beliefs of the author himself.[10]

As a Christian, Chaucer knew the hierarchies of truth and the obligations of moral choice, and he incorporated that knowledge—as one sort of knowledge among many—into his art: through the iconographic narrative image, even in his most apparently bold and autonomous fictions, and through narrative sequence, in the articulated larger structures of his art. He stood at a point of momentous change in the history of narrative. In his verse the richest traditions of the past and the most liberating possibilities of the future spoke together in one common tongue.

Notes

Only author's surname and title, the latter frequently shortened, are given in references in these notes. Complete citations appear in the Works Cited, pp. 505–34; the principles of its arrangement are explained on p. 505 and are followed by a list of abbreviations. Unless more than one edition of a primary work is cited or the editor's name appears first in the bibliographical listing, editors' names are not given in the notes.

INTRODUCTION

1. R. Cohen, *Art of Discrimination*, p. 247. Chaucer himself experimented in this mode within several poems: in an early translation (*RR*, 135–478, describing the paintings on the garden wall), and in two poems that will figure in our present discussion (his descriptions of the images that decorate the Temple of Glass in *The House of Fame* and of the wall paintings that decorate the temples of the gods in *The Knight's Tale*). Cunningham, "Literary Form of the Prologue," suggests that the allegorical wall portraits in the *Romaunt* furnished the formal antecedent for the pilgrim portraits in *The General Prologue*; if that is true, Chaucer's early exercise in the tradition led to a dazzling transformation of it in his maturity. Hagstrum, *Sister Arts*, p. 18, uses the term "iconic poetry" to designate this tradition, in which a poet "contemplates a real or imaginary work of art that he describes or responds to in some other way." He derives the term from the practice of Lucian and Philostratus, who called their prose works in that genre *eikones*, and prefers it to adjectives derived from the word *ecphrasis*, which he would restrict to poems that give voice and language to otherwise mute works of art (p. 18, n. 34). On medieval literary pictorialism, see his Chap. 2, and p. 40 (n. 14) for medieval knowledge of Horace's dictum. He thinks it finally less influential than Ovid's poetic practice (i.e., models like Ovid's description of the temple of Sol). Essential studies of this tradition include Lee, "*Ut Pictura Poesis*"; Praz, *Mnemosyne*; and a valuable introduction by Graham, "Ut Pictura Poesis." Trimpi, "The Meaning of Horace's *Ut Pictura Poesis*," offers an important reinterpretation. *NLH* 3 (1972), an issue entitled "Literary and Art History," contains several essays that deal critically with the larger topic; see especially those by the Alpers, and by Fowler. Salter, "Medieval Poetry and the Visual Arts," offers useful criticism of casual

comparisons, though she too ends in an attempt to discover comparable aesthetic problems "across" the arts—for example, how to "properly adjust border material to main subjects" (p. 30). See also a bracing book by Pickering, *Literature and Art in the Middle Ages*, and Merriman, "The Parallel of the Arts."

2. Muscatine, "*Canterbury Tales*," p. 91, notes Chaucer's characteristic preference for simile over metaphor, "as if the more discursive syntax of simile and its less pretentious reach of statement were more congenial to his rhythm and his personality," and suggests that a range of reference favoring the rural, the domestic, and the colloquial is especially characteristic of *The Canterbury Tales*. He offers a brief but telling account of such imagery. The iconographic image I cite as an example has been studied by Kaske, "The Summoner's Garleek, Oynons, and eek Lekes," who correctly associates those vegetables with Num. 11:5, in which the children of Israel, rebelling against God and Moses, think longingly of the past: "We remember the fish that we ate in Egypt. . . . The cucumbers come into our mind, and the melons, and the leeks, and the onions, and the garlic." The pilgrim portraits of *The General Prologue* are especially dense with this kind of detail, as Reiss has demonstrated in a richly learned two-part study, "The Symbolic Surface of the *Canterbury Tales*."

3. De Bruyne, *Esthetics of the Middle Ages*, p. 207, translating "poesis materialis vocis mihi depinxit imaginem," whose point he paraphrases: both painter and poet "see or picture in their imaginations the ideal form of what they will achieve."

4. Muscatine, *Chaucer and the French Tradition*, pp. 167–73, earlier offered some brief generalizations about Gothic form. Jordan, *Chaucer and the Shape of Creation*, is concerned with medieval aesthetics of structure and draws usefully upon von Simson's brilliant study, *The Gothic Cathedral*. Tuve, *Allegorical Imagery*, though not specifically concerned with Chaucer, is also of fundamental importance. See also Fleming, "Chaucer and the Visual Arts," and (for a contrary view) H. A. Kelly, "Chaucer's Arts and Our Arts." Joan Evans, in a brief article published in 1930, "Chaucer and Decorative Art," first suggested the interest of that relationship.

5. Two essays already in print can demonstrate further what I take to be the critical consequence of these ideas. See my "Chaucer's *Second Nun's Tale* and the Iconography of Saint Cecilia," and "From Cleopatra to Alceste: An Iconographic Study of *The Legend of Good Women*." Other essays on *The Canterbury Tales* will follow in due course; a preliminary version of one of them, "Of Calendars and Cuckoldry: January and May in *The Merchant's Tale*," was presented as a lecture with slides to the Chaucer Division meeting of the MLA National Convention in Houston, 1980.

6. D. Kelly, *Medieval Imagination*, goes far to meet that need, even though Chaucer is not one of his major subjects (see however, pp. 195–99). He studies the French poetry of courtly love in the terms of 12th- and 13th-century arts of poetry, with their special emphasis on the invention of images to express central ideas. He does not significantly concern himself with the visual arts, nor with my particular subject in this book: images that emerge from, rather than originate, fictions. For a larger historical survey, see Clifford, *Transformations of Allegory*, Chap. 2, pp. 71–93.

7. For a brief analysis of such an image in the *Troilus*, see my study of Pandarus leading Troilus to possession of Criseyde's body through a "stuwe doore," in "Chaucer's *Second Nun's Tale*," pp. 146–48.

8. I owe this formulation to Thomas F. Cannon, Jr., in "Chaucer's Pilgrims as Artists," a dissertation it was my pleasure to supervise.

CHAPTER I

1. "En veillant avoie lëu / Consideré et bien vëu / Le biau roumans de la Rose." Guillaume de Deguileville, *Le Pelerinage de vie humaine*, is the first poem in a vast trilogy completed by *Le Pelerinage de l'ame* and *Le Pelerinage Jhesucrist*. Since I shall often cite this work, I wish to introduce it carefully here. All three French texts have been edited by Stürzinger for the Roxburghe Club, editions that are unfortunately very rare. The first of them (p. 1) is quoted here. The *Vie* exists in two forms: one written in 1330 (or 1332); the other, much longer and involving some major revision of material, written in 1355. The second of these has had no modern edition, but may be read in Verard's 1511 (Paris) printed book. The work was widely known and highly influential: some 73 MSS. of the poems survive, and many translations and adaptations were made, into Latin and the several vernaculars, within the Middle Ages itself. Both versions of the *Vie* were translated into medieval English: the earlier into prose (in about 1400) as *The Pilgrimage of the Lyf of the Manhode*, from which (p. 1) I quote in my text above; the later into verse by John Lydgate in 1426, as *The Pilgrimage of the Life of Man*. For information about Guillaume's life and bibliographical facts about the poems, the introduction to the Lydgate edition remains valuable; there is further material in an excellent introduction to "The Middle English 'Pilgrimage of the Soul,'" ed. Clubb. Schirmer, *Lydgate*, pp. 120–26, includes a useful summary of the poem's action and offers an account of the rhetorical expansion—amplifications, circumlocutions, expletives, repetitions, flourishes—that made Guillaume's 18,123 lines grow to 24,832 lines in Lydgate's version. The English poet made almost no substantive additions. See also Pearsall, *Lydgate*, pp. 172–77. The poem's relationship to *The Romance of the Rose* is discussed in the introduction to the Lydgate edition, pp. ix–xii; on the pictorial quality of the earlier poem, see Gunn, *Mirror of Love*, pp. 108–13, and Fleming, "*Roman de la Rose*." Tuve, *Allegorical Imagery*, Chap. 3 ("Guillaume's Pilgrimage"), offers an important study of the *Vie* and its consequence for the poetry of the Renaissance. Chaucer seems to have known Guillaume's poem intimately. He translated its lyric ABC poem to the Virgin early in his career (see *Works*, ed. Robinson, pp. 524–26 for the text, and pp. 520, 855 on its probable date), a version famous in its time: the English prose translator (ca. 1400) incorporated it, naming Chaucer as author, and Lydgate left space for its inclusion (pp. 527–28) with verses commending Chaucer by way of introduction. As later chapters of this book and its succeeding volumes will demonstrate, the *Vie* furnishes a most useful gloss, sometimes an essential gloss, on several of Chaucer's tales, as well as on the idea of a pilgrimage poem as such.

2. Lydgate, in his translator's prologue, commends Guillaume's poem to his audience in precisely those terms: "And that folk may the Ryhte weye se

/ Best assuryd to-warde ther passage, / *Lat hem be-holden in the pylgrymage,* / Which callyd ys pylgrymage de movnde" (*Pilgrimage,* p. 3 [74–77]). Italics added.

3. "Quant on ot .i. romans lire, on entent les aventures, ausi com on les veïst en present." Figure 1: Oxford, Bodley MS. Douce 308, fol. 86d v. I discuss the Prologue to *Li Bestiaires d'amours,* and use another illumination from its manuscript tradition, on pp. 25–26 and figure 8: the full text of the present passage may be found there. Though Richard de Fournival died in 1260, his poem was very popular in the later medieval centuries: there survive three versions in rhyme as well as his original prose, which I quote from the critical edition by Segre, *Li Bestiaires d'amours,* p. 5.

4. St. Augustine, *Letters,* I, 16–17. Augustine offers another account of how we "see" what another describes to us, whether in a book or an oral narration, in *The Trinity,* XI.8, pp. 334–35. Cf. ll. 1073–83 of *The House of Fame.*

5. Sartre, *L'Imaginaire,* trans. as *Psychology of Imagination,* and Ryle, *Concept of Mind,* are the most important documents in the 20th-century attack on traditional concepts of mental imagery. See also Brown, *Words and Things,* Chap. 3 ("Reference and Meaning"). Ryle affirms (Chap. 8, "Imagination") that "imaging occurs, but images are not seen. . . . A person picturing his nursery is . . . not being a spectator of a resemblance of his nursery, but he is resembling a spectator of his nursery" (pp. 247–48). Warnock, *Imagination,* offers in turn a substantial critique of Sartre, Ryle, and the phenomenologists (see especially Part IV, "The Nature of the Mental Image"), which bids fair to rival their influence in the field. She writes, "Though we may exaggerate the possibility of accurately describing our images, there is so far no reason to deny that we have them, neither does Ryle deny this. What he does deny is that images are *like* material objects. . . . To imply that we never visualize things or attempt to recall things by 'seeing' them or 'hearing' them, or even 'smelling' them . . . is manifestly absurd. . . . Our problem is what images are, not whether they exist or not. It is certain that the word 'image' is a word we shall want to retain." (P. 154.) At the end of a long and acute argument, she concludes: "Imagination is our means of interpreting the world, and it is *also* our means of forming images in the mind. The images themselves are not separate from our interpretations of the world; they are our way of thinking of the objects in the world. We see the forms in our mind's eye and we see these very forms in the world. We could not do one of these things if we could not do the other. The two abilities are joined in our ability to understand that the forms have a certain meaning, that they are always significant of other things beyond themselves." (P. 194.) See also Hannay, *Mental Images,* and G. Cohen, *Psychology of Cognition,* Chap. 2 ("Visual Imagery in Thought"), which offers a useful bibliography and a sensible review of recent experimental work on this question, reaching two conclusions of interest to us here: "Many of the objections which apply to naive realist pictorial imagery do not apply to a more sophisticated, conventionalized pictorial imagery" (p. 39); and "The attempts to deny images their role in thinking run counter to intuitive and experimental evidence, and impoverish the nature of thought" (p. 43). Furbank, *Reflections on the Word "Image,"* draws upon the critique of mental

images in Sartre and Ryle to offer a modern account of what happens when one becomes audience to a poem: "What a poet produces is a certain arrangement of words, which the reader has to repeat, a certain drill which he has to perform. It is as precise and determined and rigidly designed by the author as a painted or sculptured object, but it is obviously not an 'image' in [the] everyday sense of the word. The fact that in re-enacting its meaning the reader will form private mental images (different readers forming different ones) is bringing in the word 'image' in quite a different sense." (Pp. 47–48.) Medieval authors worried far less than do modern philosophers about the way mental images formed by different persons in response to the same verbal cues may differ; they stressed instead the essential similarity of these images. I take up this matter again on p. 64.

6. "Chaucers Wordes unto Adam, His Owne Scriveyn." "Scalle" is a scabby disease of the scalp.

7. The portraits of Chaucer are reproduced by Loomis, *Mirror of Chaucer's World*, figs. 1–6. I mention the oral tradition in order to distinguish Chaucer's work from it. As Scholes and Kellogg remind us, in *Nature of Narrative*, pp. 30–31, "The method of composition, not the mode of presentation, distinguishes the genuine oral tradition from the written."

8. Figure 2: Cambridge, Corpus Christi Coll. MS. 61, fol. 1b, a full-page illumination and one of the glories of the international style in English art at the beginning of the 15th century. Its detail can be read much more easily in color, at best (because enlarged beyond the MS. size) in Bishop, *Horizon Book of the Middle Ages*, p. 282, but Evans, ed., *Flowering of the Middle Ages*, p. 324 (fig. 14), and Brewer, *Chaucer and His World*, frontispiece, also reproduce it with unusual clarity. Galway, "The 'Troilus' Frontispiece," attempts to identify specific 14th-century persons within it. Pearsall, "The *Troilus* Frontispiece," and Salter, "The 'Troilus Frontispiece,'" decisively argue against the possibility that it represents a particular moment in the history of a particular court, but Pearsall, at least, sees no reason to deny that "it is intended to create the impression of a real occasion" (p. 69). I think Salter would not disagree, though her major concern is to trace the iconographic motifs from which the picture has been constructed. (She does so quite brilliantly.) See also Salter and Pearsall, "Pictorial Illustration . . . the Role of the Frontispiece." For a judicious assessment of this new evidence, see Baker's review of the Corpus facsimile in *SAC*, 1 (1979), 187–93. David, *Strumpet Muse*, pp. 9–10, writes interestingly about the picture's meaning; he also reproduces it in color (frontispiece).

9. On Chaucer's immediate courtly milieu, see Mathew, *Court of Richard II*; Burrow, *Ricardian Poetry*; Green, *Poets and Princepleasers*; and Pearsall, "The *Troilus* Frontispiece," pp. 72–74, for some well-expressed doubts about the intimacy of the connection. See also Middleton, "The Idea of Public Poetry in the Reign of Richard II," who argues for a broader conception of Chaucer's first audiences.

10. ME "tellen" can mean "to narrate" without any specific mode of narration implied; but the phrase "er that I parte fro ye," along with other indications in the poem, confirms the sense in which I interpret it here.

11. Important studies of Chaucer's sense of a listening audience, or criticism that has endeavored to keep that audience vividly in mind, include

Crosby, "Chaucer and the Custom of Oral Delivery"; Bronson, "Chaucer's Art in Relation to His Audience," and his later *In Search of Chaucer*; Giffin, *Studies on Chaucer and His Audience*; Spearing, *Criticism and Medieval Poetry*; Ruggiers, *Art of the Canterbury Tales*; and Lawlor, *Chaucer*. For further discussion and a useful bibliography, see Jordan, "Chaucerian Narrative." Chaytor, *From Script to Print*, remains a useful background study. See also Baugh, "Middle English Romance," and Brunner, "Middle English Metrical Romances and Their Audience." Bäuml, "Varieties and Consequences of Medieval Literacy and Illiteracy," makes a number of new distinctions.

12. Figures 3 and 4: London, Brit. Lib. MS. Harley 2897, fols. 157v, 160 (a Burgundian breviary); see also figure 22. Cf. a miniature showing the preaching of St. Stephen in the breviary of Martin d'Aragon (ca. 1400), Paris, Bibl. Natl. MS. Rothschild 2529, fol. 293v, likewise full of animation and social interaction. A more sedate audience is shown listening to Archbishop Arundel preaching in the cause of Henry IV, London, Brit. Lib. MS. Harley 1319, fol. 12 (French, early 15th century). Randall, *Images in Margins*, fig. 638, also shows a sermon audience, quite interesting and varied. See Oxford, MS. Bodley 264, fol. 79 (*The Romance of Alexander*) for another sermon audience (Flemish, 1339–44), facsimile ed. James; and Meiss, *The Limbourgs*, II, fig. 563, for an audience to two apostles preaching. Salter, "The 'Troilus Frontispiece,'" reproduces three comparable scenes (figs. 3–5), as well as several scenes of poets reading or reciting to their audiences (figs. 6–11). See also Pearsall, "The *Troilus* Frontispiece," pls. II–IV, and the many examples he notes on p. 71 (n. 3).

13. The functional necessity of certain other stylistic features has long been recognized: rhetorical techniques to gain an audience's attention, to open and close a narration, to indicate with maximum clarity transitions within a narrative, to achieve a certain diffuseness of structure. To such needs we must attribute some part of the medieval fondness for rhetorical "amplification"—let one thing be said in many ways—and some part of the value that was then placed upon the conventional in poetry. In learning to read medieval narrative, we learn to accept such things, though in listening to such narrative we would need them even more.

14. From *Des Deux Bordeors Ribauz*, quoted by Baugh, "Middle English Romance," p. 21. The jongleur's notion of memory *par cuer* was doubtless less strict than our own, and allowed for the improvisation of verses we would call merely "like" those he had heard. See Chaytor, *From Script to Print*, Chap. 6 ("Publication and Circulation").

15. Spurgeon, *Five Hundred Years of Chaucer Criticism and Allusion*, I, 146.

16. *Caxton's Book of Curtesye*, p. 35.

17. Figure 5: a detail from the title page of the *Ars memoriae* in Robert Fludd's *Utriusque cosmi maioris scilicet et minoris, metaphysica, physica atque technica historia*, Vol. 2, Oppenheim, 1619, p. 47. (I print from the Bodleian Library copy.) For commentary on this figure, see Yates, *Art of Memory*, pp. 326–27, along with Clarke and Dewhurst, *Brain Function*, p. 29. On the provenance of the Latin terms, see Yates, *Art of Memory*. Chaucer's phrase occurs in *The Man of Law's Tale* (II.551), describing the old blind Christian healed by Hermengyld: "That oon of hem was blynd and myghte nat see, / But it were with thilke eyen of his mynde / With whiche men

seen, after that they ben blynde." The metaphor "eye of the mind" goes back to Plato (*Republic*, 533d), whose use of it, in Hagstrum's nice phrase (*Sister Arts*, p. 5), "exalted both sense and intellect." On such metaphors of the body, see Curtius, *European Literature and the Latin Middle Ages*, pp. 136–38. "Mynde" in the passage quoted above can mean "memory" specifically, but it should not be limited to that sense alone.

18. Because Boethius's discussion uses highly technical terms and is difficult to follow out of context, I have paraphrased it in my text. Here is the original in Chaucer's translation: if the thing to be understood is, for example, a man, "the wit comprehendith withoute-forth the figure of the body of the man that is establisschid in the matere subgett; but the ymaginacioun comprehendith oonly the figure withoute the matere; resoun surmountith ymaginacioun and comprehendith by an universel lokynge the comune spece that is in the singuler peces; but the eighe of the intelligence is heyere, for it surmountith the envyrounynge of the universite, and loketh over that bi pure subtilte of thought thilke same symple forme of man that is perdurablely in the devyne thought. . . . The heyeste strengthe to comprehenden thinges enbraseth and contienith the lowere strengthe; but the lowere strengthe ne ariseth nat in no manere to the heyere strengthe." (V, pr. 4.)

19. Bartholomaeus, *Properties*, p. 98. A masterly study by Bundy, *Theory of Imagination*, p. 179, takes such a three-part division as normative for the period as a whole. Harvey, *Inward Wits*, offers a brief and lucid introduction to medieval faculty psychology; see also D. Kelly, *Medieval Imagination*, Chap. 3.

20. The Augustine example is from *De Genesi ad litteram*, XII.c.vi., and is quoted by Peter Clemoes in an essay that has much material relevant to this chapter, "*Mens absentia cogitans* in *The Seafarer* and *The Wanderer*," pp. 65–66. On *fantasia*, see Bundy, *Theory of Imagination*, esp. pp. 183, 190–92, 278.

21. Bundy, *Theory of Imagination*, p. 189. The analysis is based on that of Albertus Magnus. On the function of this middle cell, Gilson, *Aquinas*, pp. 205–6, is also helpful. Here is Bartholomaeus's expanded definition (*Properties*, p. 99): "By þe vertu estimatiue, þat is also iclepiþ *racio sensibilis*, we beþ war to voide yuel and folwe þat is good and so in a maner by þis vertu beþ war and wys. And þis vertu and þe ymaginatiue is comyn to vs and to oþir bestis, as it is iseie in houndis and wolfes, but propirliche to speke he vsiþ no resoun but he vsith a busy and strong estimacioun."

22. Since the imagination can summon up the image of things apart from their immediate sensual cause, it has already a capacity for retention—it is a kind of memory—and certain medieval thinkers therefore sought to define the activity of the third-cell "memory" in a different way. Whereas in Aristotelian and Neoplatonic psychology the memory receives the products of fantasy and imagination more or less directly, in medieval faculty psychology it tends to become especially the receiver of ideas—intentions—from the second cell; on this change, see Bundy, *Theory of Imagination*, esp. pp. 179–80. But not all of Bundy's examples support this view very clearly, and for our purposes it could easily be overstressed: the images remain available for recall, by whichever cell; the *intentiones* are discovered within

them, and cannot be separated from them. More to our point, the popular understanding of memory, as the quotations and pictures I draw from that tradition will show, largely ignored these scholastic refinements; it describes the memory as not only dependent upon images, but as the storehouse of them, as does indeed Bartholomaeus himself (*Properties*, p. 98): "*Memoratiua . . . holdiþ and kepiþ in þe tresour of mynde þingis þat beþ apprehendid and iknowe bi þe ymaginatif and racio*." (In the passage I quote in n. 21 above, he makes clear that by *racio* here he means *racio sensibilis*, i.e., the middle cell, the "estimatiue" power.) For an extensive vernacular treatment of memory, see "*The Chess of Love*" (Commentary to *Les Eschez amoureuse*), pp. 1157–65.

23. Figure 6: from Paris, Bibl. Natl. MS. lat. 11229, fol. 37v (Paris, ca. 1400), a collection of treatises on health and medicine. Figure 7: from Triumphus Augustinus de Anchona, *Opusculum perutile de cognitione animae . . .* , an anatomy text revised by Alessandro Achillini, Bologna, 1503, sig. f. [viii]. For fuller commentary on these plates, see Clarke and Dewhurst, *Brain Function*, who reproduce them as figs. 7 and 34; the 11th-century illustration is reproduced and discussed as their fig. 3. The book is rich in information and images: figs. 1–56 are all relevant to this discussion. (Note that figure 5 of the present book also includes a three-cell diagram, though the cells are unlabeled.) Sudhoff, "Die Lehre von den Hirnventrikeln," remains an important study; on p. 180 he offers a convenient tabulation of the varying functions attributed to the three cells by a long list of medieval authorities. Pecock, *The Donet*, pp. 8–11, offers an unusually clear vernacular account of brain function, written ca. 1443–49, in the form of a teaching dialogue. It is a "five-inward-wits" version, locating the common sense in the forehead, with imagination, fantasy, estimation, and memory following in that order; fantasy and estimation share the second cell (p. 11). His definition of "estimacioun": "it is forto perceiue accordaunt þingis or discordaunt þingis, to kynde freendeful or odiose, þou3 þei mowe not be perceyued bi outward bodili wittis" (p. 10). The lamb-and-wolf example follows, along with swallows building their nests, and bees choosing their king (*sic*). Mure, *Aristotle*, pp. 121–23, has a clear account of the technical meaning of "motion" in Aristotelian psychology, a concept necessary to explain the fact that in a brute animal there is "no distinction between what a thing is and what action it demands," "the reaction issuing in a movement of pursuit or avoidance" (p. 121).

24. Baugh, in his edition *Chaucer's Major Poetry*, p. 507, likewise glosses "engyn" as "imagination," whereas Robinson, in his general glossary, offers only "skill; contrivance, device; machine," none of which is appropriate to Chaucer's use of the word in this line. (In a note, p. 759, Robinson remarks that the three faculties are ordered differently in the Latin source.) Davis et al., eds., *A Chaucer Glossary*, err, I think, in glossing this occurrence as "intelligence" (p. 46), for that risks redundancy with "intellect" in Chaucer's original. A commentary attributed to Bernard Silvester can point us toward a better definition: it names the three cells of the brain as *ingenium, ratio*, and *memoria*, defining *ingenium* as a means of finding, discovering, inventing (*est instrumentum inveniendi*), whereas *ratio* is the power of judging those findings (*est instrumentum discernendi inventa*), and *memoria* preserves them (*est instru-*

mentum conservandi inventa). See O'Donnell, "Sources and Meaning of Bernard Silvester's Commentary on the Aeneid," pp. 242–43, and the edition of Bernard's *Commentary* by Jones and Jones, e.g., p. 47 (VI.68), pp. 114–15 (VI.631–36). (Bernard's authorship is now considered doubtful.) Wetherbee, "Theme of Imagination," extensively documents the use of *ingenium* to stand for imagination in medieval psychological contexts. Hanning, *The Individual in Twelfth-Century Romance*, pp. 29–32, studies Abelard's concept of *ingenium* (in opposition to *usus*), and, pp. 105–38, includes a substantial study of "Engin" in 12th-century courtly texts. There it means chiefly intelligence, trickery, or cunning; but see pp. 111–12 for its connection with imagination. See St. Augustine, *The Trinity*, for many three-in-one analogies for the Trinity, such as that St. Cecilia uses here, and esp. pp. 311–13 (and 315–44 *passim*) for material based on faculty psychology that is interesting in relation to memory.

25. See, for instance, Boethius's commentary on Porphyry concerning the tripartite soul, *PL* 64, col. 71; in McKeon, ed. and trans., *Selections from Medieval Philosophers*, I, 70–71.

26. Gower, *Complete Works*, II, 43 (Bk. I, preceding l. 289). Peck, in his abridged edition of the *Confessio amantis*, traces the Platonic sources of the idea, p. 501 (n. 6): "These two senses enable man to perceive the numbers, motions, harmonies, and rhythms of the universe, whereby the soul is illuminated. The other three senses [Plato] ignores entirely." For an interesting commentary on *Timaeus*, 47a–c, see A. B. Chambers, "Wisdom at One Entrance Quite Shut Out." See also de Bruyne, *Esthetics of the Middle Ages*, pp. 115–17.

27. Figure 8: Paris, Bibl. Natl. MS. fr. 1951, fol. 1 (one of the rhymed versions mentioned in n. 3 above); cf. MS. fr. 12469, fol. 1 (beginning 14th century), which shows Memory as a woman standing between two tower gates, holding a banner in each hand. The same library's MS. fr. 412, fol. 228 (dated 1285) shows just the gates, one with an eye, one with an ear. The original of the text translated above reads: "Et pour chu Diex, ki tant aime l'omme qu'il le velt porveoir de quant ke mestiers lui est, a donné a homme une vertu de force d'ame ki a non memoire. Ceste memoire si a .ij. portes, vcïr ct oïr, ct a cascune de ces .ij. portes si a un cemin par on i puet aler, che son painture et parole. // Painture sert a l'oel et parole a l'oreille. Et comment on puist repairier a le maison de memoire et par painture et par parole, si est apparant par chu ke memoire, ki est la garde des tresors ke sens d'omme conquiert par bonté d'engien, fait chu ki est trespassé ausi comme present. Et a che meïsme vient on per painture et per parole. Car quant on voit painte une estoire, ou de Troies ou d'autre, on voit les fais des preudommes ki cha ariere furent, ausi com s'il fussent present. // Et tout ensi est il de parole. Car quant on ot .i. romans lire, on entent les aventures, ausi com on les veïst en present. Et puis c'on fait present de chu ki est trespassé par ces .ij. coses, c'est par painture et par parole, dont pert il bien ke par ces .ij. coses poet on a memoire venir" (ed. Segre, pp. 4–5). The original MS. (now lost) was certainly illuminated, as evidenced by the author's words, "je vous envoie en cest escrit et painture et parole" (p. 6).

28. The power and immediacy of sight, even in ordinary vision of ordinary things, leads us naturally in many vernaculars still to say "I see" when

we wish to indicate complete understanding. See Gombrich, *Symbolic Images*, p. 167.

29. St. Thomas Aquinas, *Summa theologiae*, 3.30.3, Blackfriars ed., vol. 51, p. 79, defends the mode of the angel's appearance in these terms (among others): "Taken alone intellectual vision is better than vision either of the imagination or the eyes. Yet Augustine also says that prophecy is better if it comes with vision both in the intellect and in the imagination rather than in only one of them. The blessed Virgin saw not only physically but intellectually as well, so hers was a better vision. Granting that it would have been better if she had seen the angel directly in his substantial self through an intellectual vision, it simply was not compatible with her pilgrim state to see the essence of an angel."

30. "Et in carne mea videbo Deum, Salvatorem meum. Quem visurus sum ego ipse, et non alius; et oculi mei conspecturi sunt" (Matins, first Nocturn).

31. See the discussion in Gilson, *Aquinas*, pp. 203–4. In his *Christian Philosophy in the Middle Ages*, p. 75, Gilson paraphrases St. Augustine (*De musica*, VI.2–9) concerning the way memory manifests the spirituality of the soul: "A certain redemption of matter from multiplicity and from time is achieved by memory even in the simplest of sensations." Augustine, in *De Genesi ad litteram*, had likewise stressed the power of the imagination to find access to divine truths, even to an experience of the divine. On the full scope of Augustine's contributions to a medieval theory of the imagination, see Bundy, *Theory of Imagination*, p. 172 and Chap. 8, along with Yates, *Art of Memory*, pp. 46–49, commenting on the *Confessions*, Bk. X.

32. Hugh of St. Victor, *Selected Spiritual Writings*, p. 158. The images that Reason causes the Soul to "see" include people at sea who are overtaken by a tempest (pp. 160–61), a merchant caravan that is overtaken by robbers (pp. 162–63), a rich man's house and wealth that cause him care and fearfulness (pp. 163–65), a wedding whose promise for future happiness is far from certain (pp. 165–67), and so on. All are used to point the same moral: "This too is vanity, and vanity of vanities." Henry, Duke of Lancaster (father to Chaucer's Duchess Blanche), in *Le Livre de seyntz medicines*, written in 1354, also works through great meditative images; he compares the human heart, for instance, to the vortex of the sea (pp. 90–95), a fox's hole (pp. 103–16), and a city marketplace (pp. 117–23). On this work see Legge, *Anglo-Norman Literature*, pp. 216–20.

33. Hugh of St. Victor, *Selected Spiritual Writings*, p. 183 (from Hugh's unfinished commentary on Ecclesiastes). Cf. "Contemplation is the alertness of the understanding which, finding everything plain, grasps it clearly with entire comprehension" (pp. 183–84). St. Edmund Rich (Edmund of Canterbury), author of *The Mirror of Holy Church*, a widely known Anglo-Norman treatise of the 13th century, defines the three objects of "contemplation" (his inclusive word) as being "created beings," the Scriptures, and "God Himself and His nature." In the first you "look at God in everything and in every creature," but in the third and highest kind, such images must be put away: "If your way of thinking is distracted by corporeal images [*corporeles ymaginacyouns*] you will never be able to enquire into the

nature of God. . . . Put every corporeal image outside your heart, and let your naked intention fly up above all human reasoning, and there you shall find such great sweetness and such great secrets that without special grace there is no-one who can think of it except only him who has experienced it." I quote from Colledge, ed., *The Mediaeval Mystics of England*, pp. 129, 131, 136–37, and 139. On this treatise, see Legge, *Anglo-Norman Literature*, pp. 211–12. Cf. also the discussion of the highest kind of vision in *The Chastising of God's Children*, pp. 169–70 (from the end of the 14th century): "Þe þridde principal kynde of vision is clepid an intellectual vision, whanne no bodi ne image ne figure is seen, but whanne in suche a rauysshyng þe insiȝt of þe soule bi a wondirful myȝt of god is clierli fastned in vnbodili substaunce wiþ a sooþfast knowyng. . . . Þis þridde kynde of visions is most excelent, and more worþi þan corporal or spiritual or any oþer." The most important and beautifully written of the English treatises on the *via negativa*, declaring the awesome unlikeness of God to any image we can frame, is *The Cloud of Unknowing*. St. Augustine and his mother at Ostia experienced a comparable ravishment; see *Confessions*, IX.10.

34. On this accommodation, see Bundy, *Theory of Imagination*, pp. 177–78, 199, and on the Victorines, pp. 200–207. The whole of his Chap. 10, "The Psychology of the Mystics," is of interest. For representative discussions of the role played by memory in the mystical ascent, see Hilton, *The Ladder of Perfection*, pp. 50–51, 56; St. Aelred of Rievaulx, *The Mirror of Love*, pp. 107–10; St. Bonaventura, *The Mind's Road to God*, pp. 22–27. Important background studies include Knowles, *English Mystical Tradition*, and Milosh, *Scale of Perfection*, esp. Chaps. 5 and 6, which seek to indicate very precisely the differences between Hilton's work and the religious handbook tradition.

35. See also Gray, *Themes and Images*, for a survey of popular devotional tradition that properly assesses the place of images within it, pp. 18–30, and for many interesting readings of individual lyric poems.

36. Figure 9: London, Brit. Lib. MS. Add. 37049, fol. 20 (1/2 15th century). Woolf, *English Religious Lyric*, Appendix A, pp. 373–76, offers a valuable account of the manuscript sources for medieval lyric, and discusses the present MS. on p. 375; her pls. 1, 2, and 3b are drawn from it. For her commentary on "O man unkynde" (which she reproduces as pl. 1), see pp. 184–87. Gray, *Themes and Images*, reproduces this page as pl. 2, discussing the wound on p. 34 and transcribing the lyric text on pp. 53–54; his pls. 1, 5, 7, 8, and 10 give a further sampling of the MS.'s riches, which he treats more generally on pp. 51–52 and in n. 73 (p. 243), which includes a bibliography. Oxford, Bodley MS. Douce 1, minuscule in size, is another MS. of this type, discussed by Gray, *Themes and Images*, pp. 51–52, and n. 72 (p. 243).

37. See Woolf, *English Religious Lyric*, p. 185.

38. For a brief account of the sorts of images available in the churches, see Gray, *Themes and Images*, pp. 42–44.

39. From *The Ladder of Perfection*, a work that lacks a modern scholarly edition (I elsewhere cite a readily available translation, as in n. 34). Here I quote the M.E.D. article on "imaginacioun," sense 1 (c), p. 81, which prints

from London, Brit. Lib. MS. Harl. 6579. Cf. this citation (sense 1a) from the same work: "Þouʒ þou see me nouʒt wiþ þi bodili eiʒe, þou maiʒt see me wiþ þi sowle bi ymaginacion."

40. See Macrobius, *Commentary on the Dream of Scipio*, pp. 87–92, and Curry, *Chaucer and the Mediaeval Sciences*, pp. 195–240, for a discussion of this and other medieval authorities on dreams. Koonce, *Chaucer and the Tradition of Fame*, pp. 46–57, provides a learned survey of the several traditions, and Spearing, *Medieval Dream-Poetry*, a fine critical assessment. The chapters on the dream vision poems in Rowland, ed., *Companion to Chaucer Studies*, pp. 403–45, 464–76, contain bibliographies of other recent work in this field. For Chaucer's adaptation of Cicero's *Dream of Scipio*, see *PF*, 29–84; l. 111 makes it clear he knew his Cicero through Macrobius's commentary. He uses dream lore in *The Nun's Priest's Tale*, as well, *CT*, VII.2921–39, where Pertelote discusses the causes of untrustworthy dreams, and in *The House of Fame*, 1–58, where the narrator professes himself unable to decide among all the theories that would explain them, concluding only (as he began) "God turne us every drem to goode!" Chaucer occasionally uses a dream that is true—Chauntecleer's old examples (*CT*, VII.2984–3150), or Troilus's dream of Criseyde in the arms of a boar, which oppresses him because he believes "that the boor was shewed hym in figure" (*TC*, V, 1449). The latter is indeed a *somnium*, an access to true knowledge in an ambiguous form: Cassandra explains its connection with Diomede in V, 1457–1519.

41. Faculty psychology could explain dreams, both the true and the false, as caused by intelligences—angels or demons—working through the mental faculties to cause a certain dream ("yf that spirites have the myght / To make folk to dreme a-nyght," *HF*, 41). But the angels or demons essential to this theory of cognition were not the proper business of faculty psychology. For the Christian version see, for instance, Bundy, *Theory of Imagination*, pp. 221–22 (and the quotation from St. Thomas Aquinas), or *The Chastising of God's Children*, pp. 169–83, or the substantial discussion in *Dives and Pauper*, I.1, pp. 174–81 (I, xliii–lv).

42. Chaucer briefly narrates Scipio's dream in *PF*, 29–84. See Loomis, *Mirror of Chaucer's World*, fig. 57, for a relevant illustration.

43. Lydgate, *Pilgrimage*, p. 165 (6301–3). The entire passage, pp. 164–73, is relevant, and includes a full account of faculty psychology. (It does not occur in the first French version; see p. xix.) There is a further discussion of spiritual sight and "ghostly eyen" on pp. 266–67 of Lydgate, parallel to p. 92 in the English prose.

44. Figure 10: Paris, Bibl. Natl. MS. fr. 1584, fol. D; the illumination is attributed to the Maître aux Boqueteaux. This picture and its companion piece showing Dame Nature presenting her children (with the poet standing outside his house, rather than at his writing desk) are reproduced in color by Avril, *Manuscript Painting at the Court of France*, pls. 29, 30, with a full description of their subject matter. There are similar portraits in New York, Pierpont Morgan MS. M.396, from the 2d quarter of the 15th century, fols. 1, 1v. On fol. 2 there is a conventional picture of the poet at his lectern, with no "subjects" visible. D. Kelly, *Medieval Imagination*, pp. 3–12, writes interestingly about the meaning of Machaut's Prologue.

45. Guillaume de Machaut, *Œuvres*, I, 4. He wrote the Prologue near the

end of his career; only the best and most complete MSS. have it. See the editor's introduction, I, lii–iv.

46. Figure 11: Paris, Bibl. Natl. MS. fr. 1586, fol. 30v, illustrating the *Remede de Fortune*, ll. 897–1208 (*Œuvres*, II, 33–44). On fol. 49 of the same MS., the poet is shown kneeling in the path that leads to the manor house of his lady, writing a 12-stanza prayer to Amour and Dame Esperance, with a vision of the latter (Lady Hope) in the trees before him; she is the answer to the vagaries of Fortune, and constitutes the other great subject of his poem. It illustrates ll. 3181–358 of the same poem (II, 117–23); fol. 46v shows a similar scene. For a summary of the poem's action, see Wimsatt, *Chaucer and the French Love Poets*, pp. 107–10; he goes on to assess Chaucer's indebtedness to this poem, among others, in *The Book of the Duchess*. See also Calin, *Poet at the Fountain*, pp. 55–74, and D. Kelly, *Medieval Imagination*, pp. 130–37.

47. Figure 12: London, Brit. Lib. MS. Royal 14 E.v, fol. 291, illuminated for Edward IV of England. I quote from Boccaccio, *The Fates of Illustrious Men*, p. 137. For related illuminations of Lady Fortune, see Meiss, *Boucicaut Master*, figs. 393, 394; Pleister, *Der Münchener Boccaccio*, p. 106, reproducing a French MS. dated 1458; and New York, Pierpont Morgan MS. M.343, fol. 35. For the throng of those who have fallen from her favor, see, e.g., Pleister, pp. 72, 144; Geneva, Bibl. Univ. MS. fr. 191, fol. 249v; London, Brit. Lib. MS. Add. 35321, fol. 107v. Boccaccio's conversation with the dead Petrarch, who rebukes his sloth and instructs him in the true meaning of fame (Bk. VIII), is also presented as a "seeable" event: e.g., London, Brit. Lib. MS. Royal 14 E.v., fol. 391, and Meiss, *Boucicaut Master*, figs. 388, 389.

48. Figure 13: from a MS. formerly in the Kettaneh Collection, New York (French, late 14th century). Reproduced by Meiss, *Boucicaut Master*, fig. 379 and described on p. 102. New York, Pierpont Morgan MS. G.35, fol. 1 (ca. 1480) is of comparable power, and includes several other scenes, among them the deaths of Abel and Cain; in the bottom left corner, Adam and Eve, bent with age, stand directly before Boccaccio at his writing desk, pen in hand. The same library's MS. M.343, fol. 35, ca. 1475, shows Boccaccio contemplating several of his subjects, with a large Hell Mouth below. In an engraving by the *Hausbuch* Master, ca. 1476, Boccaccio writes about Adam and Eve as they stand before him in an elaborately decorated room whose wall paintings show the Creation of Eve, and Eve receiving the apple. See Hutchison, *Master of the Housebook*, p. 158 (described pp. 73–74).

49. Figure 14: Paris, Bibl. de l'Arsenal MS. 5070, fol. 18. Reproduced in color by Branca in a deluxe edition of the *Decameron*, illustrated with hundreds of pictures from medieval and Renaissance sources: see I, 40, and on pp. 41, 42, two other manuscript illustrations of the same scene.

50. Figure 15: London, Brit. Lib. MS. Royal 15 D.iii, fol. 526, a *Bible historiale*, early 15th century, from the Egerton workshop. Paris, Bibl. Natl. MS. fr. 10, fol. 593v, illustrating the same text, has two such pictures on the same page, one of them showing the lamb, the book with seven seals, and the rider on a white horse, all in the sky above; see related pictures on fols. 592v, 594, 596v, 598, 598v. The Belleville Breviary (ca. 1325) likewise shows St. John writing in waking vision, seeing his subject before him, though with an angel dictating into his ear; see Morand, *Jean Pucelle*,

pl. VIIc. *The Cloisters Apocalypse*, I, fol. 3, in contrast, shows St. John "in the spirit" by presenting him in the iconographic posture of dream vision, his hand on a book, his eyes closed, with an angel above him unfurling a scroll: "Quod vides, in libro scribe." Fol. 15v again shows John asleep on a grassy knoll. Here even the pictures that show him writing at divine command, e.g., fols. 16, 27v, are part of the vision being granted him, not waking auctorial events. Nolan, *Gothic Visionary Perspective*, offers a suggestive study of the influence of Apocalypse commentary and illumination upon vision literature in the later medieval period. A very different tradition developed in explanation of John 13:23–26 ("Now there was leaning on Jesus' bosom one of his disciples, whom Jesus loved"). It identified John as the beloved disciple, and suggested that in those moments (often specifically named as sleep) he drew secret wisdom from Christ's breast. In the version that descends from Bede (Homily 92, on the Feast of St. John), those secrets are the secrets of apocalypse: "Postea vero nocte illa. . . . vidit secreta coelestia, quae postea scripsit, et vocavit Apocalypsim" (*PL* 92, col. 810). This version significantly enters the pictorial tradition through the *Bible moralisée*, where it is paired with Jacob's dream of a ladder reaching heaven, as Old Testament prefiguration; see for instance, Oxford, Bodley MS. 270ᵇ, fol. 17v (French, mid-13th century), or *La Bible moralisée*, I, pl. 17. Haussherr, "Christus-Johannes-Gruppen in der Bible Moralisée," p. 135, reproduces the two pictures from a Toledo MS. The episode is treated at length in *The Northern Passion*, where John falls asleep on Christ's breast and sees many wonders: "Alle þat he saughe he vndir stude / whane þat he woke fayre and wele / he couthe it recordene euiry delle / he wrote it alle in lettirrouree / als clerkes hafe wretyne in scrippture / his buke es called appocalipsis / a full selcouthe thynge it es" (I, 30, from MS. Add. 31042). Greenhill, "The Group of Christ and St. John as Author Portrait," offers some guidance to this tradition.

51. Figure 16: For a discussion of the picture and a color reproduction, see Holbrook, *Portraits of Dante*, pp. 172–81. It may also be seen in color in Evans, ed., *Flowering of the Middle Ages*, pp. 324–25 (fig. 15).

52. Jacobus de Voragine, *Golden Legend*, trans. Caxton, VI, 58. Luke's gospel is not an eyewitness account: he was converted by St. Paul, whom he accompanied on travels in Greece and Italy. The most famous of the paintings of the Virgin attributed to him is venerated at Santa Maria Maggiore in Rome, but it is in fact a 12th-century Byzantine icon. The earliest known Western example of St. Luke as painter, 1368, is an illumination by the Bohemian artist John of Troppau in a gospel book, published in a superb facsimile, *Das Evangeliar des Johannes von Troppau*, ed. Trenkler, pl. 5 and pp. 55–56. Egbert, *The Mediaeval Artist at Work*, reproduces in color the part of the picture that specifically concerns us on her title page and again (enlarged) as pl. 26, with commentary on p. 72. The illumination is not, strictly speaking, a version of St. Luke as portrait painter of the Virgin, for he is shown painting the Crucifixion, with Mary and John at the foot of the cross. He is shown writing the gospel elsewhere on the same page.

53. Figure 17: London, Brit. Lib. MS. Add. 20694, fol. 14. It has been reproduced by Martindale, *Rise of the Artist*, as fig. 12; his fig. 13 shows a detail from a painting by Roger van der Weyden, ca. 1435, on the same

theme. Martindale's text was first published as a chapter in Evans, ed., *Flowering of the Middle Ages*, with a different set of illustrations; p. 284 (fig. 2) reproduces a late-15th-century Flemish miniature not included in the separately reprinted text. The beautiful Bodmer Hours painted by Michelino da Besozzo, ca. 1405–10, shows St. Luke with paint cups at his lectern, painting the Virgin and Child (New York, Pierpont Morgan MS. M.944, fol. 75); see Thomas, *Golden Age*, pl. 3, for a color repro-duction. For other examples, see the same library's MS. M.105, fol. 35 (Rouen, ca. 1420–25, for a Lincolnshire patron); London, British Library MS. Add. 18850, fol. 20v (the Bedford Book of Hours, French, ca. 1423); Mâle, *Les Heures d'Anne de Bretagne*, pl. 6 (painted ca. 1508); Oxford, Bod-ley MS. Gough Liturg. 14, fol. 16 (workshop of Jean Colombe, ca. 1500), reproduced by Pächt and Alexander, *Illuminated Manuscripts in the Bodleian Library*, I, pl. 59 (812); and Schwarz, "Mirror of the Artist," pp. 94–98, figs. 6–10. For a discussion of this tradition, and earlier Greek examples, see Klein, *St. Lukas als Maler der Maria*; see also Réau, *Iconographie de l'art chrétien*, III.ii.827–32; and the article "Lukasbilder" in *Lexikon der Christ-lichen Ikonographie*, III, cols. 119–22. Martindale has an interesting discus-sion of the Festival of St. Luke as it was celebrated by the painters' guild in Siena (*Rise of the Artist*, p. 13). The ox, as the symbol of St. Luke, should not be thought naturalistic; it became associated with him either because his gospel especially stresses the priesthood of Christ, and the ox is the ancient animal of sacrifice (see, e.g., *Dives and Pauper*, I.1, pp. 96–98 [I, ix]) or be-cause the ox corresponds to the first letter of the Hebraic alphabet, aleph, and Luke reports that Christ is alpha and omega, the beginning and the end (see Réau, p. 829).

54. London, Brit. Lib. MS. Add. 18852, fol. 184 (Flemish, ca. 1500). Paris, Bibl. Natl. MS. fr. 245, fol. 141, a late-15th-century *Légende dorée*, presents a similar scene, St. Luke writing the gospel with a portrait of the Virgin on a painter's easel to his left.

55. Figure 18: London, Brit. Lib. MS. Harley 4335, fol. 1. Reproduced by Courcelle, *La Consolation*, pl. 44 and discussion pp. 88–89, though Courcelle does not remark the picture-frame motif. For the later MS. (Paris, Bibl. Natl. MS. lat. 6643, fol. 1, dated 1497), see his pl. 45. Evans, ed., *Flowering of the Middle Ages*, p. 192 (fig. 38), offers a color reproduction of our figure. The manuscript is bound in five volumes, one for each book: MS. Harley 4335, fol. 27, contains the miniature to Bk. I described in my text; MS. 4336, fol. 1v (Bk. II: a picture of Lady Fortune, half-beautiful, half-ugly, a prosperous family on one side of her, a family wretched and suffer-ing on the other, Lady Philosophy and Boethius looking on); MS. 4337, fol. 2 (Bk. III: a lord or magistrate, with rich treasure spread out before him, hears petitions by a prosperous family on one side, and by three [evil?] men on the other; in the foreground, a man digs in the earth); MS. 4338, fol. 1v (Bk. IV: Lady Fortune again, with richly dressed petitioners to one side and cadavers lying in darkness before her, perhaps to indicate that death puts an end to Fortune's power); MS. 4339, fol. 2 (Bk. V: as described in my text; in the lower margin, a laborer discovers jars full of gold coins in a field). These are reproduced by Courcelle as pls. 56, 87, 89, 91, and 127, re-spectively. (Cf. pls. 57, 88, 90, 92, 128.) There is also a miniature (MS. 4335,

fol. 10) preceding Jean de Meun's prologue as translator (the fifth prologue in this MS.), which shows him presenting his translation to Philip IV.

56. One other interpretation of this picture seems possible: it may show the translator or a hypothetical reader pondering Boethius's book—"visualizing" it—in an act exemplary to the real reader of the manuscript. In that case, the picture would properly belong to a prior stage of my argument, where I deal with reader response—such as that of the man in the *Bestiaire d'Amours* illumination. Even there it would possess unusual interest, for in it (uniquely to my knowledge) the mental image becomes a framed picture on the wall. But I think the picture is more likely intended to show us Boethius. The costume is not religious: its rich red gown, blue sleeves, white cowl, and black hat suggest the garb of a scholar or philosopher, no more. Nor are we prevented from identifying the man at the desk as author simply because he is not presently engaged in writing. As several of the pictures examined above make clear, a medieval author could readily be shown standing with, or sitting at, his open book, with a scene from that book made visible before him. Machaut and the children of Love, Boccaccio with Adam and Eve outside Paradise garden, St. John at his scroll, and Dante with his opened book are all in that tradition. Finally, although Boethius wrote the *Consolation* while in prison—a fact made clear in many illustrations to his book, some of which we shall examine in Chapter III—other illustrations show him in a situation we might better call "house arrest," a situation more probable, given his dignity and prior service to the state, and more likely to have permitted the composition of *The Consolation of Philosophy*. Courcelle likewise thinks the present figure represents "Boèce occupé à lire dans sa bibliothèque" (*La Consolation*, p. 88).

57. Ringbom, "Some Pictorial Conventions," p. 65 (and figs. 23–27), discusses briefly the tradition surveyed above as a variant of the *Assistenzporträt*, as though it were the solution to a formal problem only—i.e., in the creation of pictorial narrative, how to integrate the author with the action. That is certainly part of the explanation, though other purposes are served as well, and ideas concerning mental imagery are necessary to explain precisely its origin and development. Ringbom's fig. 23 differs from his others in one important respect: the author is not shown at his book. Salter and Pearsall, "Pictorial Illustration," pp. 115–18, include such pictures in their survey of the frontispiece tradition in illuminated manuscripts (they distinguish eight types of frontispiece, of which this is number four). Both essays derive from a conference in Odense in 1979, whose recently published proceedings, Andersen et al., eds., *Medieval Iconography and Narrative*, must now be added to any bibliography of essential works on the subject.

58. Froissart, *Poésies*, I, 323 (l. 3441); see also p. 287. Lydgate's poem "Mesure is Tresour" may also be of this kind, surveying the implications of its theme—moderation is best—against an "imagined" panorama of the several estates, often with historical examples: popes and prelates, kings and princes, judges and sergeants of the law, mayors and burgesses, merchants and artists, tradesmen and craftsmen, and common laborers. It concludes: "But vnto alle that wyl doo reuerence, / To alle the staatys sett here in portrature, / I shall to hem make no resistence, / That be gouernyd iustly be mesure." See Lydgate, *Minor Poems*, II, 780; the same claim to having "the

staatis alle set here in portrature" is made earlier, p. 779. Pearsall, *Lydgate*, p. 181, assumes it was written in honor of, or as guide to, a building containing paintings of the sort described, but that is nowhere made explicit in the poem, nor does London, Brit. Lib. MS. Harley 2255 leave space for any miniatures. It may equally well explore what Pearsall calls that "borderland of word and picture" (p. 179) into which Lydgate's highly visual imagination so often led him, and which in this instance may simply postulate word becoming picture in the mind. Smalley, in *English Friars and Antiquity*, has studied the "verbal pictures" invented by John Ridevall (see pp. 112ff) and Robert Holcott (see pp. 165ff), intended for visualization by the reader; there is an index of such pictures on pp. 393–94. On these see also J. B. Allen, *Friar as Critic*, pp. 105–16; Yates, *Art of Memory*, pp. 96–98; and Gombrich, *Symbolic Images*, pp. 135–37. Ridevall's allegorization of Juno as memory is summarized, with a relevant illumination, by Seznec, *Survival of the Pagan Gods*, pp. 94–95.

59. Hawes, *The Pastime of Pleasure*, p. 52. This particular passage concerns "the .v. parte" of rhetoric, which is memory—a relationship we shall examine in some detail in the next section of this chapter. I have included the passage here because it involves at most a pragmatic reduction of the formal *ars memoriae*, and because of its stress on images as a means of creating new "tales" as well as remembering those already heard. "Ymaginacioun" is also treated under the topic of *invention*; see pp. 33–37, esp. l. 708. Gower, *Confessio amantis*, V, 5551–6047 (*Complete Works*, III, 98–111), tells how Philomela wove the story of her rape by Tereus into "lettres and ymagerie" (5771), thus treating them as complementary modes of language. So too in Chaucer's version of the story, *LGW*, 2363, where "al the thyng that Tereus hath wrought, / She waf it wel, and wrot the storye above." For an ambitious survey of poetry's historical relation to other intellectual disciplines, see Hardison, *Enduring Monument*, Chap. 1, "The Classification of Systems of Criticism."

60. *Aeneid*, I, 446–93, itself provides a formal antecedent: upon his arrival in Carthage, Aeneas visits the temple of Juno and sees depicted there scenes from the Trojan War, including himself in combat—history made into art. Chaucer refers to that part of the poem in his Legend of Dido, *LGW*, (F) 1023–32, but only as the occasion for a brief lament by Aeneas; the pictures themselves are not described. Iconic poetry has always tended to include a variety of nonvisual elements, as Hagstrum, *Sister Arts*, p. 20, makes clear concerning Homer's description of Achilles' shield: "There is obviously much that is non-pictorial: sound, motion, and sociological detail all 'appear' on the surface of Hephaestus' masterpiece." We might note as well that in *The Knight's Tale* temple paintings a storm and a woman crying for help in childbirth are "heard" as well as "seen" (1.1979, 2085). But there is nothing in that tradition like the sustained and shifting ambiguity of mode that we are examining here—it even includes Chaucer's awareness that he is dreaming (l. 313)—nor is there a thematic relationship to fame within which it must be understood. For a learned account of the narrative content of this passage, see Bennett, *Chaucer's Book of Fame*, pp. 9–51. On pp. 13–15, Bennett attempts to reconcile all the details as a description of painted murals, but admits, concerning the figure of Venus and her attendant de-

ities, "it is hardly clear—and it hardly matters—whether these are to be envisaged as painted merely, or carved"; he finally chooses to see her as a statue in a niche decorated with paintings. I think the question matters, but that the ambiguity is itself the answer. Chaucer would not have found it hard to be clear in such a description, had he wished. He is seeing/ dreaming/remembering an epic poem. Koonce, *Chaucer and the Tradition of Fame*, pp. 103–7, describes the whole *Aeneid* redaction as though it were "portrayed on a 'table of bras' in the temple" (p. 103)—ignoring the complexity noted above—in order to write a learned commentary on copper and brass in the mythographic tradition, as metals especially associated with Venus.

61. Cicero, *De oratore*, II.lxxxvi.351–54; quoted by Yates, *Art of Memory*, p. 2. Quintilian, *Institutes*, XI.ii, likewise narrates the story of Simonides, as do most later writers on artificial memory (Yates, pp. 2, 28). Zinn, "Hugh of Saint Victor and the Art of Memory," offers an important supplement to Yates in stressing a Quintilian alternative to a "place and image" method and in surveying the rich range of memory techniques commended or employed by Hugh in his writings. Gray, *Themes and Images*, pp. 40–41, briefly discusses the arts of memory as background to the medieval religious lyric.

62. From *De anima*, 432a 17, 432a 9, quoted by Yates, *Art of Memory*, p. 32. Sorabji, *Aristotle on Memory*, offers a new translation of the *De memoria et reminiscentia*, with an important introduction and notes.

63. Chaucer refers to Martianus in *The House of Fame*, l. 985, and to this work specifically in *The Merchant's Tale* (IV.1732–35). Martianus transmits in brief the *Ad Herennium* version; Yates, *Art of Memory*, pp. 51–52, offers a translation of the passage, and suggests that the personifications of the Seven Liberal Arts are themselves intended as memorial images. Stahl et al., in a new translation and study of the entire work, *Martianus Capella and the Seven Liberal Arts*, II, 203 (n. 230), correct Yates's reading in one important passage. Chaucer refers to Bishop Bradwardine in *The Nun's Priest's Tale* (VII.3242) as an authority on free will and necessity; in this tale he also claims knowledge of Geoffrey de Vinsauf's work (VII.3347–49). Petrarch's *Rerum memorandarum libri* (ca. 1343–45) is discussed by Yates, p. 102. Pratt, "Chaucer and the Visconti Libraries," p. 195, notes that this book was in the library of Galeazzo Visconti at Pavia, and might have been seen, borrowed, or copied by Chaucer during his 1378 journey to Milan. (I am grateful to Lloyd J. Matthews for this reference.) Saxl, "A Spiritual Encyclopaedia of the Later Middle Ages," describes a vast moral and theological handbook that uses complex images on page after page as a means of making difficult concepts memorable. The trees of Vices and Virtues in such manuscripts are widely known, but many other symbolic pictures and diagrams were current as well; for an example, see figure 110 of the present volume. Compare St. Bonaventure, *The Tree of Life*, Prologue, pp. 97–100: "Now, in order to enkindle an affection of this sort, to assist the mind and stamp the memory, . . . [and] because imagination assists understanding. . . . Picture in your imagination a tree. Suppose its roots to be watered by an eternally gushing fountain that becomes a great and living river. . . . Suppose next that from the trunk of this tree there spring forth twelve branches," etc.

64. I quote from the translation by Nims, p. 89; on memory as "a cell of delights," see p. 87.

65. Howard, *Idea of the Canterbury Tales*, pp. 139–58, in an argument of great subtlety and power, locates that "idea" precisely in the concept of memory: memory as the work's "central fiction" and "the controlling principle of its form" (p. 139). On pp. 147–55, he suggests that *The General Prologue* portraits may have been consciously arranged as a memory system.

66. Boccaccio, *Il Teseida*, pp. 342–48 (stanzas 70–91).

67. Quoted by Caplan, in a richly learned essay, "Memoria: Treasure-House of Eloquence," in *Of Eloquence*, p. 232.

68. On this important change, see Yates, *Art of Memory*, pp. 54–81. Chaucer's knowledge of the tripartite nature of Prudence (who sees past, present, and future) is attested to in the *Troilus*, V, 743–49; he might have found it in many places, including Dante's *Convivio* IV, 27, and *Purgatorio* XXIX, 130–32. For a later explanation of Prudence's three eyes, see Lydgate, *Minor Poems*, II, 686 (from "A Mumming at London").

69. Yates, *Art of Memory*, p. 57.

70. On the defense of images, see Owst, *Literature and Pulpit*, pp. 136–48; Caiger-Smith, *English Medieval Mural Paintings*, pp. 102–17; and most recently, Woolf, *English Mystery Plays*, pp. 86–101, which brings together many of the central documents and has an extensive bibliography. For the Gregory quotation, from his 2d letter to Serenus, Bishop of Marseilles, *PL* 77, col. 1128, see Woolf, pp. 87, 365 n. 32. The problem, of course, was the Second Commandment: "Thou shalt not make to thyself a graven thing, nor the likeness of any thing that is in heaven above, or in the earth beneath. . . . Thou shalt not adore them, nor serve them." (Exod. 20:4–5.) Such defenses are relevant here, as part of memory theory and because they too credit images with the power to move the soul. But because their authors were explicitly trying to justify real images—painted, carved, engraved—against the view that would authorize only the word, spoken or written, they do not explore the question of mental images, the images we make when (in Deguileville's phrase) we put eyes in our ears. A fascinating and little-known treatise on imagery, Reginald Pecock's *The Repressor of Over Much Blaming of the Clergy*, written ca. 1449 against Lollard attack, defends images in churches (along with pilgrimages and sacraments) as being "seable rememoratijf signes," which together with "heereable rememoratijf signes (as ben Holi Scripture and othere deuoute writingis)" may do man's soul the maximum good: "the hool profite of remembring which mai come bi hem both to gidere." Pecock is unusual in discussing a third kind, those made by a man who must "wrastle withinneforth in his owne ymaginaciouns withoute leding withouteforth had bi biholding upon ymagis." He thinks such mental images, made without benefit of a public tradition, much more difficult—as men who "haunte daili contemplacioun" bear witness. The whole discussion may be read with pleasure; see vol. I, esp. 208–16. I quote from pp. 209, 212, 214; there is further discussion of mental images on p. 268. See also Lydgate, *Pilgrimage*, pp. 559–60.

71. Yates, *Art of Memory*, p. 64. The Justice example is her own. The author of *Dives and Pauper* refers to this motive power as the second of his three justifications for the use of imagery in churches: "Þey seruyn of thre

thynggys. For þey been ordeynyd to steryn manys mende to thynkyn of Cristys incarnacioun and of his passioun and of holye seyntys lyuys. Also þey been ordeynyd to steryn mannys affeccioun and his herte to deuocioun, for often man is more steryd be syghte þan be heryng or redyngge. Also þey been ordeynyd to been a tokene and a book to þe lewyd peple, þat þey moun redyn in ymagerye and peynture þat clerkys redyn in boke" (p. 82 [I.i]). The chapters that follow explore the question "How shulde I rede in þe book of peynture and of ymagerye?" (p. 83), and offer a rich vernacular introduction to that subject. The work was written ca. 1405–10.

72. St. Thomas Aquinas, *Summa theologiae*, 2.2.49, 1, quoted by Yates, *Art of Memory*, p. 74; for her discussion of the "devotional" transformation of the rules, see p. 76. In a less technical sense, Forgetfulness was one of the branches of the deadly sin of Sloth, especially in relation to the sacrament of confession: "Rechelesnesse and forȝetfulnesse blyndeþ so þe synful man þat he can no þing see in þe book of schrifte" (*Book of Vices and Virtues*, p. 28). See also *Jacob's Well*, p. 109; and on this tradition, with other references, Wenzel, *Sin of Sloth*, pp. 81, 94–95. Gower's *Confessio amantis*, IV, 530–883, treats Forgetfulness as a secular sin (*Complete Works*, II, 315–25).

73. Yates, *Art of Memory*, p. 67, quoting Albertus Magnus, *De bono*, Solution, point 17. On ethical aspects of classical Greek conceptions of memory, see Caplan, *Of Eloquence*, pp. 197–200.

74. In Gower, *Complete Works*, I, 11. The passage is discussed in a forthcoming book on Gower's moral art by Kurt Olsson.

75. See *Vita nuova*, p. 205, for the passages quoted, including "del libro della mia memoria"; and pp. 205, 206, 208, 209, 210, 212, 213, 217–18, 219, 221–22, 223, 228, and 231 for other passages relating images and memory. Bundy, *Theory of Imagination*, pp. 225–56, in a valuable study of Dante's "theory of vision, which is his theory of poetry," judges the *Vita nuova* to be an essential document, exemplifying "the belief that material vision is the necessary condition for spiritual vision, the empirical bases of which Neoplatonists, and with them Augustine, had recognized through their study of the Aristotelian psychology" (p. 225). See also Singleton, *Essay on the Vita Nuova*, esp. Chaps. 2 and 5.

76. Yates, *Art of Memory*, pp. 94–96; there are 16th-century precedents for so construing these texts. Purgatory mountain in figure 16 of the present book offers a reduced example.

77. Figures 19, 20: Oxford, Bodley MS. Holkham misc. 48, pp. 75, 79; formerly Holkham Hall MS. 514. For other examples see Brieger et al., *Illuminated Manuscripts of the Divine Comedy*, II, pls. 356–61 and 365–69; those I reproduce (pls. 359a and 365a) are most fully responsive to the text, though pls. 357a and 361a manage to include Michal scorning David's dance as well as the ark he dances before (in the example I reproduce, only the ark is shown). The authors, I, 255, mistakenly identify Nimrod (Dante's "Nembrot") as Rehoboam.

78. Yates, *Art of Memory*, p. 65, quoting *De bono*, Solution, points 16 and 18. For an account of modern experimental work on differences between the linguistic and pictorial memories, see Haber, "How We Remember What We See." Hunter, *Memory*, also draws upon a wide range of recent scientific inquiry.

79. See *Speculum humanae salvationis*, ed. Lutz and Perdrizet, and a facsimile, same title, ed. James and Berenson. Occasionally, "figural" materials deriving from sources other than the Old Testament are pictured as well. Lutz and Perdrizet, I, 72, print the Latin text of Chap. 35, of which the following lines chiefly concern us: "Omnia loca Filii sui, quae attingere potuit, devote visitavit / Et prae dulcedine amoris singula osculabatur, / Cum genuflexionibus et orationibus venerabatur. / Multa lacrimarum effusione ipsa loca irrigabat, / Quando mellifluam praesentiam Filii sui recogitabat." A closely related chapter, 44 (I, 95), concerns the Seven Sorrows of the Virgin and often uses a similar—or identical—picture for the seventh sorrow. For a 15th-century English translation of the work, see *The Miroure of Mans Saluacionne*, pp. 121–22 and 159.

80. For Mary standing before a real house, see Paris, Bibl. Natl. MS. fr. 6275, fol. 36v. Figure 21: Paris, Bibl. de l'Arsenal MS. 593, fol. 29 (cf. fol. 40v). The MS. reproduced in *Speculum humanae salvationis*, ed. James and Berenson (Chap. 35), places the memorial images in eight compartments in a wooden cupboard or press, before which Mary stands grieving, holding her hands to her face; the picture for Chap. 44 arranges the Instruments of the Passion about her, without reference to verisimilar space. Oxford, MS. Corpus Christi Coll. 161, p. 184, also uses a compartment design. For other versions, see *Speculum humanae salvationis*, ed. Lutz and Perdrizet, II, pl. 69 (cf. pl. 92), and Codex Cremifanensis 243, published in facsimile as *Speculum humanae salvationis*, ed. Neumüller, fol. 40v (cf. fol. 52). Note that the text mentions many more places than any of the pictures show: "Omnia haec loca et plura alia cum lacrimis visitavit" (Chap. 35, l. 35). The artists had to decide what to include, and their selection varies to some degree, as does the way they arrange the images into a system.

81. Jacobus de Voragine, *Golden Legend*, trans. Caxton, VI, 57–58.

82. Lydgate, *Pilgrimage*, p. 9; the French original is printed for purposes of comparison by Lydgate's editor, pp. xiii–xiv, with its first version on p. xxi. The prose translation of the latter reads, "Me thowhte as I slepte that I was a pilgrime and that I was stired to go to the citee of jerusalem in a mirour" (*Pilgrimage of the Lyf of the Manhode*, p. 1).

83. Lydgate, *Pilgrimage*, p. 664; I have emended MS. *is* to *in* in the second line and repunctuated; the French original is printed on p. 665. For the first version, see Guillaume de Deguileville, *Vie*, ed. Stürzinger, p. 420 (13469–72); its English prose translation reads: "Thou shalt anoon come to the citee to whiche thou hast ment. Thou art at the wiket and at the dore that thou seygh sum time in the mirrour." (*Pilgrimage of the Lyf of the Manhode*, p. 206.)

84. Figure 22: Paris, Bibl. Natl. MS. fr. 376, fol. 1. The same library's MS. fr. 377 (Paris, end of the 14th century) displays a similar interest: the usual first picture of the author dreaming, with the mirror image placed on a stand, is here the third (fol. 1v), whereas two pictures set side by side on fol. 1 show (a) the author writing at his desk, with the framed mirror image on a stand before him, and (b) the author reciting his poem to a listening audience. For other standard scenes with the mirror image at the foot of the bed, see Paris, Bibl. Natl. MS. fr. 823, fol. 1 (dated 1393), or London, Brit. Lib. MS. Add. 38120, fol. 1v (ca. 1400). New York, Pierpont Morgan MS.

M.772, fol. 1 (ca. 1360–70) shows the mirror above the dreamer's bed; cf. also Oxford, Bodley MS. Douce 300, fol. 1. For the lines from the translator's prologue, see Lydgate, *Pilgrimage*, p. 3 (86–87), and for the poem's discussion of how a man's eye resembles a mirror, p. 157. Hagen, "*The Pilgrimage of the Life of Man*: A Medieval Theory of Vision and Remembrance," a Ph.D. dissertation written under my direction, examines further Guillaume's use of imagery and makes interesting use of medieval optical theory in understanding Grace Dieu's initial instructions to the pilgrim.

85. Figure 23: Geneva, Bibl. Univ. MS. fr. 182, fol. 109v. Tuve, *Allegorical Imagery*, reproduces woodcuts of this type from the Lyons (Nourry) edition of 1504; see her figs. 47, 70, 84, 85, all of which show an image of the city within the mirror. (For the relevant text, see Lydgate, *Pilgrimage*, p. 176, ll. 6697–715.) The French prose translation printed on vellum by Verard, Paris, 1499, now in the Huntington Library, has illuminations that show a similar mirror, but without an image drawn within it. It may be seen in facsimile, *Le Pelerinage de vie humaine*, ed. Pollard; the picture on sig. X5ᵛ establishes the mirror on the staff as equivalent to the mirror of the opening vision, despite the fact it does not repeat that mirror's image.

86. *Pilgrimage of the Lyf of the Manhode*, p. 162. Figure 24: Paris, Bibl. Natl. MS. fr. 823, fol. 74v. On fol. 74, the pilgrim is shown prostrate, attacked by four hags with fists, a club, and a lance (the latter is plunged into his side, from which he bleeds). He still has his staff in this picture, but his hand lies across it without strength; he does not have hold of it. For the French text, see *Vie*, ed. Stürzinger, ll. 10741–52; cf. the miniature reproduced opp. p. 334 (from a Gibbs MS.). On the absence of this episode from the second version, see Lydgate, *Pilgrimage*, p. xxviii (item 8).

87. For the episode in Lydgate, see *Pilgrimage*, pp. 398–418; for the quotation, p. 413 (15354). A comparable illustration may be seen in Tuve, *Allegorical Imagery*, fig. 55 (from Bodley MS. Douce 300, fol. 73v; the position of the daughters is reversed).

88. Lydgate, *Pilgrimage*, pp. 202–28 (7225–8193); the difficulties with the gambeson occur on p. 208. For the equivalent passage in *Vie*, ed. Stürzinger, see pp. 118–39 (3799–4492). Figure 25: Paris, Bibl. Natl. MS. fr. 823, fol. 27. Figure 26: the same, fol. 27v (on fol. 28, he wears the gambeson under his pilgrim's gown, with the anvil showing outside). Figure 27: the same, fol. 29. As in all illustrated MSS. of the poem, these are merely part of a much longer sequence (here extending to fol. 35v): e.g., London, Brit. Lib. MS. Add. 22937, a beautiful copy made ca. 1450, uses twelve pictures to illustrate the full action, fols. 22v–29v; MS. Add. 25594, 14th century, fols. 6–12, uses thirteen; and Paris, Bibl. Natl. MS. fr. 376, fols. 25–33, uses fourteen. Stürzinger includes relevant examples in plates opp. pp. 118, 132. In MS. fr. 823 (from which my present figures are drawn) the pictures often alternate between the pilgrim in armor and the pilgrim dressed as a pilgrim, to establish that this is inner armor, its nature spiritual rather than material. Cambridge, Fitzwilliam Mus. MS. 62, the so-called "Cambridge Hours" (Rohan workshop, beginning of the 15th century), depicts the arming sequence in the margins of its text, in a series of small, exquisite paintings, fols. 106–11; the absence of any identifying text suggests a fairly wide-

spread knowledge of the poem and its visual tradition. On this MS., see Tuve, *Allegorical Imagery*, pp. 192–94.

89. Lydgate, *Pilgrimage*, p. 229. Figure 28: Paris, Bibl. Natl. MS. fr. 823, fol. 34. Cf. Oxford, Bodley MS. Douce 300, fol. 42 (French, ca. 1400), reproduced by Tuve, *Allegorical Imagery*, fig. 44. Although the illustrations to this MS. have no real artistic merit, they possess a wit and vigor all their own. One notes, for example, that the pilgrim—who to this point has been of a size with Grace Dieu—becomes very small indeed when no longer dressed either as pilgrim or as Christian soldier. Tuve, figs. 45a, 45b, reproduces parallel illuminations from London, Brit. Lib. MS. Add. 38120. (The poem briefly discusses an alternative kind of armor as well, David's five stones and sling, each part of which is also carefully moralized: see Lydgate, *Pilgrimage*, pp. 231, 234–40.)

90. Lydgate, *Pilgrimage*, p. 232. "Hyr courtyne" is apparently a kind of tent into which she disappears.

91. *Ibid.*, p. 242. In the following lines, as the pilgrim tries to recover from his confusion he remembers a similar grotesquerie: that Grace Dieu put eyes in his ears. For the French text concerning Lady Memory, see *Vie*, ed. Stürzinger, pp. 148–53 (4779–958).

92. Figures 29, 30 complete the sequence I have chosen to illustrate from Paris, Bibl. Natl. MS. fr. 823, fols. 34v, 35v; in the former, notice the pilgrim's armor still lying beside him on the ground. In New York, Pierpont Morgan MS. M.772, fol. 37v (French, ca. 1360–70), Lady Memory has closed (or empty) eyes at the front of her head, as well as an enormous eye at the back. On fol. 66 of this MS., when the pilgrim lies prostrate under attack from three of the sins, Memory reappears to remind him of his spiritual armor. Cf. Paris, Bibl. Natl. MS. fr. 376, fols. 31v–33, ca. 1430–40, which show her with a whole second face at the back of her head; her eyes in front are closed. London, Brit. Lib. MS. Harley 4399, fol. 32 (French, 15th century), reveals an artist's trouble in trying to illustrate this text: though the image is suitably startling, Memory's single eye appears to be in her neck.

CHAPTER II

1. See, e.g., the *Rhetorica ad Herennium*, pp. 342, 376, 380, 384, 404, 408, discussing *translatio, similitudo, exemplum, demonstratio*, etc., as figures of speech that notably possess this power. Though Chaucer may have learned some techniques of description from the handbooks of rhetoric or poetics, such books do not begin to account for the way the more complex of his descriptions function: for that I think one must look elsewhere, to ideas of the image current in other areas of medieval thought and culture. Richardson, *Blameth Nat Me*, pp. 18–54, seeks to locate "The Medieval Concept of Imagery" (her chapter title) in the rhetorical tradition exclusively, and offers therein a necessary supplement to the materials I survey in this book. But that tradition does not yield a great deal; the bulk of her book consists of interesting essays on individual fabliaux that focus on a technique she admits (pp. 173–74) Chaucer could not have learned from the rhetoricians, "a technique in which figurative comparisons are given ironic ramification

which extends their meanings beyond the immediate points of reference and causes them to function organically within the aesthetic whole of the narrative" (p. 170). Payne, *Key of Remembrance*, offers a judicious study of the rhetorical tradition and its larger consequence for Chaucer's art. Nims, "*Translatio*," gives promise of some striking reassessments to come. Rowland's chapter on "Chaucer's Imagery," in her *Companion to Chaucer Studies*, pp. 117–42, offers an interesting survey of critical thought on this subject; it concludes with a basic bibliography.

2. Loomis, *Mirror of Chaucer's World*; Hussey, *Chaucer's World*; Seraillier, *Chaucer and His World*; Halliday, *Chaucer and His World*; Chaucer, *The Canterbury Tales*, trans. Coghill (1977 ed.); Brewer, *Chaucer*, 3d ed., and *Chaucer and His World* (a particularly rich collection). See also Spencer, *Chaucer's London* (catalogue of an exhibition at the London Museum, 1972). Robertson, *Preface to Chaucer*, includes a selection of pictures integral to his argument. Pratt, in his edition of *The Tales of Canterbury*, uses several pictures to illustrate narrative.

3. As the only visual "glosses" to be offered for *The Miller's* and *Reeve's Tales* respectively, those pictures are grotesquely inadequate—as is Loomis's decision to illustrate *The Shipman's Tale* with a picture of the punishment of Ganelon, on the strength of nothing more than a two-line allusion in the text. (See Loomis, *Mirror of Chaucer's World*, figs. 128–30.) Elsewhere the book is more generous and more pertinent—a resourceful collection from which one would not wish to lose a single picture. But more pictures are needed, especially pictures of a different kind. Loomis explicitly excluded one major source of images, the illuminated manuscripts ("service books") made for churches and private devotion, even though they were the finest and most numerous produced in England at the time. In his judgment they "offer little to illuminate the *Canterbury Tales*, the *House of Fame*, or even *The Legend of Good Women*" (p. 3). I shall argue instead that such images constitute a major resource in any true "illustration" of Chaucer's art. The consequence of these different views may be easily assessed. Loomis offers no images at all for *The Man of Law's Tale*, for instance, on the grounds that "suitable illustrative material" is "scanty or nonexistent" (p. 5), whereas in Chapter VII of this book, I read the tale in terms of many such pictures, chosen from many more like them, that seem to me not only relevant but essential in kind to its full understanding.

4. I take this useful definition of iconographic likeness from Pickering, *Literature and Art*, pp. 91–92.

5. St. Thomas Aquinas, *Summa theologiae*, 1.1.10, Resp., quoted by Singleton, *Commedia*, p. 88. See also Gombrich, *Symbolic Images*, pp. 13–14, and his concluding essay, which offers a magisterial introduction to iconographic theory. It may be supplemented by Schapiro, *Words and Pictures*, a work of comparable distinction.

6. Discussed by Nims, "*Translatio*," p. 218. For the whole lyric, see Raby, ed., *Oxford Book of Medieval Latin Verse*, pp. 369–70, or Brittain, ed., *Penguin Book of Latin Verse*, pp. 204–6, whose prose translation I quote above. The poem goes on to explore the brief life of a rose as a figure for all human lives.

7. Hugh of St. Victor, *Selected Spiritual Writings*, p. 51 (*De arca Noe morali*, I, 6).

8. *Ibid.*, pp. 49–50 (I, 4, 5).

9. For an example of this double interest in both scientific classification and the hidden meanings of a divinely created world, see the opening paragraphs of the Proem to Bartholomaeus, *Properties*, p. 41, or this statement of procedure announced for Bk. XVII of that work, which concerns trees and plants: "Now somwhat schal be seyde oonliche of trees and herbes of þe whiche mencioun is ymade by name in holy writte in text oþer in glose, and þat we schull do as we may by [þe] ordre of a.b.c." (p. 882). On one of the traditions drawn upon, see Cronin, "The Bestiary and the Medieval Mind." Von Simson, *Gothic Cathedral*, p. xix, contrasts the 12th and 13th centuries with our own: "We find it necessary to suppress the symbolic instinct if we seek to understand the world as it is rather than as it seems. Medieval man conceived the symbolic instinct as the only reliable guide to such an understanding."

10. For similar categories, see Droulers, *Dictionnaire des attributs, allégories, emblèmes et symboles*, p. viii; or Anderson, *History and Imagery*, p. 92n. As an example of the third kind, one might adduce this figure from Venus's temple in *The Knight's Tale*: "Jalousye, / That wered of yelewe gooldes a gerland, / And a cokkow sittynge on hir hand" (1.1928).

11. Gray, *Themes and Images*, pp. 42–51, offers an interesting brief account; and see Phillips, *Reformation of Images*, esp. Chap. 1, "The Medieval Fabric."

12. See Josipovici, *World and the Book*, pp. 74–78, for such a description of the strategy, and an interesting interpretation of it.

13. Figure 31: Chest front, Museum of London (formerly in a private collection; it was first exhibited in 1972).

14. Many illuminators, of course, read only marginal instructions or rubrics, not the full text; others read the text, but not always with the closest attention to detail; still others followed conventional models—earlier picture cycles, or designs from pattern books. The quality of their work, moreover, varies from the banal and clumsy to the sublime. But even the poorest of their pictures are at least *medieval* "imaginings," products of a culture that enjoined upon readers and listeners a related task, the active framing of images in their minds.

15. For the Ellesmere portraits, see Loomis, *Mirror of Chaucer's World*, figs. 1, 80–101 (in black-and-white reproduction), or better, a useful bibliographical pamphlet by Schulz, *Ellesmere Manuscript*, which reproduces them in color. The Cambridge MS. portraits were first published in *Autotypes of Chaucer Manuscripts* (1879). Later, they appeared in Garnett, *English Literature* (1926). They have been largely ignored since then. Loomis disdained to include them on the ground that the painter "drew horses of such a peculiar anatomy and with such vicious eyes as to give the effect of caricature to all his figures" (intro. to fig. 80). But the colors are exceptionally vivid and interesting, and the designs are responsive to the meaning of the text, sometimes in subtle ways: e.g., the covered mystery of the Monk, all cloak and hat and averted face, in colors restricted almost entirely to rich blacks and

browns. He is not the corpulent, sociable, hunting monk of *The General Prologue* portrait, but that figure complicated by his performance on the pilgrimage, where he appears as a man of learning and authority—one who will take part in Harry Bailly's "game" only on his own very dignified terms, but whose tale is nevertheless curiously limited for one of his calling. The artist has painted the sum of portrait and performance—a man whose inner "condicioun" becomes increasingly mysterious. Loomis reproduces the Vices and Virtues pictures from this MS. as figs. 177–79. On fols. 130v–31, there were once full-page miniatures, very likely a double-page design: it would be interesting to know what was once shown there. The despoiler cut as near to the edge of the folios as he could manage, but on fol. 130v there remains part of an architectural column, in pale green, running nearly the length of the page.

16. Margaret Rickert's survey of the illuminated Chaucer MSS., published in Chaucer, *The Text of the Canterbury Tales*, ed. Manly and Rickert, I, 561–605, remains an indispensable guide. See pp. 583–604 for a description of the seven MSS. of the *Tales* that contain pictures. *The Tales of Canterbury*, ed. Pratt, reproduces the Rosenbach portrait of the Cook, p. 479. The picture of Mars, Venus, and Jupiter referred to above is from Oxford, Bodley MS. Fairfax 16, fol. 14v (ca. 1440–50); it may be seen in Brewer, *Chaucer*, 3d ed., p. 52. Woodcut illustrations are reproduced by Hodnett, *English Woodcuts*, figs. 149, 151, 170 (*CT*), 158 (*TC*), 160, 169 (*HF*), 171 (*PF*).

17. Spaces are left in Bk. I for 23 pictures; Bk. II, 36 pictures; Bk. III, 13 pictures; Bk. IV, 8 (possibly 9) pictures; Bk. V, 14 pictures. There is a note in one margin saying "neuer Foryeteth anne neuyll"; Skeat identified her as the granddaughter of John of Gaunt, and thought it "reasonable to infer that the MS. was actually written for one of John of Gaunt's family." (Chaucer, *Complete Works*, ed. Skeat, II, lxix.) For other possible candidates, see Parkes, "Palaeographical Description and Commentary," pp. 11–12, and for further commentary, Salter, "The 'Troilus Frontispiece,'" p. 23.

18. On English manuscript painting in this period, see M. Rickert, *Painting in Britain: The Middle Ages*, pp. 165–94, and Mathew, *Court of Richard II*, pp. 38–52. Millar, *English Illuminated Manuscripts*, offers many full-page reproductions; Harrison, *Treasures of Illumination*, remains a useful introduction. Pächt and Alexander, *Illuminated Manuscripts in the Bodleian Library*, Vol. III (*British, Irish, and Icelandic Schools*), catalogues a distinguished collection, and reproduces many miniatures.

19. For *Piers*, see Oxford, Bodley MS. Douce 104 (dated 1427): 68 pictures from it are reproduced in Bodleian Library Filmstrips nos. 168-I and 234; Oxford, Corpus Christi College MS. 201, fol. 1 (now in the Bodleian), has a small picture of the dreamer asleep. The illustrations to Brit. Lib. MS. Cotton Nero A.x. may be seen in a facsimile volume: *Pearl, Cleanness, Patience, and Sir Gawain*. Two copies of the *Confessio amantis* are more generously illustrated than most: Oxford, New College MS. 266 (now in Bodley), 1/4 15th century, which once had more than 30 pictures (some have been cut out, and those that remain are often badly rubbed); and New York, Pierpont Morgan MS. M.126, late 15th century, with 70 illustrations (though they are artistically undistinguished, their content is sometimes interesting). Figure 137 of the present book, illustrating Gower's version of the Constance story,

is taken from that MS.; the equivalent illustration in the New College MS. has been removed. We must, of course, allow for the fact that countless medieval MSS. have disappeared. In 1481, for instance, Peterhouse, Cambridge owned a total of 439 volumes, of which only 200 have survived; of the 87 MSS. that were given to St. Catherine's College, Cambridge, by its founder in 1473, none is still there. In the French Royal Library, 188 volumes recorded in 1373 were no longer there in 1411; St. Paul's Cathedral inventory shows 171 MSS. in 1458, only 52 in 1476; and so on. See Bühler, *Fifteenth-Century Book*, pp. 19 and 100–101, n. 39; concerning the many early printed books we know by title but which have not survived, he concludes: "Such works were practically always popular or profane works in the vernacular, which were quite literally 'read to pieces' by avid readers." That may well have been true for MSS. as well.

20. It is now possible to study the Dantean continuities in full detail, with the publication by Brieger et al. of *Illuminated Manuscripts of the Divine Comedy*. Fleming, "*Roman de la Rose*," approaches that text through its pictures and reproduces a generous number from many MSS.; Dahlberg, in his translation *The Romance of the Rose*, publishes a full cycle of illuminations from a 13th century MS. They supplement and continue Kuhn's pioneering work, still valuable, "Die Illustration des Rosenromans." Tuve, *Allegorical Imagery*, Chap. 3, has begun the modern study of Deguileville's pictorial cycle, and reproduces parallel scenes from MSS. of several periods.

21. Salter and Pearsall, "Pictorial Illustration," pp. 103–4, take proper note of this fact, and on pp. 105–14, survey the Chaucer manuscripts in particular.

22. In his edition *The Anglo-Norman Text of the "Holkham Bible Picture Book,"* Pickering has studied a reverse instance, in which a writer was commissioned to make a text that explained a long and highly sophisticated book of pictures. His conclusion: "Even when so commissioned, authors do not in fact write about and explain pictures put before them. Unless instructed to provide mere rubrics and *tituli* they write about the *themes* treated in pictures. In so doing they draw on and contribute to a verbal rather than a pictorial tradition. The characteristic opening of a passage of *Holkham* text is indeed 'here he shows how. . . .' What follows is nevertheless the writer's own contribution to the themes of the *Holkham* book, and as such it merits consideration." Morever: "The text does not describe the pictures in anything approaching the detail which the art historian would wish. It tells us, on the other hand, more about the themes as these were apprehended by the contemporary textator, possibly indeed by all members of the group of workers involved, including the commissioner of *Holkham*." (Pp. ix, xi.)

23. "Ymagynatyf," who says he has followed the dreamer for 45 years, dominates Passus XII of the poem (B-text). He claims often to have stirred the dreamer to think upon his end by imagining death and Doomsday (a product of the creative imagination), as well as upon his misspent youth (a product of the reproductive, or memorial imagination). "Ymagynatyf" employs many parables and images in his teaching, all of them exploring spiritual meaning through the data of sense experience: e.g., the parable of the swimmers, heaven as a dining hall, the rich and the poor as peacock and

lark. Harwood, "Imaginative in *Piers Plowman*," offers a learned discussion and a guide to earlier controversy on this subject, concluding (I think correctly): "If we associate Imaginative simply with that faculty of the mind which makes similitudes, we shall be able to understand not only his ability to foreshadow and prophesy but also the unity of his speech and his special relationship to clergy" (p. 255).

24. The grammatical triad Dowel–Dobet–Dobest also functions in this way, though it is not visual: it is a verbal "given," deduced from a text, whose true meaning the action then seeks to discover throughout the *Vita* section of the poem.

25. See also *BD*, 783, and ABC Poem, 81. Consult Tatlock and Kennedy, *Concordance to Chaucer*, for other instances.

26. *CT*, I.1899; *LGW*, 1760. For further instances, see Tatlock and Kennedy, *Concordance to Chaucer*, particularly citations from *RR* and *HF* for "image" meaning work in the plastic or visual arts, and from *Boece* for "image" as a mental conception. Chaucer's use of the term "figures" is closely allied, and equally inclusive in terms of media; *TC*, I, 365–66, and *The Man of Law's Tale* (II.187) use it to name mental images. Lydgate, *Minor Poems*, II, 778, in "Mesure is Tresour," includes a stanza devoted to "artificerys" (artists of all kinds), asking: "What may avaylle al your ymagynynges, / Withoute proporciouns of weyghte and iust mesour?" (The word "ymagynynges" is used generically to stand for the images an artist makes.) Artists as a group are wittily accommodated to the poem's moral theme by virtue of the text from Wisdom 11:21, central to medieval aesthetic theory, that said that God (as First Artist) had created the world in "mensura et numero et pondere"; Lydgate puns on this text in the second line quoted above. On this idea, see, e.g., Curtius, *European Literature and the Latin Middle Ages*, pp. 544–46. In what is evidently a failure to understand the sense of the stanza, the M.E.D. glosses this occurrence of the word as "scheming, plotting, intrigue; design" ("imagining[e]," sense 2a). The M.E.D. entries for "image" document in rich detail the applicability of that word to all media.

27. Edward, 2d Duke of York, *Master of Game*, pp. 3–4. A treatise on hunting, it was written sometime between 1406 and 1413. Edward here paraphrases the Prologue to *The Legend of Good Women* ([F] 25): "And yf that olde bokes were aweye, / Yloren were of remembraunce the keye."

28. Hoccleve, *Minor Poems*, p. 181 (written ca. 1421, when he was 53 years old; see p. xxii). His source is the *Horologium sapientiae* of Heinrich Suso, written in 1334; it was translated by Caxton as well; see Suso, "Orologium Sapientiae." The words "liknesse" and "figure" used in the first line offer important medieval synonyms for "image": they translate Suso's "Vide ergo nunc similitudinem hominis morientis et tecum pariter loquentis" (I quote from the Paris [Lefèvre] edition, ca. 1480 [Lib. II, cap. ii].) *Similitudo* is Suso's usual term, but *imago* occurs in the passage Hoccleve translates (p. 196) as "Than spak thymage / 'the best purueance,'" (etc). Figure 32: Oxford, Bodley MS. Selden Supra 53, fol. 118, illustrates the lines from Hoccleve's poem that I quote in my text. The MS. dates from ca. 1430. Hoccleve also uses "liknesse" as a word for the painting that he causes to be made alongside verses commending Chaucer in his *Regement of Princes*. For the picture and the text, see Loomis, *Mirror of Chaucer's World*, fig. 2. (In the

following stanza—a defense of images in churches—"ymages" and "lyk-nesse" are used together.) Machaut's *Confort d'Ami*, vv. 2185–90, uses the word "ymage" for the mental image of the beloved lady that the lover is advised to make in his heart; see D. Kelly, *Medieval Imagination*, pp. 50–51.

29. For the phrases I quote, see Hoccleve, *Minor Poems*, p. 184 (cf. p. 191) and pp. 206, 208, 189 (in that order). A similar imaging of death is advised Petrarch by St. Augustine in the former's *De secreto curarum conflictu*: "It will not do that we hear that name [Death] but lightly, or allow the re-membrance of it to slip quickly from our mind. No, we must take time to realise it. We must meditate with attention thereon. We must picture to our-selves the effect of death on each several part of our bodily frame." A vivid imagining of the signs of death follows, built upon memories of real death-bed scenes, "for things seen cling closer to our remembrance than things heard." (*Petrarch's Secret*, pp. 32–33.) Cf. the image of Death that illustrates Lydgate's poem "Death's Warning to the World," in Oxford Bodley MS. Douce 322, fol. 19v (in Loomis, *Mirror of Chaucer's World*, fig. 170). On the *ars moriendi* tradition in general, see M. C. O'Connor, *Art of Dying Well*.

30. Furbank, *Reflections on the Word "Image,"* challenges the indiscrimi-nate use of the term in literary criticism of the past several decades, particu-larly in criticism concerned with modern poetry. Examining the confusion that has resulted from the tendency to call metaphors images, he insists on this essential distinction: a metaphor is a comparison, an image is a picture; comparisons are not pictures. Properly limited, the term does of course re-main useful: it describes accurately the kind of image that is my subject in this book—large commanding pictures that we are invited to construct in our minds through an elaborate series of verbal cues. Certainly the Middle Ages used the term so, in ways that have consequence for both rhetorical organization and poetic function. (For Furbank's account of how we frame such an image, see Chapter I, n. 5, above.)

31. First published in 1953, Owen's essay has been reprinted in Wagen-knecht, ed., *Chaucer*, and in a collection edited by Owen himself, *Discus-sions of the Canterbury Tales*, from which I quote (pp. 79, 88).

32. Leyerle, "The Heart and the Chain," p. 113.

33. Tuve, *Allegorical Imagery*. Her subject is "the kinds of relations Eliza-bethans had with early materials" (p. 3), and Spenser is the Elizabethan poet she has most often in mind. Murrin, *Veil of Allegory*, studies the function of Spenser's imagery against some of the same backgrounds I employ in these chapters; it is a brilliant book, which I came upon only after my own studies were in full first draft.

34. Panofsky, *Early Netherlandish Painting*, I, Chap. 5: "Reality and Sym-bol in Early Flemish Painting: 'Spiritualia Sub Metaphoris Corporalium.'" See Kolve, "Chaucer's *Second Nun's Tale* and the Iconography of St. Cecilia," for an account of parallel techniques in Chaucer—the use of concealed Chris-tian symbolism within explicitly Christian story. My forthcoming study of *The Prioress's Tale* will furnish another example.

35. See Robertson, *Preface to Chaucer* (e.g., p. 258, on "iconographic set-tings"), and Pickering, *Literature and Art*, *passim*. Pickering, like myself, ex-plicitly disavows stylistic comparisons between the arts.

36. Important works arranged on dictionary principles include: Schiller,

Iconography of Christian Art; *Reallexikon zur Deutschen Kunstgeschichte*; *Lexikon der Christlichen Ikonographie*; and Réau, *Iconographie de l'art chrétien*. Van Marle, *Iconographie de l'art profane*, though ambitious, is synoptic and out of date; it has no successors. Bialostocki, "Iconography and Iconology," offers a brief history of the discipline and a useful bibliography. The beginning student might start there; he will find Mâle, *Gothic Image*, Anderson, *History and Imagery in British Churches*, and Chew, *Pilgrimage of Life*, attractive introductions to the more central iconographic traditions. The work of Emile Mâle, Adolf Katzenellenbogen, Erwin Panofsky, E. H. Gombrich, Millard Meiss, Meyer Schapiro, Edgar Wind, and Jean Seznec is often of interest to the student of literature. Salter and Pearsall, "Pictorial Illustration," touch upon many essential matters within a brief space, and begin by considering the limitations and dangers of three favored approaches to the interrelationship of literature and the arts (stylistic, structural, and iconographic). R. E. Kaske is preparing a volume entitled *Sources and Methodology for the Interpretation of Medieval Imagery* for the Toronto Medieval Bibliography Series.

37. See Gombrich, *Symbolic Images*, pp. 11–13, on what he calls "the dictionary fallacy." Kaske, "Chaucer and Medieval Allegory," a review of Robertson's *Preface to Chaucer*, makes a similar point (pp. 177–78): "Surely . . . the most important 'criterion of corrigibility' for any symbol proposed in a literary work will be its own total context within the work itself. In practical terms, it would be difficult even to suspect the existence of such a symbol without considerable guidance from its context." For an eloquent defense of context, see R. H. Green, "Classical Fable and English Poetry," esp. pp. 123–25. Green's subject is the use of mythographic materials in the interpretation of medieval literature: "If we were to assume that the poem says what the commentaries say its images signify, we would reduce the poem to the status of another commentary, and the poem itself would escape us. For the poem's life, and the poet's achievement, reside in a new *mirabilis concinna mutatio* by which the traditional and conventional are transformed into a new and unique existence which alters and extends the tradition. What knowledge of traditional meanings gives us is a share in the point of departure with the medieval poet and his reader." (P. 124.)

38. Geoffrey de Vinsauf, *Poetria nova*, ll. 1761–62, which in Nims's published translation reads: "A word that is uttered alone is, as it were, the raw material of discourse—a thing rough and shapeless" (p. 79). The paraphrase is from her essay, "*Translatio*," p. 216.

39. Furbank, *Reflections on the Word "Image,"* p. 12, makes this point well.

40. Cf. Howard, *The Three Temptations*, p. 31: "It is in the nature of literature and indeed of understanding to be symbolic, to find the general in the particular, the universal in the concrete. But in the criticism of literature one does not grasp only, with a kind of metaphysical leap, at the general and the universal; one attempts to experience the poet's wrangle with the particular and the concrete, to live with him the *vita activa* of his art."

41. Figure 33: Rouen, Cathedral of Notre-Dame, misericord carving, 15th century; see Kraus, *Hidden World of Misericords*, fig. 51. On bagpipes in the iconography of the "old song," see Block, "Chaucer's Millers and Their

Bagpipes"; Robertson, *Preface to Chaucer*, p. 243, and figs. 15, 33, 35, 41, 42, 117; Scott, "Sow-and-Bagpipe Imagery in the Miller's Portrait"; and Randall, *Images in Margins*, fig. 462 (a naked man playing bagpipes that cover the entire middle portion of his body—a very literal way of talking about carnal music). Cf. Cambridge, Trinity Hall MS. 12 (a French Boethius, ca. 1406), which shows Orpheus playing the bagpipes in Hades (fol. 51), seeking to win back his Eurydice; after he has lost her again (fol. 52), the bagpipes are shown detumescent.

42. Figure 34: from the upper border. The tapestries were designed by Jean Bondol and made by Nicolas Bataille, ca. 1375–80, for Louis of Anjou. A 15th-century illustration to Guillaume de Deguileville's *Le Pelerinage de l'ame* (opp. p. 92) shows the souls of the blessed being welcomed into heaven, and there, too, five angels are playing bagpipes; Remnant, *Misericords in Great Britain*, pl. 30 (c), shows an angel with bagpipes on a misericord from the Royal Foundation of St. Katharine, Butcher Row, London, which he dates 1377 (pp. 93–94); Paris, Bibl. Natl. MS. nouv. acq. lat. 3145, fol. 39, the Hours of Jeanne de Navarre, includes bagpipes in the angelic music that accompanies its Annunciation scene. Cave, *Roof Bosses in Medieval Churches*, figs. 28 (a pig playing bagpipes), 107 (an angel playing bagpipes), and 260 (a man playing bagpipes), offers a comprehensive range of examples. For Archbishop Arundel's defense of bagpipes in the trial of the Lollard priest William Thorpe, see Pollard, ed., *Fifteenth Century Prose and Verse*, p. 141: "I say to thee that it is right well done that pilgrims have with them both singers and also pipers, that when one of them that goeth barefoot striketh his toe upon a stone and hurteth him sore and maketh him to bleed, it is well done, that he or his fellow, begin then a song or else take out of his bosom a bagpipe for to drive away with such mirth the hurt of his fellow. For with such solace, the travail and weariness of pilgrims is lightly and merrily brought forth." (Punctuation added.) On the fact that even in Holy Scripture one sign can signify different things—sometimes contradictory things—in different places, see St. Augustine, *On Christian Doctrine*, III.xxv–xxviii, trans. Robertson, pp. 99–102. Two other examples may serve to reinforce this point. Though a peacock is often a symbol of pride—and functions so in Chaucer's *Reeve's Tale*, for instance—yet in the earlier Christian centuries peacocks are frequently depicted in the company of Christ the Redeemer, as inhabitants of Paradise. In the 6th-century mosaics of the Basilica of San Vitale in Ravenna, for instance, or the 12th-century mosaics of the Basilica of San Clemente in Rome, they mean only themselves, birds whose plumage is paradisiacally beautiful and whose flesh was said not to putrefy. On the former, see Bovini, *Ravenna Mosaics*, p. 45 and pl. 40. Rowland, *Birds with Human Souls*, surveys the tradition, pp. 127–30. For an extended moralization of the peacock, *in malo*, see Langland, *Piers Plowman*, B. XII, 240–69. The painting of the Last Judgment by Fra Angelico (1387–1455) now in the Museum of San Marco in Florence, which shows the saved being welcomed into the company of heaven by entering a carol dance of the saints—a dance that normally figures erotic rather than spiritual love (as in MSS. of *The Romance of the Rose*), offers a comparable example, for in this painting it images the joy of paradise directly, with-

out retrospective irony. If it has any concern at all with other possible mean-
ings of the figure, it is a wish to "redeem" them, to rediscover them within a
sacred context.

43. The examples range from drunkards' masses to scholastic burlesques
of erotic love ideas to satires on the poetry of incompetent minstrels—the
latter exemplified by Chaucer's own *Sir Thopas*.

44. Three articles by Glending Olson, prefatory to his *Literature as Rec-
reation*, break new ground in this matter: "Deschamps' *Art de Dictier* and
Chaucer's Literary Environment"; "The Medieval Theory of Literature for
Refreshment"; and "Making and Poetry."

45. Robertson, *Preface to Chaucer*, offers a learned though highly contro-
versial study of this tradition; see also Huppé and Robertson, *Fruyt and
Chaf*. For reviews and other views, see Bloomfield, "Symbolism in Medi-
eval Literature"; Kaske, "Chaucer and Medieval Allegory"; Payne, reviews
of *Preface to Chaucer* and *Fruyt and Chaf*; Utley, "Robertsonianism Redi-
vivus"; Howard, *The Three Temptations*, Chap. 1; Silverstein, "Allegory and
Literary Form"; Beichner, "Allegorical Interpretation of Medieval Litera-
ture"; and an important essay, too little known, by Crane, "On Hypotheses
in 'Historical Criticism.'" The essays by Donaldson, Kaske, and Donahue
in Bethurum, ed., *Critical Approaches to Medieval Literature*, grew out of a
conference devoted to this issue; that by Donahue, "Patristic Exegesis in the
Criticism of Medieval Literature," is notable for its historical range and dis-
crimination, and on pp. 71–74, especially, offers essential support for my
argument. Useful too are his nondogmatic definitions of what constituted a
"higher sense" (*profundior intelligentia, sensus altior, subtilior interpretatio*) in
scriptural exegesis; J. B. Allen, *Friar as Critic*, reaches like conclusions,
on the basis of a great deal of new material, and with a different group of
exegetes chiefly in mind—English friars who wrote in the first half of the
14th century.

46. Note that Chaucer sometimes uses "fruyt" (as a literary term) in a
most minimal way, to mean simply the essential narrative action, stripped of
inessential details. See *The Man of Law's Tale*, 11.411 and 701–6; in the latter
instance, it appears as "the corn" in opposition to "the chaf" and "the stree"
(straw). Such evidence, on its own, should caution us against thinking that
Chaucer meant always and only one thing when he invoked the formula, or
that a single gloss upon it can constitute a critical imperative.

47. See the "Commentary" in *Chaucer's Poetry*, ed. Donaldson, pp. 1104–
8. J. B. Allen, *Friar as Critic*, pp. 128–29, offers a subtle interpretation of
the theological language of the tale. He sees it as an "allegorical trap" in-
tended to catch overzealous exegetes: "The joke is on everybody who thinks
the tale a 'folly'—who is not content with the delight of simple foolish-
ness. . . . But even more clearly, the joke, in all its richness, would not have
been possible if there had not been an exegetical tradition in which the cock
was a figure of the preacher."

48. G. Olson, "Making and Poetry," pp. 277–78, documents one further
sense of the term, in which "poetry" stands for classical and philosophical
material, whether in verse or prose; thus "making" involves the creation of
verses that may or may not incorporate "poetry." The works of Dante and

Petrarch earn them the dignified title of "poet" on these grounds as well.

49. For representative but interesting "maker/make" usages, see: *Boece*, III, pr. 6 (first gloss); *BD*, 1157, 1159; *HF*, 622; *TC*, V, 1627; *LGW*, (G) 342, (F) 549, 562, 573, 579, 614, 618; *CT*, 1.95. And for "endyte": *PF*, 119; *TC*, I, 6; II, 257; *CT*, 1.1872; VII.1980, 3207; and the *Retraction*'s "translacions and enditynges of worldly vanitees." (A full display of the evidence is readily available in Tatlock and Kennedy, *Concordance to Chaucer*.) "Endyte" comes from late Latin *indicare* (*dictare*) and means, in general, "to declare, to dictate, to say something with authority"; its specific senses include the making of legal accusations, letter writing (*ars dictaminis*), and the writing of poetry. In Chaucer's English, the verbs "make" and "endite" are often used synonymously, though a distinction may be intended concerning the Squire, "He koude songes make and wel endite" (1.95). In *The Legend of Good Women*, Chaucer uses three verbs for his activity as poet: "ryme," "make," and "reherce" ([F] 570, 573, 574). Glending Olson, "Making and Poetry," examines these usages, and more, against a rich range of continental evidence.

50. For the reference to Otes de Granson, see the Envoy to the so-called "Complaint of Venus," which consists of three ballades translated from Granson's French; the poem was probably written in the 1390's (Granson received a handsome annuity from Richard II in 1393). The Dunbar quotation is from his "Lament for the Makaris," an elegy for dead poets that becomes a kind of continuing dance of death:

> I se that makaris amang the laif
> Playis heir ther pageant, syne gois to graif;
> Sparit is nocht ther faculte;
>   *Timor mortis conturbat me.*
> He hes done petuously devour,
> The noble Chaucer, of makaris flour,
> The Monk of Bery, and Gower, all thre;
>   *Timor mortis conturbat me.*

The maker identified only as "the Monk of Bery" is Lydgate. I quote from Dunbar, *Poems*, p. 21.

51. For information concerning the social, economic, and professional status of artists in medieval times, see Martindale, *Rise of the Artist*: pp. 9–34 concern civic artists; pp. 35–64, artists in the courts; and pp. 65–78, artists in the cloister.

52. The first is an elegy on the death of the Duchess Blanche, wife to Chaucer's patron, John of Gaunt. The arguments of Giffin, *Studies on Chaucer and His Audience*, Chap. 2, persuade me that *The Second Nun's Tale* was probably written at the request of Richard II, for Cardinal Easton to bear to Rome.

53. The idea of poetic inspiration as a kind of numinous madness did not entirely disappear, but nearly so. On some survivals, see Curtius, *European Literature and the Latin Middle Ages*, Excursus VIII, "The Poet's Divine Frenzy." Excursuses VII–XII, which Curtius termed "fragments toward a 'History of the Theory of Poetry'" (p. 468), are all of interest here. Excursus XXI ("God as Maker") might also be included under that rubric, and is

of particular relevance to the idea of poetry explored above. For a brief introduction to medieval aesthetics and poetics, Wimsatt and Brooks, *Literary Criticism*, esp. pp. 127–31, 139–46, is clear and helpful.

54. Figure 35: Brussels, Bibl. Royale MS. 9505–6, fol. 115v. Trimpi, "The Quality of Fiction," in an important appendix, pp. 113–18, discusses the consequences for medieval poetry of Aristotle's distinction between the "productive" and the "prudential" faculties, which issue in art and morality respectively. See also de Bruyne, *Esthetics of the Middle Ages*, pp. 131–38, and the three-volume work in French from which this shorter version (by de Bruyne himself) was made. On the place of the *Ethics* in university curricula, see Leff, *Paris and Oxford Universities*, e.g., pp. 131, 136, 139, 142, 143, 146. Chaucer refers to the *Ethics* in *LGW*, (F) 166, in discussing the Golden Mean.

55. I quote Mure, *Aristotle*, p. 131, n. 2., whose summary of this aspect of Aristotle's thought, pp. 131–36, is particularly lucid. Note that even Butcher's famous study, *Aristotle's Theory of Poetry and Fine Art*, for all the apparent confidence of its title, begins: "Aristotle, it must be premised at the outset, has not dealt with fine art in any separate treatise, he has formulated no theory of it, he has not marked the organic relation of the arts to one another . . . he nowhere classifies the various kinds of poetry; still less has he given a scientific grouping of the fine arts and exhibited their specific differences" (p. 113). "In the history of Greek art we are struck rather by the union between the two forms of art [the fine arts and the useful] than by their independence" (p. 115).

56. Aristotle, *Ethica Nicomachea*, VI.3 (1139ᵇ). The discussion of art is in VI.4 (1140ᵃ). Aristotle's *Poetics* were known to the late Middle Ages only through Averroes's Arabic commentary, an extended paraphrase full of misunderstandings, which was translated into Latin by Hermannus Alemannus in 1256 and gained a certain academic currency in Europe. Twenty-four MSS. of this work are extant, and it was quoted by St. Thomas Aquinas and Roger Bacon, among others, but it never exerted an influence comparable to that of the *Ethics*. On it, see Hardison, *Enduring Monument*, pp. 12ff, and Boggess, "Aristotle's *Poetics* in the Fourteenth Century." There is a translation of Alemannus by Hardison, in Preminger et al., eds., *Classical and Medieval Literary Criticism*, pp. 349–82.

57. Pickering, *Literature and Art*, pp. 38–39, forcefully emphasizes the many interests and concerns of artists that are extrinsic to substantive meaning.

58. The *Melibee*, of course, *is* assigned to the "pilgrim" Chaucer, as a means of atoning for *The Tale of Sir Thopas*, whose high art as literary parody has escaped Harry Bailly utterly. *Sir Thopas* is nothing but art, the *Melibee* almost nothing but doctrine—a double performance in which the poet radically bifurcates his own voice (as I use that term in my text above) as a comic means of establishing the true aesthetic of his poetry, in which doctrine and delight are inextricably one. See R. F. Green, *Poets and Prince-pleasers*, for an explanation of why a courtly writer might (without irony) translate a work such as the *Melibee* in his capacity as an advisor to kings, a counselor to princes (Chap. 5, esp. pp. 142–43).

59. Hugh of St. Victor, in the *Didascalicon*, pp. 87–88, says there are two

kinds of writings, those that are philosophic and systematic (i.e., the Seven Liberal Arts, *trivium* and *quadrivium*), and those that are best called "appendages," for they are "only tangential to philosophy. What they treat is some extra-philosophical matter. Occasionally, it is true, they touch in a scattered and confused fashion upon some topics lifted out of the [liberal] arts, or, if their narrative presentation is simple, they prepare the way for philosophy. Of this sort are all the songs of the poets—tragedies, comedies, satires, heroic verse and lyric, iambics, certain didactic poems, fables and histories," and so on. I don't think Chaucer would have quarreled with the basic terms in which literature is here described, only with the value placed upon it within its kind. On the Liberal Arts (so-called because they are worthy of a "free" man, and have no pecuniary purpose), see Curtius, *European Literature and the Latin Middle Ages*, esp. pp. 36–42; from ancient Greece on, the *artes mechanicae* had been excluded from the company of seven. Poetry, it is true, had always managed to keep a foot in the door through its connection with grammar and rhetoric (which could be understood as "sciences"), but poetry as substantive statement, as imaginative vision, had no formal status within the system.

60. I here paraphrase a judgment made by Markman, "The Meaning of *Sir Gawain and the Green Knight*," p. 586, concerning recent criticism devoted to that poem.

61. Gombrich, *Symbolic Images*, pp. 165–66 (citing *De oratore*, III.155). Cf. St. Augustine, *On Christian Doctrine* (II.i–ii), pp. 34–35: "A sign is a thing which causes us to think of something beyond the impression the thing itself makes upon the senses. . . . Among signs, some are natural [smoke signifies fire] and others are conventional. . . . Conventional signs are those which living creatures show to one another for the purpose of conveying, in so far as they are able, the motion of their spirits or something which they have sensed or understood." Dante, in the Letter to Can Grande (if it is authentically his), makes the point most clearly: "We perceive many things by the intellect for which language has no terms—a fact which Plato indicates plainly enough . . . by his employment of metaphors; for he perceived many things by the light of the intellect which his everyday language was inadequate to express." (*Epistolae*, pp. 209–10.)

62. Smalley, *Study of the Bible*, p. 372. See also her *English Friars and Antiquity*.

63. Southern, *Medieval Humanism and Other Studies*, esp. pp. 29–132.

64. J. B. Allen, *Friar as Critic*, pp. 98–99.

65. Bloomfield, "Allegory as Interpretation," p. 317; his earlier essay, "Symbolism in Medieval Literature," also makes a powerful case for the priority of the literal (pp. 77–78).

66. Singleton, "On *Meaning* in the Decameron," p. 119; cf. Auerbach's essay on Boccaccio in *Mimesis*, esp. pp. 216–31. Mazzotta, "The *Decameron*," argues a contrary view. Marcus, "Ser Ciappelletto," examines the means by which Boccaccio discredits the tradition of the moral *exemplum* in the very first of his tales.

67. For a long period, Boccaccio repudiated the work himself, moved by the deathbed warning of a religious fanatic in 1362 that caused him great fears and religious scruples about his early writings. But in 1370 or 1371,

during his last years at Certaldo, he revised and recopied the *Decameron*, which suggests renewed respect for his earlier achievement. See Branca, *Boccaccio*, pp. 129–31, 172. Petrarch's letter concerning the former event can be read in *Letters from Petrarch*, pp. 225–28 (*Epistolae seniles*, I, 5, May 28, 1362).

CHAPTER III

1. I do not mean by this description to deny that the narrator is some-times amused by some part of his material, especially in his representation of the young knights as lovers and philosophers. As Theseus says within the tale, "Who may been a fool, but if he love?" (1.1799). And I do not deny that "what passes for tragedy in the chivalric view of things can be at times funny, at times nasty" when seen from other perspectives (David, *Strumpet Muse*, p. 87). The tale is, after all, lengthy and capacious; it is not made less serious as a work of art by regarding human experience from a number of points of view, whatever occasional problems in the management of tone may arise. (I think there are a few.) But I do not think the larger purpose and dominant effect of this poem is comic (*pace* Neuse, "The Knight: The First Mover in Chaucer's Human Comedy"), or that it is meant to expose its teller as a mercenary killer paying inept lip service to chivalric values he nei-ther understands nor in his own life serves. Jones, *Chaucer's Knight*, argues the latter view in a book-length study that, for all its learned information, seems to me to misread convention and misjudge tone at many crucial junc-tures. Two early reviews of Jones's book raise the necessary objections: see Burrow, "The Imparfit Knight," and that by David Aers. That Chaucer re-fers to a poem on Palamon and Arcite as among his works written prior to *The Canterbury Tales* (*LGW*, [F] 420–21) ought perhaps to dissuade us from assuming too intimate a connection between the tale and its pilgrim-teller; it ought even more to prevent us from making that teller the hidden subject of the tale and its only coherent explanation. (I comment further on this matter in Chapter IV, n. 1.) Benson and Leyerle, eds., *Chivalric Literature*, argues against the prevailing view that the later Middle Ages was a period of de-cline in chivalry; Leyerle's concluding essay provides an elegant summary.

2. Boccaccio, *Teseida delle nozze d'Emilia*, III, v. 11: "Arcita si levò, ch'era in prigione / allato allato al giardino amoroso." The *Teseida* has been translated by McCoy as *The Book of Theseus*, including most of Boccaccio's own glosses (*Chiose*) to the text; throughout this chapter I quote McCoy's translation, sometimes slightly modified. Havely, *Chaucer's Boccaccio*, ap-peared after this chapter was in its final form; pp. 103–52 translate those parts of the *Teseida* that correspond most closely to Chaucer's poem, with linking summaries of the rest. Pratt, "Chaucer's Use of the *Teseida*," remains a study of fundamental interest and importance; see also his chapter on *The Knight's Tale* in Bryan and Dempster, eds., *Sources and Analogues*. Wilson, "*The Knight's Tale* and the *Teseida* Again," assesses the larger literary identi-ties of the two works.

3. Figure 36: Oxford, Bodley MS. Douce 371, fol. 40v, shows the tradi-tion at its simplest. For a more elaborate version, see Valencia, Bibl. de la Universidad MS. 387, fol. 42v (French, ca. 1420); it has been reproduced by

Fleming, "*Roman de la Rose*," fig. 31. For the text, see Dahlberg's translation, *Romance of the Rose*, pp. 121–22, of ll. 6049–144 of Jean de Meun's poem; no Middle English translation of this part of the poem has survived. Jean's House of Fortune is based upon that of Alain de Lille in the *Anticlaudianus*, Bk. VIII, which Chaucer also knew at first hand; see the translation by Sheridan, p. 189. Lydgate, "A Mumming at London," *Minor Poems*, II, 683 (40–58), paraphrases Jean's description, and attributes it to him; the ruined portion of the house is called "þat doungeoun" (l. 47). Chrétien de Troyes' *Cligés* also links a prison tower and garden in complex, emblematic ways; see the edition by Micha, p. 185 (6079) to the end, or, in translation, Chrétien de Troyes, *Arthurian Romances*, pp. 171–79. Gottfried von Strassburg, *Tristan*, pp. 261–66, also uses a bipartite setting and includes explicit commentary on its meaning. Panofsky, *Early Netherlandish Painting*, I, Chap. 5, brilliantly interprets certain architectural juxtapositions in the visual arts as vehicles of symbolic meaning. For interesting speculations on Chaucer's use of open and closed spaces, see Joseph, "Chaucerian 'Game'—'Earnest.'"

4. Figure 37: Vienna, Natl. Lib. MS. 2617, fol. 53; the manuscript has sixteen miniatures, half of them by the anonymous master, half by a less talented hand. On this MS., see Chmelarz, "Eine Französische Bilderhandschrift"; his 15 plates reproduce all the illuminations, with the historiated initial on fol. 17v placed at the beginning of his own text. Six of the illuminations were reproduced in fine color facsimile under the title of an associated MS., René d'Anjou, *Livre du Cuer d'Amours espris*, III, pls. XIX–XXIV, a facsimile unfortunately very rare. The present picture may be seen in color in Brewer, *Chaucer and His World*, opp. p. 17. The MS. is of exceptional interest, and since I do not reproduce all its pictures or use them in their precise manuscript order, I list the full sequence here: fol. 14v: the author's presentation of the book to his lady (figure 56); fol. 17v: the translator at his writing desk (historiated initial); fols. 18v–19: the battle with the Amazons, painted across two MS. pages; fol. 39: the entry of Teseo into Athens, with the Theban widows (figure 59); fol. 53: the knights in prison looking upon Emilia in the garden (figure 37); fol. 64: the release of Arcita from prison (figure 38); fol. 76v: Emilia riding out hunting (figure 46); fol. 77: Palemone and Arcita fighting in the wooded grove (figure 47); fol. 91: the two knights with followers before Teseo at the tournament lists (figure 45); fol. 102: Arcita, Emilia, and Palemone praying at the altars of the three gods (figure 48); fol. 121: the tournament battle (figure 55); fol. 138v: the appearance of the fury, and Arcita's fall (figure 53); fol. 139: the betrothal of Emilia and the dying Arcita, in Arcita's bedchamber; fol. 152: the funeral pyre of a knight killed in the tournament; fol. 169: the death of Arcita, with mourners; fol. 182: the marriage of Emilia and Palemone (figure 62). I know of only three other illustrated MSS. of the *Teseida*. The pictures in Naples, Bibl. Oratoriana dei Gerolamini MS. C.F.2.8, Florentine, ca. 1450, have been published by Degenhart and Schmitt, *Corpus der Italienischen Zeichnungen*, I.ii, 414–15, and figs. 287d–290d (a reference I owe to William Coleman). Florence, Bibl. Nazionale MS. II.II.27, from the 15th century, has three ink-and-wash drawings: on fol. 51, Palemone and Arcita fight before Emilia, who rides with hounds and falcon; on fol. 91v there is another

scene of combat; and on fol. 127v, Teseo joins the hands of Palemone and Emilia in marriage, in a company standing between two temples. The drawings are not unskillful, but they lack imaginative resonance. Cambridge, Harvard Univ. MS. Typ. 227 H (Ferrara, ca. 1471), has a small miniature on its first page showing Arcita and Palemone side by side.

5. On Mariotto di Nardo (active 1394–1431), see Berenson, *Italian Pictures of the Renaissance*, I, 129–33; he reproduces this tray, which would have been used to offer gifts at a marriage or a birth, as pl. 527. Berenson did not recognize its narrative subject, labeling it simply "*Desco da Nozze*: Garden of Love." Now in the Staatsgalerie, Stuttgart, it has been recently published (and correctly identified) by Watson, *The Garden of Love*, pp. 73–74, and pl. 60. The Florentine drawing is from the Gerolamini MS. described above; see Degenhart and Schmitt, *Corpus der Italienischen Zeichnungen*, fig. 290a (fol. 31).

6. Cupid shoots his arrows in the Florentine drawing described above, and in an interesting 16th-century woodcut reproduced by Crisp, *Mediaeval Gardens*, I, fig. 108, where it is described as an illustration to Panfillo [Pamillo] Sasso's *Strambotii*, without further bibliographical reference. Crisp was an amateur, in the old-fashioned sense of the word, and his book, though vast and useful, is not scholarly. I have searched through editions of the *Strambotii* published in various cities in 1501, 1506, and 1511, and have not succeeded in finding this woodcut; the woodcuts vary, however, and it seems likely that the reference, though incomplete, could be proved correct. Crisp did not know that the scene derives ultimately from the *Teseida*, illustrating Bk. III, vv. 15–17: "Arcita said: 'O Palemone, do you see what I behold in those beautiful immortal eyes? . . . I see in them the one who wounded the father of Phaeton because of Daphne. . . . In his hands he holds two golden arrows and now he is placing one on his bowstring as he looks at no one else but me.' . . . Then Palemone, utterly astonished, cried out, 'Alas, the other has wounded me.'"

7. In the *Teseida*, the way the young knights fall in love is developed less interestingly, though the character of Emilia is, in compensation, richer and more fully detailed. (Like Creseida in the *Filostrato*, she is to be associated with the woman Boccaccio loves, and to whom he dedicates the poem. On this, more below.) When Palemone sees her and cries "Alas!" (*Omè!*), she looks up at the window, realizes what that cry signifies, and is torn between her virginal modesty and her vanity. (The latter is said to be innate in women, who delight in having their beauty seen.) From that time forward, she adorns herself the more carefully when she goes into the garden; and whenever she knows she is looked upon, she sings most beautifully and walks with slow, graceful steps (III, vv. 17–19, 28–30). Chaucer kept none of this material.

8. *Teseida*, III, vv. 23, 24: "E dicoti che giá sua prigionia / m'è grave piú che quella di Teseo"; "anzi mi veggo qui imprigionato / e ispogliato d'ogni mia possanza." After Palemone's defeat, Teseo presents him to Emilia as her prisoner (IX, v. 60), and Palemone says he has been her prisoner since he first saw her (IX, v. 63).

9. Figure 38: Vienna, Natl. Lib. MS. 2617, fol. 64. For a color reproduc-

tion, see Unterkircher, *A Treasury of Illuminated Manuscripts*, pl. 49, with a discussion of the MS., pp. 210–12.

10. *Teseida*, III, vv. 82–85.

11. Figure 39: Cambridge, Fitzwilliam Mus. MS. 368 (a single leaf). For other examples of Honoré's work illustrating this moral text, see Millar, *The Parisian Miniaturist, Honoré*. Millar edited the French text, written by Friar Lorens of Orléans in 1279, as *La Somme le roy* (with many plates) for the Roxburghe Club. The treatise was translated three times into medieval English, once by Dan Michel of Northgate, in 1340, as the *Ayenbite of Inwyt*; again as *The Book of Vices and Virtues*, ca. 1375; and finally by William Caxton, ca. 1486, as the *Royal Book*, STC 21429. Francis's edition of *The Book of Vices and Virtues* has a substantial introduction; see also Tuve, *Allegorical Imagery*, Chap. 2. Another early-14th-century illumination to this text, Milan, Bibl. Ambrosiana MS. H.106 Sup. (S.P. 2), fol. 70, shows Lechery with manacles in one hand and fire radiating from the other. Allen, *Friar as Critic*, p. 74, discusses Robert Holcott's exposition of a picture of Cupid in his commentary on Hosea 2:3, in which chains of adamant are said to show that *per amorem cor hominis et sensus eius multipliciter alligantur* ("the heart and sense of man are fettered by love in many ways").

12. Alain de Lille, *The Complaint of Nature*, p. 47 (m. V).

13. Andreas Capellanus, *The Art of Courtly Love*, p. 124.

14. See *RR*, 1927–45, 1967–69, 2028–32, and 3799–4614, for further use of the love-prison theme. For recent discussion of the poem, see Robertson, *Preface to Chaucer*, pp. 91–110; Tuve, *Allegorical Imagery*, Chap. 4; and Fleming, "*Roman de la Rose*." The tradition is wittily used in a triple roundel attributed to Chaucer, "Merciles Beaute": "Sin I fro Love escaped am so fat, / I never thenk to ben in his prison lene; / Sin I am free, I counte him not a bene" (ll. 27–29). Barney, "Troilus Bound," examines Chaucer's use of these and several associated traditions in that longer poem, and has a valuable account of the antecedents. Cf. *Petrarch's Lyric Poems*, no. 89 ("Fuggendo la pregione ove Amor m'ebbe"), pp. 192–93.

15. Baudouin de Condé and Jean de Condé, *Dits et contes*, I, 267–377. See Wimsatt, *Chaucer and the French Love Poets*, pp. 32–36, for a more extensive description of the poem's action. For the *balades*, see Guillaume de Machaut, *Poésies lyriques*, I, 50, 103, 127, 137. On Froissart, see Fourrier's introduction to his edition of *La Prison amoureuse*, along with Whiting, "Froissart as Poet" (pp. 199–201 concern that poem), and Wimsatt, pp. 118–33. Froissart spent 1361–69 in England, as poet and secretary to the Queen, and he visited again in 1395, to be received with great honor by Richard II. Chaucer probably knew him personally, and certainly knew some of his writings; *The Book of the Duchess*, for instance, is based in part upon his *Paradis d'amour*. Loomis, *Mirror of Chaucer's World*, fig. 7, shows Froissart presenting a book of his poems to Richard II in 1395.

16. Figures 40–42 are from Vienna, Natl. Lib. MS. 2621. On this MS., see Hermann, *Die Westeuropäischen Handschriften und Inkunabeln*, II, 62–66 and pl. 19.

17. Figure 40: fol. 23v (Baudouin de Condé and Jean de Condé, *Dits et contes*, p. 280). Figure 41: fol. 25v (p. 288). Figure 42: fol. 29 (p. 303). For

the term "la douce prison d'amor" see, e.g., l. 1894, p. 333. On rabbits as symbols of lechery, see Robertson, *Preface to Chaucer*, pp. 113, 128, 255, 264; and see Wood, *Chaucer and the Country of the Stars*, pp. 139–40, on the linguistic pun involved.

18. Froissart, *La Prison amoureuse*, pp. 152 (61–69), 171 (25–31, 32–37, 43–49). For an extensive study of the poem see D. Kelly, *Medieval Imagination*, pp. 155–69.

19. The Knight of La Tour-Landry, instructing his daughters in virtuous manners, recounts a conversation he had with a young woman who was being offered to him in marriage: "And I beheld her of whome I was spoken to, and I set my self in commynycacyon with her of many thynges for to know the better her mayntenyng & gouernaunce. And so we fill in spekyng of prysoners, and thenne I said to her, damoysell, I wold wel and had leuer be youre prysoner than ony others, & I thenke that youre pryson shold not be so hard ne cruell as is the pryson of englissh men. And she ansuerd me that she had late sene such one that she wold wel that he were her prysoner. And I demanded her yf she wold yeue hym euyl pryson, & she answerd me nay, but that she wold kepe hym as derworthely as her owne body. And I said to her that he who someuer he was he was wel happy & eurous for to haue so swete & noble a pryson." Privately, he thought her manners and conversation too forward and rejected her as a possible wife. (*The Book of the Knight of the Tower*, p. 27.)

For the French texts of Charles d'Orléans, see his *Poésies*; for English versions, possibly his own (the attribution is uncertain), see his *English Poems*, from which I quote ballade no. 40, p. 49; cf. ballade no. 18 (p. 25), and chanson no. 16 (p. 112). Fox, *Lyric Poetry of Charles d'Orléans*, offers an interesting study, and prints in color, as frontispiece, a famous illumination showing Charles as prisoner in the Tower of London (London, Brit. Lib. MS. Royal 16 F.ii, fol. 73). When Charles disembarked in France in 1440, he was greeted by the Duke and Duchess of Burgundy, who had negotiated his ransom and release, and is recorded as having said to the Duchess: "Madame, vu ce que vous avez fait pour ma délivrance, je me rends votre prisonnier" (Fox, p. 16). See also William Dunbar, *Poems*, "Bewty and the Presoneir," pp. 104–7.

20. Cf. the "free" Arcite's complaint in the grove, ll. 1550–54, in which he describes himself as "so caytyf and so thral" that he is willing to serve Theseus, his mortal enemy. (Cf. l. 1717.)

21. Leyerle, "The Heart and the Chain," pp. 118–21, has noted this extension of the literal prison in a study of the verbal nucleus "*cage, cheyn, dongeon, fettre, laas,* and *tour.*" He counts more than fifty occurrences of these terms within the tale.

22. *Teseida*, II, v. 99: "E questi due furon riservati / per farli alquanto piú ad agio stare, / perché di sangue reale eran nati; / e felli dentro al palagio abitare / e cosí in una camera tenere, / faccendo lor servire a lor piacere." I have slightly modified McCoy's translation. For details concerning the servants and the escape, see IV, v. 89 and V, vv. 24–26.

23. Webb, "A Reinterpretation of Chaucer's Theseus."

24. Christine de Pisan, *Book of Fayttes of Armes*, pp. 238–39.

25. Bonet, *Tree of Battles*, pp. 152–53.

26. *Ibid.*, pp. 158–59. It was, however, apparently considered honorable policy to ransom a ruler at such an exorbitant rate that his nation could not afford to wage war. The policy worked well against the Scots and to a lesser degree against the French, though English intentions were clearer in relation to France.

27. Christine de Pisan, *Book of Fayttes of Armes*, pp. 237–38.

28. Froissart, *Chronicle*, I, 384, 385, 393. Halliday, *Chaucer and His World*, reproduces manuscript illustrations of this event: on p. 27, King John surrenders to the Black Prince; on p. 28, a steward (?) removes his hat in respect before the captive king. See also Martindale, *Rise of the Artist*, pp. 43–45, for details of the court that King John maintained in his captivity.

29. Froissart, *Chronicle*, I, 394.

30. See Loomis, *Mirror of Chaucer's World*, note to fig. 16.

31. The poems of Charles d'Orléans, written during his captivity in England, 1415–40, are perhaps representative of earlier decades as well. No complaint against his physical imprisonment will be found in them: instead they testify to suffering of a purely spiritual kind, most often of love-longing. His tormentors are of an allegorical cast, and in English bear such names as "Sadnesse" and "Melancholye," in French "Douleur, Courroux, Desplaisir et Tristesse." Fox, *Lyric Poetry of Charles d'Orléans*, p. 62.

32. *Gilbert of the Haye's Prose Manuscript*, p. 159 (a Scots translation made in 1456 of Honoré Bonet's *L'Arbre des batailles*). Palamon, in his earlier prayer to Venus, describes their lineage as brought low "by tirannye" (1.1111), clearly a word from Theseus's treatment of them to this point.

33. Macrobius, *Commentary on the Dream of Scipio*, trans. Stahl, pp. 130–31; for the passage from Cicero, see pp. 71–72. Stahl's n. 4, p. 130, lists several Pythagorean and Neoplatonist texts that describe the body as the prison of the soul. See also n. 35 below.

34. The Vulgate reads "Infelix ego homo, quis me liberabit de corpore mortis huius?" (Rom. 7:24). Chaucer makes the prison image explicit.

35. Two learned studies by Courcelle will guide anyone wishing to study these matters further: "Tradition platonicienne et traditions chrétiennes du corps-prison," and "L'Ame en cage." The Latin sources include the *Psychomachia* of Prudentius, numerous writings of the Fathers, Pope Innocent III's *De miseria humanae conditionis* (a work Chaucer himself translated), Petrarch's *Secretum meum*, and others.

36. Among English vernacular texts one may note *The Harley Lyrics*, p. 67 ("Mayden moder milde," l. 8); *Pearl*, p. 43, l. 1187, which names the world as "þys doel-doungoun"; an extended meditation in "A Tretyse of Ghostly Batayle," in Horstmann, ed., *Yorkshire Writers*, II, 434–35; and David's speech of prophecy in the *Processus prophetarum* of *The Towneley Plays*, p. 61 (149–50). In Spanish, Juan Ruiz's *Book of Good Love* (ca. 1330–43), pp. 33–34, also uses the image. One might note, too, the cult of St. Leonard, patron saint of prisoners: for a representative life, see *The South English Legendary*, II, 476–83, where he is called "prisones louerd" (ll. 11, 75), shows power "as maister" over prisons in ways that are typologically related to Christ's Harrowing of Hell (e.g., ll. 143–47), helps the Queen of France in a difficult childbirth (the womb as metaphoric prison for the child, ll. 25–50), and heals sick men (sickness as prison, ll. 85–86); for love of St.

Leonard, moreover, God may save us from "þe prisoun of helle" (l. 186). The literal term is not disdained: St. Leonard also breaks fetters and has them hung up in churches (ll. 105–22). Lydgate's prayer to St. Leonard, in *Minor Poems*, I, 135–36, is similarly comprehensive. Near the beginning of *The House of Fame*, Chaucer falls asleep like a weary pilgrim traveling to the shrine of St. Leonard, ll. 111–18; on this see Koonce, *Chaucer and the Tradition of Fame*, pp. 70–72. Visual images of the saint are also important: there is a splendid picture of St. Leonard freeing prisoners in London, Brit. Lib. MS. Add. 17275, fol. 218v (an early-14th-century French MS. of saints' lives). See also Meiss, *Boucicaut Master*, figs. 1, 474, and *The Hours of Catherine of Cleves*, pl. 141. The latter (made ca. 1440) shows St. Leonard holding a crozier, a holy book, and fetters—a counter-image, so to speak, to the painting of Luxure by Honoré that I reproduce as figure 39. The prison of this world turns up in another tradition, as well: the "commendation of death" that the medieval *ars moriendi* teaches should be spoken to a dying man to help him wish to die; see "The Boke of the Craft of Dying," in Horstmann, ed., *Yorkshire Writers*, II, 407.

37. *The Knight's Tale* was almost certainly written during the years Chaucer and his wife lived in the dwelling-house above Aldgate (1374–86). Such gate-houses were sometimes used as prisons—e.g., prisoners for debt, trespass, account, and contempt were kept in Ludgate, prisoners for felony and maiming in Newgate—and it is interesting to note that in the lease to Aldgate, the Mayor and Aldermen of London explicitly promise that they will not cause any jail to be made of it, for the keeping of prisoners, during the tenancy of the said Geoffrey. See Crow and Olson, eds., *Chaucer Life-Records*, pp. 144–47, for the lease, and Robertson, *Chaucer's London*, pp. 22–23, on Ludgate and Newgate. The experience of living in a house potentially a prison may account, in some small way, for Chaucer's interest in the prison/garden setting he found in his literary source.

38. *Book of Vices and Virtues*, pp. 126–27, although speaking of Christian sin rather than romantic love, defines an otherwise analogous situation: "And ȝit more it fareþ be þe synful as be hym þat is in a prisoune in feteres and gyues and in an hard kepynge, as seynt Petre was in Herodes prisoune, & ȝit þilke wrecche ne purueieþ hym not ne biþenkeþ hym not how he schal do to-fore justices, ne how þe galewes abideþ hym, but slepeþ and meteþ þat he is at weddynges and grete festes." For another version of the same, see Dan Michel of Northgate, *Ayenbite of Inwyt*, p. 128.

39. The theme of order has been much discussed, most notably by Muscatine, "Form, Texture, and Meaning in Chaucer's *Knight's Tale*," and in his *Chaucer and the French Tradition*, pp. 175–90; by Frost, "An Interpretation of Chaucer's Knight's Tale"; and by Underwood, "The First of *The Canterbury Tales*." Underwood pays close attention to the symbolic function of the amphitheatre, and I owe much in my understanding of this image to ideas and suggestions that I found in his essay years ago, when I first began teaching this tale. Jordan, *Chaucer and the Shape of Creation*, pp. 152–84, likewise writes well on this aspect of the poem. Kean, *Chaucer and the Making of English Poetry*, II, 1–52, which I read after completing the first version of this chapter, also compares Boccaccio's and Chaucer's amphitheatres. McCall, *Chaucer among the Gods*, offers a learned and judicious account of the tale,

with particular emphasis on the amphitheatre (see especially pp. 64, 72). Elbow, *Oppositions in Chaucer*, pp. 73–94, is full of good sense and critical perception. Severs, "The Tales of Romance," includes a brief but discriminating survey of *Knight's Tale* criticism.

40. Bk. VII, v. 1, refers in passing to "the grandeur of the theater," and v. 2 calls it "the magnificent theater." But it is not described before the passage I quote.

41. Figure 43: a model in the possession of the Deutsches Archäologisches Institut in Rome. Pratt, "Chaucer's Use of the *Teseida*," p. 600 (n. 7), likewise thinks that Boccaccio had the Roman Colosseum in mind, adducing Boccaccio's gloss to a theatre reference in Bk. II, v. 20: "A theater was generally every public place, such as the galleries and auditoriums, although some one of these, because of its superiority, might merit that name more than the others, such as the Colosseum of Rome which was a common theater for everybody" (trans. McCoy, p. 74). Pratt suggests further that "Boccaccio may have known even better the great amphitheater at Capua, about fifteen miles from Naples and nearly as large as the Colosseum."

42. For an abbreviated version of this text in modern French, see René d'Anjou, *Traité de la forme et devis d'un tournoi*, ed. Pognon, with superb reproductions, many in color. Our figure 44 is from a manuscript on paper, which served as sketchbook for two deluxe copies of the manuscript; it is from Paris, Bibl. Natl. MS. fr. 2695, fols. 48v–49. The picture is reproduced in Pognon's edition, pp. 22–23, and described on p. 34. For a discussion of the treatise and its MSS., see pp. 67–69.

43. Figure 45: Vienna, Natl. Lib. MS. 2617, fol. 91. Note that each of the young knights has behind him followers who will fight in his cause.

44. One might illustrate the fighting of wild boars (the concluding image) from Paris, Bibl. Natl. MS. fr. 619, fol. 17v, a *Livre de chasse* of Gaston Phebus; or, in illustration of their essential nature, draw upon London, Brit. Lib. MS. Add. 49622, fol. 210, a border decoration to the Gorleston Psalter (East Anglia, ca. 1310–25), showing a boar chasing a stag, or London, Brit. Lib. MS. Add. 42130, fol. 187 (the Luttrell Psalter). Oxford, Bodley MS. 764, fol. 38v, shows a boar standing over a prostrate hunter, who knifes him in the stomach; a dog is impaled on his tusks, and he is held at bay by another hunter, who pierces his side with a dagger on a long pole (from an English bestiary, mid-13th century).

45. Figure 46: Vienna, Natl. Lib. MS. 2617, fol. 76. In the *Teseida*, Teseo and Emilia and many others ride out together, and it is only in the "dense grove"—*lo folto boschetto*—that they separate, going briefly where they please. As a result, Emilia is alone when she comes upon the two knights fighting (V, vv. 77–81), and she quickly summons Teseo. The illustrator errs in omitting Teseo from this picture.

46. Figure 47: *ibid.*, fol. 77. Even here the armor and the trained horses testify that these are men rather than wild beasts who fight.

47. Bartholomaeus, *Properties*, pp. 1040–41. Cf. "þe woode þat hatte *lucus* is thikkenesse of trees and letteþ light to come to þe ground, and comeþ *per antiphrasim* 'by contrarye' of *luce*[o], -*ces* 'to schyne,' and so *lucus* is yseyde as it were 'nouȝt schynyng'" (p. 1040). Piehler, *Visionary Land-*

scape, says many interesting things about "the basic psychic polarity of city and wilderness" in medieval literature (p. 73), paying special attention to commentaries on the forest (*silva*) in which the Golden Bough is concealed (*Aeneid*, VI, 131): e.g., Servius, in the 4th century, declared that by *silvas, tenebras, et lustra* ("forests, darksome places, and wildernesses"), Virgil signifies "those things where wild animal nature and the passions dominate" (pp. 75–76). See also pp. 111–17, on the *selva selvaggia* of Dante. The tradition, according to Piehler, goes back to Plato, whose conception of "the universe as created by the interaction of *nous* and *ananke* (Reason and Necessity or Mind and Matter) was developed by Aristotle into the more familiar conjunction of *nous* and *hyle*, where *hyle* denotes the chaos antecedent to the operation of Form, but literally means 'forest'" (p. 75). In the 12th century, Bernardus Silvestris develops this idea fully in his *De mundi universitate*, using the Latin word *silva* for Greek *hyle*. For an extended account see Stock, *Myth and Science in the Twelfth Century*, pp. 97–118. An iconographic use of woods and forest can be found in popular religious writing of the later Middle Ages, as well. Deguileville's pilgrim, for instance, at the moment of his greatest despair, rides off into "a valeye deep ful of busshes, hidous, horrible and wylde . . . bi which passe I muste if I wolde go forth. Wher of I was a basht. For bi wodes hauen men lost al here wey, and many periles ben in hem to pilgrimes that goon alloone. Theeves, murderers, wylde bestes duellen in hem in hydeles. And many disgise thinges ther ben ofte times founden in hem." (*Pilgrimage of the Lyf of the Manhode*, p. 136.) Emelye describes herself to Diana, in her temple prayer, as one who loves "huntynge and venerye, / And for to walken in the wodes wilde, / And noght to ben a wyf and be with childe" (1.2308). Howard, *Idea of The Canterbury Tales*, pp. 162–65, writes about the way the pilgrims' journey "progresses at a remove, as if displaced from geographical locations," and thinks it related to an allegorical conception of human life as a journey through a wilderness, the wilderness of this world.

48. Figure 48: Vienna, Natl. Lib. MS. 2617, fol. 102.

49. In the *Teseida*, we are merely told that Arcita and Palemone go to the temples of Mars and Venus to make their offerings (VII, vv. 23, 42). The temple of Diana, in contrast, is described briefly (it is "adorned with beautiful hangings"), and the rites Emilia performs within it are versified at length. Emilia's prayer alone is not described as traveling to the "house" of the goddess: Diana's "choir" appears to her in the temple instead (VII, vv. 70–93).

50. In the house of Mars, for instance, we meet Mad Impulses, Blind Sin, Wrath red as fire, pale Fear, Betrayals with their secret weapons, Discord, Difference, Harsh Threats, Cruel Design, and so on; they are Mars's companions. The wall paintings include "enchained peoples, iron gates, and demolished fortresses" (VII, vv. 33–36).

51. On the mythographic sources, see Wilkins, "Descriptions of Pagan Divinities"; Steadman, "Venus' *Citole*"; Quinn, "Venus, Chaucer, and Peter Bersuire"; and Twycross, *Medieval Anadyomene*. Brewer, *Chaucer*, 3d ed., pp. 55, 69, 71, reproduces mythographic illuminations of Venus and Mercury, Mars and Apollo, and Saturn and Jupiter, from Oxford, Bodley MS. Rawlinson B. 214 (English, mid-15th century). Robertson, *Preface to Chau-*

cer, p. 110, suggests a mythographic reading of the tale, working in part from Boccaccio's own elaborate glosses on Mars and Venus in the *Chiose* to the *Teseida*. The *Chiose*, however, have no privileged status in this matter. There is no evidence that Chaucer knew those glosses, and a fair amount to suggest he did not. See Pratt, "Conjectures Regarding Chaucer's Manuscript of the *Teseida*." Hollander, "Validity of Boccaccio's Self-Exegesis," provides a close study of the *Chiose*. R. H. Green, "Classical Fable and English Poetry," pp. 128–33, discusses Theseus's significance in mythographic terms.

52. I quote from Klibansky et al., *Saturn and Melancholy*, p. 205; on the Arab texts and their influence, see pp. 178–95. Their figs. 31–33, from an Arab manuscript dated 1399 and from 14th-century frescoes in the Sala della Ragione, Padua, show the "professions of the planets" arranged in serial rows. Though *Saturn and Melancholy* focuses upon just one planet, the complex history of a pagan deity and its postclassical metamorphosis has never been better written; it is useful background to any of the others. Seznec, *Survival of the Pagan Gods*, a work of comparable distinction, is concerned with the entire pantheon; pp. 69–76 deal with the children of the planets. The standard work on the planet-children is Hauber, *Planetenkinderbilder*; it remains essential. Curry, *Chaucer and the Mediaeval Sciences*, pp. 119–63, made the first sustained application of astrological lore to the understanding of *The Knight's Tale*; those pages can be read with profit still. Wood, *Chaucer and the Country of the Stars*, pp. 69–76, writes about the combination of astrological and mythological traditions in the tale.

53. On my chosen series see Bossert and Storck, eds., *Mittelalterliche Hausbuch*; Graf Waldburg-Wolfegg, *Mittelalterliche Hausbuch*; and Hutchison, *Master of the Housebook*, which concerns his engravings only, but is useful on the identity of the artist and has a full bibliography (Section E) on the *Hausbuch* drawings. The MS. is a miscellany, and includes genre scenes, designs for military equipment, drawings of battles, etc., as well as the planet-children. The artist, one of the great masters of the later 15th century, was German or Netherlandish and worked in the region of the Middle Rhine around Mainz. For a brief notice in English, see Shestack, *Fifteenth Century Engravings*, no. 139. Hussey, *Chaucer's World*, reproduces four of these drawings (figs. 77, 78, 100, 116); I add Luna and Jupiter. For the Tübingen series (Univ. MS. M. d. 2), see Hauber, *Planetenkinderbilder*, pls. 13 (Saturn), 17 (Jupiter), 20 (Mars), 25 (Venus), 28 (Mercury), and 33 (Luna), and for descriptions, pp. 93–103; the MS. was made at Ulm. Klibansky et al., *Saturn and Melancholy*, reproduce the Tübingen Saturn page (fig. 40), along with those from two other series (fig. 38, from a German block book, and fig. 39, from an Italian set of engravings). There is also an English series, 3/4 15th century, made for a treatise on the planets and their influence: Oxford, Bodley MS. Rawlinson D. 1220, fols. 33ff. The Venus picture from this MS. is reproduced in Chaucer, *Tales of Canterbury*, ed. Pratt, p. 270, in connection with *The Wife of Bath's Prologue*. A variant tradition is associated with MSS. of the *Epître d'Othéa* of Christine de Pisan, in which the planet-children are engaged in only one activity, highly decorous, under the influence of the god or goddess above. They are most often seated, and the planet's influence descends in a fashion related to traditional depictions of the

Pentecost. See Klibansky et al., *Saturn and Melancholy*, figs. 35, 36; and Meiss, *The Limbourgs*, I, pp. 23–41, and II, figs. 62, 75, 76, 146. Christine's text, written ca. 1400, was translated by Stephen Scrope, ca. 1440–59, as *The Epistle of Othea*; see pp. 16–23, 35–36, 63–64 of Bühler's edition. The illustrations to the French text in London, Brit. Lib. MS. Harley 4431, are of exceptional beauty. For a more generalized treatment of the planets, see, e.g., Bartholomaeus, *Properties*, pp. 473–95, and Gower, *Confessio amantis*, VII, 670–946 (*Complete Works*, III, 251–58).

54. Figure 49: Wolfegg, *Hausbuch* MS., fol. 13 (in the collection of Graf Waldburg-Wolfegg). Curry, *Chaucer and the Mediaeval Sciences*, p. 123, quotes the Arab astrologer Albohazen Haly: "Mars is a planet by nature hot and dry, fiery, nocturnal, feminine, and violent; he is a destroyer and a conqueror, delighting in slaughter and death, in quarrels, brawls, disputes, contests, and other contraventions; he is stupid, quickly moved to vehement and devastating anger, abandoning himself completely to the execution of whatever he plans. . . . He is instrumental in stirring up seditions; he inspires wars and battles and rules over the ravaging and laying waste of lands, over pillage, plundering, ruin, and destruction by land and sea. He rejoices in the outpouring of blood, in the afflictions of the miserable, and in all kinds of oppression." In the present picture, the identity and purpose of the man with a bird cage (lower right corner) is unclear to me.

55. Figure 50: Wolfegg, *Hausbuch* MS., fol. 15.

56. Figure 51: *ibid.*, fol. 17. Hauber, *Planetenkinderbilder*, pp. 121–22, thinks the rather elegant gentleman in the left foreground may be the medicine man's accomplice, bringing him customers. That is possible, though his interlocutors do not seem especially infirm. The shell game (with two inverted tumblers) is represented in the Tübingen and Modena series as well: see Hauber, pls. 33 and 35; cf. pl. 34 (fig. 48).

57. Wood, *Chaucer and the Country of the Stars*, p. 72, has also remarked this fact. McCall, *Chaucer among the Gods*, p. 72, writes of Diana: "Given a medieval context, one might assume that the goddess of chastity, at least, would seem virtuous; but she has instead been made the embodiment of that flight from *all* bodily delights which Aristotle and the medieval schoolmen judged to be 'insensitive or savage.'" (See further his n. 22, pp. 171–72).

58. In the *Teseida*, the young knights make offerings at many temples, to many gods: "It was already the day before the one on which the battle was to be fought, when Palemone and Arcita went humbly and with pious sentiments to pray to the gods. Placing bright fires on their altars, they offered incense, and with fervent desires they prayed that the gods would help each of them in their needs on the following day. / But after he had visited the others and placed fire and incense everywhere, Arcita also returned to the temple of Mars and illuminated it much more than any of the others." (VII, vv. 22, 23.) "Palemone had also smoked up every temple in Athens and he had not omitted a god or goddess in heaven whom he had not constrained to intercede for him. But that day it pleased him to honor Cytherea more than any of the others." (VII, v. 42.) Emilia alone goes only to a single temple, to make offering to a single goddess.

59. Figure 52: Wolfegg, *Hausbuch* MS., fol. 11. Wood, *Chaucer and the Country of the Stars*, figs. 13a, b, reproduces a superb double-page painting

of Saturn's children from a *De sphaera* MS. in Modena, Biblioteca Estense. The flaying of the horse in the *Hausbuch* version is peculiar, unless the man is a tanner: tanning and leather working are professions governed by Saturn. Boars are common in Saturn pictures, sometimes being fed, sometimes being slaughtered; this boar seems attracted by the foul and stinking clothing said to be characteristic of Saturn's children (Bartholomaeus, *Properties*, p. 479).

60. Bartholomaeus, *Properties*, p. 480. Alain de Lille, *Anticlaudianus*, IV, p. 134, offers a similar characterization: "Here the star of Jupiter glows, brings tidings of safety to the world, checks Mars' rage and fury and opposes his madness with serene peace. Even if a star that is a herald of evil and a precursor of misfortune is joined to him, Jupiter makes friends with the unfriendly star and brings about a change in him, turning gloom to laughter, lament to applause, bitter tears to joy." For the well-known picture of Mars and Venus with Jupiter above, illustrating Chaucer's *Complaint of Mars* in Oxford, Bodley MS. Fairfax 16, fol. 14v, see Wood, *Chaucer and the Country of the Stars*, fig. 14, and pp. 130–41; on the poem, see Merrill, "Chaucer's *Broche of Thebes*."

61. *Paradiso* XXII, 145–46.

62. Figure 53: Vienna, Natl. Lib. MS. 2617, fol. 138. In Boccaccio's poem, the fury is sent by Venus rather than by Saturn, but since Chaucer simply shifted the responsibility from one to the other, this picture will serve to illustrate my point. The *Teseida* describes the fury: "Erinys came forth with her long serpent-tresses, and her ornaments were green hydras whose lives she had restored in the Elisos, and the sulphurous flames that they flashed forth from their mouths made them more foul-smelling as they made her more fearsome. And this Goddess carried a whip of snakes in her hand. / Her arrival into the theater caused such horror in everyone who saw her, that each man trembled in his heart, and yet no one was able to explain why. The winds made a strange noise and the sky began to seem blacker. The theater shook and every gate writhed and rattled on its hinges." (IX, vv. 5, 6.) The Angevin illuminator painted instead a flying dragon breathing fire. Chaucer does not describe the fury at all: "Out of the ground a furie infernal sterte, / From Pluto sent at requeste of Saturne, / For which his hors for fere gan to turne, / And leep aside, and foundred as he leep" (1.2684). There is no suggestion in *The Knight's Tale* that anyone has seen the fury except the horse; Chaucer creates an event that the spectators must seek to explain in purely natural terms. (Interestingly enough, Boccaccio himself explains the fury in a naturalistic way in the *Chiose*, commenting on IX, v. 5, pp. 257–58: "It is a very certain thing that animals shy at some frightening object that they seem to see, but what they see, or what they think they see, no one knows. So the author imagines that it was Erinys, one of the infernal Furies.") For the several deaths in Boccaccio's poem, see Bk. VIII, which chronicles the battle, and see Bk. X, vv. 1–8, for the funeral ceremonies.

63. Kean, *Chaucer and the Making of English Poetry*, II, 29–34, in an argument of central importance to her reading of the whole poem, seeks to explain this in a very different way. She works from Neoplatonic ideas of the soul's descent through the planetary spheres when it is born, acquiring rea-

son and understanding (*logistikon* and *theoretikon*) in the outermost sphere, the sphere of Saturn, and the power to act (*praktikon*) in the next, the sphere of Jupiter. Kean's preferred source for these identifications of the planets is Macrobius's *Commentary on the Dream of Scipio*, which Chaucer certainly knew, but whose materials are not, I think, reflected here. Indeed, the facts are almost exactly the opposite. In the poem, it is Jupiter who possesses the deepest wisdom and understanding (*theoretikon*, in Macrobius's terms), whereas Saturn acts (*praktikon*) out of a practical wisdom based on experience and age. The materials that Kean introduces on pp. 3–4 are, I think, more to the point: "Jupiter and Saturn are, respectively, *Fortuna Major* and *Infortuna Major*, the greatest of the fortunate and unfortunate planets, and Jupiter is, therefore, the only planet which can 'master' Saturn. Venus and Mars have the same relationship, to a lesser degree; they are *Fortuna Minor* and *Infortuna Minor*. Venus, like Jupiter in relation to Saturn, can overcome the bad influence of her partner in the scheme."

64. Figure 54: Wolfegg, *Hausbuch* MS., fol. 12. Hauber, *Planetenkinderbilder*, p. 119, thinks both foreground scenes concern justice: *die Juristerie in Theorie und Praxis*. The equivalent picture from the Modena *De sphaera* may be seen in Salmi, *Italian Miniatures*, fig. 98. Brooks and Fowler, "Meaning of Chaucer's *Knight's Tale*," make many ingenious connections between the planets and the characters of the poem, including that between Theseus and Jupiter's "children" (p. 125). To my mind, their most important discovery is that the lists may represent a zodiac correct in most details for a sunrise on May 7 in the late 14th century (pp. 128–29). Their larger interpretation of the poem, which invokes systems of the Four and Seven Ages of Man, does not convince me.

65. The German text is printed in Bossert and Storck, eds., *Mittelalterliche Hausbuch*, p. vi. Alcabitius writes of Jupiter's influence: "In his magisterial capacity Jupiter possesses adequate knowledge pertaining to law, delivers just decisions, and judges with integrity. When he beholds men engaged in altercations and litigations, he has the happy faculty of restoring peace and establishing concord among them." (Quoted by Curry, *Chaucer and the Mediaeval Sciences*, p. 127.) A *Calendrier des bergers*, ca. 1486, Cambridge, Fitzwilliam Mus. MS. 167, fols. 68v–69, describes those born under Jupiter in the following verses: "Qui soub Jupiter sera ne / Begnin et gracieux trouve / Sera riche de grant substance / Saige discret plain de science / Il aymera paix et concorde / Bon iugement misericorde / Joyeuse vie, vraye verite / Religion et equite."

66. Robertson, *Preface to Chaucer*, pp. 261–62, interprets in this fashion all such movements from justice to mercy in the poem.

67. I owe the terms "inclusive order" and "exclusive order" to an unpublished seminar paper by Jeanne Martin Vanecko.

68. Figure 55: Vienna, Natl. Lib. MS. 2617, fol. 121.

69. Pratt, "Chaucer's Use of the *Teseida*," p. 603, offers a mostly negative judgment: "Torn between presumptuous epic designs and the subjective vividness of his own waning amour with Maria d'Aquino, Boccaccio created neither an epic nor a pure romance, but rather a leisurely and variegated pseudo-epic, lacking unity and power of theme, design, and execution, and lacking strong characterization, but possessing numerous effective descrip-

tions and elevated passages of poetry." Chaucer, as Pratt sees it (p. 621), "unified the plot of Boccaccio's pseudo-epic, preserving much of the ornamentation and oratory; and by subordinating and transforming the epic material, he so fused it with the conflict of the lovers as to give his medieval romance an artistic integrity not achieved in the *Teseida*." On Boccaccio's own estimation of his achievement, see the work's *envoy*: XII, vv. 84–86. H. S. Wilson, "*The Knight's Tale* and the *Teseida* Again," pp. 137–39, discusses the *Teseida*'s philosophical content, such as it is, focusing on the relationship between flesh and spirit, and the interaction of passion and destiny.

70. *The Book of Theseus*, trans. McCoy, unfortunately misrepresents this aspect of the work by printing the Dedicatory Epistle after the poem, rather than at the beginning where it belongs; I quote from pp. 336–37. The dedication's narrow address is also reflected in the work's full Italian title: in a witty conceit at the poem's end we are told that the lady wishes the poem to be called the *Teseida delle nozze d'Emilia*—the "Theseid of the Nuptials of Emilia." Only under that name does it become a public poem. Pratt remarks, "here again the title and the theme fall into the dichotomy resulting from Boccaccio's double motivation, the literary and the personal" ("Chaucer's Use of the *Teseida*," p. 601).

71. Dedicatory Epistle, *The Book of Theseus*, trans. McCoy, p. 338. Boccaccio's *Filostrato*—the source for Chaucer's *Troilus and Criseyde*—also has a lengthy dedication to this lady, telling her that she should understand Troilus's suffering as expressing his own, and the history of Criseida as embodying his fears concerning their separation. That poem, too, for all its length and variety of interest, is sent forth as though it were a lyric plea, seeking a lover's response. (For a translation, see Gordon, trans., *The Story of Troilus*, pp. 25–30.) The *Filocolo* is also dedicated to Fiammetta; see H. S. Wilson, "*The Knight's Tale* and the *Teseida* Again," p. 132.

72. Figure 56: Vienna, Natl. Lib. MS. 2617, fol. 14. Note the intimacy of the setting: he presents the book in her private chamber.

73. Branca, *Boccaccio*, p. 29, summarizes the case made by modern scholarship for thinking her merely "a shining creature of the imagination, in which a great artist combined and sublimated his various and impassioned experiences of youthful love." Boccaccio gives one to understand she is an illegitimate daughter of King Robert of Naples.

74. Jordan, *Chaucer and the Shape of Creation*, p. 179.

75. Cf. Underwood, "First of *The Canterbury Tales*," p. 466: "At what I think we must now call its divine level of order, the 'seer' and maker is no longer Theseus or the Knight, but the poet who conceives and makes them both. The poem is finally, then, the poet's theatre, world, and tale."

76. Rand, *Founders of the Middle Ages*, pp. 159–60. He names Sir Thomas More, John Bunyan, and John Milton as among those who have worked significantly within this prison-literature tradition. The *Consolation* was written in 524. For the Latin text, see Boethius, *The Theological Tractates*; for a lucid and elegant modern translation, see that of Richard Green. Patch, *Tradition of Boethius*, and Barrett, *Boethius*, offer studies of his influence, as does a magisterial work by Courcelle, *La Consolation de Philosophie dans la tradition littéraire*. F. A. Payne, *King Alfred and Boethius*, offers an interesting literary analysis, giving proper emphasis to the figure of the prisoner.

Elbow, *Oppositions in Chaucer*, uses the *Consolation* as his central text, and writes brilliantly about it. Piehler, *Visionary Landscape*, pp. 31–45, offers a sophisticated study of Lady Philosophy and her allegorical mode. See also Jefferson, *Chaucer and the Consolation of Philosophy of Boethius*. Pickering, *Literature and Art*, pp. 168–91, has a valuable discussion of the differences between the Augustinian and Boethian traditions; it lends support to the theories I put forward here. Boethius's book had many literary progeny, including Thomas Usk's *Testament of Love*, which is modeled on it and borrows whole passages from Chaucer's translation. Usk wrote the *Testament* sometime between his first imprisonment in 1384 and his second (he was executed in 1388). It was printed as Chaucer's by Thynne in his edition of 1532, and can be read in Skeat, ed., *Chaucerian and Other Pieces*, pp. xviii–xxxi, 1–145. Skeat thought Usk's use of a prison setting metaphorical in intention (p. xxx and p. 453, n. 15); see, for instance, pp. 5 (15), 6 (37, 41), 9 (22–33), 14 (178–81), 17 (115ff), 18 (125), 27 (76–81), 38 (135–38), 77 (123–27).

77. Oxford, Bodley MS. Auct. F.6.5, fol. 1v (2/4 12th century), shows Boethius chained by the neck; it may be seen in Brewer, *Chaucer*, 3d ed., p. 45. Figure 57: Florence, Bibl. Laurenziana MS. Plut. 78.15, fol. 1. Barrett, *Boethius*, pp. 51–54, discusses the sources of our knowledge of Boethius's imprisonment apart from the *Consolation* itself, e.g., the *Anonymus Valesii* and Procopius. Boethius was both exiled and imprisoned, terms readily interchangeable as metaphors for the wretchedness of human life, separated from its true home and its ideal freedom. In the *Prologue* to *The Second Nun's Tale*, for example, "flemed" ("exiled," VIII.58) and "in prison" (VIII.71) are nearly synonymous; see Robinson's notes, p. 757, for further sources. Arcite's exile from Athens, and thus from the object of his desire, brings that metaphor into *The Knight's Tale* as well. In manuscript illuminations to the *Consolation*, an "exile" or "open prison" is often preferred to scenes set unambiguously in barred prisons, but the latter are current throughout the medieval period. Courcelle, *Histoire littéraire*, publishes many miniatures showing Boethius's imprisonment: pls. 37–51 contain 28 examples, of which pls. 41b, 42a, 43a, b, 44a, b, 45a, b, 46a, b, 48a, b, and 49c are all unequivocally prison scenes (barred windows, fetters, chains, or stocks): they include the two I discuss above. For commentary on the plates, see pp. 365–78; p. 375 describes the humanist movement away from scenes specifically set in prison. In Courcelle's later study, *La Consolation*, he increased this collection of miniatures considerably: see especially pls. 12 (2), 37, 58, 60, 61, 81, 83, 84, 94, 95, 96, 104, 105, 129. The "open prison" is a useful convention, as it allows the scene to be displayed more generously; one sees through more than a cell window. For an analogous instance, see the St. Catherine picture in *The Belles Heures of Jean, Duke of Berry*, fol. 17v (ca. 1410–13). We know from the saint's legend that she is incarcerated, but the architecture is nonspecific; only a man holding a key at the far right gives any indication the house is in fact a prison.

78. Robertson, *Preface to Chaucer*, p. 270.

79. Figure 58: Paris, Bibl. Natl. MS. Néerlandais 1, fol. 212v. Note the open book on Philosophy's arm, and the fact that God wears a three-tiered papal crown; the latter is a fairly common detail in these illustrations. We see

illustrated the first prose and meter of Bk. IV, in which Lady Philosophy promises to give his mind wings: "I schal fycchen fetheris in thi thought, by whiche it mai arisen in heighte" and "I have, forthi, swifte fetheris that surmounten the heighte of the hevene. Whanne the swifte thoght hath clothid itself in tho fetheris, it despiseth the hateful erthes." Philosophic thought, she tells him, flies upward, through the regions of air and fire, through the spheres of the planets and the fixed stars, passing beyond even the "laste hevene," until it finally "schal be makid parfit of the worschipful lyght of God. There halt the lord of kynges the septre of his myght and atemprith the governementz of the world, and the schynynge juge of thinges, stable in hymself, governeth the swifte wayn (*that is to seyn, the circuler moevynge of the sonne*)." (IV, m.1; italics indicate the gloss.) For Platonic and Augustinian backgrounds to the idea of such wings, see Courcelle, *La Consolation*, p. 197.

80. In the *Teseida*, death itself is called "the eternal prison" (X, v. 14). The great physician who has been summoned to treat Arcita concludes that the case is beyond medical aid, saying "any efforts made to heal him would be wasted. Just keep him happy and comfortable so that he may depart with as much contentment as possible to the eternal prison, where Dis keeps every light extinguished, and where we shall follow him when we cannot live here any longer." In Bk. X, vv. 95–99, Arcita prays to Mercury, "Carry me, therefore, into the midst of the holy souls who dwell in Elysium; for my deeds, if you examine them well, have not made me deserving of that dead air as were the wicked souls of my ancestors. . . . I do not believe that I ought to dwell among blackened souls, and I am not worthy of heaven and do not ask for it. It is precious enough for me to stay in Elysium. I pray you for this." In the *Chiose*, Boccaccio's most extensive gloss concerning the pagan afterlife is attached to Bk. II, v. 31: "It was the opinion of the ancients that every soul went to hell, except those of persons whom they deified; and they believed that to each one was appointed a specific place, in which the sins which he had committed in life were punished. When these sins were punished, they believed that the souls went into a delightful place, which was called Elysium, and then after a period of time the persons returned to the world." (Trans. McCoy, p. 74.) The *Chiose* gloss "the eternal prison," "the dead air," and "blackened souls" in the passages I have quoted above as referring unequivocally to hell: see pp. 284, 286, 287. Within the poem, however, Boccaccio stresses how tentative are all pagan hypotheses concerning the afterlife. Arcita, in his dying speech, says to Emilia: "I still do not know what place will be mine there, beyond in that uncertain life, but even if I should be with Jove and yet without you, I do not believe that I could ever feel joy" (X, v. 105). In *The Knight's Tale*, Arcite's deathbed references to an afterlife are limited to an oath as he commends Palamon to Emelye, "So Juppiter have of my soule part" (1.2792), and to a promise that even after death his spirit will serve her still: "But I biquethe the servyce of my goost / To yow aboven every creature" (1.2768). He can conceive no destiny after death significantly different from his life on earth.

81. The *Theological Tractates* include treatises *On the Trinity* and *On the Person and Two Natures in Christ* (the treatise *On the Catholic Faith* is less certainly his). The authenticity of the Christian treatises was established in

1877 with the discovery of a text by Cassiodorus that refers to four of them. On St. Severinus, see Rand, *Founders of the Middle Ages*, pp. 179–80, 323–24, and Knowles, "Boethius." Boethius's cult as St. Severinus may have been provincial, but knowledge of it was not. Cf. Lydgate, *Fall of Princes*, Part III, p. 897 (2657–60), after narrating the downfall of Boethius and his father-in-law Symmachus: "Bot touchyng Boys, as bookis specefie, / Wrot dyuers bookis of philosophie, / Of the Trynite mateeres þat wer dyuyne, / Martird for Crist & callid Seueryne."

82. The names for God are taken from Chaucer's translation: IV, pr. 1; IV, pr. 5; V, pr. 1; V, pr. 5; the problems from IV, pr. 6. Courcelle, whose *La Consolation* supersedes all previous accounts of Boethius's thought and its medieval tradition, sees the work as the literary testament of a Neoplatonic philosopher who was also a Christian (pp. 340–41): "Si la culture grecque de Boèce est une culture païenne, la *Consolation* ne contient pas non plus un seul indice prouvant que Boèce n'était pas chrétien de coeur. . . . Boèce espérait préserver le néo-platonisme dans l'Occident chrétien." In his concluding pages, Courcelle stresses a medieval tradition running counter to that of the *interpretatio christiana*, one that understood Boethius as working deliberately within the limits of the rationally knowable and is represented most powerfully by Conrad of Hirsau and John of Salisbury—a tradition Courcelle believes understood Boethius correctly (pp. 343–44). The *Consolation*, of course, posed certain problems for orthodox Christian belief, especially in its assumptions concerning the prior existence of souls, their memory of that prior existence, the concept of the World Soul, the idea of the perpetuity of the world, and so on. On the commentators' response to these ideas, see Courcelle, *La Consolation*, pp. 276–78, 337–38, and *passim*. In Courcelle's view, the fact that Boethius's philosophy was "pleine d'attraits ou de dangers" (p. 338) was one source of its continuing vitality for medieval thinkers.

83. For God with a crossed nimbus, see Courcelle, *La Consolation*, pl. 99 (1), from a printed book, 1501; pl. 100 (1), from the 12th century; pl. 101 (1), from the 14th century. Pl. 100 (1) is unique in showing five wounds: its God is unequivocally Christ. Pickering, *Essays on Medieval German Literature and Iconography*, pp. 46–58, in a study of the theme "*Trinitas Creator*," has discussed the relation of the crossed nimbus to *Sapientia*, the Son as Wisdom of the Father, though without reference to the present text or pictures; see also Heimann, "Trinitas creator mundi." In Paris, Bibl. Natl. MS. fr. 1098, fol. 96v (2/2 15th century), God holds an orb topped by a small cross; it furnishes pl. 103 (2) in Courcelle, *La Consolation* (there is a Christian church in the far landscape). New York, Pierpont Morgan MS. M.222, fol. 87, resembles this picture but surrounds God with the souls of the blessed. For other orbs with a cross, see Courcelle, pls. 93 (2), 100 (2), 122, 124. Paris, Bibl. Natl. MS. fr. 12459, fol. 55 (also 15th century) shows God as three identical persons; its fols. 61, 64, however, show Boethius's "winged mind" contemplating only the stars. Courcelle, pls. 101 (2) and 101 (3) show only stars or a generalized radiance above. Plate 103 (1) is the most comprehensive of the Christianized images: it shows Three Persons, with a chalice and host at their bosom, in an aureole of tongued flames, sur-

rounded by angels and the souls of the blessed. It is an image of the Trinity common in contemporary Books of Hours, and I suspect that it found its way into this scene without anyone in the workshop taking much thought in the matter: it was an elegant way of showing God. For a more careful illustration, see Courcelle, *Histoire littéraire*, pl. 40b, a 12th-century illumination in which Christ is shown in a stylized cloud above Philosophy's head. He has a crossed nimbus, holds the Gospels, and raises his fingers in blessing. Philosophy too holds a book, and Boethius, recumbent, gazes upon her alone. A similar configuration can be seen in pl. 38, from the 10th century, and in pl. 39, where the figure above Lady Philosophy is labeled *Sapiencia* (understood as Divine Wisdom) and is personified as a woman; she is located outside Boethius's range of vision. (The MSS. from which pls. 39 and 40 are drawn both contain a poem on Wisdom who is God, along with a text of the *Consolation*. On the relation of those MSS., see pp. 366–68.)

84. The strong claim that pagan religion had once made upon the minds and souls of men, so vividly felt in the pages of the early Fathers, had become a dim memory; the threats to the True Faith were now quotidian sin and Christian heresy. This distance permitted men in the later Middle Ages a certain compassion for, and sympathetic imagining of, earlier cultures to which their own owed much, but which lacked knowledge of the Christian God. *The Book of Vices and Virtues*, p. 124, states eloquently the relation between virtuous paganism and virtuous Christianity, in which the concluding remarks about "charity" mean doing good because of one's love for God:

A, God, how we schulde be a-ferd, whan þei þat weren heþen and wiþ-out any lawe y-write, þat wisten no þing of þe verray grace of God ne of þe Holi Gost, and 3it clombe þei vp to þe hil of parfi3tnesse of lif bi strengþe of here owne vertue, and deyned not to loke on þe world; & we þat ben cristene and hadde þe grace and þe bileue veraliche and conen þe comaundementes of God and han þe grace of þe Holi Gost, 3if we wolen, and more we my3t do profi3t in on day þan þilke my3ten in an hole 3ere, we lyuen as swyn here byneþe in þis grottes of þis world! And þerfore seiþ seynt Poule þat þe heþen þat ben wiþ-out lawe, at domes day schul jugge vs, þat han þe lawe & don it nou3t; but for þey ne hadden not þe ri3t bileue ne þe 3efte of þe Holi Gost, þei my3t not haue no lyueliche ne verrey vertue, al-þei3 þei weren faire. For as moche as þer is bitwexe a cole of fier and a ded coole, oþere a ded man and a quek man, ri3t so moche is þer bitwexe vertue wiþ-oute charite and vertue wiþ charite.

For an eloquent description of Chaucer's sense of the pagan past, see Mc-Call, *Chaucer among the Gods*, pp. 111–12; McCall's exploration of this theme in *The Legend of Good Women*, pp. 113–17, likewise harmonizes with my own (see Kolve, "From Cleopatra to Alceste").

85. Figure 59: Vienna, Natl. Lib. MS. 2617, fol. 39. It is reproduced in color by S. Mitchell, *Medieval Manuscript Painting*, pl. 155, with an enlarged detail on the back cover.

86. Teseo misunderstands even the literal results of the tournament, as anyone might, concluding that it was "foreseen long ago in the limpid and holy divine intellect . . . that Emilia was kept for our dear Arcita and he was destined to be her bridegroom. For this you [who have been defeated] ought to be as happy as you can." (IX, v. 57.)

87. Kean, *Chaucer and the Making of English Poetry*, II, 41–48 (and also I, 71–75) sees in the maker of this speech a far more comprehensive and

convincing philosopher than do I. Like myself, Burlin, *Chaucerian Fiction*, pp. 99–100, 105–8, stresses the limitations of Boethius as a model, and the problematic nature of Theseus's speech.

88. Kean, *Chaucer and the Making of English Poetry*, II, 25, 26. Kean has argued the position more fully and with greater learning than anyone else.

89. *Ibid.*, p. 50 (cf. pp. 48–59).

90. Figure 60: Philadelphia, Mus. of Art MS. 45-65-1, fol. 64, by the Orosius Master, ca. 1400 (reproduced in Meiss, *Boucicaut Master*, fig. 488, and briefly discussed on p. 45). Cf. McCall, *Chaucer among the Gods*, pp. 16–17.

91. Figure 61: Paris, Bibl. Natl. MS. fr. 244, fol. 4. The picture is based upon the *Antiphonae majores* or "Great O's" (seven in number) of the Advent liturgy, which are incorporated into the text here illustrated—the Advent chapter of Jacobus de Voragine's *Legenda aurea*, in French translation. It may be read in Caxton's English as *The Golden Legend*, I, 7–25, or trans. Ryan and Ripperger, pp. 2–6. For the original, see Graesse, pp. 3–5. The antiphons furnish the prayers spoken in abbreviated (sometimes variant) form in banderoles by the seven groups in the painting. The antiphons are conveniently printed, and their tradition surveyed, by Burlin, *Old English Advent*, pp. 40–45. The names of God are closely related to the specific prayers that are prayed: for instance, those "seated in darkness" pray to *Oriens* (the east, the sun), and those in the prison house to the "key of David." The full text of the *O Rex gentium* antiphon, in naming Christ as the cornerstone of the Church (the phrase *lapsique angularis* is omitted here) may mean that the otherwise anomalous ship at sea represents the Ship of the Church. (On the latter tradition, see Chapter VII, below.) This painting concentrates upon Christ's First Advent, as Redeemer, though the liturgy concerns as well his Second Advent, as Judge. Cambridge, Fitzwilliam Mus. MS. 22, p. 6, in contrast, illustrates the chapter by showing contemporary prisoners behind a barred window, one in stocks in a basement, and another seated outside with manacles on his legs; the last of these opens his hands in prayer to God, shown in the sky above. The MS. is French, made ca. 1480. Christian use of the metaphor was widespread and various. In Alain de Lille's *Anticlaudianus*, p. 154, Christ comes to enter "the penitentiary of our flesh"; Robert Grosseteste's "Castel of Love," pp. 361–69, has Christ enter the castle (Mary's body) in order to ransom man from the prison of hell. For other instances, see *Book of Vices and Virtues*, p. 27; Herrtage, ed., *The Early English Versions of the "Gesta Romanorum,"* p. 320 (cf. Hoccleve, *Minor Poems*, I, 175); and Julian of Norwich, *A Book of Showings*, p. 693 (Chap. 77, l. 41). *Book of Vices and Virtues*, p. 85, can exemplify the Christian use of this theme at its most comprehensive. After discussing man's free will, and the freedom that is man's in a state of grace, it names a third and greater kind of freedom: "But ʒit al þis fredom is but þraldom, to regard of þe þridde fraunchise þat þei haue þat ben delyuered al out of þe body and ben wiþ his [Christ's] swete companye. Þilke ben verrely free. For þei ben delyuered of alle turmentes of wepyng, of deeþ and of synne, of perel, of deceytes of þe world, of wrechednesse, & of al penaunce of body and soule, and neuere to turne aʒeyn. Of alle þes þinges þer nys no man free in þis world, be he neuere so good ne so parfiʒt."

92. Cf. the confrontation between the pagan and Christian faiths in *The*

Second Nun's Tale, where conversion properly turns upon an explanation of the Trinity (VIII.320–32). The martyrdom of St. Cecilia, Tiburce, and Valerian stems from their refusal to worship "the ymage of Juppiter" (VIII.364), to "doon sacrifice, and Juppiter encense" (VIII.413). They object to the worship of an idol, of course—"myghty God is in his hevenes hye"—but the more profound truth is that he is One God in Three Persons.

93. See *Teseida*, XI, vv. 1–3, and *Troilus*, V, 1807–27. If the *Troilus* was written before *The Knight's Tale*, a chronology unlikely on artistic grounds, then Chaucer had already versified this material and could not use it again. But a similar journey might easily have been invented, since the *Teseida* offered as well Arcita's hope that his soul might dwell in Elysium and not in the place of punishment (X, vv. 95, 107). Chaucer chooses to speak instead of the limitations on what he knows, misrepresenting his source in order to do so; there are essentially no hypotheses concerning the pagan afterlife in his poem.

94. Cf. Christine de Pisan, *Epistle of Othea*, p. 17, talking about the virtues that a knight or ruler ought to possess in imitation of Jupiter: "Therfore Othea seith, that is to seye Prudence, that a good knyghte scholde haue the condicion of Jubiter. . . . To [which] purpos seith Pictagoras that a kyng scholde be graciouslye conuersant with [his] pepill and schewe to theym a gladde visage." And see Elbow, *Oppositions in Chaucer*, pp. 78–88, on the highest values affirmed by the poem.

95. See Gordon, trans., *Story of Troilus*, p. 25: "A young man ardently loves a lady, but fortune grants him no happiness with her except that he may sometimes see her, or sometimes speak of her, or meditate sweetly upon her. Which then of these three things gives the most delight? And it never happened that each of these three things failed to be defended by many. . . . I remember that I, deluded by false seeming, . . . urged and maintained that to be able to think sometimes of the loved person was a greater delight by far. . . . O foolish judgment, O ignorant verdict. . . . Bitter experience makes that clear now." (His lady had since departed from Naples.) Cf. the love questions in Boccaccio's *Il Filocolo*, trans. H. G., rev. Carter, as *Thirteen Most Pleasant and Delectable Questions of Love*. For a brief but useful introduction to the genre, see Chaucer, *The Parlement of Foulys*, ed. Brewer, pp. 10–13.

96. Christine de Pisan, *Epistre de la prison de vie humaine*, pp. 284–85 (the section beginning "pour laquel chose te puis faire une tel question et demande"). See also p. 285, nn. 2, 3.

97. Figure 62: Vienna, Natl. Lib. MS. 2617, fol. 182.

98. *Teseida*, XII, vv. 48, 67–68. When Robertson, *Preface to Chaucer*, p. 265, argues that the marriage of Theseus and Hippolyta has a symbolic import ("He conquered al the regne of Femenye"), he is, I think, correct: a verbal cue is in the poem; we are asked to think of such things. But his discovery of a comparable symbolism in the concluding marriage, seeing in it a wedding of carnality to wisdom, with wisdom ascendent, does not convince me: "the marriage of Palamon and Emelye establishes Thebes, the city of Venus and Bacchus, in a position of 'obeisance' to Athens, the city of Minerva." The two cities are not given those values in Chaucer's poem, nor are the characters of Palamon and Emelye strong enough to suggest such identifications without the poet's specifically assigning them. (Boccaccio's

Chiose, be it noted, offer no substantive comment on the marriage.) Mc-Call, *Chaucer among the Gods*, pp. 83–86, writes beautifully about poetic patterning as the ultimate resolution of the questions raised by the poem.

99. For evidence on how a poet nearly contemporary with Chaucer read this work, one may turn to *The Kingis Quair* (The King's Book), a poem attributed to James I of Scotland, imprisoned by the English from 1406 until his marriage to Joan Beaufort in 1424—a marriage politically propitious, but, on the evidence of the poem at least, a love union as well. The poet describes himself as reading "Boece" one sleepless night, as the poem begins, but the poem's setting and initial action are modeled upon Chaucer's *Knight's Tale* directly. James first sees his lady in a garden next to ("fast by") his prison window; he falls deeply in love with her, and senses himself imprisoned in a new way ("sudaynly my hert became hir thrall / For euer, of free wyll"). In the course of the poem, and in comment upon this new happiness, he is shown a terrifying vision of Fortune and her wheel, with a sinister pit below. But given that the poem's primary purpose is to celebrate his good fortune in marriage and the recovery of his political freedom, he joyfully mounts that wheel at the poem's end. He concludes, as it were, in the character of Palamon, praising the Wheel of Fortune, preferring the partial truth: "thankit be Fortunys exil[tr]ee / And quh[e]le, that thus so wele has quhirlit me." The prison image and the vision of Fortune's destructive power are allowed no overriding authority: as truths they have not been denied, but neither are they allowed to dominate the mood of the poem's ending, where another truth, the possibility of earthly happiness, is found more appropriate. I quote from the Norton-Smith edition, ll. 285–86, 1322–23. For the prison/garden setting, see ll. 211–308; for the vision of Fortune's wheel, ll. 1107–1204. Norton-Smith discusses the controversy over the poem's authorship, pp. xix–xx.

100. Nims, "*Translatio*," pp. 226–27, has noted Chaucer's extension of the pilgrimage metaphor in terms similar to my own. See also Westlund, "The *Knight's Tale* as an Impetus for Pilgrimage." Baldwin, *Unity of the Canterbury Tales*, was the first to address this subject seriously; his monograph remains essential reading. Two recent books by Howard, *Idea of the Canterbury Tales* and *Writers and Pilgrims*, along with Zacher, *Curiosity and Pilgrimage*, have significantly extended our understanding of both the institution and its literary progeny. See also Turner and Turner, *Image and Pilgrimage*. I have postponed my own account of the poem's framing fiction for another occasion, when I shall write about *The General Prologue* and *The Parson's Prologue and Tale* together, under the title "The Image of the Pilgrim."

CHAPTER IV

1. Unless, of course, we take Chaucer's portrait of the Knight in *The General Prologue* to be totally ironic in its praise, as Jones does in *Chaucer's Knight*, pp. 31–140. He has written a valuable commentary on the Knight's military campaigns that puts (sometimes troublesome) flesh to the skeletal list in *The General Prologue*. But it is often difficult to determine how much of this information would have been known to Chaucer and his first audiences or to guess in any confident way their probable attitudes toward it.

(Aers's review of the book, pp. 171–72, offers some striking counter-evidence.) Most readers will be skeptical of the analogies with modern-day warfare that provide Jones's commentary with its emotional color. Certainly, his pejorative glossing of the great value words that describe the Knight's character—his love of "chivalrie," "trouthe and honour, fredom and curteisie," his meekness, his "worthynesse," and so on—denies the ordinary medieval significance of those terms to a degree that amounts to special pleading. (For example, many of the same words are used in praise of Hector, the greatest Trojan hero, in the *Troilus*, II, 153–89; it is because Troilus too embodies values such as "alle trouth and alle gentilesse, / Wisdom, honour, fredom, and worthinesse" that he is called "the wise, worthi Ector the secounde.") For a learned statement of the more traditional view, see Mann, *Chaucer and Medieval Estates Satire*, pp. 106–15, 127, and 262 (nn. 42, 43).

2. In terms of plot, character, and formulaic language, the ways in which the Miller reviews and revises *The Knight's Tale* have been widely understood. *The Miller's Tale*, ed. Hieatt, pp. 4–5, offers a brief summary and, on pp. 55–60, a useful bibliography.

3. For the oaths "by seint Thomas," see 1.3291, 3461. The Miller's joking promise to "telle a legende and a lyf" (1.3141) is perhaps an implicit admission of what ought to be expected (construing "legende" as meaning a "saint's life").

4. Howard, *Idea of the Canterbury Tales*, p. 243, terms "unimpersonated artistry" all that is "in the tale" but could not credibly have been "put there by its teller." I shall have more to say on this matter at the beginning of Chapter V.

5. See the discussion by Hirsch, *Aims of Interpretation*, pp. 32–34, which uses Piaget's concept of "corrigible schemata" as a means of defining the function of genre.

6. The standard works on fabliaux are Bédier, *Fabliaux*, and Nykrog, *Fabliaux*; Muscatine's *Chaucer and the French Tradition* is the most important account in English. Cooke and Honeycutt, *Humor of the Fabliaux*, and Cooke, *Old French and Chaucerian Fabliaux*, are of value, as is Brewer, "Fabliaux." See also Benson and Andersson, eds., *Literary Context of Chaucer's Fabliaux*; in their introduction, pp. 26–27, they focus on the one essential difference between the two national traditions—fabliaux are erotic stories in verse, "*novelle*" erotic stories in prose—and offer a useful list of the major early collections of the latter. For recent translations from the French repertory, see Hellman and O'Gorman, trans., *Fabliaux*; Eglesfield, trans., *Bawdy Tales*; and Brians, ed. and trans., *Bawdy Tales*. Williams, "French Fabliau Scholarship," surveys the field as of 1981.

7. The example is from Boccaccio's *Decameron*, IV.2. Another instance from the same work, offering a partial exception to the above generalization, is discussed on p. 211 of the present chapter.

8. See Bryan and Dempster, eds., *Sources and Analogues*, pp. 106–23, and Benson and Andersson, eds., *Literary Context of Chaucer's Fabliaux*, pp. 3–77.

9. Muscatine, *Chaucer and the French Tradition*, p. 224. Bennett, *Chaucer at Oxford and at Cambridge*, p. 116, demonstrates the historical accuracy of

its detail, the product of Chaucer "grinding the rough grain of fabliau into the fine flour of local character and local story."

10. See Chapter II of the present book, especially p. 59. Muscatine, "*Canterbury Tales*," p. 91, remarks Chaucer's "marked preference for similes over metaphors, as if the more discursive syntax of simile and its less pretentious reach of statement were more congenial to his rhythm and his personality." I think that part of the explanation, though perhaps not the whole.

11. On parish clerks, see Coulton, *Medieval Panorama*, pp. 144–47; Bennett, *Chaucer at Oxford and at Cambridge*, pp. 42–47 (on pp. 46–47 Bennett discusses Absolon's probable education—grammar hall, not university); and Severs, "Chaucer's Clerks," p. 143.

12. See Beichner, "Characterization in *The Miller's Tale*" and "Absolon's Hair."

13. Some of these occupations are explored by Bennett, *Chaucer at Oxford and at Cambridge*, pp. 45–52.

14. For background to this portrait, see *ibid.*, pp. 31–40, and Severs, "Chaucer's Clerks," pp. 140–43.

15. There is a pun on "lycorys" as well, which embodies the rhetorical sequence dominant in these portraits, a movement from the natural image ("licorice root") to an echo ("lecherous") that is potentially moral.

16. In "Heile of Bersele," a 14th-century Flemish fabliau that is the nearest contemporary analogue, Heile is a whore, visited by a miller, a priest, and a smith in turn; see Bryan and Dempster, eds., *Sources and Analogues*, pp. 112–18. *The Miller's Tale*, ed. Hieatt, pp. 51–54, offers a more idiomatic translation. In Masuccio's *Il novellino* (1476)—"Viola e li suoi amanti"—the woman is a carpenter's wife, but "not at all averse or disdainful to the suits of her almost countless lovers," three of whom she favors above the others—a smith, a merchant, a friar; see Benson and Andersson, eds., *Literary Context of Chaucer's Fabliaux*, pp. 28–29, for a text and translation.

17. For the Bartholomaeus version of the Six Ages, see *Properties*, pp. 291–93. In this scheme, *infancia* lasts for seven years, *puericia* another seven, and *adholoscencia* yet another seven (i.e., to the age of 21). But Isidore of Seville, Bartholomaeus notes, extends the latter to the age of 28 (a fourth seven), and physicians regard it as lasting yet another seven years, to 35. *Adholoscencia* is followed by the ages he terms *iuuentus*, *senecta*, and *senectus*. For an early Christian version of the Six Ages, see "On the Ages of the World and of Man" in Whitbread, trans., *Fulgentius the Mythographer*, pp. 187–221; in his introduction, pp. 182–83, Whitbread compares Fulgentius's version to Bede's. The bestiary, too, often includes a Six-Age analysis; see *The Book of Beasts*, pp. 219–25, translating a Latin bestiary made in England in the 12th century.

18. See McNeill and Gamer, trans., *Medieval Handbooks of Penance*, pp. 113, 158, 185, 272, 376, for instances in which youthfulness lessens the seriousness of sin or misdemeanors (categorized as *ludis* on p. 112).

19. On the full tradition, and its varying number of ages, see Chew, *Pilgrimage of Life*, pp. 144–73. "Aristotle had made three divisions; Pythagoras, Horace, and Ovid, four; Marcus Varro, five; Solon, Saint Augustine, Avicenna, Isidore of Seville, and the Venerable Bede, six; Hippocrates . . . seven" (p. 146).

20. *Peter Idley's Instructions to His Son*, p. 85 (281–82).

21. Figure 63: London, Brit. Lib. MS. Arundel 83, fol. 126v. Reproduced by Chew, *Pilgrimage of Life*, fig. 104 (described, p. 150). I follow Lucy Freeman Sandler, "The Psalter of Robert de Lisle," Ph.D. diss., New York Univ., 1964, in dating the work of the "Madonna Master" (responsible for the picture before us) ca. 1308–10; the other major miniaturist of the manuscript worked ca. 1339. Sandler identifies its provenance as Westminster/ London rather than East Anglian (pp. 230–31). The inscription encircling the image of the youth with comb and mirror reads *Numquam ero labilis: etatem mensuro*, while that around the image of the youth with balance scales reads *Vita decens seculi: speculo probatur*. The first of these inscriptions suits its picture in a general way, but the second inscription, with its reference to *speculum*, suits it better. It is possible the pictures have been reversed, or that the inscriptions and the pictorial sequence derive from slightly different traditions. As Chew (p. 362, n. 18) remarks laconically: "Not all the inscriptions seem obviously appropriate." Kaske, "*Piers Plowman*," pp. 162–65, has also argued the two figures should be reversed, suggesting some interesting correspondences between this mirror and Langland's "Mirour þat hiȝte middelerþe" (B. XI, 8). On this picture, see Sandler's dissertation, pp. 175–83. Following Rushforth, she writes (p. 183): "Youth is the age of beauty and narcissism. The mirror is one of the symbols of the goddess Venus, who, as a planet in the Ptolemaic astrological system, presides over the age of puberty." Dante, *Convivio*, IV, Chaps. 23–28, likewise uses a four-age division (*l'adolescenza, la gioventute, la senettute, lo senio*), though to a different end: he describes how one can recognize the truly noble person at any of these ages. For an English translation, see that by Wicksteed, pp. 341–75. Tristram, *Figures of Life and Death*, Chaps. 2 and 3, surveys medieval ideas of "Youth and Its Mentors" and "Age and Its Perspectives."

22. See New York, Pierpont Morgan MS. (Glazier) G.50, fol. 29 (English, ca. 1316–31). In each of the Seven Ages, of which this picture represents the first, the man is shown alongside a lady instructress or Wisdom figure. In the second age, he holds what I take to be a ball, light green in color (fol. 50); the other ages are shown on fols. 58v, 64, 68, 72, 81. Here, as in figure 63, the mirror and comb almost certainly derive from the standard portrait of *Oiseuse* ("Ydelnesse") in MSS. of *The Romance of the Rose*— a beautiful young woman, gatekeeper to the garden of Deduit, who holds in her hand "a gay mirrour" and whose only concerns are pleasure and the combing of her golden hair: "For I entende to nothyng / But to my joye and my pleying, / And for to kembe and tresse me." (*RR*, 567, 597–99.) Brewer, *Chaucer*, 3d ed., p. 18, reproduces a fine late-14th-century illumination. See also Robertson, *Preface to Chaucer*, fig. 68; and Randall, *Images in Margins*, figs. 246, 249, where grotesque figures are shown similarly engaged. A wall painting of the Seven Ages (ca. 1275) survives at Leominster, Herefordshire, and another (early 14th century) at Longthorpe Tower, near Peterborough; on the latter, see Tristram, *English Wall Painting*, pp. 27–28, 219. He quotes (p. 28) from Lydgate's *Reson and Sensuallyte* an explanation of wheel symbolism pertinent to our figure 63: "Thy lyff . . . ys lyk a cercle that goth aboute, round and swyfft as any thouht, wych in hys course ne cesset nouht . . . tyl he kam to hys restyng place wych ys in God."

23. "*The Chess of Love*," p. 758.

24. *Ibid.*, pp. 758–63, 768–69.

25. *Ibid.*, p. 757. The poem describes images that decorate the outside wall of the Garden of Mirth, among them that of Age; that topic brings Youth into the commentary as well, and thus this division into Youth and Age, each with two parts. See p. 753.

26. Dante, *Convivio* IV, 24, p. 348. In a long allegorical poem, called by its editor "The Mirror of the Periods of Man's Life," written ca. 1430, the portrait of youth is organized around the following details (ll. 79, 81–82, 101–2, 229–30, 273–76):

> Course of kynde is for ȝouþe to be wilde. . . .
> Thus at vij ȝeer age childhood bigynnes,
> And folowith folies many foold.
>
> . . .
>
> Quod lust to conscience, "ȝouþe so muste;
> ȝouþe can not kepe him chast."
>
> . . .
>
> ȝouþe ful of corage wole be;
> þou must haue helpe, or ellis spille.
>
> . . .
>
> Quod man to Conscience, "ȝouþe axiþ delice;
> For ȝouþe þe course of kinde wole holde;
> But ȝouþe were a foole and nyce,
> How schulde wijsdom be founde in oolde."

Some of these statements are in the author's voice; others are spoken by "lust," the "wicked aungil," or man in self-excuse. They enunciate an idea of youth to whose currency the poem bears witness, but which it obviously cannot approve: its perspectives are those of eternity, as it follows its figure for mankind from birth to his death at the age of 100, giving him ample time to regret the follies of his youth, along with the vices of his maturity. The latter gain the upper hand when he is 20; see ll. 113–248. (In Furnivall, ed., *Hymns to the Virgin and Christ*, pp. 58–78.) As John Burrow has shown in a fascinating study, "'Young Saint, Old Devil,'" there were two ways in which medieval moralists thought about the order of human development set out in schema of the Ages of Man: as a norm to be transcended, or as a norm to be achieved (p. 391). He locates Chaucer within the latter position, even in *The Prioress's Tale*, which portrays "a young saint who is so pointedly *not*, in the proverb's sense, a 'young saint'" (p. 394). Burrow stresses the aspects of the little clergeoun's character that make him less *puer senex* than real boy. Tristram, *Figures of Life and Death*, pp. 27–28, writes about the Squire as "Chaucer's personification of Youth," and catalogues the various attitudes toward that condition embodied in the *Tales* themselves: "To the Miller, Youth is a healthy joke, to the Merchant and Reeve a sour one; to the Franklin it is romantically nostalgic, to the Wife of Bath a challenge to her vigour."

27. Figure 64: Brussels, Bibl. Royale MS. 10176–78, fol. 98. In Paris, Bibl. Natl. MS. fr. 376, fols. 76v, 77 (ca. 1430–40), Youth has wings at her heels so large the tips reach to her shoulders. For related illuminations, see New York, Pierpont Morgan MS. M.772, fols. 86, 86v (ca. 1360–70); Lon-

don, Brit. Lib. MS. Cotton Tiberius A.vii, fols. 41v, 79v (the Lydgate translation), and MS. Harley 4399, fols. 76v, 77, 78; see also that reproduced in Guillaume de Deguileville, *Vie*, ed. Stürzinger, facing p. 369 (from a Huth MS). For the text, see Lydgate, *Pilgrimage*, pp. 303–6 (esp. ll. 11140–48, 11191–210); I quote ll. 11073–74 and 11145 above. For "Youthe" still with the pilgrim at the age of 30, see p. 338 (12448); cf. pp. 344–46 (12679–748). Her animal wildness is clear: like Alisoun, she winces "ageyn the prykke, / As wylde coltys in Arras" (p. 304 [11136–37]). In Guillaume's first version, trans. as *The Pilgrimage of the Lyf of the Manhode*, she is called "Jolyfnesse" (pp. 180ff). Her relation to the French original of "Youthe" in *The Romaunt of the Rose* is direct: Guillaume dreams his dream one night after having read in *The Romance of the Rose*; see p. 9 of the present book. Her relation to wisdom may be gauged from the following (Lydgate, p. 306, ll. 11202–10):

> "And the ffyn of myn entent ys
> To folwe the lust off my corage,
> And to spende my yonge age
> In merthe only, & in solace,
> ffolwe my lustys in ech place;
> Ther-to hooly I me enclyne,
> Rather than to han doctryne
> Off ffader, moder, thogh they be wyse,
> Al ther techyng I despyse."

28. Figure 65: New York, Pierpont Morgan MS. M.132, fol. 102v.

29. *Roman de la rose*, ed. Lecoy, II, 173–74 (13911–22). I quote Dahlberg's trans., p. 239. Boccaccio, in the *Decameron*, postulates a similar necessity in his preface to the stories of the Fourth Day, where he tells in his own person a tale demonstrating that the "natural affections" (instinctive desires) of young people will out, in spite of anything one can do to repress them: see the trans. by McWilliam, pp. 326–31. Juan Ruiz, *Book of Good Love*, pp. 52–53, offers further 14th-century testimony to the power of natural desire, citing Aristotle as authority.

30. "Mirror of the Periods of Man's Life," in Furnivall, ed., *Hymns to the Virgin and Christ*, p. 71 (425–28).

31. Corsa, *Chaucer*, p. 114. My sentence closely paraphrases her original, but also extends it; she refers only to Alisoun in this way. In the words of Chaucer's contemporary, Thomas Usk, in his *Testament of Love* (Bk. III, Chap. 8): "These than unrightful appetytes and unthrifty lustes whiche the flesh desyreth, in as mokel as they ben in kynde, ben they nat bad; but they ben unrightful and badde for they ben in resonable creature, where-as they being, in no waye shulde ben suffred. In unresonable beestes neyther ben they yvel ne unrightful; for there is their kynde being." (In Skeat, ed., *Chaucerian and Other Pieces*, p. 142.) Cf. *The Merchant's Tale* (IV.1281–82), where old January speaks of bachelors as persons able to imagine "they lyve but as a bryd or as a beest, / In libertee, and under noon arreest." In the inclusive first etymology of *The Book of Beasts* (p. 7) we are reminded that animals "are known as 'wild' (*ferus*) because they are accustomed to freedom by nature and are governed (*ferantur*) by their own wishes. They wander hither and thither, fancy free, and they go wherever they want to go." Similarly,

we are told birds are called *aves* "because they do not follow straight roads (*vias*), but stray through any byway" (pp. 103–4).

32. Walter Hilton, *The Scale of Perfection*, II, 14. This important work still awaits a scholarly edition; I print from that of Wynkyn de Worde (1494), STC no. 14042, with emendations based on his editions of 1525, 1533 (transcribed from University Microfilms no. 1400). Underhill edited the work from MSS., but modernized the spelling; for the present passage, see pp. 276–78. Bloomfield, *Seven Deadly Sins*, pp. 245–49, presents a synoptic list of the various animals used to symbolize the sins, with many references drawn from literature and the visual arts. Three books by Rowland, *Blind Beasts*, *Animals with Human Faces*, and *Birds with Human Souls*, offer richly learned guides to the larger subject; the latter two volumes include many medieval illustrations. For the beast-fable and beast-epic traditions (not described above), consult *Blind Beasts*, pp. 2–3, and for the sins, pp. 18–19, along with the relevant annotation. Klingender, *Animals in Art and Thought*, is magisterial in its sweep and authority; it includes a magnificent collection of animal illustrations, 306 in all, from prehistory to the end of the Middle Ages. See also Fischer, "Handlist of Animal References."

33. Figures 66–68: Cambridge, Univ. Lib. MS. Gg.iv.27, fols. 416, 432, 433. In keeping with the tale, the remedial virtues are given equal place. In the first picture, Envy is opposed by Charity, wearing a triple crown, who holds in her hands a sceptre and a flaming heart; in the second, Gluttony is opposed by Abstinence, who holds in her hands a sceptre and a water pitcher; in the third, Lechery is opposed by Chastity, who transfixes the monster at her feet with a spear topped by a cross. The MS. once contained a complete set of seven such pairs.

The sparrow had been thought lascivious since Roman times; for medieval evidence, see, e.g., Bartholomaeus, *Properties*, p. 639, and the survey, with many references, in Rowland, *Birds with Human Souls*, pp. 157–60. For commentary on these figures, see Loomis, *Mirror of Chaucer's World*, figs. 177–79. Oxford, MS. Bodley 283, an English translation of the *Somme le roi*, has a complete set of the Seven Sins, most portrayed as riding on symbolic animals (3/4 15th century). Mâle, *L'Art religieux de la fin du moyen âge*, figs. 178–84, reproduces an elegant set of the same.

34. Figures 69, 70: Cambridge, Trinity Hall MS. 12, fols. 40v, 41.

35. Cf. Bartholomaeus, *Properties*, p. 1237: "A swyn hatte *porcus* as it were *sporcus* 'vile and defouled', as Isidorus seiþ. . . . And froteþ and walweþ in drytte and in fenne and dyueþ in slyme and bawdeþ himself þerwiþ and resteþ in stynkyng place." Chaucer uses this figure again in *The Man of Law's Tale*, where the drunken messenger "sleep as a swyn" (II.745). See Anderson, *History and Imagery*, pl. 56, for a similar subject on a misericord seat from Norwich Cathedral: a merry drunkard rides along on a sow, tipping back his tankard, in imminent danger of falling off.

36. *The Book of Beasts*, pp. 142, 146 (White reproduces pictures from the manuscript he translates). The bestiary tradition ultimately derives from the *Physiologus*, an anonymous work of natural history made sometime between the second and fifth centuries A.D., probably in Greek, though we know it only through its translations, the earliest being in Latin and dating from the 8th century. (There is a recent trans. by Curley.) Chaucer refers to

it in *The Nun's Priest's Tale* (VII.3271). The *Physiologus* is a compilation, drawing upon the writings of Herodotus, Aristotle, Pliny the Elder, and others; in its later medieval form it is enriched with lore from St. Ambrose, Isidore of Seville, Hugh of Folieto (on birds), Giraldus Cambrensis, and so on. Natural history is made to yield "lessons" in even the earliest versions, though not all are intended to shape human action: some are meant to illuminate divine and doctrinal mysteries. And in some entries moralizations *in bono et in malo* exist side by side, just as they do in the *Allegoriae sacram scripturam*, where eight symbolic meanings are given to the lion, including both Christ and Anti-Christ; on this see Rowland, *Blind Beasts*, pp. 4–5. See also McCulloch, *Mediaeval Latin and French Bestiaries*; Klingender, *Animals in Art and Thought*, pp. 339–402 (cogent, with many illustrations); and Debidour, *Le Bestiaire sculpté*.

37. Langland, *Piers Plowman*, B. XI, 320ff (pp. 457ff). Cf. Walter Map, in *De nugis curialium*, pp. 2–3: "Now how comes it that we men have degenerated from our original beauty, strength, and force, while other living creatures in no way go astray from the grace first given to them? . . . The creatures of earth, sea and air—everything except man—rejoice in the life and powers with which they were created. They, it seems, have not fallen out of their Maker's favour. And what should this mean but that they still keep the obedience enjoined upon them, while we have spurned it from the beginning." On pp. 24–25, he again raises the matter: "It is a wholesome thing to guide ourselves by the reason of unreasoning creatures, to which nature dictates a better rule of life than our own wisdom can devise"; he praises wholly wild creatures above the domesticated in this regard, for the latter, he says, live a little less naturally than they did before their lives were brought into contact with our own. When Nature confesses to Genius in *The Romance of the Rose*, she takes comparable care to exempt the plants and animals from her complaint against man and his behavior (ed. Lecoy, III, 69–71 [18951–19024]; trans. Dahlberg, pp. 314–15).

38. Figure 71: from *Queen Mary's Psalter*, London, Brit. Lib. MS. Royal 2 B.vii, fol. 2; there is a facsimile of this early-14th-century MS., ed. Warner. It is closely related to the corresponding page in *The Holkham Bible Picture Book*, London, Brit. Lib. MS. Add. 47682, fol. 2v, from 1/2 14th century; see the facsimile, ed. Hassall. Both MSS. are English. The two pages are reproduced opposite each other by Klingender, *Animals in Art and Thought*, pp. 410–11. For a relevant creation of Eve, see New York, Pierpont Morgan MS. M.769, fol. 9 (a *Christ-Herre Chronik*, Bavarian, ca. 1375). Cf. the exquisite illumination of the sixth day in the same library's MS. M.638, fol. 1v (reproduced in facsimile as *Old Testament Miniatures*, p. 29); it is from Paris, ca. 1250. Figure 72: Cambridge, Fitzwilliam Mus. MS. 251, fol. 16 (a *Livre de la propriété des choses*); the picture is reproduced in color by Meiss, *Boucicaut Master*, fig. 457. There are closely related scenes in Meiss, *The Limbourgs*, figs. 167, 169. See also New York, Pierpont Morgan MS. 833, fol. 5, for three medallions of considerable beauty showing (respectively) the creation of the trees and plants, the birds, and the animals (from a Bible illustrated in Bohemia in 1391 in the court atelier); and Paris, Bibl. Natl. MS. lat. 757, fols. 45, 49, 53, for three superb paintings of the Creation (Lombard, 1380). For bestiary Creation scenes, see Rowland, *Animals with Hu-*

man Faces, frontispiece (from Oxford, Bodley MS. Ashmole 1511, fol. 6v, ca. 1200); and Oxford, Bodley MS. Douce 151, fols. 3, 3v (ca. 1300). On fol. 5, Adam is shown naming the animals in Eden (Rowland, *Animals with Human Faces*, p. 1, reproduces the equivalent scene from London, Westminster Abbey MS. 22, fol. 4, 13th century); see also *A Thirteenth Century Bestiary*, pl. 7; and *A Peterborough Psalter and Bestiary of the Fourteenth Century*, fig. 32.

39. Langland, *Piers Plowman*, B. XI, 369–71 (pp. 459–60). Schmidt, "Langland and Scholastic Philosophy," discusses the sources of this tradition; see esp. pp. 145–50.

40. Cf. Klingender, *Animals in Art and Thought*, p. 385: "The English bestiary illustrators confined themselves from first to last to the natural history side of the *Physiologus* text and of the additions that were made to it from time to time, for the chapter on the Creation and Naming of the Animals . . . was also, of course, for the medieval reader natural history in the strict sense." Klingender describes on pp. 391–96 the growth of naturalism in the bestiary illuminations—a tendency, discernible from the 12th through the 14th centuries, to incorporate detail based on direct observation.

41. Bks. XII, XVII, and XVIII of Bartholomaeus, *Properties*, treat birds, plants, and animals respectively. For information on the encyclopedic tradition, see Collison, *Encyclopaedias*, and Klingender, *Animals in Art and Thought*, pp. 351–59, 380. Collison describes Bartholomaeus's work as "the most popular encyclopaedia in Europe for three centuries" (pp. 57–58). It was a monastic product, like the encyclopedias of his great contemporaries, Alexander Neckham and Vincent de Beauvais, and its formal arrangement is governed by theological ideas: Book I concerns the nature and names of God; II, the angels, both good and evil; III, the human soul; and so on, descending through the chain of being. Where the subject matter of the book is doctrinal, doctrine is, of course, to be found; even in the books of natural history, Bartholomaeus says (in the prefatory remarks to each) he will mention only the creatures named in the Bible or "in the gloss." In the proem (p. 41), he declares the purpose of the whole is to furnish materials with which "to vndirstonde redels and menynges of scriptures and of writinges þat þe holy gost hath iȝeue derkliche ihid and wrapped vndir liknes and fygures of propirtees of þinges." But "the gloss" is a capacious reference point, excluding little, and the declared higher purpose does not significantly color the treatment of creatures below man. They yield information chiefly about themselves. Rowland, too, *Blind Beasts*, p. 5, remarks that Bartholomaeus is unusually free of explicit moralizing. In 1266, Brunetto Latini produced in French *Li Livres dou tresor*, "the first vernacular encyclopaedia with a basis of Cicero rather than Aquinas, and a public of merchants and officials rather than scholars and theologians" (Collison, p. 65). For an account of earlier medieval encyclopedic traditions, see Saxl, *Lectures*, pp. 228–54.

42. On the latter, see Klingender, *Animals in Art and Thought*, pp. 400–2, and Randall, *Images in Margins*, esp. pp. 16–17. After the near-collapse of English book illustration in the mid-14th century, the bestiary tradition flourished chiefly in ecclesiastical wood carving, especially misericords, roof bosses, and bench ends; see Klingender, pp. 432–38. For nearly comprehen-

sive indexes of extant examples, see Cave, *Roof Bosses*, and Remnant, *A Catalogue of Misericords*.

43. Bartholomaeus, *Properties*, p. 1229.

44. Figure 73: New York, Pierpont Morgan MS. M.81, fol. 46v, an English bestiary; cf. Oxford, MS. Bodley 764, fol. 51 (13th century), reproduced in Rowland, *Animals with Human Faces*, p. 52; and London, Brit. Lib. MS. Harl. 4751, fol. 30v (13th century). *The Luttrell Psalter* (English, ca. 1340), fol. 190, displays a charming example. Cf. Oxford, Bodley MS. Ashmole 1525, fol. 14 (an English psalter, 1/4 13th century); Oxford, MS. New Coll. 130, fol. 41, and MS. Balliol Coll. 238E, fol. 56v. For an example from the margins of the Hours of Jeanne d'Evreux (French, ca. 1325), see Randall, *A Cloisters Bestiary*, p. 27.

45. Bartholomaeus, *Properties*, p. 1197. The notation concerning Old Testament sacrifice represents information included for the sake of Scriptural understanding. For a bestiary entry, see *The Book of Beasts*, pp. 75–76.

46. Bartholomaeus, *Properties*, pp. 1114–15. Cf. *The Book of Beasts*, p. 74.

47. Figure 74: Oxford, MS. Bodley 764, fol. 41v. Fol. 42 shows two calves running and leaping. Bartholomaeus says of the calf, "whan he is fulle and haþ wel ysouked þanne he is glad and mery and lepeþ and sterteleþ, lepynge aboute, and goþ nouȝt oute of his moder fores" (*Properties*, p. 1259). Figure 75: Oxford, MS. Bodley 764, fol. 35v. See also Rowland, *Animals with Human Faces*, pp. 114–15, and *Blind Beasts*, Chap. 9.

48. Bartholomaeus, *Properties*, pp. 1227–28 (I have quoted the phrases out of order). Figure 76: New York, H. P. Kraus collection (formerly MS. Dyson Perrins 26), fol. 93v, a bestiary fragment. For other examples, see Oxford, Bodley MS. Laud. Misc. 720, fol. 163 (from a 13th-century MS. of Giraldus Cambrensis), and Cambridge, Corpus Christi Coll. MS. 53, fol. 197v (a Peterborough bestiary of the early 14th century). Rowland, *Animals with Human Faces*, p. 159, reproduces another, as does *The Book of Beasts*, p. 92. For a related Anglo-Norman text, see Guillaume le Clerc, *The Bestiary*, written ca. 1210, p. 69 (2419–49). For a full account of weasel lore, see Rowland, *Animals with Human Faces*, pp. 158–60. In her *Blind Beasts*, pp. 25–29, this material is used to explicate other details in Chaucer's description of Alisoun, not always convincingly.

49. Oxford, MS. Bodley 764, fol. 81v, for instance, shows the swallows flying to their nests under the eaves. For a bestiary description, see *The Book of Beasts*, pp. 147–48, and the picture there; cf. Bartholomaeus, *Properties*, pp. 631–32, and see the illuminations in Oxford, Bodley MS. Douce 308, fols. 96, 98. Rowland, *Blind Beasts*, p. 24, comments usefully on the swallow's song, a subject she has treated more fully in "Chaucer's 'Throstil Old'" (see esp. p. 383); she finds evidence of personal observation in his bird descriptions. See also her *Birds with Human Souls*, pp. 163–69. Absolon twice addresses Alisoun in a more generalized way: "My faire bryd" (I.3699), and "sweete bryd" (I.3805).

50. Bartholomaeus, *Properties*, p. 1190.

51. Figure 77: Oxford, MS. Bodley 264, fol. 107. In the opposite corner of the page, a blacksmith forges a shoe while a man holds the reins of a horse. See also Oxford, Bodley MS. Douce 88, fol. 51 (a treatise on the care

of horses, English, 13th century). Alisoun is twice compared to a colt (1.3263, 3282). In Lydgate's "Testament," the poet looks back to the time when he was "lyke a yong colt that ran without brydell" (*Minor Poems*, I, 352 [626]; the whole passage concerning his youth, ll. 607–69, is relevant to this chapter).

52. Figure 78: London, Brit. Lib. MS. Add. 42130, fol. 73, the Luttrell Psalter. Cf. two such scenes in Randall, *Images in Margins*, figs. 325, 326, and another (showing an ape dancing to a frame drum) in *The Hours of Jeanne d'Evreux*, fig. 17 (fol. 76). (Its main miniature shows the Presentation in the Temple.) Janson, *Apes and Ape Lore*, pp. 262–63, reproduces and comments upon a Nuremberg woodcut, ca. 1480, showing a woman making an ape of a young man by simultaneously embracing him and taking money from his purse; the metaphor is contributed by a monkey shown looking at itself in a mirror in the background. On apes, see Bartholomaeus, *Properties*, pp. 1246–47, e.g.: "We clepen hem *simias* and ʒiuen hem þat name for liknesse of resoun, for in many þynges he counterfeteþ þe dedes of men. . . . Þe ape is a beste wonderliche yschape but he haþ som likenesse of mankynde and is ylerned and taught, and so he is taught to lepe and pleye in dyuers manere wise." Flood miniatures often make a point of showing an ape within the ark, as in figure 91 below; or being loaded into it, as in London, Brit. Lib. MS. Egerton 1894, fol. 3 (the MS. has been published in facsimile, *Illustrations of the Book of Genesis*); or departing therefrom, as in Pierpont Morgan MS. M.638, fol. 2v (ca. 1250). The latter is reproduced in facsimile, *Old Testament Miniatures*, p. 33.

53. Figure 79: London, Brit. Lib. MS. Add. 18850, fol. 16v; it shows several other events as well, including Noah's sacrifice, his discovery of the art of fermenting grapes, and his drunkenness. New York, Pierpont Morgan MS. M.769, fol. 23 (a *Christ-Herre Chronik*, Bavarian, ca. 1375), shows the animals and birds rushing from the ark with a wonderful wild joy. Klingender, *Animals in Art and Thought*, fig. 160, reproduces the beautiful mosaic of this subject from St. Mark's in Venice. See also *Old Testament Miniatures*, p. 33, for the Flood page from Pierpont Morgan MS. M.638, fol. 2v (ca. 1250): the animals and the humans depart the ark on separate ladders. In Chaucer's use of the tradition, the reversal of gender may be poetically deliberate, a comic reflection on the nature of uxoriousness. Note, too, the sequence of Nicholas's persuasion: like the rhetoric of the tale's formal portraits, it moves from a natural image to a specifically human (potentially moral) notation; a sense of the "natural" as prior and more urgent becomes stylistically determinant.

54. Figure 80: New York, Pierpont Morgan MS. M.88, fol. 156v (border decoration from a psalter). I take the darker birds to be ducks, and the white birds geese or swans.

55. Cf. three historiated initials and their associated border decoration in a Lombard MS. of Pliny's *Natural History* (made in 1389), depicting the animal, avian, and botanical kingdoms in turn: Milan, Bibl. Ambrosiana MS. E.24 Inf., fols. 84v, 106, 129. Klingender, *Animals in Art and Thought*, p. 355 (fig. 211) reproduces an "animal kingdom" miniature from a MS. of the French translation of Bartholomaeus, ca. 1480.

56. Figure 81: Cambridge, Magdalene Coll. MS. Pepys 1916, fol. 9v;

fol. 19v offers an even greater number of animals randomly displayed. Two pages filled with birds, from the same MS., have been reproduced by Bennett, *The Parlement of Foules*, pl. 4; a third may be seen in Rickert, *Painting in Britain*, pl. 164, or in Brewer, *Chaucer*, p. 63. The entire MS. has been published in facsimile by James, ed., "An English Medieval Sketchbook"; see this for a tentative identification of the birds and animals depicted, many of which have their names written in English alongside. In figure 81, these include the sheep, the horse, the cat, the coney, and the talbott (a dog). On the difficult question of provenance, see Bennett's discussion and bibliography, pp. 20–21 (n. 3); he dates the MS. ca. 1400 in his list of plates. See also Klingender, *Animals in Art and Thought*, pp. 421–26. If, as seems likely, the manuscript was intended as a pattern book for an artists' workshop, its bird and animal pages must have been intended for use in marginal decoration rather than in the great Scriptural programs: like the writings of the encyclopedists, these pages display an interest in animals almost entirely divorced from moral or doctrinal systems. The illustration of Adam naming the animals in *A Thirteenth-Century Bestiary*, pl. 7, offers an equally dense field image.

57. For a comparable instance in the visual arts, see the exquisite landscape reproduced by Avril, *Manuscript Painting in the Court of France*, pl. 26, illustrating Machaut's *Le Dit du lion* (ca. 1350). Where the text calls for an enchanted garden, the manuscript painter has depicted a forest bounded by a river that is full of bird and animal life. Avril writes: "All human presence has been banished from the serene vision, which shows the increased attention artists began to pay to the study of nature toward the end of the Middle Ages. This may be one of the oldest independent landscapes in European painting." (P. 90.)

58. Lydgate, *Pilgrimage*, p. 305 (11145–48). She is playing with a ball against a wall when the pilgrim first sees her, p. 303 (11080–83); she describes her preferred games, pp. 305–6 (11150–201). In Chaucer's *Parliament of Fowls*, the dreamer sees among Cupid's company "Youthe, ful of game and jolyte" (226). Images representing persons at play, both children and adults, are numerous in the borders of manuscripts, some of which aspire to an almost encyclopedic comprehensiveness. Among the latter are two of the greatest English psalters of the 14th century—*Queen Mary's Psalter* and *The Luttrell Psalter*—along with the incredibly rich borders of *The Romance of Alexander*. Randall, *Images in Margins*, reproduces numerous examples; see her index entry "Games, sports, and pastimes," pp. 103–4.

59. For a brilliant investigation of "game" as a mode of action, see Huizinga, *Homo Ludens*, esp. Chap. 1; for an application of its insights to the medieval drama, see Kolve, *Play Called Corpus Christi*, Chaps. 2 and 8. Josipovici, *World and the Book*, pp. 87–99, writes interestingly about this subject in relation to *The Canterbury Tales* as a whole. See also Lanham, "Game, Play, and High Seriousness in Chaucer's Poetry."

60. Figure 82: from the transept roof (ca. 1509). Anderson, *Drama and Imagery*, pp. 87–104, argues for the connection between these bosses and local drama tradition, and publishes the present example as fig. 11b. Doob, *Nebuchadnezzar's Children*, Chap. 3, offers a learned study of Herod as a type of the Mad Sinner, and reproduces this roof boss (pl. 10). See also Skey,

"Iconography of Herod." I quote from Craig, ed., *Two Coventry Corpus Christi Plays*, p. 27 (779–81); the stage direction follows two lines after.

61. See Donaldson, "Idiom of Popular Poetry," and Kaske, "*Canticum Canticorum*." Kaske's elaborate exegesis of Absolon's wooing speech perhaps exaggerates its importance; I think it a matter of local comic effect, not "a profoundly comic association of Absolon with the *Sponsus* and of Alisoun with the *sponsa*" meant to govern our whole reading of the tale (p. 479).

62. Alisoun once refers to him as jealous: "'Myn housbonde is so ful of jalousie / That but ye wayte wel and been privee, / I woot right wel I nam but deed,' quod she" (1.3294); and at the tale's end, we're told she has been "swyved," "for al his kepyng and his jalousye" (1.3851). But these notations are not elaborated in terms of either action or characterization, and they are undercut by the other facts I discuss above. Paul Olson's summary of the relation of character to action, in his essay "Poetic Justice in the *Miller's Tale*," p. 229, ignores all such complexity: "John is a possessive *jaloux* from the first static portrait, and he acts like one until he goes to sleep. Nicholas is a lecher; he does strictly what lechery demands—all of his intellectual cleverness is put to its purposes. And Absolon does only what the fastidious vanity implicit in his portrait would suggest." In fact, John does not behave possessively; lechery does not "demand" intellectual cleverness; and fastidious vanity accounts for only a small part of what makes Absolon interesting. Olson's interpretation is one of three from Princeton that see in the tale a nexus of three sins (in which "jalousie," for instance, becomes a name for avarice). See n. 122 below.

63. M.E.D. "jelous" (sense 2a): "fond, amorous, ardent." For Chaucer's version of the other kind of jealousy, see *The Merchant's Tale*, esp. IV.2072–92.

64. Joseph, "Chaucerian 'Game'—'Ernest,'" pp. 88–89, discusses this aspect of *The Miller's Tale*; McClintock, "Games and the Players of Games," writes provocatively about the importance of "gaming, or games-playing" to fabliau as a genre, pp. 113–14. For a learned commentary on Nicholas's style of loving, see Reiss, "Chaucer's *deerne love* and the Medieval View of Secrecy in Love."

65. Nicholas cries out "A berd! a berd!" (1.3742), meaning "A fine trick! a great trick!," naming Alisoun's intention and saluting her as gamester; Absolon meanwhile ponders the fact that he has kissed "a beard."

66. Trevet, "Life of Constance," p. 36; see Bryan and Dempster, eds., *Sources and Analogues*, p. 176, for the Anglo-Norman text alone.

67. The former is reproduced by Randall, *Images in Margins*, fig. 533 (Tournai, Cathedral Treasury, the Psalter of Louis le Hutin, dated 1315). For the Gorleston Psalter example (East Anglian, ca. 1310–25), see London, Brit. Lib. MS. Add. 49622, fol. 61; fols. 63, 66, 78, 82, 83v, 102v, 104, 108, 124, 157v, display related obscenities.

68. Figure 83: Oxford, MS. Bodley 264, fol. 56. The man apparently breaks wind or defecates as well. The manuscript is the famous *Romance of Alexander* (1344). Its borders include a number of bared bottoms: see also fols. 3, 79, 90v in the facsimile, ed. James; of our present example, James says only "boy, indecorous: nun kneels on [right]" (p. 18).

69. Reproduced by Randall, *Images in Margins*, figs. 535, 536 (from a

Glazier MS. of the *Voeux du paon*). See figs. 526–42 for a representative collection of bum-baring motifs, and index entries under "Obscaena: exposing hindquarters" and "kissing or peering at hindquarters," pp. 192–93, for others not reproduced.

70. See Oxford, Bodley MS. Laud Misc. 751, fol. 173v (from a Flemish MS. of a French version of Quintus Curtius's *Historia Alexandri Magni*, illuminated ca. 1470–80).

71. See Randall, *Images in Margins*, fig. 543, and index entries under "Obscaena: trumpet aimed at hindquarters" and "tube blown at hindquarters," p. 193.

72. Figure 84: a roof boss from Sherborne Abbey, reproduced by Cave, *Roof Bosses*, fig. 202. See Randall, *Images in Margins*, figs. 502, 539, 540, 541, for related manuscript examples, and index entries under "Obscaena: pole aimed at hindquarters," "shooting hindquarters," and "spear aimed at hindquarters," for still others (p. 193). Oxford, Bodley MS. Laud Misc. 751, shows a young gallant shooting a bow and arrow at another young man, who bares his arse to him as target (fol. 208, bottom border).

73. Muscatine, *Chaucer and the French Tradition*, p. 227, writes (with reference to Donaldson's "Idiom of Popular Poetry"), "Linguistic analysis has shown how much the Oxford idiom of love is the idiom of English rather than of French romance. It is the native version of the imported heresy that is parodied here. More congenial to the setting, it is also funnier than Continental love would have been, for it is exposed to the laughter of the sophisticated, who know better, as well as of the Miller's kind, who know worse."

74. Figure 85: Cambridge, Trinity Coll. MS. B.11.22, fol. 30 (from a Flemish Book of Hours). For a similar scene or scenes involving a lover and the God of Love alone, see MSS. of *The Romance of the Rose*; Dahlberg illustrates his translation with a standard sequence of three (figs. 14, 15, 16). Randall, *Images in Margins*, prints the Trinity Coll. example above as fig. 398; cf. figs. 395, 396. See also Robertson, *Preface to Chaucer*, fig. 60.

75. Figure 86: London, Brit. Lib. MS. Add. 49622, fol. 199. Reproduced by Randall, *Images in Margins*, as fig. 260; see also her figs. 268, 467, 550, 600, 604, 645, 677, some of them showing the veneration of saints. Cf. Tristram, *English Wall Painting*, pl. 57 (from Clifton Campville, Staffordshire).

76. Figure 87: an ivory writing tablet from the Detroit Institute of Arts (42.136); published as pl. 4 (fig. 74), and fully described, p. 112, in Levin, ed., *Images of Love and Death*. The subject often appears in ivory carvings (cf. pl. 4 [fig. 64] and pl. 7 [fig. 70], along with Robertson, *Preface to Chaucer*, figs. 59, 63), and frequently appears in MS. illumination; see Randall, *Images in Margins*, figs. 400, 402, 403, and Robertson, fig. 25 (with his commentary, p. 113, concerning the canopy of stone). On the possible erotic symbolism of the animals held by ladies in such scenes, see Robertson, p. 191 ("a small furry creature which . . . represents the object of the lover's quest"); see also his pp. 113, 128, 193, 203, 255, 263–64. But we should in fact distinguish between two such traditions, one involving rabbits, the other small dogs. Whereas the first (through a pun on the French *con* and *conin*—English "coney") is almost certainly erotic, the dog is more plausibly interpreted as a symbol of fidelity. (Levin, p. 112, suggests this is its meaning in the present example.) Certainly a dog is far more common in

such scenes. We might note that Yolande of Soissons is shown in her Psalter praying in church to the Virgin and Child with just such a dog at her knees—clearly without irony intended. See Gould, *Psalter and Hours*, pl. 19; she dates the Psalter ca. 1275–85.

77. In "Heile of Bersele," p. 116, it is the priest; so too in the versions by Hans Sachs, Schumann, and Cropacius (see Benson and Andersson, eds., *Literary Context of Chaucer's Fabliaux*, pp. 63, 67, 75); only in Wittenweiler (a Swiss version, author otherwise unknown, date wholly uncertain) and in Hanz Folz (late 15th or early 16th century) is the woman's arse presented (*ibid.*, pp. 43, 49).

78. *Harley Lyrics*, p. 62 (23); the MS. is dated ca. 1314–25 (see p. 3).

79. Figure 88: Cambridge, Fitzwilliam Mus. MS. 22, p. 181, from a French *Légende dorée* of 1480, illustrating the Ten Commandments; on p. 182, the devil stands like an exultant stage manager before the bed in which the naked lovers embrace. Absolon notes this fact about the carpenter's window earlier in the tale as well (1.3677), reminding himself that it "stant ful lowe upon his boures wal." Bennett, *Chaucer at Oxford and at Cambridge*, in his sketched reconstruction of the carpenter's house puts the shot-window too high for kneeling (see p. 28, fig. 2b). Pantin's guess (also sketched) is, in that respect, to be preferred (Bennett, fig. 2a). The architecture and window are discussed on pp. 36–39.

80. Figure 89: New York, Pierpont Morgan MS. G.24, fol. 54, the *Voeux du paon*. Randall, *Images in Margins*, reproduces it as fig. 537; her fig. 576, from the same MS., shows a similar garment at issue (this time without buttocks) between a husband and wife quarreling over who gets to wear the pants.

81. "Coold" is grammatically ambiguous and can be read as either adjective or past participle; the meaning is essentially the same. For a similar pun on "queynt," cf. Troilus addressing the house of the absent (and false) Criseyde, "O thow lanterne of which queynt is the light" (*TC*, V, 543). But the tone there is not remotely comic: Troilus's idealization of erotic love ultimately destroys him. Beidler, "Art and Scatology," p. 94, has suggested that Chaucer's purpose is "to show this parish clerk worshipping, not the Virgin Mary whom he should have been worshipping, but an earthly woman."

82. Woolf, *English Mystery Plays*, offers a learned guide to the tradition in general, and on pp. 132–45, detailed commentary on the extant plays of Noah's Flood; see also the present author's *Play Called Corpus Christi*. Chambers, *Mediaeval Stage*, remains essential for its collection of local dramatic records, arranged by locality in Appendix W. It will eventually be replaced by the multi-volumed *Records of Early English Drama*, executive editor Alexandra F. Johnston; volumes devoted to York, Chester, Coventry, and Newcastle have already appeared. The quotation in my text (a defense of imagery in general) is from *Dives and Pauper*, I.i.82. For a defense of the plays, see I.i.292–96.

83. From "A Tretise of Miraclis Pleyinge," in Hudson, ed., *English Wycliffite Writings*, p. 100. Cf. the record of *tableaux vivants* staged in Paris in 1424, quoted by Woolf, *English Mystery Plays*, p. 97 (trans., p. 368, n. 76).

84. Hudson, ed., *English Wycliffite Writings*, p. 100.

85. See D. C. Allen, *Legend of Noah*, p. 72, on the prohibition against

intercourse, and Lewis, *Noah and the Flood*, for a comprehensive survey of the whole tradition in commentary and apocrypha. The English drama normally attributes the Flood to sin in general, to the Seven Deadly Sins as a group, or to man's disobedience, though in *The Chester Mystery Cycle*, p. 42 (6), God initially says man has become his foe "through fleshe-likinge," and in N-Town Sem, his wife, and Japhet at one point all identify lechery as the specific cause (*Ludus Coventriae*, p. 42 [218–35]). The French tradition is far more emphatic. In the *Mistère du Viel Testament*, I, 199 (5206–17), Noah deplores the forbidden coupling of the sons of Seth with the daughters of Cain, and on pp. 203–6, 213–15, we see three pairs in their courtship and love making; later we will see them (and some others) drown. For a highly sophisticated version of the Flood as caused by man's sexual sin, see the northern English poem *Cleanness*, late 14th century, pp. 18–26 (249–556). Huppé, *A Reading of the Canterbury Tales*, p. 80, remarks interestingly on Nicholas's preference for elaborate means to a simple end, as does Thro, "Chaucer's Creative Comedy," esp. pp. 98–99.

86. See 1.3514–20, and on the tradition, J. J. O'Connor, "Astrological Background."

87. There was no other "Pilate's voice" to be heard in medieval England. See Parker, "'Pilates Voys,'" and Ellinwood, "A Further Note on 'Pilates Voys.'" Miller, "The *Miller's Tale* as Complaint," p. 150, suggests that the Miller's affectation of this voice is part of his antichivalric antipathy to the Knight and to the ethos of his tale. Harder, "Chaucer's Use of the Mystery Plays," was the first (to my knowledge) to bring dramatic materials to bear upon a reading of the tale, with a sense of their true priority. He calls attention to a number of interesting details, including the fact that as a carpenter old John belongs to one of the two guilds (the shipwrights were the other) most often charged with producing the play of the Flood (p. 194). Rowland, "The Play of the *Miller's Tale*," has recently reasserted the primacy of drama traditions, but with reference to a wholly different pageant—the Annunciation to Mary. She develops her argument, based on typology, at greater length in "Chaucer's Blasphemous Churl."

88. Figure 90: Cambridge, St. John's Coll. MS. 231, fol. 8. Figure 91: London, Brit. Lib. MS. Add. 28162, fol. 7v, a MS. of the *Somme le roi*, probably from Lorraine. A parallel miniature illuminated in Paris ca. 1300 by Honoré can be seen in Cambridge, Fitzwilliam Mus. MS. 192 (a single leaf): it is reproduced by Tuve, *Allegorical Imagery*, p. 95 (fig. 18). Brussels, Bibl. Royale MS. 11041, fol. 81v (the same text, dated 1415) uses arched windows to display the full company; for another version of the same, see Milan, Bibl. Ambrosiana MS. H.106 Sup. (S.P. 2), fol. 51 (early 14th century). For other miniatures that include a docile Mrs. Noah, see London, Brit. Lib. MS. Royal 17 E.vii, Part I, fol. 11v (French, from a *Bible historiale* dated 1357), and MS. Royal 14 B.ix, a roll chronicle of the genealogy of Christ (early 14th century), along with those reproduced by Sandler, *Peterborough Psalter*, p. 24; Meiss, *Boucicaut Master*, fig. 459, and *The Limbourgs*, II, figs. 287–88; and Klingender, *Animals in Art and Thought*, fig. 137 (a 12th-century miniature of great beauty, highly schematic in design, showing the animals two by two in separate compartments, with the family of Noah in full dignity above). See also figure 108 of the present volume. On the great variety of

architectural structures used to depict the ark, and the authorities that justify them, see D. C. Allen, *Legend of Noah*, pp. 155–73.

89. See Oxford, MS. Bodley 270b, fol. 9v, or its facsimile, *La Bible moralisée*, I, pl. 9. The page contains two Flood pictures of great beauty.

90. London, Brit. Lib. MS. Egerton 1894, fol. 2v; on fol. 3 she assists Noah in loading the ark. See the facsimile ed., *Illustrations of the Book of Genesis*; the MS. has not been closely dated (M. R. James thought it 14th century but "not early").

91. See the immensely learned article by Mill, "Noah's Wife Again," and another by Utley, "The One Hundred and Three Names of Noah's Wife." Concerning the Swedish paintings, see the references in Mill, pp. 622–23, of which Lindblom, *La Peinture gothique*, pp. 210–14, is the most readily available. See his pl. 42 (6) for a painting from Edshult (the devil rides on Mrs. Noah's shoulder) and fig. 55 for one from Villberga (the devil stands behind her on the ladder leading into the ark). Both Lindblom (p. 212) and Mill (p. 626) think the examples from the visual arts are more likely to reflect drama tradition than vice versa.

92. Figures 92–95: London, Brit. Lib. MS. Royal 2 B.vii, fols. 5v, 6, 6v, 7. On this East Anglian MS., see Rickert, *Painting in Britain*, pp. 142–43. Warner, in his facsimile ed., *Queen Mary's Psalter*, transcribes the Anglo-Norman text below each picture, and provides on pp. 56–57 the translation I quote (with some modifications) above.

93. The play survives only in an 18th-century copy that both modernized and corrupted its original. I quote the text reconstructed by Davis, ed., *Non-Cycle Plays and Fragments*, pp. 29–31 (136–39, 184–85, 186–89); he also prints the version published in 1736. See pp. xl–xlvii for a history of the text, whose original he thinks dated from the mid-15th century or earlier. The oldest guild records of drama in Newcastle date from 1427.

94. Garvin, "A Note on Noah's Wife," seconding a suggestion first made by Sir Israel Gollancz, argues that an English drawing from Oxford, Bodley MS. Junius 11, fol. 66 (ca. 1000), illustrating an Anglo-Saxon poem on Genesis, represents the reluctant wife: one of Noah's sons, standing on the ladder to the ark, gestures toward a woman who stands at its foot; her hand is raised in return. But we know so little how to read expressive gesture in visual art of this period that no confident interpretation is possible. (Cf. the gesture of the son who stands before Noah at the other end of the ship.) Unless we declare the meaning of her gesture to be hesitancy or refusal, however, we lose all reason for identifying her as Mrs. Noah; she may equally well be one of the daughters-in-law, and the son's gesture indicative merely of concern. The picture is well known; there is a good reproduction in M. Rickert, *Painting in Britain*, pl. 44.

95. Figure 96: New York, Pierpont Morgan MS. M.302, fol. 1v (detail). Sandler, *Peterborough Psalter*, has published the opening miniatures of the MS.: for this folio, see p. 40, and for the date, pp. 116–17; see also pp. 39–47, 147–50. She does not comment on the presence of the devil in this scene. The picture conflates two separate events, for the devil is simultaneously shown leaving the ark, through a hole in its bottom. The full sequence of pictures offers a possible clue as to why this motif was chosen. Fol. 1 shows in four compartments (a) the Creation, (b) the Creation of Eve, (c) the Fall

of Man, and (d) the Expulsion from Eden; fol. 1v shows (a) the Flood, (b) Joachim and the Lord, (c) the Marriage of Joachim and Anna, and (d) the Birth of the Virgin; fol. 2 depicts (a) the Annunciation, (b) the Nativity, (c) the Adoration of the Magi, (d) the Presentation in the Temple. The sequence leaps from the Flood to the history of the Virgin and Christ, and just as Christ is typologically related to Adam, so the presence of the devil relates Mrs. Noah typologically to Eve, whose significance Mary reverses.

96. The windows have been reproduced by Anderson, *Drama and Imagery*, pls. 14a, 14b. That in Great Malvern Priory (late 15th century) shows Noah and his wife at the foot of the ladder to the ark, and he is stroking or pulling at his beard. Anderson, p. 108, writes "there is no mistaking the way in which Noah fingers his beard with rueful embarrassment and his wife's stiffly raised hand is poised like a chopper, ready to cut off any further argument." This description may be correct, but the meaning of the gestures is not really clear, and the presence of a daughter-in-law behind Mrs. Noah suggests that the glass may be a perfectly decorous rendering of the ark-loading scene. The window's text reads simply "Ingressus est noe & filii & uxor eius," only slightly altered from Genesis 7:7, which seems another reason for doubting unusual content in the picture. On Malvern Priory's full Noah sequence—there were once eleven scenes—see Rushforth, *Medieval Christian Imagery*, pp. 16, 159–65, and figs. 68–73. The York Minster panel is from the great East Window, which John Thornton, a glazier of Coventry, contracted to complete during the years 1405–8 (on his work, see M. Rickert, *Painting in Britain*, p. 188). Coventry had an important cycle drama, as did York. This window too is difficult to interpret: either of its two women might be Mrs. Noah, and all the persons shown are dignified and sober (Noah indeed is shown praying). In no text known to me does Mrs. Noah continue to be troublesome *after* boarding the ark, which constitutes another reason for doubting Anderson's belief that we are here shown "one of the sons apparently still reasoning with his mother" (*Drama and Imagery*, p. 108). On this window see also Davidson and O'Connor, *York Art*, p. 25; they offer a better reproduction, p. 26 (fig. 7). In my judgment, neither window illustrates Noah's troubles with his wife. Anderson suggests (p. 107) that a roof boss in the nave of Norwich Cathedral may also illustrate those troubles; I have not seen it, nor, so far as I know, has it ever been published, though Cave, *Roof Bosses*, figs. 149, 150, includes two others from that Flood sequence.

97. Figure 97: Misericord seat, from the Church of St. Mary, Fairford (Gloucestershire); see Remnant, *A Catalogue of Misericords*, pl. 14 (d), and p. 49 (no. 14). A woman is beating the man with some kind of kitchen implement, while holding him by the hair. See Remnant's index, p. 211, under "Domestic scenes: brawls," for a list of further examples. Anderson, *History and Imagery*, pl. 90, reproduces a spirited example (1520) from Bristol Cathedral (described by Remnant, p. 47, no. 11), and in her *Misericords*, pl. 43, yet another, from Henry VII's Chapel at Westminster Abbey. Hussey, *Chaucer's World*, fig. 76, publishes a version from Carlisle Cathedral. For illuminations of this subject, see Randall, *Images in Margins*, index entries under "Man beaten by woman," p. 157, and figs. 394, 576 (cf. figs. 708–10).

98. Bennett, *Chaucer at Oxford and at Cambridge*, p. 49.

99. Chambers, *Mediaeval Stage*, II, 379–82, prints the London records. These cycles at Skinners Well (also called Clerkenwell) were produced by the parish clerks of London—clerks in minor orders, like Absolon in our tale.

100. On the architecture of the ark, see D. C. Allen, *Legend of Noah*, pp. 71–72; the Anglo-Saxon drawing discussed in n. 94 above offers a fine early example of the three-tiered ark. For a picture of a dough tray being put to its proper use, see Baltimore, Walters Gallery MS. W.88, fol. 15, from a calendar; on the page opposite, a man and woman are shown baking bread. Both pages are reproduced by E. Rickert, ed., *Chaucer's World*, p. 26.

101. See *Cursor Mundi*, I, 106 (Cotton MS. ll. 1701–6); *The Chester Mystery Cycle*, p. 42 (5–8); *Mistère du Viel Testament*, I, 197–98 (5155–60).

102. "And thoughte, 'Allas, now comth Nowelis flood!'" (1.3818); "He was agast so of Nowelis flood" (1.3834). I assume Chaucer intends this as comic mispronunciation, the error of a "lewede" carpenter. But note the form of Noah's name in figure 91, from the French *Somme le roi*: *Larche Noel qui senefie pes*. So too the equivalent picture in Cambridge, Fitzwilliam Mus. MS. 368, though not in Brussels, Bibl. Royale MS. 11041, fol. 81v, where it is spelled *Noe*. (In the *Mistère du Viel Testament*, his name is likewise *Noé*.)

103. I refer to the version in Valentin Schumann's *Nachtbüchlein*; the husbands in Hans Sachs's version (written in 1537) and in that by Caspar Cropacius (late 16th century) are similarly selfish. All three may be read in Benson and Andersson, eds., *Literary Context of Chaucer's Fabliaux*, pp. 64–67, 60–63, 72–77. Bloomfield, "The Miller's Tale," p. 206, also urges a kinder view of this particular *senex amans* than has been common in recent criticism.

104. *York Plays*, p. 41 (41–44), and for the phrase quoted in the next sentence, p. 46 (40).

105. *Ibid.*, p. 48 (89–92). For my views on Mrs. Noah's refusal to board the ark in the Chester and Wakefield plays, see Kolve, *Play Called Corpus Christi*, pp. 145–51.

106. The complete cycle can be read only in *The Towneley Plays*, ed. England and Pollard, but plays attributed to the Wakefield Master (including the *Processus Noe cum filiis*) have been more recently edited by Cawley, *The Wakefield Pageants in the Towneley Cycle*, whose text I cite here. See pp. 14–16 (1–72).

107. *Ludus Coventriae*, pp. 35–38 (1–91). Gibson, "Bury St. Edmunds, Lydgate, and the *N-Town Cycle*," has convincingly argued the new provenance.

108. *Ludus Coventriae*, p. 39 (138–39). Cf. Mrs. Noah, p. 36 (30): "Ffor synfull levyng oure sowle xal spyll." On why Noah was chosen to be saved, Genesis 6:8–9 tells us only that "Noe found grace before the Lord. . . . Noe was a just and perfect man in his generations; he walked with God." Petrus Comestor explained the meaning of this in his *Historia scholastica*: "Noah was in truth perfect in his generations, which is not to say of that perfection found in man's true homeland [heaven], but perfect within the limits of his generations, that is, earthly in his perfection." And Rabanus Maurus, in his important commentary on Genesis, urged a similar interpretation: "Certain

persons are here called perfect—not perfect in the way the saints are to become perfect in that immortal state in which they will be made equal with the angels of God, but perfect in the way men can be perfect in this earthly pilgrimage." It is a modest specification, and proved congenial to the dramatists. They explored its human probabilities in a number of ways, one of which was to imagine fully Noah's relationship with his wife. I have discussed these matters at some length in *Play Called Corpus Christi*, pp. 145–51, 253–57, 262–64; the Comestor and Maurus quotations will be found in the original Latin on pp. 246–47.

109. *The Chester Mystery Cycle*, pp. 50–53; I quote from p. 50 (203–4).

110. *York Plays*, p. 53 (269–70). Cf. p. 49 (143–44): "My commodrys and my cosynes bathe, / þam wolde I wente with vs in feere"; and p. 50 (151–52): "My frendis þat I fra yoode / Are ouere flowen with floode." After the speech quoted in my text, Noah firmly directs his wife's attention to the present moment and its obligations; but even in that speech, the pronoun he chooses, "we," testifies to fellowship with those now drowned (p. 53 [271–74]): "Dame, all ar drowned, late be thy dyne, / And sone þei boughte þer synnes sore. / Gud lewyn latte vs be-gynne / So þat we greue oure god nomore."

111. Woolf, *English Mystery Plays*, pp. 139–40.

112. In the Chester cycle, Noah tells God he has "tarryed" 120 winters making the ship for that explicit reason—the exact period of time God announced at the beginning that He would wait to see if sinful man "will blynne"; *The Chester Mystery Cycle*, pp. 42 (8) and 48 (149–52). God's will and Noah's are as one. In N-Town, Noah says God has waited 100 years for man to amend: see *Ludus Coventriae*, pp. 41–42 (206–11). In the *Mistère du Viel Testament*, Noah pleads for all: see I, 199 (5186–97). The *Cornish Ordinalia*, p. 27, offers an even bolder version of Noah's fellow feeling for those who will be drowned. In *Cursor Mundi*, when Noah preaches repentance to the people, they scoff at him and scorn the ark: "Qui es þis carl sua ferd?" (p. 108, Cotton MS., l. 1736). But his charity survives their scorn, and he prays for their souls as they lie beneath the waters (p. 112, Cotton MS., ll. 1817–26):

> He fined noþier night ne day
> For þat caitiue folk to prai,
> For mans kind, sua sais þe bok
> · · ·
> He praid to godd for þam alsua
> O þair saulus na vegeance ta;
> · · ·
> Sin þai ware ded sua reufulli,
> þe saulus he wald haf of merce.

113. *Mistère du Viel Testament*, I, 228 (s.d.): "Icy surmonteront les eaues tout le lieu, la ou l'en joue le mistère, et y pourra avoir plusieurs hommes et femmes qui feront semblant d'eulx noyer, qui ne parleront point." The particular deaths begin on p. 226.

114. Boccaccio, *Decameron*, III.4, trans. McWilliam, p. 257.

115. *Ibid.*, p. 262.

116. Figure 98: Paris, Bibl. de l'Arsenal MS. 5070, fol. 108v. Boccaccio, *Decameron*, ed. Branca, reproduces it in color, I, 251, along with parallel illuminations on p. 253 (an upper and lower room, with Friar Puccio in a simple posture of prayer), and on p. 255 (adjoining rooms, but a cruciform posture); an early woodcut showing the latter configuration is reproduced on the same page.

117. Boccaccio, *Decameron*, trans. McWilliam, p. 262.

118. *Ludus Coventriae*, p. 41 (s.d. and 199). Noah and his family exit to build the ark on p. 39 (s.d. after 141); the death of Cain follows; the stage direction quoted above brings Noah and family back into the playing space, where their speeches presuppose the waters already covering the earth (hence my translation of *cum* as "in"). Noah's lines just after the stage direction (198–99) suggest it may have been a song of sorrow and mourning.

119. *The Chester Mystery Cycle*, p. 53 (s.d. after 252 and 260). The Latin stage direction is from London, Brit. Lib. MS. Harley 2124, and is quoted from the textual variants at the bottom of the page.

120. Robertson, *Preface to Chaucer*, pp. 127–30, 194 (and fig. 64), 243 (on the Miller and his bagpipes). On snoring as carnal music, see p. 250, below.

121. J. B. Allen, *Friar as Critic*, pp. 129–30, writes sensibly about Chaucer's use of religious parody, judging it a technique of looking at "the human" without seeking to serve devotional or didactic ends.

122. This reading is suggested by Robertson, *Preface to Chaucer*, pp. 382–86, and has been worked out in detail by two of his students, Bolton, "The 'Miller's Tale,'" and Paul Olson, "Poetic Justice." Hieatt, in her edition of *The Miller's Tale*, pp. 18–19, offers some trenchant criticism of their view.

123. In *The Knight's Tale* (1.1307–23: Palamon's lament), men cannot bear to think that they may be no more than just another animal species in God's eyes:

> "What is mankynde moore unto you holde
> Than is the sheep that rouketh in the folde?
> For slayn is man right as another beest,
> And dwelleth eek in prison and arreest, . . .
> And yet encresseth this al my penaunce,
> That man is bounden to his observaunce,
> For Goddes sake, to letten of his wille,
> Ther as a beest may al his lust fulfille.
> And whan a beest is deed he hath no peyne;
> But man after his deeth moot wepe and pleyne,
> Though in this world he have care and wo.
> Withouten doute it may stonden so.
> The answere of this lete I to dyvynys.

The Miller demonstrates, within the limits of his tale, another response to this perplexity: if we are no more than beasts, what delights become available to us! Cf. Lydgate, "The Floure of Curtesye," ll. 50–70, on the freedom allowed birds (*Minor Poems*, II, 412); he is influenced by both *The Parliament of Fowls* and *The Knight's Tale* passage quoted above. As Meyer Schapiro has written concerning drolleries in medieval manuscripts, "The alternatives are not, as is often supposed, religious meaning or no meaning, but religious or secular meanings, both laden with affect. Like metaphor in poetry, such marginal decoration is also a means of dwelling in an enjoyed feeling or desire." (*Late Antique, Early Christian and Mediaeval Art*, pp. 179–81.) This sort of art, in his opinion, offers "a process of desublimation through which the distance between the natural and the civilized is abolished. . . . [and as a result] we are not limited to the alternatives: symbolic or decorative. There are other kinds of meaning (as in metaphor, parody, and humor) which need not be symbolic in the coded manner of mediaeval religious symbolism." (*Ibid.*, p. 198.)

124. Reiss, "Chaucer's Parodies of Love," p. 40. Beichner, too, in "Characterization in *The Miller's Tale*," underestimates the matter when he suggests (p. 124) that the natural similes used to describe Alisoun serve simply to link her with country values and manners, and thus make more plausible her invention of the arse trick. I am by no means the first to think these similes do important work. Cf. Muscatine, *Chaucer and the French Tradition*, p. 224 (the fabliau, he argues, is here made virtually philosophical, illustrating not only "the binding, practical sequentiality of all events," but also "the sovereignty of animal nature"). Ruggiers, *Art of the Canterbury Tales*, pp. 59–60, briefly expresses a similar sense of their function, as does Corsa, *Chaucer*, p. 114 (in a passage I have already cited), along with Rowland, *Blind Beasts*, p. 167, and Dean, "Imagery in the *Knight's Tale* and the *Miller's Tale*," p. 162.

125. In *The Chester Mystery Cycle*, the entry of the animals into the ark is elaborately staged as a great roll call of the creatures, brought on in the form of "bordes" on which "all the beastes and fowles hereafter reahersed muste bee paynted," with which the ark is then "borded rownde aboute." Each member of Noah's family takes a turn at cataloguing the creatures as they arrive, with Sem speaking first: "Syr, here are lions, leopardes in; / horses, mares, oxen, and swynne, / geates, calves, sheepe, and kyne / here sytten thou may see." In the course of these speeches (which occupy 32 lines) nearly 50 different creatures are named and pictures of them brought forward to be hung upon the ark's superstructure. (See pp. 48–50, ll. 161–92.) This would have created a stage property similar to many manuscript illuminations portraying an ark with multiple chambers or windowlike compartments that display a great number of animals, with Noah and his wife at the center. (Cf. our figures 90 and 91.) For the animals' entry as depicted in the visual arts, see Meiss, *Patronage*, II, figs. 393, 394, and *The Visconti Hours*, fol. LF 72. Rushforth, *Medieval Christian Imagery*, fig. 71, reproduces the scene from the Flood window in Great Malvern Priory (described, pp. 161–62); the portico mosaics (13th century) of St. Mark's Cathedral in Venice include three scenes of the loading, one with animals, two with birds (Klingender, *Animals in Art and Thought*, fig. 159, reproduces one of the latter). *The Cornish Ordinalia*, pp. 29–30, has Noah's sons lead in the "horses, cattle, pigs, and sheep," whereas the birds are described as flying in on their own (p. 30); after the waters recede, Noah and his family offer a tithe of all the birds and beasts as a sacrifice, including a cow, a dove, a pheasant, a goose, a mallard, a partridge, two larks, and a capon (pp. 33–34).

CHAPTER V

1. Cannon, "Chaucer's Pilgrims as Artists." Pratt and Young, "Literary Framework," remains a useful survey of the prior tradition.

2. See especially Hoffman, "Chaucer's Prologue to Pilgrimage," Baldwin, *Unity of The Canterbury Tales*, and Zacher, *Curiosity and Pilgrimage*, Chap. 5.

3. Figure 99: San Marino, Huntington Lib. MS. 26.C.9, fol. 34v. Cf. Hussey's description of this portrait (*Chaucer's World*, p. 131): "A rough lout with a heavy sword and no evidence of grace anywhere in him."

4. For a brilliant and provocative rethinking of these issues, see Leicester, "Art of Impersonation," and his reply to Robert Burlin's criticism of some of his assumptions. Working from certain deconstructionist axioms—i.e., "in writing, voice is first of all a function not of persons but of language," and "we can assign an 'I' to any statement" since "language is positional"— Leicester would urge us to "see the pilgrims as the products rather than as the producers of their tales," and the poet as "the creation rather than the creator of his poem" (pp. 217–18). Leicester's essay necessarily implies that all tales are equally voiced, since they share exactly the same sort of "textuality." But that is to blur a distinction between tales that I suspect most readers of Chaucer have always felt necessary. I agree with Leicester that all voices are ultimately Chaucer's own, and in that sense explore a variety of value systems and points of view, each of which can be distinguished from any other. But I cannot agree that *The Knight's Tale* generates a knight-narrator in the same way and to the same degree as *The Wife of Bath's Prologue and Tale* (or *The Reeve's Tale*) generate their particular narrators. There are differences in kind (the presence of a personal prologue in the latter two examples), as well as degree. The question is finally whether Chaucer took as his primary goal in the *Tales* the creation of "speakers"—in all cases, and everywhere to equal effect. I do not think he did. No small part of the interest of *The Canterbury Tales* for its own time as well as for our own derives from the fact that it has *themes*: it is about subjects, and actions, and ideas, and the world at large. It is never *simply* about "voices"—the idiosyncrasies of interiority—even in those places where "voice" does invite our close attention. Indeed, part of the work's real "textuality"—a word Leicester uses chiefly in its fashionable modern sense—is its nature as a "collection": as a *compilatio*, a manuscript miscellany, a portable library, a pilgrimage chronicle (see Doyle and Parkes's subtle survey of the various sorts of *ordinatio* used to make formal sense of the work in its earliest manuscripts, "The Production of Copies of the *Canterbury Tales*," esp. pp. 190–94).

5. Figure 100: London, Brit. Lib. MS. Royal 2 B.vii, fol. 78v. Hussey, *Chaucer's World*, fig. 99, has associated this picture with Chaucer's Reeve before me. For recent studies of the Reeve's social and economic background, see Mann, *Chaucer and Medieval Estates Satire*, pp. 163–67, and Robertson, "Some Disputed Chaucerian Terminology," pp. 573–76.

6. Figure 101: Cambridge, Univ. Lib. MS. Gg.iv.27, fol. 186. Figure 102: San Marino, Huntington Lib. MS. 26.C.9, fol. 42. Curry, *Chaucer and the Mediaeval Sciences*, Chap. 4, discusses the portraits of the Reeve and the Mil-

ler in terms of physiognomy and humoral psychology; he quotes (p. 72) from the *Secreta secretorum* in commenting on the Reeve as a type of the choleric man: "The colerike [man] by kynde he sholde be lene of body; his body is light and drye, and he shal be sumwhat rogh; and lyght to wrethe and lyght to peyse; of sharpe witt, wyse and of good memorie, a greete entremyttere; he louyth hasty wengeaunce; desyrous of company of women moore than hym nedyth." Cf. two poems on the complexions of men in Robbins, ed., *Secular Lyrics*, nos. 76, 77.

7. Paul Olson, "The *Reeve's Tale*," offers an important exception: he writes closely about the strategies of persuasion that shape the Reeve's ser-moning. I owe more to former students, especially to Steven Marx and Zeese Papanikolas, than to any published writing on this prologue.

8. In Luke 7:32, Christ describes the resentment of the Pharisees and other worldly men toward him and his followers as being like that of chil-dren who say (in the Wycliffite translation) "we han sungun to you with pipis, and ye han not daunsid" (Skeat's annotation). *The Parson's Tale* also uses imagery of "gleedes" and "coles" in discussing the sin of anger (*Ira*), one of the emotions that govern the Reeve's performance: "Ne at this tale I saugh no man hym greve, / But it were oonly Osewold the Reve. / By cause he was of carpenteris craft, / A litel ire is in his herte ylaft; / He gan to grucche, and blamed it a lite." (I.3859.) Here is the beginning of the Parson's recapitulation of the image: "For certes, right so as fir is moore mighty to destroyen erthely thynges than any oother element, right so Irc is myghty to destroyen alle spiritueel thynges. / Looke how that fir of smale gleedes, that been almost dede under asshen, wollen quike agayn when they been touched with brymstoon; right so Ire wol everemo quyken agayn, whan it is touched by the pride that is covered in mannes herte" (x.547). "In this forseyde develes fourneys ther forgen three shrewes," i.e., Pride, Envy, and Contumely (x.554).

9. Figure 103: from a health manual by Aldebrandius of Sienna, London, Brit. Lib. MS. Sloane 2435, fol. 44v; it is reproduced in color by Evans, ed., *Flowering of the Middle Ages*, p. 54 (fig. 43). Cf. a fine late-15th-century cel-larer misericord from the Church of St. Lawrence in Ludlow, described by Remnant, *A Catalogue of Misericords*, p. 135 (no. 11), and reproduced by Brewer, *Chaucer and His World*, p. 27; see also the misericord from Heming-ton, Northants, reproduced by Remnant as pl. 33d and described on p. 115 (no. 4). Milan, Bibl. Ambrosiana MS. E 24 inf., fol. 141 (a copy of Pliny's *Naturalis historia* dated 1389), is ornamented with a cellarer initial.

10. Bodel, *Jeu de Saint Nicholas*, p. 52 (1050–51); ll. 1038–39 make it clear the cask is a literal stage property. See Axton and Stevens, trans., *Medi-eval French Plays*, for a full translation, from which I quote above; the tavern action occupies pp. 114–21. The drinking leads to dicing and brawling, but none of them thinks the worse of it for that. The play was written ca. 1199–1202.

11. Figure 104: Paris, Bibl. Natl. MS. fr. 9221, fol. 16 (a MS. of Machaut's poetry made for the Duc de Berry in the late 14th century). Cf. the minia-ture on fol. 107, where a similar group sings in a flowering garden. The text of the *rondeau* can be found in Guillaume de Machaut, *La Louange des dames*,

p. 108 (no. 236); its full refrain reads "Gentils cuers, souveingne vous / Des maus que li miens senti, / Quant de vous se departi." Wilkins dates the MS. on pp. 10–12 (MS. "E").

12. Figure 105: London, Brit. Lib. MS. Egerton 3307, fol. 72v; the MS. also contains hymns, passions, and carols. The text of this drinking song appears first in the *Carmina Burana* MS. of the late 13th century; ed. Meyers, Hilka, and Schumann, I, pt. 3, no. 202. (Waddell, trans., *Mediaeval Latin Lyrics*, pp. 196–99, offers a facing-page translation/re-creation.) Cf. the lyric "In taberna quando sumus" from the same collection (no. 196). Remnant, *A Catalogue of Misericords*, pl. 22a and p. 48 (no. 4), reproduces a late-15th-century misericord from Fairford (Gloucestershire) that shows a man and woman seated, drinking from a cask between them; they hold hands to their heads, perhaps in laughter, perhaps as a sign the wine is doing its natural work. For another powerful tavern image, see London, Brit. Lib. MS. Add. 27695, fol. 14—a late-14th-century Italian treatise on the Seven Sins. It shows a tapster below passing drink to carousers above, one of whom is being sick in the corner. That part of the image at least was not intended to make drunkenness seem attractive. It is reproduced in color by Evans, ed., *Flowering of the Middle Ages*, p. 263 (fig. 55), and by Brewer, *Chaucer and His World*, opp. p. 16. See also *The Hours of Catherine of Cleves*, pl. 110, for a tapster and a merry drunk in the bottom margin.

13. It is possible that Chaucer took his cue for the Reeve's use of the image from a French fabliau that tells the Reeve's very story, for it has one of the students boast, when he has returned from the bed of the host's daughter, "I took her from the front and from the side; I tapped her tun [*aforé li ai son tonel*] and gave her the ring from the iron cooking pan!" See Jean Bodel, "De Gombert et des II clers," in Benson and Andersson, eds., *Literary Context of Chaucer's Fabliaux*, p. 96 (150–55); I have slightly altered their translation, p. 97. Chaucer may have taken a further cue from the two casks of Jupiter that Reason speaks of in *The Romance of the Rose*: "Jupiter, in every season, says Homer, has two full casks on the threshold of his house. There is no old man or boy, no lady or girl, old or young, ugly or beautiful, who may receive life in this world and not drink from these two casks. It is a tavern full of people, where Fortune, the hostess, draws absinthe and sweetened wine in cups, to make sops for everybody." (Ed. Lecoy, ll. 6783–94; trans. Dahlberg, p. 131.) The image recurs at l. 10597 (Dahlberg, p. 188). Chaucer also uses the tun image in relation to worldly pleasures in *The Parson's Tale* (X.859): "And for that many man weneth that he may nat synne, for no likerousnesse that he dooth with his wyf, certes, that opinion is fals. God woot, a man may sleen hymself with his owene knyf, and make hymselve dronken of his owene tonne." A bold and beautiful transformation of the image, to stand for the joys of heaven that can be earned by sobriety on earth, descends in the *Somme le roi* tradition (here, from *Book of Vices and Virtues*, p. 274): "Þei schulle see & come to þat gret tauerne where þat þe tunne is made al comune, þt is in þe lif wiþ-outen ende, where þe wyne of loue, of pees, and of ioie and solas schal be ȝeue so largeliche to euery wiȝt þat comeþ þider þat alle schul be fulfilled." Cf. Michel of Northgate, *Ayenbite of Inwyt*, p. 247.

14. Cicero, *De senectute*, pp. 13, 77, 79; the work was written ca. 44 B.C.

Chaucer translates a single passage ("And Tullius seith") in *The Tale of Melibee*, VII.1165, but a series of images suggests he may have had access to it as a whole: on p. 83 (*ed. cit.*) old age is likened to a fire going out, to a fruit falling after it has ripened, and to a voyage reaching its end. Chaucer has subtly altered each, if he had that text in mind. (Note that Cicero testifies to a belief in the afterlife as at least a possibility, p. 97.) Pratt, "Chaucer and the Hand That Fed Him," argues for Chaucer's knowledge of John of Wales's *Communiloquium*, which brings together many quotations concerning old age from both classical authors and the Church Fathers.

15. *The Book of Beasts*, pp. 224–25.

16. Bartholomaeus, *Properties*, pp. 292–93; he continues with a description of the wretchedness of age that is of comparable power, but places its emphasis almost entirely upon the physical condition of the body.

17. "*The Chess of Love*," pp. 763–84. Two brief passages (pp. 771, 773) are especially suggestive here: the old "are honorable above all, and should be honored above all" because they are "the ones who are most just, reasonable, and moderate, because they are naturally, unlike the young, not passionate" and "The right office, then, of the old . . . is to undertake virtue and to give good counsel to everyone, especially to the young and to their good friends. The young should also . . . believe their counsel . . . and there take an example of living well." Petrarch, in a famous letter, offers a personal account: "I admit that I am an old man. I read my years in my mirror, others read them on my brow. My familiar expression has changed; the bright look of my eyes is veiled, but I feel the clouding with no distress. My falling hair, my roughened skin, my snowy crown, testify that my winter has come. But I render my thanks to him who watches and guides us at dawning and at evening, from childhood to decrepitude. In this state I feel my mental powers undiminished, and I notice no dwindling in my bodily vigor, in my application to familiar studies, in my capacity for honest activities. For other activities I am incompetent, and thereat I rejoice. . . . I feel that I have triumphed over my body, that old enemy which waged many a cruel war on me. . . . Life never seemed so beautiful as it does now, when to many others it begins to be a burden. May God, who has brought me to this age, transport me from this vain mortal life to the true eternal life, as now I prize higher one day of this ripeness than do most young men prize a year of their bloom." (*Epistolae rerum senilium*, VIII/2; in *Letters from Petrarch*, pp. 254–55.)

18. For a convenient text of the antiphon, see Brittain, ed., *Penguin Book of Latin Verse*, p. 183; it was widely used in the medieval liturgy, though (according to Brittain) it now survives in the Dominican Breviary alone. For St. Augustine, see *The City of God*, XIII.10–11, pp. 419–21; and for "Toure of All Toures," *The Book of the Craft of Dying*, p. 128. *The Book of Vices and Virtues*, in its *ars moriendi* section, phrases the lesson with equal power: "For whan þou bygynnyst to lyue, þou bigynnist to dye . . . for þou seist þou hast fifty or sixty wynter; þat is not soþ, deþ haþ hem, for neuere wole he ȝelde þe aȝen" (p. 69). Cf. "*The Chess of Love*," p. 778; *The Dicts and Sayings of the Philosophers*, p. 274; and also Chaucer's own *Parliament of Fowls* (50–56), paraphrasing Cicero's *Dream of Scipio*.

19. Written ca. 1291–92; I have used an unpublished edition by Bour-

neuf, "The 'Testament' of Jean de Meun," p. 112 (1710–11) and p. 10 (165). In Jean's text, the four sins are all branches of Envy. Robinson, in his edition of Chaucer, has annotated these parallels. Many mss. of *The Romance of the Rose* conclude with the *Testament* (perhaps as its ultimate correction and completion), and it is therefore highly probable that Chaucer had access to the work. Coffman, "Old Age from Horace to Chaucer," offers a magisterial study of that entire subject; he pays special attention to the second elegy of Maximian (and its transmission) as a possible source for the coals-into-embers passage. Robinson notes a parallel in Alain de Lille's *Parabolae* as well.

20. Gower, *Confessio amantis, Complete Works*, III, 448–78 (VIII, 2301–3172). I quote ll. 2416, 2824–33, 3162–72. My other main subject in this chapter is touched upon in l. 2407, when Venus tells Gower cruelly that love and gray hair go ill together, and he'll not be mistaken for a young colt ("olde grisel is no fole").

21. Figure 106: Brussels, Bibl. Royale ms. 10176–78, fol. 108v. For the text, see Lydgate, *Pilgrimage*, pp. 646–52. Guillaume de Deguileville's first version, *Pilgrimage of the Lyf of the Manhode*, in its closing pages is also relevant; the speech comparing man to green grass that has become hay and must be cut with scythe (p. 206) contrasts interestingly with the Reeve's meditation on ripeness and rottenness. Hugh of St. Victor, *De arca Noe morali* (III.14), also writes on "How the fruit of divine wisdom is harvested by death" (*Selected Spiritual Writings*, p. 119). The Reeve's prologue incorporates a version of the Signs of Old Age, which is a variant upon a far more common tradition, the Signs of Death, whose origin has been traced to a medical list, the *Prognosticon* of Hippocrates. Woolf, *English Religious Lyric*, Chap. 3, surveys the tradition and notes its double potential: "The figure of the old man could be seen as a moral warning to all of the closeness of death; but it could also serve as a type for the satirical treatment of the characteristic, or supposedly characteristic, vices of old age" (p. 104). See also her Chap. 9. Eustache Deschamps wrote a fine *ballade* on the subject, with the refrain "Ce sont les signes de la mort"; it may conveniently be read (with prose translation) in Woledge, ed., *Penguin Book of French Verse*, I, pp. 245–47. For an English example from the 15th century that intercalates a Latin moral line by line with the list of "signs," see that printed by Woolf, p. 82. In the central tradition, the Signs of Death were "thought of as a solemn and prophetic warning from which the Christian should appropriately take fright" (*ibid.*, p. 80).

22. Cf. two poems from the early 15th century in Furnivall, ed., *Hymns to the Virgin and Christ*: "The Mirror of the Periods of Man's Life," pp. 58–78, and "God Send Us Paciens in Oure Oolde Age," pp. 79–82. The former displays some remarkable parallels in language and imagery to *The Reeve's Prologue*, as well as a view of age and death as only parts of a whole. The portrait of "Elde" in *The Romaunt of the Rose* presents a generalized portrait of old age as one of the categories excluded from the game of love, but describes it fairly, without despair or a morbid emphasis on vice, and indeed urges compassion for the weakness and sufferings of the old. See *RR*, 349–412. In ll. 381–84, "The tyme, that may not sojourne, / But goth, and

may never retourne, / As watir that doun renneth ay, / But never drope retourne may" we have another possible source for the tun image.

23. Lothario dei Segni (Pope Innocent III), *On the Misery of the Human Condition*, p. 3. See the introduction, esp. pp. xviii, xxix, xliii, for remarks germane to the present discussion, and on p. 13 (I.x), Innocent's treatment of the discomforts of old age. Chaucer translated the work as "the Wreched Engendrynge of Mankynde, / As man may in pope Innocent yfynde" (*LGW*, [G] 414–15); the translation has not survived. Though Innocent never wrote the book "concerning man's dignity," he could not, as a Christian, discourse on man's misery without promising an equal treatment of that other truth.

24. The Monk never gets to the saint's life, for the Knight and Harry Bailly halt his recital of tragic tales early on. We should note that the *de casibus* tradition requires a fall from good fortune and high estate, but does not absolutely demand that the action conclude in misery. The Monk narrates Adam's fall, for instance, but that fall was elsewhere understood to be (because of Christ's ensuing sacrifice) "fortunate," a happy fall in a divine comedy. Nebuchadnezzar, too, after a period of terrible suffering, earns God's grace and is restored to his kingdom and his happiness (VII.2170–82).

25. The honesty of the local miller was a matter of real economic consequence for any medieval community, and the reputation of millers as a class was not high. Witness the two gilded thumbs in the Ellesmere MS. portrait of Chaucer's Miller (our figure 99), unfortunately not legible in black-and-white reproduction. Mill scenes are common in medieval manuscript art (mostly in borders): see, e.g., *The Luttrell Psalter*, fol. 158; *The Romance of Alexander*, fols. 49, 81; London, Brit. Lib. MS. Stowe 17, fol. 89v (among those reproduced by Randall, *Images in Margins*, figs. 696–99); Cambridge, Fitzwilliam Mus. MS. 165, fol. 48v (a water mill, reproduced by Hussey, *Chaucer's World*, fig. 96); and New York, Pierpont Morgan MS. M.705, fol. 38v.

26. "Deynous Symkyn," which is what he's called in the town, is itself a moral name. Friedman, "A Reading of Chaucer's *Reeve's Tale*," pp. 13–17, would relate the miller and his wife to the *processio vitiorum*, which is tonally plausible but structurally strained: two persons do not readily suggest an allegorical progress of seven sins. To think of them as a comic Satan and Superbia, as Friedman goes on to do, may come nearer to the mark, but I would stop short of that identification as well. The point is local evil in a small village, and its scale must be respected. Friedman's essay is distinguished; see especially his analysis of the peacock image, pp. 11–12, and the matter discussed in note 54 below.

27. Langland, *Piers Plowman*, B. XV, 94–95 (p. 539); the entire passage through l. 148 is relevant, including the long quotation in Latin from St. John Chrysostom that follows l. 117 (p. 541): "Just as all good springs from the Temple, so out of the Temple issues all that is evil. If the priesthood is sound, the whole Church will flourish; but if it is corrupt, the faith of all men will be rotten. Likewise if the priesthood is full of errors, the whole people turns to error. . . . and so when you see a people undisciplined and irreligious, you can be sure the priesthood is unsound." I quote from Lang-

land, *Piers the Ploughman*, trans. Goodridge, p. 182. Cf. also B. X, 272–96.

28. Figure 107: Oxford, MS. Bodley 764, fol. 46. Rowland, *Animals with Human Faces*, p. 107, explains this picture with some bestiary lore: "Horses are called *equi* in Latin because when they are teamed in four, as they are here, they are made equal, matched in shape and pace."

29. Figure 108: New York, Pierpont Morgan MS. M.638, fol. 2v (detail); it is reproduced in color in *Old Testament Miniatures*, p. 33, which dates the pictures ca. 1250. (The horse shown departing the ark in the bottom-left frame of that page—not reproduced here—is, in contrast, literal and representative merely.) The raven was understood as a figure of apostasy, guilty of returning to and feeding upon the past, the carnal world that had been destroyed. In my figure 95, from *Queen Mary's Psalter*, fol. 7, the raven also feeds on a horse's head, a fact duly noted by the accompanying text: "Le corbeu si ad troue la teste de vn Chiual ou il se arreste" (facsimile, ed. Warner, p. 57). *The Holkham Bible Picture Book*, fol. 8, employs the same motif, as does a *Bible moralisée* illuminated by Paul and Jean de Limbourg in 1402 (reproduced by Meiss, *The Limbourgs*, II, fig. 287); see also Oxford, Bodley MS. Canon. Liturg. 99, fol. 57 (French, ca. 1500). In the Carew-Poyntz Book of Hours (English, ca. 1350–60), now Cambridge, Fitzwilliam Mus. MS. 48, the raven feeds on an ass (fol. 18v); Psalm 31:9 may offer an explanation. Near the end of the Book of Apocalypse (19:17–21) an angel calls all the birds to a great feast, to eat the carrion of kings, tribunes, and horses. That text may also have influenced the treatment of the raven in these Flood illuminations, for the Flood was understood to prefigure the end of the world. Cambridge, Corpus Christi Coll. MS. 20, fol. 51v, early 14th century, gives horses prominence in the scene; cf. Cambridge, Magdalene Coll. Pepys MS. 1803, fol. 41 (English, mid-14th century).

30. Figure 109: Bocchi, *Symbolicae quaestiones*, 117 ("Semper libidini imperat prudentia"). Attributed to G. Bonasone. Bartsch, XV.165.294. On Bocchi's work, see Wind, *Pagan Mysteries in the Renaissance*, p. 71 (n. 68); he reproduces this engraving as fig. 41, and discusses it pp. 145–46 (and n. 15).

31. Figure 110: Munich, Staatsbibl. MS. Cod. lat. 10570, fol. 8v, a text of Ramon Lull's *Ars generalis*; for other examples see Cambridge, Fitzwilliam Mus. MS. 252, fol. 9v (Italian, 14th century), and those reproduced by Yates, "Art of Ramon Lull," pl. 18a, and Ong, *Ramus*, p. 78. Lull died ca. 1316. Evans, *Medieval Drawings*, pl. 70, publishes a 12th-century example from Paris, in which a regal Lady Dialectic holds an *arbor Porphyrii* in her hand; he describes the drawing on p. 32. For the Porphyrian texts of Boethius, see Migne, *PL* 64, cols. 1–158, or better, *Porphyrii Isagoge, translatio Boethii, Aristoteles Latinus*. Bk. I of Boethius's second edition of the commentaries on the *Isagoge* may be conveniently read in McKeon, ed. and trans., *Selections from Medieval Philosophers*, I, 70–99; the horse is named as representative animal on p. 89. See also "De Trinitate," in Boethius, *The Theological Tractates*, p. 6 (19–20).

32. The 17th-century summary is from the *Monitio logica: or, An Abstract and Translation of Burgersdicius His Logick* (London, 1697), quoted by Crane, "Houyhnhnms, Yahoos, and the History of Ideas," in *The Idea of the Humanities*, p. 277. Aristotle himself, in *Categories, and De interpretatione*, used

the horse as a representative animal, e.g., pp. 4, 5, 7; but sometimes an ox or other animal is used, as on pp. 3, 7.

33. I quote from Porphyry, *Isagoge*, trans. Warren, pp. 42, 47; on pp. 40, 48, 51, the horse is likewise used as a contrast to rational man. Warren's introduction includes a discussion of the text's importance, and essential bibliography. St. Augustine, *Confessions*, X.7, p. 213, pairs "the horse and the mule, senseless creatures" as categorically different from himself, a creature with a soul capable of loving God—the specific animals deriving (more than likely) from Psalm 31, but used with a logical rigor that suggests the influence of Porphyry as well. (The passage is an object lesson in how difficult it can be to determine a line of descent for any single use of the horse as image or sign.) Cf. St. Aelred of Rievaulx, *Mirror of Love*, p. 109, and *Vices and Virtues*, ed. Holthausen, p. 88.

34. Figure 111: New York, Pierpont Morgan MS. M.638, fol. 9; reproduced in color in *Old Testament Miniatures*, p. 59. Moses closes the parted waters with a staff (God looking down from above), as the forces of Pharaoh fall from their horses into the sea. On representations of Pride as a man falling from a horse, see, e.g., Katzenellenbogen, *Allegories of the Virtues and Vices*, pp. 76, 83, and fig. 72a. (The "Quo vadis?" conversion of St. Paul is sometimes represented in the same terms.) Rowland, "The Horse and Rider Figure," cites Philo Judaeus (p. 246) in her survey of the background; see also her *Animals with Human Faces*, pp. 103–12. For a general introduction, see Vogel, *Some Aspects of the Horse and Rider Analogy*.

35. I quote here two texts adduced by Robertson, *Preface to Chaucer*, p. 254. That from St. Gregory may be read in Migne, *PL* 76, col. 588; the other is from *In proverbia Salomonis* (Paris, 1515), fol. ix.

36. Figure 112: London, Wellcome Mus. MS. 49, fol. 68, a manuscript miscellany from Germany with more than three hundred illustrations, many of them moral diagrams (fols. 32, 62, 69 also use emblematic horses). It dates from ca. 1420. On this MS. see Saxl, "A Spiritual Encyclopaedia"; a sister MS. from Rome, Bibl. Casanatensis MS. 1404, fol. 29, includes the same picture. For a late-13th-century illustrated MS. of the *Anticlaudianus*, see Verona, Bibl. Cap. MS. 251, esp. fols. 15, 15v, 16, 16v. For Alain's text, see the edition by Bossuat, and the translation by Sheridan; the chariot and its horses are described at length in Bk. IV (Sheridan, pp. 120–26). Wetherbee, *Platonism and Poetry*, pp. 211–19, offers a brief critical reading of the poem.

37. Figure 113: Lilienfeld, Austria, Stiftsbibl. MS. 151, fol. 253. Twenty-four MSS. of this work are known; six of them are illustrated. Cambridge, Trinity Hall MS. 12 (*De la regale du monde*, ca. 1406), has splendid full-page horse and rider drawings; see fol. 109v (the sinful passions) and fol. 111 (the virtuous passions).

38. "For lyke as ane horse welle-taughte beryth hys mastere over many peryllys and saueth hym fro perysshyng, so the body welle-rewled bereth the soule ouer many peryllys off thys wrecched worlde. . . . [But] yeff he be wylde and off euylle condycions, he ys lyke to be hys masters confusyone and to cast hym in to the handes off hys enemyes, and therfore hit ys nedeffulle that he be brydelyde." In Horstmann, ed., *Yorkshire Writers*, II,

420–36; I quote from p. 421. Cf. Langland, *Piers Plowman*, B. XVII, 110, where the Good Samaritan rides "on my Capul þat highte *caro*—of man-kynde I took it." For other emblematic uses of the horse, see the many in-stances cited by Robertson, *Preface to Chaucer*, and Rowland, *Animals with Human Faces*, along with *The Book of Vices and Virtues*, p. 226 (15–18); "The Land of Cokaygne," in Bennett, Smithers and Davis, eds., *Early Middle En-glish Verse and Prose*, pp. 143–44 (160–70); Gower, *Confessio amantis*, IV, 1340–446; also Boccaccio, *Decameron*, VII.2. For the tradition among Chaucer's immediate heirs, see for example, Hoccleve, *Minor Poems*, pp. 27 (78), 177, 186–87 (236–38); Lydgate, *Minor Poems*, II, 414 (134–37); Dun-bar, *Poems*, p. 93 (353–57) and p. 122 (73–75, 79–80). Compare Villon's *Lais* (Legacy), in *Complete Works*, ed. Bonner, p. 14 (255): "Carmes chevau-chent noz voisines" ("Carmelite friars ride our neighbor ladies").

A parable and its associated pictures in *Le Mortifiement de vaine plaisance*, written by King René of Anjou some fifty years after Chaucer's death, can represent the full tradition with a characteristic late-medieval verisimilitude and grace. A rich and powerful seigneur promises a high reward to a wag-oner (*charretier*) if he will bring the seigneur's wife to the door of his distant manor, without overturning the wagon or straying too much along the way. The poor man is attracted by the offer, but perplexed too, for the well-fed horses are wild and restless, one of them distracted by every sound it hears, the other inclined to wander off toward anything that takes its fancy. A friend advises the wagoner to stop the ears of the first, blindfold the second, and cut the rations of both by two-thirds; by this means the wife will be safely conveyed to her husband. René then tells us that the seigneur is to be understood as God, the spouse as man's soul, and the road as the path of life. The horses are the senses of sight and hearing, which move the wagon of the will, and the wagoner, whose whip is holy doctrine, is none other than Reason itself. An attractive Christian humility informs the parable in its de-tails. Neither of these horses is magnificent, much less winged; Reason is a poor man, not notably quick of mind; and the journey spoken of is no stately progress of the soul, but a hard journey along a rough road with an unpredictable team. Yet in the end those horses and that driver can bear the soul to God. The poem was written in 1453–55, on the death of Isabella, the king's first wife. Eleven MSS. survive, most of them illuminated in a costly fashion: Cambridge, Fitzwilliam Mus. MS. 165, fol. 46 (late 15th century); New York, Pierpont Morgan MS. M.705, fol. 33 (ca. 1470); and Brussels, Bibl. Royale MS. 10308, fol. 43 (ca. 1458), all offer interesting versions of this scene. The latter is reproduced by Lyna in his edition of the work, pl. V; for the text of this parable, see pp. 27–32.

The moral play *Mankind* also uses the figure extensively; it survives in the drama tradition into Ben Jonson's *Bartholomew Fair*, IV.v.20–26, Shake-speare's *Winter's Tale*, I.ii.94–96, 276, 288, II.i.134–35 (see also his *Venus and Adonis*), and Tourneur's *The Revenger's Tragedy*, I.ii.131–43, II.ii.138— to name just three examples.

39. Figure 114: Rome, Vatican Lib. MS. pal. lat. 1066, fol. 232v, illustrat-ing a treatise on the Four Cardinal Virtues. For Prudence controlling the libido, cf. the motto of the Bocchi engraving (figure 109, and n. 30 above). The book of Prudence displays this text: *Memorare preterita / Intellige pre-*

sentia / Provide futura. Rome, Bibl. Casanatensis MS. 1404, fol. 34v, includes a nearly identical picture.

40. The cardinal virtue of Temperance is sometimes shown as a beautiful woman wearing a horse's bridle, with the bit in her mouth, the reins in her hands, and spurs on her feet. Tuve, *Allegorical Imagery*, figs. 16, 17, reproduces two examples, and discusses the tradition, pp. 71–77, building upon her earlier study, "Notes on the Virtues and Vices," which remains essential reading. I join Tuve in thinking the accompanying verses almost certainly later than the pictorial tradition, an after-the-fact attempt to explain them, sometimes unduly narrow or even off the point; she too thinks the bridle stands for control over all the appetites, not merely the tongue alone ("Notes," p. 284). For another such figure, see a French Book of Hours (ca. 1435), New York, Pierpont Morgan MS. M.359, fol. 117v, and for similar literary versions of the bridle image, see Chaucer's translation of Boethius, I, pr. 5 (25), and Usk, *Testament of Love*, p. 58 (43ff).

41. Figure 115: London, Victoria and Albert Museum. It has been reproduced by Robertson, *Preface to Chaucer*, fig. 63, though he describes it in a somewhat contradictory fashion: on p. 194, he suggests a reading such as the one I offer above, but on p. 394, the horses have become "recalcitrant" (I would describe them as "under control") and thereby grist for his ironic mill: they are said to illustrate a condition like that of Andreas's Walter, who cannot manage the reins of his passion. There is a virtually identical carving on a mirror back in the Muzeo Nationale in Florence. An ivory writing-tablet cover, Rhenish, mid-14th century, also from the Victoria and Albert Museum, shows two such lovers on horseback, with the lady holding her horse tightly by the reins and keeping the whip ready at his flank. Her lover, in contrast, has dropped his reins, and allows his horse to move at will. He carries a falcon on one hand, and strokes his lady under the chin with the other. I read the image as both complimentary and exemplary to well-born women: as long as at least one horse does not run free the idealized nature of this love will not be in danger. Cf. the fine initial reproduced by Brewer, *Chaucer and His World*, p. 82.

42. *TC*, I, 953; III, 429, 1635; IV, 1678; V, 90–92. Rowland, "The Horse and Rider Figure," pp. 252–53, has an interesting analysis. See also Chaucer's "Complaint of Mars" (41–42), "Anelida and Arcite" (183–87), and *The Wife of Bath's Prologue* (III.813–15). The name Bayard seems on occasion specifically to invite a symbolic reading; cf. *Cleanness*'s description of the Sodomites at the gates, stunned by the angels' spell (l. 886): "Þay blustered as blynde as Bayard watȝ euer." But sometimes, as in *Piers Plowman*, A. IV, 40, it is simply a name often given to horses. It signified "bay," and in literature was attached to a magic horse given by Charlemagne to Renaud or Rinaldo; thence it became a mock-heroic name for any horse, and was eventually associated with blindness, heedlessness, and recklessness (so the O.E.D.). To that list one must surely add lechery.

43. Bartholomaeus, *Properties*, p. 1188. Cf. Bernardus Silvestris, *Commentary on the Aeneid*, VI, 515–16: "The horse has this meaning because in this animal lechery flourishes especially" (trans. Schreiber and Maresca, p. 96). The whole commentary on the Trojan horse (pp. 95–97), identifying it first with the will, then (overwhelmingly) with lechery, is relevant to

this chapter. Virgil's *Georgics*, Bk. III, in treating the care and breeding of horses, frequently notes their vigor in mating season.

44. Langland, *Piers Plowman*, B. VII, 90–93 (p. 375). Compare St. Thomas Aquinas, *Summa theologiae*, 1.98.2: "Animals lack reason. So what makes man like the animals in copulation is the inability of reason to temper the pleasure of copulation and the heat of desire." (Blackfriars ed., vol. 13, p. 157.)

45. See Andreas Capellanus, *The Art of Courtly Love*, "Author's Preface," p. 27; and cf. *Pamphilus, De amore*, p. 131 (697–98).

46. Guillaume de Lorris and Jean de Meun, *Le Roman de la rose*, ed. Lecoy, II, 177 (ll. 14023–46) and III, 94 (ll. 19757–58), trans. Dahlberg, pp. 241, 326 (see also his note, p. 418).

47. Figure 116: Paris, Bibl. Natl. MS. fr. 25526, fol. 111v (14th century). The borders of this MS. are frequently obscene: on fol. 106, for instance, a nun leads a man by a string tied to his genitals; on fol. 111, they copulate standing, their gowns thrown back; in the present border they copulate lying down. The nun wears a brown habit with a black wimple; he is secular and golden-haired. There is another scene of copulation on fol. 132v, with a dog facing a rabbit on the opposite page (fol. 133)—further evidence, perhaps, that the horse before us is no unconsidered addition to the border. Fleming, "*Roman de la Rose*," p. viii, directed me to this manuscript.

48. As in these lines from the *Ars amatoria*: "But when delay is not safe, it is useful to drive with full power, / Useful to give your mount spirited prick of the spur" (II, 731–32; "Cum mora non tuta est, totis incumbere remis / Utile, et admisso subdere calcar equo"). I quote from Ovid, *Art of Love*, trans. Humphries, p. 152. The context is entirely sympathetic to sexual pleasure.

49. The translation is by Dronke, *Medieval Lyric*; see pp. 109–11. Cf. an English lyric that uses the refrain "Turn vpe hyr haltur & let hyr goo!" in Robbins, ed., *Secular Lyrics*, no. 181. Boccaccio, *Decameron*, IX.10, likewise puts the tradition to witty use: in summary, "Father Gianni is prevailed upon by Neighbour Pietro to cast a spell in order to turn his wife into a mare; but when he comes to fasten on the tail, Neighbour Pietro, by saying that he didn't want a tail, completely ruins the spell." (Trans. McWilliam, p. 726.) Although no one would accuse Boccaccio of having a moral purpose in this tale—it enters the collection under the rubric of "Dioneo's privilege"—its full comic resonance depends upon the existence of a moral tradition closely allied. Two 15th-century illustrations to the story, published in color in the *Decameron*, ed. Branca, III, 825, 828, use real mare's tails in the attempt (which is not what Father Gianni uses). Paris, Bibl. Natl. MS. fr. 239, fol. 264v, in contrast, depicts the action without benefit of metaphor.

50. Figure 117: from the Metropolitan Museum, New York (accession no. 17.190.173). Two panels not shown here depict aged men and women journeying to the Fountain of Youth. A similar casket showing Phyllis and Aristotle (Koechlin no. 1282) is preserved at the Victoria and Albert Museum, London, as is an ivory *gravoir* from the same period (accession no. 286–1867), topped with a sculpture of Phyllis firmly astride her philosopher-steed. Dalton, "Two Mediaeval Caskets," publishes an exam-

ple from the British Museum; see also Ross, "Allegory and Romance on a Mediaeval French Marriage Casket," and the encyclopedic work of Koechlin, *Les Ivoires gothiques français*, esp. figs. 1138 (a knife handle?), 1150 (a comb), 1285 (a casket). Randall, *Images in Margins*, figs. 554, 555, 557, reproduces examples from manuscript illumination; see also Meiss, *The Limbourgs*, II, fig. 10. For an exquisite 15th-century German engraving of the subject, see Hutchison, *Master of the Housebook*, p. 134 (no. 54), and her interesting discussion of its social and intellectual backgrounds, pp. 50–52. The Metropolitan Museum, New York (Robert Lehman Collection), has a superb bronze aquamanile cast in the form of Phyllis riding Aristotle, ca. 1400; it may be seen in Hoving, Husband, and Hayward, eds., *The Secular Spirit*, p. 61, or in Levin, ed., *Images of Love and Death*, pl. 18 (fig. 90), very fully described, pp. 122–23. Its provenance is probably south Netherlandish or east French. (An aquamanile is a pitcher used to hold water for washing hands, in this case most likely at the banquet table of a great lord.) For Henri's text, see *Le Lai d'Aristote*; the English version quoted here is from Hellman and O'Gorman, trans., *Fabliaux*, pp. 167–79; their afterwords, pp. 177–79 and p. 191, have valuable information. Gower, *Confessio amantis*, briefly rhymes the story: VIII, 2705–13. On the iconography, see Mâle, *Gothic Image*, pp. 334–35; van Marle, *Iconographie de l'art profane*, II, 491–95, and figs. 509–20; Smalley, *English Friars and Antiquity*, pp. 167–68; and most important, Storost, "Femme chevalchat Aristotte," with six plates.

51. Figure 118: Paris, Bibl. de l'Arsenal MS. 5070, fol. 337. Figure 119: Paris, Bibl. Natl. MS. fr. 239, fol. 256v. They illustrate the sixth tale of the Ninth Day. Both are reproduced in color in Boccaccio, *Decameron*, ed. Branca, III, 803, 807, along with several other representations of the same scene. A German analogue, "Irregang und Girregar," in Benson and Andersson, eds., *Literary Context of Chaucer's Fabliaux*, pp. 141–43, makes interesting use of the darkness; Joseph, "Chaucerian 'Game'—'Earnest,'" pp. 88–91, writes well about the function of the narrow space.

52. Chaucer's word "fnorteth" ("snores") is difficult: some manuscripts read "snorteth" and one reads "frontith" ("kicks"), but in all cases we are left seeing the miller "as an hors." Kraus, *Living Theatre of Medieval Art*, p. 174, cites the St. Bernard anecdote. For St. Jerome's commentary on the neighing of horses in Jeremiah, see Miller, "Venus, Adonis, and the Horses," p. 253 (n. 7), or Migne, *PL* 24, col. 715. See also Correale, "Chaucer's Parody of Compline."

53. Gower, *Confessio amantis*, VIII, 159–63 (*Complete Works*, III, 390).

54. I am not the first to make a connection between the two halves of the tale, though I first did so independently. Copland, "*The Reeve's Tale*," p. 23, briefly relates the clerks' love making and the horse's energies; he is followed by Ruggiers, *Art of the Canterbury Tales*, p. 76, and by Richardson, *Blameth Nat Me*, pp. 89–93, but none of these indicates that a learned tradition lies behind the verbal association. Robertson, *Preface to Chaucer*, pp. 253–55, introduces the tradition, but without reference to *The Reeve's Tale*, and Rowland, "Horse and Rider Figure," notices the line "he priketh harde and depe as he were mad" on p. 249, but makes no reference to the runaway horse. Rowland's chapter "The Horse" in *Blind Beasts* gathers together all

the necessary materials, but never decisively applies them to the present tale: she comes nearest on p. 126. Dent, "Chaucer and the Horse," and Fisher, "Chaucer's Horses," are exclusively concerned with literal horses—their type, breed, harness equipment, and function as signs of social status. Friedman, "A Reading of Chaucer's *Reeve's Tale*," alone (to my knowledge) brings learned material to bear upon a critical reading of the Bayard figure, borrowing some evidence from Robertson and Rowland, but making (as they do not) the essential connection between that learning and Chaucer's *Reeve's Tale*: see his pp. 9–11. Delasanta, "Horsemen of the *Canterbury Tales*," an essay of uncommon perception and good sense, offers learned commentary on horses as an index to pride and humility, esp. p. 33.

55. Benson and Andersson, eds., *Literary Context of Chaucer's Fabliaux*, pp. 79–201, provide the basic documents, and a four-page comparison, feature by feature, of the related versions. They conclude: "As the analogues show, every action in the plot of 'The Reeve's Tale' has its parallel in some earlier form of the story, and from a superficial viewpoint it therefore seems that Chaucer's plot is controlled by the tradition" (p. 86). But in fact the *runaway* horse is in none of the analogues.

56. Muscatine, *Chaucer and the French Tradition*, p. 66.

57. The Reeve says to the Miller "ful wel koude I thee quite / With bleryng of a proud milleres ye" (I.3864), just as the miller in his tale will say of the clerks, "But by my thrift, yet shal I blere hir ye" (I.4049).

58. The scholars possibly quote a point of law rather than a folk proverb in I.4180–82, but its form is colloquial, not learned, and their introduction of it ambiguous.

59. See especially Owst, *Literature and Pulpit in Medieval England*, pp. 323–26. The *Somme le roi* translations (Michel of Northgate, *Ayenbite of Inwyt*, p. 39; *Book of Vices and Virtues*, p. 33) promulgated the idea that reeves are typical of those who steal (the second branch of avarice), holding back the rents of their lords, overstating debts and expenses, and understating receipts and rents. Men of religion who acquire private property are there said to be of the same kind.

60. Michel of Northgate, *Ayenbite of Inwyt*, pp. 27–28; *Book of Vices and Virtues*, p. 23.

CHAPTER VI

1. With the notable exception of Hengwrt; due to the tentative nature of its compilation, its nonsequential production, and the accidental misplacement of several quires, its ordering of the tales carries no authority. See Chaucer, *Text of the Canterbury Tales*, ed. Manly and Rickert, I, 270–75, and Chaucer, *Canterbury Tales*, ed. Ruggiers, pp. xxii–xxxiii.

2. The Man of Law's declared intention to "speke in prose, and lat him [Chaucer] rymes make" (II.96) has long been thought to record an earlier stage in the writing of *The Canterbury Tales*, when Chaucer intended the Man of Law to tell the prose *Tale of Melibee* rather than the rhyme-royal tale of Custance (for the logic of this guess, see my n. 57 below). That assumption seems proper still, despite a recent essay by Martin Stevens, "The Royal Stanza," which uses the text of a 1486 royal entry ceremony in York to dem-

onstrate that "prose" could be used (by that date at least) to name rhyme-royal verse—a special sense of the word developing from the Latin *prosa*, meaning rhythmic poem or sequence. Stevens goes on to limit Chaucer's use of the word "ryme" to iambic pentameter rhymed in couplets (the primary verse form of the *Tales*) and the tail-rhyme stanzas of *Sir Thopas*, in order to interpret the statement as meaning the Man of Law will tell a tale in rhyme-royal form, while letting Chaucer rhyme on in his usual, less ambitious way. The line thus becomes relevant to the tale as we have it, and hypotheses concerning revision and imperfect cancellation become unnecessary. But even if Stevens were able to produce a text written before 1486 that unequivocally uses the term in that sense, there is no contextual support for thinking it implied here. The context indeed implies the opposite, the ordinary sense of the term. The Man of Law explicitly *declines* to engage Chaucer in a contest of poetry—that is the larger meaning of the passage—for he has no wish, he tells us, to be likened to the Pierides, the foolish daughters of King Pierus of Emathia who challenged the Muses to a singing contest and were turned into magpies for their presumption and their failure ("*Methamorphosios* woot what I mene"; II.93). If, in comparison to Chaucer, he seems to offer only the plainest fare ("hawebake," baked hawthorn fruit, a dish just barely edible), he doesn't care: "I speke in prose, and lat hym rymes make" (II.95–96). The context clearly requires that prose be something generally thought inferior to (and less ambitious than) rhyme—i.e., plain prose—whereas Stevens's interpretation requires that it be thought something finer, more "royal." The same prose/rhyme dichotomy is central to the exchange in which the Host halts Chaucer's own *Tale of Sir Thopas*, saying "Thou doost noght elles but despendest tyme. / Sire, at o word, thou shalt no lenger ryme," which leads Chaucer to begin a new tale (described as "a litel thyng in prose"), the plain-prose *Melibee* (VII.931, 937). It is most unlikely that Chaucer would use the same set of literary terms to mean something wholly different in this later context. (The Parson too tells "a myrie tale in prose" [X.46], having nothing to do with rhyme royal.) Though Stevens has brilliantly rewritten the history of the royal stanza, I think the Man of Law's promise to speak "in prose" is not part of it.

3. The idea goes back to Furnivall, seconded by Skeat (though both allowed for the other possibility); see Chaucer, *Complete Works*, ed. Skeat, V, 132. Robinson's headnote says it "is usually taken to be the second day" but concludes, because of the unfinished state of the tales, that "the satisfactory settlement of such questions is hardly possible" (pp. 689–90). Albert Baugh, in his widely used edition *Chaucer's Major Poetry*, surveys the problem briefly and concludes "but in the existing text it is necessary to regard *The Man of Law's Introduction and Tale* as beginning a new day" (p. 313). Three other recent editors, Pratt, *Tales of Canterbury*, Donaldson, *Chaucer's Poetry*, and Fisher, *Complete Poetry and Prose of Geoffrey Chaucer*, choose not to declare themselves on the matter, though Fisher judges it "appropriate that the Man of Law's Tale be Part II of the Canterbury collection because its prologue sets the date of the pilgrimage . . . and recapitulates the terms of the story-telling context" (p. 80).

4. Figure 120: San Marino, Huntington Lib. MS. 26.C.9, fol. 47. Loomis, *A Mirror of Chaucer's World*, commenting on this picture (his

fig. 91), writes, "The horse turns his head around in disgusted curiosity to see what kind of fool he has on his back."

5. Curry, *Chaucer and the Mediaeval Sciences*, pp. 50–51; the documents are quoted on pp. 48–49.

6. Oxford, MS. Bodley 264, fol. 204 (the *Romance of Alexander*), made 1338–44, shows tented cookshops selling baked goods and roast pig, the kind that might have been set up at a fair. Geese would have been roasted in a fashion similar to pigs; see from Bodley MS. 264, fol. 84, the scene reproduced in E. Rickert, ed., *Chaucer's World*, opp. p. 27. They were no doubt often sold in the same shops; see the 1378 London ordinance printed by Rickert, pp. 30–31. For other bakeshop pictures, see *The Hours of Catherine of Cleves*, pl. 111, and Arano, *Medieval Health Handbook*, figs. 211, 212, 214.

7. Bowden, *Commentary on the General Prologue*, pp. 187–88, summarizing researches by Earl D. Lyon, C. Jamison, and Edith Rickert.

8. Figure 121: described in Remnant, *A Catalogue of Misericords*, p. 74 (pl. 28c). Photo courtesy of Mr. Remnant. Kraus, *Hidden World of Misericords*, pl. 25, shows a cook with bellows blowing up flames under a grill.

9. The Pardoner refers to "the fyr of lecherye, / That is annexed unto glotonye" (VI.481), citing drunken Lot lying with his daughters and Herod at the feast ordering the death of John the Baptist as a favor to Salome for her sensual dance. The Parson begins his treatment of *Luxuria*: "After Glotonye thanne comth Lecherie, for thise two synnes been so ny cosyns that ofte tyme they wol nat departe" (X.836). The connection is made everywhere in medieval writing on the Deadly Sins. The Pardoner's portrait of cooks laboring to feed a glutton's belly is also to our present point: "Thise cookes, how they stampe, and streyne, and grynde, / And turnen substaunce into accident, / To fulfille al thy likerous talent!" (VI.538.)

10. Figure 122: London, Brit. Lib. MS. Add. 42130, fol. 207.

11. Figure 123: Oxford, Bodley MS. Douce 62, fol. 95 (a Book of Hours). For several variants on this scene by the same painter (the "Brussels Initial Master"), see Meiss, *Patronage*, figs. 787–90 (the last in color). Cf. Avril, *Manuscript Painting at the Court of France*, pl. 37. Hughes, *Heaven and Hell*, has many relevant pictures; see esp. pp. 183, 185, 186, 189, 207, 209, 210, 212, 213, 214, 271, 272, 273. D. D. R. Owen, *Vision of Hell*, offers a guide to the visionary texts (including the Latin and Celtic) upon which the iconography of hell is ultimately based.

12. *The Chester Mystery Cycle*, p. 325 ("The Cookes Playe"). An alewife left behind in hell because of fraudulent trade practices ends the play (pp. 337–39), offering an image by which an allied craft sought to govern itself: "Tavernes, tapsters of this cittye / shalbe promoted here with mee / for breakinge statutes of this contrye, / hurtinge the commonwealth." For the Beverley list of plays and guilds (no playing text survives), see Chambers, *Mediaeval Stage*, II, 341. Such an assignment was not universal: in York, the Cooks and Waterleaders were in charge of the Second Trial before Pilate, the Remorse of Judas, and the Purchase of the Field of Blood; in Dublin, they contributed to the Pharaoh pageant (i.e., the Crossing of the Red Sea) (*ibid.*, II, 411, 364). But where Cooks staged the Harrowing of Hell, certain witty connections were being made. See also n. 36 below.

13. The crucial lines are these: "Non altrimenti i cuoci a' lor vassalli / fanno attuffare in mezzo la caldaia / la carne con li uncin, perché non galli." (Dante, *Divine Comedy*, ed. Singleton, I, 216–17 [*Inferno* XXI, 55–57; see also XXII, 133–51].) Figure 124: Rome, Vatican Lib. MS. lat. 4776, fol. 72. For other versions of the scene, see Brieger et al., *Illuminated Manuscripts of the Divine Comedy*, I, 142–44, and II, 229–43. Cf. the use of fleshhooks, ladle, and spit in Giotto's *Last Judgment* (Padua, Scrovegni Chapel), in Martindale and Baccheschi, *Complete Paintings of Giotto*, pls. 39–41.

14. Figure 125: London, Brit. Lib. MS. Add. 47682, fol. IIv; cf. fol. 23. Brewer, *Chaucer and His World*, p. 53, shows a devil using a fleshhook on a courtier. See also van Alsloot, *Isabella's Triumph*, pl. 5, where a devil does battle with St. Michael, demonic fleshhook matched against the angel's shining sword; though the pageant recorded is late (1615), it employs late-medieval pageant cars and costumes.

15. Figure 126: Cambridge, Univ. Lib. MS. Gg.iv.27, fol. 193v. Chaucer, *Tales of Canterbury*, ed. Pratt, p. 479, reproduces the portrait of the Cook in the fragment of the Oxford MS. (1440–50) now owned by the Rosenbach Foundation; he is youthful, curly-headed, and well dressed, and holds a large cleaver in his hand. Though Pratt makes no more of it, he notes that in this picture the Cook "has so far preserved a sort of flamboyant dignity."

16. *Text of the Canterbury Tales*, ed. Manly and Rickert, I, 591–92.

17. The Cambridge portrait of the Reeve is discussed in Chapter V.

18. Hieatt, "'To boille the chiknes,'" has researched these skills in detail; see also Cosman, *Fabulous Feasts*, esp. Chaps. 2 and 3.

19. Mann, *Chaucer and Medieval Estates Satire*, p. 103. It has been noted, however, that the guildsmen are drawn from those nonvictualing trades, under the protection of John of Gaunt, that managed to remain essentially neutral in the bitter struggle between victuallers and nonvictuallers for control of London in 1386, a year in which Chaucer served in Parliament; *The Cook's Tale*, in contrast, concerns a master victualler and his apprentice. See Kuhl, "Chaucer's Burgesses," pp. 652–59. Robertson, *Chaucer's London*, p. 80, notes the unlikelihood that any of these particular guildsmen would become aldermen, since other, more powerful crafts furnished the vast majority of men elected to that office. He has figures for 1377–94 that are reasonably comprehensive: Grocers, a victualing trade, furnished the greatest number (108).

20. Unwin, *Gilds and Companies of London*, remains the standard study; on the Cooks' ordinances see p. 88 (also pp. 167, 370–71). The number of organized crafts grew enormously in the reign of Edward III, from 25 in a list made in 1328 to at least 60 by his death. In 1422, 111 crafts are listed as practicing in London, though not all would have had ordinances (pp. 87–88).

21. Though the Cook calls himself "Hogge of Ware," taking his name from his place of birth (a village in Hertfordshire), Chaucer calls him "the Cook of Londoun" (I.4325), and the fact that he owns his own shop makes it certain he was a citizen. (Apprentices were drawn from all over England; see Thrupp, *Merchant Class*, pp. 210–22.) His self-characterization in offering to tell the next tale—"And therfore, if ye vouche-sauf to heere / A tale of me, that am a povre man, / I wol yow telle, as wel as evere I kan, / A litel

jape that fil in oure citee" (1.4340)—should be read chiefly as a literary disclaimer, not as a precise index to economic status.

22. Skeat's note to the line (1.4357) remains useful; see his edition, Chaucer, *Complete Works*, V, 128–29.

23. Lyon, "The Cook's Tale," p. 148. So too Robinson in his edition (p. 5) and Donaldson in his (p. 1071), along with Howard, *Idea of the Canterbury Tales*, pp. 244–47, Burlin, *Chaucerian Fiction*, p. 152, and David, *Strumpet Muse*, pp. 118–19, to name just a few. Lyon, however, p. 152, makes one remark in passing that suggests he may have sensed another possibility. "Rogues, doubtless, there have always been in literature. But tales of rogues in a bourgeois setting became common only with the development and formulation of a bourgeois morality."

24. Thrupp, *Merchant Class*, pp. 14–17. See also Veale, "Craftsmen and the Economy of London."

25. Brentano, "On the History and Development of Gilds," pp. cxxix–xxx.

26. On this see Thrupp, *Merchant Class*, p. 164 and n. 21.

27. *Ibid.*, pp. 16–17 and 166. Further (p. 16): "The central psychological prop of the economic and political inequalities that developed was in the individual's inescapable respect for authority. Attitudes to authority oscillated between extremes and, whether subservient or resentful, were likely to be extraordinarily emotional."

28. *Ibid.*, p. 169.

29. *Ibid.*, p. 167.

30. Toulmin Smith, ed., *English Gilds*, pp. 31, 35, 38.

31. In 1385, for instance, Sir William Walworth left a will distributing substantial legacies to his present and former apprentices, and a sum much larger to the Carthusians for a chantry to be dedicated to the soul of his former master, John Lovekyn. See Myers, *London in the Age of Chaucer*, p. 154. Robertson, *Chaucer's London*, p. 79, cites a similar bequest by one John de Croydon, fishmonger.

32. Figure 127: Geneva, Bibl. Publ. et Univ. MS. fr. 160, fol. 82, illustrating Aristotle's *Ethics* in its French translation. Lady Fortitude (*Force*) is dressed in armor and holds a diamond; Lady Justice bears an emerald and a sword, with a pair of scales alongside. The picture is reproduced in color, together with many other relevant images, in *Marchands et métiers au moyen âge*, p. 42. Salmi, *Italian Miniatures*, pl. 12, prints in color a comparable scene showing the market of Porta Ravegnana in Bologna painted for the Register of the Drapers' Guild (1411). It is printed in black and white by Brooke, *Structure of Medieval Society*, p. 98. For scenes of the grain trade in 14th-century Florence, see Formaggio and Basso, *A Book of Miniatures*, pl. 25. Evans, ed., *Flowering of the Middle Ages*, Chap. 7, has a useful text (by Donald King) and a rich collection of relevant pictures; those on pp. 262–63 are of special interest (note fig. 53 in particular). An earlier chapter (pp. 18–19) reproduces Ambrogio Lorenzetti's allegorical fresco in Siena depicting Good Government, whose benefits include a well-organized life of trade, there shown in handsome detail (dated 1337–39). It may be seen in Brewer, *Chaucer and His World*, as well, between pp. 120–21, described pp. 125–26; see also the pictures on pp. 118, 132, 137. For a recent syn-

thesis of archaeological research and documentary records, see Platt, *English Medieval Town*; Carus-Wilson, "Towns and Trade," remains a useful introduction.

33. *The Très Riches Heures* offers all three kinds: the city as scene of miracle (pls. 73–74, "The Procession of St. Gregory"), as background to the labors of the month (pls. 6, 7, for May and June), and as monument map (pl. 106, a plan of Rome). Brewer, *Chaucer and His World*, p. 123, includes a similar plan of Florence. Lavedan, *Représentations des villes*, shows nothing of trade except the Lorenzetti fresco; the same is true of Buttafava, *Visioni di città*. Lehmann-Haupt, "The Book of Trades in the Iconography of Social Typology," offers a brief introduction to this neglected subject.

34. Figure 128: Paris, Bibl. Natl. ms. fr. 2092, fol. 35v. All these borders have been published by Egbert, *On the Bridges of Mediaeval Paris*; for her commentary on the present picture (pl. 28), see p. 78. As this royal manuscript illustrates, pride in civic achievement was not limited to the merchant and tradesman classes.

35. Its pictures have been published in beautiful facsimile as *Der Krakauer Behaim Codex*.

36. Figure 129: London, Brit. Lib. ms. Add. 18850, fol. 15v. Noah could be read as either master carpenter or master shipwright at this stage of the ark's construction. Brussels, Bibl. Royale ms. 9231, fol. 11v, displays a similar influence: Noah holds a staff and directs the work of five apprentices and sons. London, Brit. Lib. ms. Royal 15.D.iii, fol. 12, is also in this tradition. To adduce a few instances from Chambers, *Mediaeval Stage*, "Noah's Flood" was played, or staged in dumb-show procession, by Shipwrights in Dublin, Newcastle, and York (the Building of the Ark only; the Fishers and Mariners, with equal propriety, staged Noah and the Flood); see II, 364, 424, 410. In Hereford, the Carpenters were responsible for "Noye ship" (II, 368), and in Hull, the Master Mariners and Pilots (II, 370). Note, however, that in Chester and Beverley it was played by the Watermen (II, 340)—a witty connection still—and that in Dublin the Vintners were also involved, which suggests Noah's drunkenness was either an actual subject or one held in mind. Related instances are not far to seek. The Glovers were often in charge of the Adam and Eve pageant, probably because the actors were usually costumed in skin suits of white leather to represent nakedness before the Fall; see records from Dublin (II, 364) and Hereford (II, 368), and the specification "in whytt lether" from Cornwall (II, 391). In Shrewsbury that subject was the responsibility of the Tailors, presumably because fig leaves were the first human clothing (II, 395), and in Norwich it fell to the Grocers, perhaps because an apple figures in the action (II, 425). In Dublin, the Weavers presented Abraham and Isaac (a connection between the sacrificial lamb and wool?), whereas in York this subject fell to the Parchment-makers and Bookbinders (something, no doubt, to do with vellum): see II, 364, 410. In York, the Chaundelers (candle-makers) played the Angel and the Shepherds (the Nativity announcement), presumably because a construction of candles was needed for the blazing star (II, 410), whereas in Coventry the Shearmen (along with the Tailors) played it, shearmen like shepherds depending upon sheep for a livelihood. The Goldsmiths' Guild frequently presented the Adoration of the Magi, where gold is one of the gifts pre-

sented (e.g., Dublin and York, II, 364, 410). In Beverley, Chester, and York, the Bakers presented Maundy Thursday and the Last Supper, with the bread of the Eucharist furnishing the essential connection (II, 340, 411). (For the Chester assignments, see *The Chester Mystery Cycle*, table of contents; and for Coventry, Craig, ed., *Two Coventry Corpus Christi Plays*.)

37. One reason boundaries between the crafts are blurred is that several of them often provided the same service: witness the Cook himself, who is clearly also a Pasteler ("For many a pastee hastow laten blood"; 1.4346). Compare the 1378 Cooks' ordinance from London, which sets prices for "divers flesh-meat and poultry, as well roasted as baked in pasties" (E. Rickert, ed., *Chaucer's World*, p. 30). Toulmin Smith, ed., *English Gilds*, p. 405, publishes a document dated 1467 that prohibits butchers from practicing the cooks' craft in Worcester, on penalty of a fine—which is to say some butchers did. And Cosman, *Fabulous Feasts*, p. 70, notes that four different kinds of bakers, each with a different name, had shops in Bread Street (see also her pl. 15). Perkyn Revelour's master, if only because of his evident wealth and self-assurance, seems likely to belong to one of the four greater victualing crafts—the Grocers, Fishmongers, Vintners, or Brewers. The first seems most likely, but we cannot know for sure. For a list of other possible contenders, see Unwin, *Gilds and Companies of London*, pp. 370–71.

38. In his film *I racconti di Canterbury* (1972), Pier Paolo Pasolini invented a merry continuation of the story, in which Perkyn remains happy and irresponsible to the very end. The screenplay has been published as part of his *Trilogia della vita*; pp. 70–73 and figs. 47–54 represent *The Cook's Tale*. M. Green, "The Dialectic of Adaptation," p. 50, describes well the centrality of Perkyn Revelour to Pasolini's larger vision: "Pasolini makes Perkyn into a sympathetic and engaging figure. His sexuality and carefree attitudes are the expression of a liberated and innocent personality; his rascality and buffoonery are engaging rather than repulsive." Pasolini's view of the larger work is distinctly partial: the film ends with these words appearing on the screen: "Qui finiscono i Racconti di Canterbury raccontati per il solo piacere di raccontare" ("Here conclude the Tales of Canterbury told for the sole pleasure of telling tales"), and then "Amen."

39. Printed in Chaucer, *Text of the Canterbury Tales*, ed. Manly and Rickert, II, 169.

40. *Ibid.*, V, 434–37, from Oxford, MS. Bodley 686 (the full 44 lines must be reconstructed from the list of variants beginning on p. 432, "*Spur. ll. bef.* 4383"). I have added some light punctuation.

41. For images of capital punishment, see, for instance, those reproduced by Fremantle, *Age of Faith*, pp. 90–91, and Robertson, *Chaucer's London*, p. 98, or that in *Queen Mary's Psalter*, pl. 108 (fol. 61v). For lesser punishments, see a baker being punished for selling bread that is unsavory or underweight by being drawn through the streets on a hurdle-sled, a faulty loaf tied around his neck, in Cosman, *Fabulous Feasts*, p. 69; or a woman being drawn through the streets in an open cart, her skirts hauled up to show her genitals (presumably as punishment for fornication) in a Glasgow MS. of the *Cent Nouvelles nouvelles*, reproduced by Coghill in the illustrated edition of his translation of *The Canterbury Tales* (1977), p. 71. Robertson, *Chaucer's*

London, pp. 95–115, writes well about such matters: "The attitude toward both murderers and thieves reveals far less sensitivity to the 'sanctity of human life,' which was not a medieval concept, than we have. The treatment of minor offenses, on the other hand, reveals a great deal of confidence in the efficacy of public shame." (I quote from pp. 106–7.) For background studies, see Bellamy, *Crime and Public Order*; McCall, *Medieval Underworld*; and Hanawalt, *Crime and Conflict*.

42. Figure 130: Rouen, Bibl. Mun. MS. 927, fol. 127v. The illuminations have been published by van Moé, "Les *Ethiques, Politiques* et *Economiques* d'Aristote." The *Ethics* was the earliest complete work of Aristotle to be rendered into a modern vernacular; it survives in 17 MSS. For that text, see Oresme, *Livre de Ethiques d'Aristote* (I quote from pp. 417, 419). Books VIII–IX are devoted to Friendship (*amistié*). Although there is no evidence that Chaucer knew the work, Cook, "Chaucer's Pandarus and the Medieval Ideal of Friendship," surveys the full classical and medieval tradition, and notes many parallel distinctions in works accessible to Chaucer and his first audiences. Here for instance is Aelred of Rievaulx on the subject (*De spirituali amicitia*): "Spiritual friendship, which we call true friendship, is not desired because of the prospect of any worldly advantage, nor because of anything external, but arises from the dignity of one's own nature and the feelings of the human heart" (quoted in Cook, p. 409, n. 8).

43. Just as *The Pardoner's Tale* responds to a dual request—for "som myrthe or japes" as well as for "som moral thyng" (VI.319, 325)—so it is possible to speak morally about a "jape" such as that the Cook takes as his subject: "I wol yow telle, as wel as evere I kan, / A litel jape that fil in oure citee" (I.4342). Indeed, in the fragment as it stands, the gaiety originates entirely in Perkyn Revelour; the narrative that surrounds him is sober. The word "jape" designates a subject, not necessarily the mood or manner of its telling.

44. Stanley, in a substantial essay, "'Of This Cokes Tale Maked Chaucer Na Moore,'" has suggested that the tale indeed *is* finished. In his view (p. 59), the Cook's response to the Miller's and Reeve's common interest in the dangers of giving lodging to strangers—"herberwynge by nyghte is perilous" (I.4332)—is to create a situation in which no real risks are run. "The last few lines of *The Cook's Tale* give the recipe for carefree *herbergage*: though the lodger be a thief, no loss if a thief in cahoots with him puts him up; though the lodger be a swiver, no danger if the landlady is a whore, and no honour to lose if the pimping landlord is her husband. . . . There is no more for him to say on that subject: *Of this Cokes Tale maked Chaucer na moore*." Although this is an ingenious way of emphasizing the carefully worked degeneration of the "herbergage" theme in *The Canterbury Tales* to this point—no one has written about it better—I do not think anyone, modern or medieval, could come to that ending for the first time without feeling puzzlement, surprise, and frustration. There is no preparation for it; both rhythm and proportion are wrong. This is not how tales end, and certainly not how medieval tales end.

45. Chaucer, *Text of the Canterbury Tales*, ed. Manly and Rickert, II, 49, 165. In their view, "since all the MSS that lack these parts were to some extent

eclectic or were made up from various sources, in them the text may have been intentionally omitted because the tale was incomplete"—provisional support for an argument soon to be made above.

46. So *ibid.*, II, 479; Doyle and Parkes, "Paleographical Introduction," judge Hengwrt to be "probably the earliest surviving copy" (p. xix), but add (p. xx): "We cannot determine on purely paleographical evidence whether Hg was written before El or vice versa, or how long may separate them; it is conceivable that to some extent the scribe's work on them over-lapped, as the variations in his practices do. The time taken cannot have been less than several months on each, more if the copying was not a full-time occupation and if, as appears to have happened with [Hengwrt], the supply of exemplars was interrupted." They append a significant footnote (p. xx, n. 4): "The arguments over whether Hengwrt or Ellesmere was copied first are so complex that the present writers are not in complete agreement on this particular issue."

47. See Chaucer, *Text of the Canterbury Tales*, ed. Manly and Rickert, esp. II, 41, 489, and Benson, "Order of *The Canterbury Tales*," a bold reconsidera-tion of the Manly and Rickert conclusions. Benson argues that inconsisten-cies and contradictions do not preclude Chaucer as the compiler of the lost MS. upon which the Ellesmere MS. is ultimately based (see esp. pp. 110–17).

48. The so-called *Endlink* is a stray piece of writing, left over from some earlier stage of composition. It makes no specific address to any preceding tale (the Host's "This was a thrifty tale for the nones!" [II.1165] could follow anything), and the rough joking with the Parson that follows immediately after is entirely unlikely as a sequel to *The Man of Law's Tale*. All but six of the MSS. that contain this piece designate it a "Prologue," most often "The Squire's Prologue," and the other six have no heading at all. Nowhere in the MS. tradition does a rubric link it to *The Man of Law's Tale*. The Hengwrt and Ellesmere MSS. lack it altogether, as do the three MSS. that follow the Ellesmere order (*Text of the Canterbury Tales*, ed. Manly and Rickert, II, 478; III, 452–53). The only good early MS. that contains these lines (Harley 7334, written ca. 1410) assigns the next tale to the "sompnour," though *The Wife of Bath's Prologue and Tale* follow immediately after. The assignment to the Summoner (Manly and Rickert, II, 481) may once have been correct, for an attack on the Parson by that corrupt member of the ecclesiastical establish-ment would be in character; and Manly and Rickert conjecture that it was assigned to him at a time when the Man of Law was charged with the *Tale of Melibee* rather than the tale of Constance ("This was a thrifty tale for the nones!" would then become a rather barbed formula of praise). If these con-jectures are correct, then the link bears no substantive relation to the Con-stance story, nor to the later sequence of tales, having been made redundant by the present *Summoner's Prologue*, written when the Friar/Summoner quarrel was invented. Manly and Rickert print the Summoner version (III, 230), but term it "a mere vestigial organ, a sort of literary vermiform ap-pendix" (II, 190) of no present relevance. Robinson's procedure in his edi-tion (p. 697) is more bewildering: "Although the MSS. strongly support the theory that Chaucer abandoned the *Epilogue*, there can be no doubt of its genuineness or of its interest to the reader of the *Canterbury Tales*. It is there-fore included, but bracketed, in the present text." Not only does Robinson

print it where he admits it does not belong, but he titles it—on no MS. authority, and *without* brackets— *The Epilogue of the Man of Law's Tale,* choosing the version that names the Shipman as the next teller (a variant supported only by the poorest MSS.), while in fact printing *The Shipman's Tale* as beginning Fragment VII, without prologue, following the Ellesmere arrangement. Baugh, in his edition *Chaucer's Major Poetry,* is more tidy: he brings *The Shipman's Tale* forward, to make of this a proper unit (prologue and tale). But either procedure masks the real fact—that we have nothing from Chaucer's hand meant to follow *The Man of Law's Tale* directly—and in doing so masks the real design of the tales that begin the journey. Benson, "Order of *The Canterbury Tales,*" argues decisively that the *Endlink* was meant to be canceled (pp. 100–101, n. 14).

49. Figure 131: Aberystwyth, Natl. Lib. of Wales MS. Peniarth 392, fol. 57v. For a facsimile edition, see *Canterbury Tales,* ed. Ruggiers. Figure 132: San Marino, Huntington Lib. MS. 26.C.9, fols. 47v, 48. See *The Ellesmere Chaucer Reproduced in Facsimile.* Doyle and Parkes, "Production of Copies of the *Canterbury Tales* and the *Confessio Amantis,*" pp. 163–210, greatly refine our knowledge of the possible relationships between Hengwrt and Ellesmere, emphasizing that "the differences between the texts . . . can only be explained by the fact that [Scribe] B was copying from different exemplars, and that Ellesmere's exemplar had been prepared by an editor" (p. 186). They propose regarding Ellesmere as a *compilatio* (i.e., a manuscript emphasizing the tales as repositories of *auctoritates* and *sententiae*), an arrangement with apparatus (generically called an *ordinatio*) much more ambitious than Hengwrt (pp. 186–91); in Corpus Christi Coll. MS. 198, they find yet another kind of presentation, this one emphasizing the *Tales* "as a sequence of stories on different topics" (p. 193). "No one attempt has any special authority. . . . Since different interpretations occur in copies produced by the same scribes it seems more likely that the scribes were following different instructions or different exemplars whilst executing different commissions than that they were responsible for the different interpretations themselves." (*Ibid.,* p. 194.) On the yellow-brown ink, see *Text of the Canterbury Tales,* ed. Manly and Rickert, I, 271–74, and Doyle and Parkes, "Paleographical Introduction," pp. xxvi–xxxiii, who offer a minute description of changes in the inks throughout the manuscript. They write about *The Cook's Tale,* p. xxvii, noting that a slight change in the style of the minims in the last line may indicate the scribe even then "thought [no continuation] was likely"; "nonetheless he, or his director, did not give up all hope or obstruct continuation at a later date, since they did not fill the space with an explicit as done elsewhere in the manuscript."

50. Figure 133: Vienna, Natl. Lib. MS. 2554, fol. 1v (from an Old Testament); reproduced in color by Evans, ed., *Flowering of the Middle Ages,* p. 83.

51. On these ideas see "God as Maker," Excursus XXI in Curtius, *European Literature and the Latin Middle Ages,* pp. 544–46, and de Bruyne, *Esthetics of the Middle Ages,* Chap. 2, esp. parts 1 and 3.

52. The anonymous conclusion that follows l. 4058 can be read in the Ernest Langlois edition, or in Robbins's translation *The Romance of the Rose,* pp. 89–90; it is very swift and summary, a program for a poem. Dahlberg

omits it from his translation "since it exhibits a marked lessening of literary skill" (p. 371). *The Tale of Beryn* and Lydgate, *Siege of Thebes*, may be read in EETS editions. Caxton's ending (ca. 1483) for *The House of Fame* deserves to be better known: it follows upon the authentic line announcing "A man of gret auctorite" (*HF*, 2158).

> And wyth the noyse of them wo [*sic*]
> I Sodeynly awoke anon tho
> And remembryd what I had seen
> And how hye and ferre I had been
> In my Ghoost / and had grete wonder
> Of that the god of thonder
> Had lete me knowen / and began to wryte
> Lyke as ye haue herd me endyte
> Wherfor to studye and rede alway
> I purpose to doo day by day
> Thus in dremyng and in game
> Endeth thys lytyl book of Fame.

He appends a prose epilogue: "I fynde nomore of this werke to fore sayd / For as fer as I can vnderstonde / This noble man Gefferey Chaucer fynysshyd at the sayd conclusion of the metyng of lesyng and sothsawe / where as yet they ben chekked and maye not departe / whyche werke as me semeth is craftyly made / and dygne to be wreton & knowen." Printed in Chaucer, *A Parallel-Text Edition of Chaucer's Minor Poems*, pp. 240–41. Caxton makes no guess at the great riddle—Who is the man of authority, and what is he going to say?—but he does "finish" the poem. Thynne in his 1532 edition copied Caxton's ending, but improved its opening lines: "And therwithal I abrayde / Out of my slepe halfe a frayde." In Oxford, Bodley MS. Fairfax 16, which furnishes our best text of the poem, the scribe left blank the rest of the page and the three folios (six sides) that follow—clearly in hope that the rest of the poem might be supplied from some other source. Since that was never found, someone around the year 1600 copied the Caxton/Thynne conclusion, no doubt thinking it Chaucer's, in the space immediately following the authentic text. (R. E. Alton kindly dated for me that later hand.)

53. *Text of the Canterbury Tales*, ed. Manly and Rickert, II, 171.

54. *Ibid.*, pp. 170–71. The tale is an ancestor, at some remove, of Shakespeare's *As You Like It*.

55. *Ibid.*, p. 168.

56. The tale is vestigial, in a way different from all but one of his other unfinished works. If *The House of Fame* was planned to end where it does, in announcing a man of great authority, then its shape is that of a joke or riddle; if it is unfinished, it is nevertheless lengthy and substantial, for in its three "books" (2,158 lines), several important matters are brought to substantive conclusion. *The Legend of Good Women*, after 2,723 lines (in the F version), is likewise unfinished, though it is possible to guess from its prologue and the finished legends what its conclusion was meant to be; see my essay "From Cleopatra to Alceste." Within *The Canterbury Tales* itself, Chaucer terminates *Sir Thopas* for dramatic and thematic reasons, so that the *Tale of Melibee* (which is its reverse image) may begin. He clearly meant

to finish *The Squire's Tale* (672 lines exist), though its gaucheries may have grown tiresome, for he writes as though he had: the Franklin tactfully praises it before beginning his own tale of courtesy. *The Monk's Tale* is broken off for a number of reasons, chief among them Chaucer's wish to review its central concerns through *The Nun's Priest's Tale*, a comedic beast fable. In each of these three pairs, the answering narrative offers the essential conclusion. (*The Monk's Tale*, moreover, *is* finished in its shape if the Croesus episode is placed last, as Robinson does in his edition, for that episode ends with general remarks on tragedy and fortune, which are picked up again in the prologue that follows. Since the order of the tragedies varies in the manuscripts, however, Chaucer's intention remains uncertain: see Robinson's headnote, pp. 746–47, and Fry, "The Ending of the *Monk's Tale*," for an interesting defense of the arrangement that would place the "modern instances" last.) "Anelida and Arcite" is very different from these—a fragmentary poem of 357 lines, partly narrative, partly lyric, uneven in quality and unsure in its progress. It was doubtless found among Chaucer's posthumous papers and copied out; I do not think anyone imagines that Chaucer had released it for publication. In that regard it is like our present subject, *The Cook's Tale*: 58 lines of a narrative poem whose major action is not even begun. Cf. *TC*, II, 260: "sithen th'ende is every tales strengthe."

57. See Robinson's headnote to Fragment II, pp. 689–90, for references. Carleton Brown, "The Man of Law's Head-link," concludes that *The Man of Law's Introduction* was originally written as the prologue to the first tale of the first day, which was to be the *Tale of Melibee*, and that the present Fragment I was invented later, to replace it in the opening position. In *Text of the Canterbury Tales*, II, 491, Manly and Rickert suggest simply that it is proper to the first day. C. A. Owen, *Pilgrimage and Storytelling*, resumes and amplifies views published in several essays dating from 1951 to 1968 (references, p. 220, n. 1). He argues, counter to prevailing orthodoxies, that Chaucer's first conception of the *Tales* stressed religious ideas of pilgrimage—each pilgrim telling a single tale on a one-way journey, with the Man of Law offering the *Tale of Melibee* as first tale—and that he later conceived of the narrative contest ("play and game"), in which each pilgrim is meant to tell four tales on a five-day journey, three days out and two returning (pp. 21–41). When Owen disposes the finished tales within this hypothetical five-day journey, the Man of Law no longer figures in the design of the first day (see his Chap. 4). Owen's book is full of insight and intelligence, but I think it more likely that Chaucer moved from overambition (four tales for each pilgrim, 120 tales in all) to something nearer possibility (one tale for each); that he conceived the work, from the beginning, as a dialectical interplay between the pleasures of the narrative contest and the religious imperatives of human life, i.e., between the pastimes that "shorten" the pilgrims' way and the majesty of the shrine they seek; and that the most important change in his program for the poem was the one Ralph Baldwin (*Unity of the Canterbury Tales*) has analyzed so brilliantly—the decision to end with the pilgrims just outside the walls of Canterbury, contemplating by means of *The Parson's Prologue and Tale* the way of penance and the allegorical pilgrimage of the soul. As I shall argue in my concluding chapter, I think that the design of

the first day, in its movement to *The Man of Law's Tale*, expresses that prog-ress in small, and bears a modular relation to the whole. Wood, *Chaucer and the Country of the Stars*, pp. 161–72, argues that the tale belongs on the sec-ond day of the pilgrimage (which would then be dated April 18), in order that we might think of the pilgrimage as beginning on April 17, the day on which Noah began his journey in the ark. But I see no compelling reason here for thinking of Noah, nor do I see any need for assuming that the poem is going to divide the journey into distinct days; on the latter score, How-ard, *Idea of the Canterbury Tales*, pp. 165–66, is convincing. Furthermore, as I shall argue later in this chapter and in the following one, there is good rea-son to think the tale integral to the opening design—an assignment that E. S. Cohen, "The Sequence of the *Canterbury Tales*," p. 193, and Martin Stevens, "Malkyn in the Man of Law's Headlink," have made in print be-fore me.

58. Carleton Brown, "The Man of Law's Head-Link," p. 33, points out that *The Reeve's Prologue* is placed at Deptford at "half-wey pryme" (i.e., 7:30), which assumes that *The Knight's* and *Miller's Tales* have been told be-tween "Thomas a Watering," where the tale telling begins, and Deptford, which amounts to more than 3,000 lines in one and one-half hours (assum-ing they started telling tales as early as 6:00). This would imply an impossi-ble rate of 2,000 lines per hour. Chaucer's concern was to create the fiction of a chronology, not a realistic chronology per se. Cf. *Text of the Canterbury Tales*, ed. Manly and Rickert, II, 491. Howard, *Idea of the Canterbury Tales*, p. 166, postulates for the poem a dual time scheme that in one of its aspects creates the "poetical image" of a single day's passing.

59. Davis et al., eds., *A Chaucer Glossary*, p. 78, are misleading in offer-ing only "indolence" and "inactivity" as the meaning of "idelnesse." Cf. Wenzel, *Sin of Sloth*: "The shift from a state of mind (*taedium*) to external behavior (*ydelnesse in servitio Dei*) pervades and informs the entire popular image of *acedia*, which emphasizes, not the emotional disorientation of dis-gust for the divine good, but rather the numerous observable faults which derive from such a state" (p. 88). "Beyond doubt, popular *acedia* was a vice which, first and foremost, led to the neglect of spiritual or religious duties" (p. 90). Chap. 4 of Wenzel's magisterial study concerns the popular image of Sloth, and Chap. 5 its iconography.

60. This formula either derives from or parallels the portrait of *Oiseuse*, doorkeeper to the Garden of *Deduit* ("Delight"), quoted just above.

61. The tale is in prose and manages almost entirely without the aid of a narrative plot, employing the briefest of quasi-allegorical events—a man has his home broken into by three enemies, who beat his wife and wound his daughter—as an occasion for a long, elaborate debate on the wisdom of taking revenge upon those who do one injury. It avoids both rhyme and "story," in the way the *Introduction* suggests the Man of Law means to do. And its *sic et contra* of proverb, precept, and legal maxim, its great burden of learning, and its close imitation of formal counsel giving would all suit the Man of Law's profession well. But we must note, as well, that Trevet's *Chroniques*, Chaucer's source for the existing *Man of Law's Tale*, is written in Anglo-Norman prose. It is just possible that Chaucer originally planned to translate it in the same medium.

62. Criseyde, for instance, as a means of assuring Troilus that she will be true during the time they are apart, speaks this apostrophe to the river Simoïs that runs through Troy:

> "And thow, Symois, that as an arwe clere   (IV, 1548)
> Thorugh Troie rennest ay downward to the se,
> Ber witnesse of this word that seyd is here,
> That thilke day that ich untrewe be
> To Troilus, myn owene herte fre,
> That thow retourne bakward to thi welle,
> And I with body and soule synke in helle!"

The image here is likewise positive in its connotations: the fact of order in the physical universe affirms the possibility of order in the realm of human affairs.

63. *Summa theologiae*, 3.89.3.1 (noted by Robinson, p. 690).

64. Cf. other popular diminutives of the time: Jankyn, Perkyn, Haukyn, Symkyn. The quotation is from Langland, *Piers Plowman*, A. I, 158 (ed. Kane, p. 201). On the evidence of the *Promptorium parvulorum*, "Malkyn" most commonly served as a diminutive of "Matilda" (col. 280, and p. 648, n. 1347); but if one wanted an English diminutive for "Malyne"—a pretentious, Frenchified sort of name, ignorantly chosen (it is etymologically linked to *malin* and *maligne*)—"Malkyn" would readily suggest itself. Davis et al., eds., *A Chaucer Glossary*, p. 183, glosses "Malin/Malkin/Malle" as variants of the same name.

65. Stevens, "Malkyn in the Man of Law's Headlink." As the next chapter will make clear, my reading of *The Man of Law's Tale* does not depend upon this interpretation of the Host's remarks, but this interpretation of those remarks does depend upon such a reading of the *Tale*.

66. Figure 134: San Marino, Huntington Lib. MS. 26.C.9, fol. 50v.

67. Mann, *Chaucer and Medieval Estates Satire*, pp. 89–91. After sketching the stereotypical portrait of a lawyer that emerges from the moral and complaint literature of the period, she distinguishes Chaucer's purposes as different: "Although these sources may have influenced Chaucer in selecting a Sergeant for description, the fact that he has *not* taken over the complaints about bribery and corruption is the most striking feature of the Sergeant's portrait. . . . To read the statement [about gifts of robes and fees] only as a way of saying that the Sergeant is corruptible is to destroy the ambiguity that Chaucer has carefully created, and to miss the point he makes by its means. . . . We are forced to take the Sergeant on the terms of his façade. It is, of course, a façade. . . . The point is that we do not know what lies behind it. To suggest a front without giving away the reality is a feat which Chaucer manages with dexterity."

68. Some further details from Manly, *Some New Light on Chaucer*, pp. 133–35: "They ranked socially immediately after knights bachelors and took precedence of Companions of the Bath, younger sons of knights, and even younger sons of great nobles. Professionally, they ranked immediately after the judges of the king's bench and common pleas and took precedence of both the attorney-general and the solicitor-general and also the barons of the exchequer, except the chief. . . . The king himself in the writ addressed to one of them [used] the respectful plural *vos* instead of the *tu* and *te* com-

monly used in addressing officials and other inferiors. . . . As would natu-
rally be inferred, the sergeants at law have always been few in number. . . .
For the reign of Richard II Foss lists only fifteen sergeants, all but two of
whom were later appointed judges." (Though the records are incomplete,
scholars judge the total number to have been about twenty; see Robinson's
note, pp. 658–59.) Manly quotes as well Sir John Fortescue's fascinating ac-
count of the rituals of their appointment and investiture (from *De laudibus
legum Angliae*) on pp. 136–40. Hassall, *How They Lived*, pp. 268–69,
includes Sir John's account of the professional life of judges (the rank
to which any sergeant of the law aspired). See also McKenna, "Making of a
Fourteenth-Century Sergeant of the Lawe," and Hastings, *Court of Common
Pleas*, esp. pp. 59–80.

69. Figure 135: A miniature in the collection of the Library of the Inner
Temple, London. It may be seen in color as frontispiece to Hastings, *Court
of Common Pleas*, where its detail is much easier to read; she describes it on
pp. 28–30. A later copy of this picture, from a Cambridge MS., is re-
produced by Hussey, *Chaucer's World*, fig. 56; in his fig. 57, showing the
Chancery Court, presided over by the Lord Chancellor, sergeants of the law
are also represented.

70. On this identification, see Manly, *Some New Light on Chaucer*, pp.
147–57; he lists several reasons Chaucer would have known of Pynchbek
and might have thought ill of him (not all of the latter are compelling); in
addition, one of several writs to arrest Chaucer for small debt in 1388 was
signed by Pynchbek as chief baron of the Exchequer (Robinson, p. 659;
Crow and Olson, eds., *Chaucer Life-Records*, p. 386). But even the latter fact
must be kept within proportion: Pynchbek himself was not suing Chaucer,
and the whole affair—in that extremely litigious period—must have seemed
to Chaucer small beer indeed. The gesture toward Pynchbek is a joke, quick
and deft, not a massive retaliation, and only a small part of Chaucer's first
audiences would have made any sense of the identifying pun at all.

71. The Man of Law as pilgrim-narrator has fared exceedingly badly at
the hands of recent critics. Wood, *Chaucer and the Country of the Stars*,
pp. 192–244, mounts a large-scale attack, seeing him as sentimental, inter-
ested only in love tales, confused about Boethian issues (thinking Christ
ought to send only good fortune), concerned with astrology to the neglect
of Providence, and so on. In trying to hear a very specific narrative voice, I
think Wood has exaggerated a few details, neglected the shape of the larger
narrative sequence, and ultimately misread the poem. Greater exaggerations
are to be found in Delasanta's "And of Great Reverence," which sees the tale
as continuing a "pattern of demolition" of the narrator's character that is be-
gun in the *General Prologue* portrait. Delasanta's procedure is to examine a
minutely "interstitial pattern of errors about things literary" (p. 291), a
"spate of mini-errors" (p. 296) made by "the pilgrim of vaunted memory"
(p. 293), exposing mere "intellectual posturing and didactic gesture" (p.
294). If Chaucer's aim was satire, it is pitched so high that few would have
heard it; in several instances, I suspect he merely "got it wrong." (There are
comparable errors in *HF*, 177–78 and 1844, which are surely unintentional;
the former is "got right" in *LGW*, 941–42.) The highly rhetorical passages
in the tale—perfectly conventional and decorous exercises in medieval "art

poetical"—are termed "pharisee" by Delasanta, reflecting "that peculiar combination of law and self-righteous religion" that suggests an even more dire "pharisaical schizophrenia" afflicting the Man of Law (pp. 303–4). We are meant to see him as "a self-righteous, militant, rectitudinous, and unmerciful Christian" (p. 307). Despite occasional excess, both Wood and Delasanta are useful reading, however, the more so (in the present context) since their sense of the tale differs so radically from my own. Though I ultimately differ as well from E. T. Donaldson, who thinks the tale "exceedingly—even excessively—pietistic," he expresses a sense of its teller nearer to my own when he writes, "While scarcely suited to the Man of Law's moral character, it seems suited to the sense of decorum that such a character might be expected to have—a conviction that stories should be historically true (as Trivet asserted Custance's was) and morally edifying, to the hearer if not to the teller: stories should, that is, have the appearance of worth" (*Chaucer's Poetry*, pp. 1073–74). Clogan, "Narrative Style of The Man of Law's Tale," offers what seems to me a definitive account of the poem's rhetoric; it is deeply learned, draws upon the appropriate literatures, and points toward a nonironic reading of the poem. For further comment on these views, see n. 64 of the following chapter.

72. See Hoffman, "Chaucer's Prologue to Pilgrimage," for an analysis of this ambiguity.

73. The tradition goes back to John Cassian (ca. 425), and has a long and flourishing history; see Wenzel, *Sin of Sloth*, pp. 20, 74, 76 (and *passim*). Chaucer uses it directly in *The Parson's Tale*: see x.713–16 for "ydelnesse" as a branch of *Acedia*, and x.728–38 for fortitude as its *remedium*: "Agayns this horrible synne of Accidie, and the branches of the same, ther is a vertu that is called *fortitudo* or strengthe," which has several species, among them "constaunce, that is, stablenesse of corage" (x.737). This description of Custance, "She was so diligent, withouten slouthe, / To serve and plesen everich in that place" (ii.530), derives extra meaning from that fact. On proper "busynesse" as yet another virtue remedial to Sloth—it is the Second Nun's Choice—see Wenzel, p. 89.

74. The list may even include Criseyde—as "Brixseyde," her name in Benoît de Sainte-Maure's *Roman de Troie*, one of Chaucer's sources for the *Troilus* (Alfred David's suggestion, *Strumpet Muse*, p. 124). In "From Cleopatra to Alceste," I read the omissions in Chaucer's program for the *Legend* as being likewise thematically significant; that poem too is preceded by a prologue in which Chaucer wittily attacks his own oeuvre.

75. David, *Strumpet Muse*, Chap. 8, incorporating a very influential article, "The Man of Law vs. Chaucer." He reads the catalogue of Chaucer's works as the poet's own rueful assessment of his public fame—it is as a love-poet he is chiefly known—and sees the Man of Law as an ironic portrait of those members of Chaucer's first audiences, highly placed or highly born, who "favored him with condescending praise and gratuitous advice" (p. 123). I would add to those readings the explanation that follows in my text above.

76. Cf. W. H. Auden on the subject of poets and their oeuvre: "Our works are often in better taste than our lives."

77. Since the learned Man of Law is one of a handful of pilgrims who

would not have needed to learn his tale by oral tradition, the purpose of that claim in the Prologue is obscure: "I were right now of tales desolaat, / Nere that a marchant, goon is many a yeere, / Me taughte a tale, which that ye shal heere" (II.131). Again one has a sense of work not fully revised—like the "I speke in prose" promise earlier—for the *Introduction* and *Prologue* together create an awkward redundancy. Both are complete in their own right, and both introduce the tale directly, the *Introduction* concluding "And with that word he, with a sobre cheere, / Bigan his tale, as ye shal after heere" (II.97), and the *Prologue* finishing with the lines quoted above ("Me taughte a tale, which that ye shal heere"). I suspect they were composed for separate occasions and never intended to be used together. The *Introduction*, as we have seen, is intimately related to the pilgrimage occasion, whereas the *Prologue* seems to have been written for a listening audience of merchants whom Chaucer addresses directly ("O riche marchauntz, ful of wele been yee, / O noble, o prudent folk, as in this cas!" etc. [II.122]), addressing them, moreover, in his customary ironic and self-deprecating voice. It would be a witty joke for the famous poet Chaucer to present himself to a merchant company as entirely dependent upon them for material. It is a puerile joke, making no sense (comic or otherwise), in the voice of the Man of Law, spoken to a company of fellow pilgrims. The same may be said of the *Prologue*'s complacent praise of the life of rich merchants—a point of view the tale will undercut profoundly, in its presentation of voyages that are wholly unlike those made for pecuniary profit, and which find their reward in a very different kind of feast. (Even in terms of this Chaucer-and-an-audience-of-merchants hypothesis, the tale complicates its introduction far more than the introduction complicates the tale.) I suspect that the earliest scribe or his director came upon copies of both the *Introduction* and the *Prologue* among Chaucer's papers and decided to transcribe them consecutively rather than choose between them, seeing them both linked to the tale of Custance and wishing to preserve as much of Chaucer's finished writing as could be found. The result, unfortunately, comes close to being nonsense, formally and thematically, though it has been read over and over as central to Chaucer's intended characterization of the Man of Law. (If we must read it so, then the explanation I suggest in my text above seems to me more likely: it simply transfers to the Man of Law something of Chaucer's own preference for ironic self-presentation.) Giffin, *Studies on Chaucer and His Audience*, Chap. 4, likewise argues the tale was first written for an audience of merchants, though less plausibly that it was composed ca. 1383 in support of the cause of Costanza of Castile, wife of John of Gaunt. Lewis, "Chaucer's Artistic Use of *De miseria*," offers a very different account of the opening sequence and its logic, but likewise assumes discontinuous composition; see esp. pp. 485–88.

78. There is nothing suspect about the *Prologue*'s dispraise of poverty: it is a translation, almost word for word, from Pope Innocent III's *De miseria*, I.15, which is quoting in turn from the Bible (Ecclus. 40:29, Prov. 14:20, 15:15, 19:7). Chaucer's *Melibee* likewise praises wealth and dispraises poverty (VII.1547–676), with no irony intended, for reasons that *The Chess of Love* commentary makes particularly clear: "Religious poverty is marvelous, not natural, and mentioned only to be excluded from the general

condemnation of penury on ethical grounds" (translator's introduction, p. v; see pp. 790–811). What the loathly lady in *The Wife of Bath's Tale* praises as "glad poverte" (III.1183) is another subject altogether, and part of the counsel of perfection. The prologue that is our present subject speaks of involuntary poverty instead—poverty that damages rather than ennobles the spirit. The only implausible theme in our prologue is its complacent praise of wealth as a kind of bliss: Innocent III continues (in the very same chapter) to talk about the misery of being rich. That praise functions ironically in relation to the Custance story, as I suggest in my note above; the dispraise of poverty does not.

79. On Long Will's self-portrait, based upon theological conceptions of the will (a central pun in the poem) and of sloth as a defect of the will, see a distinguished doctoral dissertation by John M. Bowers, "Langland's *Piers Plowman*: *Acedia* and the Crisis of Will" (Univ. of Virginia, 1978).

CHAPTER VII

1. Giffin, *Studies on Chaucer and His Audience*, p. 68, citing Schlauch, *Chaucer's Constance and Accused Queens*.

2. E.g., the general description by MacLaine, *Student's Comprehensive Guide to The Canterbury Tales*, p. 87, summarizing an extensive bibliography of critical writing on the tale: "GENRE: Sentimental tale, with some elements of saint's legend, based on folk tale motif of the Calumniated Wife." Block, "Originality, Controlling Purpose, and Craftsmanship in Chaucer's *Man of Law's Tale*," p. 581, thinks that Chaucer suppressed certain precise information about names, places, and dates that he found in his source in order "to lift Trevet's pedestrian story . . . into the realms of romance, remote in time and space." Paull, "Influence of the Saint's Legend Genre," provides a useful study of the features Chaucer's tale shares with legends of female saints, but Chaucer's audiences knew of no St. Custance, and would have heard her tale as uncanonized history. Luria, "Dame Custance's Voyages Re-examined," a brief paper presented to the Chaucer Group of the Modern Language Association meeting in Chicago, 1965, touched upon several of the themes I here attempt to bring together into a critical reading of the poem. Though my own researches were already substantially underway, I owe the interpretation on p. 324 and n. 47 to Luria's paper. More recent criticism will be noted where pertinent below.

3. The relevant Trevet text may be read in Bryan and Dempster, eds., *Sources and Analogues*, pp. 165–81, or with a modern translation by Brock in Furnivall, Brock, and Clouston, eds., *Originals and Analogues*, 2d series, I, 2–53; for a mid-15th-century translation into English, see in the same series III, 222–50, in which the editor begins at a point earlier in the Trevet text and makes its historical nature even more clear. The full text has no printed edition in either Anglo-Norman or Middle English. For the *Confessio amantis* version, see Gower, *Complete Works*, II, 146–73, or Bryan and Dempster, eds., *Sources and Analogues*, pp. 181–206. Lines 77–89 of *The Man of Law's Introduction* are generally thought to be a comic attack on the author Chaucer elsewhere calls "moral Gower," who was indeed his friend; they refer to stories told in the *Confessio amantis*. On the dating of the first

version of that work, see Fisher, *John Gower*, pp. 116–17; he suggests it was begun ca. 1385. Isaacs, "Constance in Fourteenth-Century England," compares as well the romance version known as *Emare*, whose provenance and date are conjectural, and whose treatment of the material is popular and unlearned, a folktale in rhyme.

4. On the historical identifications, see Bryan and Dempster, eds., *Sources and Analogues*, pp. 156–58. John Capgrave's *Solace of Pilgrimes*, a pilgrim's guide to Rome written ca. 1450, in its summary of Roman history records (p. 58) the reign of Tiberius and then of "Mauricius [who] regned aftir him xx ʒere euene. In his tyme was seynt gregorie pope be whom inglond was neuly conuerted on to þe feith." The tradition that descends through Trevet makes Tiberius emperor at that time, rather than Maurice, but it implicitly lays claim to the same kind of historical truth. Pratt, "Chaucer and *Les Cronicles* of Nicholas Trevet," records (p. 304) the section heading I quote in my text, and suggests (p. 301) Chaucer's larger indebtedness to the work, whose "theme and drama . . . consists partly in the opposition and continuous struggle of the Christian and pagan worlds for control of the earth and of the minds and souls of men. Into this struggle Trevet fitted the story of Constance. . . . Chaucer preserves this perspective."

5. See Legge, *Anglo-Norman Literature*, pp. 298–302. Trevet's Latin histories are the *Annales sex regum Angliae* and a *Historia ab orbe condito ad Christi nativitatem*. Smalley, *Historians in the Middle Ages*, pp. 191–92, writes briefly on Trevet's range and on the importance of his commentary on Livy to the new kind of interest in the past (conscious of the distortions of anachronism) that begins in the 14th century. Much of our knowledge of Trevet's work rests on the scholarship of Ruth J. Dean, most recently summarized in her essay, "Nicholas Trevet, Historian." His patron, Princess Mary, although a nun, was by no means out of touch with the courtly and sophisticated world. She entered the convent of Amesbury at the age of seven (an enforced vocation) as companion to the dowager Queen Eleanor, widow to Henry III—an event Trevet takes care to chronicle. She was already forty at the time of Trevet's writing, and because of her rank and royal duties, enjoyed a fair amount of freedom of movement. The book Trevet wrote for her is announced as a brief history that will seek to avoid tedium and be easily remembered; unlike his two earlier works, it does not name sources or attempt to account for events year by year. Dean writes, "Like most of Trevet's work, the *Cronicles* are didactic, but their intention is practical and moral rather than intellectual" (p. 343); they devote a good deal of attention to miracles, legends, and ecclesiastical matters such as questions of hierarchy, sanctuary, celibacy, and the history of the liturgy, along with the history of the Angevin dynasty and the Dominican order. That the book is written in Anglo-Norman suggests Mary was educated but not scholarly; that Trevet had in mind an audience beyond his immediate patroness is suggested by the fact that he continued to work on it after her death (pp. 344, 348). Indeed the number and variety of extant manuscripts (nine of the original, one in Middle English) reveal that it was copied at many centers and for readers "of differing demands and tastes" (p. 349). For further information, see also R. J. Dean, "The Manuscripts of Nicholas Trevet's Anglo-Norman *Cronicles*."

6. Gower, *Confessio amantis*, *Complete Works*, II, 146 (597), 173 (1586). The tale that follows, of Demetrius and Perseus, sons of Philip of Macedonia, is called by Gower "a tale soth" (1610) and begins: "In a Cronique, as thou schalt wite." The Latin summaries in the margin of the MS. often emphasize historical details, e.g.: "consilio Pelagii tunc pape" (p. 146); "in partes Anglie, que tunc pagana fuit, prope Humber sub quodam castello Regis, qui tunc Allee vocabatur" (p. 149); "Arcennus Romanorum Consul" (pp. 160–61); "De coronacione Mauricii, qui adhuc in Cronicis Mauricius Imperator Cristianissimus nuncupatus est" (p. 173).

7. As Richard Firth Green has recently demonstrated, "the interest of the aristocracy in the late middle ages in historical works was considerably greater than its interest in belles-lettres. The testimony of library catalogues and book inventories points to a strong preference for historical fact—or at least for works that were taken to be factual—over romantic fiction. . . . The line between the historical and the fabulous was, furthermore, by no means as clearly drawn in the middle ages as it is today, and there is little doubt that the numerous 'histories' of Troy, Thebes, and Alexander, or even of Arthur, Charlemagne, and Godfrey of Bouillon, were read largely as sober, factual accounts" (*Poets and Princepleasers*, pp. 136–37). What seems to us most "fabulous" in the life of Constance was, moreover, the very stuff of hagiography—the history of the saints. Jeanette Beer's study of "the truth assertion" in medieval literature (*Narrative Conventions of Truth in the Middle Ages*, pp. 10–11) declares central an assumption she finds most clearly expressed in Isidore of Seville's *Etymologiae*: "Isidore posited for truth a hierarchy of values by word-class, in which 'true' was subordinate to 'truth' because the adjective 'verus' derived from, and was chronologically subordinate to, the substantive 'veritas.' Such theorizing had metaphysical implications—it extolled pure abstraction ('veritas') over the attribute derived therefrom ('verus'). . . . The facts were subordinate to the 'truth.'" All this evidence points to the same conclusion: we must not allow modern notions of the historically probable to limit and distort our sense of the medieval genre.

8. There are enough verbal echoes between Gower's and Chaucer's versions to make it certain one of them was written with knowledge of the other, but no confident conclusion about priority seems possible. Macaulay, in his edition of Gower, *Complete Works*, II, 483–84, sets out the evidence and concludes (not very convincingly) that Chaucer preceded Gower; on pp. 482–83, he offers a summary of Gower's alterations of Trevet.

9. I have suggested elsewhere (Chapter VI, n. 77) that the *Prologue* was probably never intended for the Man of Law, but dates from an earlier, independent occasion. Here I wish only to emphasize that the claim to have learned the tale from a merchant does not necessarily undercut the historical claim made later in lines 1121–27, quoted in my text above. Oral authority was real authority in the Middle Ages: most people heard what history they knew. And merchant-voyagers were, as the *Prologue* says, an important source of news of distant lands, able to report on the state of kingdoms ("al th'estaat / Of regnes"; II.128) and on matters of peace and strife ("tidynges / And tales, bothe of pees and of debaat"; II.129). The Sultan of the tale will call upon his Syrian merchants for just such information ("tidynges of son-

dry regnes"; II.181), as do (on occasion) the intelligence agencies of modern states. "Tidynges" is a neutral term in medieval usage, as is "tales." The former means "news" or "reports"—word of what has been happening—whereas the latter simply implies a narrative account of something. They may be true, or false, or a mixture of the two. Chaucer's largest comment on this matter is to be found in *The House of Fame*, ll. 1916–2137; lines 2122–24 are of special interest because they link shipmen and pilgrims as persons whose wallets are full of "lesinges, / Entremedled with tydynges" (lies mixed up with news—trustworthy news, presumably, because of the grammatical opposition). The Constance story is clearly of the trustworthy kind, for (as the Man of Law later makes clear) Roman "geestes" confirm it and furnish further detail. That term too needs to be understood precisely. "Geestes" means literally "things done," particularly those important enough to be worth remembering, deeds worthy of "fame"—and thus, by extension, the accounts that preserve those deeds. Though the word was sometimes used loosely, to mean a poem or song of any kind, the citations assembled in the M.E.D. amply establish its more customary claim as authentic historical narrative. See for example (under "gest[e," p. 92) quotations referring to "the gestes of the apostles" and to the "gestes of Englonde" told by St. Bede. Chaucer himself refers to Flavius Josephus, the great Jewish historian, as author of "Jewes gestes" in *The House of Fame*, l. 1434. Although historical tradition could sometimes be confusing and self-contradictory—as Trevet testifies in choosing between two traditions and as Chaucer implicitly acknowledges in *The House of Fame*, ll. 1514–19—I think there can be no question that for both authors "geestes" (the history of things done) address truth in a way different from that of fiction (the narrative of things consciously invented, of things "made up"). See also *The Merchant's Tale* (IV.2284–85) on "Romayn geestes," and cf. the M.E.D. definition of "cronical": "Of a fact; recorded in chronicles, historical."

10. Burrow, *Ricardian Poetry*, p. 79 (the first quotation is from Lewis, *The Allegory of Love*, cited by Burrow, p. 155, n. 76). Burrow's discussion continues to p. 92.

11. Important studies include de Lubac, *Exégèse médiévale*; Smalley, *Study of the Bible* and *English Friars and Antiquity*; Tuve, *Allegorical Imagery*; J. B. Allen, *Friar as Critic*. MacQueen, *Allegory*, offers a brief introduction and basic bibliography. Clifford, *Transformations of Allegory*, and Barney, *Allegories of History, Allegories of Love*, are securely rooted in medieval theory and practice, but extend to Renaissance and modern adaptations as well.

12. Sometimes only three senses are postulated, as by Hugh of St. Victor, *On the Sacraments*, p. 5, or in his *Didascalicon*, pp. 120–21; sometimes as many as seven, as by one Angelom of Luxeuil. But a fourfold division was most commonly assumed—by Cassian, Aldhelm, Rabanus Maurus, Bede, John of Salisbury, St. Thomas Aquinas, Dante, Hugh of St. Cher, and many others. On these varying traditions, see Caplan, *Of Eloquence*, pp. 93–104.

13. On the tag, made famous by Nicholas of Lyra, see Caplan, *Of Eloquence*, p. 99 (*speres* occasionally appears for *tendas*); see also Owst, *Literature and Pulpit*, whose notes, pp. 59–60, quote versions in English from sermon MSS.: (1) "Sence historial": "whan a man understondith the story that spekith of a bodili doynge even aftur the lettre sowneth." (2) "Sence alle-

gorik": "whan a man understondith bi a bodili thyng that he redith of in story an other gostli thyng that is bitokened therbi." (3) "Sence tropologik": "whan a man redith a story that spekith moche of my3ti dedis or of gode worchyng, and understondith that he shuld have stronge gostli dedis of holi lyvyng." (4) "Sence anagogik": "whan a man undirstondeth an hevenli thyng bi a bodili thyng seid in story" (from another MS.: "that bitokneth thyng to hope in blis"). The "Prolog for Alle the Bokis of the Oolde Testament" included in the Wycliffite translation of the Bible (second version, ca. 1395) includes similar definitions and an example: "The literal understonding techith the thing don in dede, and literal undirstonding is ground and foundament of thre goostly undirstondingis. . . . Allegorik is a goostly undirstonding that techith what thing men owen for to bileeve of Crist either of Hooly Chirche. Moral is a goostly understonding that techith men what vertues thei owen to sue and what vices thei owen to flee. Anagogik is a goostly undirstonding that techith men what blisse thei schal have in Hevene. // And these foure undirstondingis moun be taken in this word 'Jerusalem,' for-whi, to the literal undirstonding, it signefieth an erthly citée, as Loundoun either such another. To allegorie, it signefieth Hooly Chirche in erthe, that fightith ayens synnes and fendis. To moral undirstondinge, it signefieth a Cristen soule. To anagogik it signefieth Hooly Chirche regnynge in blisse either in Hevene and tho that be therinne." I quote from the version of the "Prolog" published by Dunn and Byrnes, eds., *Middle English Literature*, pp. 485-86. The nouns most often used in Latin exegesis are *significatio* and *sensus*; see Barney, *Allegories of History, Allegories of Love*, p. 46.

14. Robinson, p. 694 (note to l. 519).

15. "'Deus,' dist li reis, 'si penuse est ma vie!' / Pluret des oilz, sa barbe blanche tiret." ("'God,' says the king, 'how painful is my life!' Tears come to his eyes, he pulls at his white beard.") (*La Chanson de Roland*, p. 276 [4000-4001].)

16. See esp. II.264-94, 516-18, 645-51, 708-14, 822-26, 855-63, 1055-58, 1112, most of which are Chaucer's additions to his source.

17. In *The Parson's Tale*, Chaucer defines *constantia* as: "Constaunce, that is, stablenesse of corage; and this sholde been in herte by stedefast feith, and in mouth, and in berynge, and in chiere, and in dede." (X.737.) It is part of the cardinal virtue *fortitudo*, called: "Strengthe, that is an affeccioun thurgh which a man despiseth anoyouse thinges. . . . it dar withstonde myghtily and wisely kepen hymself fro perils that been wikked, and wrastle agayn the assautes of the devel. . . . For this *fortitudo* may endure by long suffraunce the travailles that been covenable." (X.728.)

18. Figure 136: Oxford, Bodley MS. Laud Misc. 570, fol. 21v, made for Sir John Fastolf and illustrating the *Livres des quatre vertus*, abridged (possibly by Christine de Pisan) from the *Breviloquium de virtutibus* of John of Wales. On the iconography of the Virtues, see Tuve, *Allegorical Imagery*, pp. 57-143; she describes this MS. on p. 71, and her figs. 14, 15, 16 are drawn from it. Cf. the closely related *Force* illustrated in her fig. 17.

19. Figure 137: New York, Pierpont Morgan MS. M.126, fol. 32v, containing Gower's first version of the poem, dedicated to Richard II. There was once a Constance illumination in the Oxford, New College MS. 266

Confessio amantis (fol. 39), but it has been cut out, along with many others. The Bauchon Chapel bosses of Norwich Cathedral, carved ca. 1450, apparently illustrate scenes from an analogue to the Trevet/Gower/Chaucer version, though there are significant differences. Alan H. Nelson and Anne Spiselman are preparing a study of these bosses, and have generously allowed me to consult their photographs.

20. See Beichner, "Chaucer's Man of Law and *Disparitas Cultus.*"

21. See Oman, *Medieval Silver Nefs*, pp. 11–12. He writes: "The piece was of the richest sort and was adorned with religious subjects which it is not easy to link together into a coherent theme." *Nefs* were fitted out variously as incense boats, drinking vessels, saltcellars, and reliquaries.

22. In Horstmann, ed., *Yorkshire Writers*, II, 67–70. I quote only ll. 153–59, 175–78, 181–86, 201–4, though the entire passage is of interest. (Other portions of this poem's allegory will be noted in their proper places: it furnishes a comprehensive gloss to Chaucer's narrative.) On "gods vitayles" in l. 154, cf. *Book of Vices and Virtues*, interpreting "our daily bread" in the *Pater noster* to mean the body and blood of Christ in the Eucharist: "Þis is þe bisquit wher-wiþ he vitaileþ his schip, þat is holi chirche, for to passe wiþ þe grete see, out of þis perilous world" (p. 110, ll. 19–22). Owst, *Literature and Pulpit*, discusses ship imagery as an example of the way such figures were used in preaching, and offers many instances thereof, pp. 68–76. There are powerful moments in Anglo-Saxon poetry built upon this figure, especially in the *Andreas*, ll. 359–81, 469–536, 822–26, 851–56; for a translation, see Gordon, ed. and trans., *Anglo-Saxon Poetry*, pp. 185–89, 195. Kaske, "A Poem of the Cross in the Exeter Book," argues that the Ship of the Church figure is to be found in "The Husband's Message"; his n. 33 cites a number of patristic sources for the tradition. It probably developed as an analogue of the ship of state image, first used by Alcaeus, from Miylene on Lesbos, but familiar to the Middle Ages from Horace's *Ode* I, 14. See Dronke, *Fabula*, p. 94, n. 1, for a general bibliography.

23. Figure 138: New York, Pierpont Morgan MS. M.799, fol. 234v (a Lombard breviary made for the use of the Hermits of St. Augustine). A beautiful German lyric by Ezzo, a priest at Bamberg, composed for a grand German pilgrimage to the Holy Sepulchre in 1065, includes a stanza, *O crux salvatoris*, in which Christ is hymned as "the mast-tree of our ship . . . the sail of true belief"; discussed and trans. by Dronke, *Medieval Lyric*, p. 49.

24. See Jacobus de Voragine, *Legenda aurea*, p. 409, or its translation as *The Golden Legend* by Caxton, IV, 76, or by Ryan and Ripperger, p. 357, from which I quote above. Reinhard, "Setting Adrift in Mediaeval Law and Literature," p. 40, prints a versified Magdalen legend (early 14th century), which includes these details: "Huy weren in a schip ipult withouten ster and ore, / þat huy scholden beon furfaren and ne libben nomore; / þare nas noþur ido with heom noþur watur ne bred, / For huy scholden of-hongrede beon and sone þare-afturward ded. / Huy schypeden in þe salte se, ase Jesu Crist it wolde."

25. Figure 139: from the Magdalen Chapel in the lower Basilica of S. Francesco, Assisi; it is held to be School of Giotto at the least, though recent opinion has tended to favor the master's direct participation: see Martindale

and Baccheschi, *Complete Paintings of Giotto*, pp. 111–12, and Palumbo, ed., *Giotto e i Giotteschi in Assisi*, pp. 106–27 (figs. 98, 100 reproduce the painting under discussion). The scene is also depicted in 13th-century stained glass at Chartres, and on an altar retable painted by Lukas Moser in 1432/33 in Tiefenbronn; the latter can be seen in Mâle, *Saints Compagnons*, p. 67 (cf. the woodcut on p. 63). Another 13th-century window depicting the journey is published by du Ranquet, *Vitraux de la cathédrale de Clermont-Ferrand*, pl. opp. p. 100. See also Réau, *Iconographie de l'art chrétien*, III, 847, 852–55. A simpler version from a French MS. of the early 14th century shows Saints Martha, Mary Magdalen, and Maximinus standing alone in a small boat afloat upon the open sea (London, Brit. Lib. MS. Add. 17275, fol. 341). The modesty and scale of this representation is nearer to Cus-tance's second and third journeys than to her first. The ship journey of St. Andrew to Murgundia (or Mermedonia), recounted in the *Legenda aurea* and treated poetically in the Old English *Andreas*, is illustrated in a 15th-century window at Greystoke; Andrew's sailing companions, unrecognized by him, are in fact Christ and two angels. See n. 22 above. Anderson, *Drama and Imagery*, writes about the window, pp. 204–7, and reproduces the scene of Andrew's arrival by boat, pl. 19a.

26. Figure 140: A New Year's greeting, made in Switzerland or Alsace, now in the Vienna National Library; see Schreiber, *Manuel de l'amateur de la gravure*, no. 795. He titles it "The Christchild as Steersman." It turns a ship of the Church into a ship of good wishes. For a ship of the Church contain-ing Mary with the infant Christ and two angels with trumpets appearing before a donor, see a French Book of Hours made ca. 1500, formerly on loan to Colchester, Castle Museum MS. 217–32. I print the German poem from Kiepe and Kiepe, eds., *Epochen der deutschen Lyrik*, and the translation (by Mabel Cotterell) from Flores, ed., *Anthology of Medieval Lyrics*, pp. 450–51.

27. Figure 141: Schreiber, *Manuel de l'amateur de la gravure*, no. 1709, now in Paris, the Louvre (Collection E. de Rothschild, inv. no. 15LR). Re-produced in color by Blum, *Primitifs de la gravure sur bois*, pl. 15, described p. 70. Cf. also Schreiber, no. 1711. The St. Ursula picture in *The Belles Heures of Jean, Duke of Berry* (fol. 178v) shows the martyrdom occurring on shipboard, amid turbulent waters, with Cologne in the distance; *The Golden Legend*, in contrast, locates it in Cologne, after the pilgrimage to Rome is completed: see Jacobus de Voragine, *Legenda aurea*, pp. 701–5, or the trans. by Ryan and Ripperger, pp. 627–31. Randall, *Images in Margins*, fig. 627 (from Queen Mary's Psalter) has the murder take place upon the bank. See also de Tervarent, *Légende de Sainte Ursule*, II, pls. 118, 119, which treat the mast as a cross.

28. Guillaume de Deguileville, *Pilgrimage of the Lyf of the Manhode*, pp. 190–92. The whole passage should be read, for the idea is richly devel-oped. In Lydgate's translation, the corresponding passage begins on p. 579, with the ship described on pp. 588–91. In Dante, *Purgatorio* XXXII, the Church is represented as a triumphal chariot, but is nevertheless twice de-scribed (ll. 116, 129) as a ship.

29. Figure 142: Oxford, Bodley MS. Douce 300, fol. 113v. Cf. New York, Pierpont Morgan MS. M.772, fol. 92 (French, ca. 1360–70), which

shows on board Grace Dieu, Fear of God, and the pilgrim; on fol. 90, the pilgrim sees the ship for the first time, and on fol. 91v, Fear of God inhibits his entry. London, Brit. Lib. MS. Cotton Tiber. A. vii, fols. 81, 81v, illustrates Lydgate's version of the event. See also Paris, Bibl. Natl. MS. fr. 377, fol. 91v (end of the 14th century), for a fine cathedral ship, with a white dove standing on the sail. Brussels, Bibl. Royale MS. 10176–78, fol. 102 (Flemish, ca. 1380–90), offers an exquisite illustration. Tuve, *Allegorical Imagery*, reproduces Oxford, Bodley MS. Laud misc. 740, fol. 118v (her fig. 88, p. 212); it is a MS. of the English prose translation, 2/4 15th century. On the symbolism of cathedral architecture, see von Simson, *Gothic Cathedral*. Guillaume de Deguileville was in fact a Cistercian monk at the Abbey of Chalis in Valois, near Senlis.

30. Gower, *Confessio amantis*, V, 1871; cf. also the Prologue, ll. 234–35, and his *Vox clamantis*, III, 14 (p. 140): "Peter's ship is faltering; set it right before it perishes, O Christ, and do not let pride swallow it up" (*Major Latin Works*, p. 144). For the commentary by St. Hippolytus, see Rush, *Death and Burial in Christian Antiquity*, pp. 60–61. Cf. the moralization of the story of Jonathas in Hoccleve, *Minor Poems*, p. 242. *The Rohan Master: A Book of Hours*, ed. Meiss and Thomas, fol. 3 (pl. 3), develops the theme of the Church surrounded by the sea of the world in a novel way, without ship imagery. The *Ovide moralisé en prose*, ed. de Boer, pp. 294–95, discovers in the story of Ceyx and Alcyone an allegory of the Ship of the Church.

31. Figure 143: Oxford, Bodley MS. Douce 313, fol. 290v; cf. also fol. 46. For the fresco by Andrea da Firenze, see Meiss, *Painting in Florence and Siena*, fig. 97, and discussion pp. 94–100. The Spanish Chapel paintings in fact were not executed until 1366–68. M. Rickert, *Reconstructed Carmelite Missal*, pl. 12b, shows Peter's ship and Christ walking on the water within an initial (English, 1390's).

32. E.g., a drawing by Parri Spinelli (1397–1453), now in the Metropolitan Museum of Art, New York. The *Navicella* mosaic was about 33 feet high and 52 feet wide. On this and other versions of the design, see Virch, "A Page from Vasari's Book of Drawings." A large-scale cartoon (1628) by Cosimo Bartoli also survives; it is reproduced by Oakeshott, *Mosaics of Rome*, pl. 222, and discussed pp. 328–32. For reconstructions of the facade of the old St. Peter's with the *Navicella* in place, see Martindale and Baccheschi, *Complete Paintings of Giotto*, p. 110.

33. See St. Augustine, *Sermons*, p. 337 (Sermon 25). See also Sermon 26: "The Apostle Peter, who as he was walking, tottered through fear, and sinking in distrust, rose again by confession, gives us to understand that the sea is the present world, and the Apostle Peter the type of the One Church" (p. 340).

34. Figure 144: London, Brit. Lib. MS. Add. 11639, fol. 521, a Hebrew Miscellany, with School of Paris miniatures; on this MS., see Gutmann, *Hebrew Manuscript Painting*, p. 22 and commentary to pls. 20, 21. Figure 145: London, Brit. Lib. MS. Royal 14 B.ix (a genealogical roll, illustrating a text by Peter of Poitiers); cf. the closely related Bodley MS. reproduced by Pächt and Alexander, *Illuminated MSS.*, III, fig. 429b. For other arks of Noah assimilated to the Ship of the Church tradition, see Paris, Bibl. Natl. MS. fr. 28,

fol. 66v, illustrating Book XV of *The City of God* (French, ca. 1460); *Holkham Bible Picture Book*, fol. 8; an early-15th-century *Speculum humanae salvationis* in New York, Pierpont Morgan MS. M.140, fol. 5; the Genesis page of the Winchester Bible, ca. 1160–70, in Smalley, *Historians in the Middle Ages*, fig. 12 (p. 28); that from a *Somme le roi* in Robertson, *Preface to Chaucer*, fig. 79; *The Rohan Master*, pl. 26; and a carving in Ely Cathedral (ca. 1338), in Anderson, *Misericords*, pl. 13. On this development in illustrating the ark, see Allen, *Legend of Noah*, esp. pp. 158–59. For other instances identifying the ark allegorically as the Church, see Kolve, *Play Called Corpus Christi*, pp. 69–70, to which might be added: *Vices and Virtues*, pp. 43–45; Langland, *Piers Plowman*, B. X, 405–16; Lydgate, *Pilgrimage*, p. 587 (21992–94). Trevet's version of the story directly links Constance's boat to Noah's ark: "Then, in the eighth month of the fourth year, God, who steered the ship of the holy man Noah in the great flood, sent a favourable wind." (Bryan and Dempster, eds., *Sources and Analogues*, p. 168; here in Brock's trans., p. 12.) The *Pange, lingua* hymn of Venantius Fortunatus, written in honor of a fragment of the True Cross and sung in churches on Good Friday, concludes with lines praising the cross as being "like a ship, to prepare for the shipwrecked world a refuge" ("Atque portum praeparare nauta mundo naufrago"). On this poem see Raby, *A History of Christian-Latin Poetry*, pp. 88–91, and for an English translation, Brittain, ed., *Penguin Book of Latin Verse*, pp. 124–25.

35. Figure 146: Paris, Bibl. Natl. MS. fr. 19, fol. 55v, illustrating Book XV of *The City of God*. St. Augustine writes (here in the Dods trans.): "When these two cities began to run their course by a series of deaths and births, the citizen of this world was the first-born, and after him the stranger in this world, the citizen of the city of God, predestinated by grace, elected by grace, by grace a stranger below, and by grace a citizen above. . . . Accordingly, it is recorded of Cain that he built a city, but Abel, being a sojourner, built none. For the city of the saints is above, although here below it begets citizens, in whom it sojourns till the time of its reign arrives." (XV.1, p. 479.) I base my description of the picture primarily upon XV.20, which puzzles over the discrepancy in generations; see esp. p. 508. I presume the single dead man to be Adam, who brought death into the world. The ark was the first sign of mercy shown to man after the Fall.

36. Figure 147: Verona, Basilica of San Zeno Maggiore; cf. that of San Fermo Maggiore in the same city (a roof even more elaborately keeled) and, in Padua, the Churches of the Eremitani and of Santa Maria dei Servi (all four roofs date from the 14th century). In France, the Church of Sainte-Catherine at Honfleur has such a roof, as does the entry to the chapel in the house of Jacques Coeur in Bourges (both 15th century): the latter perhaps also makes reference to his richly successful career as a merchant. A church in Schermerhorn, North Holland, has a three-vault ship's keel roof and two votive ship models suspended in its aisles; it may be seen in Sitwell, *Netherlands*, fig. 76.

37. A kind of underground Christianity survives from an earlier Celtic mission, driven by pagan conquest to take refuge in Wales. Three secret Christians still live near the castle (II.540–50).

38. The *Crescentia* form of the story focuses on her power to cure and heal, rather than on baptism. See Schlauch, *Chaucer's Constance and Accused Queens*, pp. 109–10.

39. Figure 148: London, Brit. Lib. MS. Royal 15 D.iii, fol. 398v (a *Bible historiale*, Egerton Workshop). For characteristic Jonah pictures see, e.g., London, Brit. Lib. MS. King's 5, fols. 19 and 20 (a *Biblia pauperum*, Flemish or Rhenish, ca. 1400); Brit. Lib. MS. Royal 1 E.ix, fol. 232v (the "Richard II" Bible); and Brit. Lib. MS. Harl. 4382, fol. 122v (a *Bible historiale*, ca. 1400, once owned by Jean de Berry). See also Cockerell and James, eds., *Two East Anglian Psalters*, Ormesby, pl. 10; James, *Bohun Manuscripts*, pl. 45; and Randall, *Images in Margins*, figs. 290, 291.

40. Figure 149: Oxford, Bodley MS. Douce 313, fol. 146. Cf. our figure 111. The *Biblia pauperum* commonly shows this subject as one of its types of the Baptism of Christ: see the facsimile ed. Soltész, pl. 9. Cf. also Sandler, *The Peterborough Psalter*, fol. 24v and p. 113.

41. Tertullian, *Homily on Baptism*, pp. 19–21; on its influence, see pp. xxxiii–vi. The essential link was made by Saint Paul (I Cor., 10:1–2): "For I would not have you ignorant, brethren, that our fathers were all under the cloud: and all passed through the sea. And all in Moses were baptized, in the cloud and in the sea." The Easter hymn *Ad coenam agni*, originally intended for those newly baptized on that day, contains the following stanza: "Prepared for the supper of the Lamb, / Radiant in our white robes, / Having passed through the Red Sea, / Let us sing to Christ the Lord." (Quoted by Hardison, *Christian Rite and Christian Drama*, p. 95.) As noted above, Noah's Flood and the story of Jonah were likewise understood as types of the Baptism, involving delivery/salvation through water. On these three types, see Daniélou, *The Bible and the Liturgy*, Chaps. 4–6.

42. Daniélou, *The Bible and the Liturgy*, Chaps. 1–3 (a brilliant study of the early ceremonies). For a primary text, see Hugh of St. Victor, *On the Sacraments*, who describes the primacy of the rite (p. 282); its meaning as purification (p. 283), as rebirth (p. 290), and as exorcism (p. 298); its figures and types (pp. 296, 301–2); and its relation to Christ's death (p. 299). For these associated reasons, the early Church baptized only on Easter and Pentecost. See also Hardison, *Christian Rite and Christian Drama*, pp. 81, 154–55.

43. Figure 150: Poitiers, the Baptistery of St. John, whose architecture dates from the 4th, 7th, and 13th centuries; the sarcophagi and moldings are Merovingian. On this building, see Hubert et al., *Europe of the Invasions*, pp. 38–40, figs. 45–53.

44. Figure 151: Cambridge, Trinity Coll. MS. B.11.7, fol. 22v (from an English *Horae*). Cf. Oxford, Bodley MS. Auct. D. inf. 2.11, fol. 36v, ca. 1440–50, and the many examples spanning the Christian centuries reproduced by Schiller, *Iconography of Christian Art*, I, pls. 349–88. Figure 152: Cambridge, Fitzwilliam Mus. MS. 3-1954, fol. 70v (a French *Horae* made for the Duke of Burgundy; the pictures are in the style of the Maître aux Boqueteaux). On the baptism of pagans, see that of St. Augustine as shown in *The Très Riches Heures*, pl. 32; or that administered by Saints Peter and Paul in *Les Grandes Heures*, pl. 94 (cf. fig. 8); or that of Constantine in

New York, Pierpont Morgan MS. M.769, fol. 322v (a *Christ-herre Chronik*, ca. 1375–80); or the baptisms shown in a *L'Ystoire de Helayne* MS. dated 1448 (Brussels, Bibl. Royale MS. 9967), ed. Van den Gheyn, pls. 8, 10, 23; or the baptism of King Clovis, the first Christian king of France, in an illumination ca. 1480, in Laborde, *MSS. à peintures de la Cité de Dieu*, pl. 105. All are shown naked and waist-deep in the font; despite the historical reference, the costumes and architecture that surround them are contemporary. Cf. *Queen Mary's Psalter*, pls. 283, 301 (early 14th century). The early Church baptized by submersion (water completely covering the body) or immersion (water covering part of the body, with water poured over the rest) rather than by affusion or infusion (water poured over the head), as is most common today.

45. Figure 153: London, Brit. Lib. MS. Add. 29704-5, fol. 36v. Published by M. Rickert, *Reconstructed Carmelite Missal*, pl. 5 (described p. 101). Even ordinary pictures of infant baptism often convey a feeling of submission to water, as in Oxford, Bodley MS. Laud Misc. 740, fol. 5v (Guillaume de Deguileville's *Pilgrimage of the Lyf of the Manhode*), or Paris, Bibl. Natl. MS. fr. 823, fol. 4v, or London, Brit. Lib. MS. Harl. 2278, fol. 77.

46. Chaucer, *The Man of Law's Tale*, p. 35.

47. Luria, "Dame Custance's Voyages Re-examined,"; see n. 2 above. The steward is treated with a special contempt, greater even than that accorded the wicked Sultaness. Although she worships the wrong god, she refuses to deny her faith, fearing "afterward in helle to be drawe, / For we reneyed Mahoun oure creance" (II.339). For Apostacy in Guillaume de Deguileville's revised poem, see Lydgate, *Pilgrimage*, pp. 643–46. See also Michel of Northgate, *Ayenbite of Inwyt*, pp. 19, 43, and Gower's *Confessio amantis*, VIII, 11, where Lucifer and the fallen angels are described as "al the route apostazied." In some of the earliest ceremonies of baptism, the catechumen was anointed with oil: "Unctus et quasi athleta Christi, quasi luctam hujus saeculi luctaturus" ("anointed also, like an athlete of Christ, like one about to fight the battle of the world"); see Villien, *History and Liturgy of the Sacraments*, pp. 34–35, and Daniélou, *The Bible and the Liturgy*, pp. 40–42.

48. See McNeill and Gamer, *Medieval Handbooks of Penance*, pp. 18–20. Langland, *Piers Plowman*, B. XV, 443–51, describes the process of England's conversion, stressing miracles more than preaching, deeds more than words.

49. Bryan and Dempster, eds., *Sources and Analogues*, p. 175.

50. Reinhard, "Setting Adrift," pp. 35–36. Cf. Gottfried von Strassburg, *Tristan*, pp. 73–74, in which Norwegian merchants kidnap the young Tristan and endure great peril at sea until they resolve to put him ashore. The history of Jonah illustrates this idea as well.

51. Reinhard, "Setting Adrift," p. 58: "Ut venator [Beorn] in illa navicula in qua saepe dictus Lothebrocus in Angliam applicuit, poneretur et in medio maris solus sine omni instrumento navali dimissus probetur, si illum Deus velit a periculo liberare."

52. Figure 154: London, Brit. Lib. MS. Harl. 2278, fol. 46, made for presentation to Henry VI. Other boat journeys that figure in the poem are illustrated on fols. 16v, 20, 41v. For Lydgate's text see Horstmann, ed., *Alten-*

glische Legenden: Neue Folge, pp. 376–445; I quote from p. 401. *Corolla Sancti Eadmundi* contains the poem (pp. 409–524), along with many other versions of the saint's history.

53. Reinhard, "Setting Adrift," p. 47.

54. In Horstmann, ed., *Yorkshire Writers*, II, 68 (59–64). The poem immediately following in the MS. is titled "Þo whele of fortune" (*ibid.*, p. 70). A poem in London, Brit. Lib. MS. Add. 37049, also northern, 1/2 15th century, develops a similar image ("Þis warld may lykkynd be / Most propyrly vnto þe see") on fol. 72.

55. Alain de Lille, *Anticlaudianus*, VII.405–VIII.62 (ed. Bossuat), trans. Sheridan, pp. 186–91. Chaucer refers to the work in *HF*, 986.

56. *Roman de la rose*, ll. 5891–6144, ed. Lecoy (trans. Dahlberg, pp. 118–22). Cf. Cambridge, Fitzwilliam Mus. MS. 169, fol. 30 (15th century), which offers a minimal iconographic version. Christine de Pisan, in *La Mutacion de Fortune*, written in 1403, invents a variant *Château de Fortune*, suspended by four chains and surrounded by sea; newcomers to the castle arrive by boat. On this text, see Meiss, *Limbourgs*, I, 9–12, and for illustrations, II, figs. 14–16.

57. Figure 155: London, Brit. Lib. MS. Cotton Tiber. A. vii, fol. 58v. Figure 156: *ibid.*, fol. 59v. For this action, see Lydgate, *Pilgrimage*, pp. 508–25, and for the verses quoted, ll. 19437–46. This long section on the sea of the world comes just before the ABC hymn to the Virgin that Chaucer translated, which is followed by a long discourse on astrology, the power of the stars, and God's governance of them—another significant theme in our tale. (Lydgate incorporates Chaucer's translation of the ABC poem, pp. 528–33.) For other images of Fortune and her wheel in the midst of the sea, see London, Brit. Lib. MS. Add. 10341, fol. 31v (Lady Philosophy shows this image to Boethius in a vision), from the 15th century, and Oxford, Bodley MS. Douce 332, fol. 58, from a 14th-century *Romance of the Rose*, supremely simple and beautiful, reproduced by Fleming, "*Roman de la Rose*," fig. 30; see also MS. Douce 195, fol. 43 (15th century) in *The Romance of the Rose*, ed. Dahlberg, fig. 30.

58. Figure 157: Paris, Bibl. Natl. MS. fr. 916, fol. 74v. This work, which Chaucer translated as "Of the Wreched Engendrynge of Mankynde" (*LGW*, [G] 414), furnishes four passages in the *Man of Law's Tale* (II.421–27, 771–77, 925–31, 1132–38), plus much of the "poverty" prologue. After Trevet's *Chroniques*, it is the most prominent literary source for the poem. See Lotario dei Segni, *On the Misery of the Human Condition*; Chaucer's translation has been lost.

59. On the tradition of *Fortuna Redux*, see Panofsky, *Iconography of Correggio's Camera di San Paolo*, pp. 58–59, and figs. 28, 29 (the coin of Vespasian), 35, 36. The coin of Domitian (A.D. 81–96) was reported, with photo, in *The Times*, August 7, 1963. Chaucer's *Canticus Troili*, based on Petrarch's "S'amor non è," uses the image of a rudderless boat in the sea of fortune to express Troilus's condition as a lover: "Thus possed to and fro, / Al stereles withinne a boot am I / Amydde the see, bitwixen wyndes two, / That in contrarie stonden evere mo" (*TC*, I, 415). Patch, *Goddess Fortuna*, remains a valuable introduction to the subject as a whole; see also Pickering, *Literature and Art*, pp. 168–222.

60. Among the Renaissance pictures, see an engraving by Nicoletto da Modena in which Fortune's cloak billows behind her like a ship's sail, as she stands in the sea, one foot upon a globe representing the earth and its inherent instability (cf. Chaucer's ballade "Trouthe," in which he advises against trust in "hir that turneth as a bal") and her other foot upon a rudder. (See van Marle, *Iconographie de l'art profane*, II, 185–91, and fig. 215.) And consider a decorated pavement in the Cathedral of Siena, designed by Pinturicchio (1504, laid 1506), whose subject is a mountain in the midst of a sea, with Socrates and Crates at its top serving a goddess who is either Virtue or Wisdom. Still other philosophers ascend the slope, leaving behind them Lady Fortune, her cloak a sail, one foot on a ball, the other on a ship, governing the sea of this world. Crates pours out jewels and gold, as worthless things, upon the lovely Lady Fortune below. Old documents name the mosaic *La storia della Fortuna*, though it could as well be named "The Reward of Virtue" or "The Pursuit of Wisdom." See van Marle, II, fig. 213, and Cust, *Pavement Masters of Siena*, pp. 25–28. See also 16th-century engravings by Albrecht Dürer, Sebald Beham, and Heinrich Aldegrever, in *Symbols in Transformation*, figs. 43, 45–47, discussed pp. 51–52, employing the symbolism of the turning ball, the sail, the ship, and the sea.

61. Figure 158: Paris, Bibl. Natl. MS. fr. 990, fol. 2. Discussed by Mâle, *L'Art religieux*, p. 307.

62. Trevet, in Bryan and Dempster, eds., *Sources and Analogues*, p. 168.

63. *Cleanness*, p. 23, ll. 413–24. In *Wakefield Pageants*, Noah invokes God as steersman ("Help, God, in this nede! / As thou art stere-man good, and best, as I rede, / Of all, / Thou rewle vs in this rase") before issuing a practical command ("Wife, tent the stere-tre") as he sounds the depth of the sea (p. 25, ll. 427–33). *Cursor Mundi*, I, 112 (1803–12) has a strong description of the ark lost on the waters. In *The Miller's Tale* (1.3532–34) Nicholas says to John, "I undertake, withouten mast and seyl, / Yet shal I saven hire and thee and me. / Hastow nat herd hou saved was Noe?" Troilus invites Criseyde to become his "steere" when he pledges her his love (III, 1291).

64. Wood, *Chaucer and the Country of the Stars*, in a lengthy chapter, "Astrology in the *Man of Law's Tale*," pp. 192–244, argues from this rhetoric that the narrator displays a marked concern for astrology to the neglect of Providence; that this grows out of the avaricious, mercantile obsessions commonly attributed to lawyers (p. 242); and that the whole tale displays an "anti-Boethian, anti-humanistic, anti-religious approach to life" (p. 195), which must be intended as an ironic exposure of its pilgrim teller. Loomis, "Constance and the Stars," has convincingly challenged his reading on astrological grounds (see esp. p. 217, for her critical conclusions). The present chapter presents an alternative reading of virtually all Wood's other evidence. I would, for example, emphasize the serial nature of the rhetorical apostrophes, seeing in them a traditional means of strengthening the tale's emotional effect by responding to its events as they occur, subject to later correction as the patterns and purposes of the whole emerge. The Man of Law moves his audience through the narrative and on their behalf comments on it, asks questions of it, and decorates it poetically to make a maximally effective work of art. Here he asks an obviously pragmatic question when the story itself cannot yet yield an answer, in order to heighten the

power of that answer when it comes. He leaves the question unresolved as a deliberate strategem; we should not fix him there, as though he were incapable of perceiving the point of his own story—a point that he makes beautifully clear by the end.

65. Cf. also Bk. II, pr. 2, in which Fortune defends herself against Philosophy by an analogy with the sea, saying it is her nature to be unstable: "The see hath eek his ryght to ben somtyme calm and blaundysschyng with smothe watir, and somtyme to ben horrible with wawes and with tempestes." (Chaucer's trans.)

66. See esp. II.822–26, 866–68, 950–52.

67. For the Latin text, see *Navigatio Sancti Brendani Abbatis*, ed. Selmer. There is a translation in Webb, *Lives of the Saints*, pp. 31–68. Webb adds a useful introduction on the distinctive features of Celtic Christianity.

68. Webb, *Lives of the Saints*, p. 37. See also pp. 50–51.

69. Figure 159: Oxford, Queen's College MS. 305, fol. 148. For the vernacular texts, see Waters, ed., *Anglo-Norman Voyage of St. Brendan*, and *The South English Legendary*, I, 180–204; on the former, see Legge, *Anglo-Norman Literature*, pp. 8–18. Owen, *Vision of Hell*, summarizes the story and speculates on its relationship to the pagan *Voyage of Bran*, pp. 22–27.

70. Figure 160: Oxford, Bodley MS. Laud Misc. 720, fol. 226v. The relevant text may be read in Giraldus Cambrensis, *First Version of the Topography of Ireland*, trans. O'Meara. The men shown are from Connacht and are pagan; the chapter is headed "Many in the island have never been baptized, and have not yet heard of the Faith" (pp. 94–95). Smalley, *Historians in the Middle Ages*, shows the picture in color (pl. 6, opp. p. 148).

71. *The Anglo-Saxon Chronicle*, p. 53. Later the three voyagers (according to Æthelweard) went toward Rome, en route to Jerusalem (*ibid.*, n. 7).

72. See Reinhard, "Setting Adrift," pp. 36, 37.

73. Quoted by Henry, *Early English and Celtic Lyric*, p. 33; see p. 36 for a Welsh instance and a discussion of Dorothy Whitelock's interpretation of the Anglo-Saxon *Seafarer*, and Chap. 3 for a study of this kind of pilgrimage (called *ailithre*).

74. *Ibid.*, p. 32, n. 1.

75. Webb, trans., *Lives of the Saints*, p. 51.

76. A few examples across the medieval centuries must suffice. The *Sermons* of St. Augustine, already cited, establish the sea through which the Ship of the Church sails as one of temptation and danger (p. 342; also pp. 337–38): "Consider the world to be the sea; the wind is boisterous, and there is a mighty tempest. Each man's peculiar lust is his tempest." Dronke, *Medieval Lyric*, p. 49, translates a relevant 11th-century German lyric by the priest Ezzo, cited in n.23 above. In the 12th century the image may be found, e.g., in Alain de Lille, *The Complaint of Nature*, p. 85 ("the shipwreck of the human race"); in the Archpoet's "Confession" ("Feror ego veluti sine nauta navis"), in Raby, ed., *Oxford Book of Medieval Latin Verse*, p. 263; and it is explicated by Bernardus Silvestris, *Commentary on the Aeneid*, ed. Jones and Jones, pp. 11, 20–21, 30–31 (trans. Schreiber and Maresca, pp. 12, 22, 33). In the early 13th century, it occurs, e.g., in Guillaume le Clerc, *Bestiary*, pp. 21, 40–42, in moralizations of the sawfish and the ibis; also in *Vices and Virtues*, pp. 43–45. Some 14th-century uses

are: *Pricke of Conscience*, p. 34 (II, 1212–24); *Book of Vices and Virtues*, pp. 126 (25–31), 127 (28–35), working with the text from Proverbs; in a variant form in Gower's *Vox clamantis*, I, 17–21 (pp. 66–81), in which the Peasants' Revolt is imaged as a terrible storm on a sea of vice and rebellion and the Tower of London becomes the ship in which good men seek safety (*Major Latin Works*, pp. 84–95); and "Of þo flode of þo world," in Horstmann, ed., *Yorkshire Writers*, II, 67. For some 15th-century occurrences, see *Dicts and Sayings of the Philosophers*, ed. Bühler, p. 101 (where the simile is credited to Socrates); Herrtage, ed., *Early English Versions of the "Gesta Romanorum,"* p. 321; Owst, *Literature and Pulpit*, p. 71 (quoting from a sermon); Christine de Pisan, *Epistle of Othea*, p. 45 (an allegory of Neptune, which London, Brit. Lib. MS. Harl. 4431, fol. 110v, illustrates beautifully).

77. The Psalter is divided into eight sections for recital in the daily liturgy: seven sections are assigned to the seven days of the week, and the eighth is distributed across them all. Figure 161: London, Brit. Lib. MS. Royal 17 E.vii, Pt. I, fol. 243v (a *Bible historiale*); cf. the same library's MS. Add. 35311, fol. 53v (ca. 1415). Likewise New York, Pierpont Morgan MS. M.75, fol. 34 (3/4 14th century), and the examples reproduced by Meiss, *Patronage*, II, fig. 79 (which includes a ship) and *Boucicaut Master*, fig. 460 (which includes a mermaid in the water). All the above include God. Psalm 41:8 also speaks of waters of tribulation: "Deep calleth on deep, at the noise of thy flood-gates. All thy heights and thy billows have passed over me." In London, Brit. Lib. MS. Royal 2 B.viii, fol. 64 (an English Psalter, 1/4 14th century), David is nearly pulled under by the water and God is absent. Guillaume de Deguileville, *Pilgrimage of the Lyf of the Manhode*, pp. 32, 171, speaks of the waters of contrition; on p. 172, they are called "a secunde cristeninge."

78. See London, Brit. Lib. MS. Royal 1 E.ix, fol. 149v, a Bible possibly owned by Richard II. St. Augustine read the psalm as foretelling the Passion of Christ and interpreted its details in those terms: the waters are the multitudes who prevailed upon Christ even unto death. See St. Augustine, *Expositions on the Book of Psalms*, III, 357–59, 362–63. According to Harrison, *Treasures of Illumination*, in England the psalm was most often illuminated with a picture of Jonah and the whale (see p. 20, and pls. 14, 17 [5]); Burrow, *Ricardian Poetry*, reproduces a Bohun MS. page with Jonah as his frontispiece. But David in the water is also a common subject, and if the census is extended to Northern Europe as a whole, by far the more frequent one— as a glance at the summary Tables appended to Haseloff, *Psalterillustration*, will make clear.

79. Figure 162: Paris, Bibl. Natl. MS. Lat. 10483, fol. 37 (the Belleville Breviary, illuminated by Jean Pucelle). On this MS., see Morand, *Jean Pucelle*, pp. 43–45, with many plates. The present page is reproduced in color by Avril, *Manuscript Painting at the Court of France*, pl. 12 (with commentary). He correctly reads the picture as symbolizing "the Church's trust in God in spite of tribulations" (p. 62). Madrid, Bibl. Natl. MS. I.i.77 (late 14th century) includes this description of the subject and its allegorical meaning, intended as a guide to the illuminator: "David est in mari in navi et tempestas oritur et ipse orat Dominum.—Ecclesia flagellatur et Petrus plorat." See Berger, "Les Manuels pour l'illustration du Psautier," p. 108.

80. Figure 163: London, Brit. Lib. MS. Cotton Tiber. A.vii, fol. 52v, illustrating the Lydgate translation; the pilgrim is shown in his solitary swimming on fol. 58 as well. See Lydgate, *Pilgrimage*, pp. 509–18, for the text (cf. *Pilgrimage of the Lyf of the Manhode*, pp. 174–80). For another text in which devils fish for men see "Of þo flode of þo world," in Horstmann, ed., *Yorkshire Writers*, II, 69. For other representative illuminations, see Tuve, *Allegorical Imagery*, figs. 86, 87; New York, Pierpont Morgan MS. M.772, fols. 83, 87v, 89 (ca. 1360–70); London, Brit. Lib. MS. Add. 38120, fol. 92v (ca. 1400); Paris, Bibl. Natl. MS. fr. 376, fol. 74 (ca. 1430–40), MS. fr. 377, fols. 78v, 80, 83v (end of 14th century), and MS. fr. 823, for a particularly rich sequence, fols. 79, 79v, 82v, 83, 85, 86v (Parisian, dated 1393). Henry of Lancaster, *Le Livre de seyntz medicines*, pp. 90–95, explores the figure of the sea of this world at length; he was father to Chaucer's Duchess Blanche. See also *Lanterne of Light*, pp. 44–47.

81. Hugh of St. Victor, *Selected Spiritual Writings*, p. 45.

82. *Ibid.*, p. 143; see also pp. 160–61, 175–76 (from *De vanitate mundi*).

83. I quote from Lydgate, *Pilgrimage*, p. 511 (19144, 19156).

84. Langland, *Piers Plowman*, B. VIII, 26–50.

85. A variant of this image occurs in *The Parson's Tale* (x.362–65).

86. Guillaume de Deguileville, *Pilgrimage of the Lyf of the Manhode*, pp. 177–78. The pressure of this moral meaning is so strong that in the lines describing Custance's journey to England—"She dryveth forth into oure occian / Thurghout oure wilde see, til atte laste / Under an hoold that nempnen I ne kan, / Fer in Northhumberlond the wawe hire caste" (II.505)—the phrase "oure wilde see" (the English Channel or North Sea) suggests as well a sense of specifically English passion, sin, and error.

87. King Alla slays his mother for her crime (II.893–96), an event that apparently occasions no sense of sin at the time, though later he does penance by making a pilgrimage to the Pope in Rome (II.988–96).

88. Cf. Brunetto Latini, *Li Livres dou tresor*, pp. 208–9: "Li constans est millour que li mouvables, porce ke li movables se torne a cascun vent, mais li hom ferm et constans ne sera ja esmeus par force de desiriers" ("the constant [man] is better than the changeable [man], because the changeable turns with every wind, but the firm and constant man will never be moved by the power of desire"). See also pp. 269–70. Cf. the images of tower and tree used to define Constancy in *Book of Vices and Virtues*, p. 168: "Þe fifþe degree of prowesse is cleped constaunce, þat is continuaunce. Þis is þe vertue þat makeþ þe herte as stedefast and tristy to God as a tour þat is founded vpon þe harde roche and as a tree þat is roted harde in good erþe, þat schakeþ ne boweþ for no wynde þat may come ne blowe, þat is to seie for non auenture þat may come, good ne euele."

89. Heb. 13:14, as translated in *The Lanterne of Light*, a 15th-century Wycliffite treatise, p. 40 (31–32). Cf. *Pricke of Conscience*, p. 38 (1370–73): "*Non habemus manentem civitatem, / sed futurum inquirimus.* / 'Na syker wonnyng-sted here haf we, / Bot we seke ane, þat sal ay be.'"

90. In the legend of Judas Iscariot incorporated into *The Golden Legend*'s life of St. Matthias, Judas's mother dreams that the child she has conceived will be the destroyer of the Jewish people, and so his father sets the child adrift at sea in a little basket-boat to meet his death (Jacobus de Voragine,

Legenda aurea, p. 184; *The Golden Legend*, trans. Ryan and Ripperger, pp. 172–73). The story is told in *The South English Legendary*, as well (p. 693), and is narrated by Judas himself in the Wakefield "Hanging of Judas" (*Towneley Plays*, pp. 394–95). On this tradition, see Baum, "The Mediaeval Legend of Judas Iscariot," esp. pp. 482, 485, 591–93. (Baum records 42 Latin texts of the separate legend, and versions in every likely vernacular. It was extremely popular in the late 13th and 14th centuries.)

91. *Aeneid*, VI, 295–330, 384–416. Boccaccio uses the figure of Acheron's shore in *De casibus*, Bk. III, p. 80; *Fates of Illustrious Men*, p. 87.

92. Figure 164: London, Brit. Lib. MS. Egerton 943, fol. 7v. "Then, weeping bitterly, they drew all together to the accursed shore which awaits every man that fears not God. . . . Thus they depart over the dark water." (*Inferno* III, 106–20, trans. Sinclair, p. 53.) See *Inferno*, ed. and trans. Singleton, II, 52–56, for commentary on the Virgilian echoes and borrowings; and Brieger et al., *Illuminated Manuscripts of the Divine Comedy*, II, 53, 55–61, 64–66, for many other illustrations of this voyage, and (for Brieger's commentary) I, 119–20. In Brieger's judgment, "It seems that the earliest illuminators started on their new task with an illustrated codex of Virgil's *Aeneid* before them" (I, 86; fig. 107, from the 13th century, offers interesting evidence). Cf. the moment in *Piers Plowman*, B. XVIII, 307, when Christ comes to harrow hell, and a devil says: "I se wher a soule comeþ silynge hiderward."

93. *Purgatorio* II, 40–51, trans. Sinclair, p. 35; see *Purgatorio*, ed. and trans. Singleton, II, 30–32, for commentary. Figure 165: London, Brit. Lib. MS. Egerton 943, fol. 65 (companion picture to my figure 164; cf. the two pictures of disembarkment on fol. 65v). For other pictures see Brieger et al., *Illuminated Manuscripts of the Divine Comedy*, II, 18–25, 332–35.

94. Eilhart von Oberge, *Tristrant*, pp. 60–61; for the original, see the edition by Buschinger, pp. 88–93. Gottfried von Strassburg, *Tristan*, handles the matter very differently (pp. 139–41): Tristan knows he must go to Ireland to be cured, and sails for it deliberately. So too Malory (*Works*, pp. 286–87).

95. Figure 166: Wienhausen Embroidery, I, 2d row, scene 9, discussed by Loomis and Loomis, *Arthurian Legends in Medieval Art*, pp. 50–52. Tristan is put to sea like someone dead or dying. Cf. their fig. 48, a tile from Chertsey Abbey, ca. 1270, which once had a full Tristan cycle decorating its floor (figs. 25–59). The garment Tristan wears in the boat, where he is shown harping, seems to be a shroud; it is unlike what he wears in his illness, when King Mark visits him (fig. 47), or while teaching Iseult to harp (fig. 49). A tile fragment reading "sans governail" ("without a rudder") probably belongs to this scene.

96. Malory, *Works*, pp. 721–22; for the French original, more detailed in the loading of the ship, see *La Queste del Saint Graal*, pp. 241–42, trans. as *The Quest of the Holy Grail*, pp. 249–50.

97. Malory, *Works*, pp. 779–82 ("Astolat"—Fr. *Escalot*—is modern Guilford); for the French text see *La Mort le Roi Artu*, pp. 87–92, trans. as *The Death of King Arthur*, pp. 92–96. Arthur's own death journey is by ship, under the mysterious charge of Morgan the Fay; see *La Mort le Roi Artu*, pp. 250–52; *The Death of King Arthur*, pp. 224–26. Manchester, John Ry-

lands Lib. MS. French 1, fol. 226, illustrates the arrival of the lady "morte en vne nef deuant le chastel le roy artu" (at Camelot, in the French version, rather than at Westminster, as in Malory); there is a related illustration in London, Brit. Lib. MS. Royal 14 E.iii, fol. 153v. Both MSS. date from ca. 1316. See also Loomis and Loomis, *Arthurian Legends in Medieval Art*, figs. 247, 338, and their discussion of these MSS., pp. 97–98. Stones, "A Short Note on Manuscripts Rylands French 1 and Douce 215," argues that the Bodley Douce MS. was originally part of the Rylands MS; it also shows a corpse afloat on the water, fol. 35 (from the prose *Lancelot* cycle). In all three pictures, the man who (in the text) steers the ship is not shown; the image is generalized as a ship of death journeying at random upon the water. A related tradition, derived from late-classical romance, involves the disposal of a corpse at sea, perhaps the best-known example being the story of Appollonius of Tyre, extant in several English versions including that told by Gower in the *Confessio amantis*. In this story, the prince's wife, thought to have died in childbirth during a tempest at sea, is buried with treasure in a watertight coffin that floats to land, where she is miraculously restored to life by a physician. In Gower's version (its incest episode is obliquely referred to in *The Man of Law's Introduction*) she wakes to ask, as if from death, "Ha, wher am I? / Where is my lord, what world is this?" (VIII, 1206–7, in *Complete Works*, II, 418.) The story involves many journeys, chiefly emblematic of fortune; its one death journey is quickly undone, as she is restored to life. But cf. ll. 1539–40, where the daughter's unwarranted epitaph concludes, "Fourtiene yer sche was of Age, / Whan deth hir tok to his viage." In the Cornish plays, on the advice of Veronica, Pilate's corpse, which has polluted the Tiber, is sent to hell in a boat committed to the open sea; that boat and its freight are there received by devils. See *The Cornish Ordinalia*, pp. 236–40, 267. The boat ending is a variant on the story as narrated in Jacobus de Voragine, *The Golden Legend*, trans. Ryan and Ripperger, p. 215 (*Legenda aurea*, p. 234), as part of the Passion of Our Lord. Cf. James, trans., *Apocryphal New Testament*, pp. 157–58.

98. Jacobus de Voragine, *The Golden Legend*, trans. Ryan and Ripperger, pp. 371–72; trans. Caxton, IV, 102; *Legenda aurea*, p. 424. See also *The South English Legendary*, I, 331–32.

99. Figure 167: London, Brit. Lib. MS. Royal 20 D.vi, fol. 20. The alabaster retable is in five parts, with both outer panels showing the saint in a boat: the one on the left showing Christ calling James and John, who are holding fishing nets, the one on the right his death ship. It is illustrated and described by Chamoso Lamas, *Santiago de Compostela*, pp. 95–96. One might compare the scene in the St. James cycle painted by Altichiero in the San Felice Chapel of San Antonio da Padua, ca. 1379, which shows the saint's body being readied by his followers, while an angel sits in the death ship, hand on the rudder; see Mellini, *Altichiero*, who publishes the full cycle, with commentary. Mâle, *Saints Compagnons*, pp. 135–68, reproduces several medieval versions of the subject, including a silver altar carving from Pistoia, Italy (14th century, p. 144), showing the corpse with ten followers in the boat, sail and rudder untended, with the mast forming a protective cross above them. Bottineau, *Chemins de Saint-Jacques*, is also rich in illustrations: see esp. pp. 17, 34, 42, 43. For other MS. illuminations, see

Paris, Bibl. Natl. MS. lat. 17294, fol. 515 (made between 1424 and 1435), and Rome, Bibl. Vaticana MS. lat. 8541, fol. 29 (a Passional, 1/2 14th century). See also Vázquez de Parga et al., *Las peregrinaciones a Santiago de Compostela*, esp. III, pl. 35 (2) and 37.

100. Figure 168: from the Magdalen Chapel in the lower Basilica of S. Francesco, Assisi; on the cycle, see Palumbo, ed., *Giotto e i Giotteschi in Assisi*, pp. 106–28; this painting is reproduced as color pl. 16; cf. color pl. 15. Baccheschi, in Martindale and Baccheschi, *Complete Paintings of Giotto*, p. 112, identifies the subject simply as "The Magdalen receives Communion and Her Soul is carried to Heaven"; he also reproduces the lunette that shows her daily contemplation of the bliss of heaven. For the text quoted, see Jacobus de Voragine, *The Golden Legend*, trans. Ryan and Ripperger, p. 362; *Legenda aurea*, p. 414. For other versions of the scene, see the references in Réau, *Iconographie de l'art chrétien*, III, 852–53, 857–58.

101. Trevet, "Life of Constance," trans. Brock, pp. 10–12; Bryan and Dempster, eds., *Sources and Analogues*, pp. 167–68.

102. II.470–76, 484–504, 639–44, 932–45.

103. Yunck, "Religious Elements," pp. 253–56. The prayers he adduces either include persons not mentioned by Chaucer or exclude others Chaucer does name; the correspondence is not exact. Yunck associates these prayers with the theme of martyrdom; I think instead they point to the death journey of the soul. Farrell, "Chaucer's Use of the Theme of the Help of God," associates many of the same figures (again the correspondence is not one to one) with an iconographic series C. R. Morey discovered in the art of the earliest Christian sarcophagi, which he termed "the Help of God" and whose common theme is deliverance from death and sin and suffering. I would stress the fact that this is (in Morey's words) "catacomb symbolism."

104. The ancient Egyptians thought of the heavens as a large ocean on which the sun and stars traveled in ships. The Sun God, Ra, traveled in the greatest of these, and the kings of Egypt, who claimed descent from him, were imagined as being conducted after death to the east to shine among the gods; magnificent funeral ships were placed in temples for this purpose. In time, the idea was democratized: anyone, royal or not, might travel to the east with the god, and once there would need yet another ship because the fields of Iaru, the fields of the blessed, were surrounded by water. Mourners sought to supply the dead with boats for that passage, so that they might be independent of the celestial ferryman, a frightening and malevolent creature. Such burial myths and customs probably lie behind the Roman myth of Charon and Acheron noted above, with *Aeneid*, Bk. VI, its classic literary expression. See Rush, *Death and Burial*, pp. 44–54. For visual evidence from Egypt, see Panofsky, *Tomb Sculpture*, figs. 8, 13, 21a (commentary, pp. 13, 14, 17).

105. Figure 169: a stele from the Kelsey Museum of Archaeology, Univ. of Michigan, Ann Arbor; reproduced by Panofsky, *Tomb Sculpture*, fig. 170 (cf. also figs. 171, 172), with commentary, pp. 44–45. On the museum's collection, see Hooper, *Funerary Stelae from Kom Abou Billou*, and Bonner, "The Ship of the Soul on a Group of Grave-Stelae"; Bonner describes the present example (his fig. 3) on p. 85. It is a monument to a young man named Apion, who died in his 26th year. He stands with his hands raised in

an attitude of prayer (conventional in both Greek and Roman monuments); the boat is small, with a steering paddle but without sail. Rush, *Death and Burial*, pp. 54–71, provides a learned account of both the literary and the archaeological evidence for the idea of death as a *migratio ad Dominum*. Perret, *Catacombes de Rome*, V, pl. 69 (7), shows the ship and the *chi-ro* monogram. Glob, *Mound People*, fig. 51 (commentary, p. 148), reproduces a ship carved on a Bronze Age tombstone from Himmerland, Denmark, dating before 1000 B.C. Farrell, "Chaucer's Use of the Theme of the Help of God," alone among Chaucer critics has sensed the importance of the figure of the "orant" for an understanding of Custance (p. 242); he found it described in Morey.

106. Perhaps the most famous example is the burial ship of a mid-seventh-century East Anglian king, excavated in this century at Sutton Hoo. Its grave goods suggest that he was a Christian, for they include silver bowls and scabbard bosses decorated with crosses, and two silver christening spoons engraved with the names Saulus and Paulus, in memory of that earlier conversion. See Bruce-Mitford, *Sutton Hoo Ship Burial*, for a general account. His frontispiece shows the excavation in progress, pl. 22a the christening spoons, and pl. 28 the silver bowls. The burial is dated ca. 625–50; see pp. 44–51. The latest testings of soil from the burial chamber reveal phosphate concentrations that suggest (contrary to earlier opinion) that a body was part of the original burial. Oxenstierna, *Norsemen*, pp. 107–9, translates a remarkable eyewitness account by an Arab, Ibn Fadlan, of a ship funeral on the shore of the Volga in 922.

107. Oxenstierna, *Norsemen*, fig. 6. See Wilson, *Vikings and Their Origins*, figs. 24, 87, for similar burial grounds, and pp. 47–52 for commentary thereon, along with Brøndsted, *Vikings*, pp. 298–305. See *Beowulf*, ed. Klaeber, note to ll. 4–52 (esp. p. 122), on the three stages of ship burials. The account of the funeral of Scyld Scefing at the beginning of the poem as well as the funeral of Beowulf at its end are both relevant here. Meaney, *A Gazetteer of Early Anglo-Saxon Burial Sites*, pp. 15–21, "The Burial Customs of the Heathen English," is helpful, as is the detailed survey that follows. Ship burials were not common—they seem to have been reserved for chieftains and men of wealth—but the evidence of Caister-on-Sea, where only parts of the sides of boats were laid over graves, suggests the importance not just of aristocratic tradition but of "some symbolism, probably that of a journey to the world of the dead" (p. 19). She describes Snape and Sutton Hoo on pp. 232 and 233–35.

108. See Smithers, "Meaning of *The Seafarer* and *The Wanderer*," pp. 137–40. He also argues for the MS. reading *wælweg* (*Seafarer*, 63) as meaning "corpse road" (the path traveled by the dead) rather than an emendation yielding "whale's road" as the poem's intended kenning for "ocean."

109. Kennedy, trans., *An Anthology of Old English Poetry*, p. 140 (punctuation mine).

110. See Henry, *Early English and Celtic Lyric*, pp. 58–63, for a text and translation ("Uga Corbmaic meic Cuilendain"), esp. stanzas 10, 11 (p. 60). *The Anglo-Saxon Chronicle*'s account of the three Irishmen who arrived at Alfred's court in 891 (see above, p. 333) follows it with this brief item: "& Swifneh se betsta lareow þe on Scottum wæs gefor" ("and Suibhne, the

best teacher among the Irish, died"). The linking is suggestive. They voyage in one way, he in another, for the literal sense of "gefor" is simply "set forth," "traveled," "went out." Henry (whose translation I quote) notes the sequence (p. 29, n. 1), but without comment. (In the translation by Whitelock et al., p. 53, "on Scottum" is translated as "among the Scots.")

111. Guillaume de Deguileville, *Le Pelerinage de l'ame*, p. 94 (2715–18).

112. Hoccleve, *Minor Poems*, p. 212 (911–17).

113. Lydgate, *Minor Poems*, I, 335 (165–67).

114. Bryan and Dempster, eds., *Sources and Analogues*, p. 174; Trevet, "Life of Constance," trans. Brock, p. 30.

115. Bryan and Dempster, eds., *Sources and Analogues*, pp. 168, 175, 177, 178; and Trevet, "Life of Constance," trans. Brock, pp. 10, 12, 34, 38, 42.

116. These two numbers appear in Trevet without symbolic implication, and Chaucer may have meant to transmit them in the same mode. But the elimination of all numbers *except* the 3 and the 5, and the decision to make the two voyages occur in the same boat, suggest he meant us to think about them in relation to other anagogic tendencies in his poem. For a general introduction to the symbolic meaning of numbers, see Hopper, *Medieval Number Symbolism*; Fowler, ed., *Silent Poetry*; and two essays by Peck, "Numerology and Chaucer's *Troilus and Criseyde*," esp. pp. 1–13, and "Number as Cosmic Language." On the octagonal shape of baptismal fonts, see Mâle, *Gothic Image*, p. 14 (nn. 2 and 3), and Daniélou, *The Bible and the Liturgy*, p. 37; there is an example from the 5th century in Fréjus, pictured in Huyghe, ed., *Larousse Encyclopedia of Byzantine and Medieval Art*, p. 243 (fig. 506). Augustine summarizes his eight-age schema in the penultimate paragraph of *The City of God* (trans. Dods, p. 867). Cf. Hugh of St. Victor, "De arca Noe morali," *Selected Spiritual Writings*, pp. 120–21, on 7 as the number of this present life and 8 as the number of eternity: "Let wisdom grow, then, through seven and eight." In *Emaré*, a romance analogue to Chaucer's tale, the heroine on her second journey floats at random for "a full sevene nyght and more" before arriving at Rome, and her husband makes his penitential journey to that city after "fully seven yere" of grief; see Rumble, ed., *Breton Lays in Middle English*, pp. 120 (673–82) and 125 (805–16). The number 8 likewise figures heavily (and symbolically) in the *Voyage of St. Brendan*, in his quest for the blessed isles: see Webb, trans., *Lives of the Saints*, pp. 41, 43, 45, 52, 60–61, 67, 68.

117. Coghill and Tolkien, in their edition of *The Man of Law's Tale*, p. 36, draw this parallel; see *Early English Versions of the "Gesta Romanorum,"* ed. Herrtage, e.g., pp. 4, 6, 11, 13, 16, 22, 30, 36, 41, for stories in which the Roman Emperor is said to represent God or Christ, and pp. 25, 44, 125, 144, 164, 173, 222, 236, 430, 437, for stories in which his daughter stands for man's soul. An analogue to the Constance story appears in this collection, in which the Emperor is differently named and the ship journeys not important, but where he is identified in the "moralite" as "our lord ihesu crist; the wife is þe sowle of man" (p. 319; the story begins on p. 311).

118. In Augustine's *The City of God*, Rome is at once the glory of the past and the type of the earthly city; but even in its degeneracy and defeat, the City of God exists within it in the hearts of the faithful, a greater city that

will be separated from the other only at the end of time. The schematic image of Rome painted ca. 1413–16 by the Limbourgs for Jean de Berry shows the monuments of that city, classical and Christian, side by side, as a complex treasury of human aspiration and achievement, intermingled until time's end: see pl. 106 in the facsimile *Très Riches Heures*, or Meiss, *The Limbourgs*, II, fig. 721 (for commentary, I, 209–14). On the importance of Rome in medieval times, see Homo, *Rome médiévale*, esp. pp. 168–75, on pilgrimages, religious festivals, and jubilees; and Mazzolani, *Idea of the City*. Carney, trans., *Medieval Irish Lyrics*, p. 81, presents a 9th-century lyric concerning a pilgrimage to Rome that is explicitly anagogical in mood. Geoffrey de Vinsauf, *Poetria nova*, p. 16 (30–31), plays wittily with the idea that a journey to Rome is like a journey to heaven because the Pope is in that city; see also p. 91. In Dante, *Purgatorio* II (101), the ship of souls has sailed from the Tiber, from the port of Rome; the musician Casella explains that they often have to wait there until there is room for their passage. Most daringly (and movingly), *Purgatorio* XXXII (100–2) allows Beatrice to promise Dante that after he has been for some time longer a forester (*silvano*), he will, like her, become forever a citizen of "that Rome in which Christ is Roman": "Qui sarai tu poco tempo silvano; / et sarai meco sanza fine cive / di quella Roma onde Cristo è romano" (trans. Sinclair). There is almost certainly a pun on "Rome" in *Piers Plowman*, C. VI, 331, when the pilgrimage is being planned: "'Be þe rode,' quod Repentaunce, 'thow romest toward heuene.'" A 15th-century miracle play, the *Miracle de la fille du roy de Hongrie* from the collection *Miracles de Nostre Dame par personnages*, offers a very close analogue to the Constance story; its concluding reunion scene takes place not merely in Rome but in St. Peter's Church (V, 82–88). I learned of this text from an unpublished paper by Anne Spiselman.

119. St. Augustine, *On Christian Doctrine*, p. 40.

120. London, Brit. Lib. MS. Royal 2 A.xviii, fol. 34. Smithers, "Meaning of *The Seafarer* and *The Wanderer*," discusses the patristic conception of exile as pilgrimage.

121. E.g., Schlauch in Bryan and Dempster, eds., *Sources and Analogues*, p. 160.

122. *De mortalitate*, 26, quoted by Rush, *Death and Burial*, p. 57.

123. The concluding paragraph is apparently Chaucer's own; it does not appear in any extant copy of his sources.

124. Figure 170: Paris, Bibl. Natl. MS. fr. 19, fol. 232, illustrating Bk. XXII. Figure 171: by Giovanni di Paolo, in New York, The Metropolitan Museum of Art. On this painting see Pope-Hennessy, *Giovanni di Paolo*, pp. 17–22. Hughes, *Heaven and Hell*, pp. 26–27, reproduces in color another painting by Giovanni on the same subject now in the Pinacoteca Nazionale in Siena. Cf. also the pictures on pp. 148, 149 (the former is closely related to our figure 170). A symbolic Tree of the Joys of Heaven, included as a memorial diagram in London, Brit. Lib. MS. Add. 37049, fol. 66 (northern English, 1/2 15th century), includes among its branches "luf & frenschyp," "acorde & onehede." And the "Toure of all Toures" describes the holy men who have died to the world and desire only to be in heaven in this fashion: "There they have conversation, as Saint Paul saith:

their place, their joy, their comfort and their desiring." (*The Book of the Craft of Dying*, p. 129.)

125. Figure 172: London, Brit. Lib. MS. King's 5, fol. 30; Cambridge, Corpus Christi Coll. MS. 164, is a sister MS. (for its version, see fols. 31v, 32). A metrical "Story of the Lady and Thomas" in Cambridge, Univ. Lib. MS. Ff.v.48, fol. 125v, concludes with these lines (15th century): "Jesu crowned with thorne so clere / Bryng vs to thy hall on hye." In the N-Town drama cycle, heaven is named to Christ in the Temptation play as "þi faderys halle" (*Ludus Coventriae*, p. 197 [123]; see also p. 374 [42]). Cf. Guillaume de Deguileville's *Pilgrimage of the Soul* (ed. Clubb, p. 283): "Ful soth it is þat oure blisful Lord Ihesu seid þat in his [Fadiris] hows wer many mansiones and dyuers. And this fonde I veari trewe, for this hows is chief and principall of alle othir houses." Cf. the illumination from the Taymouth Hours, reproduced by Harthan, *Book of Hours*, p. 47.

126. *Book of Vices and Virtues*, pp. 99–101 (the whole discussion is relevant).

127. See Job 1:4, where his seven sons each give a feast for the others (and for their three sisters) as a sign of Job's prosperity and the favor he has found before God; his restoration to God's grace at the end is also marked by feasting (Job 42:11) and by the birth of seven new sons and three new daughters. There is besides an intervening feast whose meaning is death (Job 1:13–19) like that the Sultaness gives for the Roman wedding party in the first part of *The Man of Law's Tale*. For another example see the facsimile *Biblia pauperum*, p. 39, where the central picture shows Christ holding the souls of the blessed in a large cloth; the feasting of the children of Job is on the left, Jacob's dream of the heavenly ladder on the right.

128. Figure 173: New York, Pierpont Morgan MS. M.385, fol. 45, illustrating Esther 1:3–4. Cf. the same library's MS. M.140 (German, late 14th century), fol. 45, and the facsimile *Speculum humanae salvationis*, ed. James and Berenson, Chap. 42 (3, 4). The 15th-century English translation expresses the meaning thus:

> The thredde figure may be taken / in the feestes of the sons of Jope
> Ffor of so contynuel feestyng / of othere we ne rede I hope
> Of Job the sons seven / ilkone about his day
> Calling thaire thre Systres / contynuyd ffeestis alway
> Be whilk ffeestes vnderstande / hevenly ffelicitee
> Be the Cyrcuyt of seven dayes / perpetuel eternitee.

Of Ahasuerus's feast it says:

> The feest of kyng Aswere / was ix^{xx} dayes duryng
> Bot the ffeest of Jhesu crist / shalle be euremore lasting.

(The number "ix^{xx}" means "nine score.") See *The Miroure of Mans Saluacionne*, p. 146. See Oxford, Corpus Christi Coll. MS. 161, fol. 168 (now at the Bodleian), for an excellent drawing of the children of Job from a *Speculum* MS. of the early 15th century. Katzenellenbogen, *Allegories of the Virtues and Vices*, pl. 22, reproduces an elaborate page from the Floreffe Bible (ca. 1155) that features the feast. The iconography of the heavenly feast, to which the feasting of Job's children is typologically related, derives from Greek and Roman traditions of the afterlife. Many of the grave stelae found at Terenouthis show the deceased person reclining upon a couch at a banquet; our figure 169, showing the ship of the soul, comes from that collection (late 4th or early 5th century). On these see Bonner, "Ship of the Soul," p. 85 (fig. 2 and n. 1), and fig. 5 (which conflates the two motifs). The pagan *refrigerium*, a "refreshment" meal eaten at the tomb of a deceased by his family and friends on the anniversary of his death, served the early Church as a conveniently ambiguous image for the Eucharist; the miracle of the loaves and the fishes is assimilated to it. See Gough, *Origins of Christian Art*, pp. 45–47 (figs. 44–46), and Grabar, *Christian Iconography*, pp. 8–9 (figs. 6–9).

129. Figure 174: Cambridge, Magd. Coll. MS. Pepys 1803, fol. 39v (an Apocalypse); cf. Cambridge, Corpus Christi Coll. MS. 20, fol. 49v (early 14th century), which shows the Lamb on a trestle table set with knives, bowls, and saltcellars, and three women who feast. Cf. M. Rickert, *Reconstructed Carmelite Missal*, color pl. B, opp. p. 46, which juxtaposes two other feasts, the Last Supper and the elevation of the Host, in an initial "C" introducing the introit of the Mass for Corpus Christi (commentary, pp. 101–2).

130. The English tradition goes back as far as the Anglo-Saxon *Dream of the Rood*, ll. 140–41, which describes the Lord's *folc* seated at banquet ("ᵹeseted to symle"), where there is perpetual joy. Cf. Dante, *Paradiso* XXIV, 1–9. For 14th-century examples, see, e.g.: Walter Hilton's *The Ladder of Perfection*, I, 44 (pp. 54–55), taking his text from Cant. 5:1, "Eat, my friends, and drink deep, my best-beloved"; Julian of Norwich, *A Book of Showings*, pp. 351–52 (Chap. 14, the long text); the wedding feast in *Cleanness*, esp. ll. 105–8 and 161–62 (pp. 15, 16); *St. Erkenwald*, ll. 332–38 (p. 64); Herrtage, ed., *Early English Versions of the "Gesta Romanorum,"* p. 16; *Piers Plowman*, B. XII, 196–209 (pp. 477–78); *Book of Vices and Virtues*, p. 73, which links feasts and royal weddings ("euere-more festes grete, and realle weddynges, wiþ songes and ioye wiþ-outen ende"); and the Halliwell MS. continuation of Grosseteste's "Castel of Loue," I, 404–5, which from l. 1763 to its end talks specifically of families and friends reunited in joy. Ruggiers, *Art of the Canterbury Tales*, p. 173, briefly suggests the anagogical sense of Chaucer's ending.

131. In comparison, the *Knight's Tale* vision of Palamon and Emelye "in alle wele, / Lyvynge in blisse, in richesse, and in heele" (1.3101) offers an ending superficial and unexamined.

132. Christianity is careful to establish Christ's dominion over the sea—he must sleep in a storm at sea, walk upon the waters, command Peter to walk upon water in trust of him—as well as his power to transform the meaning of water: he will be baptized with water, turn water to wine, pour blood and water from his side as he dies. As Tertullian says, at the end of a long enumeration of examples from both Testaments, "Wherever Christ is, there is water" (*Homily on Baptism*, p. 21). Bartholomaeus, *Properties*, describes the sea as a natural phenomenon at considerable length (pp. 665–72), but earlier (p. 88) credits storms at sea to the devil: "Also al þe entent of fendes is to do euel and to greue and disese goode men, and þerfore ofte þey makeþ tempest in þe see and in þe aier."

133. Hugh of St. Victor, *Selected Spiritual Writings*, pp. 59–60. Cf. *The Lanterne of Light*, pp. 85–87, discussing six kinds of true pilgrimage—a

similarly meditative exfoliation (the first and last kinds are anagogically relevant to *The Man of Law's Tale*). [James I of Scotland], *The Kingis Quair*, in part an imitation of Chaucer's *Knight's Tale*, likewise works a rich vein of ship imagery: in st. 15, the ship of Fortune; in 16, reason as rudder to the will (the moral ship), and the sea of this world; in 18, the ship journey as equivalent to the act of writing a long poem (cf. Dante beginning the *Purgatorio*, and Chaucer beginning Bk. II of the *Troilus*); in 22–24, the literal ship in which the narrator was captured by the English. That ship turns out to be the source of the others; they are metaphoric discoveries about its meaning as event.

134. St. Thomas Aquinas, *Summa theologiae*, 1.1.10. reply obj. 1, as quoted by Caplan, *Of Eloquence*, p. 100.

135. I borrow this phrase from J. B. Allen, *Friar as Critic*, p. 133, discussing the Anglo-Saxon *Phoenix*; see his full discussion, pp. 135–36, of the priority of literal things over the spiritual senses to be discovered within them.

136. *Book of Vices and Virtues*, p. 69.

137. London, Brit. Lib. MS. Add. 18850, fol. 50; cf. also the two scenes on fol. 47v (French, 1423).

CONCLUSION

1. Muscatine, "*Canterbury Tales*," pp. 90–92.

2. Payne, *Key of Remembrance*, pp. 46, 73.

3. Henke, *Joyce's Moraculous Sindbook*, p. 14 (n. 11).

4. Rowland, *Blind Beasts*, p. 126. See also her note on "Chaucer's *The Wife of Bath's Prologue*, D. 389." For an equivalent joke in the visual arts, the only example known to me, see London, Brit. Lib. MS. Royal 10 E.iv, fol. 115 (Gregory IX's *Decretals*, early 14th century), where a marginal illustration juxtaposes a mill and a couple fornicating upon a bank.

5. In the formal arts of memory, this advice had always been given: choose images that are particularly striking, active, beautiful, or ugly, and ornament them with uncommon care, for such images will remain longest in memory. In Cicero's words, "imaginibus autem agentibus, acribus, insignitis, quae occurrere celeriterque percutere animum possint" (*De oratore*, II.lxxxvii.358), quoted by Yates, *Art of Memory*, p. 18 (see also her pp. 10, 17, 52, 74, 87).

6. Zacher, *Curiosity and Pilgrimage*, has greatly enriched our understanding of pilgrimage as a metaphor and an institution; see his Chap. 5 for a reading of *The Canterbury Tales* in those terms.

7. Kolve, "From Cleopatra to Alceste."

8. Figure 175: a map of the pilgrims' way published in *Chaucer's Major Poetry*, ed. Baugh, p. 229.

9. Bateson, "Style, Grace, and Information in Primitive Art," in his *Steps to an Ecology of Mind*; see esp. pp. 129, 151–52.

10. This sense of the poem's development is powerfully argued by Howard, *Writers and Pilgrims*, pp. 96–99. Within sight of the shrine, as he puts it, "everything 'modern' in the work—its verisimilitude, its attention to individual character, its literary gamesmanship, its self-consciousness about language and fictionality and art—all this is wiped away" (p. 96).

Works Cited

THIS LIST does not constitute a complete bibliography of the subject, but merely records works cited in the notes. To help a reader find any given reference with a minimum of fuss, all works, both primary and secondary, have been combined in a single alphabetical listing.

In listing primary works, I have followed these principles: (1) Works of known authorship are always listed under the author's name. (Medieval names whose second element is less a distinctive surname than a designation of place of origin—Alain de Lille, for example—are alphabetized under the first element, the Christian name.) (2) Editions of anonymous works, including facsimiles, are listed under title if the title of the edition is substantially the same as that of the original work. (3) If the modern author or translator is responsible for the title (as, for example, in a collection of poems), the work is listed under his name. Modern collections of essays are listed under the editor's name; modern works (such as exhibition catalogues) for which no editor is given are listed under title. In every case, the short form of the note will lead one to the alphabetized entry in the Works Cited.

The following abbreviations have been used in the Works Cited and notes:

ChauR	*Chaucer Review*
CFMA	*Classiques Français du Moyen Age*
CL	*Comparative Literature*
E&S	*Essays and Studies by Members of the English Association*
EETS	Early English Text Society
ELH	*English Literary History*
ES	*English Studies*
HAB	*The Humanities Association Review/La Revue de l'Association des Humanités*
ISLL	*Illinois Studies in Language and Literature*
JAAC	*Journal of Aesthetics and Art Criticism*
JEGP	*Journal of English and Germanic Philology*
JWCI	*Journal of the Warburg and Courtauld Institutes*
LeedsSE	*Leeds Studies in English*
LFQ	*Literature/Film Quarterly*
MÆ	*Medium Ævum*
M&H	*Medievalia et Humanistica*
ME	Middle English
M.E.D.	Middle English Dictionary
MLN	*Modern Language Notes*
MLQ	*Modern Language Quarterly*
MLR	*Modern Language Review*

MP	*Modern Philology*
MS	*Mediaeval Studies*
NLH	*New Literary History*
NM	*Neuphilologische Mitteilungen*
PAPS	*Proceedings of the American Philosophical Society*
PL	*Patrologia Latina*
PMLA	*Publications of the Modern Language Association of America*
PQ	*Philological Quarterly*
RELat	*Revue des Etudes Latines*
RES	*Review of English Studies*
RPh	*Romance Philology*
SAC	*Studies in the Age of Chaucer*
SAQ	*South Atlantic Quarterly*
SARev	*South Atlantic Review*
SATF	Société des Anciens Textes Français
SP	*Studies in Philology*
STS	Scottish Text Society
TLS	*Times Literary Supplement*
TWA	*Transactions of the Wisconsin Academy of Sciences, Arts, and Letters*
UTQ	*University of Toronto Quarterly*
YES	*Yearbook of English Studies*
YSE	*Yale Studies in English*
ZFSL	*Zeitschrift für Französische Sprache und Literatur*

St. Aelred of Rievaulx. *The Mirror of Love*. In Colledge, ed., *The Mediaeval Mystics of England*, pp. 103–21.

Aers, David. Review of Terry Jones, *Chaucer's Knight: The Portrait of a Medieval Mercenary*. *SAC*, 4 (1982), 169–75.

Alain de Lille. *Anticlaudianus*. Ed. R. Bossuat. Paris: J. Vrin, 1955.

———. *Anticlaudianus or the Good and Perfect Man*. Trans. James J. Sheridan. Toronto: Pontifical Institute, 1973.

———. *The Complaint of Nature*. Trans. Douglas M. Moffat. *YSE*, 36 (1908); repr. Hamden, Conn.: Shoe String Press, 1972.

Allen, Don Cameron. *The Legend of Noah*. 1949; repr. Urbana: Univ. of Illinois Press, 1963.

Allen, Judson Boyce. *The Friar as Critic*. Nashville: Vanderbilt Univ. Press, 1971.

Alpers, Svetlana, and Paul Alpers. "*Ut Pictura Noesis?*: Criticism in Literary Studies and Art History." *NLH*, 3 (1972), 437–58.

Alsloot, Denis van. *Isabella's Triumph*. Ed. James Laver. London: Faber, 1947.

Andersen, Flemming G., et al., eds. *Medieval Iconography and Narrative: A Symposium*. Odense, Denmark: Odense Univ. Press, 1980.

Anderson, M. D. *Drama and Imagery in English Medieval Churches*. Cambridge: Cambridge Univ. Press, 1963.

———. *History and Imagery in British Churches*. London: John Murray, 1971.

———. *Misericords: Medieval Life in English Woodcarving*. Harmondsworth: Penguin, 1954.

Andreas, and The Fates of the Apostles. Ed. Kenneth R. Brooks. Oxford: Clarendon, 1961.

Andreas Capellanus. *The Art of Courtly Love*. Trans. John Jay Parry. New York: Ungar, 1941.

The Anglo-Norman Text of the "Holkham Bible Picture Book." Ed. F. P. Pickering. Oxford: Blackwell, 1971.

The Anglo-Saxon Chronicle. Rev. trans. Dorothy Whitelock, David C. Douglas, and Susie I. Tucker. London: Eyre and Spottiswoode, 1961.

Aquinas, St. Thomas. *Summa theologiae*. Blackfriars ed., 60 vols. New York: McGraw-Hill, 1964–76.

Arano, Luisa Cogliati. *The Medieval Health Handbook: Tacuinum Sanitatis*. Trans. Oscar Ratti and Adele Westbrook. New York: Braziller, 1976.

Aristotle. *Categories, and De interpretatione*. Trans. J. L. Ackrill. Oxford: Clarendon, 1963.

———. *Ethica Nicomachea*. Trans. W. D. Ross. Oxford: Clarendon, 1925.

———. *The Ethics of Aristotle*. Trans. J. A. K. Thomson. 1953; repr. Harmondsworth: Penguin, 1955.

Auerbach, Erich. *Mimesis: The Representation of Reality in Western Literature*. Trans. Willard R. Trask. Princeton: Princeton Univ. Press, 1953.

St. Augustine. *The City of God*. Trans. Marcus Dods. New York: Modern Library, 1950.

———. *Confessions*. Trans. R. S. Pine-Coffin. Harmondsworth: Penguin, 1961.

———. *Expositions on the Book of Psalms*. Trans. J. Tweed, T. Scratton, et al. 6 vols. A Library of Fathers of the Holy Catholic Church, 24, 25, 30, 32, 37, 39. Oxford: Parker, 1847–84.

———. *Letters*. Trans. Sister Wilfrid Parsons. *The Writings of St. Augustine*, Vols. 9–13. New York: Fathers of the Church, 1951–56.

———. *On Christian Doctrine*. Trans. D. W. Robertson, Jr. Indianapolis: Bobbs-Merrill, 1958.

———. *Sermons*. Ed. Philip Schaff. Nicene and Post-Nicene Fathers of the Christian Church, 6. New York: Scribner's, 1908.

———. *The Trinity*. Trans. Stephen McKenna. Fathers of the Church, 45. Washington, D.C.: Catholic University of America Press, 1963.

Autotypes of Chaucer Manuscripts. 1st series, vol. XVI. London: Chaucer Society Publications, 1879.

Avril, François. *Manuscript Painting at the Court of France: The Fourteenth Century (1310–1380)*. New York: Braziller, 1978.

Axton, Richard, and John Stevens, trans. *Medieval French Plays*. New York: Barnes and Noble, 1971.

Baker, Donald C. Review of Geoffrey Chaucer, *Troilus and Criseyde: A Facsimile of Corpus Christi College Cambridge MS. 61*. In *SAC*, 1 (1979), 187–93.

Baldwin, Ralph. *The Unity of the Canterbury Tales*. Anglistica, 5 (1955).

Barney, Stephen A. *Allegories of History, Allegories of Love*. Hamden, Conn.: Shoe String Press, 1979.

———. "Troilus Bound." *Speculum*, 47 (1972), 445–58.

Barrett, Helen M. *Boethius: Some Aspects of His Times and Work*. Cambridge: Cambridge Univ. Press, 1940.

Bartholomaeus Anglicus. *On the Properties of Things*. Trans. John Trevisa. Ed. M. C. Seymour et al. 2 vols. Oxford: Clarendon, 1975.

Bateson, Gregory. *Steps to an Ecology of Mind*. New York: Chandler, 1972; repr. Ballantine.

Baudouin de Condé and Jean de Condé. *Dits et contes*. Ed. Auguste Scheler. 3 vols. Brussels: Devaux, 1866–67.

Baugh, Albert C. "The Middle English Romance: Some Questions of Creation, Presentation, and Preservation." *Speculum*, 42 (1967), 1–31.

Baum, Paull Franklin. "The Mediaeval Legend of Judas Iscariot." *PMLA*, 31 (1916), 481–632.

Bäuml, Franz H. "Varieties and Consequences of Medieval Literacy and Illiteracy." *Speculum*, 55 (1980), 237–65.

Bédier, Joseph. *Les Fabliaux*. Paris: Champion, 1893; 5th ed., 1925.

Beer, Jeanette M. A. *Narrative Conventions of Truth in the Middle Ages*. Geneva: Droz, 1981.

Beichner, Paul E., C.S.C. "Absolon's Hair." *MS*, 12 (1950), 222–33.

———. "The Allegorical Interpretation of Medieval Literature." *PMLA*, 82 (1967), 33–38.

———. "Characterization in *The Miller's Tale*." In Richard J. Schoeck and Jerome Taylor, eds., *Chaucer Criticism: The Canterbury Tales*, pp. 117–29. Notre Dame, Ind.: Univ. of Notre Dame Press, 1960.

———. "Chaucer's Man of Law and *Disparitas Cultus*." *Speculum*, 23 (1948), 70–75.

Beidler, Peter G. "Art and Scatology in the *Miller's Tale*." *ChauR*, 12 (1977), 90–102.

Bellamy, John G. *Crime and Public Order in England in the Later Middle Ages*. London: Routledge and Kegan Paul, 1973.

The Belles Heures of Jean, Duke of Berry. Ed. Millard Meiss and Elizabeth H. Beatson. New York: Braziller, 1974.

Bennett, J. A. W. *Chaucer at Oxford and at Cambridge*. Toronto: Univ. of Toronto Press, 1974.

———. *Chaucer's Book of Fame: An Exposition of "The House of Fame."* Oxford: Clarendon, 1968.

———. *The Parlement of Foules: An Interpretation*. Oxford: Clarendon, 1957.

———, G. V. Smithers, and Norman Davis, eds. *Early Middle English Verse and Prose*. Oxford: Clarendon, 1966.

Benson, Larry D. "The Order of *The Canterbury Tales*." *SAC*, 3 (1981), 77–120.

———, and Theodore M. Andersson, eds. *The Literary Context of Chaucer's Fabliaux: Texts and Translations*. Indianapolis: Bobbs-Merrill, 1971.

———, and John Leyerle, eds. *Chivalric Literature: Essays on Relations between Literature and Life in the Later Middle Ages*. Kalamazoo, Mich.: Medieval Institute, 1980.

Beowulf and the Fight at Finnsburg. Ed. F. Klaeber. 3d ed. Boston: D. C. Heath, 1950.

Berenson, Bernard. *Italian Pictures of the Renaissance: Florentine School*. 2 vols. London: Phaidon, 1963.

Berger, Samuel. "Les Manuels pour l'illustration du Psautier aux XIIIe siècle." *Mémoires de la Société Nationale des Antiquaires de France*. 6th series, VII (1898), 95–134.

Bernardus Silvestris. *The Commentary on the First Six Books of the* Aeneid *of Vergil*. Ed. Julian Ward Jones and Elizabeth Frances Jones. Lincoln, Nebr.: Univ. of Nebraska Press, 1977.

———. *Commentary on the First Six Books of Virgil's "Aeneid."* Trans. E. G. Schreiber and Thomas E. Maresca. Lincoln, Nebr.: Univ. of Nebraska Press, 1980.

Bethurum, Dorothy, ed. *Critical Approaches to Medieval Literature*. New York: Columbia Univ. Press, 1960.

Bialostocki, Jan. "Iconography and Iconology." *The Encyclopaedia of World Art*, 1963 ed.

La Bible moralisée conservée à Oxford, Paris et Londres; reproduction intégrale du manuscrit du XIII siècle, accompagnée d'une notice par le comte A. de Laborde. Facsimile ed. A. de Laborde. Paris: Société Française de reproductions de manuscrits à peintures, 1911–27.

Biblia pauperum. Facsimile ed. Elizabeth Soltész. Hanau/Main: Verlag Werner Dausien, 1967.

Bishop, Morris. *The Horizon Book of the Middle Ages*. New York: American Heritage, 1968.

Block, Edward A. "Chaucer's Millers and Their Bagpipes." *Speculum*, 29 (1954), 239–43.

———. "Originality, Controlling Purpose, and Craftsmanship in Chaucer's *Man of Law's Tale*." *PMLA*, 68 (1953), 572–616.

Bloomfield, Morton W. "Allegory as Interpretation." *NLH*, 3 (1972), 301–17.

———. "The Miller's Tale—An UnBoethian Interpretation." In Jerome Mandel and

Bruce A. Rosenberg, eds., *Medieval Literature and Folklore Studies: Essays in Honor of Francis Lee Utley*, pp. 205–11. New Brunswick: Rutgers Univ. Press, 1970.

———. *The Seven Deadly Sins*. East Lansing: Michigan State Univ. Press, 1952.

———. "Symbolism in Medieval Literature." *MP*, 56 (1958), 73–81.

Blum, André. *Les Primitifs de la gravure sur bois*. Paris: Gründ, 1956.

Boccaccio, Giovanni. *Decameron*. Ed. Vittore Branca. 3 vols. Naples: Alberto Marotta, 1966.

———. *Decameron*. Trans. G. H. McWilliam. Harmondsworth: Penguin, 1972.

———. *De casibus illustrium virorum*. Facsimile of the Paris ed. of 1520, ed. Louis Brewer Hall. Gainesville, Fla.: Scholars' Facsimiles, 1962.

———. *The Fates of Illustrious Men*. Trans. and abridged Louis Brewer Hall. New York: Ungar, 1965.

———. *Il Teseida*. Ed. Salvatore Battaglia. Florence: Sansoni, 1938.

———. *Teseida*. Trans. as *The Book of Theseus* by Bernadette Marie McCoy. New York: Medieval Text Association, 1974.

———. *Teseida delle nozze d'Emilia*. Ed. Aurelio Roncaglia. Bari: Laterza, 1941.

———. *Thirteen Most Pleasant and Delectable Questions of Love [Il Filocolo]*. Trans. H. G. (1566). Rev. Harry Carter. New York: Potter, 1974.

Bodel, Jean. *Le Jeu de Saint Nicolas*. Ed. Alfred Jeanroy. CFMA. Paris: Champion, 1967.

Boethius. *The Consolation of Philosophy*. Trans. Richard Green. Indianapolis: Bobbs-Merrill, 1962.

———. *The Second Edition of the Commentaries on the Isagoge of Porphyry*. In McKeon, ed., *Selections from Medieval Philosophers*, I, 70–99.

———. *The Theological Tractates; The Consolation of Philosophy*. Trans. H. F. Stewart, E. K. Rand, and S. J. Tester. Loeb Classical Library, 74. London: Heinemann, 1973.

Boggess, William F. "Aristotle's *Poetics* in the Fourteenth Century." *SP*, 67 (1970), 278–94.

"The Boke of the Craft of Dying." In Horstmann, ed., *Yorkshire Writers*, II, 406–20.

Bolton, Whitney F. "The 'Miller's Tale': An Interpretation." *MS*, 24 (1962), 83–94.

St. Bonaventura. *The Mind's Road to God*. Trans. George Boas. Indianapolis: Bobbs-Merrill, 1953.

[St. Bonaventure.] *The Tree of Life*. In *The Works of Bonaventure*, Vol. I. Trans. Jose de Vinck. Paterson, N.J.: St. Anthony Guild Press, 1960.

Bonet, Honoré. *The Tree of Battles*. Trans. G. W. Coopland. Liverpool: Univ. Press of Liverpool, 1949.

Bonner, Campbell. "The Ship of the Soul on a Group of Grave-Stelae from Terenuthis." *PAPS*, 85 (1941), 84–91.

The Book of Beasts. Trans. T. H. White. London: Jonathan Cape, 1954.

The Book of the Craft of Dying. Ed. F. M. M. Comper. London: Longmans, Green, 1917.

The Book of the Knight of the Tower. Trans. William Caxton. Ed. M. Y. Offord. EETS, s.s. 2. London: Oxford Univ. Press, 1971.

The Book of Vices and Virtues. Ed. W. Nelson Francis. EETS, o.s. 217. London: Oxford Univ. Press, 1942.

Bossert, Helmuth Th., and Willy F. Storck, eds. *Das Mittelalterliche Hausbuch*. Leipzig: Deutscher Verein für Kunstwissenschaft, 1912.

Bottineau, Yves. *Les Chemins de Saint-Jacques*. Paris: Arthaud, 1964.

Bovini, Giuseppe. *Ravenna Mosaics*. Trans. Gustina Scaglia. Greenwich, Conn.: New York Graphic Society, 1956.

Bowden, Muriel. *A Commentary on the General Prologue to the Canterbury Tales*. New York: Macmillan, 1948.

Bowers, John Mathews. "Langland's *Piers Plowman*: *Acedia* and the Crisis of Will." Ph.D. diss., Univ. of Virginia, 1978.

Branca, Vittore. *Boccaccio: The Man and His Works*. Trans. Richard Monges and Dennis J. McAuliffe. New York: New York Univ. Press, 1976.

Brentano, Lujo. "On the History and Development of Gilds." In Toulmin Smith, ed., *English Gilds*, pp. xlix–cxcviii.

Brewer, Derek S. *Chaucer*. 3d ed. London: Longman, 1973.

———. *Chaucer and His World*. London: Eyre Methuen, 1978.

———. "The Fabliaux." In Rowland, ed., *Companion to Chaucer Studies*, pp. 296–325.

———, ed. *Chaucer and Chaucerians: Critical Studies in Middle English Literature*. University, Ala.: Univ. of Alabama Press, 1966.

———, ed. *Geoffrey Chaucer: Writers and Their Background*. Athens: Ohio Univ. Press, 1975.

Brians, Paul, ed. and trans. *Bawdy Tales from the Courts of Medieval France*. New York: Harper and Row, 1972.

Brieger, Peter, Millard Meiss, and Charles S. Singleton. *Illuminated Manuscripts of the Divine Comedy*. 2 vols. Princeton: Princeton Univ. Press, 1969.

Brittain, Frederick, ed. *The Penguin Book of Latin Verse*. Harmondsworth: Penguin, 1962.

Brøndsted, Johannes. *The Vikings*. Trans. Kalle Skov. Harmondsworth: Penguin, 1965.

Bronson, Bertrand H. "Chaucer's Art in Relation to His Audience." In *Five Studies in Literature*, Univ. of Calif. Publ. in English, 8, pp. 1–53. Berkeley: Univ. of California Press, 1940.

———. *In Search of Chaucer*. Toronto: Univ. of Toronto Press, 1960.

Brooke, Christopher. *The Structure of Medieval Society*. London: Thames and Hudson, 1971.

Brooks, Douglas, and Alastair Fowler. "The Meaning of Chaucer's *Knight's Tale*." *MÆ*, 39 (1970), 123–46.

Brown, Carleton. "The Man of Law's Head-link and the Prologue of the Canterbury Tales." *SP*, 34 (1937), 8–35.

Brown, Roger W. *Words and Things*. Glencoe, Ill.: The Free Press, 1958.

Bruce-Mitford, R. L. S. *The Sutton Hoo Ship Burial: A Handbook*. London: The British Museum, 1968.

Brunner, Karl. "Middle English Metrical Romances and Their Audience." In Mac-Edward Leach, ed., *Studies in Medieval Literature in Honor of Prof. Albert Croll Baugh*, pp. 219–27. Philadelphia: Univ. of Pennsylvania Press, 1961.

Bryan, W. F., and Germaine Dempster, eds. *Sources and Analogues of Chaucer's Canterbury Tales*. London: Routledge and Kegan Paul, 1941.

Bühler, Curt F. *The Fifteenth-Century Book: The Scribes, the Printers, the Decorators*. Philadelphia: Univ. of Pennsylvania Press, 1960.

Bundy, Murray Wright. *The Theory of Imagination in Classical and Mediaeval Thought*. *ISLL*, 12, nos. 2, 3 (1927).

Burlin, Robert B. *Chaucerian Fiction*. Princeton: Princeton Univ. Press, 1977.

———. *The Old English Advent*. New Haven: Yale Univ. Press, 1968.

Burrow, J. A. "The Imparfit Knight." Review of Terry Jones, *Chaucer's Knight: The Portrait of a Medieval Mercenary*. *TLS*, 15 Feb. 1980, p. 163.

———. *Ricardian Poetry*. New Haven: Yale Univ. Press, 1971.

———. "'Young Saint, Old Devil': Reflections on a Medieval Proverb." *RES*, n.s. 30 (1979), 385–96.

Butcher, S. H. *Aristotle's Theory of Poetry and Fine Art*. 4th ed., corr. London: Macmillan, 1911.

Buttafava, Claudio. *Visioni di città nelle opere d'arte del medioèvo e del rinascimento.* Milan: Libreria Salto, 1963.

Caiger-Smith, A. *English Medieval Mural Paintings.* Oxford: Clarendon, 1963.

Calin, William. *A Poet at the Fountain: Essays on the Narrative Verse of Guillaume de Machaut.* Lexington: Univ. of Kentucky Press, 1974.

Cannon, Thomas F., Jr. "Chaucer's Pilgrims as Artists." Ph.D. diss., Univ. of Virginia, 1973.

Capgrave, John. *Ye Solace of Pilgrimes.* Ed. C. A. Mills. London: Oxford Univ. Press, 1911.

Caplan, Harry. *Of Eloquence: Studies in Ancient and Mediaeval Rhetoric.* Ed. Anne King and Helen North. Ithaca: Cornell Univ. Press, 1970. Esp. "The Four Senses of Scriptural Interpretation and the Medieval Theory of Preaching," pp. 93–104; "Memoria: Treasure-House of Eloquence," pp. 196–246.

Carmina Burana. Ed. Wilhelm Meyers, Alfons Hilka, Otto Schumann, and Bernhard Bischoff. 2 vols. in 4 parts. Heidelberg: Winter, 1930–70.

Carney, James, trans. *Medieval Irish Lyrics.* Dublin: Dolmen, 1967.

Carus-Wilson, E. M. "Towns and Trade." In Austin Lane Poole, ed., *Medieval England,* 2 vols., rev. ed., I, 209–63. Oxford: Clarendon, 1958.

Cave, C. J. P. *Roof Bosses in Medieval Churches.* Cambridge: Cambridge Univ. Press, 1948.

Caxton's Book of Curtesye. Ed. F. J. Furnivall. EETS, e.s. 3. London: Trübner, 1868.

Chambers, A. B. "Wisdom at One Entrance Quite Shut Out: *Paradise Lost,* III.1–55." *PQ,* 42 (1963), 114–19.

Chambers, E. K. *The Mediaeval Stage.* 2 vols. London: Oxford Univ. Press, 1903.

Chamoso Lamas, Manuel. *Santiago de Compostela.* Guías Artísticas de España. Barcelona: Aries, 1961.

La Chanson de Roland. Ed. Gérard Moignet. New York: Larousse, 1969.

Charles d'Orléans. *The English Poems of Charles of Orleans.* Ed. Robert Steele and Mabel Day. EETS, o.s. 215, 220. London: Oxford Univ. Press, 1941; repr. with Bibliographical Supplement, 1970.

———. *Poésies.* Ed. Pierre Champion. 2 vols. CFMA 34, 56. Paris: Champion, 1923–27.

The Chastising of God's Children. Ed. Joyce Bazire and Eric Colledge. Oxford: Blackwell, 1957.

Chaucer, Geoffrey. *The Canterbury Tales.* Trans. Nevill Coghill. Harmondsworth: Penguin, illustrated ed., 1977.

———. *The Canterbury Tales: A Facsimile and Transcription of the Hengwrt Manuscript, with Variants from the Ellesmere Manuscript.* Ed. Paul G. Ruggiers. Intro. Donald C. Baker, A. I. Doyle, and M. B. Parkes. Norman: Univ. of Oklahoma Press, 1979.

———. *Chaucer's Major Poetry.* Ed. Albert C. Baugh. New York: Appleton-Century-Crofts, 1963.

———. *Chaucer's Poetry.* Ed. E. T. Donaldson. 2d ed. New York: Ronald, 1975.

———. *The Complete Poetry and Prose of Geoffrey Chaucer.* Ed. John H. Fisher. New York: Holt, Rinehart, and Winston, 1977.

———. *The Complete Works of Geoffrey Chaucer.* Ed. Walter W. Skeat. 2d ed. 6 vols. 1899; repr. Oxford: Clarendon, 1963.

———. *The Ellesmere Chaucer Reproduced in Facsimile.* Preface by Alix Egerton. 2 vols. Manchester: Manchester Univ. Press, 1911.

———. *The Man of Law's Tale.* Ed. Nevill Coghill and Christopher Tolkien. London: Harrap, 1969.

———. *The Miller's Tale.* Ed. Constance B. Hieatt. New York: Odyssey, 1970.

———. *A Parallel-Text Edition of Chaucer's Minor Poems.* Ed. F. J. Furnivall. Chaucer Society First Series 21, 57, 58. London: Trübner, 1871, 1879.

———. *The Parlement of Foulys*. Ed. D. S. Brewer. London: Thomas Nelson, 1960.

———. *The Tales of Canterbury. Complete.* Ed. Robert A. Pratt. Boston: Houghton Mifflin, 1974.

———. *The Text of the Canterbury Tales, Studied on the Basis of All Known Manuscripts.* Ed. J. M. Manly and Edith Rickert. Chicago: Univ. of Chicago Press, 1940.

———. *Troilus and Criseyde: A Facsimile of Corpus Christi College Cambridge MS. 61.* Intro. M. B. Parkes and Elizabeth Salter. Cambridge: Brewer, 1978.

———. *The Works of Geoffrey Chaucer.* Ed. F. N. Robinson. 2d ed. Boston: Houghton Mifflin, 1961.

Chaytor, H. J. *From Script to Print: An Introduction to Medieval Literature.* Cambridge: Cambridge Univ. Press, 1945.

"*The Chess of Love.*" Trans. Joan Martin Jones. Ph.D. diss., Univ. of Nebraska, 1968.

The Chester Mystery Cycle. Ed. R. M. Lumiansky and David Mills. EETS, s.s. 3. London: Oxford Univ. Press, 1974.

Chew, Samuel C. *The Pilgrimage of Life.* New Haven: Yale Univ. Press, 1962.

Chmelarz, Eduard. "Eine Französische Bilderhandschrift von Boccaccio's Theseide." *Jahrbuch der Kunsthistorischen Sammlungen des Allerhöschsten Kaiserhauses*, 14 (1893), 318–28.

Chrétien de Troyes. *Arthurian Romances.* Trans. W. W. Comfort. London: Dent, 1914.

———. *Cligés.* Ed. Alexandre Micha. CFMA 84. Paris: Champion, 1965.

Christine de Pisan. *The Book of Fayttes of Armes and of Chyualrye.* Trans. William Caxton. Ed. A. T. P. Byles. EETS, o.s. 189. London: Oxford Univ. Press, 1932; corr. 1937.

———. *The Epistle of Othea.* Trans. Stephen Scrope. Ed. Curt F. Bühler. EETS, o.s. 264. London: Oxford Univ. Press, 1970.

———. *L'Epistre de la prison de vie humaine.* Ed. S. Solente. *Bibliothèque de l'Ecole des Chartres*, 85 (1924), 263–301.

Cicero. *De senectute, De amicitia, De divinatione.* Ed. and trans. W. A. Falconer. Loeb Classical Library. London: Heinemann, 1923.

Clarke, Edwin, and Kenneth Dewhurst. *An Illustrated History of Brain Function.* Oxford: Sandford Publications, 1972.

Cleanness. Ed. J. J. Anderson. Manchester: Manchester Univ. Press, 1977.

Clemoes, Peter. "*Mens absentia cogitans* in *The Seafarer* and *The Wanderer.*" In Derek A. Pearsall and R. A. Waldron, eds., *Medieval Literature and Civilization: Studies in Memory of G. N. Garmonsway*, pp. 62–77. London: Athlone, 1969.

Clifford, Gay. *The Transformations of Allegory.* London: Routledge and Kegan Paul, 1974.

Clogan, Paul M. "The Narrative Style of The Man of Law's Tale." *M&H*, n.s. 8 (1977), 217–33.

The Cloisters Apocalypse. Facsimile ed. Florens Deuchler, Jeffrey M. Hoffeld, and Helmut Nickel. 2 vols. New York: Metropolitan Museum of Art, 1971.

The Cloud of Unknowing. Ed. Phyllis Hodgson. EETS, o.s. 218. London: Oxford Univ. Press, 1944.

Cockerell, S. C., and M. R. James, eds. *Two East Anglian Psalters.* Roxburghe Club. Oxford, 1926.

Coffman, George R. "Old Age from Horace to Chaucer: Some Literary Affinities and Adventures of an Idea." *Speculum*, 9 (1934), 249–77.

Cohen, Edward S. "The Sequence of the *Canterbury Tales.*" *ChauR*, 9 (1974), 190–95.

Cohen, Gillian. *The Psychology of Cognition.* New York: Academic Press, 1977.

Cohen, Ralph. *The Art of Discrimination: Thomson's "The Seasons" and the Language of Criticism.* Berkeley: Univ. of California Press, 1964.

Colledge, Eric, ed. *The Mediaeval Mystics of England*. New York: Scribner, 1961.

Collison, Robert Lewis. *Encyclopaedias: Their History Throughout the Ages*. 2d ed. New York: Hafner, 1966.

Cook, Robert G. "Chaucer's Pandarus and the Medieval Ideal of Friendship." *JEGP*, 69 (1970), 407–24.

Cooke, Thomas D. *The Old French and Chaucerian Fabliaux*. Columbia: Univ. of Missouri Press, 1978.

———, and B. L. Honeycutt. *The Humor of the Fabliaux*. Columbia: Univ. of Missouri Press, 1974.

Copland, Murray. "*The Reeve's Tale*: Harlotrie or Sermonyng?" *MÆ*, 31 (1962), 14–32.

The Cornish Ordinalia: A Medieval Dramatic Trilogy. Trans. Markham Harris. Washington, D.C.: Catholic Univ. of America Press, 1969.

Corolla Sancti Eadmundi. Ed. Lord Francis Hervey. New York: Dutton, 1907.

Correale, Robert M. "Chaucer's Parody of Compline in the *Reeve's Tale*." *ChauR*, 1 (1967), 161–66.

Corsa, Helen Storm. *Chaucer: Poet of Mirth and Morality*. Notre Dame, Ind.: Univ. of Notre Dame Press, 1964.

Cosman, Madeleine Pelner. *Fabulous Feasts: Medieval Cookery and Ceremony*. New York: Braziller, 1976.

Coulton, G. G. *Medieval Panorama: The English Scene from Conquest to Reformation*. Cambridge, 1938; repr. New York: Meridian, 1955.

Courcelle, Pierre. "L'Ame en cage." In Kurt Flasch, ed., *Parusia. Studien zur Philosophie Platons und zur Problemgeschichte des Platonismus: Festgabe für J. Hirschberger*, pp. 103–16. Frankfurt/Main: Minerva, 1965.

———. *La Consolation de Philosophie dans la tradition littéraire: antécédents et postérité de Boèce*. Paris: Etudes Augustiniennes, 1967.

———. *Histoire littéraire des grandes invasions germaniques*. 3d ed. Paris: Etudes Augustiniennes, 1964.

———. "Tradition platonicienne et traditions chrétiennes du corps-prison." *RELat*, 43 (1965), 406–43.

Cox, Lee Sheridan. "A Question of Order in the *Canterbury Tales*." *ChauR*, 1 (1967), 228–52.

Craig, Hardin, ed. *Two Coventry Corpus Christi Plays*. 2d ed. EETS, e.s. 87. London: Oxford Univ. Press, 1957.

Crane, R. S. *The Idea of the Humanities and Other Essays Critical and Historical*. 2 vols. Chicago: Univ. of Chicago Press, 1967. Esp. "Houyhnhnms, Yahoos and the History of Ideas," II, 261–82; "On Hypotheses in 'Historical Criticism': Apropos of Certain Contemporary Medievalists," II, 236–60.

Crisp, Frank. *Mediaeval Gardens*. Ed. Catherine Childs Paterson. 2 vols. London, 1924; repr. New York: Hacker Art Books, 1966.

Cronin, Grover, Jr. "The Bestiary and the Mediaeval Mind—Some Complexities." *MLQ*, 2 (1941), 191–98.

Crosby, Ruth. "Chaucer and the Custom of Oral Delivery." *Speculum*, 13 (1938), 413–32.

Crow, Martin M., and Clair C. Olson, eds. *Chaucer Life-Records*. Oxford: Clarendon, 1966.

Cunningham, J. V. "The Literary Form of the Prologue to the *Canterbury Tales*." *MP*, 49 (1952), 172–81.

———. *Tradition and Poetic Structure*. Denver: Alan Swallow, 1960.

Curry, Walter Clyde. *Chaucer and the Mediaeval Sciences*. 2d ed. New York: Barnes and Noble, 1960.

Cursor mundi. Ed. Richard Morris. EETS, o.s. 57, 59, 62, 66, 99, 101. London: Paul, Trench, Trübner, 1874–93.

Curtius, Ernst Robert. *European Literature and the Latin Middle Ages*. Trans. Willard R. Trask. New York: Pantheon, 1953.

Cust, Robert H. Hobart. *The Pavement Masters of Siena (1369–1562)*. London: Bell, 1901.

Cynewulf. *The Fates of the Apostles*. In Kennedy, trans., *An Anthology of Old English Poetry*, p. 140.

Dalton, Osborne M. "Two Mediaeval Caskets with Subjects from Romance." *Burlington Magazine*, 5 (1904), 299–309.

Daniélou, Jean, S.J. *The Bible and the Liturgy*. Notre Dame, Ind.: Univ. of Notre Dame Press, 1956.

Dante Alighieri. *The Convivio of Dante Alighieri*. Trans. Philip H. Wicksteed. Temple Classics. 4th ed. London: Dent, 1924.

———. *The Divine Comedy*. Trans. John D. Sinclair. 3 vols. 1939–46; repr. New York: Oxford Univ. Press, 1961.

———. *The Divine Comedy*. Ed. and trans. Charles S. Singleton. 3 vols., 6 parts. Princeton: Princeton Univ. Press, 1970–75.

———. *Epistolae*. Ed. and trans. Paget Toynbee. 2d ed. Oxford: Clarendon, 1966.

———. *Vita nuova*. In E. Moore and Paget Toynbee, eds., *Le opere di Dante Alighieri*. Oxford: Nella Stamperia dell' Università, 1894; repr. 1963.

David, Alfred. "The Man of Law vs. Chaucer: A Case in Poetics." *PMLA*, 82 (1967), 217–25.

———. *The Strumpet Muse: Art and Morals in Chaucer's Poetry*. Bloomington: Indiana Univ. Press, 1976.

Davidson, Clifford, and David E. O'Connor. *York Art: A Subject List of Extant and Lost Art Including Items Relevant to Early Drama*. Kalamazoo, Mich.: Medieval Institute, 1978.

Davis, Norman, ed. *Non-Cycle Plays and Fragments*. EETS, s.s. 1. London: Oxford Univ. Press, 1970.

———, et al., eds. *A Chaucer Glossary*. Oxford: Clarendon, 1979.

Dean, Christopher. "Imagery in the *Knight's Tale* and the *Miller's Tale*." *MS*, 31 (1969), 149–63.

Dean, Ruth J. "The Manuscripts of Nicholas Trevet's Anglo-Norman *Cronicles*." *M&H*, 14 (1962), 95–105.

———. "Nicholas Trevet, Historian." In J. J. G. Alexander and M. T. Gibson, eds., *Medieval Learning and Literature: Essays Presented to Richard William Hunt*, pp. 328–52. Oxford: Clarendon, 1976.

The Death of King Arthur. Trans. James Cable. Harmondsworth: Penguin, 1971.

Debidour, V. H. *Le Bestiaire sculpté du moyen âge en France*. Paris: Arthaud, 1961.

de Bruyne, Edgar. *The Esthetics of the Middle Ages*. Trans. Eileen B. Hennessy. New York: Ungar, 1969.

"De clerico et puella." In *The Harley Lyrics*, ed. Brook, pp. 62–63.

Degenhart, Bernard, and Annegrit Schmitt. *Corpus der Italienischen Zeichnungen 1300–1450*. 2 parts in 7 vols. Berlin: Gebr. Mann Verlag, 1968.

Delasanta, Rodney. "And of Great Reverence: Chaucer's Man of Law." *ChauR*, 5 (1971), 288–310.

———. "The Horsemen of the *Canterbury Tales*." *ChauR*, 3 (1968), 29–36.

Dent, A. A. "Chaucer and the Horse." *Proceedings of the Leeds Philosophical and Literary Society*, IX, i (1959), 1–12.

The Dicts and Sayings of the Philosophers. Ed. Curt F. Bühler. EETS, o.s. 211. London: Oxford Univ. Press, 1941.

Dives and Pauper. Ed. Priscilla Heath Barnum. 2 vols. EETS, o.s. 275, 280. London: Oxford Univ. Press, 1976, 1980.

Donahue, Charles. "Patristic Exegesis in the Criticism of Medieval Literature: Summation." In Bethurum, ed., *Critical Approaches to Medieval Literature*, pp. 61–82.

Donaldson, E. Talbot. "Idiom of Popular Poetry in the Miller's Tale." In his *Speaking of Chaucer*, pp. 13–29. New York: Norton, 1970.

Doob, Penelope B. R. *Nebuchadnezzar's Children: Conventions of Madness in Middle English Literature*. New Haven: Yale Univ. Press, 1974.

Doyle, A. I., and M. B. Parkes. "Paleographical Introduction." See Chaucer, *The Canterbury Tales: A Facsimile and Transcription of the Hengwrt Manuscript, with Variants from the Ellesmere Manuscript*, pp. xix–xlix.

———. "The Production of Copies of the *Canterbury Tales* and the *Confessio Amantis* in the Early Fifteenth Century." In M. B. Parkes and Andrew G. Watson, eds., *Medieval Scribes, Manuscripts and Libraries: Essays Presented to N. R. Ker*, pp. 163–210. London: Scolar Press, 1978.

The Dream of the Rood. Ed. Bruce Dickins and Alan S. C. Ross. 3d ed. London: Methuen, 1951.

Dronke, Peter. *Fabula: Explorations into the Uses of Myth in Medieval Platonism*. Leiden: Brill, 1974.

———. *The Medieval Lyric*. London: Hutchinson, 1968.

Droulers, Eugène. *Dictionnaire des attributs, allégories, emblèmes et symboles*. Turnhout: Brepols, [1949].

Dunbar, William. *The Poems of William Dunbar*. Ed. W. Mackay Mackenzie. 1932; repr. Bath: Pitman, 1950.

Dunn, Charles W., and Edward T. Byrnes, eds. *Middle English Literature*. New York: Harcourt Brace Jovanovich, 1973.

St. Edmund Rich (Edmund of Canterbury). *The Mirror of Holy Church*. In Colledge, ed., *The Mediaeval Mystics of England*, pp. 123–40.

Edward, Second Duke of York. *The Master of Game*. Ed. W. A. and F. Baillie-Grohman. London: Ballantyne, Hanson, 1904.

Egbert, Virginia Wylie. *The Mediaeval Artist at Work*. Princeton: Princeton Univ. Press, 1967.

———. *On the Bridges of Mediaeval Paris: A Record of Early Fourteenth-Century Life*. Princeton: Princeton Univ. Press, 1974.

Eglesfield, Robert, trans. *Bawdy Tales of the Middle Ages*. London: Tandem, 1967.

Eilhart von Oberg. *Tristrant*. Ed. Danielle Buschinger. Göppingen: Kümmerle, 1976.

———. *Tristrant*. Trans. J. W. Thomas. Lincoln: Univ. of Nebraska Press, 1978.

Elbow, Peter. *Oppositions in Chaucer*. Middletown, Conn.: Wesleyan Univ. Press, 1975.

Ellinwood, Leonard. "A Further Note on 'Pilates Voys.'" *Speculum*, 26 (1951), 482.

Emaré. In Rumble, ed., *The Breton Lays in Middle English*, pp. 97–133.

Das Evangeliar des Johannes von Troppau. Ed. Ernst Trenkler. Vienna: Klagenfurt, 1948.

Evans, Joan. "Chaucer and Decorative Art." *RES*, 6 (1930), 408–12.

———, ed. *The Flowering of the Middle Ages*. New York: McGraw-Hill, 1966.

Evans, M. W. *Medieval Drawings*. London: Hamlyn, 1969.

Farrell, Robert T. "Chaucer's Use of the Theme of the Help of God in the *Man of Law's Tale*." *NM*, 71 (1970), 239–43.

Fischer, Nancy. "Handlist of Animal References in Middle English Religious Prose." *LeedsSE*, 4 (1970), 49–110.

Fisher, John H. "Chaucer's Horses." *SAQ*, 60 (1961), 71–79.

———. *John Gower: Moral Philosopher and Friend of Chaucer*. London: Methuen, 1965.

Fleming, John V. "Chaucer and the Visual Arts of His Time." In Rose, ed., *New Perspectives in Chaucer Criticism*, pp. 121–36.

———. *The "Roman de la Rose": A Study in Allegory and Iconography*. Princeton: Princeton Univ. Press, 1969.

Flores, Angel, ed. *An Anthology of Medieval Lyrics.* New York: Modern Library, 1962.

Formaggio, Dino, and Carlo Basso. *A Book of Miniatures.* Trans. Peggy Craig. New York: Tudor, 1962.

Fowler, Alastair. "Periodization and Interart Analogies." *NLH,* 3 (1972), 487–509.

———, ed. *Silent Poetry.* London: Routledge and Kegan Paul, 1970.

Fox, John Howard. *The Lyric Poetry of Charles d'Orléans.* Oxford: Clarendon, 1969.

Fremantle, Anne. *Age of Faith.* New York: Time-Life Books, 1965.

Friedman, John Block. "A Reading of Chaucer's *Reeve's Tale.*" *ChauR,* 2 (1967), 8–19.

Froissart, Jean. *The Chronicle of Froissart.* Trans. Sir John Bourchier, Lord Berners. Ed. William Paton Ker. 6 vols. London: D. Nutt, 1901–3.

———. *Poésies.* Ed. Auguste Scheler. 3 vols. Brussels, 1870–72.

———. *La Prison amoureuse.* Ed. Anthime Fourrier. Paris: Klincksieck, 1974.

Frost, William. "An Interpretation of Chaucer's *Knight's Tale.*" *RES,* 25 (1949), 289–304.

Fry, Donald K. "The Ending of the *Monk's Tale.*" *JEGP,* 71 (1972), 355–68.

Furbank, P. N. *Reflections on the Word "Image."* London: Secker and Warburg, 1970.

Furnivall, F. J., ed. *Hymns to the Virgin and Christ, The Parliament of Devils, and Other Religious Poems.* EETS, o.s. 24. London: Trübner, 1867.

———, Edmund Brock, and W. A. Clouston, eds. *Originals and Analogues of Some of Chaucer's Canterbury Tales.* Chaucer Society, 2d series, Parts I and III. London: Trübner, 1872, 1876.

Galway, Margaret. "The 'Troilus' Frontispiece." *MLR,* 44 (1949), 161–77.

Garnett, Richard. *English Literature: An Illustrated Record.* New York: Macmillan, 1926.

Garvin, Katherine. "A Note on Noah's Wife." *MLN,* 49 (1934), 88–90.

Geoffrey de Vinsauf. *Poetria nova.* Trans. Margaret F. Nims. Toronto: Pontifical Institute, 1967.

Gibson, Gail McMurray. "Bury St. Edmunds, Lydgate, and the *N-Town Cycle.*" *Speculum,* 56 (1981), 56–90.

Giffin, Mary. *Studies on Chaucer and His Audience.* Quebec: Editions L'Eclair, 1956.

Gilbert of the Haye's Prose Manuscript: The Buke of the Law of Armys. Ed. J. H. Stevenson. STS 44. Edinburgh: Blackwood, 1901.

Gilson, Etienne. *The Christian Philosophy of St. Thomas Aquinas.* Trans. L. K. Shook. New York: Random House, 1956.

———. *History of Christian Philosophy in the Middle Ages.* New York: Random House, 1955.

Giraldus Cambrensis. *The First Version of the Topography of Ireland.* Trans. John J. O'Meara. Dundalk: Dundalgan Press, 1951.

Glob, P. V. *The Mound People.* Trans. Joan Bulman. London: Faber, 1974.

"God send us Paciens in oure Oolde Age." In Furnivall, ed., *Hymns to the Virgin and Christ,* pp. 79–82.

Gombrich, E. H. *Symbolic Images: Studies in the Art of the Renaissance.* London: Phaidon, 1972.

Gordon, R. K., ed. and trans. *Anglo-Saxon Poetry.* London: Dent, 1926; rev. ed. 1954.

———, trans. *The Story of Troilus.* 1934; New York: Dutton, 1964.

Gottfried von Strassburg. *Tristan.* Trans. A. T. Hatto. Baltimore: Penguin, 1960.

Gough, Michael. *The Origins of Christian Art.* London: Thames and Hudson, 1973.

Gould, Karen. *The Psalter and Hours of Yolande of Soissons.* Speculum Anniversary Monographs, 4. Cambridge, Mass.: Mediaeval Academy of America, 1978.

Gower, John. *Confessio amantis.* Ed. Russell A. Peck. New York: Holt, Rinehart, and Winston, 1968.

———. *Confessio amantis*. In *The Complete Works of John Gower*, vols. 2 and 3, ed. G. C. Macaulay. EETS, e.s. 81, 82. London: Oxford Univ. Press, 1957.

———. *The Major Latin Works of John Gower*. Trans. Eric W. Stockton. Seattle: Univ. of Washington Press, 1926.

———. *Mirour de l'omme*. In *The Complete Works of John Gower*, vol. 1, ed. G. C. Macaulay, pp. 1–334. Oxford: Clarendon, 1899.

———. *Vox clamantis*. In *The Complete Works of John Gower*, vol. 4, ed. G. C. Macaulay, pp. 3–313. Oxford: Clarendon, 1902.

Grabar, Andre. *Christian Iconography: A Study of Its Origins*. Princeton: Princeton Univ. Press, 1968.

Graham, John. "Ut Pictura Poesis." *Dictionary of the History of Ideas*, 5 vols., IV, 465–76. New York: Scribner's, 1973.

Les Grandes Heures de Jean de France, Duc de Berry. Ed. Marcel Thomas. Paris: Draeger, 1971.

Gray, Douglas. *Themes and Images in the Medieval English Religious Lyric*. London: Routledge and Kegan Paul, 1972.

Green, Martin. "The Dialectic of Adaptation: *The Canterbury Tales* of Pier Paolo Pasolini." *LFQ*, 4 (1976), 46–53.

Green, Richard Firth. *Poets and Princepleasers: Literature and the English Court in the Late Middle Ages*. Toronto: Univ. of Toronto Press, 1980.

Green, Richard Hamilton. "Classical Fable and English Poetry in the Fourteenth Century." In Bethurum, ed., *Critical Approaches to Medieval Literature*, pp. 110–33.

Greenhill, Eleanor S. "The Group of Christ and St. John as Author Portrait: Literary Sources, Pictorial Parallels." In Johanne Autenrieth and Franz Brunhölzl, eds., *Festschrift Bernard Bischoff*, pp. 406–16. Stuttgart: Hiersemann, 1971.

Grosseteste, Robert. "The Castel of Loue." In Carl Horstmann, ed., *The Minor Poems of the Vernon MS.*, Part I, pp. 355–406. EETS, o.s. 98. London: Paul, Trench, Trübner, 1892.

Guillaume de Deguileville. "The Middle English *Pilgrimage of the Soul*: An Edition of MS. Egerton 615." Ed. Merrel Dare Clubb, Jr. Ph.D. diss., Univ. of Michigan, 1954.

———. *Le Pelerinage de l'ame*. Ed. J. J. Stürzinger. Roxburghe Club. London, 1895.

———. *Le Pelerinage de vie humaine*. Facsimile ed. Alfred W. Pollard. Roxburghe Club. Manchester, 1912.

———. *Le Pelerinage de vie humaine*. Ed. J. J. Stürzinger. Roxburghe Club. London, 1893.

———. *Le Pelerinage Jhesucrist*. Ed. J. J. Stürzinger. Roxburghe Club. London, 1897.

———. *The Pilgrimage of the Life of Man*. Trans. John Lydgate. *See* Lydgate, John.

———. *The Pilgrimage of the Lyf of the Manhode*. Ed. William A. Wright. Roxburghe Club. London, 1869.

Guillaume de Lorris and Jean de Meun. *Le Roman de la rose*. Ed. Félix Lecoy. 3 vols. CFMA, 92, 95, 98. Paris: Champion, 1965–70.

———. *The Romance of the Rose*. Trans. Charles Dahlberg. Princeton: Princeton Univ. Press, 1971.

———. *The Romance of the Rose*. Trans. Harry W. Robbins. Ed. Charles W. Dunn. New York: Dutton, 1962.

Guillaume de Machaut. *La Louange des dames*. Ed. Nigel Wilkins. New York: Barnes and Noble, 1973.

———. *Œuvres*. Ed. Ernest Hœpffner. 3 vols. SATF. Paris: Firmin Didot, 1908–21.

———. *Poésies lyriques*. Ed. V. Chichmaref. 2 vols. Paris: 1909; repr. Geneva: Slatkine, 1973.

Guillaume le Clerc. *The Bestiary of Guillaume le Clerc*. Trans. George Claridge Druce. Ashford, Kent: Headley Brothers, 1936.

Gunn, Alan M. F. *The Mirror of Love: A Reinterpretation of "The Romance of the Rose."* Lubbock: Texas Tech Press, 1952.

Gutmann, Joseph. *Hebrew Manuscript Painting.* New York: Braziller, 1978.

Haber, Ralph Norman. "How We Remember What We See." *Scientific American,* May 1970, pp. 104–12.

Hagen, Susan Kathleen. "*The Pilgrimage of the Life of Man*: A Medieval Theory of Vision and Remembrance." Ph.D. diss., Univ. of Virginia, 1976.

Hagstrum, Jean. *The Sister Arts.* Chicago: Univ. of Chicago Press, 1958.

Halliday, F. E. *Chaucer and His World.* London: Thames and Hudson, 1968.

Hanawalt, Barbara A. *Crime and Conflict in English Communities, 1300–1348.* Cambridge: Harvard Univ. Press, 1979.

Hannay, Alastair. *Mental Images: A Defense.* New York: Humanities Press, 1971.

Hanning, Robert W. *The Individual in Twelfth-Century Romance.* New Haven: Yale Univ. Press, 1977.

Harder, Kelsie B. "Chaucer's Use of the Mystery Plays in the *Miller's Tale.*" *MLQ,* 17 (1956), 193–98.

Hardison, O. B., Jr. *Christian Rite and Christian Drama in the Middle Ages.* Baltimore: Johns Hopkins Univ. Press, 1965.

———. *The Enduring Monument.* Chapel Hill: Univ. of North Carolina Press, 1962.

The Harley Lyrics. Ed. G. L. Brook. Manchester: The University Press, 1948.

Harrison, Frederick. *Treasures of Illumination: English Manuscripts of the Fourteenth Century (c. 1250 to 1400).* London: The Studio, 1937.

Harthan, John. *The Book of Hours.* New York: Crowell, 1977.

Harvey, E. Ruth. *The Inward Wits: Psychological Theory in the Middle Ages and in the Renaissance.* Warburg Institute Surveys, 6. London: Warburg Institute, 1975.

Harwood, Britton J. "Imaginative in *Piers Plowman.*" *MÆ,* 44 (1975), 249–63.

Haseloff, Günther. *Die Psalterillustration im 13. Jahrhundert.* Kiel, Germany: privately printed, 1938.

Hassall, W. O. *How They Lived: An Anthology of Original Accounts Written Before 1485.* Oxford: Blackwell, 1962.

Hastings, Margaret. *The Court of Common Pleas in Fifteenth Century England.* Ithaca: Cornell Univ. Press, 1947.

Hauber, A. "Planetenkinderbilder und Sternbilder." *Studien zur Deutschen Kunstgeschichte,* 194. Strassburg: Heitz, 1916.

Haussherr, Reiner. "Christus-Johannes-Gruppen in der Bible Moralisée." *Zeitschrift für Kunstgeschichte,* 27 (1964), 133–52.

Havely, N. R. *Chaucer's Boccaccio: Sources of "Troilus" and the "Knight's" and "Franklin's" Tales.* Chaucer Studies, 5. Cambridge: Brewer, 1980.

Hawes, Stephen. *The Pastime of Pleasure.* Ed. William Edward Mead. EETS, o.s. 173. London: Oxford Univ. Press, 1928.

"Heile of Bersele." In Bryan and Dempster, eds., *Sources and Analogues,* pp. 112–18.

Heimann, Adelheid. "Trinitas creator mundi." *JWCI,* 2 (1938–39), 42–52.

Hellman, Robert, and Richard O'Gorman, trans. *Fabliaux: Ribald Tales from the Old French.* New York: Crowell, 1965.

Henke, Suzette A. *Joyce's Moraculous Sindbook: A Study of "Ulysses."* Columbus: Ohio State Univ. Press, 1978.

Henri d'Andeli. *Le Lai d'Aristote.* Ed. Maurice Delbouille. Paris: "Les Belles Lettres," 1951.

Henry, Duke of Lancaster. *Le Livre de seyntz medicines.* Ed. E. J. Arnould. Anglo-Norman Text Society, 2. Oxford: Blackwell, 1940.

Henry, P. L. *The Early English and Celtic Lyric.* London: Allen and Unwin, 1966.

Hermann, Hermann Julius. *Die Westeuropäischen Handschriften und Inkunabeln der Gotik und der Renaissance. Englische und Französische Handschriften des XIV Jahrhunderts,* 2. Leipzig, 1936.

Herrtage, J. H., ed. *The Early English Versions of the "Gesta Romanorum."* EETS, e.s. 33. London: Oxford Univ. Press, 1879.

Hieatt, Constance B. "'To boille the chiknes with the marybones': Hodge's Kitchen Revisited." In Vasta and Thundy, eds., *Chaucerian Problems and Perspectives*, pp. 149–63.

Hilton, Walter. *The Ladder of Perfection.* Trans. Leo Sherley-Price. Harmondsworth: Penguin, 1957.

———. *The Scale of Perfection.* Ed. Evelyn Underhill. London: Watkins, 1923.

Hirsch, E. D., Jr. *The Aims of Interpretation.* Chicago: Univ. of Chicago Press, 1976.

Hoccleve, Thomas. *The Minor Poems.* Ed. F. J. Furnivall and Israel Gollancz. Rev. in one vol. by J. Mitchell and A. I. Doyle. EETS, e.s. 61/73. London: Oxford Univ. Press, 1970.

———. *Regement of Princes.* Ed. F. J. Furnivall. EETS, e.s. 72. London: Paul, Trench, Trübner, 1897.

Hodnett, Edward. *English Woodcuts, 1480–1535.* London: Oxford Univ. Press, 1935.

Hoffman, Arthur W. "Chaucer's Prologue to Pilgrimage: The Two Voices." *ELH*, 21 (1954), 1–16. Repr. in Wagenknecht, ed., *Chaucer: Modern Essays in Criticism*, pp. 30–45.

Holbrook, R. T. *Portraits of Dante from Giotto to Raffael.* London: Warner, 1911.

The Holkham Bible Picture Book. Facsimile ed. W. O. Hassall. London: Dropmore Press, 1954.

Hollander, Robert. "The Validity of Boccaccio's Self-Exegesis in His *Teseida.*" *M&H*, n.s. 8 (1977), 163–83.

Homo, Léon Pol. *Rome médiévale, 476–1420.* Paris: Payot, 1934; repr. 1956.

Hooper, F. A. *Funerary Stelae from Kom Abou Billou.* Ann Arbor: Kelsey Museum of Archaeology, 1961.

Hopper, Vincent Foster. *Medieval Number Symbolism.* New York: Columbia Univ. Press, 1938.

Horstmann, Carl, ed. *Altenglische Legenden: Neue Folge.* Heilbron, Germany: Henninger, 1881.

———, ed. *Yorkshire Writers: Richard Rolle of Hampole . . . and His Followers.* 2 vols. London: Sonnenschein; New York: Macmillan, 1895–96.

The Hours of Catherine of Cleves. Ed. John Plummer. New York: Braziller, 1966.

The Hours of Jeanne d'Evreux. Facsimile ed. James J. Rorimer. New York: Metropolitan Museum of Art, 1957.

Hoving, Thomas, Timothy B. Husband, and Jane Hayward, eds. *The Secular Spirit: Life and Art at the End of the Middle Ages.* New York: Dutton, 1975.

Howard, Donald R. *The Idea of the Canterbury Tales.* Berkeley: Univ. of California Press, 1976.

———. *The Three Temptations: Medieval Man in Search of the World.* Princeton: Princeton Univ. Press, 1966.

———. *Writers and Pilgrims: Medieval Pilgrimage Narratives and Their Posterity.* Berkeley: Univ. of California Press, 1980.

Hubert, J., J. Porcher, and W. F. Volbach. *Europe of the Invasions.* Trans. Stuart Gilbert and James Emmons. New York: Braziller, 1969.

Hudson, Anne, ed. *Selections from English Wycliffite Writings.* Cambridge: Cambridge Univ. Press, 1978.

Hugh of St. Victor. *Didascalicon.* Trans. Jerome Taylor. New York: Columbia Univ. Press, 1961.

———. *On the Sacraments of the Christian Faith.* Trans. Roy J. Deferrari. Cambridge, Mass.: Mediaeval Academy of America, 1951.

———. *Selected Spiritual Writings.* Trans. "A Religious of C.S.M.V." Intro. Aelred Squire, O.P. London: Faber, 1962.

Hughes, Robert. *Heaven and Hell in Western Art*. London: Weidenfeld and Nicolson, 1968.

Huizinga, Johan. *Homo Ludens*. Boston: Beacon Press, 1950.

Hunter, Ian M. L. *Memory*. Rev. ed. Harmondsworth: Penguin, 1964.

Huppé, Bernard F. *A Reading of the Canterbury Tales*. New York: State Univ. of New York Press, 1964.

———, and D. W. Robertson, Jr. *Fruyt and Chaf: Studies in Chaucer's Allegories*. Princeton: Princeton Univ. Press, 1963.

Hussey, Maurice. *Chaucer's World: A Pictorial Companion*. Cambridge: Cambridge Univ. Press, 1967.

Hutchison, Jane C. *The Master of the Housebook*. New York: Collectors Editions, 1972.

Huyghe, René, ed. *Larousse Encyclopedia of Byzantine and Medieval Art*. Trans. Dennis Gilbert, Ilse Schreier, and Wendela Schurmann. London: Hamlyn, 1963.

Idley, Peter. *Peter Idley's Instructions to His Son*. Ed. Charlotte d'Evelyn. Boston: Heath, 1935.

Illustrations of the Book of Genesis. Facsimile ed. Montague Rhodes James. Roxburghe Club. Oxford, 1921.

Isaacs, Neil D. "Constance in Fourteenth-Century England." *NM*, 59 (1958), 260–77.

Jacob's Well. Ed. Arthur Brandeis. EETS, o.s. 115. London: Paul, Trench, Trübner, 1900.

Jacobus de Voragine. *The Golden Legend of Jacobus de Voragine*. Trans. Granger Ryan and Helmutt Ripperger. New York: Longmans, Green, 1941; repr. Arno, 1969.

———. *The Golden Legend or Lives of the Saints*. Trans. William Caxton. Ed. F. S. Ellis. 7 vols. London: Dent, 1900.

———. *Legenda aurea*. Ed. Th. Graesse. 3d ed. 1890; repr. Osnabruck: Otto Zeller, 1969.

[James I of Scotland.] *The Kingis Quair*. Ed. John Norton-Smith. Oxford: Clarendon, 1971.

James, Montague Rhodes. *The Bohun Manuscripts*. Roxburghe Club. Oxford, 1936.

———, ed. "An English Medieval Sketch-book, No. 1916 in the Pepysian Library, Magdalene College, Cambridge." *Walpole Society Publications*, 13 (1925), 1–17.

———, trans. *The Apocryphal New Testament*. Oxford: Clarendon, 1924.

Janson, H. W. *Apes and Ape Lore in the Middle Ages and the Renaissance*. London: Warburg Institute, 1952.

Jefferson, Bernard L. *Chaucer and the Consolation of Philosophy of Boethius*. 1917; repr. New York: Haskell House, 1965.

Jones, Terry. *Chaucer's Knight: The Portrait of a Medieval Mercenary*. Baton Rouge: Louisiana State Univ. Press, 1980.

Jordan, Robert M. *Chaucer and the Shape of Creation*. Cambridge: Harvard Univ. Press, 1967.

———. "Chaucerian Narrative." In Rowland, ed., *Companion to Chaucer Studies*, pp. 95–116.

Joseph, Gerhard. "Chaucerian 'Game'—'Earnest' and the 'Argument of Herbergage' in *The Canterbury Tales*." *ChauR*, 5 (1970), 83–96.

Josipovici, Gabriel. *The World and the Book: A Study of Modern Fiction*. London: Macmillan, 1971.

Julian of Norwich. *A Book of Showings to the Anchoress Julian of Norwich*. Ed. Edmund Colledge, O.S.A., and James Walsh, S.J. 2 vols. Toronto: Pontifical Institute, 1978.

Kaske, R. E. "The *Canticum Canticorum* in the *Miller's Tale*." *SP*, 59 (1962), 479–500.

———. "Chaucer and Medieval Allegory." *ELH*, 30 (1963), 175–92.

———. "*Piers Plowman* and Local Iconography." *JWCI*, 31 (1968), 159–69.

———. "A Poem of the Cross in the Exeter Book: 'Riddle 60' and 'The Husband's Message.'" *Traditio*, 23 (1967), 41–71.

———. "The Summoner's Garleek, Oynons, and eek Lekes." *MLN*, 74 (1959), 481–84.

Katzenellenbogen, Adolf. *Allegories of the Virtues and Vices in Mediaeval Art from Early Christian Times to the Thirteenth Century*. Trans. Alan J. P. Crick. London, 1939; repr. New York: Norton, 1964.

Kean, P. M. *Chaucer and the Making of English Poetry*. 2 vols. London: Routledge and Kegan Paul, 1972.

Kelly, Douglas. *Medieval Imagination: Rhetoric and the Poetry of Courtly Love*. Madison: Univ. of Wisconsin Press, 1978.

Kelly, Henry Ansgar. "Chaucer's Arts and Our Arts." In Rose, ed., *New Perspectives in Chaucer Criticism*, pp. 107–20.

Kennedy, Charles W., trans. *An Anthology of Old English Poetry*. New York: Oxford Univ. Press, 1960.

Kiepe, Eva, and Hansjürgen Kiepe, eds. *Epochen der deutschen Lyrik: 1300–1500*. Munich: Deutscher Taschenbuch, 1972.

King, Donald. "Currents of Trade: Industry, Merchants and Money." In Evans, ed., *The Flowering of the Middle Ages*, pp. 245–80.

Klein, Dorothea. *St. Lukas als Maler der Maria: Ikonographie der Lukas-Madonna. . . .* Berlin: O. Schloss, 1933.

Klibansky, Raymond, Erwin Panofsky, and Fritz Saxl. *Saturn and Melancholy*. New York: Basic Books, 1964.

Klingender, Francis. *Animals in Art and Thought to the End of the Middle Ages*. Ed. Evelyn Antal and John Harthan. Cambridge, Mass.: M.I.T. Press, 1971.

Knowles, David. "Boethius, Anicius Manlius Severinus." *The Encyclopedia of Philosophy*. New York: Collier-Macmillan, 1967.

———. *The English Mystical Tradition*. New York: Harper, 1961.

Koechlin, Raymond. *Les Ivoires gothiques français*. 3 vols. Paris: A. Picard, 1924.

Kolve, V. A. "Chaucer and the Visual Arts." In Brewer, ed., *Geoffrey Chaucer*, pp. 290–320.

———. "Chaucer's *Second Nun's Tale* and the Iconography of St. Cecilia." In Rose, ed., *New Perspectives in Chaucer Criticism*, pp. 137–74.

———. "From Cleopatra to Alceste: An Iconographic Study of *The Legend of Good Women*." In John P. Hermann and John J. Burke, Jr., eds., *Signs and Symbols in Chaucer's Poetry*, pp. 130–78. University, Ala.: Univ. of Alabama Press, 1981.

———. *The Play Called Corpus Christi*. Stanford: Stanford Univ. Press, 1966.

Koonce, B. J. *Chaucer and the Tradition of Fame*. Princeton: Princeton Univ. Press, 1966.

Der Krakauer Behaim Codex. Facsimile ed. Friedrich Winkler. Berlin: Deutscher Verein für Kunstwissenschaft, 1941.

Kraus, Dorothy, and Henry Kraus. *The Hidden World of Misericords*. New York: Braziller, 1975.

Kraus, Henry. *The Living Theatre of Medieval Art*. London: Thames and Hudson, 1967.

Kuhl, Ernest P. "Chaucer's Burgesses." *TWA*, 18 (1916), 652–75.

Kuhn, Alfred. "Die Illustration des Rosenromans." *Jahrbuch der Kunsthistorischen Sammlungen des Allerhöchsten Kaiserhauses*, 31 (1913), 1–66.

Langland, William. *Piers Plowman: The A Version. Will's Visions of Piers Plowman and Do-Well*. Ed. George Kane. London: Univ. of London, Athlone Press, 1960.

———. *Piers Plowman: The B Version. Will's Visions of Piers Plowman, Do-Well, Do-Better, and Do-Best*. Ed. George Kane and E. Talbot Donaldson. London: Univ. of London, Athlone Press, 1975.

———. *Piers Plowman: An Edition of the C-text.* Ed. Derek Pearsall. Berkeley: Univ. of California Press, 1979.

———. *Piers the Ploughman.* Trans. J. F. Goodridge. Rev. ed. Baltimore: Penguin, 1966.

Lanham, Richard A. "Game, Play, and High Seriousness in Chaucer's Poetry." *ES,* 48 (1967), 1–24.

The Lanterne of Light. Ed. Lilian M. Swinburn. EETS, o.s. 151. London: Paul, Trench, Trübner, 1917.

Latini, Brunetto. *Li Livres dou tresor.* Ed. Francis J. Carmody. Berkeley: Univ. of California Press, 1948.

Lavedan, Pierre. *Représentations des villes dans l'art du moyen âge.* Paris: Van Oest, 1954.

Lawlor, John. *Chaucer.* London: Hutchinson Univ. Library, 1968.

Lee, Rensselaer W. "*Ut Pictura Poesis*: The Humanistic Theory of Painting." *Art Bulletin,* 22 (1940), 197–269; repr. New York: Norton, 1967.

Leff, Gordon. *Paris and Oxford Universities in the Thirteenth and Fourteenth Centuries.* New York: Wiley, 1968.

Legge, M. Dominica. *Anglo-Norman Literature and Its Background.* Oxford: Clarendon, 1963.

Lehmann-Haupt, Hellmut. "The Book of Trades in the Iconography of Social Typology." Bromsen Lecture (April 28, 1973). Boston: The Public Library, 1976.

Leicester, H. Marshall, Jr. "The Art of Impersonation: A General Prologue to the *Canterbury Tales.*" *PMLA,* 95 (1980), 213–24.

———. Reply to a letter from Robert B. Burlin. *PMLA,* 95 (1980), 881–82.

Levin, William R., ed. *Images of Love and Death in Late Medieval and Renaissance Art.* Catalogue. Ann Arbor: Univ. of Michigan Museum of Art, 1975.

Lewis, Jack P. *A Study of the Interpretation of Noah and the Flood in Jewish and Christian Literature.* Leiden: Brill, 1968.

Lewis, Robert Enzer. "Chaucer's Artistic Use of Pope Innocent III's *De Miseria Humane Conditionis* in the Man of Law's Prologue and Tale." *PMLA,* 81 (1966), pp. 485–92.

Lexikon der Christlichen Ikonographie. Ed. Engelbert Kirschbaum. 8 vols. Freiburg: Herder, 1968–76.

Leyerle, John. "The Heart and the Chain." In Larry D. Benson, ed., *The Learned and the Lewed,* Harvard English Studies, 5, pp. 113–45. Cambridge: Harvard Univ. Press, 1974.

Lindblom, Andreas. *La Peinture gothique en Suède et en Norvège.* Stockholm: Wahlström and Widstrand, 1916.

Loomis, Dorothy Bethurum. "Constance and the Stars." In Vasta and Thundy, eds., *Chaucerian Problems and Perspectives,* pp. 207–20.

Loomis, Roger Sherman. *A Mirror of Chaucer's World.* Princeton: Princeton Univ. Press, 1965.

———, and Laura Hibbard Loomis. *Arthurian Legends in Medieval Art.* New York: MLA, 1938.

Lorens of Orléans, Friar. *La Somme le roy.* Ed. Eric G. Millar. Roxburghe Club. Oxford, 1953.

Lothario dei Segni (Pope Innocent III). *On the Misery of the Human Condition.* Trans. M. M. Dietz. Ed. Donald R. Howard. Indianapolis: Bobbs-Merrill, 1969.

Lubac, Henri de. *Exégèse médiévale.* 4 vols. Paris: Aubier, 1959–64.

Ludus Coventriae or The Plaie Called Corpus Christi. Ed. K. S. Block. EETS, e.s. 120. London: Oxford Univ. Press, 1922.

Luria, Maxwell S. "Dame Custance's Voyages Re-examined: Some Traditional Associations of the Christian Exile." Paper presented to the Chaucer Group, MLA Convention, Chicago, 1965.

The Luttrell Psalter. Facsimile ed. Eric G. Millar. London: The British Museum, 1932.

Lydgate, John. *Fall of Princes*. Ed. Henry Bergen. 4 vols. EETS, e.s. 121–24. London: Oxford Univ. Press, 1924–27.

———. *The Minor Poems of John Lydgate*. Ed. Henry Noble MacCracken. 2 vols. EETS, e.s. 107, o.s. 192. London: Oxford Univ. Press, 1911, 1934.

———. *The Pilgrimage of the Life of Man*. Ed. F. J. Furnivall and Katharine B. Locock. EETS, e.s. 77, 83, 92. London: 1899, 1901, 1904; repr. Millwood, N.Y.: Kraus, 1978.

———. *Siege of Thebes*. Ed. A. Erdmann. 2 vols. EETS, e.s. 108, 125. London: Paul, Trench, Trübner, 1911; and Oxford Univ. Press, 1930.

Lyon, Earl DeWitt. "The Cook's Tale." In Bryan and Dempster, eds., *Sources and Analogues*, pp. 148–54.

McCall, Andrew. *The Medieval Underworld*. London: Hamish Hamilton, 1979.

McCall, John P. *Chaucer among the Gods: The Poetics of Classical Myth*. University Park, Pa.: Pennsylvania State Univ. Press, 1979.

McClintock, Michael W. "Games and the Players of Games: Old French Fabliaux and the *Shipman's Tale*." *ChauR*, 5 (1970), 112–36.

McCulloch, Florence. *Mediaeval Latin and French Bestiaries*. Rev. ed. Chapel Hill: Univ. of North Carolina Press, 1962.

McKenna, Isobel. "The Making of a Fourteenth-Century Sargeant of the Lawe." *Revue Universitaire d'Ottawa*, 45 (1975), 244–62.

McKeon, Richard, ed. and trans. *Selections from Medieval Philosophers*. 2 vols. New York: Scribner's, 1929–30.

MacLaine, Allan H. *The Student's Comprehensive Guide to the Canterbury Tales*. Great Neck, N.Y.: Barron's Educational Series, 1964.

McNeill, John T., and Helena M. Gamer, trans. *Medieval Handbooks of Penance*. New York: Columbia Univ. Press, 1938.

MacQueen, John. *Allegory*. Critical Idiom Series, 14. London: Methuen, 1970.

Macrobius. *Commentary on the Dream of Scipio*. Trans. William Harris Stahl. New York: Columbia Univ. Press, 1952.

Mâle, Emile. *L'Art religieux de la fin du moyen âge en France*. 5th ed. Paris: Armand Colin, 1949.

———. *The Gothic Image: Religious Art in France of the Thirteenth Century*. Trans. Dora Nussey. 1913; London: Fontana Library, 1961.

———. *Les Heures d'Anne de Bretagne*. *Verve*, 4, 1946.

———. *Les Saints Compagnons du Christ*. Paris: P. Hartmann, 1958.

Malory, Thomas. *The Works of Sir Thomas Malory*. Ed. Eugene Vinaver. London: Oxford Univ. Press, 1954.

Mankind. In *The Macro Plays*, ed. Mark Eccles, pp. 153–84. EETS, o.s. 262. London: Oxford Univ. Press, 1969.

Manly, John Matthews. *Some New Light on Chaucer*. New York: Henry Holt, 1926.

Mann, Jill. *Chaucer and Medieval Estates Satire*. Cambridge: Cambridge Univ. Press, 1973.

Manning, Stephen. "Chaucer's Constance, Pale and Passive." In Vasta and Thundy, eds., *Chaucerian Problems and Perspectives*, pp. 13–23.

Map, Walter. *De nugis curialium*. Trans. Montague Rhodes James. Oxford: Clarendon, 1914.

Marchands et métiers au moyen âge. La Documentation Photographique, 6009. Paris: La Documentation Française, 1974.

Marcus, Millicent. "Ser Ciappelletto: A Reader's Guide to the *Decameron*." *HAB*, 26 (1975), 275–88.

Markman, Alan M. "The Meaning of *Sir Gawain and the Green Knight*." *PMLA*, 72 (1957), 574–86.

Marle, Raimond van. *The Development of the Italian Schools of Painting.* 19 vols. The Hague: Nijhoff, 1923–38.

––––––. *Iconographie de l'art profane.* 2 vols. The Hague: Nijhoff, 1931–32.

Martindale, Andrew. *The Rise of the Artist in the Middle Ages and Early Renaissance.* London: Thames and Hudson, 1972.

––––––, and Edi Baccheschi. *The Complete Paintings of Giotto.* New York: Abrams, 1966.

Masuccio. "Viola e li suoi amanti," from *Il novellino.* In Benson and Andersson, eds., *The Literary Context of Chaucer's Fabliaux,* pp. 26–37.

Mathew, Gervase. *The Court of Richard II.* London: John Murray, 1968.

Mazzolani, Lidia Storoni. *The Idea of the City in Roman Thought: From Walled City to Spiritual Commonwealth.* Trans. S. O'Donnell. Bloomington: Indiana Univ. Press, 1970.

Mazzotta, Giuseppe. "The *Decameron*: The Marginality of Literature." *UTQ,* 42 (1972), 64–81.

Meaney, Audrey. *A Gazetteer of Early Anglo-Saxon Burial Sites.* London: Allen and Unwin, 1964.

Meiss, Millard. *French Painting in the Time of Jean de Berry: The Boucicaut Master.* London: Phaidon, 1968.

––––––. *French Painting in the Time of Jean de Berry: The Late Fourteenth Century and the Patronage of the Duke.* London: Phaidon, 1967.

––––––. *French Painting in the Time of Jean de Berry: The Limbourgs and Their Contemporaries.* 2 vols. London: Thames and Hudson, 1974.

––––––. *Painting in Florence and Siena after the Black Death.* 1951; repr. New York: Harper and Row, 1964.

Mellini, Gian Lorenzo. *Altichiero e Jacopo Avanzi.* Milan: Edizioni de Comunità, 1965.

Merrill, Rodney. "Chaucer's *Broche of Thebes*: The Unity of 'The Complaint of Mars' and 'The Complaint of Venus.'" In Eric Rothstein, ed., *Literary Monographs,* 5, pp. 1–61. Madison: Univ. of Wisconsin Press, 1973.

Merriman, James D. "The Parallel of the Arts: Some Misgivings and a Faint Affirmation." *JAAC,* 31 (1972–73), 153–64, 309–22.

Michel of Northgate, Dan. *Ayenbite of Inwyt.* Ed. Richard Morris, corr. Pamela Gradon. EETS, o.s. 23. London: Oxford Univ. Press, 1965.

Middleton, Anne. "The Idea of Public Poetry in the Reign of Richard II." *Speculum,* 53 (1978), 94–114.

Mill, Anna Jean. "Noah's Wife Again." *PMLA,* 56 (1941), 613–26.

Millar, Eric G. *English Illuminated Manuscripts of the XIVth and XVth Centuries.* Paris and Brussels: Van Oest, 1926.

––––––. *The Parisian Miniaturist, Honoré.* London: Faber, 1959.

Miller, Robert P. "The *Miller's Tale* as Complaint." *ChauR,* 5 (1970), 147–60.

––––––. "Venus, Adonis, and the Horses." *ELH,* 19 (1952), 249–64.

Milosh, Joseph E. *The Scale of Perfection and the English Mystical Tradition.* Madison: Univ. of Wisconsin Press, 1966.

Miracles de Nostre Dame par personnages. Ed. Gaston Paris and Ulysse Robert. 8 vols. SATF. Paris: Firmin Didot, 1876–93.

The Miroure of Mans Saluacionne. Ed. Alfred H. Huth. Roxburghe Club. London, 1888.

"The Mirror of the Periods of Man's Life." In Furnivall, ed., *Hymns to the Virgin and Christ,* pp. 58–78.

Le Mistère du Viel Testament. Ed. Baron James de Rothschild. 6 vols. SATF. Paris: Firmin Didot, 1878–91.

Mitchell, Jerome, and William Provost, eds. *Chaucer the Love Poet.* Athens: Univ. of Georgia Press, 1973.

Mitchell, Sabrina. *Medieval Manuscript Painting*. Compass History of Art. New York: Viking Press, 1965.

Moé, Emile van. "Les *Ethiques, Politiques* et *Economiques* d'Aristote, traduits par Nicole Oresme, manuscrit de la Bibliothèque de la Ville de Rouen." In R. Cantinelli and Emile Dacier, eds., *Les Trésors des Bibliothèques de France*, III, 3–15. Paris: Van Oest, 1930.

Morand, Kathleen. *Jean Pucelle*. Oxford: Clarendon, 1962.

La Mort le Roi Artu. Ed. Jean Frappier. 3d ed. Paris: Minard, 1936.

Mure, G. R. G. *Aristotle*. London: Benn, 1932.

Murrin, Michael. *The Veil of Allegory: Some Notes Toward a Theory of Allegorical Rhetoric in the English Renaissance*. Chicago: Univ. of Chicago Press, 1969.

Muscatine, Charles. "*The Canterbury Tales*: Style of the Man and Style of the Work." In Brewer, ed., *Chaucer and Chaucerians*, pp. 88–113.

———. *Chaucer and the French Tradition*. Berkeley: Univ. of California Press, 1957.

———. "Form, Texture, and Meaning in Chaucer's *Knight's Tale*." *PMLA*, 65 (1950), 911–29.

Myers, A. R. *London in the Age of Chaucer*. Norman, Okla.: Univ. of Oklahoma Press, 1972.

Navigatio Sancti Brendani Abbatis. Ed. Carl Selmer. Notre Dame, Ind.: Univ. of Notre Dame Press, 1959.

Neuse, Richard. "The Knight: The First Mover in Chaucer's Human Comedy." *UTQ*, 31 (1962), 299–315.

Nims, Margaret F., IBVM. "*Translatio*: 'Difficult Statement' in Medieval Poetic Theory." *UTQ*, 43 (1974), 215–30.

Nolan, Barbara. *The Gothic Visionary Perspective*. Princeton: Princeton Univ. Press, 1977.

The Northern Passion. Ed. Frances A. Foster. EETS, o.s. 145, 147. London: Paul, Trench, Trübner, 1913; Oxford Univ. Press, 1916.

Nykrog, Per. *Les Fabliaux: etude d'histoire littéraire et de stylistique médiévale*. Copenhagen: Ejnar Munksgaard, 1957.

Oakeshott, Walter F. *The Mosaics of Rome: From the Third to the Fourteenth Centuries*. London: Thames and Hudson, 1967.

O'Connor, John J. "The Astrological Background of the *Miller's Tale*." *Speculum*, 31 (1956), 120–25.

O'Connor, Mary Catharine, Sister. *The Art of Dying Well*. New York: Columbia Univ. Press, 1942.

O'Donnell, J. Reginald. "The Sources and Meaning of Bernard Silvester's Commentary on the Aeneid." *MS*, 24 (1962), 233–49.

Old Testament Miniatures. Intro. Sydney C. Cockerell. Pref. John Plummer. New York: Braziller, n.d.

Olson, Glending. "Deschamps' *Art de Dictier* and Chaucer's Literary Environment." *Speculum*, 48 (1973), pp. 714–23.

———. *Literature as Recreation in the Later Middle Ages*. Ithaca, N.Y.: Cornell Univ. Press, 1982.

———. "Making and Poetry in the Age of Chaucer." *CL*, 31 (1979), 272–90.

———. "The Medieval Theory of Literature for Refreshment and Its Use in the Fabliau Tradition." *SP*, 71 (1974), 291–313.

Olson, Paul A. "Poetic Justice in the *Miller's Tale*." *MLQ*, 24 (1963), 227–36.

———. "The *Reeve's Tale*: Chaucer's *Measure for Measure*." *SP*, 59 (1962), 1–17.

Oman, Charles. *Medieval Silver Nefs*. Victoria and Albert Museum Monograph no. 15. London: H.M. Stationery Office, 1963.

Ong, Walter J. *Ramus, Method, and the Decay of Dialogue*. Cambridge: Harvard Univ. Press, 1958.

Oresme, Nicole. *Le Livre de Ethiques d'Aristote.* Ed. Albert D. Menut. New York: Stechert, 1940.

Ovid. *The Art of Love.* Trans. Rolfe Humphries. Bloomington: Indiana Univ. Press, 1957.

Ovide moralisé en prose. Ed. C. de Boer. Amsterdam: North-Holland Publishing Co., 1954.

Owen, Charles A., Jr. "The Crucial Passages in Five of the *Canterbury Tales*: A Study in Irony and Symbol." *JEGP*, 52 (1953), 294–311.

————. *Pilgrimage and Storytelling in the Canterbury Tales: The Dialect of "Ernest" and "Game."* Norman, Okla.: Univ. of Oklahoma Press, 1977.

————, ed. *Discussions of the Canterbury Tales.* Boston: Heath, 1961.

Owen, D. D. R. *The Vision of Hell: Infernal Journeys in Medieval French Literature.* New York: Barnes and Noble, 1970.

Owst, G. R. *Literature and Pulpit in Medieval England.* 2d ed. Oxford: Blackwell, 1961.

Oxenstierna, Count Eric. *The Norsemen.* Ed. and trans. Catherine Hutter. Greenwich, Conn.: New York Graphic Society, 1965.

Pächt, Otto, and J. J. G. Alexander. *Illuminated Manuscripts in the Bodleian Library, Oxford.* 3 vols. Oxford: Clarendon, 1966–73.

Palumbo, Giuseppe, ed. *Giotto e i Giotteschi in Assisi.* Rome: Canesi, 1969.

Pamphilus, De amore. Trans. Thomas Jay Garbáty. *ChauR,* 2 (1967), 108–34.

Panofsky, Erwin. *Early Netherlandish Painting: Its Origins and Character.* 2 vols. Cambridge: Harvard Univ. Press, 1953.

————. *The Iconography of Correggio's Camera di San Paolo.* London: Warburg Institute, 1961.

————. *Tomb Sculpture.* New York: Abrams, 1964.

Parker, Roscoe E. "'Pilates Voys.'" *Speculum,* 25 (1950), 237–44.

Parkes, M. B. "Palaeographical Description and Commentary." In Chaucer, *Troilus and Criseyde: A Facsimile,* pp. 1–13.

Pasolini, Pier Paolo. *Trilogia della vita.* Ed. Giorgio Gattei. Bologna: Cappelli, 1975.

Patch, Howard Rollin. *The Goddess Fortuna.* London, 1927; repr. New York: Octagon, 1974.

————. *The Tradition of Boethius.* New York: Oxford Univ. Press, 1935.

Paull, Michael R. "The Influence of the Saint's Legend Genre in the *Man of Law's Tale.*" *ChauR,* 5 (1971), 179–94.

Payne, F. Anne. *King Alfred and Boethius.* Madison: Univ. of Wisconsin Press, 1968.

Payne, Robert O. *The Key of Remembrance: A Study of Chaucer's Poetics.* New Haven: Yale Univ. Press, 1963.

————. Review of D. W. Robertson, Jr., *A Preface to Chaucer: Studies in Medieval Perspectives. CL,* 15 (1963), 269–71.

————. Review of Bernard F. Huppé and D. W. Robertson, Jr., *Fruyt and Chaf: Studies in Chaucer's Allegories. CL,* 15 (1963), 272–76.

Pearl. Ed. E. V. Gordon. Oxford: Clarendon, 1953.

Pearl, Cleanness, Patience, and Sir Gawain. Facsimile ed. Sir Israel Gollancz. EETS, o.s. 162. London: Oxford Univ. Press, 1923.

Pearsall, Derek. *John Lydgate.* Charlottesville: Univ. Press of Virginia, 1970.

————. "The *Troilus* Frontispiece and Chaucer's Audience." *YES,* 7 (1977), 68–74.

Peck, Russell A. "Number as Cosmic Language." In David L. Jeffrey, ed., *By Things Seen: Reference and Recognition in Medieval Thought,* pp. 47–80. Ottawa: Univ. of Ottawa Press, 1979.

————. "Numerology and Chaucer's *Troilus and Criseyde.*" *Mosaic,* 5, no. 4 (1972), 1–29.

Pecock, Reginald. *The Donet.* Ed. Elsie Vaughan Hitchcock. EETS, o.s. 156. London: Oxford Univ. Press, 1921.

————. *The Repressor of Over Much Blaming of the Clergy*. Ed. Churchill Babington. Rolls Series 19. 2 vols. London: Longman, Green, Longman and Roberts, 1860.

Perret, Louis. *Les Catacombes de Rome*. 6 vols. Paris: Gide et J. Bavdry, 1851–55.

A Peterborough Psalter and Bestiary of the Fourteenth Century. Facsimile ed. Montague Rhodes James. Roxburghe Club. Oxford, 1921.

Petrarch, Francesco. *De secreto curarum conflictu*. Trans. as *Petrarch's Secret, or The Soul's Conflict with Passion*, by William H. Draper. London: Chatto and Windus, 1911.

————. *Letters from Petrarch*. Trans. Morris Bishop. Bloomington: Indiana Univ. Press, 1966.

————. *Petrarch's Lyric Poems: The "Rime Sparse" and Other Poems*. Ed. and trans. Robert M. Durling. Cambridge: Harvard Univ. Press, 1976.

Phillips, John. *The Reformation of Images: Destruction of Art in England, 1535–1660*. Berkeley: Univ. of California Press, 1973.

Physiologus. Trans. Michael J. Curley. Austin: Univ. of Texas Press, 1979.

Pickering, F. P. *Essays on Medieval German Literature and Iconography*. Cambridge: Cambridge Univ. Press, 1980.

————. *Literature and Art in the Middle Ages*. Coral Gables, Fla.: Univ. of Miami Press, 1970.

Piehler, Paul. *The Visionary Landscape: A Study in Medieval Allegory*. London: Arnold, 1971.

Plato. *Phaedrus*. Trans. R. Hackforth. Cambridge: Cambridge Univ. Press, 1952.

Platt, Colin. *The English Medieval Town*. London: Secker and Warburg, 1976.

Pleister, Werner. *Der Münchener Boccaccio*. Munich: Suddeutscher Verlag, 1965.

Pollard, Alfred W., ed. *Fifteenth Century Prose and Verse: An English Garner*. 1903; New York: Cooper Square, 1964.

Pope-Hennessy, John. *Giovanni di Paolo: 1403–1483*. New York: Oxford Univ. Press, 1938.

Porphyry. *Isagoge*. Trans. Edward W. Warren. Toronto: Pontifical Institute, 1975.

————. *Porphyrii Isagoge, translatio Boethii, Aristoteles Latinus*. Ed. Lorenzo Minio-Paluello. Bruges/Paris: Desclée de Brouwer, 1966.

Pratt, Robert A. "Chaucer and *Les Cronicles* of Nicholas Trevet." In E. Bagby Atwood and Archibald A. Hill, eds., *Studies in Language, Literature, and Culture of the Middle Ages and Later*, pp. 303–11. Austin: Univ. of Texas Press, 1969.

————. "Chaucer and the Hand That Fed Him." *Speculum*, 41 (1966), 619–42.

————. "Chaucer and the Visconti Libraries." *ELH*, 6 (1939), 191–99.

————. "Chaucer's Use of the *Teseida*." *PMLA*, 62 (1947), 598–621.

————. "Conjectures Regarding Chaucer's Manuscript of the *Teseida*." *SP*, 42 (1945), 745–63.

————. "The Knight's Tale." In Bryan and Dempster, eds., *Sources and Analogues*, pp. 82–105.

————, and Karl Young. "The Literary Framework of the Canterbury Tales." In Bryan and Dempster, eds., *Sources and Analogues*, pp. 1–81.

Praz, Mario. *Mnemosyne: The Parallel Between Literature and the Visual Arts*. Princeton: Princeton Univ. Press, 1970.

Preminger, Alex, O. B. Hardison, Jr., and Kevin Kerrane, eds. *Classical and Medieval Literary Criticism*. New York: Ungar, 1974.

The Pricke of Conscience. Ed. Richard Morris. Berlin: Asher, 1863.

Promptorium parvulorum. Ed. A. L. Mayhew. EETS, e.s. 102. London: Paul, Trench, Trübner, 1908.

Queen Mary's Psalter. Facsimile ed. Sir George Warner. London: The British Museum, 1912.

The Quest of the Holy Grail. Trans. P. M. Matarasso. Harmondsworth: Penguin, 1969.

La Queste del Saint Graal. Ed. Albert Pauphilet. CFMA, 33. Paris: Champion, 1972.

Quinn, Betty Nye. "Venus, Chaucer, and Peter Bersuire." *Speculum*, 38 (1963), 479–80.

Raby, F. J. E. *A History of Christian-Latin Poetry: From the Beginnings to the Close of the Middle Ages.* 2d ed. Oxford: Clarendon, 1953.

———, ed. *The Oxford Book of Medieval Latin Verse.* 1959; corr. repr. Oxford: Clarendon, 1966.

Rand, E. K. *Founders of the Middle Ages.* Cambridge, Mass., 1928; repr. New York: Dover, 1957.

Randall, Lilian M. C. *Images in the Margins of Gothic Manuscripts.* Berkeley: Univ. of California Press, 1966.

Randall, Richard H., Jr. *A Cloisters Bestiary.* New York: Metropolitan Museum of Art, 1960.

Ranquet, Henri du. *Les Vitraux de la cathédrale de Clermont-Ferrand.* Clermont-Ferrand: Paul Vallier, 1932.

Reallexikon zur Deutschen Kunstgeschichte. Ed. Otto Schmitt et al. 7 vols. Stuttgart, Munich: J. B. Metzlersche et al., 1937–75.

Réau, Louis. *Iconographie de l'art chrétien.* 6 parts in 3 vols. Paris: Presses Universitaires de France, 1955–59.

Reinhard, J. R. "Setting Adrift in Mediaeval Law and Literature." *PMLA*, 56 (1941), 33–68.

Reiss, Edmund. "Chaucer's *deerne love* and the Medieval View of Secrecy in Love." In Vasta and Thundy, eds., *Chaucerian Problems and Perspectives*, pp. 164–79.

———. "Chaucer's Parodies of Love." In Mitchell and Provost, eds., *Chaucer the Love Poet*, pp. 27–44.

———. "The Symbolic Surface of the *Canterbury Tales*: The Monk's Portrait." *ChauR*, 2 and 3 (1968), 254–72, 12–28.

Remnant, G. L. (with M. D. Anderson). *A Catalogue of Misericords in Great Britain.* Oxford: Clarendon, 1969.

René d'Anjou. *Livre du Cuer d'Amours espris.* Ed. O. Smital and E. Winkler. 3 vols. Vienna: L'Imprimerie de l'Etat Autrichien, 1926.

———. *Le Mortifiement de vaine plaisance.* Ed. Frédéric Lyna. Brussels: J. E. Goossens, 1926.

———. *Traité de la forme et devis d'un tournoi.* Ed. Edmond Pognon. *Verve*, 4, no. 16. Paris, 1946.

Rhetorica ad Herennium. Ed. and trans. Harry Caplan. Loeb Classical Library, 403. Cambridge: Harvard Univ. Press, 1954.

Richard de Fournival. *Li Bestiaires d'amours di Maistre Richart de Fornival.* Ed. Cesare Segre. Documenti di Filologia, no. 2. Milan: R. Ricciardi, 1957.

Richardson, Janette. *Blameth Nat Me: A Study of Imagery in Chaucer's Fabliaux.* The Hague: Mouton, 1970.

Rickert, Edith, ed. *Chaucer's World.* London: Oxford Univ. Press, 1948.

Rickert, Margaret. *Painting in Britain: The Middle Ages.* London: Penguin, 1954.

———. *The Reconstructed Carmelite Missal.* London: Faber, 1952.

Ringbom, Sixten. "Some Pictorial Conventions for the Recounting of Thoughts and Experiences in Late Medieval Art." In Andersen et al., eds., *Medieval Iconography and Narrative*, pp. 38–69.

Robbins, Rossell Hope, ed. *Secular Lyrics of the XIVth and XVth Centuries.* Oxford: Clarendon, 1952.

Robertson, D. W., Jr. *Chaucer's London.* New York: Wiley, 1968.

———. *A Preface to Chaucer: Studies in Medieval Perspectives.* Princeton: Princeton Univ. Press, 1963.

———. "Some Disputed Chaucerian Terminology." *Speculum*, 52 (1977), 571–81.

The Rohan Master: A Book of Hours. Facsimile ed. Millard Meiss and Marcel Thomas. New York: Braziller, 1973.

The Romance of Alexander. Facsimile ed. Montague Rhodes James. Oxford: Clarendon, 1933.

Rose, Donald M., ed. *New Perspectives in Chaucer Criticism.* Norman, Okla.: Pilgrim Books, 1981.

Ross, David J. A. "Allegory and Romance on a Mediaeval French Marriage Casket." *JWCI,* 11 (1948), 112–42.

Rowland, Beryl. *Animals with Human Faces: A Guide to Animal Symbolism.* Knoxville: Univ. of Tennessee Press, 1973.

————. *Birds with Human Souls: A Guide to Bird Symbolism.* Knoxville: Univ. of Tennessee Press, 1973.

————. *Blind Beasts: Chaucer's Animal World.* Kent, Ohio: Kent State Univ. Press, 1971.

————. "Chaucer's Blasphemous Churl: A New Interpretation of the Miller's Tale." In Rowland, ed., *Chaucer and Middle English Studies,* pp. 43–55.

————. "Chaucer's Imagery." In Rowland, ed., *Companion to Chaucer Studies,* pp. 117–42.

————. "Chaucer's *The Wife of Bath's Prologue,* D. 389." *Explicator,* 24 (1965), 14.

————. "Chaucer's 'Throstil Old' and Other Birds." *MS,* 24 (1962), 381–84.

————. "The Horse and Rider Figure in Chaucer's Works." *UTQ,* 35 (1966), 246–59.

————. "The Play of the *Miller's Tale:* A Game Within a Game." *ChauR,* 5 (1970), 140–46.

————, ed. *Chaucer and Middle English Studies in Honor of Rossell Hope Robbins.* London: Allen and Unwin, 1974.

————, ed. *Companion to Chaucer Studies.* Rev. ed. New York: Oxford Univ. Press, 1979.

Ruggiers, Paul G. *The Art of the Canterbury Tales.* Madison: Univ. of Wisconsin Press, 1965.

Ruiz, Juan. *The Book of Good Love.* Trans. Rigo Mignani and Mario A. DiCesare. Albany: State Univ. of New York Press, 1970.

Rumble, Thomas C., ed. *The Breton Lays in Middle English.* Detroit: Wayne State Univ. Press, 1965.

Rush, Alfred C. *Death and Burial in Christian Antiquity.* Catholic Univ. of America Studies in Christian Antiquity, 1. Washington, D.C.: Catholic Univ. of America Press, 1941.

Rushforth, G. McN. *Medieval Christian Imagery as Illustrated by the Painted Windows of Great Malvern Priory.* Oxford: Clarendon, 1936.

Ryle, Gilbert. *The Concept of Mind.* London, 1949; repr. New York: Barnes and Noble, 1965.

St. Erkenwald. Ed. Ruth Morse. Totowa, N. J.: Rowman and Littlefield, 1975.

Salmi, Mario. *Italian Miniatures.* Trans. Elisabeth Borgese-Mann. Ed. Milton S. Fox. New York: Abrams, 1954.

Salter, Elizabeth. "Medieval Poetry and the Visual Arts." *E&S,* n.s. 22 (1969), 16–32.

————. "The 'Troilus Frontispiece.'" In Chaucer, *Troilus and Criseyde: A Facsimile,* pp. 15–23.

————, and Derek Pearsall. "Pictorial Illustration of Late Medieval Poetic Texts: The Role of the Frontispiece or Prefatory Picture." In Andersen et al., eds., *Medieval Iconography and Narrative,* pp. 100–23.

Sandler, Lucy Freeman. *The Peterborough Psalter in Brussels and Other Fenland Manuscripts.* London: Harvey Miller, 1974.

————. "The Psalter of Robert de Lisle." Ph.D. diss., New York Univ., 1964.

Sartre, Jean-Paul. *L'Imaginaire*. Trans. as *The Psychology of Imagination*, by Bernard Frechtman. New York: Washington Square Press, 1948.

Saxl, Fritz. *Lectures*. 2 vols. London: Warburg Institute, 1957.

————. "A Spiritual Encyclopaedia of the Later Middle Ages." *JWCI*, 5 (1942), 82–134.

Schapiro, Meyer. *Late Antique, Early Christian and Mediaeval Art*. New York: Braziller, 1979.

————. *Words and Pictures: On the Literal and the Symbolic in the Illustration of a Text*. The Hague: Mouton, 1973.

Schiller, Gertrud. *Iconography of Christian Art*. Trans. Janet Seligman. 2 vols. London: Lund Humphries, 1971–72.

Schirmer, Walter F. *John Lydgate: A Study in the Culture of the XVth Century*. Trans. Anne E. Keep. London: Methuen, 1961.

Schlauch, Margaret. *Chaucer's Constance and Accused Queens*. New York: New York Univ. Press, 1927.

Schmidt, A. V. C. "Langland and Scholastic Philosophy." *MÆ*, 38 (1969), 134–56.

Scholes, Robert, and Robert Kellogg. *The Nature of Narrative*. New York: Oxford Univ. Press, 1966.

Schreiber, W. L. *Manuel de l'amateur de la gravure sur bois et sur métal au XVe siècle*. 8 vols. Berlin: A. Cohn, 1891–1911.

Schulz, Herbert C. *The Ellesmere Manuscript of Chaucer's Canterbury Tales*. San Marino, Calif.: The Huntington Library, 1966.

Schwarz, Heinrich. "The Mirror of the Artist and the Mirror of the Devout." In *Studies in the History of Art Dedicated to William E. Suida*, pp. 90–105. London: Phaidon, 1959.

Scott, Kathleen L. "Sow-and-Bagpipe Imagery in the Miller's Portrait." *RES*, n.s. 18 (1967), 287–90.

Serraillier, Ian. *Chaucer and His World*. London: Lutterworth, 1967.

Severs, J. Burke. "Chaucer's Clerks." In Rowland, ed., *Chaucer and Middle English Studies*, pp. 140–52.

————. "The Tales of Romance." In Rowland, ed., *Companion to Chaucer Studies*, pp. 271–95.

Seznec, Jean. *The Survival of the Pagan Gods*. Trans. Barbara F. Sessions. 1953; repr. New York: Harper, 1961.

Shestack, Alan. *Fifteenth Century Engravings of Northern Europe*. Catalogue. Washington, D.C.: National Gallery of Art, 1968.

Silverstein, Theodore. "Allegory and Literary Form." *PMLA*, 82 (1967), 28–32.

Simson, Otto von. *The Gothic Cathedral*. London: Routledge and Kegan Paul, 1956.

Singleton, Charles S. *Commedia: Elements of Structure*. Cambridge: Harvard Univ. Press, 1954.

————. *An Essay on the Vita Nuova*. Cambridge: Harvard Univ. Press, 1949.

————. "On *Meaning* in the Decameron." *Italica*, 21 (1944), 117–24.

Sitwell, Sacheverell. *The Netherlands*. 2d ed., rev. London: Batsford, 1952.

Skeat, Walter W., ed. *Chaucerian and Other Pieces . . . A Supplement to the Complete Works of Geoffrey Chaucer*. 1897; repr. Oxford: Clarendon, 1963.

Skey, Miriam Anne. "The Iconography of Herod the Great in Medieval Art." *The EDAM Newsletter*, 3 (1980), 4–10.

Smalley, Beryl. *English Friars and Antiquity in the Early Fourteenth Century*. Oxford: Blackwell, 1960.

————. *Historians in the Middle Ages*. London: Thames and Hudson, 1974.

————. *The Study of the Bible in the Middle Ages*. 2d ed. Oxford, 1952; repr. Notre Dame, Ind.: Univ. of Notre Dame Press, 1964.

Smithers, G. V. "The Meaning of *The Seafarer* and *The Wanderer*." *MÆ*, 26 (1957), 137–53, and 28 (1959), 1–22.

Sorabji, Richard. *Aristotle on Memory*. London: Duckworth, 1972.

The South English Legendary. Ed. Charlotte d'Evelyn and Anna J. Mill. 3 vols. EETS, o.s. 235, 236, 244. London: Oxford Univ. Press, 1956–59.

Southern, R. W. *Medieval Humanism and Other Studies*. Oxford: Blackwell, 1970.

Spearing, A. C. *Criticism and Medieval Poetry*. 2d ed. London: Arnold, 1972.

———. *Medieval Dream-Poetry*. Cambridge: Cambridge Univ. Press, 1976.

Speculum humanae salvationis. Facsimile ed. Montague Rhodes James and Bernhard Berenson. Oxford: Oxford Univ. Press, 1926.

Speculum humanae salvationis. Ed. J. Lutz and P. Perdrizet. 2 vols. Mulhouse: Meininger, 1907, 1909.

Speculum humanae salvationis. Ed. Willibrord Neumüller, O.S.B. Graz: Akadem. Druck- u. Verlagsanst., 1972.

Spencer, Brian. *Chaucer's London*. Catalogue. London: London Museum, 1972.

Spurgeon, Caroline F. E. *Five Hundred Years of Chaucer Criticism and Allusion, 1357–1900*. 3 vols. Cambridge: Cambridge Univ. Press, 1925.

Stahl, William Harris, with Richard Johnson and E. L. Burge. *Martianus Capella and the Seven Liberal Arts*. 2 vols. New York: Columbia Univ. Press, 1971, 1977.

Stanley, E. G. "'Of This Cokes Tale Maked Chaucer Na Moore.'" *Poetica*, 5 (1976), 36–59.

Steadman, John M. "Venus' *Citole* in Chaucer's *Knight's Tale* and Berchorius." *Speculum*, 34 (1959), 620–24.

Stevens, Martin. "Malkyn in the Man of Law's Headlink." *LeedsSE*, 1 (1967), 1–5.

———. "The Royal Stanza in Early English Literature." *PMLA*, 94 (1979), 62–76.

Stock, Brian. *Myth and Science in the Twelfth Century: A Study of Bernard Silvester*. Princeton: Princeton Univ. Press, 1972.

Stones, M. A. "A Short Note on Manuscripts Rylands French 1 and Douce 215." *Scriptorium*, 22 (1968), 42–45.

Storost, Joachim. "Femme chevalchat Aristotte." *ZFSL*, 66 (1956), 186–201.

Sudhoff, Walther. "Die Lehre von den Hirnventrikeln in textlicher und graphischer Tradition des Altertums und Mittelalters." *Archiv für Geschichte der Medizin*, 7 (1913), 149–205.

Suso, Heinrich. "Orologium Sapientiae, or The Seven Poyntes of Trewe Wisdom." Trans. William Caxton. Ed. Carl Horstmann. *Anglia*, 10 (1888), 323–89.

Symbols in Transformation: Iconographic Themes at the Time of the Reformation. An Exhibition of Prints in Memory of Erwin Panofsky. Intro. Craig Harbison. Catalogue. Princeton: Princeton Art Museum, 1969.

The Tale of Beryn. Ed. F. J. Furnivall and W. G. Stone. EETS, e.s. 105. London: Paul, Trench, Trübner and Oxford Univ. Press, 1909.

Tatlock, S. P., and Arthur G. Kennedy. *A Concordance to the Complete Works of Geoffrey Chaucer*. 1927; repr. Gloucester, Mass.: Peter Smith, 1963.

Tertullian. *Homily on Baptism*. Ed. and trans. Ernest Evans. London: S.P.C.K., 1964.

Tervarent, Guy de. *La Légende de Sainte Ursule dans la littérature et l'art du moyen-âge*. 2 vols. Paris: Van Oest, 1931.

"The 'Testament' of Jean de Meun." Ed. Aimée Céleste Bourneuf. Ph.D. diss., Fordham Univ., 1956.

A Thirteenth-Century Bestiary. Facsimile ed. Eric G. Millar. Roxburghe Club. Oxford, 1958.

Thomas, Marcel. *The Golden Age: Manuscript Painting at the Time of Jean, Duke of Berry*. New York: Braziller, 1979.

Thro, A. Booker. "Chaucer's Creative Comedy: A Study of the *Miller's Tale* and the *Shipman's Tale*." *ChauR*, 5 (1970), 97–111.

Thrupp, Sylvia L. *The Merchant Class of Medieval London [1300–1500]*. Ann Arbor: Univ. of Michigan Press, 1948.

Toulmin Smith, J., ed. *English Gilds: The Original Ordinances of More Than One Hundred Early English Gilds*. EETS, o.s. 40. London: Trübner, 1870.

The Towneley Plays. Ed. George England and Alfred W. Pollard. EETS, e.s. 71. London: Oxford Univ. Press, 1897.

The Très Riches Heures of Jean, Duke of Berry. Ed. Jean Longnon, Raymond Cazelles, and Millard Meiss. New York: Braziller, 1969.

"A Tretyse of Gostly Batayle." In Horstmann, ed., *Yorkshire Writers*, II, 420–36.

Trevet, Nicholas. "The Life of Constance." See Bryan and Dempster, eds., *Sources and Analogues*, pp. 165–81; and Furnivall et al., eds., *Originals and Analogues*, 2d series, I, 2–53 (trans. Brock), and III, 222–50.

Trimpi, Wesley. "The Meaning of Horace's *Ut Pictura Poesis*." *JWCI*, 36 (1973), 1–34.

———. "The Quality of Fiction: The Rhetorical Transmission of Literary Theory." *Traditio*, 30 (1974), 1–118.

Tristram, E. W. *English Wall Painting of the Fourteenth Century*. London: Routledge and Kegan Paul, 1955.

Tristram, Philippa. *Figures of Life and Death in Medieval Literature*. London: Elek, 1976.

Turner, Victor, and Edith Turner. *Image and Pilgrimage in Christian Culture*. New York: Columbia Univ. Press, 1978.

Tuve, Rosemond. *Allegorical Imagery: Some Mediaeval Books and Their Posterity*. Princeton: Princeton Univ. Press, 1966.

———. "Notes on the Virtues and Vices." *JWCI*, 26 (1963), 264–303, and 27 (1964), 42–72.

Twycross, Meg. *The Medieval Anadyomene: A Study in Chaucer's Mythography*. Medium Aevum Monographs, n.s. 1. Oxford: Blackwell, 1972.

Underwood, Dale. "The First of *The Canterbury Tales*." *ELH*, 26 (1959), 455–69.

Unterkircher, Franz. *A Treasury of Illuminated Manuscripts*. New York: Putnam, 1967.

Unwin, George. *The Gilds and Companies of London*. 4th ed. London: Cass, 1963.

Usk, Thomas. *The Testament of Love*. In Skeat, ed., *Chaucerian and Other Pieces*, pp. 1–145.

Utley, Francis Lee. "The One Hundred and Three Names of Noah's Wife." *Speculum*, 16 (1941), 426–52.

———. "Robertsonianism Redivivus." *RPh*, 19 (1965), 250–60.

Vasta, Edward and Zacharias P. Thundy, eds. *Chaucerian Problems and Perspectives: Essays Presented to Paul E. Beichner, C.S.C.* Notre Dame, Ind.: Univ. of Notre Dame Press, 1979.

Vázquez de Parga, Luis, José-Maria Lacarra and Juan Uría Ríu. *Las peregrinaciones a Santiago de Compostela*. 3 vols. Madrid: Escuela de Estudios Medievales, 1948–49.

Veale, Elspeth M. "Craftsmen and the Economy of London in the Fourteenth Century." In A. E. J. Hollaender and William Kellaway, eds., *Studies in London History Presented to Philip Edmund Jones*, pp. 133–51. London: Hodder and Stoughton, 1969.

Vices and Virtues. Ed. F. Holthausen. EETS, o.s. 89. London: Oxford Univ. Press, 1888.

Villien, Antoine. *The History and Liturgy of the Sacraments*. London: Burns, Oates, 1932.

Villon, François. *The Complete Works of François Villon*. Ed. and trans. Anthony Bonner. New York: Bantam, 1964.

Virch, Claus. "A Page from Vasari's Book of Drawings." *Metropolitan Museum of Art Bulletin*, 19 (1961), 185–93.

Virgil. *The Aeneid of Virgil.* Trans. Allen Mandelbaum. Berkeley: Univ. of California Press, 1971; repr. New York: Bantam, 1972.

The Visconti Hours. Facsimile ed. Millard Meiss and Edith W. Kirsch. New York: Braziller, 1972.

Vogel, M. U. *Some Aspects of the Horse and Rider Analogy in the Debate Between the Body and the Soul.* Washington, D.C.: Catholic Univ. of America Press, 1948.

Waddell, Helen, trans. *Mediaeval Latin Lyrics.* Rev. ed. 1929; repr. Harmondsworth: Penguin, 1952.

Wagenknecht, Edward, ed. *Chaucer: Modern Essays in Criticism.* New York: Oxford Univ. Press, 1959.

The Wakefield Pageants in the Towneley Cycle. Ed. A. C. Cawley. Manchester: Manchester Univ. Press, 1958.

Waldburg-Wolfegg, Johannes Graf von. *Das Mittelalterliche Hausbuch.* Munich: Prestel-Verlag, 1957.

Warnock, Mary. *Imagination.* Berkeley: Univ. of California Press, 1976.

Waters, E. G. R., ed. *The Anglo-Norman Voyage of St. Brendan, by Benedeit.* Oxford: Clarendon, 1928.

Watson, Paul F. *The Garden of Love in Tuscan Art of the Early Renaissance.* Philadelphia: Art Alliance Press, 1979.

Webb, Henry J. "A Reinterpretation of Chaucer's Theseus." *RES*, 23 (1947), 289–96.

Webb, J. F., trans. *Lives of the Saints.* Baltimore: Penguin, 1965.

Wenzel, Siegfried. *The Sin of Sloth: "Acedia" in Medieval Thought and Literature.* Chapel Hill: Univ. of North Carolina Press, 1960.

Westlund, Joseph. "The *Knight's Tale* as an Impetus for Pilgrimage." *PQ*, 43 (1964), 526–37.

Wetherbee, Winthrop. *Platonism and Poetry in the Twelfth Century.* Princeton: Princeton Univ. Press, 1972.

———. "The Theme of Imagination in Medieval Poetry and the Allegorical Figure 'Genius.'" *M&H*, n.s. 7 (1976), 45–64.

Whitbread, Leslie George, trans. *Fulgentius the Mythographer.* Columbus: Ohio State Univ. Press, 1971.

Whiting, B. J. "Froissart as Poet." *MS*, 8 (1946), 189–216.

Wilkins, Ernest H. "Descriptions of Pagan Divinities from Petrarch to Chaucer." *Speculum*, 32 (1957), 511–22.

Williams, Harry F. "French Fabliau Scholarship." *SARev*, 46 (1981), 76–82.

Wilson, David M. *The Vikings and Their Origins.* London: Thames and Hudson, 1970.

Wilson, H. S. "*The Knight's Tale* and the *Teseida* Again." *UTQ*, 18 (1949), 131–46.

Wimsatt, James. *Chaucer and the French Love Poets.* Chapel Hill: Univ. of North Carolina Press, 1968.

Wimsatt, William K., Jr. and Cleanth Brooks. *Literary Criticism: A Short History.* New York: Knopf, 1957.

Wind, Edgar. *Pagan Mysteries in the Renaissance.* 1958; rev. ed. Harmondsworth: Penguin, 1967.

Woledge, Brian, ed. *The Penguin Book of French Verse.* Vol. I: *To the Fifteenth Century.* Harmondsworth: Penguin, 1961.

Wood, Chauncey. *Chaucer and the Country of the Stars: Poetic Uses of Astrological Imagery.* Princeton: Princeton Univ. Press, 1970.

Woolf, Rosemary. *The English Mystery Plays.* Berkeley: Univ. of California Press, 1972.

———. *The English Religious Lyric in the Middle Ages.* Oxford: Clarendon, 1968.

Yates, Frances A. *The Art of Memory*. London: Routledge and Kegan Paul, 1966.

———. "The Art of Ramon Lull." *JWCI*, 17 (1954), 115–73.

The York Plays. Ed. Lucy Toulmin Smith. Oxford: Clarendon, 1885.

L'Ystoire de Helayne. Ed. J. Van den Gheyn, S.J. Brussels: Vromant, 1913.

Yunck, John A. "Religious Elements in Chaucer's *Man of Law's Tale*." *ELH*, 27 (1960), 249–61.

Zacher, Christian K. *Curiosity and Pilgrimage: The Literature of Discovery in Fourteenth Century England*. Baltimore: Johns Hopkins Univ. Press, 1976.

Zinn, Grover A., Jr. "Hugh of Saint Victor and the Art of Memory." *Viator*, 5 (1974), 211–34.

Illustration Sources and Credits

I AM INDEBTED to the following museums, galleries, libraries, and other institutions for supplying photographs and for permission to reproduce in this volume illustrations from works in their possession: in Aberystwyth, the National Library of Wales; in Ann Arbor, the Kelsey Museum of Archaeology at the University of Michigan; in Brussels, the Bibliothèque Royale Albert Ier; at Cambridge, Corpus Christi College, the Fitzwilliam Museum, the Master and Fellows of Magdalene College, the Master and Fellows of St. John's College, the Master and Fellows of Trinity College, the Master and Fellows of Trinity Hall, the Syndics of Cambridge University Library; in Detroit, the Detroit Institute of Arts; in Florence, the Biblioteca Medicea-Laurenziana; in Geneva, the Bibliothèque Publique et Universitaire; in Lilienfeld, Austria, the Stiftsbibliothek; in London, the British Library, the Courtauld Institute of Art, the Masters of the Bench of the Inner Temple, the Museum of London, the Victoria and Albert Museum, the Wellcome Institute Library; in Munich, the Bayerische Staatsbibliothek; in New York, the Metropolitan Museum of Art, the Pierpont Morgan Library, Praeger Publishers, Prentice-Hall, Inc. (Englewood Cliffs, N.J.); at Oxford, the Bodleian Library, Phaidon Press, the Queen's College Library; in Paris, the Bibliothèque de l'Arsenal, the Bibliothèque Nationale, the Musée du Louvre; in Philadelphia, the Philadelphia Museum of Art; in Rome, the Deutsches Archäologisches Institut; in Rouen, the Bibliothèque Publique et Municipale; in San Marino, California, the Huntington Library; in Schloss Wolfegg, Germany, Fürstlich zu Waldburg-Wolfegg; in Vatican City, the Biblioteca Apostolica Vaticana; in Vienna, the Österreichische Nationalbibliothek; in Wienhausen, Germany, the Cistercian Convent Museum.

I am similarly indebted to the following persons and art-photographic collections: Alinari/Art Resource, Florence; the National Monuments Record, London; the Société de la propriété artistique et des dessins et modèles, Paris; the Visual Artists and Galleries Association, Inc., New York; and G. L. Remnant, Esq.

Date and provenance are specified in the legend printed with each illustration, together with a reference to the endnote in which it is discussed.

1. A man reading (from the *Bestiaires d'amours*). Oxford, Bodley MS. Douce 308, fol. 86d v.

2. Chaucer reading to a courtly audience. Cambridge, Corpus Christi Coll. MS. 61, fol. 1b.

3. A bishop preaching to a congregation. London, Brit. Lib. MS. Harley 2897, fol. 157v.

4. A bishop preaching to a congregation. London, Brit. Lib. MS. Harley 2897, fol. 160.

5. The eye of the imagination. Robert Fludd, *Ars memoriae* (Oppenheim, 1619), p. 47.

6. Brain diagram (a "disease man"). Paris, Bibl. Natl. MS. lat. 11229, fol. 37v.

7. Three-cell diagram of the brain. Triumphus Augustinus de Anchona, *Opusculum perutile de cognitione animae* . . . , rev. Achillini (Bologna, 1503), sig. f [viii].

8. Lady Memory and the doors of sight and hearing. Paris, Bibl. Natl. MS. fr. 1951, fol. 1.

9. *Imago pietatis*, illustrating "O man unkynde." London, Brit. Lib. MS. Add. 37049, fol. 20.

10. The God of Love presents his children to Guillaume de Machaut. Paris, Bibl. Natl. MS. fr. 1584, fol. D.

11. Guillaume de Machaut writes a poem about Lady Fortune and her wheel. Paris, Bibl. Natl. MS. fr. 1586, fol. 30v.

12. Boccaccio writes about Lady Fortune. London, Brit. Lib. MS. Royal 14 E.v, fol. 291.

13. Boccaccio writes about Adam and Eve. *De casibus*, ex coll. Kettaneh, N.Y. Reproduced from Meiss, *Boucicaut Master*, fig. 379.

14. A Christian and a Jew discuss their faiths. Paris, Bibl. de l'Arsenal MS. 5070, fol. 18.

15. St. John writes the book of Apocalypse. London, Brit. Lib. MS. Royal 15 D.iii, fol. 526.

16. Dante and the landscape of his book. Domenico di Michelino, the Duomo, Florence. Courtesy Fratelli Alinari, Florence.

17. St. Luke as painter and writer. London, Brit. Lib. MS. Add. 20694, fol. 14.

18. Boethius and Lady Philosophy. London, Brit. Lib. MS. Harley 4335, fol. 1.

19. Dante and Virgil contemplate images of humility. Oxford, Bodley MS. Holkham misc. 48, p. 75. Photo courtesy of the Courtauld Institute of Art.

20. Dante and Virgil tread upon images of the proud. Oxford, Bodley MS. Holkham misc. 48, p. 79.

21. Mary revisits in her mind the sacred places. Paris, Bibl. de l'Arsenal MS. 593, fol. 29.

22. Guillaume's dream: the image in the mirror. Paris, Bibl. Natl. MS. fr. 376, fol. 1.

23. Guillaume's pilgrimage: Envy, Treason, and Detraction. Geneva, Bibl. Univ. MS. fr. 182, fol. 109v.

24. Guillaume's dream: Grace Dieu restores the Staff of Hope. Paris, Bibl. Natl. MS. fr. 823, fol. 74v.

25. Grace Dieu shows the pilgrim a suit of armor. Paris, Bibl. Natl. MS. fr. 823, fol. 27.

26. Grace Dieu offers the pilgrim the gambeson of Patience. Paris, Bibl. Natl. MS. fr. 823, fol. 27v.

27. Grace Dieu offers the pilgrim further armor. Paris, Bibl. Natl. MS. fr. 823, fol. 29.

28. The pilgrim throws off his suit of armor. Paris, Bibl. Natl. MS. fr. 823, fol. 34.

29. The pilgrim is introduced to Lady Memory. Paris, Bibl. Natl. MS. fr. 823, fol. 34v.

30. Lady Memory takes up the pilgrim's armor. Paris, Bibl. Natl. MS. fr. 823, vol. 35v.

31. Scenes from *The Pardoner's Tale*. A chest front, Museum of London.

32. Hoccleve's dialogue with the image of a dying man. Oxford, Bodley MS. Selden Supra 53, fol. 118.

33. A bagpiper with small dogs. Misericord, Cathedral of Notre-Dame, Rouen. Photo Pascal Corbierre. Courtesy Henry and Dorothy Kraus.

34. An angel with bagpipes. Tapestry border, Angers, the Chateau. Courtesy ARCH. PHOT/VAGA, New York/SPADEM.

35. Art and Wisdom (illustrating Aristotle's *Ethics*). Brussels, Bibl. Royale MS. 9505-6, fol. 115v.

36. The House of Fortune (from *The Romance of the Rose*). Oxford, Bodley MS. Douce 371, fol. 40v.

37. Emilia in the pleasure garden; Palemone and Arcita in prison. Vienna, Natl. Lib. MS. 2617, fol. 53.

38. Arcita released from prison. Vienna, Natl. Lib. MS. 2617, fol. 64.

39. Lady Lechery and her manacles. Cambridge, Fitzwilliam Mus. MS. 368.

40. The Prison of Love (illustrating Baudouin de Condé). Vienna, Natl. Lib. MS. 2621, fol. 23v.

41. The lover walking the road to the prison. Vienna, Natl. Lib. MS. 2621, fol. 25v.

42. The torments of the Prison of Love. Vienna, Natl. Lib. MS. 2621, fol. 29.

43. A modern model of the Roman Colosseum. Rome, Deutsches Archäologisches Institut.

44. A medieval tournament lists. Paris, Bibl. Natl. MS. fr. 2695, fols. 48v–49.

45. Palemone and Arcita kneel before Teseo at the tournament lists. Vienna, Natl. Lib. MS. 2617, fol. 91.

46. Emilia rides out hunting. Vienna, Natl. Lib. MS. 2617, fol. 76.

47. Palemone and Arcita fight in the grove. Vienna, Natl. Lib. MS. 2617, fol. 77.

48. Arcita, Emilia, and Palemone pray to the gods. Vienna, Natl. Lib. MS. 2617, fol. 102.

49. The children of Mars. Wolfegg, Fürstlich zu Waldburg-Wolfegg, *Hausbuch* MS., fol. 13.

50. The children of Venus. Wolfegg, Fürstlich zu Waldburg-Wolfegg, *Hausbuch* MS., fol. 15.

51. The children of Luna. Wolfegg, Fürstlich zu Waldburg-Wolfegg, *Hausbuch* MS., fol. 17.

52. The children of Saturn. Wolfegg, Fürstlich zu Waldburg-Wolfegg, *Hausbuch* MS., fol. 11.

53. The fury frightens Arcita's horse. Vienna, Natl. Lib. MS. 2617, fol. 138.

54. The children of Jupiter. Wolfegg, Fürstlich zu Waldburg-Wolfegg, *Hausbuch* MS., fol. 12.

55. The tournament underway. Vienna, Natl. Lib. MS. 2617, fol. 121.

56. Boccaccio presents to Fiammetta the book of his poem. Vienna, Natl. Lib. MS. 2617, fol. 14.

57. Boethius writes his book, behind a prison window. Florence, Bibl. Laurenziana MS. Plut. 78.15, fol. 1.

58. Lady Philosophy and the mind's wings. Paris, Bibl. Natl. MS. Néerlandais 1, fol. 212v.

59. The Theban widows interrupt Teseo's triumph. Vienna, Natl. Lib. MS. 2617, fol. 39.

60. Pagans and Christians point to their different temples. Philadelphia, Mus. of Art MS. 45-65-1, fol. 64, the Philip S. Collins Collection.

61. The Advent of Christ to those who wait in prison, in darkness, and in hell. Paris, Bibl. Natl. MS. fr. 244, fol. 4.

62. The marriage of Palemone and Emilia. Vienna, Natl. Lib. MS. 2617, fol. 182.

63. The Ages of Man. London, Brit. Lib. MS. Arundel 83, fol. 126v.

64. Youth transports the pilgrim across the sea of this world. Brussels, Bibl. Royale MS. 10176-78, fol. 98.

65. Bird in cage and monk in cloister. New York, Pierpont Morgan MS. M.132, fol. 102v.

66. Envy. Cambridge, Univ. Lib. MS. Gg.iv.27, fol. 416.

67. Gluttony. Cambridge, Univ. Lib. MS. Gg.iv.27, fol. 432.

68. Lechery. Cambridge, Univ. Lib. MS. Gg.iv.27, fol. 433.

69. Boethius and two lovers courting. Cambridge, Trinity Hall MS. 12, fol. 40v.

70. A boar mounting a sow. Cambridge, Trinity Hall MS. 12, fol. 41.

71. The creation of the animals. London, Brit. Lib. MS. Royal 2 B.vii, fol. 2.

72. The wedding of Adam and Eve. Cambridge, Fitzwilliam Mus. MS. 251, fol. 16.

73. Cats and mice. New York, Pierpont Morgan MS. M.81, fol. 46v.

74. A cow and calf. Oxford, MS. Bodley 764, fol. 41v.

75. Sheep and lambs. Oxford, MS. Bodley 764, fol. 35v.

76. A weasel. New York, H. P. Kraus collection (formerly MS. Dyson Perrins 26), fol. 93v.

77. The shoeing of a horse. Oxford, MS. Bodley 264, fol. 107.

78. A man training an ape. London, Brit. Lib. MS. Add. 42130, fol. 73.

79. The animals leaving the ark. London, Brit. Lib. MS. Add. 18850, fol. 16v.

80. Ducks and geese swimming. New York, Pierpont Morgan MS. M.88, fol. 156v.

81. Animals on a sketchbook page. Cambridge, Magdalene Coll. MS. Pepys 1916, fol. 9v.

82. Herod ranting. Roof boss, Norwich Cathedral. Courtesy Natl. Monuments Record, London.

83. Arse baring, with kneeling nun. Oxford, MS. Bodley 264, fol. 56.

84. Shooting at a bared arse with a crossbow. Roof boss, Sherborne Abbey. Courtesy Natl. Monuments Record, London.

85. A man and woman kneel before the God of Love. Cambridge, Trinity Coll. MS. B.11.22, fol. 30.

86. Two monks kneel before the cross. London, Brit. Lib. MS. Add. 49622, fol. 199.

87. A lover kneels before his lady. Ivory writing tablet, Detroit Institute of Arts (42.136). Gift of Robert H. Tannahill.

88. A lover climbs in through the bedroom window, assisted by the devil. Cambridge, Fitzwilliam Mus. MS. 22, p. 181.

89. An ape reveres an arse and breeches. New York, Pierpont Morgan MS. G.24, fol. 54.

90. Noah and his family enter the ark. Cambridge, St. John's Coll. MS. 231, fol. 8.

91. The ark and its inhabitants. London, Brit. Lib. MS. Add. 28162, fol. 7v.

92. The angel commands Noah to build the ark. London, Brit. Lib. MS. Royal 2 B.vii, fol. 5v.

93. The devil and Mrs. Noah; Mrs. Noah and her husband; the angel's reprimand. London, Brit. Lib. MS. Royal 2 B.vii, fol. 6.

94. The loading of the ark. London, Brit. Lib. MS. Royal 2 B.vii, fol. 6v.

95. The release of the dove; the escape of the devil. London, Brit. Lib. MS. Royal 2 B.vii, fol. 7.

96. The devil on Mrs. Noah's back. New York, Pierpont Morgan MS. M.302, fol. 1v.

97. A domestic quarrel. Misericord, Church of St. Mary, Fairford, Gloucestershire. Courtesy G. L. Remnant.

98. Friar Puccio's devotions. Paris, Bibl. de l'Arsenal MS. 5070, fol. 108v.

99. The Miller (Ellesmere MS.). San Marino, Huntington Lib. MS. 26.C.9, fol. 34v.

100. The labor of August: a reeve in the field. London, Brit. Lib. MS. Royal 2 B.vii, fol. 78v.

101. The Reeve. Cambridge, Univ. Lib. MS. Gg.iv.27, fol. 186.

102. The Reeve (Ellesmere MS.). San Marino, Huntington Lib. MS. 26.C.9, fol. 42.

103. A monk cellarer. London, Brit. Lib. MS. Sloane 2435, fol. 44v.

104. Singing around a wine cask. Paris, Bibl. Natl. MS. fr. 9221, fol. 16.

105. "O potatores exquisiti" (carousing around a wine cask). London, Brit. Lib. MS. Egerton 3307, fol. 72v.

106. The pilgrim meets Infirmity and Old Age. Brussels, Bibl. Royale MS. 10176-78, fol. 108v.

107. Four horses (from a bestiary). Oxford, MS. Bodley 764, fol. 46.

108. The raven feeds on a horse (Noah's Flood). New York, Pierpont Morgan MS. M.638, fol. 2v.

109. Prudence controlling the horses of Lechery. Engraving, Achille Bocchi, *Symbolicae quaestiones*, 117.

110. Porphyry's tree. Munich, Staatsbibl. MS. Cod. lat. 10570, fol. 8v.

111. The drowning of Pharaoh's host. New York, Pierpont Morgan MS. M.638, fol. 9.

112. The chariot of Prudence. London, Wellcome Mus. MS. 49, fol. 68.

113. The arming of the soul. Lilienfeld (Austria), Stiftsbibl. MS. 151, fol. 253.

114. *Ymago Prudencie*. Rome, Vatican Lib. MS. pal. lat. 1066, fol. 232v.

115. A lover presents his heart to his lady. Ivory mirror back, London, Victoria and Albert Museum.

116. A horse walks away from a man copulating with a nun. Paris, Bibl. Natl. MS. fr. 25526, fol. 111v.

117. Phyllis rides Aristotle. Ivory casket panel (detail), New York, Metropolitan Mus. of Art (accession no. 17.190.173). Gift of J. Pierpont Morgan, 1917.

118. The Boccaccio analogue. Paris, Bibl. de l'Arsenal MS. 5070, fol. 337.

119. The Boccaccio analogue. Paris, Bibl. Natl. MS. fr. 239, fol. 256v.

120. The Cook (Ellesmere MS.). San Marino, Huntington Lib. MS. 26.C.9, fol. 47.

121. Portrait of a cook. Misericord, Kent, Minster-in-Thanet. Courtesy G. L. Remnant.

122. Kitchen scenes (from the Luttrell Psalter). London, Brit. Lib. MS. Add. 42130, fol. 207.

123. Demons torture the damned in hell. Oxford, Bodley MS. Douce 62, fol. 95.

124. Barrators punished in hell. Rome, Vatican Lib. MS. lat. 4776, fol. 72.

125. Disputation between Christ and Satan. London, Brit. Lib. MS. Add. 47682, fol. 11v.

126. The Cook. Cambridge, Univ. Lib. MS. Gg.iv.27, fol. 193v.

127. A street of shops, between figures representing Fortitude and Justice. Geneva, Bibl. Publ. et Univ. MS. fr. 160, fol. 82.

128. Commercial life on a Paris bridge. Paris, Bibl. Natl. MS. fr. 2092, fol. 35v.

129. Noah as master shipwright. London, Brit. Lib. MS. Add. 18850, fol. 15v.

130. Three kinds of friendship (illustrating Aristotle's *Ethics*). Rouen, Bibl. Mun. MS. 927, fol. 127v.

131. The end of *The Cook's Tale* (Hengwrt MS.). Aberystwyth, Natl. Lib. of Wales MS. Peniarth 392, fol. 57v.

132. The end of *The Cook's Tale* (Ellesmere MS.). San Marino, Huntington Lib. MS. 26.C.9, fols. 47v, 48.

133. God as *artifex*, creating the world. Vienna, Natl. Lib. MS. 2554, fol. 1v.

134. The Man of Law (Ellesmere MS.). San Marino, Huntington Lib. MS. 26.C.9, fol. 50v.

135. The Court of Common Pleas, with Sergeants of the Law (coiffed) in the

foreground. London, Library of the Inner Temple, detached folio (photo A. C. Cooper, Ltd.).

136. Fortitude, attended by Constancy, Magnificence, Patience, and Perseverance. Oxford, Bodley MS. Laud Misc. 570, fol. 21v.

137. Scenes from Gower's tale of Constance. New York, Pierpont Morgan MS. M.126, fol. 32v.

138. The Ship of the Church. New York, Pierpont Morgan MS. M.799, fol. 234v.

139. The arrival of St. Mary Magdalen and her fellows at Marseilles. Fresco, School of Giotto, Magdalen Chapel, lower Basilica of San Francesco, Assisi. Courtesy Fratelli Alinari, Florence.

140. Mary and the Christ Child aboard a ship. Vienna National Library (woodcut, Alb 50.433).

141. St. Ursula rescuing sinners. Paris, Louvre, Collection E. de Rothschild, inv. no. 15 Rés.

142. The pilgrim sees the Ship of the Church. Oxford, Bodley MS. Douce 300, fol. 113v.

143. Christ, walking on the water, bears up Peter. Oxford, Bodley MS. Douce 313, fol. 290v.

144. Noah's ark. London, Brit. Lib. MS. Add. 11639, fol. 521.

145. Noah's ark. London, Brit. Lib. MS. Royal 14 B.ix.

146. Noah's ark and the City of Cain. Paris, Bibl. Natl. MS. fr. 19, fol. 55v.

147. A "ship's keel" roof. Basilica of San Zeno Maggiore, Verona. Courtesy Fratelli Alinari, Florence.

148. Jonah cast up by the whale. London, Brit. Lib. MS. Royal 15 D.iii, fol. 398v.

149. The crossing of the Red Sea. Oxford, Bodley MS. Douce 313, fol. 146.

150. Interior. Baptistery of St. John, Poitiers. ARCH. PHOT/VAGA, New York/SPADEM.

151. The Baptism of Christ. Cambridge, Trinity Coll. MS. B.11.7, fol. 22v.

152. The baptism of pagans. Cambridge, Fitzwilliam Mus. MS. 3-1954, fol. 70v.

153. Initial for Trinity Sunday, with infant baptism. London, Brit. Lib. MS. Add. 29704-5, fol. 36v.

154. St. Edmund sets Beorn adrift, in judgment for murder. London, Brit. Lib. MS. Harl. 2278, fol. 46.

155. The sea of this world, with the tree of human life, and the pilgrim caught on the wheel of Fortune. London, Brit. Lib. MS. Cotton Tiber. A.vii, fol. 58v.

156. The pilgrim and Lady Fortune in the sea of this world. London, Brit. Lib. MS. Cotton Tiber. A.vii, fol. 59v.

157. Life as a storm-tossed ship. Paris, Bibl. Natl. MS. fr. 916, fol. 74v.

158. The mount of contemplation amid the sea of this world. Paris, Bibl. Natl. MS. fr. 990, fol. 2.

159. The voyage of St. Brendan. Oxford, Queen's College MS. 305, fol. 148.

160. Two Irishmen in a coracle. Oxford, Bodley MS. Laud Misc. 720, fol. 226v.

161. David amid the waters of tribulation. London, Brit. Lib. MS. Royal 17 E.vii, Pt. I, fol. 243v.

162. St. Peter praying from aboard a ship. Paris, Bibl. Natl. MS. Lat. 10483, fol. 37.

163. Satan as fisherman in the sea of the world. London, Brit. Lib. MS. Cotton Tiber. A.vii, fol. 52v.

164. Charon and the souls of the damned. London, Brit. Lib. MS. Egerton 943, fol. 7v.

165. Souls ferried to Purgatory. London, Brit. Lib. MS. Egerton 943, fol. 65.

166. Tristan put to sea. The Wienhausen Embroidery, I, 2d row, scene 9. Wienhausen, Cistercian Convent Museum (photo Rheinländer).

167. The death ship of St. James the Greater. London, Brit. Lib. MS. Royal 20 D.vi, fol. 20.

168. The soul of St. Mary Magdalen borne by angels to heaven. School of Giotto. Magdalen Chapel, lower Basilica of San Francesco, Assisi. Courtesy Fratelli Alinari, Florence.

169. A soul arrives in the harbor of eternity. Ann Arbor, Kelsey Mus. of Archaeology, no. 21188, Univ. of Michigan.

170. Paradise. Paris, Bibl. Natl. MS. fr. 19, fol. 232.

171. Paradise. Giovanni di Paolo, New York, Metropolitan Mus. of Art (accession no. 06.1046). Rogers Fund, 1906.

172. The house of many mansions, right; and left, the feasting of the children of Job. London, Brit. Lib. MS. King's 5, fol. 30.

173. The feasts of Ahasuerus and of Job's children. New York, Pierpont Morgan MS. M.385, fol. 45.

174. The marriage supper of the Lamb. Cambridge, Magdalene Coll. MS. Pepys 1803, fol. 39v.

175. The route of the Canterbury pilgrims. Albert C. Baugh, *Chaucer's Major Poetry*, © 1963, p. 229. Reprinted by permission of Prentice-Hall, Inc., Englewood Cliffs, N.J.

Index